D0370987

Sources of Japanese Tradition

SECOND EDITION

VOLUME 1

INTRODUCTION TO ASIAN CIVILIZATIONS

Introduction to Asian Civilizations

Wm. Theodore de Bary, General Editor

Sources of Japanese Tradition
(1958; 2nd ed., 2001)

Sources of Indian Tradition
(1958; 2nd ed., 1988)

Sources of Chinese Tradition
(1960; issued in 2 vols., 1964;
vol. 1, 2nd ed., 1999;
vol. 2, 2nd ed., 2000)

Sources of Korean Tradition
(vol. 1, 1997; vol. 2, 2001)

Sources of Japanese Tradition

SECOND EDITION

VOLUME ONE: FROM EARLIEST TIMES TO 1600

Compiled by Wm. Theodore de Bary, Donald Keene,
George Tanabe, and Paul Varley

WITH COLLABORATION OF

William Bodiford, Jurgis Elisonas, and Philip Yampolsky

and contributions by

Yoshiko Dykstra, Allan Grapard, Paul Groner, Edward Kamens,
Robert Morrell, Charles Orzech, Rajyashree Pandey,
Denis Twitchett, and Royall Tyler

COLUMBIA UNIVERSITY PRESS

NEW YORK

Columbia University Press
Publishers Since 1893
New York Chichester, West Sussex
Copyright © 2001 Columbia University Press
All rights reserved

Library of Congress Cataloging-in-Publication Data
Sources of Japanese tradition / compiled by Wm. Theodore de Bary . . . [et al.] ; with
collaboration of William Bodiford, Jurgis Elisonas, Philip Yampolsky ; and contributions by
Yoshiko Dykstra . . . [et al.]. — 2nd ed.
    p. cm. — (Introduction to Asian civilizations)
    Includes bibliographical references and index.
    Contents: v. 1. From earliest times through the sixteenth century
    ISBN 0–231–12138–5 (cloth)   ISBN 0–231–12139–3 (paper)
    1. Japan—Civilization—Sources. 2. Japan—History—Sources. I. De Bary, William
Theodore, 1919– II. Dykstra, Yoshiko Kurata. III. Series.

DS821 . S68 2001
952—dc21   00-060181

Casebound editions of Columbia University Press books are printed on permanent and
   durable acid-free paper.
Printed in the United States of America
c 10 9 8 7 6 5 4 3   p 10 9 8 7 6 5 4

Acknowledgment is gratefully made for permission to reprint from the following:

Anesaki Masaharu. *Nichiren, the Buddhist Prophet.* Cambridge, MA: Harvard University Press,
1916, pp. 83–85.

Aoki Michiko, tr. *Izumo no Kuni Fudoki.* Monumenta Nipponica Monographs. Tokyo: Sophia
University Press, 1971, pp. 80, 82.

From pp. 71–75 of *Conversations with Shôtetsu,* translated by Robert H. Brower, with an introduction and notes by Stephen H. Carter, Michigan Monograph Series in Japanese Studies,
Number 7 (Ann Arbor: Center for Japanese Studies, The University of Michigan, 1992). Used
with permission.

Reprinted from *Japanese Court Poetry,* by Robert H. Brower and Earl Miner, with the permission
of the publishers, Stanford University Press. © 1961 the Board of Trustees of the Leland Stanford
Junior University.

Delmer Brown, and Ichiro Ishida. *Future and the Past: A Translation and Study of the Gukanshô.*
Copyright © 1979 The Regents of the University of California.

Thomas Conlan, tr. *In Little Need of Divine Intervention: Scrolls of the Mongol Invasions of
Japan, Translation with an Interpretive Essay of the Invasions.* Forthcoming 2000, Cornell East
Asia Series, East Asia Program, Cornell University, 140 Uris Hall, Ithaca, NY 14853–7601.

James Dobbins. *Jôdo Shinshu: Shin Buddhism in Medieval Japan.* Bloomington: Indiana University Press, 1989, pp. 141–142, 145.

Yoshiko Kurata Dykstra. "Jizô, the Most Merciful: Tales from the *Jizô Bosatsu Reigenki*." *Monumenta Nipponica* 33.2 (1978), pp. 27–29, 192, 197–200.

Yoshiko Kurata Dykstra. *Miraculous Tales of the Lotus Sutra from Ancient Japan.* Hirakata City,
Japan: Intercultural Research Institute, Kansai University of Foreign Studies, 1983, pp. 27–29.

Continued on page 517

Dedicated to the memory of
Ryūsaku Tsunoda
Pioneer teacher of Japanese
Studies in America

CONTENTS

PREFACE

This volume, part of a series dealing with the civilizations of Japan, China, Korea, India, and Pakistan, contains source readings revealing what the Japanese have thought about themselves, the world they lived in, and the problems they faced living together. These readings help provide an understanding of the background of contemporary Japanese civilization, especially as reflected in traditions of thought that remain alive today. Accordingly, we devote much of our attention to the religious and philosophical developments in early times that are still part of the Japanese heritage and affect people's thinking today. More attention is given to political and social questions ordinary histories of philosophy or religion do not treat. Also, since the arts of Japan have a unique importance in the modern world—indeed, to many people, are the embodiment of Japanese civilization—we have made room for a discussion of Japanese aesthetic concepts. Accordingly, we have made brief excursions into theories of literature and dramatic art, even though we cannot hope to take full stock of the arts in a book focused more on society

Western readers attempting to understand Japanese civilization should take care not to assume that one or another of its more striking aspects represents the whole or to select mainly those items that appear important as parallels to developments in the West. To avoid such misconceptions, we have tried to let the Japanese speak for themselves—to let the criteria of selection be those that emerge internally from the dialogue among successive generations of Japanese as they commented on or took issue with one another. At the same time, it is true that this process has been repeatedly influenced by external challenges. Thus the traditions represented here reflect their continued interactions with other developments in continental Asia and, in modern times, with the West. "Tradition" as represented here is therefore a hybrid growth—diverse, dynamic, and complex rather than monolithic or unchanging.

Another requirement of a book such as this is to achieve balance and perspective. It is unlikely that we have succeeded completely in doing this, but knowing our aim, critical readers will at least understand why we have spread ourselves so thin over the length and breadth of Japanese history and civilization and have dealt summarily with subjects that might call for more extended treatment or for contextualization in greater detail. To a limited extent, we have tried to explain the circumstances that prompted or conditioned these writings and have included more historical and explanatory material in some cases than in others, but those readers not familiar with Japanese history who seek a fuller historical and institutional background may do well to supplement this text by reading a general or cultural history along with it. Given the limitations of an introductory text, we have not sought the coverage of an intellectual history or tried to deal with every thinker or movement of importance but, instead, have selected examples that we think best illustrate the relation of divergent currents to the mainstreams of Japanese thought or that indicate the relevance of intellectual and religious attitudes toward the most persistent problems of Japanese society. In the modern period, for instance, we have bypassed some of the more obvious examples of either Western influence or apparent Japanese idiosyncrasy in favor of others better illustrating trends or tendencies of central importance. Thus, when describing recent trends, we have often focused on persons active in public life or organized political movements, close to the great events of their time, rather than intellectuals or scholars in the narrow sense.

These readings were originally compiled in the 1950s and based on a series of essays and translations prepared by Ryusaku Tsunoda, for many years the curator of the Japanese collection at Columbia University and a lecturer on Japanese religion and thought. In this second edition, these readings have been considerably supplemented, revised, and adapted. In the process we have solicited, and benefited from, the collaboration of others who have contributed their expertise in special fields.

This series was originally produced in the 1950s in connection with the Columbia College General Education Program in Oriental Studies, which was encouraged and supported by the Carnegie Corporation of New York. For the wide use of these sources over the years since then, we would like to acknowledge the debt owed to Deans Harry J. Carman and Lawrence H. Chamberlain of Columbia College. Their foresight and leadership were responsible for the progress toward a goal long sought by members of the Columbia College faculty, who even before World War II recognized the need for the college's core curriculum to include other world civilizations.

EXPLANATORY NOTE

The consonants of Japanese words or names are read as in English (with "g" always hard) and the vowels as in Italian. There are no silent letters. The name Abe, for instance, is pronounced "Ah-bay." The long vowels "ō" and "ū" are indicated except in the names of cities already well known in the West, such as Tokyo and Kyoto. All romanized terms have been standardized according to the Hepburn system for Japanese, pin-yin for Chinese, and the McCune-Reischauer for Korean. Chinese philosophical terms used in Japanese texts are given in their Japanese readings (e.g., *ri* instead of *li* for "principle," "reason") except where attention is specifically drawn to the Chinese original. Sanskrit words appearing in italics follow the standard system of transliteration found in Louis Renou's *Grammaire sanskrite* (Paris 1930), pp. xi–xiii. Sanskrit terms and names appearing in roman letters follow *Webster's New International Dictionary*, second edition unabridged, except that a macron is used to indicate long vowels and the Sanskrit symbols for ś (ç) are uniformly transcribed as "sh" in the text itself. Personal names also are spelled in this manner except when they occur in the titles of works.

Japanese names are given in their Japanese order, with the family name first and the personal name last. The dates given after personal names are those of birth and death except in the case of rulers, whose reign dates are preceded by "r." Generally, the name by which a person was most commonly known in

Japanese tradition is the one used in the text. Since this book is intended for general readers rather than specialists, we have not burdened the text with a list of the alternative names or titles that usually accompany biographical references to a scholar in Chinese or Japanese historical works. For the same reason, the sources of translations given at the end of each selection are as concise as possible. There is a complete bibliography at the end of the book.

Contributors are identified with their work in the table of contents; unattributed chapters are the responsibility of the editors. Unless otherwise indicated, in the reference at the end of each selection, the author of the book is the writer whose name precedes the selection. The initials following the source citation are those of the translator or the compiler of the section. Excerpts from existing translations have often been adapted and edited to suit our purposes. In particular, we have removed unnecessary brackets and footnotes and have inserted essential commentary in the text whenever possible rather than add a footnote. Those interested in the full text and annotations may, of course, refer to the original translation cited with each such excerpt. As sources for our own translations, we have tried to use standard editions that would be available to other scholars.

W. T. de B.

CONTRIBUTORS

Identified by initials following original translations

YD	Yoshiko Dykstra: Kansai Gaidai University
JSAE	Jurgis S. A. Elisonas, Indiana University
AG	Allan Grapard, University of California, Santa Barbara
PG	Paul Groner, University of Virginia
EK	Edward Kamens, Yale University
JPL	Jeroen Pieter Lamers, Royal Dutch Ministry of Economic Affairs
RM	Robert Morrell, Washington University in St. Louis
RP	Rajyashree Pandey, La Trobe University
TR	Thomas Rimer, University of Pittsburgh
DS	Daniel Stevenson, University of Kansas
GT	George Tanabe, University of Hawaii, Manoa
RT	Royall Tyler, Australian National University
TH	Tsay Heng-ting, Columbia University
PV	Paul Varley, University of Hawaii, Manoa

CHRONOLOGICAL TABLE

First century B.C.E.	First reference to Japan (called land of Wa) in Chinese dynastic histories.
C.E. 57	Envoy from country of Nu in land of Wa makes tributary visit to Han court. First exact date concerning Wa in dynastic histories.
239	Envoy sent by Queen Himiko of Yamatai in land of Wa to Wei court.
538	Recognized as date for formal introduction of Buddhism to Japan.
562	Kingdom of Silla destroys Mimana, Japanese enclave at tip of Korean Peninsula (present-day Korean scholars disclaim existence of such an enclave).
592–628	Reign of Empress Suiko. Prince Shōtoku serves as regent.
600	First Japanese embassy to Sui Court.
604	Prince Shōtoku's Seventeen-Article Constitution. First official use in Japan of Chinese calendar.
630	First Japanese embassy to Tang court.
645	Taika reform.
668	Tenchi becomes emperor, Silla unifies Korea.
672	Tenmu becomes emperor after armed succession dispute (Jinshin War).

702   Promulgation of Taihō Code.

Nara Period

710   Establishment of first permanent capital at Nara.

712   *Records of Ancient Matters* (*Kojiki*).

720   *Chronicles of Japan* (*Nihongi* or *Nihon shoki*).

741   Copies of *Golden Light Sūtra* distributed to all provinces.

751   *Kaifūsō* (*Fond Recollections of Poetry*), first collection of Chinese verse by Japanese poets.

752   Dedication of Great Buddha (*Daibutsu*) at Tōdaiji Temple in Nara.

754   Chinese monk Ganjin arrives in Japan and establishes ordination center at Tōdaiji.

c. 759   Compilation of *Man'yōshū* (*Collection of a Myriad Generations*), oldest anthology of *waka* (or *tanka*) poetry.

764   Empress Kōken reascends throne as Empress Shōtoku; appoints priest Dōkyō as prime minister.

770   Death of Empress Shōtoku and fall of Dōkyō from power.

781   Kanmu becomes emperor.

788   Saichō founds Enryakuji Temple on Mt. Hiei.

Heian Period

794   Court moves capital to Heian (Kyoto).

805   Saichō returns from study in China.

806   Kūkai returns from study in China.

815   *New Compilation of the Register of Families* (*Shinsen shōjiroku*).

816   Kōyasan Monastery founded by Kūkai.

817   Saichō codifies regulations for monks at Enryakuji Temple on Mt. Hiei.

838   Last official mission to Tang China.

847   Ennin returns from China to found Tendai esotericism in Japan.

858   Beginning of Fujiwara regency at court. Enchin returns from China and founds study center at Miidera Temple.

905   *Kokinshū* (*Collection of Ancient and Modern Poems*), first imperially authorized anthology of *waka* (or *tanka*) poetry.

972   Death of Kūya, early popularizer of devotion to Amida Buddha.

c. 990–1020 Classical age of Japanese court prose: *Tale of Genji, Pillow Book, Izumi Shikibu Diary, Honchō monzui* (Chinese prose by Japanese).

1017	Death of Genshin, author of *Essentials of Salvation*.
1068	Accession of Emperor Go-Sanjō and beginning of attempt to curb power of Fujiwara regents.
1086	Abdication of Emperor Shirakawa and commencement of age of ascendancy of senior retired emperors at court (1086–1156).
1132	Death of Ryōnin, early popularizer of Pure Land Buddhism.
1156	Beginning of rise to power at court of Taira warrior family under Kiyomori.
1180–1185	Minamoto-Taira (*Genpei*) War. Victory of Minamoto.

Kamakura Period

1185	*De facto* founding of Kamakura Shogunate by Minamoto Yoritomo.
1191	Eisai (Yōsai), founder of Rinzai branch of Zen sect, returns from second trip to China; introduces tea to Japan.
1192	Yoritomo receives title of shogun.
1205	Beginning of rise to power of Hōjō as shogunal regents.
1212	Death of Hōnen.
1220	*Gukanshō* by Jien.
1223	Dōgen, founder of Sōtō branch of Zen sect, goes to China.
1232	*Jōei shikimoku* (basic law code of Kamakura Shogunate).
1260	Nichiren first predicts a foreign invasion.
1262	Death of Shinran, founder of True Pure Land sect.
1268	Nichiren warns of impending Mongol invasion.
1271	Nichiren sentenced to death, escapes, and is banished.
1274	First Mongol invasion.
1281	Second Mongol invasion.
1289	Death of Ippen, popularizer of Amida cult.
1325	At suggestion of Zen master Musō Soseki, Emperor Go-Daigo sends first official embassy to China since Tang dynasty.
c. 1331	*Essays in Idleness* (*Tsurezuregusa*).
1333	Overthrow of Kamakura Shogunate. Beginning of Kenmu Restoration (1333–1336).

Muromachi (Ashikaga) Period

1336	*De facto* founding of Muromachi Shogunate in Kyoto by Ashikaga Takauji. Beginning of period of War Between Northern and Southern Courts (1336–1392).
1338	Takauji receives title of shogun.

1339   *Chronicle of the Direct Succession of Divine Sovereigns (Jinnō shō-tōki)* by Kitabatake Chikafusa.

1368   Ashikaga Yoshimitsu becomes shogun; fosters diplomatic and trade relations with China.

1384   Death of Kan'ami, early master of Nō drama.

1443   Death of Zeami, greatest master of Nō drama.

1467–1477   Ōnin War. Much of Kyoto destroyed.

1478   Commencement of Age of War in Provinces (*Sengoku*, 1478–1568).

1488   Death of Nisshin, evangelizer of Nichiren sect.

1499   Death of Rennyo, leader of True Pure Land sect.

1511   Death of Yoshida Kanetomo of the "Primal Shinto" movement.

1543   Portugese merchants land on Tanegashima—first Europeans to visit Japan. Introduce European guns (arqubuses).

1549   St. Francis Xavier arrives in Japan and founds Jesuit mission.

1568   Oda Nobunaga enters Kyoto and begins process of military unification of Japan.

1571   Nobunaga's army destroys Enryakuji Temple on Mt. Hiei.

1582   Nobunaga assassinated; Toyotomi Hideyoshi succeeds him as unifier.

1591   Death of Sen no Rikyū, greatest of tea masters.

1592   Hideyoshi's first invasion of Korea.

1597   Hideyoshi's second invasion of Korea.

1598   Death of Hideyoshi.

1600   Battle of Sekigahara and founding of Tokugawa Shogunate by Ieyasu.

1603   Ieyasu receives title of shogun.

Sources of Japanese Tradition

SECOND EDITION

VOLUME 1

PART I

Early Japan

Chapter 1

THE EARLIEST RECORDS OF JAPAN

The oldest extant annals in Japanese are the *Records of Ancient Matters* (*Kojiki*, 712 C.E.) and the *Chronicles of Japan* (*Nihon shoki* or *Nihongi*, 720). The *Records* opens with chapters on the mythological Age of the Gods and continues the story of Japan to about 500 C.E..[1] Although this book reveals early Japanese ways of thinking and patterns of behavior, it contains little that can be taken as historical fact. The *Chronicles*, a much longer work, covers the same story from the Age of the Gods to 500 but continues for some two hundred years more until the end of the seventh century (697). The *Chronicles* becomes increasingly reliable as history after about the late sixth century. Indeed, the bestowal of the posthumous name of Suiko, meaning "conjecture the past," on an empress who reigned from 592 to 628 seems to suggest that it was around this time that the Japanese, no doubt under Chinese influence, first began the serious writing of history, albeit often in the interests of the ruling house that the historians served.

An important source of written information about Japan before the sixth century is the Chinese dynastic histories. By the time Japan first came into the Chinese purview, about the first century B.C.E., the writing of history had left far behind the foundation myths of the *Classic of Documents*, and Chinese

---

1. The *Records of Ancient Matters* also provides genealogical data for the sovereigns of the sixth and early seventh centuries.

historians were compiling generally reliable records of the past. In the first century B.C.E., Japan was called Wa by the Chinese[2] and was described as a land comprising more than a hundred tribal communities. As late as the Chinese Three Kingdoms period (220–265), according to the dynastic accounts, Wa was still divided into some thirty communities (although we know from the archaeological record in Japan that the country was then evolving into its first centralized state).

The Chinese histories do not tell us how the people now known as the Japanese first found their way to the islands. Without conclusive evidence on this subject, modern scholars have expounded various theories based on linguistics, archaeology, architecture, and a great many criteria, with some contending that the Japanese originally came from Southeast Asia and others insisting that they were a northern people. The Japanese probably had diverse origins, with various peoples entering from different directions. The mainstream of cultural influence came from the continent by way of Korea. When the first Qin emperor (247–210 B.C.E.) unified China and built the Great Wall to prevent the northern barbarians from making incursions on the fertile plains of the Yellow River, it seems likely that his actions helped direct the migrations of different peoples eastward or westward along the wall. Disturbances resulting from the movement of tribes were sometimes so severe that Emperor Wu (r. 140–87 B.C.E.) of the Han dynasty was compelled to send expeditionary forces to restore order. An outpost of the Han empire thus was established in northern Korea and served as a model of organized government to the surrounding tribes, possibly including the Japanese.

It may seem surprising that Japanese were in Korea in the first century C.E., but there appears to have been no fixed boundary at the time between the territory of the Koreans and that of the Japanese. Very likely there was a fairly steady eastward migration from north of China to the Korean peninsula and thence to the Japanese archipelago. During the third century, the Chinese withdrew from Korea, and the country was divided into three states, Koguryŏ, Paekche, and Silla, and beginning in the fourth century, Japanese periodically fought in Korea, usually siding with Paekche against Koguryŏ and Silla. Japanese historians claim that Japan established a territorial enclave at the tip of the Korean peninsula called Mimana sometime during the fourth century, although nationalistic Korean historians vigorously deny that such an enclave ever existed. Whatever interests the Japanese may have had in Korea were finally destroyed in 562. During the seventh century, Silla, with Chinese aid, subjugated the rival kingdoms of Koguryŏ and Paekche and unified the peninsula. These successes of the combined forces of Silla and Tang China drove the Japanese from the continent into the relative isolation of their islands, an event

---

2. Wa is the Japanese pronunciation. In Chinese, it is Wo.

that may have helped bring about the birth of the historical Japanese state. That is, the rise of powerful dynasties in China and Korea impelled Japan to achieve a unified government in order not to be overwhelmed.

To understand some of the important influences on Japanese thought since earliest times, we turn next to the islands' geographical features. The Chinese account of Japan in the *History of the Latter Han Dynasty* opens with the words "The people of Wa live on mountainous islands in the ocean," and in fact, the two elements of water and mountains, together with a kind of sun worship, have always been very close to the Japanese. Although we are likely to find in any country's religious beliefs a worship of noticeable or beneficial aspects of nature, the combination of these three elements is especially characteristic of Japan. The numerous clear streams and the ever-present ocean have always delighted the Japanese, as we can tell from their earliest poetry. To their love of water the Japanese joined a passion for lustration and cleanliness and, in our own day, for swimming. The Japanese love of mountains is not surprising in a country renowned for its numerous peaks, especially the incomparable Mount Fuji, and the worship of the sun is not unnatural in a country blessed with a temperate climate. Today we can still appreciate what an awe-inspiring experience it must have been for the Japanese of any age to stand on the summit of Mount Fuji and greet the sun as it rose from the waters of the Pacific. Other characteristics of the Japanese recorded in the early Chinese accounts that are still noticeable today include honesty, politeness, gentleness in peace and bravery in war, a love of liquor, and religious rites of purification and divination.

The Japanese accounts of the birth of the gods and of the foundation of their country belong, of course, to the realm of mythology rather than history, but they afford us a glimpse of Japanese attitudes toward the world and nature. Also, since later Japanese attached importance to these legends, some knowledge of them is indispensable to understanding Japanese thought.

JAPAN IN THE CHINESE DYNASTIC HISTORIES

The following extracts are from the official histories of successive Chinese dynasties, beginning with the Latter Han (25–220 C.E.), although the first of these accounts was written for the Kingdom of Wei (220–265) and compiled about 297 C.E.. The *History of the Latter Han* was compiled about 445 and incorporates much from the earlier description of the Japanese.

These accounts are contained in a section devoted to the barbarian neighbors of China at the end of each history. Thus they do not occupy a prominent place in these works, being more in the nature of an afterthought or footnote. Particularly in the earlier accounts, the information is apt to be scattered and disconnected and, not surprisingly, is presented by official chroniclers who viewed Japanese affairs with an eye to Chinese interests and prestige.

Nevertheless, we can discern some of the main outlines of Japan's development in these early centuries. In the first accounts, Japan appears to be a heterogeneous group of communities in contact with China, with one ruling house bidding for Chinese recognition of its supremacy over the others. In one case, the influence of the Chinese ambassador is said to have been the decisive factor in settling a dispute over the succession to the Yamato throne. The kings of Wa, as the Yamato rulers were known, also made strong claims to military supremacy in Korea, which were at times acknowledged by the Chinese court. In the later accounts, the unification of Japan has progressed noticeably. The sovereignty of the Yamato house has been asserted over hitherto autonomous regions, and its government displays many of the trappings of the Chinese imperial structure. On occasion, the Japanese court is rebuked for its pretensions to equality with the Chinese and even for its hinted superiority, as when the Japanese ruler addressed the Chinese, "The Child[3] of Heaven in the land where the sun rises addresses a letter to the Child of Heaven in the land where the sun sets."

ACCOUNTS OF THE EASTERN BARBARIANS

HISTORY OF THE KINGDOM OF WEI (WEI ZHI) CA. 297 C.E.

The people of Wa [Japan] dwell in the middle of the ocean on the mountainous islands southeast of [the prefecture of] Daifang. They formerly comprised more than one hundred communities. During the Han dynasty, [Wa] envoys appeared at the court; today, thirty of their communities maintain intercourse with us through envoys and scribes. . . .

The land of Wa is warm and mild. In winter as in summer the people live on raw vegetables and go about barefooted. They have [or live in] houses; father and mother, elder and younger, sleep separately. They smear their bodies with pink and scarlet, just as the Chinese use powder. They serve food on bamboo and wooden trays, helping themselves with their fingers. When a person dies, they prepare a single coffin, without an outer one. They cover the graves with earth to make a mound. When death occurs, mourning is observed for more than ten days, during which period they do not eat meat. The head mourners wail and lament, while friends sing, dance and drink liquor. When the funeral is over, all members of the family go into the water to cleanse themselves in a bath of purification.

When they go on voyages across the sea to visit China, they always select a man who does not comb his hair, does not rid himself of fleas, lets his clothing get as dirty as it will, does not eat meat, and does not lie with women. This

---

3. The term *tenshi*, usually rendered as "Son of Heaven," is actually gender neutral; here, in the Japanese case, it refers to Empress Suiko.

man behaves like a mourner and is known as the "mourning keeper." When the voyage meets with good fortune, they all lavish on him slaves and other valuables. In case there is disease or mishap, they kill him, saying that he was not scrupulous in observing the taboos. . . .

Whenever they undertake an enterprise or a journey and discussion arises, they bake bones and divine in order to tell whether fortune will be good or bad. First they announce the object of divination, using the same manner of speech as in tortoise shell divination; then they examine the cracks made by fire and tell what is to come to pass.

In their meetings and in their deportment, there is no distinction between father and son or between men and women. They are fond of liquor. In their worship, men of importance simply clap their hands instead of kneeling or bowing. The people live long, some to one hundred and others to eighty or ninety years. Ordinarily, men of importance have four or five wives; the lesser ones, two or three. Women are not loose in morals or jealous. There is no theft, and litigation is infrequent. In case of violations of the law, the light offender loses his wife and children by confiscation; as for the grave offender, the members of his household and also his kinsmen are exterminated. There are class distinctions among the people, and some men are vassals of others. Taxes are collected. There are granaries as well as markets in each province, where necessaries are exchanged under the supervision of the Wa officials. . . .

When the lowly meet men of importance on the road, they stop and withdraw to the roadside. In conveying messages to them or addressing them, they either squat or kneel, with both hands on the ground. This is the way they show respect. When responding, they say "ah," which corresponds to the affirmative "yes."

The country formerly had a man as ruler. For some seventy or eighty years after that there were disturbances and warfare. Thereupon the people agreed upon a woman for their ruler. Her name was Pimiko. She occupied herself with magic and sorcery, bewitching the people. Though mature in age, she remained unmarried. She had a younger brother who assisted her in ruling the country. After she became the ruler, there were few who saw her. She had one thousand women as attendants, but only one man. He served her food and drink and acted as a medium of communication. She resided in a palace surrounded by towers and stockades, with armed guards in a state of constant vigilance. . . .

In the sixth month of the second year of Jingchu [238 C.E.], the Queen of Wa sent the grandee Nashonmi and others to visit the prefecture [of Daifang], where they requested permission to proceed to the Emperor's court with tribute. The Governor, Liu Xia, dispatched an officer to accompany the party to the capital. In answer to the Queen of Wa, an edict of the Emperor, issued in the twelfth month of the same year, said as follows:

Herein we address Pimiko, Queen of Wa, whom we now officially call a
friend of Wei. The Governor of Daifang, Liu Xia, has sent a messenger
to accompany your vassal, Nashonmi, and his lieutenant, Tsushi Gori.
They have arrived here with your tribute, consisting of four male slaves
and six female slaves, together with two pieces of cloth with designs, each
twenty feet in length. You live very far away across the sea; yet you have
sent an embassy with tribute. Your loyalty and filial piety we appreciate
exceedingly. We confer upon you, therefore, the title "Queen of Wa
Friendly to Wei," together with the decoration of the gold seal with purple
ribbon. The latter, properly encased, is to be sent to you through the
Governor. We expect you, O Queen, to rule your people in peace and to
endeavor to be devoted and obedient. . . .

When Pimiko passed away, a great mound was raised, more than a hundred
paces in diameter. Over a hundred male and female attendants followed her to
the grave. Then a king was placed on the throne, but the people would not
obey him. Assassination and murder followed; more than one thousand were
thus slain.

A relative of Pimiko named Iyo, a girl of thirteen, was [then] made queen
and order was restored. Zheng [the Chinese ambassador] issued a proclamation
to the effect that Iyo was the ruler. Then Iyo sent a delegation of twenty under
the grandee Yazaku, General of the Imperial Guard, to accompany Zheng
home [to China]. The delegation visited the capital and presented thirty male
and female slaves. It also offered to the court five thousand white gems and two
pieces of carved jade, as well as twenty pieces of brocade with variegated designs.

[Adapted from Tsunoda and Goodrich, *Japan in the Chinese
Dynastic Histories*, pp. 8–16]

HISTORY OF THE LATTER HAN DYNASTY (*HOU HAN SHU*)
CA. 445 C.E.

The Wa dwell on mountainous islands southeast of Han [Korea] in the middle
of the ocean, forming more than one hundred communities. From the time of
the overthrow of Chaoxian [northern Korea] by Emperor Wu [r. 140–87 B.C.E.],
nearly thirty of these communities have held intercourse with the Han (Chinese) court by envoys or scribes. Each community has its king, whose office is
hereditary. The King of Great Wa resides in the country of Yamadai. . . .

In the second year of the Jianwu Zhongyuan era [57 C.E.], the Wa country
Nu sent an envoy with tribute who called himself *Dafu*. This country is located
in the southern extremity of the Wa country. Emperor Guangwu bestowed on
him a seal. . . .

During the reigns of Huandi [147–168] and Lingdi [168–189] the country of

Wa was in a state of great confusion, war and conflict raging on all sides. For a number of years, there was no ruler. Then a woman named Pimiko appeared. Remaining unmarried, she occupied herself with magic and sorcery and bewitched the populace. Thereupon they placed her on the throne. She kept one thousand female attendants, but few people saw her. There was only one man who was in charge of her wardrobe and meals and acted as the medium of communication. She resided in a palace surrounded by towers and stockade, with the protection of armed guards. The laws and customs were strict and stern.

[Tsunoda and Goodrich, *Japan in the Chinese Dynastic Histories*, pp. 1–3]

HISTORY OF THE LIU SONG DYNASTY (*SONGSHU*) CA. 513 C.E.

The following extract is preceded by an account of four successive Japanese rulers who asked to be confirmed in their titles by the Chinese court. One of these titles was "Generalissimo Who Maintains Peace in the East Commanding with Battle-Ax All Military Affairs in the Six Countries of Wa, Paekche, Silla, Imna, Jinhan and Mok-han." Wa refers to Japan, and the other five names to states comprising most of the Korean peninsula. On at least two occasions in the fifth century, the Chinese court, while accepting the fealty of the Japanese "king," confirmed his claim to military supremacy in Korea.

Kō died and his brother, Bu,[4] came to the throne. Bu, signing himself King of Wa, Generalissimo Who Maintains Peace in the East Commanding with Battle-Ax All Military Affairs in the Seven Countries of Wa, Paekche, Silla, Imna, Kala, Jinhan and Mok-han, in the second year of Shengming, Shunti's reign [478], sent an envoy bearing a memorial which reads as follows: "Our land is remote and distant; its domains lie far out in the ocean. From of old our forebears have clad themselves in armor and helmet and gone across the hills and waters, sparing no time for rest. In the east, they conquered fifty-five countries of hairy men; and in the west, they brought to their knees sixty-six countries of various barbarians. Crossing the sea to the north, they subjugated ninety-five countries. The way of government is to keep harmony and peace; thus order is established in the land. Generation after generation, without fail, our forebears have paid homage to the court. Our subject, ignorant though he is, is succeeding to the throne of his predecessors and is fervently devoted to your Sovereign Majesty. Everything he commands is at your imperial disposal. In order to go by the way of Paekche, far distant though it is, we prepared ships and boats. Koguryŏ,[5] however, in defiance of law, schemed to capture them. Borders were

---

4. Yūryaku, 456–479.
5. A state in northern Korea.

raided, and murder was committed repeatedly. Consequently we were delayed every time and missed favorable winds. We attempted to push on, but when the way was clear, Koguryŏ was rebellious. My deceased father became indignant at the marauding foe who blocked our way to the sovereign court. Urged on by a sense of justice, he gathered together a million archers and was about to launch a great campaign. But because of the death of my father and brother, the plan that had been matured could not be carried out at the last moment. Mourning required the laying down of arms. Inaction does not bring victory. Now, however, we again set our armor in array and carry out the wish of our elders. The fighting men are in high mettle; civil and military officials are ready; none have fear of sword or fire.

"Your Sovereign virtue extends over heaven and earth. If through it we can crush this foe and put an end to our troubles, we shall ever continue loyally to serve [Your Majesty]. I therefore beg you to appoint me as supreme commander of the campaign, with the status of minister, and to grant to others [among my followers] ranks and titles, so that loyalty may be encouraged."

By imperial edict, Bu was made King of Wa and Generalissimo Who Maintains Peace in the East Commanding with Battle-Ax All Military Affairs in the Six Countries of Wa, Silla, Imna, Kala, Jinhan and Mok-han.

[Tsunoda and Goodrich, *Japan in the Chinese Dynastic Histories*, pp. 23–24]

HISTORY OF THE SUI DYNASTY (*SUI SHU*) CA. 630 C.E.

During the twenty years of the Kaihuang era (581–600), the King of Wa, whose family name was Ame and personal name Tarishihoko, and who bore the title of Ahakomi, sent an envoy to visit the court. The Emperor ordered the appropriate official to make inquiries about the manners and customs [of the Wa people]. The envoy reported thus: "The King of Wa deems Heaven to be his elder brother and the sun, his younger.[6] Before break of dawn he attends the court, and, sitting cross-legged, listens to appeals. Just as soon as the sun rises, he ceases these duties, saying that he hands them over to his brother." Our just Emperor said that such things were extremely senseless,[7] and he admonished [the King of Wa] to alter [his ways].

[According to the envoy's report], the King's spouse is called Kemi. Several hundred women are kept in the inner chambers of the court. The heir apparent

---

6. At variance with the later claim of the imperial line to be descended from the Sun Goddess.

7. According to Chinese tradition, a virtuous ruler showed his conscientiousness by attending to matters of state the first thing in the morning. Apparently the Japanese emperor was carrying this to a ridiculous extreme by disposing of state business before dawn.

is known as Rikamitahori. There is no special palace. There are twelve grades of court officials. . . .

There are about one hundred thousand households. It is customary to punish murder, arson and adultery with death. Thieves are made to make restitution in accordance with the value of the goods stolen. If the thief has no property with which to make payment, he is taken to be a slave. Other offenses are punished according to their nature—sometimes by banishment and sometimes by flogging. In the prosecution of offenses by the court, the knees of those who plead not guilty are pressed together by placing them between pieces of wood, or their heads are sawed with the stretched string of a strong bow. Sometimes pebbles are put in boiling water and both parties to a dispute made to pick them out. The hand of the guilty one is said to become inflamed. Sometimes a snake is kept in a jar, and the accused ordered to catch it. If he is guilty, his hand will be bitten. The people are gentle and peaceful. Litigation is infrequent and theft seldom occurs.

As for musical instruments, they have five-stringed lyres and flutes. Both men and women paint marks on their arms and spots on their faces and have their bodies tattooed. They catch fish by diving into the water. They have no written characters and understand only the use of notched sticks and knotted ropes. They revere Buddha and obtained Buddhist scriptures from Paekche. This was the first time that they came into possession of written characters. They are familiar with divination and have profound faith in shamans, both male and female. . . .

Both Silla and Paekche consider Wa to be a great country, replete with precious things, and they pay her homage. Envoys go back and forth from time to time.

In the third year of Daye [607], King Tarishihoko sent an envoy to the court with tribute. The envoy said: "The King[8] has heard that to the west of the ocean a Bodhisattva of the Sovereign reveres and promotes Buddhism. For that reason he has sent an embassy to pay his respects. Accompanying the embassy are several tens of monks who have come to study Buddhism." [The envoy brought] an official message which read: "The Child of Heaven in the land where the sun rises addresses a letter to the Child of Heaven in the land where the sun sets. We hope you are in good health." When the Emperor saw this letter, he was displeased[9] and told the official in charge of foreign affairs that this letter from the barbarians was discourteous, and that such a letter should not again be brought to his attention.

[Tsunoda and Goodrich, *Japan in the Chinese Dynastic Histories*, pp. 229–232]

---

8. Actually, in 607, Empress Suiko.

9. Because of the presumptuousness of the Japanese ruler in claiming the title of Child of Heaven, to be on a par with the Chinese emperor.

NEW HISTORY OF THE TANG DYNASTY (*XIN TANG SHU*)[10]

Japan in former times was called Wa-nu. It is 24,000 *li* distant from our capital, situated to the southeast of Silla in the middle of the ocean. It is five months' journey to cross Japan from east to west and a three months' journey from south to north. There are no castles or stockades in that country, only high walls built by placing timbers together. The roofs are thatched with grass. There are over fifty islets there, each with a name of its own but all under the sovereignty of Japan. A high official is stationed to have surveillance over these communities.

As for the inhabitants, the women outnumber the men. The people are literate and revere the teachings of Buddha. In the government there are twelve official ranks. The family name of the King is Ame. The Japanese say that from their first ruler, known as Ame-no-minaka-nushi, to Hikonagi, there were altogether thirty-two generations of rulers, all bearing the title of *mikoto* and residing in the palace of Tsukushi. Upon the enthronement of Jinmu, son of Hikonagi, the title was changed to *tennō*[11] and the palace was moved to the province of Yamato. . . .

In the fifth year of Zhenguan [631], the Japanese sent an embassy to pay a visit to the court. In appreciation of this visit from such a distance, the sovereign gave orders to the official concerned not to insist on yearly tribute. . . .

At this time, Silla was being harassed by Koguryŏ and Paekche. Emperor Gao Zong sent a sealed rescript to Japan ordering the King to send reinforcements to succor Silla. But after a short time, King Kōtoku died [654] and his son Ame-no-toyo-takara was enthroned. Then he also died, and his son Tenchi was enthroned. In the following year [663] an envoy came to the court accompanied by some Ainus. The Ainus also dwell on those islands. The beards of the Ainus were four feet long. They carried arrows at their necks, and without ever missing would shoot a gourd held on the head of a person standing several tens of steps away.

Then Tenchi died [671] and his son, Tenmu, came to the throne. He died, and his son Sōji was enthroned.[12]

In the first year of Xianheng [670] an embassy came to the court from Japan to offer congratulations upon the conquest of Koguryŏ. About this time, the Japanese who had studied Chinese came to dislike the name Wa and changed it to Nippon. According to the words of the Japanese envoy himself, that name

---

10. Compiled in the eleventh century on the basis of earlier materials relating to the Tang dynasty (618–906).

11. Still the title of Japanese emperors but applied anachronistically to earlier rulers of the claimed imperial line.

12. Actually Tenmu was succeeded by a daughter of Tenchi known as Empress Jitō (686–697).

was chosen because the country was so close to where the sun rises. Some say [on the other hand], that Nippon was a small country which had been subjugated by the Wa, and that the latter took over its name. As this envoy was not truthful, doubt still remains. Besides the envoy was boastful, and he said that the domains of his country were many thousands of square *li* and extended to the ocean on the south and on the west. In the northeast, he said, the country was bordered by mountain ranges beyond which lay the land of the hairy men.

[Tsunoda and Goodrich, *Japan in the Chinese Dynastic Histories*, pp. 38–40]

THE EARLIEST JAPANESE CHRONICLES

The great native chronicles of early Japan, the *Records of Ancient Matters* (*Kojiki*) and the *Chronicles of Japan* (*Nihongi*), were completed as late as the first decades of the eighth century C.E., when Japanese writers were already strongly influenced by Chinese traditions.[13] It is therefore difficult to distinguish any pure native traditions in these works, nor are they fully reliable as accounts of Japan's early history. Many of the events described are anachronistic, and many of the legends are selected with a view to confirming the religious or political claims of the ruling dynasty. The emphasis on ancestry is already quite apparent, although other evidence indicates that family genealogies were in a very confused state before the introduction of writing and the Chinese practice of compiling genealogical records (see chapter 4).

The following excerpts from translations by Chamberlain and Aston were selected to show what seem to be the most unsystematic and unsophisticated of legends dealing with the age of the gods and the creation of the land. In contrast to the founding myths of the Confucian *Classic of Documents* (*Shujing*), which focus on the sage-kings as the founders of civilization and culture heroes, the focus of attention here is on the creative role of numerous gods in the formation of many islands. Again in contrast to the Chinese classic account, which is unicentered and projects a single moral and political authority, the Japanese mythic world is polytheistic, polycentric, nature oriented, and alive with an almost ungovernable spiritual élan, riotous creativity, and irrepressible fertility.

BIRTH OF THE LAND

Before the land was created, there were twelve deities, whose "forms were not visible." Izanami and Izanagi were the last of these, not the first, but they were directed by the

---

13. Footnotes to translations from the *Kojiki* and *Nihongi*, unless otherwise identified, are those of Chamberlain and Aston, respectively, in some cases abbreviated or adapted to the usage in this text.

other deities in concert to solidify the drifting flotsam and jetsam on the sea to shape the land. In the subsequent profusion of creativity, many islands and regions were formed, each reflecting the Japanese people's strong sense of place and pluralism.

Izanagi and Izanami stood on the floating bridge of Heaven and held counsel together, saying, "Is there not a country beneath?" Thereupon they thrust down the jewel-spear of Heaven[14] and, groping about therewith, found the ocean. The brine which dripped from the point of the spear coagulated and became an island which received the name of Ono-goro-jima.

The two deities thereupon descended and dwelt in this island. Accordingly they wished to become husband and wife together, and to produce countries.

So they made Ono-goro-jima the pillar of the center of the land.

Now the male deity turning by the left and the female deity by the right, they went round the pillar of the land separately. When they met together on one side, the female deity spoke first and said, "How delightful! I have met with a lovely youth." The male deity was displeased and said, "I am a man, and by right should have spoken first. How is it that on the contrary thou, a woman, shouldst have been the first to speak? This was unlucky. Let us go round again." Upon this the two deities went back, and having met anew, this time the male deity spoke first and said, "How delightful! I have met a lovely maiden."

Then he inquired of the female deity, saying, "In the body is there aught formed?"

She answered and said, "In my body there is a place which is the source of femininity." The male deity said, "In my body again there is a place which is the source of masculinity. I wish to unite this source-place of my body to the source-place of thy body." Hereupon the male and female first became united as husband and wife.

Now when the time of birth arrived, first of all the island of Ahaji was reckoned as the placenta, and their minds took no pleasure in it. Therefore it received the name of Ahaji no Shima.[15]

Next there was produced the island of Ō-yamato no Toyo-aki-tsu-shima.[16] (Here and elsewhere [the characters for Nippon] are to be read Yamato.)[17]

---

14. Considered by some commentators to resemble a phallus. Compare Aston, *Nihongi*, I, p. 10.

15. "The island which will not meet"; that is, it is unsatisfactory. Ahaji may also be interpreted as "my shame." The characters with which this name is written in the text mean "foam-road." Perhaps the true derivation is "millet-land."

16. Rich-harvest (or autumn) island of Yamato.

17. Yamato probably means "mountain gate." It is the genuine ancient name for the province containing Nara and many of the other early capitals of Japan, and it was also used for the whole country. Several emperors called themselves *yamato-neko*, and it is mentioned by the historian of the Later Han dynasty of China (23–220 B.C.E.) as the seat of rule in Japan at that time.

Next they produced the island of Iyo no futa-na[18] and next the island of Tsukushi.[19] Next the islands of Oki and Sado were born as twins. This is the prototype of the twin-births which sometimes take place among mankind.

Next was born the island of Koshi,[20] then the island of Ō-shima, then the island of Kibi no Ko.[21]

Hence first arose the designation of the Great Eight-Island Country.

Then the islands of Tsushima and Iki, with the small islands in various parts, were produced by the coagulation of the foam of the salt-water.

[Adapted from Aston, *Nihongi*, I, pp. 10–14]

PREFACE TO *RECORDS OF ANCIENT MATTERS* (*KOJIKI*)

This preface, from the earlier *Kojiki*, continues the mythic account to the founding of the imperial line.

Now when chaos[22] had begun to condense but force and form were not yet manifest and there was nought named, nought done, who could know its shape? Nevertheless Heaven and Earth first parted, and the Three Deities performed the commencement of creation; yin and yang then developed; and the Two Spirits [Izanagi and Izanami] became the ancestors of all things. Therefore with [Izanagi's] entering obscurity and emerging into light, the sun and moon were revealed by the washing of his eyes; he floated on and plunged into the sea-water, and heavenly and earthly deities appeared through the ablutions of his person. So in the dimness of the great commencement, we, by relying on the original teaching, learn the time of the conception of the earth and of the birth of islands; in the remoteness of the original beginning, we, by trusting the former sages, perceive the era of the genesis of deities and of the establishment of men. Truly we do know that a mirror was hung up, that jewels were spat out, and that then a hundred kings succeeded each other; that a blade was bitten and a serpent cut in pieces, so that myriad deities did flourish. By deliberations in the Tranquil River the empire was pacified; by discussions on the Little Shore the land was purified. Wherefore His Augustness Ho-no-ni-ni-gi[23] first descended to the Peak of Takachi, and the Heavenly Sovereign Kamu-Yamato[24]

---

18. Now called Shikoku.

19. Now called Kyushu.

20. Koshi is not an island but comprises the present provinces of Etchū, Echigo, and Echizen.

21. These two are not clear. Kibi is now Bingo, Bizen, and Bitchū. Ko, "child" or "small," perhaps refers to the small islands of the Inland Sea.

22. The primordial state of nondifferentiation and dispersion.

23. The abbreviated form of the name of the Sun Goddess's grandson.

24. That is, the first "human emperor," Jinmu.

did traverse the Island of the Dragon-Fly.[25] A weird bear put forth its claws, and a heavenly saber was obtained at Takakura. They with tails obstructed the path, and a great crow guided him to Eshinu. Dancing in rows they destroyed the brigands, and listening to a song they vanquished the foeman. Being instructed in a dream, he was reverent to the heavenly and earthly deities and was therefore styled the Wise Monarch;[26] having gazed on the smoke, he was benevolent to the black-haired people,[27] and is therefore remembered as the Emperor-Sage.[28] Determining the frontiers and civilizing the country, he issued laws from the Nearer Afumi;[29] reforming the surnames and selecting the gentile names, he held sway at the Farther Asuka.[30] Though each differed in caution and in ardor, though all were unlike in accomplishments and in intrinsic worth, yet was there none who did not by contemplating antiquity correct manners that had fallen to ruin and, by illumining modern times, repair laws that were approaching dissolution.[31]

[Adapted from Chamberlain, *Ko-ji-ki*, pp. 4–7]

---

25. That is, Japan.

26. "Emperor Sūjin" must be mentally supplied as the logical subject of this clause.

27. Chinese term for the people of China, which is applied here to the Japanese.

28. That is, Emperor Nintoku.

29. That is, Emperor Seimu.

30. That is, Emperor Ingyō.

31. Characteristics of the Chinese sage-kings that are hardly appropriate here.

Chapter 2

EARLY SHINTO

From the early days of the opening of Japan, Western scholars, intrigued by what they imagined to be the indigenous nature of Shinto, have devoted considerable attention to this religion. By the turn of the twentieth century, scholars from many Western nations were studying what has been termed the "national faith of Japan" in the hope of discovering in it an explanation of Japanese characteristics long obscured to foreigners by the country's self-imposed isolation. Strictly speaking, however, Shinto is not a purely indigenous religion, for it shares continental features and absorbed foreign elements from earliest times. Thus it is both native and hybrid. Shamanistic and animistic practices similar to those of Shinto, which seem to spring from some earlier common religious ground, have been found throughout northeast Asia, especially Korea.

Shinto had diverse origins and remained an aggregate of heterogeneous cults well into historical times. Its failure to develop into a unified religion can be largely attributed to Japan's natural features and the people's strong sense of regionalism. That is, the numerous tribal communities living in the river basins held to their own beliefs even after the unified control of the central government began to be felt early in the seventh century.

The objects of worship in all Shinto cultures were known as *kami*, a term for which it is difficult to find a translation. A famous student of Shinto, Motoori Norinaga (1730–1801), wrote:

I do not yet understand the meaning of the term *kami*. Speaking in general, however, it may be said that *kami* signifies, in the first place, the deities of heaven and earth that appear in the ancient records and also the spirits of the shrines where they are worshiped.

It is hardly necessary to say that it includes human beings. It also includes such objects as birds, beasts, trees, plants, seas, mountains and so forth. In ancient usage, anything whatsoever which was outside the ordinary, which possessed superior power, or which was awe-inspiring was called *kami*. Eminence here does not refer merely to the superiority of nobility, goodness or meritorious deeds. Evil and mysterious things, if they are extraordinary and dreadful, are called *kami*. It is needless to say that among human beings who are called *kami* the successive generations of sacred emperors are all included. The fact that emperors are also called "distant *kami*" is because, from the standpoint of common people, they are far-separated, majestic and worthy of reverence. In a lesser degree we find, in the present as well as in ancient times, human beings who are *kami*. Although they may not be accepted throughout the whole country, yet in each province, each village and each family there are human beings who are *kami*, each one according to his own proper position. The *kami* of the divine age were for the most part human beings of that time and, because the people of that time were all *kami*, it is called the Age of the Gods (*kami*).[1]

Primitive Shinto embraced cults of diverse origins, including animism, shamanism, fertility cults, and the worship of nature, ancestors, and heroes. Over time, the distinctions among these various cults gradually disappeared. The Sun Goddess, for instance, became the chief deity not only of nature worshipers but of ancestor worshipers as well. She was also considered to be the dispenser of fertility and of the fortunes of the nation. Similarly, an object of animistic worship could assume the role of a fertility god or shamanistic deity or even pose as the ancestor of the land on which a community lived. Before Shinto could become the "national faith" of Japan, however, it had to be successively bolstered by the philosophical and religious concepts of Han Confucianism, Esoteric Buddhism, Neo-Confucianism, and, finally, Christianity. The forms of these influences will be discussed in later chapters. In the early period with which we are concerned here, Shinto was still a primitive and almost inarticulate group of cults.

The oldest center of Shinto worship was the Izumo Shrine on the Japan Sea coast, which was close to the Korean peninsula and by way of which continental civilization reached Japan. The Kashima and Katori Shrines in the Tone River

---

1. Holtom, *The National Faith of Japan*, pp. 23–24.

basin to the north for a long time marked the frontier between the lands of the Japanese and those of less civilized inhabitants. The shrine at Ise, that of the Sun Goddess, came to be the most important, and it was there that various symbols of the imperial power were displayed.

The buildings of the shrines were architecturally very simple, generally consisting of a single room (which was sometimes partitioned) raised off the ground and entered by steps at the side or front. The building was invariably made of wood, with whole tree trunks used for beams. A mirror, sword, or other form of "god embodiment" (*shintai*) might be enshrined within, but often the building served merely as a place where the *kami*, visible or invisible, could be worshiped.

Outside the shrine's main building, two other architectural features usually are found, a gateway called a *torii* and a water basin where worshipers could wash their mouth and hands. Indeed, the characteristic Japanese insistence on cleanliness finds its expression in many forms, and two important acts of worship at Shinto shrines, the *harai* and the *misogi*, reflect this tendency. The former apparently originated in the airing of the cave or pit dwellings of prehistoric times and came to refer to both the sweeping out of a house and the special rites of chasing out evil spirits. The latter refers to the washing of the body, an act of increasingly spiritual significance. In addition to these formal acts of religion, formulas, prayers, and ritual practices were associated with almost all human activities (but especially the arts and crafts), whereby divine power was invoked to ensure success.

Worship at a Shinto shrine consisted of "attendance" and "offering." Attendance meant not only being present and giving one's attention to the object of worship but often also performing ceremonial dances or joining in processions, which have always been an important part of Shinto ritual. The offerings usually consisted of the firstborn of a household, the first fruits of the season, or the first catch from the water but might also include booty of war, such as the heads of enemies. The shrine was in the charge of a medium who transmitted messages from both the *kami* and the political rulers. The mediums were assisted by "supplicators"—the general term for officers of the shrine—and ablutioners. Some of the texts of the prayers and rituals of this early time have been preserved and often are beautiful, with a simplicity characteristic of Shinto.

LEGENDS CONCERNING SHINTO DEITIES

There is virtually no documentary evidence to indicate the original character of Shinto belief. Before the introduction of Chinese writing and Chinese ideas, the Japanese were unable to record their religious beliefs, and there is little reason to believe that they had produced an articulate body of doctrine or dogma. The legends in the *Kojiki* and *Nihongi*, often cited as containing the original deposit of Shinto folklore, are late compilations in which political considerations and specifically Chinese conceptions intrude themselves almost everywhere. This intrusion was recognized by the great Neo-Shinto scholars of the eighteenth and nineteenth centuries who tried almost in vain to find in these texts any evidence of pure Japanese beliefs. Elements of Chinese cosmology are most apparent in rationalistic passages explaining the origin of the world in terms of the yin and yang principles, which seem to come directly from Chinese works such as the *Huainanzi*. The prevalence of paired male and female deities such as Izanagi and Izanami may also be the result of conscious selection with the yin and yang principles in mind. Also, the frequency of numerical sets of deities, such as the Five Heavenly Deities of the *Kojiki* and the Seven Generations of Heavenly Deities of the *Nihongi*, may represent an attempt at selection and organization in terms of a Chinese cosmological series, in this case the Five Elements and the Seven Heavenly Luminaries.

Chapter 1 showed us the strong sense of place in early myth and the special preoccupation with the creation of the Japanese islands. Since the first histories were produced in an era when the Yamato house was asserting its hegemony over other communities, the historians, writing at their ruler's direction, naturally were concerned with establishing the dynasty's bid for sovereignty, which they based on genealogy, claiming descent from the gods. Because we have little besides these official accounts to go by, it is easy to understand how these dynastic myths came to dominate the scene. However, even passages meant to assert dynastic supremacy or that became systematized along this line betray the existence of diverse and competing cults or inadvertently reveal traditional attitudes and practices taken for granted by all. Note, too, in the following excerpts that the names of deities and semidivine beings are composed of vivid images from nature and that often their activities suggest a concern with fertility, ritual purification, ancestor or hero worship, and animism.

BIRTH OF THE SUN GODDESS

In this account from the *Nihongi*, the Sun Goddess, Amaterasu, is identified not as the first of the gods or the creator of the world but simply as the Sun Maiden or Sun Princess, one among the many offspring of the primal pair Izanagi and Izanami.

Izanagi no Mikoto and Izanami no Mikoto consulted together saying, "We have now produced the great-eight-island country, with the mountains, rivers, herbs, and trees. Why should we not produce someone who shall be lord of the universe?" They then together produced the Sun Goddess, who was called Ō-hiru-me no muchi.[2]

---

2. Great-noon-[sun] maiden-of-possessor.

(Called in one writing Amaterasu no Ō-hiru-me no muchi.)[3]

(In one writing she is called Amaterasu-ō-hiru-me no Mikoto.)[4]

The resplendent luster of this child shone throughout all the six quarters.[5] Therefore the two deities rejoiced saying, "We have had many children, but none of them have been equal to this wondrous infant. She ought not to be kept long in this land, but we ought of our own accord to send her at once to Heaven and entrust to her the affairs of Heaven."

At this time Heaven and Earth were still not far separated, and therefore they sent her up to Heaven by the ladder of Heaven.

They next produced the Moon-god.

(Called in one writing Tsuki-yumi[6] no Mikoto or Tsuki-yomi no Mikoto.)

His radiance was next to that of the Sun in splendor. This god was to be the consort of the Sun Goddess and to share in her government. They therefore sent him also to Heaven.

Next they produced the leech child, which even at the age of three years could not stand upright. They therefore placed it in the rock-camphor-wood boat of Heaven and abandoned it to the winds.

Their next child was Susa no o no Mikoto.[7]

(Called in one writing Kami Susa-no-o no Mikoto or Haya Susa-no-o no Mikoto.)[8]

This god had a fierce temper and was given to cruel acts. Moreover he made a practice of continually weeping and wailing. So he brought many of the people of the land to an untimely end. Again he caused green mountains to become withered. Therefore the two gods, his parents, addressed Susa-no-o no Mikoto, saying, "Thou art exceedingly wicked, and it is not meet that thou shouldst reign over the world. Certainly thou must depart far away to the Nether-land." So they at length expelled him.

[Adapted from Aston, *Nihongi*, I, pp. 18–20]

THE DIVINE CREATION OF THE IMPERIAL ANCESTORS

In the following excerpt from the *Kojiki*, notice that the divine offspring from which the imperial line is traced were the joint creation of Amaterasu, the Sun Goddess, and

---

3. Heaven-illumine-of-great-noon-maiden-deity.

4. Heaven-illumine-great-noon-maiden-of-augustness.

5. North, south, east, west, above, below.

6. *Yumi* means "bow"; *yomi*, "darkness." Neither is inappropriate as applied to the moon.

7. Better known as Susa-no-o, a god particularly associated with the Izumo people, who was probably relegated to a subordinate role when these people were displaced or eclipsed in power by the Yamato group.

8. *Kami*, "deity"; *haya*, "quick."

Susa-no-o, the unruly storm god. They were produced from the mouth of Susa-no-o after he had chewed up Amaterasu's ornaments, but she claimed them as her own on the ground that the seed or stuff of which they were made came from her. Thus the ordinary male and female functions are reversed in establishing the genetic relationship, which gives priority to the Sun Goddess but suggests the absorption of Susa-no-o's power into the imperial line.

So thereupon His-Swift-Impetuous-Male-Augustness (Susa-no-o) said, "If that be so, I will take leave of the Heaven-Shining-Great-August-Deity (Amaterasu)[9] and depart." [With these words] he forthwith went up to Heaven, whereupon all the mountains and rivers shook, and every land and country quaked. So the Heaven-Shining-Deity, alarmed at the noise, said: "The reason of the ascent hither of His Augustness my elder brother is surely no good intent. It is only that he wished to wrest my land from me." And she forthwith, unbinding her august hair, twisted it into august bunches; and both into the left and into the right august bunch, as likewise into her august head-dress and likewise on to her left and her right august arm, she twisted an augustly complete [string] of curved jewels eight feet [long] of five hundred jewels; and slinging on her back a quiver holding a thousand [arrows], and adding [thereto] a quiver holding five hundred [arrows], she likewise took and slung at her side a mighty and high [-sounding] elbow-pad and brandished and stuck her bow upright so that the top shook; and she stamped her feet into the hard ground up to her opposing thighs, kicking away [the earth] like rotten snow and stood valiantly like unto a mighty man, and waiting, asked: "Wherefore ascendest thou hither?" Then Susa-no-o replied, saying: "I have no evil intent. It is only that when the Great-August-Deity [our father] spoke, deigning to inquire the cause of my wailing and weeping, I said: 'I wail because I wish to go to my deceased mother's land'; whereupon the Great-August-Deity said: 'Thou shalt not dwell in this land' and deigned to expel me with a divine expulsion. It is therefore, solely with the thought of taking leave of thee and departing, that I have ascended hither. I have no strange intentions." Then the Heaven-Shining-Deity said: "If that be so, whereby shall I know the sincerity of thine intentions?" Thereupon Susa-no-o replied, saying: "Let each of us swear, and produce children." So as they then swore to each other from the opposite banks of the Tranquil River of Heaven, the august names of the deities that were born from the mist [of her breath] when, having first begged Susa-no-o to hand her the ten-grasp saber which was girded on him and broken it into three fragments, and with the jewels making a jingling sound having brandished and washed them in the

---

9. In the following, the names of deities appearing frequently in these accounts are standardized and given an abbreviated translation or transliteration in place of the full title.

True-Pool-Well of Heaven, and having crunchingly crunched them, the Heaven-Shining-Deity blew them away, were Her Augustness Torrent-Mist-Princess, another august name for whom is Her Augustness Princess-of-the-Island-of-the-Offing; next Her Augustness Lovely-Island-Princess, another august name for whom is Her Augustness Good-Princess; next Her Augustness Princess-of-the-Torrent. The august name of the deity that was born from the mist [of his breath] when, having begged the Heaven-Shining-Deity to hand him the augustly complete [string] of curved jewels eight feet [long] of five hundred jewels that was twisted in the left august bunch [of her hair], and with the jewels making a jingling sound having brandished and washed them in the True-Pool-Well of Heaven, and having crunchingly crunched them, Susa-no-o blew them away, was His Augustness Truly-Conqueror-I-Conquer-Conquering-Swift-Heavenly-Great-Great-Ears. The august name of the Deity that was born from the mist [of his breath] when again, having begged her to hand him the jewels that were twisted in her august head-dress, and having crunchingly crunched them, he blew them away, was His Augustness Prince-Lord-of-Heaven. The august name of the deity that was born from the mist [of his breath] when again, having begged her to hand him the jewels that were twisted on her left august arm, and having crunchingly crunched them, he blew them away, was His Augustness Prince-Lord-of-Life. The august name of the deity that was born from the jewels that were twisted on her right august arm, and having crunchingly crunched them, he blew them away, was His-Wondrous-Augustness-of-Kumanu [five deities in all].

Hereupon the Heaven-Shining-Deity said to Susa-no-o: "As for the seed of the five male deities born last, their birth was from things of mine; so undoubtedly they are my children. As for the seed of the three female deities born first, their birth was from a thing of thine; so doubtless they are thy children." Thus did she declare the division.

[Adapted from Chamberlain, *Ko-ji-ki*, pp. 45–59]

LEGENDS CONCERNING SUSA-NO-O

The part of Amaterasu's unruly brother Susa-no-o in creating the imperial line has been described. His other activities are of interest because they reflect the importance of regional cults incorporated into the Yamato system of Shinto. After his banishment from Heaven, Susa-no-o is reported in one account to have gone to Korea, an indication that the gods' activities were no more limited to Japan than were those of the people themselves. In any case, this black sheep of the gods settled in Izumo, where he married the local princess and rid the land of a dreaded serpent, in whose body was found the Great Sword, which became one of the Three Imperial Regalia (another of the regalia, a curved stone or jewel, is produced in both Izumo and Korea).

SUSA-NO-O AND THE SUN GODDESS

After this Susa-no-o no Mikoto's behavior was exceedingly rude. In what way? Amaterasu [the Heaven-Shining-Deity] had made august rice fields of Heavenly narrow rice fields and Heavenly long rice fields. Then Susa-no-o, when the seed was sown in spring, broke down the divisions between the plots of rice and in autumn let loose the Heavenly piebald colts and made them lie down in the midst of the rice fields. Again, when he saw that Amaterasu was about to cele-brate the feast of first fruits, he secretly voided excrement in the New[10] Palace. Moreover, when he saw that Amaterasu was in her sacred[11] weaving hall, en-gaged in weaving garments of the gods, he flayed a piebald colt of Heaven and, breaking a hole in the roof tiles of the hall, flung it in. Then Amaterasu started with alarm and wounded herself with the shuttle. Indignant of this, she straight-way entered the Rock-cave of Heaven and, having fastened the Rock-door, dwelt there in seclusion. Therefore constant darkness prevailed on all sides, and the alternation of night and day was unknown.

Then the eighty myriads of gods met on the bank of the Tranquil River of Heaven and considered in what manner they should supplicate her. Accord-ingly Omoi-kane[12] no kami, with profound device and far-reaching thought, at length gathered long-singing birds[13] of the Eternal Land and made them utter their prolonged cry to one another. Moreover he made Ta-jikara-o[14] to stand beside the Rock-door. Then Ame no Koyane no Mikoto, ancestor of the Nak-atomi deity chieftains,[15] and Futo-dama no Mikoto,[16] ancestor of the Imibe[17] chieftains, dug up a five-hundred branched True Sakaki[18] tree of the Heavenly

---

10. For the sake of greater purity in celebrating the festival.

11. The Chinese character translated here as "sacred" has the primary meaning of "abstinence, fasting." In the *Nihongi*, however, it represents avoidance, especially the religious avoidance of impurity.

12. "Thought combining" or "thought including."

13. That is, roosters.

14. Hand-strength-male.

15. Nakatomi probably means "ministers of the middle," mediating between the gods and the emperor and the emperor and the people. In historical times, their duties were of a priestly character. Worship and government were closely associated in ancient times in more countries than Japan. *Matsurigoto*, "government," is derived from *matsuri*, "worship." It was the Nakatomi who recited the Harai or purification rituals. Here the Nakatomi stand for the Fujiwara and their hereditary claim to the prime ministership.

16. *Futo-dama*, "big jewel."

17. Imi-be or imbe is derived from *imi*, the root of *imu*, "to avoid, to shun, to practice religious abstinence," and *be*, "a hereditary corporation."

18. The *sakaki*, or *Cleyera japonica*, is the sacred tree of the Shinto religion and is still used in Shinto religious ceremonies.

Mount Kagu.[19] On its upper branches they hung an august five-hundred string of Yasaka jewels. On the middle branches they hung an eight-hand mirror.[20] . . . On its lower branches they hung blue soft offerings and white soft offerings. They recited their liturgy together.

Moreover Ame no Uzume[21] no Mikoto, ancestress of the Sarume[22] chieftain, took in her hand a spear wreathed with Eulalia grass and, standing before the door of the Rock-cave of Heaven, skillfully performed a mimic dance.[23] She took, moreover, the true Sakaki tree of the Heavenly Mount Kagu and made of it a head-dress; she took club-moss and made of it braces; she kindled fires; she placed a tub bottom upwards[24] and gave forth a divinely inspired utterance.

Now Amaterasu heard this and said, "Since I have shut myself up in the Rock-cave, there ought surely to be continual night in the Central Land of fertile reed-plains. How then can Ame no Uzume no Mikoto be so jolly?" So with her august hand, she opened for a narrow space the Rock-door and peeped out. Then Ta-jikara-o no kami forthwith took Amaterasu by the hand and led her out. Upon this the gods Nakatomi no Kami and Imibe no Kami[25] at once drew a limit by means of a bottom-tied rope[26] (also called a left-hand rope) and begged her not to return again [into the cave].

After this all the gods put the blame on Susa-no-o and imposed on him a fine of one thousand tables[27] and so at length chastised him. They also had his hair plucked out and made him therewith expiate his guilt.

[Adapted from Aston, *Nihongi*, I, pp. 40–45]

SUSA-NO-O IN IZUMO

So, having been expelled, Susa-no-o descended to a place [called] Torikami at the head-waters of the River Hi in the land of Izumo. At this time some chopsticks came floating down the stream. So Susa-no-o, thinking that there must be people at the headwaters of the river, went up it in quest of them, when he

---

19. Mount Kagu is the name of a mountain in Yamato. Here it is supposed to have a counterpart in Heaven.

20. It is said to be this mirror that is worshiped at Ise as an emblem of the Sun Goddess.

21. Terrible female of Heaven.

22. Monkey female.

23. This is said to be the origin of the Kagura, or the pantomimic dance now performed at Shinto festivals.

24. Strangely, the *Nihongi* neglects to say that—as we learn from the *Kojiki*—she danced on this and made it give out a sound.

25. These gods' names were properly Koyane no Mikoto and Futo-dama no Mikoto (see the preceding), but here the names of their human descendants are substituted.

26. A rope made of straw or rice that has been pulled up by the roots.

27. That is, tables of offerings.

came upon an old man and an old woman—two of them—who had a young girl between them and were weeping. Then he deigned to ask: "Who are ye?" So the old man replied, saying: "I am an earthly deity,[28] child of the Deity Great-Mountain-Possessor.[29] I am called by the name of Foot-Stroking-Elder, my wife is called by the name of Hand-Stroking-Elder, and my daughter is called by the name of Wondrous-Inada-Princess." Again he asked: "What is the cause of your crying?" [The old man] answered, saying: "I had originally eight young girls as daughters. But the eight-forked serpent of Koshi has come every year and devoured [one], and it is now its time to come, wherefore we weep." Then he asked him: "What is its form like?" [The old man] answered, saying: "Its eyes are like *akakagachi*, it has one body with eight heads and eight tails. Moreover on its body grows moss and also chamaecyparis[30] and cryptomerias. Its length extends over eight valleys and eight hills, and if one looks at its belly, it is all constantly bloody and inflamed." (What is here called *akakagachi* is the modern *hohozuki*.)[31] Then Susa-no-o said to the old man: "If this be thy daughter, wilt thou offer her to me?" He replied, saying: "With reverence, but I know not thine august name." Then he replied, saying: "I am elder brother to the Heaven-Shining-Deity. So I have now descended from Heaven." Then the Deities Foot-Stroking-Elder and Hand-Stroking-Elder said: "If that be so, with reverence will we offer [her to thee]." So Susa-no-o, at once taking and changing the young girl into a multitudinous and close-toothed comb which he stuck into his august hair-bunch, said to the Deities Foot-Stroking Elder and Hand-Stroking-Elder: "Do you distill some eightfold refined liquor.[32] Also make a fence round about, in that fence make eight gates, at each gate tie [together] eight platforms, on each platform put a liquor vat and into each vat pour the eightfold refined liquor and wait." So as they waited after having thus prepared everything in accordance with his bidding, the eight-forked serpent came truly as [the old man] had said and immediately dipped a head into each vat and drank the liquor. Thereupon it was intoxicated with drinking, and all [the heads] lay down and slept. Then Susa-no-o drew the ten-grasp saber that was augustly girded on him and cut the serpent in pieces, so that the River Hi flowed on changed into a river of blood. So when he cut the middle tail, the edge of his august sword broke. Then, thinking it strange, he thrust into and split [the flesh] with the point of his august sword and looked, and there was a sharp great sword [within]. So he took this great sword, and thinking it a strange

---

28. Or "Country Deity," "Deity of the Land."

29. O-yama-tsu-mi-no-kami.

30. A coniferous tree, the *Chamaecyparis obtusa*, in Japanese *hi-no-ki*. The cryptomeria is *Cryptomeria japonica*.

31. The winter cherry, *Physalis alkekengi*.

32. In Japanese, *sake*.

thing, he respectfully informed[33] Amaterasu. This is the Herb-Quelling Great Sword.[34]

So thereupon Susa-no-o sought in the land of Izumo for a place where he might build a palace. Then he arrived at a place [called] Suga and said: "On coming to this place my august heart is pure,"[35] and in that place he built a palace to dwell in. So that place is now called Suga. When this Great Deity first built the palace of Suga, clouds rose up thence. Then he made an august song. That song said:

> Eight Clouds arise. The eightfold fence
> of Izumo makes an eightfold fence
> for the spouses to retire [within]. Oh!
> that eightfold fence.
>
> [Adapted from Chamberlain, *Ko-ji-ki*, pp. 60–64]

DESCENT OF THE DIVINE GRANDSON WITH THE THREE IMPERIAL REGALIA

In this account, the Sun Goddess commissions the Divine Grandson to rule the land, bearing the so-called Three Imperial Regalia — a mirror, a sword, and a curved jewel — as symbols of divine authority. Actually the bronze mirror, long sword, and curved jewel are of continental origin (found earlier in north China and Korea), so originally they represented not native tradition but prestigious items of a higher civilization, of which the dynasty was the proud bearer among culturally less advanced tribes.

Note also that the legitimacy of the ruling house is shared with its supporting clans and service corporations, whose primal ancestors likewise received their charge from the Sun Goddess. These include the Nakatomi, from whom the Fujiwara derived their own claim to share in imperial rule. No such pluralistic arrangement was attached to Chinese conceptions of dynastic sovereignty.

"All the Central Land of Reed-Plains is now completely tranquilized." Now the Heaven-Shining-Deity gave command, saying: "If that be so, I will send down my child." She was about to do so when in the meantime an August Grandchild was born whose name was called Ama-tsu-hiko-hiko-ho-no-ninigi no Mikoto. Her son represented to her that he wished the August Grandchild to be sent down in his stead. Therefore the Heaven-Shining-Deity gave to Ama-tsu-hiko-

---

33. According to some sources, "sent it with a message to."

34. Reputedly one of the Three Imperial Regalia.

35. That is, "I feel refreshed." The Japanese term used is *suga-sugashi*, whose origin is attributed to the name of the place Suga. More probably the name gave rise to this detail of the legend.

hiko-ho-no-ninigi no Mikoto the Three Treasures, viz. the curved jewel of Ya-saka gem, the eight-hand mirror, and the sword Kusanagi and joined to him as his attendants Ame no Koyane no Mikoto, the first ancestor of the Nakatomi; Futo-dama no Mikoto, the first ancestor of the Imbe; Ame no Uzume no Mi-koto, the first ancestor of the Sarume; Ishi-kori-dome no Mikoto, the first an-cestor of the mirror makers; and Tamaya no Mikoto, the first ancestor of the jewel makers; in all gods of five *be*.[36] Then she commanded her August Grand-child, saying: "This Reed-plain-1500-autumns-fair-rice-ear Land is the region which my descendants shall be lords of. Do thou, my August Grandchild, pro-ceed thither and govern it. Go! and may prosperity attend thy dynasty, and may it, like Heaven and Earth, endure for ever."

[Adapted from Aston, *Nihongi*, I, pp. 76–77]

PRINCESS YAMATO AND PRINCE PLENTY

The shrine in Izumo, Kitsuki-no-miya, dedicated to the son of Susa-no-o, is the most ancient shrine in Japan and therefore is called "the shrine ahead of those to all other gods" (*kami-mae no yashiro*). Perhaps because it was here that Susa-no-o, from the Yamato line, married the Izumo princess and their son Prince Plenty or the Great Landlord God (Ōnamochi or Ō-mono-nushi) married a Yamato princess, this shrine is particularly thought of as symbolizing union and compromise. A visit to the Izumo Shrine is regarded therefore as especially beneficial to those with hopes of marriage or those desirous of promoting greater harmony and understanding in their own families.

After this, Yamato-toto-hi-momo-so-bime no Mikoto [Princess Yamato] became the wife of Ō-mono-nushi no Kami [Prince Plenty].[37] This god, however, was never seen in the daytime but came at night. Princess Yamato said to her hus-band: "As my Lord is never seen in the daytime, I am unable to view his august countenance distinctly; I beseech him therefore to delay a while, that in the morning I may look upon the majesty of his beauty." The Great God answered and said: "What thou sayest is clearly right. Tomorrow morning I will enter thy toilet case and stay there. I pray thee be not alarmed at my form." Princess Yamato wondered secretly in her heart at this. Waiting until daybreak she looked into her toilet case. There was there a beautiful little snake,[38] of the length and thickness of the cord of a garment. Thereupon she was frightened and uttered an exclamation. The Great God was ashamed and, changing suddenly into human form, spake to his wife and said: "Thou didst not contain thyself but

---

36. *Be*, hereditary guilds or corporations of craftsmen.
37. Or "the Great Landlord God."
38. This is one of numerous evidences of serpent worship in ancient Japan.

hast caused me shame: I will in my turn put thee to shame." So treading the Great Void, he ascended to Mount Mimoro. Hereupon Princess Yamato looked up and had remorse. She flopped down on a seat and with a chopstick stabbed herself in the pudenda so that she died. She was buried at O-chi.

[Adapted from Aston, *Nihongi*, I, pp. 158–159]

THE FOUNDING OF IZUMO

A somewhat different tone is found in the mythic account of the founding of Izumo as given in the local "history," *Izumo no kuni fudoki*, which asserts its independent creation and distinctive autonomy in relation to Yamato hegemony.

Izumo was named for the words of the God Yatsukamizu Omidzunu. The august Omidzunu, who performed the *kunihiki* (also *kunubiki*, meaning "land pulling"), spoke majestically [thus], "Clouds-Rising Izumo is a narrow strip of young land. [When the creator gods established the land of Izumo] they made it small. Therefore, it must be enlarged with the addition of more land, which is to be attached [to the original land of Izumo]."

"As I looked at the cape of white Shiragi in search of spare land," he said, "I could see that Shiragi had an overabundance." Thereupon, he took a wide spade shaped like a maiden's chest, thrust it into the land as though he had plunged it into the gill of a large fish, shook it about as if brandishing pampas grass [and broke off a piece]. Then he looped a three-ply rope around the land and began to pull it. He pulled the rope slowly as if reeling in [a fishing line]. As it came near, it looked like a huge riverboat [being] pulled by his august might. "Come land, come hither," said the god. Thus, he added [to Izumo] the portion of land called the cape of Kizuki, which protrudes from the inlet of Kozu. . . .

Similar "catches" are made by the god, incorporating other lands into Izumo, and then the account continues by claiming autonomy for Izumo and its tutelary shrine.

"Now I am finished pulling the land," said the god. Thereupon, the God Omidzunu set his cane in the ground of Ou and uttered a word, "O-e." That is why [this place] is called Ou. (What is known as the sacred woods of Ou is situated on a small hill northeast of the district office. The diameter of this mound is about forty-four feet. There is a lofty tree atop the hill.)

Township of Mori. Mori is situated 13.1 miles southeast of the district office. The Great God Ohonamuchi, when he walked along Mount Nagaye on his return from his campaign to pacify Yakuchi in the land of Koshi, said, "The land that I have opened and governed shall be entrusted hereafter to the Imperial Grandson for his peaceful administration. As for the land of Izumo, it shall be kept as my territory and I will dwell in it forever. I will protect it like a precious jewel. Green hills and mountains shall surround Izumo, and I shall protect it. Therefore, the place will be called Mori, meaning 'to defend.'" (The [new] graphs for *mori* were adopted in 726.)

Township of Yashiro. Yashiro is located thirteen miles east of the district office. "This is the shrine in which I will reside," said the God Amatsuko, the ancestor of Iki of Yashiro, when he came down from heaven with Ame no Hohi. That is why the place is called Yashiro, meaning shrine.

[Aoki, *Izumo no kuni fudoki*, pp. 80, 82]

ENSHRINEMENT OF AMATERASU

The following entries in the *Nihongi*, for the twenty-fifth year of Emperor Suinin's reign (5 B.C.E., according to traditional dating, but more probably around 260 C.E.), describe the founding of the great shrine to Amaterasu at Ise. The moving of the Sun Goddess no doubt refers to the transporting of the mirror thought to be her embodiment.

25th year, Spring, 2nd month, 8th day. The emperor commanded the five officers, Takenu Kaha-wake, ancestor of the Abe no Omi; Hiko-kuni-fuku,[39] ancestor of the imperial chieftains; O-kashima, ancestor of the Nakatomi deity chieftains; Tochine, ancestor of the Mononobe deity chieftains; and Take-hi, ancestor of the Ōtomo deity chieftains, saying: "The sagacity of our predecessor on the throne, the Emperor Mimaki-iri-hiko-inie, was displayed in wisdom: he was reverential, intelligent, and capable. He was profoundly unassuming, and his disposition was to cherish self-abnegation. He adjusted the machinery of government and did solemn worship to the gods of Heaven and Earth. He practiced self-restraint and was watchful as to his personal conduct. Every day he was heedful for that day. Thus the weal of the people was sufficient, and the empire was at peace. And now, under our reign, shall there be any remissness in the worship of the Gods of Heaven and Earth?"[40]

3rd month, 10th day. The Great Goddess Amaterasu was taken from [the princess] Toyo-suki-iri-hime[41] and entrusted to [the princess] Yamato-hime no Mikoto. Now Yamato-hime sought for a place where she might enshrine the Great Goddess. So she proceeded to Sasahata in Uda. Then turning back from

---

39. Both these men are named in Emperor Sūjin's reign, tenth year, eighty-five years earlier, according to the traditional reckoning.

40. This speech is thoroughly Chinese and Confucian. Much of the language comes from the Canon of Yao in the *Classic of Documents*.

41. To whom she had been entrusted in 92 B.C.E., eighty-seven years earlier.

thence, she entered the land of Ōmi and went round eastward to Mino, whence she arrived in the province of Ise.

Now the Great Goddess Amaterasu instructed Yamato-hime, saying: "The province of Ise, of the divine wind,[42] is the land whither repair the waves from the eternal world, the successive waves. It is a secluded and pleasant land. In this land I wish to dwell." In compliance, therefore, with the instruction of the Great Goddess, a shrine was erected to her in the province of Ise. Accordingly an Abstinence Palace[43] was built at Kawakami in Isuzu. This was called the palace of Iso. It was there that the Great Goddess Amaterasu first descended from Heaven.

[Adapted from Aston, *Nihongi*, I, pp. 175–176]

SHINTO PRAYERS (*NORITO*)

The *norito* are prayers or mantras uttered on ritual occasions or festivals. Those presented here are mostly preserved in the *Engi-shiki* of 927 C.E., a compilation of the Heian court that reflects the codification of Shinto practice in relation to the unification and bureaucratization of the state but that also records many aspects of Japanese religion long antedating the process of state building.

Most of the *norito* thus preserved are highly formulaic, ritualized, and repetitive. Typically they consist of an invocation of a god or gods; a recollection of the founding of the shrine, which is the site of the ceremony; an identification of the recitant and his status; a list of offerings; a petition for certain benefits or blessings; a promise of recompense to be made in return; and a final salutation. Along with this generalized formality, there is great specificity in regard to particular deities, places, and details of local history and myth. Here, however, the main focus is on the imperial house and its Grand Shrine at Ise.

NORITO FOR THE FESTIVAL OF THE SIXTH MONTH

This prayer was offered in the sixth month by a priest of the Nakatomi clan to pray for the well-being of the emperor and imperial house. It is similar to one offered at Ise for the success of the grain-growing season. Although much of it is addressed to the Sovereign Deities in general, the following excerpts focus on a prayer to Amaterasu on behalf of the reigning emperor, spoken of here as the Sovereign Grandchild.

---

42. This is a stock epithet (*makura kotoba*) for this province.

43. Abstinence Palace or Worship Palace: "On the accession of an Emperor, an unmarried Princess of the Imperial House was selected for the service of the Shrine of Ise, or if there was no such unmarried Princess, then another Princess was fixed upon by divination and appointed worship-princess. The Worship-Palace was for her residence" (Aston, *Nihongi*, I, p. 176).

Hear me, all of you assembled priests (*kamu-nusi*) and exorcists (*hafuri*). Thus
I speak.

> I humbly speak before you,
>> The Sovereign Deities whose praises are fulfilled as
>>> Heavenly Shrines and Earthly Shrines
>> By the command of the Sovereign Ancestral Gods and Goddesses
>>> Who divinely remain in the High Heavenly Plain. . . .

> I humbly speak with special words in the solemn presence
>> Of the deity Ama-terasu-oho-mi-kami,
>>> Who dwells at Ise:
> The lands of the four quarters, upon which you gaze out,
>> As far as the heavens stand as partitions,
>> As far as the land extends in the distance,
>> As far as the bluish clouds trail across the sky,
>> As far as the white clouds hang down on the horizon:

On the blue ocean
> As far as the prows of the ships can reach,
> Without stopping to dry their oars,
> On the great ocean the ships teem continuously;
On the roads by land
> As far as the horses' hooves can penetrate,
> The ropes of the [tribute] packages tightly tied,
> Treading over the rocks and roots of trees,
> They move over the long roads without pause, continuously;
The narrow land is made wide,
> The steep land is made level;
And you entrust the distant lands [to the Sovereign Grandchild]
> As if casting myriad ropes about them and drawing them hither.
[If you vouchsafe to do all this], then in your presence
> The first fruits of the tribute will be piled up
> Like a long mountain range,
> And of the rest [the Sovereign Grandchild] will partake tranquilly.
Also because you bless the reign of the Sovereign Grandchild

As a long reign, eternal and unmoving,
And prosper it as an abundant reign,
As my Sovereign Ancestral Gods and Goddesses,
Like a cormorant bending my neck low,
I present to you the noble offerings of the Sovereign Grandchild
And fulfill your praises. Thus I speak.

[Adapted from Philippi, Norito, pp. 36–39]

THE BLESSING OF THE GREAT PALACE

This prayer, invoking the gods' protection of the Imperial Palace, was recited by a member of the Imibe (Imbe) clan, professional abstainers whose role thus is connected with purification rituals. Note that in the absence of a supreme god, by certifying the rule of the imperial line, this polytheistic pantheon acts "in council," that is, by consensus.

The Sovereign Ancestral Gods and Goddesses,
   Who divinely remain in the High Heavenly Plain,
   Commanded the Sovereign Grandchild to occupy the heavenly high seat,
   And presenting unto him the mirror and sword, the heavenly signs [of the
    imperial succession],
   Said in blessing:
"Our sovereign noble child, oh Sovereign Grandchild,
   "Occupying this heavenly high seat,
   "[Retain] the heavenly sun-lineage for myriads of thousands of long
   autumns,
   "And rule tranquilly the Great Eight-Island Land of the Plentiful
    Reed Plains and of the Fresh Ears of Grain as a peaceful land."
Thus entrusting the land to him,
   By means of a heavenly council,
   They silenced to the last leaf
    The rocks and the stumps of the trees.
    Which had been able to speak,
   And [caused him to] descend from the heavens
    To reign over this kingdom
   [As] the Sovereign Grandchild ruling the heavenly sun-lineage. . . .
Because you protect the reign of the Sovereign Grandchild as eternal and
   unmoving,
   And prosper it as an abundant reign, an overflowing reign, a long reign;
Therefore, onto the long strings of myriad *mi-fuki* noble beads,
   Which have been purified and sanctified by the sacred bead-makers,
   Have been attached colored cloth, radiant cloth;
And I, Imibe-no-sukune So-and-so, hanging a thick sash over my weak
   shoulders,
   Bless and pacify—
Grant that any error or omission in this
   May be heard rectified and beheld rectified
    By [the rectifying deities] Kamu-naho-bi-no-mikoto and
    Oho-naho-bi-no-mikoto,

And that they may hear and receive it tranquilly and peacefully.
Thus I humbly speak.

[Philippi, *Norito*, pp. 41–43]

THE GREAT EXORCISM OF THE LAST DAY OF THE SIXTH MONTH

This *norito* is of special interest because it details the sins to be exorcised, some of them in the nature of moral faults but others simply baneful occurrences—misfortunes or things that have just gone wrong and need to be remedied. Notice again that the gods act in concert; also notice the means of purification that they use: washing away, blowing away, and "losing" them (keeping away).

By the command of the Sovereign Ancestral Gods and Goddesses,
    Who divinely remain in the High Heavenly Plain,
The eight myriad deities were convoked in a divine convocation.
    Consulted in a divine consultation,
    And spoke these words of entrusting:
        "Our Sovereign Grandchild is to rule
        "The Land of the Plentiful Reed Plains of the Fresh Ears of Grain
        "Tranquilly as a peaceful land."
Having thus entrusted the land,
    They inquired with a divine inquiry
    Of the unruly deities in the land,
    And expelled them with a divine expulsion. . . .
The lands of the four quarters thus entrusted,
    Great Yamato, the Land of the Sun-Seen-on-High,
    Was pacified and made a peaceful land;
The palace posts were firmly planted in the bed-rock below,
    The cross-beams soaring high towards the High Heavenly plain,
    And the noble palace of the Sovereign Grandchild constructed,
        Where, as a heavenly shelter, as a sun-shelter,
            he dwells hidden,
        And rules [the kingdom] tranquilly as a peaceful land.

The various sins perpetrated and committed
    By the heavenly ever-increasing people to come into existence
    In this land which he is to rule tranquilly as a peaceful land.
First, the heavenly sins:
    Breaking down the ridges,
    Covering up the ditches,
    Releasing the irrigation sluices,
    Double planting,
  Setting up stakes,

Skinning alive, skinning backwards,
Defecation—
Many sins [such as these] are distinguished and called the heavenly sins.
The earthly sins:
  Cutting living flesh, cutting dead flesh,
  White leprosy, skin excrescences,
  The sin of violating one's own mother,
  The sin of violating one's own child,
  The sin of violating a mother and her child,
  The sin of violating a child and her mother,
  The sin of transgression with animals,
  Woes from creeping insects,
  Woes from the deities on high,
  Woes from the birds on high,
  Killing animals, the sin of witchcraft—
  Many sins [such as these] shall appear.

When they thus appear,
By the heavenly shrine usage. . . .
  Pronounce the heavenly ritual, the solemn ritual words.
When he thus pronounces them . . . . the heavenly deities
  Will hear and receive [these words].

When they thus hear and receive,
Then, beginning with the court of the Sovereign Grandchild,
  In the lands of the four quarters under the heavens,
  Each and every sin will be gone.
As the gusty wind blows apart the myriad layers of heavenly clouds;
  As the morning mist, the evening mist is blown away by the
    morning wind, the evening wind; . . . .
As a result of the exorcism and the purification,
  There will be no sins left.
They will be taken into the great ocean
  By the goddess called Se-ori-tsu-hime,
  Who dwells in the rapids of the rapid-running rivers
    Which fall surging perpendicular
    From the summits of the high mountains and the summits of the
      low mountains.
When she thus takes them,
  They will be swallowed with a gulp
    By the goddess called Haya-aki-tsu-hime. . . .
When she thus swallows them with a gulp,
  The deity called Ibuki-do-nushi,

Who dwells in the Ibuki-do,[44]
Will blow them away with his breath to the land of Hades,
the under-world.
When she thus loses them,
Beginning with the many officials serving in the Emperor's court,
In the four quarters under the heavens,
Beginning from today,
Each and every sin will be gone.

[Philippi, *Norito*, pp. 45–48]

MOVING THE SHRINE OF THE GREAT DEITY AT ISE

The Grand Shrine was relocated every twenty years so that the premises could be cleansed and purified—a ritual signifying both conservation and renewal and again stressing purification as a main theme of Shinto ritual.

By the solemn command of the Sovereign Grandchild,
I humbly speak in the solemn presence of the Great Sovereign Deity:

In accordance with the ancient custom,
    The great shrine is built anew once in twenty years,
The various articles of clothing of fifty-four types,
    And the sacred treasures of twenty-one types are provided,
And exorcism, purification and cleansing are performed.

I, the functionary participating (rank, surname, name), have been dispatched
    To say the manner in which the offerings are to be presented.
        Thus I humbly speak.

[Philippi, *Norito*, p. 67]

DRIVING AWAY A VENGEFUL DEITY

In this *norito* the deities are again described as consulting together on the way to deal with unruly deities disturbing the land entrusted to the Heavenly Grandchild. The solution is to mollify them with gifts and persuade them to go elsewhere and live in peace.

By the command of the Ancestral Gods and Goddesses,
    Who divinely remain in the High Heavenly Plain,
    And who began matters,

---

44. Literally, "breath-blowing entrance."

The eight myriad deities were convoked in a divine convocation
  in the high meeting-place of Heaven,
    And consulted in a divine consultation, [saying]:
      "Our Sovereign Grandchild is to rule
      "The Land of the Plentiful Reed Plains and of
        the Fresh Ears of Grain
      "Tranquillity as a peaceful land."
Thus he left the heavenly rock-seat,
  And descended from the heavens,
    Pushing with an awesome pushing through the myriad layers
      of heavenly clouds
    And was entrusted [with the land]—
Then they consulted with a divine consultation, [saying]:
  "Which deity should first be dispatched
  "To expel with a divine expulsion and to pacify
  "The unruly deities in the Land of the Fresh Ears of Grain?"
Then the numerous deities all consulted and said:
  "Ame-no-ho-hi-no-mikoto should be sent to pacify them. . . ."

Then, after the unruly deities have been removed by a "divine expulsion," there is a ritual reenactment in which the priest speaks of the propitiatory offerings.

With this prayer I present offerings,
  Providing garments of colored cloth, radiant cloth, plain cloth,
    and coarse cloth;
  A mirror as something to see clearly with,
  A jewel as something to play with,
  A bow and arrow as something to shoot with,
  A sword as something to cut with,
  A horse as something to ride on;
  Wine, raising high the soaring necks
    Of the countless wine vessels, filled to the brim;
  In rice and in stalks;
  That which lives in the mountains—
    The soft-furred and the coarse-furred animals—
  That which grows in the vast fields and plains—
    The sweet herbs and the bitter herbs—
  As well as that which lives in the blue ocean—
    The wide-finned and the narrow-finned fishes,
    The sea-weeds of the deep and the sea-weeds of the shore—
I place these noble offerings in abundance upon tables
  Like a long mountain range and present them
Praying that the Sovereign Deities

Will with a pure heart receive them tranquilly
    As offerings of ease,
    As offerings of abundance,
And will not seek vengeance and not ravage,
But will move to a place of wide and lovely mountains and rivers,
    And will as deities dwell there pacified.
With this prayer, I fulfill your praises. Thus I humbly speak.
                                    [Philippi, *Norito*, pp. 68–70]

CONGRATULATORY WORDS OF THE CHIEFTAIN OF IZUMO

When the deities of High Heaven:
Take-mi-musu-bi
And Kamu-musu-bi-no-mikoto
Entrusted to the rule of the Sovereign Grandchild
the Great Eight-Island land,
The distant ancestor of the omi of Izumo,
Ame-no-ho-hi-no-mikoto,
Was dispatched to inspect the land.
Pushing through the myriad layers of heavenly clouds,
Flying the heavens and flying the earth,
He looked throughout the kingdom,
And then reported on his search:
"The Land of the Plentiful Reed Plains and of the Fresh
Ears of Grain
"During the day seethes as with summer flies,
"And during the night is overrun with gods which shine
as sparks of fire.
"The very rocks, the stumps of trees,
"The bubbles of water all speak,
"And it is truly an unruly land.
"But I shall pacify and subjugate it,
"And shall have it ruled tranquilly
"By the Sovereign Grandchild as a peaceful land."
Thus saying, he dispatched his son
Ame-no-hina-dori-no-mikoto,
Together with Futsu-nushi-no-mikoto,
And caused them to descend from the heavens.
The two swept away and subjugated the unruly deities,
Propitiated and pacified the great Land-creator,
And caused him to relinquish the rule
Of the visible, material things in the Great Eight-Island Land.
Then, Ō-namochi-no-mikoto said:

"The Sovereign Grandchild will dwell peacefully in the
land of Yamato."
Thus saying, he attached his peaceful spirit
To a mirror of large dimensions,
Eulogizing it by the name
Yamato-no-Ō-mono-nushi-Kushi-mika-tama-no-mikoto,
And had it dwell in the sacred grove of Ō-miwa.
He caused the spirit of his son
Aji-suki-taka-hiko-ne-no-mikoto
To dwell in the sacred grove of Kamo in Kaduraki;
Caused the spirit of Koto-shiro-nushi-no-mikoto
To dwell in Unade;
And caused the spirit of Kayanarumi-no-mikoto
To dwell in the sacred grove of Asuka.
[These deities] he presented to the Sovereign Grandchild
As his close protector-deities,
And himself dwelt peacefully
In the shrine of Kizuki of the myriad clay.
Then the Sovereign Ancestral Gods and Goddesses said:
"Do you, oh Ame-no-ho-hi-no-mikoto, bless the long reign,
the great reign of the Emperor
"As eternal and unmoving,
"And do you prosper it as an abundant reign."
Thus do I, inheriting this tradition,
Perform the worship service,
And as the morning sun rises in effulgent glory
Do present, as tokens of homage of the deities and as tokens of
homage of the omi,
The sacred treasures of blessing. Thus I humbly speak.
In the manner of wiping clean and viewing
The surface of a smooth, clear mirror,
May you, the incarnate deity, rule [clearly] the Great Eight-Island land
Together with heaven and earth, sun and moon,
Peacefully and tranquilly; as a sign thereof
I bear the divine treasures of blessing
[And present them] as tokens of homage of the deities and tokens of
homage of the omi,
And fearfully and reverently,
Do humbly speak the congratulatory words of divine blessing of
heavenly tradition. Thus I humbly speak.

                    [Philippi, *Norito*, pp. 73–75]

Chapter 3

PRINCE SHŌTOKU AND HIS CONSTITUTION

The reign of Empress Suiko (592–628 C.E.) was one of the most remarkable periods in Japanese history. A crisis had developed in Japan toward the end of the sixth century as a result of the loss of Japanese domains on the Korean peninsula and the defeat of its ally, the kingdom of Paekche. Within the country, there also was serious contention among the powerful clans, partly on account of developments in Korea. The large numbers of Korean refugees who fled to Japan from the turmoil of the peninsula added to the authorities' difficulties. Besides political and economic problems, the arrival of Buddhism some fifty years earlier had caused bitter controversies. Some of the important clans, representing traditional Shinto views, were violently opposed to what they considered a foreign and harmful religion. Above all was the fact that a unified and expanding China under the Sui and a unifying Korea under Silla were now facing a weak and decentralized Japan. Apart from whatever threat to their security that the Japanese felt to lie in the changing situation on the continent, they also, of course, wanted to emulate the superior achievements of the rising Chinese and Korean dynasties.

Accordingly, the Yamato court attempted to enhance its power and prestige in the eyes of foreigners and domestic rivals alike by adopting many features of the superior Chinese civilization and especially its political institutions. The first measures included a reorganization of court ranks and etiquette in accordance with Chinese models, the adoption of the Chinese calendar, the opening of formal diplomatic relations with China, the creation of a system of highways, the erection of many Buddhist temples, and the compilation of official chronicles. Most important, perhaps, was the proclamation of a "constitution"—a set of principles of government in seventeen articles, this number probably having been derived from the combination of eight, the largest yin number, and nine, the largest yang number.

The chief architect of this project was Prince Shōtoku (573–621), who served as "regent" during much of the reign of his aunt, Empress Suiko. The veneration of Prince Shōtoku after his death may be inferred from his name itself, which might be translated as "sage virtue" or "sovereign moral power." Shōtoku, although a member of the imperial family, was also a member of the powerful Soga family, which had been the main support of Buddhism during its early days in Japan, and he always showed a deep interest in the religion and appears to have been well read in Confucian literature. Shōtoku's military achievements were less conspicuous than his civil ones, but at one time he had under his control in Kyushu a considerable army whose function was to have been the reassertion of Japanese influence in Korea.

Although Shōtoku was a devout Buddhist, it was to Confucian models that he turned for guidance when faced with the enormous task of state building. His most crucial problem, the establishment of the court as the central authority, was well met by the teachings of Confucianism as it had developed during the great Han empire. According to these teachings, the universe consisted of three realms, Heaven, Earth, and Man, with man playing a key creative role between the other two. The basis of all authority and order lay in Heaven and was manifested to Earth by the stately progress of the sun, moon, and planets across the firmament. It was the duty of the ruler to make sure that his country was governed in accordance with the pattern established by Heaven. This is the reason for the importance of the calendar in countries dominated by Confucian thought; that is, unless the "time" was correct, the government on Earth would be out of step with the movements of Heaven.

A regular, determined system of government was exactly what was needed in Japan during Shōtoku's time. The statement of the Han Confucian ideal of government itself is found in article III of his constitution: "The lord is Heaven; the vassal, Earth. Heaven overspreads; Earth upbears. When this is so, the four seasons follow their due course, and the powers of Nature develop their efficiency." Hints of Legalist and other non-Confucian ideas may be detected elsewhere. Buddhism recognized no unvarying universal order except the law of constant change and adaptability—in this case, to the Han state system. Thus Buddhism and Confucianism were able to exist side by side in Japan for a thousand years without any serious conflict, but both had to adapt to Japanese ways.

Shōtoku's policy of internal reforms was complemented by his attitude toward China. He realized how much Japan had to learn from China and wanted to cultivate good relations with that country. To that end, Japanese students (though possibly of Chinese or Korean ancestry) were sent to Sui China to study both Confucianism and Buddhism. Shōtoku's own respect for Chinese learning is obvious from his constitution, which makes no mention of traditional Japanese religious practices or the Japanese principle of a hereditary line of emperors. Many Japanese historians, however, have professed to discover an assertion of equality with China in the letters that Shōtoku sent to the Sui court. One of them, as we saw in the excerpts from the Chinese dynastic histories, bore the superscription "The Child of Heaven in the Land of the Rising Sun to the Child of Heaven in the Land of the Setting Sun," and another, "The Eastern Emperor Greets the Western Emperor." Whether these letters represented serious attempts by Shōtoku to assert Japan's parity with China or merely reflected an ignorance of Chinese protocol and sensibilities is difficult to ascertain. In any case it is recorded that the Sui emperor was highly displeased.

INTERNAL STRIFE IN THE LATE SIXTH CENTURY

In these excerpts we get a glimpse of the struggle for power at court between the Mononobe and Soga clans just before Empress Suiko and Prince Shōtoku came to power. Against this background, the seeming platitudes of Shōtoku's constitution become more relevant to the political situation in his time. These passages also testify to a growing interest in Buddhism, which will be dealt with more fully in the next chapter. Many of the portions deleted from the account here pertain to this subject or to intercourse with the Korean kingdoms.

The episode involving Yorozu, an adherent of the defeated Mononobe, has been retained as an early example of the indomitable spirit and resourcefulness long admired in the Japanese warrior, even before these traits became systematized in recent centuries in the cult of the warrior, *bushidō*. Yorozu, though a rebel, is pictured as a loyalist at heart. The story of his tragic end is told with a sympathy for the underdog and the martyr that has continued to find expression in the literature and political life of Japan until the present day.

As in passages cited earlier from the *Nihongi*, these accounts are interspersed with comments on questionable points or alternative accounts from different sources, indicating at least a rudimentary sense of critical historiography.

The Emperor Tachibana no Toyohi[1] died in the second year of his reign [ca. 587 C.E.], Summer, the 4th month. In the fifth month the army of the Great Deity Chieftain[2] Mononobe made a disturbance thrice. The Great Deity Chief-

---

1. Yōmei *tennō*.

2. Heredity title of clan chieftains (other than that of the imperial clan) tracing their ancestry to deities of heaven and earth.

tain from the first wished to set aside the other imperial princes and to establish the Imperial Prince Anahobe[3] as emperor. He now hoped to make use of a hunting party to devise a plan for raising him to the throne instead. So he secretly sent a messenger to the Imperial Prince Anahobe to say: "I should like to hunt with the imperial prince in Awaji." The plot leaked out.

6th month, 7th day. Soga no Mumako no Sukune and other ministers, on behalf of Kashikiya hime no Mikoto, commissioned Nifute, the deity chieftain of Saheki; Iwamura, the deity chieftain of Hashi; and Makuhi, the imperial chieftain of Ikuba, saying: "Do ye with rigorous discipline of arms proceed at once to execute the Imperial Prince Anahobe and the Imperial Prince Yakabe." On this day, at midnight, Nifute, the deity chieftain of Saheki, and his colleagues surrounded the palace of the Imperial Prince Anahobe. Upon this the guardsmen, having first climbed up into the upper story, smote the Imperial Prince Anahobe on the shoulder. The imperial prince fell down from the upper story and ran away into an outhouse. Then the guardsmen, holding up lights, executed him.

8th day. The Imperial Prince Yakabe was executed. . . .

He was put to death because he approved the Imperial Prince Anahobe.

9th day. The nun Zen-shin and the others addressed the Great Imperial Chieftain, saying: "Discipline is the basis of the method of those who renounce the world; we pray thee to let us go to Paekche to receive instruction in the law of discipline."[4] This month, tribute envoys from Paekche arrived at court. The Great Imperial Chieftain addressed the envoys, saying: "Take these nuns with you, and when you are about to cross over to your country, make them learn the law of discipline. When they have done, send them off." The envoys answered and said: "When we return to our frontier state, we shall first of all inform the king of our country, and it will afterward be not too late to send them off."

Autumn, 7th month. The Great Imperial Chieftain, Soga no Mumako no Sukune, incited the imperial princes and the ministers to plot the destruction of the Great Deity Chieftain, Mononobe no Moriya. . . . [Soga, Imperial Prince Mumayado (Shōtoku), and others advanced to attack.] The Great Deity Chieftain, in personal command of the young men of his family and of a slave army, built a rice fort, and gave battle. Then the Great Deity Chieftain climbed up into the fork of an elm at Kisuri from which he shot down arrows like rain. His troops were full of might. They filled the house and overflowed into the plain. The army of the imperial princes and the troops of the ministers were timid and afraid and fell back three times. At this time the Imperial Prince Mumayado

---

3. Half brother of the reigning emperor.

4. That is, the monastic discipline of Buddhism. Paekche was the state in southwest Korea that first sent Buddhist missionaries to Japan.

(Shōtoku), his hair being tied up on the temples [the ancient custom was for boys at the age of fifteen or sixteen to tie up their hair on the temples; at the age of seventeen or eighteen it was divided and made into tufts, as is the case even now], followed in the rear of the army. He pondered in his own mind, saying to himself: "Are we not going to be beaten? Without prayer we cannot succeed." So he cut down a *nuride* tree and swiftly fashioned images of the four Heavenly Kings.[5] Placing them on his top knot, he uttered a vow: "If we are now made to gain the victory over the enemy, I promise faithfully to honor the four Heavenly Kings, guardians of the world, by erecting to them a temple with a pagoda." The Great Imperial Chieftain Soga no Mumako also uttered a vow: "Oh! all ye Heavenly Kings and great Spirit King, aid and protect us and make us to gain the advantage. If this prayer is granted, I will erect a temple with a pagoda in honor of the Heavenly Kings and the great Spirit King and will propagate everywhere the three precious things."[6] When they had made this vow, they urged their troops of all arms sternly forward to the attack. Now there was a man named Ichihi, Tomi no Obito, who shot down the Great Deity Chieftain from his branch and killed him and his children. His troops accordingly gave way suddenly. Joining their forces, they every one put on black clothes[7] and, going hunting on the plain of Magari in Hirose, so dispersed. . . .

A dependent of the Great Deity Chieftain Mononobe no Moriya named Yorozu [the personal name], of the Tottori-be, in command of one hundred men, guarded the house at Naniwa, but hearing of the chieftain's downfall, he urged his horse into a gallop and made his escape by night in the direction of the village of Arimaka in the district of Chinu where, having passed his wife's house, he at length concealed himself among the hills. The court took counsel together, saying: "Yorozu cherishes traitorous feelings and therefore has concealed himself among these hills. Let his kindred be extirpated promptly and no remissness shown." Yorozu, in tattered and filthy raiment and with a wretched countenance, came forth alone, of his own accord, bow in hand and girt with a sword. The officials sent several hundred guardsmen to surround him. Yorozu, accordingly, was afraid and hid himself in a bamboo thicket where he tied cords to the bamboos and pulled them so as to shake the bamboos and thus make the people to doubt where he had gone in. The guardsmen were deceived and, pointing to the quivering bamboos, ran forward, saying: "Yorozu is here!" Yorozu forthwith shot his arrows, not one of which missed its mark, so that the guardsmen were afraid and did not dare to approach. Yorozu then

---

5. Buddhist guardian gods.

6. The three treasures of Buddhism: Buddha, the Law, and the monastic orders.

7. It is explained here that "black" was the color of underlings' clothes and that the chiefs put on this color for disguise. The "hunting" was only a pretense.

unstrung his bow and, taking it under his arm, ran off toward the hills. The guardsmen accordingly pursued him, shooting their arrows at him from both sides of a river, but none of them were able to hit him. Hereupon one of the guardsmen ran on swiftly and got before Yorozu. Lying down by the river's side, he aimed at him and hit him on the knee. Yorozu forthwith pulled out the arrow and, stringing his bow, let fly his arrows. Then prostrating himself on the earth, he exclaimed aloud: "A shield of the emperor, Yorozu would have devoted his valor to his service, but no examination was made, and on the contrary, he has been hard pressed and is now at an extremity. Let some one come forward and speak with me, for it is my desire to learn whether I am to be slain or to be made a prisoner." The guardsmen raced up and shot at Yorozu, but he warded off the flying shafts and slew more than thirty men. Then he took the sword [and] flung it into the midst of the water of the river. With a dagger which he had besides, he stabbed himself in the throat and died. The governor of Kawachi reported the circumstances of Yorozu's death to the court, which gave an order by a stamp[8] that his body should be cut into eight pieces and disposed for exposure among the eight provinces. The governor of Kawachi accordingly, in obedience to the purport of the stamped order, was about to dismember him for exposure when thunder pealed and a great rain fell. Now, there was a white dog which had been kept by Yorozu. Looking up and looking down, he went [a]round, howling beside the corpse and, at last, taking up the head in his mouth, placed it on an ancient mound. He then lay down close by and starved to death in front of it. The governor of Kawachi, thinking that dog's conduct very strange, reported it to the court. The court could not bear to hear of it for pity and issued a stamped order to this effect: "The case of this dog is one that is rarely heard of in the world and should be shown to after ages. Let Yorozu's kindred be made to construct a tomb and bury their remains." The kindred of Yorozu accordingly assembled together and raised a tomb in the village of Arimaka, where they buried Yorozu and his dog. . . .

8th month, 2nd day. The emperor,[9] upon the advice of Kashikiya hime no Mikoto and the Ministers, assumed the Imperial Dignity. Soga no Mumako no Sukune was made Great Imperial Chieftain as before. The ministers and high officials were also confirmed in their previous ranks. . . .

4th year, Autumn, 8th month, 1st day. The emperor addressed his ministers, saying: "It is our desire to establish Imna.[10] What do ye think?" The ministers

---

8. *Oshide*: a stamp of red or black ink on the palm of the hand as a token of authority.

9. Sujun.

10. Imna is the Korean pronunciation for Mimana, which some Japanese historians claim was an outpost on the southern tip of the Korean peninsula established by the Japanese in the early fourth century and held until 562. Most Korean scholars reject this claim. In this passage Sujun suggests that Mimana be reestablished.

said to him: "The Miyake of Imna should be established. We are all of the same opinion as Your Majesty."

Winter, 11th month, 4th day. Ki no Omaro no Sukune [and others] were appointed as generals. Taking with them the imperial chieftains and deity chieftains of the various houses as adjutant generals of the divisions of the army, they marched out in command of over twenty thousand men and stationed themselves in Tsukushi.[11] Kishi no Kana was sent to Silla and Kishi no Itahiko to Imna to make inquiry respecting Imna.

5th year, Winter, 10th month, 4th day. A wild boar was presented to the emperor. Pointing to it, he said: "When shall those to whom We have an aversion be cut off as this wild boar's throat has been cut?" An abundance of weapons was provided beyond what was customary.

10th day. Soga no Mumako no Sukune, having been told of the pronouncement of the emperor and, alarmed at his detestation of himself, called together his people and conspired with them to assassinate the emperor.

In this month, the Hall of Worship and the covered gallery of the great Hōkōji Temple were built.

11th month, 3rd day. Mumako no Sukune lied to the ministers, saying: "Today I present the taxes of the eastern provinces" and sent Koma, Yamato no Aya no Atae, who killed the emperor. . . .

5th day. Mounted messengers were sent to the general's quarters in Tsukushi, saying: "Do not let foreign matters be neglected in consequence of the internal troubles."

[Aston, *Nihongi*, II, pp. 112–120][12]

THE REIGN OF SUIKO AND RULE OF SHŌTOKU

From the many entries in the *Chronicles of Japan* for Suiko's reign, we have selected a few to show how greatly this empress and Prince Shōtoku came to be revered for the accomplishments of their joint rule. Particularly noteworthy is Shōtoku's reputation as a profound student of Buddhism, such that he could expound some of the great sūtras at a time when few Japanese could read any Chinese. In addition to this prince's legendary feats are recorded the building of many temples, the adoption of Chinese court ceremonial in the form of cap ranks, the sending of embassies (including students) to China, and the first project to write an official history of Japan comparable to the great Chinese histories.

---

11. Northern Kyushu.

12. Important personal titles left untranslated by Aston are rendered here according to the usage by R. K. Reischauer in *Early Japanese History*.

THE EMPRESS SUIKO, 592–628 C.E.

The Empress Toyo-mike Kashikiya-hime[13] was the second daughter of the Emperor Ame-kuni oshi-hiraki hiro-niha[14] and a younger sister by the same mother of the Emperor Tachibana no toyo-hi.[15] In her childhood she was called the Princess Nukada-be. Her appearance was beautiful, and her conduct was marked by propriety. At the age of eighteen, she was appointed empress consort of the Emperor Nunakura futo-dama-shiki.[16] When she was thirty-four years of age, in the 5th year and the 11th month of the reign of the Emperor Hatsuse-be,[17] the emperor was murdered by the Great Imperial Chieftain Mumako no Sukune, and the succession to the Dignity being vacant, the ministers besought the empress consort of the Emperor Nunakura futo-dama-shiki, viz. the Princess Nukada-be, to ascend the throne. The empress refused, but the public functionaries urged her in memorials three times until she consented,[18] and they accordingly delivered to her the imperial seal. . . .

1st year [593 C.E.], Summer, 4th month, 10th day. The Imperial Prince Mumayado no Toyotomimi [Shōtoku] was appointed Prince Imperial. He had general control of the government and was entrusted with all the details of administration. He was the second child of the Emperor Tachibana no Toyo-hi. . . . He was able to speak as soon as he was born and was so wise when he grew up that he could attend to the suits of ten men at once and decide them all without error. He knew beforehand what was going to happen. Moreover he learned the Inner Doctrine[19] from a Koryo priest named Hye-cha and studied the Outer Classics[20] with a doctor called Kak-ka. In both of these branches of study he became thoroughly proficient. The emperor his father loved him and made him occupy the Upper Hall South of the Palace. Therefore he was styled the Senior Prince Kami-tsu-miya,[21] Muma-ya-do Toyotomimi. [pp. 121–123]

. . .

11th year [604]. 12th month, 5th day. Cap-ranks[22] were first instituted in all twelve grades:

---

13. *Toyo,* "abundant"; *mi,* "august"; *ke,* "food"; *Kashikiya,* "cook house"; *hime,* "princess."

14. Kinmei.

15. Yōmei.

16. Bidatsu.

17. Sujun.

18. It was the Chinese custom to decline such an honor twice and accept it only when offered it a third time.

19. That is, Buddhism.

20. That is, the Chinese Classics. Inner and Outer have here something of the force of our words "sacred" and "secular."

21. Kami-tsu-miya means "upper palace."

22. The Chinese custom, transmitted through Korea, of distinguishing rank by the form and materials of the official cap.

Dai-toku:	. . .	greater virtue
Shō-toku:	. . .	lesser virtue
Dai-nin:	. . .	greater humanity
Shō-nin:	. . .	lesser humanity
Dai-rei:	. . .	greater decorum
Shō-rei:	. . .	lesser decorum
Dai-shin:	. . .	greater trust
Shō-shin:	. . .	lesser trust
Dai-gi:	. . .	greater rightness
Shō-gi:	. . .	lesser rightness
Dai-chi:	. . .	greater wisdom
Shō-chi:	. . .	lesser wisdom

Each cap was made of sarcenet of a special color.[23] They were gathered up on the crown in the shape of a bag and had a border attached. Only on the first day of the year were hair flowers[24] worn.

In this year also, a Chinese-style calendar was officially adopted for the first time.[25] [pp. 127–128]

. . .

14th year [606], 5th month, 5th day. The imperial commands were given to Kuratsukuri no Tori, saying: "It being my desire to encourage the Inner Doctrines, I was about to erect a Buddhist temple, and for this purpose sought for relics. Then thy grandfather, Shiba Tattō, offered me relics. Moreover, there were no monks or nuns in the land. Thereupon thy father, Tasuna, for the sake of the Emperor Tachibana no Toyohi, took priestly orders and reverenced the Buddhist law. Also thine aunt Shimame was the first to leave her home and, becoming the forerunner of all nuns, to practice the religion of Shākya. Now, we desired to make a sixteen-foot Buddha and, to that end, sought for a good image of Buddha. Thou didst provide a model which met our wishes. Moreover, when the image of Buddha was completed, it could not be brought into the hall, and none of the workmen could suggest a plan of doing so. They were, therefore, on the point of breaking down the doorway when thou didst manage to admit it without breaking down the doorway. For all these services of thine, we grant thee the rank of Dainin, and we also bestow on thee twenty *chō* of

---

23. In imitation of China's contemporary Sui dynasty, purple was for officials of the fifth rank and upward. *Nin* was green, *rei* red, *shin* yellow, *gi* white, and *chi* black. Princes and chief ministers wore the cap of the highest rank, namely, *toku*.

24. Hair ornaments of gold or silver in the shape of flowers. Specimens are preserved in the Nara Museum.

25. Compare R. K. Reischauer, *Early Japanese History*, A, p. 140.

paddy fields in the district of Sakata in the province of Afumi." With the revenue derived from this land, Tori built for the empress the temple of Kongō-ji,[26] now known as the nunnery of Sakata in Minabuchi.

Autumn, 7th month. The empress requested the Prince Imperial to lecture on the Sūtra of Queen Śrīmālā.[27] He completed his explanation of it in three days.

In this year the Prince Imperial also lectured on the Lotus Sūtra[28] in the Palace of Okamoto. The empress was greatly pleased and bestowed on the Prince Imperial one hundred *chō* of paddy fields in the province of Harima. They were therefore added to the temple of Ikaruga. [pp. 134–135]

. . .

16th year [608], Autumn, 9th month. At this time there were sent to the land of Tang[29] the students Fukuin [and others], together with student priests Nichibun [and others], in all eight persons.

In this year many persons from Silla came to settle in Japan. [p. 139]

. . .

22nd year [614], 6th month, 13th day. Mitasuki, lord of Inugami, and Yatabe no Miyakko were sent to the land of Great Tang. [p. 145]

. . .

28th year [620]. This year, the Prince Imperial, in concert with the Great Imperial Chieftain Soga, drew up a history of the emperors, a history of the country and the original record of the imperial chieftains, deity chieftains, court chieftains, local chieftains, the one hundred eighty hereditary corporations and the common people.[30] [p. 148]

. . .

29th year [621], Spring, 2nd month, 5th day. In the middle of the night the Imperial Prince Mumayado no Toyotomimi no Mikoto died in the palace of Ikaruga. At this time all the princes and imperial chieftains, as well as the people of the empire, the old, as if they had lost a dear child, had no taste for salt and vinegar[31] in their mouths; the young, as if they had lost a beloved parent, filled the ways with the sound of their lamenting. The farmer ceased from his plow, and the pounding woman laid down her pestle. They all said: "The sun and moon have lost their brightness; heaven and earth have crumbled to ruin: henceforward, in whom shall we put our trust?"

---

26. Diamond temple.

27. Skt: Shrīmālādevīsimhanāda; J: Shōmangyō.

28. The Saddharmapuṇḍarīka Sūtra; J: Hokke-kyō.

29. When this occurred, China was ruled by the Sui dynasty, but at the time of this writing, it was ruled by the Tang dynasty.

30. Almost all of this work was burned during disturbances in 645, and the remainder is no longer extant.

31. To be understood generally of well-flavored food.

In this month the Prince Imperial Kamitsumiya[32] was buried in the Shinaga Misasagi.

At this time Hye-cha, the Buddhist priest of Koryo, heard of the death of the Prince Imperial Kamitsumiya and was greatly grieved thereat. He invited the priests and, in honor of the Prince Imperial, gave them a meal and explained the sacred books in person. On this day he prayed, saying: "In the land of Nippon there is a sage, by name the Imperial Prince Kamitsumiya Toyotomimi. Certainly Heaven has freely endowed him with the virtues of a sage.[33] Born in the land of Nippon, he thoroughly possessed the three fundamental principles,[34] he continued the great plans of the former sages. He reverenced the Three Treasures[35] and assisted the people in their distress. He was truly a great sage. And now the Prince Imperial is dead. I, although a foreigner, was in heart closely united to him. Now what avails it that I alone should survive? I have determined to die on the 5th day of the 2nd month of next year.[36] So shall I meet the Prince Imperial Kamitsumiya in the Pure Land and together with him pass through the metempsychosis of all living creatures." Now when the appointed day came, Hye-cha died, and all the people that day said one to another: "Prince Kamitsumiya is not the only sage, Hye-cha is also a sage." [pp. 148–149]

. . .

30th year [622], Autumn, 7th month. . . . At this time the Buddhist priests E-sai and E-kō, with the physicians E-jitsu and Fuku-in, students of the learning of the Great Tang, arrived in company with . . . others. Now E-jitsu and the rest together made representation to the empress, saying: "Those who have resided in Tang to study have all completed their courses and ought to be sent for. Moreover, the land of Great Tang is an admirable country, whose laws are complete and fixed. Constant communication should be kept up with it." [p. 150]

[Aston, *Nihongi*, II, pp. 121–150]

THE SEVENTEEN-ARTICLE CONSTITUTION OF PRINCE SHŌTOKU

The influence of Confucian ethical and political doctrines is apparent in this set of basic principles of government, a key document in the process of state building led by Shōtoku. The fact that most of these principles are stated in very general terms reflects the characteristic outlook of Confucianism: the ruler should offer his people

---

32. Prince Shōtoku.
33. According to the Confucian conception.
34. Namely, Heaven, Earth, and Man. The meaning is that he was a philosopher.
35. Of Buddhism.
36. The anniversary of the prince's death.

moral guidance and instruction, not burden them with detailed laws involving compulsion rather than eliciting cooperation. Therefore this constitution exhorts the people to lay aside partisan differences and accept imperial rule in order to achieve social harmony. Ministers and officials are urged to be diligent and considerate, prompt and just in the settlement of complaints or charges, careful in the selection of assistants and wary of flatterers, conscientious in the performance of their duties while not overreaching their authority, and ever mindful of the desires of the people so that public good is put above private interest. Articles XII and XV alone refer to the imperial government's specific functions or prerogatives: the power to raise taxes and the seasons in which forced labor is to be exacted, likewise an aspect of the power to tax. Both of these represent practical measures indispensable to the establishment of the imperial authority over a hitherto uncentralized society, no doubt with a view to achieving the uniformity and centralization that the Chinese empire exemplified.

12th year [604], Summer, 4th month, 3rd day. The Prince Imperial in person prepared for the first time laws. There were seventeen clauses, as follows:

I. Harmony is to be valued,[37] and contentiousness avoided. All men are inclined to partisanship and few are truly discerning. Hence there are some who disobey their lords and fathers or who maintain feuds with the neighboring villages. But when those above are harmonious and those below are conciliatory and there is concord in the discussion of all matters, the disposition of affairs comes about naturally. Then what is there that cannot be accomplished?

II. Sincerely reverence the Three Treasures. The Buddha, the Law, and the religious orders are the final refuge of all beings and the supreme objects of reverence in all countries. It is a law honored by all, no matter what the age or who the person. Few men are utterly bad; with instruction they can follow it. But if they do not betake themselves to the Three Treasures, how can their crookedness be made straight?

III. When you receive the imperial commands, fail not scrupulously to obey them. The lord is Heaven, the vassal is Earth. Heaven overspreads, and Earth upbears. When this is so, the four seasons follow their due course, and the powers of Nature obtain their efficacy. If the Earth attempted to overspread, Heaven would simply fall in ruin. Therefore is it that when the lord speaks, the vassal listens; when the superior acts, the inferior yields compliance. Consequently when you receive the imperial commands, fail not to carry them out scrupulously. Let there be a want of care in this matter, and ruin is the natural consequence.

IV. The ministers and functionaries should make ritual decorum their leading principle, for the leading principle in governing the people consists in ritual decorum. If the superiors do not behave with decorum, the inferiors are dis-

---

37. From the *Analects* of Confucius, 1:12.

orderly; if inferiors are wanting in proper behavior, there must necessarily be offenses. Therefore it is that when lord and vassal behave with decorum, the distinctions of rank are not confused; when the people behave with decorum, the governance of the state proceeds of itself.

V. Ceasing from gluttony and abandoning covetous desires, deal impartially with the suits which are submitted to you. Of complaints brought by the people, there are a thousand in one day. If in one day there are so many, how many will there be in a series of years? If the man who is to decide suits at law makes gain his ordinary motive and hears cases with a view to receiving bribes, then will the suits of the rich man be like a stone flung into water,[38] while the plaints of the poor will resemble water cast upon a stone. Under these circumstances the poor man will not know whither to betake himself. Here too there is deficiency in the duty of the minister.

VI. Chastise that which is evil and encourage that which is good. This was the excellent rule of antiquity. Conceal not, therefore, the good qualities of others, and fail not to correct that which is wrong when you see it. Flatterers and deceivers are a sharp weapon for the overthrow of the state, and a pointed sword for the destruction of the people. Sycophants are also fond, when they meet, of dilating to their superiors on the errors of their inferiors; to their inferiors, they censure the faults of their superiors. Men of this kind are all wanting in fidelity to their lord, and in benevolence towards the people. From such an origin great civil disturbances arise.

VII. Let every man have his own charge, and let not the spheres of duty be confused. When wise men are entrusted with office, the sound of praise arises. If unprincipled men hold office, disasters and tumults multiply. In this world, few are born with knowledge; wisdom is the product of earnest meditation. In all things, whether great or small, find the right man, and they will surely be well managed; on all occasions, be they urgent or the reverse, meet but with a wise man, and they will of themselves be amenable. In this way will the state be lasting and the temples of the Earth and of grain will be free from danger. Therefore did the wise sovereigns of antiquity seek the man to fill the office, and not the office for the sake of the man.

VIII. Let the ministers and functionaries attend the court early in the morning, and retire late. The business of the state does not admit of remissness, and the whole day is hardly enough for its accomplishment. If, therefore, the attendance at court is late, emergencies cannot be met; if officials retire soon, the work cannot be completed.

IX. Trustworthiness is the foundation of right. In everything let there be trustworthiness, for in this there surely consists the good and the bad, success and failure. If the lord and the vassal trust one another, what is there which

---

38. That is, they meet with no resistance.

cannot be accomplished? If the lord and the vassal do not trust one another, everything without exception ends in failure.

X. Let us cease from wrath, and refrain from angry looks. Nor let us be resentful when others differ from us. For all men have hearts, and each heart has its own leanings. Their right is our wrong, and our right is their wrong. We are not unquestionably sages, nor are they unquestionably fools. Both of us are simply ordinary men. How can any one lay down a rule by which to distinguish right from wrong? For we are all, one with another, wise and foolish, like a ring which has no end. Therefore, although others give way to anger, let us on the contrary dread our own faults, and though we alone may be in the right, let us follow the multitude and act like them.

XI. Give clear appreciation to merit and demerit, and deal out to each its sure reward or punishment. In these days, reward does not attend upon merit, nor punishment upon crime. Ye high functionaries who have charge of public affairs, let it be your task to make clear rewards and punishments.

XII. Let not the provincial authorities or the Kuni no Miyatsuko[39] levy exaction on the people. In a country there are not two lords; the people have not two masters. The sovereign is the master of the people of the whole country. The officials to whom he gives charge are all his vassals. How can they, as well as the government, presume to levy taxes on the people?

XIII. Let all persons entrusted with office attend equally to their functions. Owing to their illness or to their being sent on missions, their work may sometimes be neglected. But whenever they become able to attend to business, let them be as accommodating as if they had had cognizance of it from before and not hinder public affairs on the score of their not having had to do with them.

XIV. Ye ministers and functionaries! Be not envious. For if we envy others, they in turn will envy us. The evils of envy know no limit. If others excel us in intelligence, it gives us no pleasure; if they surpass us in ability, we are envious. Therefore it is not until after a lapse of five hundred years that we at last meet with a wise man, and even in a thousand years we hardly welcome one sage. But if we do not find wise men and sages, wherewithal shall the country be governed?

XV. To turn away from that which is private, and to set our faces towards that which is public—this is the path of a minister. Now if a man is influenced by private motives, he will assuredly fail to act harmoniously with others. If he fails to act harmoniously with others, he will assuredly sacrifice the public interest to his private feelings. When resentment arises, it interferes with order, and is subversive of law. Therefore in the first clause it was said that superiors and inferiors should agree together. The purport is the same as this.

---

39. The Kuni no Miyatsuko were the old local nobles whose power was at this time giving way to that of the central government.

XVI. Let the people be employed [in forced labor] at seasonable times. This is an ancient and excellent rule. Let them be employed, therefore, in the winter months, when they are at leisure. But from Spring to Autumn, when they are engaged in agriculture or with the mulberry trees, the people should not be so employed. For if they do not attend to agriculture, what will they have to eat? If they do not attend to the mulberry trees, what will they do for clothing?

XVII. Matters should not be decided by one person alone. They should be discussed with many others. In small matters, of less consequence, many others need not be consulted. It is only in considering weighty matters, where there is a suspicion that they might miscarry, that many others should be involved in debate and discussion so as to arrive at a reasonable conclusion.

[Ienaga, *Shōtoku taishi shū*, NST, 2:128–133; trans. adapted from Aston, *Nihongi*, II, pp. 128–133; dB]

Questions have long been asked about the actual authorship and dating of this document, but even if not everything in the Seventeen Articles is by Shōtoku's own hand, few scholars have doubted that the contents are generally representative of his thinking. Since the text appears in the *Nihon shoki* (720 C.E.), it must in any case reflect views current in the early state-building period, and as recorded in that early chronicle, it became canonical as one of the founding myths of Japan. More than that, however, there are signs of a singular intelligence at work in its composition.[40]

Besides their importance as a political document, Shōtoku's Seventeen Articles are significant as a remarkable synthesis of Confucian and Buddhist thought with native Japanese tradition. In the first article, the Confucian ideal of social harmony is set forth, and in the seventh article, the Confucian idea of having the "right man" or "wise man" (the sage) is said to be indispensable to attaining this ideal. However, in the tenth article, serious doubts are raised about the possibility of knowing right from wrong, no doubt reflecting Shōtoku's own awareness of Buddhist skepticism in this regard, as taught by the Emptiness (Three Treatise) school. Moreover in Article XIV, the extreme difficulty of finding a wise man—and, even more, the rarity of a sage—is emphasized. How then, without them, can one hope to achieve "harmony"? The answer is found in the concluding article: not by relying on one person to decide things, but by engaging in general consultation. If we recall how often in early myths the gods

---

40. Konishi, *A History of Japanese Literature*, I, p. 311, concludes his weighing of the evidence, pro and con, with: "The Constitution may well be Shōtoku's work, but Korean immigrant intellectuals in his entourage must have also made major contributions. I would like to think that the solicitation of cooperation from these intellects, and the consolidation of a composition of such speculative force, could only have been effected if Prince Shōtoku himself was the author of the work." In any case, says Konishi, "we may conclude that the extant Constitution remains essentially a work of Suiko Tennō's time."

themselves met in council and consulted together, we can see how Shōtoku's reference to concord in the discussion of affairs (in the first article) and consultation (in the last) evokes a native tradition of consensus formation that is characteristic also of the Japanese inclination, down to the present, for informal, consensual decision-making processes as a way of handling affairs. Note also that the Japanese emperor or empress is nowhere directly cited. He or she remains on a mystical plane or behind the scenes, symbolizing an ultimate authority whose mysterious power is in proportion to its not being directly used but only ritually exercised. Suiko reigns while Shōtoku rules and lays down the law.

In Shōtoku's case, we know that his promotion of constitutional law (*kenpō*) was only one aspect of an age marked by its promotion of spiritual as well as secular law. Whether or not Shōtoku is accepted as the author of all three of the sūtra commentaries attributed to him, the Lotus, Vimalakīrti, and Shrīmālā Sūtras are known to have traveled together through China and Korea and to have achieved great prominence in Japan at this time. The Lotus itself, as its title "The Lotus of the Wondrous Law" suggests, preached a universal law on a spiritual plane, which could be easily reconciled, through the principle of Emptiness and adaptive means, to the Chinese secular law and institutions that furnished the main content of the Seventeen Articles. Indeed, it was the principle of accommodation that enabled these two conceptions of law, religious and secular, to coexist in seventh-century Japan. The religious conception, with its lofty spiritual aspiration, took wings in the pagodas of temples like Shōtoku's own Hōryūji, "Temple of the Ascendancy of the Law," and numerous other temple structures that rose over the Yamato plain with the Law of Buddhism written into their names: Hōkōji, Hōrinji, Hokkiji, Hokkeji, and so on. In due time, alongside these embodiments of the religious law came the successive codifications of the secular law that gave more precise definition, at least in writing, to Shōtoku's "exemplary law" (*kenpō*).

THE LOTUS SŪTRA

The Lotus Sūtra, the chief text of the Buddhism sponsored by Shōtoku, was also one of the most influential and popular sūtras among Mahāyāna Buddhists in East Asia. Although its authorship and date are obscure, the Lotus was first translated from Sanskrit into Chinese during the third century C.E. In vivid language arousing the imagination, it relates what it claims to be the most profound teaching of Shākyamuni. More than any other sūtra, the Lotus is revered not only for its profound message but also because the text itself is sacred, with each Chinese character regarded as the embodiment of the Buddha. Nichiren Buddhists, who subsequently identified the Lotus Sūtra as their chief text, have treated the book itself as an object of worship, just as buddhas and bodhisattvas are worshiped by others.

Chinese and Japanese commentators have traditionally summarized the message of the Lotus Sūtra in three lessons. The first is that Shākyamuni was both a mortal being and a manifestation of the Eternal Buddha. As such, the questions of his demise are settled decisively in favor of his being present forever. That is, the Buddha does not die. Just as the Buddha's presence is extended throughout time, so the salvation of the Buddha extends to all beings. The second lesson is that salvation is universal and includes even women, who were regarded in other sūtras as being incapable of becoming buddhas. Third, the Lotus Sūtra encompasses all approaches to salvation in the One Vehicle, which is sometimes equated with Mahāyāna Buddhism; at other times the One Vehicle is limited to the Lotus Sūtra itself. Together these three lessons comprise a message that is eternal, universal, and comprehensive.

It is precisely on the basis of these characteristics that the Lotus Sūtra is presented as the highest truth. The highest truth is by nature a sovereign truth that stands above other teachings, and the One Vehicle is therefore supreme. This is an interesting logic that leads to the conclusion that because the Lotus Sūtra is inclusive of all times, persons, and approaches, it is the absolute truth that supersedes the messages propounded by other sūtras and teachers. It is this sūtra's dual character that makes it possible for Tendai Buddhists to accept so many other teachings and practices while Nichiren Buddhists reject them.

In the following parable of the burning house, a rich man saves his sons—who do not realize that the house they are in is on fire—by promising them a variety of wonderful carts to lure them out. Actually he has only one cart, but his deliberate misrepresentation is justified by the fact that it was an expedient device used for the boys' own salvation and by the magnificent splendor of the one kind of cart he did give them. Encompassing the virtues of all of the other carts, this One Vehicle was singularly supreme and eclipsed everything else.

This important point is made not through philosophical argumentation but by parable, a literary device that the Lotus Sūtra uses extensively. It is these stories that have endeared the Lotus Sūtra to so many people and have inspired poets, artists, and even politicians to create verse, paintings, and ideologies that make up what has been called the culture of the Lotus Sūtra.

PREACHING THE ONE GREAT VEHICLE [MAHĀYĀNA]

At that time the World-Honored One calmly arose from his samādhi and addressed Shāriputra, saying: "The wisdom of the Buddhas is infinitely profound and immeasurable. The door to this wisdom is difficult to understand and difficult to enter. . . .

Shāriputra, ever since I attained Buddhahood I have through various causes and similes widely expounded my teachings and have used countless expedient means to guide living beings and cause them to renounce their attachments.

Why is this? Because the Thus-Come One is fully possessed of both expedient means and the perfection of wisdom. . . .

Shāriputra, to sum it up: the Buddha has fully realized the Law that is limitless, boundless, never attained before. . . .

Shāriputra, the Buddhas preach the Law in accordance with what is appropriate, but the meaning is difficult to understand. Why is this? Because we employ countless expedient means, discussing causes and conditions and using words of simile and parable to expound the teachings. This Law is not something that can be understood through pondering or analysis. Only those who are Buddhas can understand it. . . .

Shāriputra, I know that living beings have various desires, attachments that are deeply implanted in their minds. Taking cognizance of this basic nature of theirs, I will therefore use various causes and conditions, words of simile and parable, and the power of expedient means and expound the Law for them. Shāriputra, I do this so that all of them may attain the one Buddha vehicle and wisdom embracing all species." . . . [pp. 23–31]

THE PARABLE OF THE BURNING HOUSE

"Shāriputra, I will now make use of similes and parables to further clarify this doctrine. For through similes and parables those who are wise can obtain understanding.

Shāriputra, suppose that in a certain town in a certain country there was a very rich man. He was far along in years and his wealth was beyond measure. He had many fields, houses, and menservants. His own house was big and rambling, but it had only one gate. A great many people—a hundred, two hundred, perhaps as many as five hundred—lived in the house. The halls and rooms were old and decaying, the walls crumbling, the pillars rotten at their base, and the beams and rafters crooked and aslant.

At that time a fire suddenly broke out on all sides, spreading through the rooms of the house. The sons of the rich man, ten, twenty, perhaps thirty, were inside the house. When the rich man saw the huge flames leaping up on every side, he was greatly alarmed and fearful and thought to himself, I can escape to safety through the flaming gate, but my sons are inside the burning house enjoying themselves and playing games, unaware, unknowing, without alarm or fear. The fire is closing in on them, suffering and pain threaten them, yet their minds have no sense of loathing or peril and they do not think of trying to escape!

Shāriputra, this rich man thought to himself, I have strength in my body and arms. I can wrap them in a robe or place them on a bench and carry them out of the house. And then again he thought, This house has only one gate, and moreover it is narrow and small.

My sons are very young, they have no understanding, and they love their games, being so engrossed in them that they are likely to be burned in the fire. I must explain to them why I am fearful and alarmed. The house is already in flames and I must get them out quickly and not let them be burned up in the fire!

Having thought in this way, he followed his plan and called to all his sons, saying, 'You must come out at once!' But though the father was moved by pity and gave good words of instruction, the sons were absorbed in their games and unwilling to heed him. They had no alarm, no fright, and in the end no mind to leave the house. Moreover, they did not understand what the fire was, what the house was, what danger was. They merely raced about this way and that in play and looked at their father without heeding him.

At that time the rich man had this thought: The house is already in flames from this huge fire. If I and my sons do not get out at once, we are certain to be burned. I must now invent some expedient means that will make it possible for the children to escape harm.

The father understood his sons and knew what various toys and curious objects each child customarily liked and what would delight them. And so he said to them, 'The kind of playthings you like are rare and hard to find. If you do not take them when you can, you will surely regret it later. For example, things like these goat-carts, deer-carts, and ox-carts. They are outside the gate now where you can play with them. So you must come out of this burning house at once. Then whatever ones you want, I will give them all to you!'

At that time, when the sons heard their father telling them about these rare playthings, because such things were just what they had wanted, each felt emboldened in heart and, pushing and shoving one another, they all came wildly dashing out of the burning house.

At this time the rich man, seeing that his sons had gotten out safely and all were seated on the open ground at the crossroads and were no longer in danger, was greatly relieved and his mind danced for joy. At that time each of the sons said to his father, 'The playthings you promised us earlier, the goat-carts and deer-carts and ox-carts—please give them to us now!'

Shāriputra, at that time the rich man gave to each of his sons a large carriage of uniform size and quality. The carriages were tall and spacious and adorned with numerous jewels. A railing ran all around them and bells hung from all four sides. A canopy was stretched over the top, which was also decorated with an assortment of precious jewels. Ropes of jewels twined around, a fringe of flowers hung down, and layers of cushions were spread inside, on which were placed vermilion pillows. Each carriage was drawn by a white ox, pure and clean in hide, handsome in form and of great strength, capable of pulling the carriage smoothly and properly at a pace fast as the wind. In addition, there were many grooms and servants to attend and guard the carriage.

What was the reason for this? This rich man's wealth was limitless and he had many kinds of storehouses that were all filled and overflowing. And he thought to himself, "There is no end to my possessions. It would not be right if I were to give my sons small carriages of inferior make. These little boys are all my sons and I love them without partiality. I have countless numbers of large carriages adorned with seven kinds of gems. I should be fair-minded and give one to each of my sons. I should not show any discrimination. Why? Because even if I distributed these possessions of mine to every person in the whole country I would still not exhaust them, much less could I do so by giving them to my sons!"

At that time each of the sons mounted his large carriage, gaining something he had never had before, something he had originally never expected. "Shāriputra what do you think of this? When this rich man impartially handed out to his sons these big carriages adorned with rare jewels, was he guilty of falsehood or not?"

Shāriputra said, "No, World-Honored One. This rich man simply made it possible for his sons to escape the peril of fire and preserve their lives. He did not commit a falsehood. Why do I say this? Because if they were able to preserve their lives, then they had already obtained a plaything of sorts. And how much more so when, through an expedient means, they are rescued from that burning house." . . .

[Adapted from Watson, *The Lotus Sūtra*, pp. 23–31, 56–63]

THE VIMALAKĪRTI SŪTRA (YUIMA-KYŌ)

The Vimalakīrti Sūtra eulogizes Buddha's lay disciple, Vimalakīrti, who lives as a householder and yet achieves a wisdom unmatched even by those following a monastic discipline. At the Japanese court, this ideal of the Buddhist layman found favor among men active in state affairs, and later under Fujiwara auspices, a date was reserved on the court calendar for reading and expounding on this sūtra. An extant commentary on the Vimalakīrti text has been traditionally ascribed to Prince Shōtoku. Although some modern scholarship has questioned this attribution, there can be little doubt that the sūtra itself and its teaching of Emptiness and Expedient Means were influential in seventh-century Japan.

At the time in the great city of Vaishali there was a rich man named Vimalakīrti. Already in the past he had offered alms to immeasurable numbers of Buddhas, had deeply planted the roots of goodness and had grasped the truth of birthlessness. Unhindered in his eloquence, able to disport himself with transcendental powers, he commanded full retention of the teachings and had attained the state of fearlessness. He had overcome the torments and ill will of the devil and entered deeply into the doctrine of the Law, proficient in the perfection of wisdom and a master in the employing of expedient means. He had successfully fulfilled his great vow and could clearly discern how the minds of others were tending. Moreover, he could distinguish whether their capacities were keen or obtuse. His mind was cleansed and purified through long practice of the Buddha Way, firm in its grasp of the Great Vehicle, and all his actions were well thought and planned. He maintained the dignity and authority of a Buddha, and his mind was vast as the sea. All the Buddhas sighed with admiration, and he commanded the respect of the disciples, of Indra, Brahma and the Four Heavenly Kings.

Desiring to save others, he employed the excellent expedient of residing in Vaishali. His immeasurable riches he used to relieve the poor, his faultless observation of the precepts served as a reproach to those who would violate prohibitions. Through his restraint and forbearance he warned others against rage and anger, and his great assiduousness discouraged all thought of sloth and indolence. Concentrating his single mind in quiet meditation, he suppressed disordered thoughts; through firm and unwavering wisdom he overcame all that was not wise. . . .

He frequented the busy crossroads in order to bring benefit to others, entered the government offices and courts of law so as to aid and rescue all those he could. He visited the places of debate in order to guide others to the Great Vehicle, visited the schools and study halls to further the instruction of the pupils. He entered houses of ill fame to teach the folly of fleshly desire, entered wine shops in order to encourage those with a will to quit them. . . .

The common people honored him as first among them because he helped them to gain wealth and power. The Brahma deities honored him as first among them because he revealed the superiority of wisdom. The Indras honored him as first among them because he demonstrated the truth of impermanence. The Four Heavenly Kings, guardians of the world, honored him as foremost because he guarded all living beings.

In this way the rich man Vimalakīrti employed immeasurable numbers of expedient means in order to bring benefit to others.

Using these expedient means, he made it appear that his body had fallen prey to illness. Because of his illness, the king of the country, the great ministers, rich men, lay believers and Brahmans, as well as the princes and lesser officials, numbering countless thousands, all went to see him and inquire about his illness.

Vimalakīrti then used this bodily illness to expound the Law to them in broad terms: "Good people, this body is impermanent, without durability, without strength, without firmness, a thing that decays in a moment, not to be relied on. It suffers, it is tormented, a meeting place of manifold ills.

"Good people, no person of enlightened wisdom could depend on a thing like this body. This body is like a cluster of foam, nothing you can grasp or handle. This body is like a bubble that cannot continue for long. This body is like a flame born of longing and desire. This body is like the plantain that has no firmness in its trunk. This body is like a phantom, the product of error and confusion. This body is like a shadow, appearing through karma causes. This body is like an echo, tied to causes and conditions. This body is like a drifting cloud, changing and vanishing in an instant. This body is like lightning, barely lasting from moment to moment.

"This body is like earth that has no subjective being. This body is like fire, devoid of ego. This body is like wind that has no set life span. This body is like water, devoid of individuality. . . .

This body is impure, crammed with defilement and evil. This body is empty and unreal; though for a time you may bathe and cleanse, clothe and feed it, in the end it must crumble and fade. This body is plague-ridden, beset by a hundred and one ills and anxieties. This body is like the abandoned well on the hillside, old age pressing in on it. This body has no fixity, but is destined for certain death. This body is like poisonous snakes, vengeful bandits or an empty village, a mere coming together of components, realms and sense-fields.

"Good people, a thing like this is irksome and hateful and therefore you should seek the Buddha body. Why? Because the Buddha is the Dharma body. It is born from immeasurable merits and wisdom. It is born from precepts, meditation, wisdom, emancipation and the insight of emancipation. It is born from pity, compassion, joy and indifference. . . .

The body of the Thus-Come One is born of immeasurable numbers of pure and spotless things such as these.

"Good people, if you wish to gain the Buddha body and do away with the ills that afflict all living beings, then you must set your minds on attaining supreme perfect enlightenment."

In this manner the rich man Vimalakīrti used the occasion to preach the Law to those who came to inquire about his illness. As a result, numberless thousands of persons were all moved to set their minds on the attainment of supreme perfect enlightenment. [pp. 32–36]

ENTERING THE GATE OF NONDUALISM

In the following passage, the sūtra deals with the question of how one enters "the gate of nondualism," that is, the entrance to "supreme perfect enlightenment."

At the time Vimalakīrti said to the various bodhisattvas, "Sirs, how does the bodhisattva go about entering the gate of nondualism? Let each explain as he understands it."

One of the bodhisattvas in the assembly, whose name was Dharma Freedom, spoke these words: "Sirs, birth and extinction form a dualism. But since all dharmas are not born to begin with, they must now be without extinction. By grasping and learning to accept this truth of birthlessness, one may enter the gate of nondualism." . . . .

The bodhisattva Delight in Truth said, "The true and the not true form a dualism. But one who sees truly cannot even see the true, so how can he see the untrue? Why? Because they cannot be seen by the physical eye; only the eye of wisdom can see them. But for this eye of wisdom there is no seeing and no not seeing. In this way one may enter the gate of nondualism."

When the various bodhisattvas had finished one by one giving their explanations, they asked Manjushri, "How then does the bodhisattva enter the gate of nondualism?"

Manjushri replied, "To my way of thinking, all dharmas are without words, without explanations, without purport, without cognition, removed from all questions and answers. In this way one may enter the gate of nondualism."

At that time Vimalakīrti remained silent and did not speak a word.

Manjushri sighed and said, "Excellent, excellent! Not a word, not a syllable; this truly is to enter the gate of nondualism."

[Adapted from Watson, *The Vimalakirti Sūtra*, pp. 32–35, 104, 110–111]

Chapter 4

CHINESE THOUGHT AND INSTITUTIONS

IN EARLY JAPAN

At this point a chapter devoted especially to Chinese influences in early Japan may seem needless, for in every topic discussed so far this influence has been quite conspicuous. As the Yamato people consolidated their position in central Japan and their rulers attempted to win undisputed supremacy over other clans of the confederacy, it was to the Chinese example that they turned more and more for political guidance and cultural direction. In Prince Shōtoku we have already seen the embodiment of this tendency to adopt and adapt all that China might contribute to the unification and pacification of a restless, turbulent people.

The most striking examples of this trend are to be found in the series of imperial edicts issued during the period of Great Reform (Taika), which began in 645. Proceeding from the theory enunciated in Shōtoku's constitution that "in a country there are not two lords; the people have not two masters," these reforms asserted the doctrine that "under the heavens there is no land which is not the king's land. Among holders of land there is none who is not the king's vassal." On this ground an ambitious program was launched to curb the powers of the clan leaders, who had frequently jeopardized the throne itself in their struggles for power. In place of the old political organization based on clan units was to be the systematic territorial administration of the Chinese, with local governors designated by the court, centrally directed and executing a uniform law to represent the paramount authority of the emperor. In keeping with this, the central administration itself was overhauled so as to provide a close replica of the great Tang empire's vast, symmetrical bureaucracy. A new aristocracy was thereby created of those who held office and court rank conferred by the throne. Thus the old and complex class structure, along with the clan hierarchy based on birth and blood, was to be replaced by a simpler division of society into two main classes, the rulers and the common people, characteristic of imperial China.

The reformers did not limit their actions to the political sphere. Indeed, implicit in the erection of this state machinery was the need for economic changes that would channel the wealth of the country toward the center of political power. Thus it was recognized from the first that the Tang tax system was indispensable to the functioning of the Tang-type administration. The Tang tax system, moreover, presupposed a system of land nationalization and redistribution such as that instituted during the early years of that dynasty by the famous monarch Taizong. Accordingly, the Japanese reformers attempted to abolish "private" property, nationalize the land, redistribute it on the basis of family size, and adopt the Chinese system of triple taxation on land, labor, and produce. In fact, so meticulously was the Chinese example followed that land and tax registers for this period, preserved in the imperial repository at Nara, are almost identical in form and terminology to contemporary Chinese registers discovered at the western outpost of the Chinese empire, Dunhuang. Furthermore, by their assertion of the imperial right to universal labor and military service, the reformers went far toward achieving for the ruling house the control over all the elements of power characteristic of the greatest Chinese dynasties. But with this wholesale imitation of China came likewise the chronic difficulties experienced by these dynasties, which tended to undermine the new state almost from the start.

In these early years, however, China exerted an influence more profound and lasting than the political changes inaugurated in the seventh century. This was the vast system of coordinated knowledge and belief of which the Chinese imperial structure was indeed the most imposing terrestrial symbol but that stretched out into realms of thought and action both transcending and penetrating the immediate political order. Like the imperial pattern itself, this far-reaching syncretism was a product of the Han dynasties (202 B.C.E.–220 C.E.), in which parallel tendencies unified and organized both the political and intellectual lives of China. In the realm of thought, this development was most apparent in the adoption of Confucianism as the state creed and cult, expounded in the imperial university, incorporated into the civil service examinations, and systematized by scholars working for the throne who tried to arrive at a definitive version of the Confucian classics.

The Confucianism of the Han dynasties, introduced to Japan at the latest by the sixth and seventh centuries C.E., represented more than the essential ethical teachings of Confucius and his early followers. Although these teachings were there, at the base of the new intellectual edifice, they had become overlaid and, to some extent, obscured by the great weight of correlative learning and doctrine that had since accumulated. This was not necessarily because many popular beliefs sought to gain respectability by associating with doctrines having the sanction of tradition and the state. Rather, Confucianism itself had to battle with other potent philosophies for official favor, and in the process its fundamental rationalism penetrated realms of thought that it had previously not explored fully. By so doing, it absorbed much from other traditions, such as the Daoist and Five Phases or Elements (or yin-yang) schools, to fill out its own lean frame.

Modern minds may find a great deal here that seems to have been poorly digested. Yet we must recognize that in terms of the knowledge then available, this synthesis is remarkable for its order and coherence, and in the hands of an articulate spokesman such as Dong Zhongshu, it served well to reinforce some of the fundamental political doctrines of the Confucian school, persuading absolute monarchs to use their power wisely and with restraint. At the heart of all such Confucian speculation is the doctrine, which Confucianism shared with other influential schools of thought, that the universe is a harmonious whole in which humankind and nature constantly interact with each other in all aspects of life. From this doctrine it was concluded that human actions, particularly those of rulers, affect the natural order, which is sensitive above all to the ethical quality of their acts. If people fail to fulfill their proper functions, nature will act or operate to restore the total balance or harmony. For this reason, it was believed that natural occurrences, especially spectacular aberrations, would reveal—when properly interpreted—the extent to which a person or ruler had lapsed from his duty or his proper course of conduct.

The importance in China of divination and other early arts or sciences is evident when we consider that the earliest Chinese writing now preserved is found on oracle bones, recording the questions and responses that the diviners obtained by scrutinizing the cracks made when the bones were heated. In later times we find that astrologers were called "historians" (*shi*) and combined the functions of both diviners and compilers of records. Their influence is apparent in the Chinese view of history as the expression of the processes and decrees of Heaven. For the early Chinese, a noteworthy event was not merely a fact to be recorded—it was to be interpreted as either a bad omen or a sign of Heaven's approval. Eclipses and comets were evident attempts of Heaven to express its desires, but the sight of an unusually shaped cloud was also sometimes considered important enough to warrant changing the name by which a part of an emperor's reign was known. The close connection between the diviner and the historian is revealed in the statement in the preface to the *True Records of Three Japanese Reigns* (901 C.E.), in which the compilers declare their intent of fully recording the "auspicious signs with which Heaven favors the Lord of Men and the portents with which Heaven admonishes the Lord of Men." The application of this method is already fully evident in such an early history as the *Chronicles of Japan* (*Nihongi*).

Behind such a statement lay the belief in the necessary correspondences between the worlds of Heaven and earth. When the astronomers reported that the heavenly bodies had reached their spring positions, the rites suitable to spring had to be performed on earth. Or if a lucky cloud indicated that some favorable change had been decreed by Heaven, a corresponding change, such as in the reign name, had to be made on earth. A failure to observe the changes in Heaven might lead to disasters on earth. If, for example, a rite suitable to winter were performed in the spring because of a faulty calendar, the crops would be destroyed in the bud by wintry weather. The proper rites, on the other hand, could ensure such blessings as seasonal rainfall. The Han philosopher Dong Zhongshu described various ways of making sure that rain fell when it was needed; one of them was to have the government employees and other subjects cohabit with their wives on a day chosen by yin-yang methods.

Different sciences were evolved to deal with events in the Three Realms of Heaven, Earth, and Humankind. These were, respectively, astrology, geomancy, and the art of "avoiding calamities." Astrology enabled people to discover what the fate of a kingdom or an individual was to be. The twelve divisions of the heavens (based on the twelve-year cycle of the planet Jupiter) had corresponding divisions on earth, so when, for example, Jupiter was in the division of the heavens "controlling" a particular country, that country was safe from invasion. By learning from the stars what Heaven decreed, one could predict events on earth. Conversely, by means of geomancy and the art of "avoiding calamities," people could cooperate with Heaven if this was in their interest. Thus, when the site of Kyoto was chosen because it possessed the "proper" number of rivers and mountains, it represented an attempt to secure by means of geomancy the most auspicious surroundings for the new capital. Heaven—understood here as Nature—had designed such a place for a capital, and humans could benefit by it. The art of "avoiding calamities" may have been especially congenial to the Japanese because, as earlier recorded in the Chinese dynastic histories, they favored the arts of prognostication.

In 602 C.E., the Korean monk Kwallŭk brought to Japan some books on geomancy and "avoiding calamities." Several members of the court were selected to study with Kwallŭk, and some of the extraordinary changes that took place in the next few years may be attributed to the influence of the new learning. In 604, a year whose astrological signs marked it for "avoiding calamities" as a "revolutionary year," Prince Shōtoku's Seventeen-Article Constitution was proclaimed. In the same year also appeared the first Japanese calendar, an event of immense importance to both the writing of history and the development of the rites of state.

It may be, of course, that these events did not actually occur in 604 but were credited to that year by later historians anxious to impart additional significance to them by their association with a "revolutionary year." It seems clear now, for example, that the events attributed to the reign of the legendary emperor Jinmu were assigned to "revolutionary years" by the compilers of the *Chronicles of Japan* for a similar reason. There is, in any case, ample evidence of the prevalence of yin-yang (by which the whole Han Confucian ideology is meant) thinking in both the *Records of Ancient Matters* (712) and the *Chronicles of Japan* (720). The preface to the former work begins:

> Now when chaos had begun to condense, but force and form were not yet manifest, and there was nought named, nought done, who could know its shape? Nevertheless Heaven and Earth first parted, and the Three Deities performed the commencement of creation; the yin and the yang then developed, and the Two Spirits became the ancestors of all things.[1]

The *Chronicles of Japan* begins:

> Of old, Heaven and Earth were not yet separated, and the yin and the yang not yet divided. They formed a chaotic mass like an egg which was of obscurely defined limits and contained germs. The purer and clearer part was thinly drawn out, and formed Heaven, while the heavier and grosser element settled down and became Earth.[2]

Perhaps the chief purpose of the compilation of the *Records of Ancient Matters* was to establish the legitimacy of the claim of Emperor Tenmu and his descendants to the throne. This was done in terms of both genealogy and virtue or accomplishment. For instance, it was declared of Tenmu that, among other things, "he held the mean between the Two Essences [yin and yang], and regulated the order of the Five Phases." We can see, then, how intimately yin-yang thinking was connected with early Japanese historiography.

Mention of the five phases brings us to the center of the art of "avoiding calamities." An elaborate system of correspondences among the planets, the elements, the directions, the seasons, the signs of the zodiac, and various other categories was created, as follows:

Planet	*Element*	*Direction*	*Season*	*Signs of the Zodiac*
Jupiter	wood	east	spring	tiger, hare
Mars	fire	south	summer	serpent, horse
Saturn	earth	center	solstices[3]	dog, ox, dragon, sheep
Venus	metal	west	autumn	monkey, cock
Mercury	water	north	winter	boar, rat

1. Chamberlain, *Ko-ji-ki*, p. 4.
2. Aston, *Nihongi*, I, pp. 1–2.
3. Summer and winter intervals between the seasons.

According to the theory of the five phases or elements, the two elements bordering any particular element were beneficial to it, whereas the two separated elements were harmful. Thus both wood and earth were beneficial to fire, but metal and water were harmful. Likewise, a person born under the sign of Mars would make a suitable spouse for one born under Jupiter and Saturn, but not for one born under Venus or Mercury. It was possible to "avoid calamity" by preventing a marriage or partnership between people born under conflicting elements.

In Japan, life came to be ruled largely by such beliefs. When we read novels of the Heian period (794–1186), we cannot help but notice the frequent mention of "unlucky directions" or "unlucky days." Depending on the planet governing a person, different directions were auspicious or inauspicious on a certain day. Diaries giving the astrological conditions of each day of the year were popular with the great men of the state, who made their plans according to the prevailing heavenly influences. To advise the government on all matters of yin-yang lore, a department of yin-yang (Onyōryō) was established as early as 675 C.E., and detailed provisions for its organization were given in the Taihō Code of 701–702.

The yin-yang attempt to explain both the physical and spiritual phenomena of the universe in terms of the five phases was increasingly successful and met little serious opposition. Some Buddhists appear to have been hostile at first to fortune-telling on the basis of the five phases but later attempted to do much the same with phases of their own choosing. By and large, however, the yin-yang teachings were widely accepted and remained unchallenged until modern times. Up to 1861, for example, the reign names continued to change regularly when one of the "revolutionary years" turned up in the cycle. The yin-yang system has been used on many occasions even in recent decades; lucky days are still chosen by yin-yang methods; and the zodiacal sign under which a person was born was rarely ignored when arranging marriages.

Yin-yang was not the only variety of Chinese thought familiar to the Japanese court of the Nara and Heian periods. The classics of Confucianism and Daoism were relatively well known, as is evinced by the poetry of the *Manyōshū*, an anthology completed in the eighth century. Here we find frequent echoes of Chinese thought in a form indicating their familiarity even at that early date. Outright imitations of Chinese thought and literature can be found in the *Kaifūsō*, a collection of poetry written in Chinese dating from 751 C.E.. It was not only in literary works that Japanese writers showed their indebtedness to Chinese style and sentiments. When, for example, the commentary on the legal code of 833 C.E. was submitted to the throne, it was accompanied by a memorial that is a tissue of allusions to Chinese literature. Thus, Japan borrowed the legal institutions of the Tang dynasty not only for its own purposes but also for the flowery phraseology in which the Chinese were accustomed to give their reasons for the existence of laws. The use of such language undoubtedly had a great influence on the development of thought in Japan, and specimens of it can be found in innumerable prefaces and memorials.

The lasting remains of the introduction of Chinese thought to early Japan are apparent in every field, but especially in the concept of imperial rule, sometimes called Tennōism. In modern times, Tennōism has been identified with the claims made for the divine ancestry of the imperial house, its unbroken succession from the Sun Goddess, and the commission of the Divine Grandson's imperial descendants to rule the land. The formulation of this idea and the title itself, however, reflect a convergence of the state-building process on the Chinese model (what might be called Han imperial absolutism) and its fusion of Chinese religious and cosmological notions with native Japanese traditions.

We mentioned earlier that when the Japanese addressed the Sui court, speaking for the "Child of Heaven in the Land of the Rising Sun" to "the Child of Heaven in the Land of the Setting Sun," the Chinese court was incensed by Japan's temerity in making this claim to parity, if not superiority. Diplomatic niceties aside, the Japanese themselves could have had some difficulty with the Chinese concept of the child or son of Heaven to which attached the Confucian idea that the emperor, out of filial respect, should conform to Heaven's mandate, that is, conduct his rule in accordance with the moral, rational, and generally human principles identified with Heaven and its mandate. Chinese emperors were thus theoretically subject to the criteria of merit, and rulers or dynasties could forfeit the mandate to rule if they did not live up to them. Japanese rule (and Japanese social life generally), however, was governed by the hereditary principle, not the merit principle, and those who represented the Japanese dynasty must have been somewhat uneasy with the language of the "Child of Heaven" and its implied basis of legitimacy in moral accountability.

For their purposes, a more convenient non-Confucian Chinese term existed in the expression (Ch: *tien-huang,* J: *tennō*) "Heavenly Emperor," which in Chinese religious cosmology (often thought of as Daoist) was identified with the North Star as patron deity of the northern quarter of the imperial capital. Moreover, since the Imperial Palace (both in China and, by now, in Nara-period Japan) was located in the northern quarter according to this cosmological scheme, imperial rule was considered to be under the aegis of this god, which conveniently bore no moral connotations.

The final step in this process linked the *tennō* concept with the claim of the imperial house to be descended from the Sun Goddess. She was not, however, first among the gods in time, generation, or seniority. As we have seen, some of the early accounts referred to her diminutively as the Sun Princess or Sun

Maiden (Ōhirume), and she was the younger sister of Susa no wo. But by referring to her as Amaterasu no Ōmikami (Great Heaven Shining Deity, her name as written in Chinese characters, *tien* or *ten* for "Ama"), the authority of Heaven as expressed by a prime Japanese religious symbol, the sun, could be invoked to legitimize imperial rule without incurring any responsibility for answering to moral, rational criteria. Such Confucian qualities might be attributed to individual rulers personally without subjecting the imperial line itself to any such accountability.

The successive steps taken toward establishing a strong central government reflect Japanese adherence to the Chinese concept of the sovereign as the sole possessor of Heaven's sanction. Prince Shōtoku's constitution, the Taika reforms, and the adoption of Chinese legal and bureaucratic institutions all were intended to strengthen the emperor's claim to be a true polar star about whom the lesser celestial luminaries turned. Symbolic of this trend is the choice of posthumous titles for the two great rulers of the late seventh century, Tenchi (or Tenji) (Heavenly Wisdom) and Tenmu (Heavenly Might).

The establishment of a more permanent capital at Nara in 710 also was necessary for the prestige of the emperor in the eyes of his people as well as in those of such Chinese or Korean emissaries as might visit the country. The capitals at Nara and then Kyoto were built in imitation of Changan, closely following yin-yang theories. Kyoto was divided by eight streets and nine avenues. The palace, situated in the north in accordance with yin-yang, was surrounded by ninefold walls. The emperor was served by a bureaucracy organized into nine departments of state, with eight ranks of officials. And as if to protect the capital from baleful influences coming from the northeast, the unlucky quarter, a Buddhist monastery was built as a spiritual bastion on Mount Hiei, which lay in that direction. But before this event, Buddhism itself had become a force to be reckoned with by the government, and to this development we shall turn in the next chapter.

CHINESE-STYLE HISTORY AND THE IMPERIAL CONCEPT

The following excerpts should be read with those from the *Records of Ancient Matters* (*Kojiki*) and the *Chronicles of Japan* (*Nihongi*), contained in the first and second chapters, which traced the legendary beginnings of the Japanese people and ruling house. The selections here, while related to the same subject, are intended to show especially how, in the writing of history on Chinese models, the imperial line is clothed with all the attributes of the ideal Chinese ruler and how the Chinese concept of sovereignty has been adapted to the Japanese situation so as to strengthen the claims of the Yamato kings.

The opening excerpt, written as a preface to the first extant book, expresses a more sober, rational, and critical attitude, reflecting the difficulty of providing a coherent and credible account from legendary sources that are quite unsystematic, diverse, and uncritically naive in their native simplicity. Nevertheless, the author does his best to measure up to the standards and forms of Chinese historiography.

FROM THE PREFACE TO *RECORDS OF ANCIENT MATTERS* (*KOJIKI*)

Hereupon, regretting the errors in the old words and wishing to correct the misstatements in the former chronicles, [Empress Genmyō], on the eighteenth day of the ninth moon of the fourth year of Wadō [November 3, 711], commanded me, Yasumaro, to select and record the old words, learned by heart by Hieda no Are according to the imperial decree, and dutifully to lift them up to her.

In reverent obedience to the contents of the decree, I have made a careful choice. But in high antiquity, both speech and thought were so simple that it would be difficult to arrange phrases and compose periods in the characters.[4] To relate everything in an ideographic transcription would entail an inadequate expression of the meaning; to write altogether according to the phonetic method would make the story of events unduly lengthy.[5] For this reason have I sometimes in the same sentence used the phonic and ideographic systems conjointly and have sometimes in one matter used the ideographic record exclusively. Moreover, where the drift of the words was obscure, I have by comments elucidated their signification, but need it be said that I have nowhere commented on what was easy? . . . All together, the things recorded commence with the separation of Heaven and Earth and conclude with the august reign at Oharida.[6] So from the Deity Master-of-the-August-Center-of-Heaven down to His Augustness Prince-Wave-Limit-Brave-Cormorant-Thatch-Meeting-Incompletely makes the first volume; from the Heavenly Sovereign Kamu-Yamato-Ihare-Biko down to the august reign of Homuda makes the second volume; from the Emperor Ō-Sazaki down to the great palace of Oharida makes the third vol-

---

4. That is, the simplicity of speech and thought in early Japan renders it too hard a task to rearrange the old documents committed to memory by Are in such a manner as to make them conform to the rules of Chinese style.

5. That is, if I adopted in its entirety the Chinese ideographic method of writing, I should often fail to give a true impression of the nature of the original documents. But if I consistently used the Chinese characters, syllable by syllable, as phonetic symbols for Japanese sounds, this work would reach inordinate proportions, on account of the great length of the polysyllabic Japanese as compared with the monosyllabic Chinese.

6. That is, commence with the creation and end with the death of Empress Suiko (628 C.E.), who resided at Oharida.

ume.[7] All together, I have written three volumes, which I reverently and re-spectfully present. I, Yasumaro, with true trembling and true fear, bow my head, bow my head.

Reverently presented by the Court Noble Futo No Yasumaro, an officer of the upper division of the first class of the fifth rank and of the fifth order of merit, on the 28th day of the first moon of the fifth year of Wadō [March 10, 712].

[Adapted from Chamberlain, Ko-ji-ki, pp. 11–13]

EMPEROR JINMU

The following extracts from the *Chronicles of Japan* deal with the reign of Emperor Jinmu, who reputedly founded the earthly domain of the imperial line. It is clear that the concept of sovereignty and pretensions to universal rule advanced here (and made much of in the emperor-centered nationalism of modern times) are based on Han Chinese models. Hence the incongruities that appear when the historian—obviously with one eye on the claims of imperial China to being the Central Kingdom of the world—makes similar claims for this remote island kingdom.

The Emperor Kami Yamato Ihare-biko's personal name was Hiko-hoho-demi. He was the fourth child of Hiko-nagisa-take-u-gaya-fuki-aezu no Mikoto. His mother's name was Tama-yori-hime, daughter of the sea god. From his birth, this emperor was of clear intelligence and resolute will. At the age of fifteen he was heir to the throne. When he grew up, he married Ahira-tsu-hime, of the district of Ata in the province of Hyūga, and made her his consort. By her he had Tagishi-mimi no Mikoto and Kisu-mimi no Mikoto.

When he reached the age of forty-five, he addressed his elder brothers and his children, saying: "Of old, Our Heavenly Deities Taka-mi-musubi no Mikoto and Ō-hiru-me no Mikoto, pointing to this land of fair rice-ears of the fertile reed-plain, gave it to Our Heavenly ancestor, Hiko-ho no ninigi no Mikoto. Thereupon Hiko-ho no ninigi no Mikoto, throwing open the barrier of Heaven and clearing a cloud path, urged on his superhuman course until he came to rest. At this time the world was given over to widespread desolation. It was an age of darkness and disorder. In this gloom, therefore, he fostered justice and so governed this western border.[8] Our imperial ancestors and imperial parent, like gods, like sages, accumulated happiness and amassed glory. Many years elapsed. From the date when Our Heavenly ancestor descended until now it is

---

7. Kamu-Yamato-Ihare-Biko is the proper native Japanese name of the emperor commonly known by the Chinese "canonical name" of Jinmu. Homuda is part of the native Japanese name of Emperor Ōjin. Ō-Sazaki is the native Japanese name of Emperor Nintoku.

8. That is, Kyushu.

over 1,792,470 years.[9] But the remote regions do not yet enjoy the blessings of imperial rule. Every town has always been allowed to have its lord, and every village its chief, who, each one for himself, makes division of territory and practices mutual aggression and conflict.

"Now I have heard from the Ancient of the Sea[10] that in the east there is a fair land encircled on all sides by blue mountains. Moreover, there is there one who flew down riding in a Heavenly Rock-boat. I think that this land will undoubtedly be suitable for the extension of the Heavenly task,[11] so that its glory should fill the universe. It is, doubtless, the center of the world.[12] The person who flew down was, I believe, Nigi-haya-hi.[13] Why should we not proceed thither, and make it the capital?"

All the imperial princes answered and said: "The truth of this is manifest. This thought is constantly present to our minds also. Let us go thither quickly." This was the year Kinoe Tora [fifty-first] of the Great Year[14] [pp. 109–111].

The year Tsuchinoto Hitsuji, Spring, 3rd month, 7th day. The emperor made an order[15] saying: "During the six years that our expedition against the east has lasted, owing to my reliance on the Majesty of Imperial Heaven, the wicked bands have met death. It is true that the frontier lands are still unpurified and that a remnant of evil is still refractory. But in the region of the Central Land,[16] there is no more wind and dust. Truly we should make a vast and spacious capital and plan it great and strong.

"At present things are in a crude and obscure condition, and the people's minds are unsophisticated. They roost in nests or dwell in caves.[17] Their manners are simply what is customary. Now if a great man were to establish laws, justice could not fail to flourish. And even if some gain should accrue to the people, in what way would this interfere with the Sage's[18] action? Moreover, it

---

9. This is in imitation of the great number of years ascribed to the reigns of the early Chinese monarchs.

10. Shiho tsutsu no oji.

11. That is, for the further development of the imperial power.

12. The world is here the six quarters north, south, east, west, zenith, and nadir. This is, of course, Chinese, as indeed is this whole speech.

13. *Nigi-haya-hi* means "soft-swift-sun."

14. The great year is the Chinese cycle of sixty years. It is needless to add that such dates are, in this part of the *Nihongi*, purely fictitious.

15. This whole speech is thoroughly Chinese in every respect, and it is preposterous to put it in the mouth of an emperor who is supposed to have lived more than a thousand years before the introduction of Chinese learning into Japan.

16. Claiming for Japan the name always used for China: "Central Kingdom."

17. The reader must not take this as any evidence of the manners and customs of the ancient Japanese. It is simply a phrase suggested by the author's Chinese studies.

18. Meaning the emperor's action, because in Chinese tradition the early rulers were "sage-kings."

will be well to open up and clear the mountains and forests, and to construct a palace. Then I may reverently assume the Precious Dignity and so give peace to my good subjects. Above, I should then respond to the kindness of the Heavenly Powers in granting me the kingdom, and below, I should extend the line of the imperial descendants and foster rightmindedness. Thereafter the capital may be extended so as to embrace all the six cardinal points, and the eight cords may be covered so as to form a roof.[19] Will this not be well?

When I observe the Kashiwa-bara plain, which lies southwest of Mount Unebi, it seems the center of the land. I must set it in order."

Accordingly he in this month commanded officers to set about the construction of an imperial residence [pp. 131–132].

[Aston, *Nihongi*, I, pp. 109–132]

NINTOKU: RULE OF BENEVOLENCE

Nintoku is a striking example of the legendary Japanese emperor, clothed in all the attributes of the Chinese sage-king, as the virtuous father of his people sacrificing his own comfort in order to provide for their welfare. The benevolent paternalism ascribed to Nintoku, a much later successor to Jinmu, became an important element in the glorification of the emperor as an embodiment not simply of awesome power but also of heavenly virtue and love.

4th year, Spring, 2nd month, 6th day. The emperor addressed his ministers, saying: "We ascended a lofty tower and looked far and wide, but no smoke arose in the land. From this we gather that the people are poor and that in the houses there are none cooking their rice. We have heard that in the reigns of the wise sovereigns of antiquity,[20] from everyone was heard the sound of songs hymning their virtue, in every house there was the ditty, 'How happy are we.' But now when we observe the people, for three years past, no voice of eulogy is heard; the smoke of cooking has become rarer and rarer. By this we know that the five grains[21] do not come up and that the people are in extreme want. Even in the home provinces[22] there are some who are not supplied; what must it be in the provinces outside of our domain?"

3rd month, 21st day. The following decree was issued: "From this time forward, for the space of three years, let forced labor be entirely abolished, and let

---

19. The character for "roof" also means the "universe." The eight cords or measuring tapes simply mean "everywhere."

20. Actually Chinese antiquity.

21. Hemp, millet, rice, wheat and barley, and legumes—the Five Grains of ancient China.

22. The territory around the capital ruled immediately by the emperor. This is a Chinese phrase, not properly applicable to Japan at this period.

the people have rest from toil." From this day forth his robes of state and shoes did not wear out, and none were made. The warm food and hot broths did not become sour or putrid and were not renewed. He disciplined his heart and restrained his impulses so that he discharged his functions without effort.

Therefore the palace enclosure fell to ruin and was not rebuilt; the thatch decayed and was not repaired; the wind and rain entered by the chinks and soaked the coverlets; the starlight filtered through the decayed places and exposed the bed mats. After this the wind and rain came in due season,[23] the five grains produced in abundance. For the space of three autumns the people had plenty, the praises of his virtue filled the land, and the smoke of cooking was also thick.

7th year, Summer, 4th month, 1st day. The emperor was on his tower and, looking far and wide, saw smoke arising plentifully. On this day he addressed the empress, saying: "We are now prosperous. What can there be to grieve for?" The empress answered and said: "What dost thou mean by prosperity?" The emperor said: "It is doubtless when the smoke fills the lands, and the people freely attain to wealth." The empress went on to say: "The palace enclosure is crumbling down, and there are no means of repairing it; the buildings are dilapidated so that the coverlets are exposed. Can this be called prosperity?" The emperor said: "When Heaven establishes a prince, it is for the sake of the people. The prince must therefore make the people the foundation. For this reason the wise sovereigns of antiquity, if a single one of their subjects was cold and starving, cast the responsibility on themselves. Now the people's poverty is no other than our poverty; the people's prosperity is none other than our prosperity. There is no such thing as the people's being prosperous and yet the prince in poverty."[24]

[Aston, *Nihongi*, I, 278–279]

THE REFORM ERA

The way was cleared for the inauguration of the Taika reforms in 645 by the overthrow of the powerful Soga clan. Before this, the *Nihongi* records many strange occurrences and calamities, as if Heaven were showing its displeasure over the Soga usurpation of imperial power. Then Fujiwara no Kamatari and the future emperor, Tenchi, appeared on the scene as the leaders of a "restoration." Kamatari, from the Nakatomi clan traditionally charged with Shinto priestly functions, is said to have declined several

---

23. The notion that the emperor's virtues have a direct influence on the weather is, of course, Chinese.

24. This whole episode is the composition of someone familiar with Chinese literature. The sentiments are throughout characteristically Chinese, and in several cases, whole sentences are copied verbatim from Chinese works.

times the post of superintendent of the Shinto religion. After his successful coup, the emperor that Kamatari installed on the throne is likewise identified in the *Nihongi* as one who "despised the Way of the Gods (Shinto)." Kamatari devoted himself to Chinese learning and is cast by the historian in the role of the duke of Zhou, the statesman instrumental in founding the Zhou dynasty in China and in establishing what was regarded by Confucians as the ideal social order.

FUJIWARA NO KAMATARI AND THE FUTURE EMPEROR TENCHI

The Deity Chieftain Nakatomi no Kamako [Fujiwara no Kamatari] was a man of an upright and loyal character and of a reforming disposition. He was indignant with Soga no Iruka for breaking down the order of prince and vassal, of senior and junior, and cherishing veiled designs upon the state. One after another he associated with the princes of the imperial line, trying them in order to discover a wise ruler who might establish a great reputation. He had accordingly fixed his mind on Naka no Ōe, but for want of intimate relations with him, he had been so far unable to unfold his inner sentiments. Happening to be one of a football[25] party in which Naka no Ōe [the future Tenchi] played at the foot of the keyaki tree of the temple of Hōkōji, he observed the [prince's] leathern shoe fall off with the ball. Placing it on the palm of his hand, he knelt before the prince and humbly offered it to him. Naka no Ōe in his turn knelt down and respectfully received it. From this time they became mutual friends and told each other all their thoughts. There was no longer any concealment between them. They feared, however, that jealous suspicions might be caused by their frequent meetings and they both took in their hands yellow rolls[26] and studied personally the doctrines of Zhou[27] and Confucius with the learned Minabuchi. Thus they at length while on their way there and back, walking shoulder to shoulder, secretly prepared their plans. On all points they were agreed.

[Aston, *Nihongi*, II, pp. 184–185]

INAUGURATION OF THE GREAT REFORM ERA

After the assassination of the Soga leaders, the reigning empress abdicated and a new government was formed with the future Tenchi as crown prince and Kamatari as chief

---

25. What kind of football—like ours or, in Chinese fashion, knocking the ball from one to another like a shuttlecock—is not clear.

26. Chinese books.

27. The duke of Zhou, the statesman and sage instrumental in founding the Zhou dynasty in China.

minister actually directing affairs. A new reign and era title was therefore announced, Taika, meaning "Great Transformation."

4th year of Kōkyoku (645), 6th month, 19th day. The emperor, the empress dowager, and the prince imperial summoned together the ministers under the great tsuki tree and made an oath appealing to the gods of Heaven and Earth, and saying:

"Heaven covers us: Earth upbears us: the imperial way is but one. But in this last degenerate age, the order of lord and vassal was destroyed, until Supreme Heaven by our hands put to death the traitors. Now, from this time forward, both parties shedding their heart's blood, the lord will eschew double methods of government, and the vassal will avoid duplicity in his service of the sovereign! On him who breaks this oath, Heaven will send a curse and earth a plague, demons will slay them, and men will smite them. This is as manifest as the sun and moon."[28]

The style 4th year of the Empress Ame-toyo-takara ikashi-hi tarashihime was altered to Taika, 1st year.

[Aston, *Nihongi*, II, pp. 197–198]

REFORM EDICTS

Only a few of the most important reform edicts are included here, outlining the major steps taken by the court to extend its political and fiscal control over the country. These steps were aimed at establishing a Chinese type of centralized administration over areas that previously had enjoyed considerable autonomy under hereditary clan chieftains.

1st year of Taika [645], 8th month, 5th day. Governors of the eastern provinces were appointed. Then the governors were addressed as follows: "In accordance with the charge entrusted to us by the gods of Heaven, We propose at present for the first time to regulate the myriad provinces.

"When you proceed to your posts, prepare registers of all the free subjects of the state and of the people under the control of others, whether great or small. Take account also of the acreage of cultivated land. As to the profits arising from the gardens and ponds, the water and land, deal with them in common with the people. Moreover it is not competent for the provincial governors while in their provinces to decide criminal cases, nor are they permitted by accepting bribes to bring the people to poverty and misery. When

---

28. Note that there is nothing Buddhist or Shinto in this vow. It is pure Chinese. Furthermore, it is not exactly an oath according to our ideas but an imprecation on rebellion.

they come up to the capital, they must not bring large numbers of the people in their train. They are only allowed to bring with them the local chieftains and the district officials. But when they travel on public business, they may ride the horses of their department and eat the food of their department. From the rank of Suke[29] upwards, those who obey this law will surely be rewarded while those who disobey it shall be liable to be reduced in cap rank. On all, from the rank of Hangan[30] downwards, who accept bribes a fine shall be imposed of double the amount, and they shall eventually be punished criminally according to the greater or less heinousness of the case. Nine men are allowed as attendants on a chief governor, seven on an assistant, and five on a secretary. If this limit is exceeded, and they are accompanied by a greater number, both chief and followers shall be punished criminally.

"If there be any persons who lay claim to a title[31] but who, not being local chieftains, imperial chieftains or custodians[32] of districts by descent, unscrupulously draw up lying memorials, saying: 'From the time of our forefathers we have had charge of this Miyake or have ruled this district,' in such cases, ye, the governors, must not readily make application to the court in acquiescence in such fictions but must ascertain particularly the true facts before making your report.

"Moreover on waste pieces of ground let arsenals be erected, and let the swords and armor, with the bows and arrows of the provinces and districts, be deposited together in them. In the case of the frontier provinces which border close on the Emishi,[33] let all the weapons be mustered together, and let them remain in the hands of their original owners. In regard to the six districts of the province of Yamato, let the officials who are sent there prepare registers of the population and also take into account the acreage of cultivated land.

"This means to examine the acreage of the cultivated ground, and then numbers, houses and ages of the people." [pp. 200–201]

. . .

9th month, 19th day. Commissioners were sent to all the provinces to take a record of the total numbers of the people. The emperor on this occasion made an edict as follows:

"In the times of all the emperors, from antiquity downwards, subjects have been set apart for the purpose of making notable their reigns and handing down their names to posterity. Now the imperial chieftains and deity chieftains, the

---

29. Assistant to a governor.
30. Assistant district chief.
31. Literally, "name."
32. Collectors and guardians of tax grain.
33. Ainu.

court chieftains, and local chieftains have each one set apart their own vassals, whom they compel to labor at their arbitrary pleasure. Moreover they cut off the hills and seas, the woods and plains, the ponds and rice fields belonging to the provinces and districts and appropriate them to themselves. Their contests are never ceasing. Some engross to themselves many tens of thousand of *shiro*[34] of rice land while others possess in all patches of ground too small to stick a needle into. When the time comes for the payment of taxes, the imperial chieftains, the deity chieftains, and the court chieftains first collect them for themselves and then hand over a share. In the case of repairs to palaces or the construction of imperial tombs, they each bring their own vassals, and do the work according to circumstances. The Classic of Changes says: 'Diminish that which is above: increase that which is below: if measures are framed according to the regulations, the resources [of the state] suffer no injury, and the people receive no hurt.'

"At the present time, the people are still few. And yet the powerful cut off portions of land and water,[35] and converting them into private ground, sell it to the people, demanding the price yearly. From this time forward the sale of the land is not allowed. Let no man without due authority make himself a landlord, engrossing to himself that which belongs to the helpless."

The people were greatly rejoiced. [pp. 204–205]

2nd year [646], Spring, 1st month, 1st day. As soon as the ceremonies of the new year's congratulations were over, the emperor promulgated an edict of reform, as follows:

"I. Let the people established by the ancient emperors, etc., as representatives of children be abolished, also the Miyake of various places and the people owned as serfs by the Wake, the imperial chieftains, and the village headmen. Let the farmsteads[36] in various places be abolished." Consequently fiefs[37] were granted for their sustenance to those of the rank of Daibu and upwards on a descending scale. Presents of cloth and silk stuffs were given to the officials and people, varying in value.

"Further we say. It is the business of the Daibu to govern the people. If they discharge this duty thoroughly, the people have trust in them, and an increase of their revenue is therefore for the good of the people.

"II. The capital is for the first time to be regulated, and governors appointed for the home provinces and districts. Let barriers, outposts, guards and post

---

34. A land measure of 15.13 acres.

35. That is, rice ground and other cultivated land.

36. Of serfs.

37. Not a true feudal domain but office lands from which these officials could draw the tax proceeds as a form of salary.

horses, both special and ordinary, be provided, bell tokens[38] made, and mountains and rivers regulated.[39]

"For each ward in the capital let there be appointed one alderman, and for four wards one chief alderman, who shall be charged with the superintendence of the population and the examination of criminal matters. For appointment as chief alderman of wards let men be taken belonging to the wards, of unblemished character, firm and upright, so that they may fitly sustain the duties of the time. For appointment as aldermen, whether of rural townships or of city wards, let ordinary subjects be taken belonging to the township or ward, of good character and solid capacity. If such men are not to be found in the township or ward in question, it is permitted to select and employ men of the adjoining township or ward.

"The home provinces shall include the region from the River Yokogawa at Nabari on the east, from Mount Senoyama in Kii on the south, from Kushibuchi in Akashi on the west, and from Mount Afusakayama in Sasanami in Afumi on the north. Districts of forty townships[40] are constituted greater districts, of from thirty to four townships are constituted middle districts, and of three or fewer townships are constituted lesser districts. For the district authorities, of whatever class, let there be taken local chieftains of unblemished character, such as may fitly sustain the duties of the time, and made Tairei and Shōrei.[41] Let men of solid capacity and intelligence who are skilled in writing and arithmetic be appointed assistants and clerks.

"The number of special or ordinary post horses given shall in all cases follow the number of marks on the posting bell tokens. When bell tokens are given to [officials of] the provinces and barriers, let them be held in both cases by the chief official, or in his absence by the assistant official.

"III. Let there now be provided for the first time registers of population, books of account and a system of the receipt and regranting of distribution land.[42]

"Let every fifty houses be reckoned a township, and in every township let there be one alderman who shall be charged with the superintendence of the population,[43] the direction of the sowing of crops and the cultivation of mul-

---

38. Signs of rank indicating the number of horses to which an official was entitled—a Chinese practice.

39. The regulation of mountains and rivers means the provision of guards at ferries and mountain passes serving as boundaries between different provinces.

40. A township consisted of fifty houses.

41. Greater and lesser governors.

42. The Denryō (Land Regulations) says, "In granting Kō-bun-den [land shared in proportion to population] men shall have two *tan*, women a third less and children under five years of age none. Lands are granted for a term of six years."

43. That is, of the registers of population.

berry trees, the prevention and examination of offenses, and the enforcement of the payment of taxes and of forced labor.

"For rice land, thirty paces in length by twelve paces in breadth shall be reckoned a *tan*.[44] Ten *tan* make one *chō*. For each *tan* the tax is two sheaves and two bundles [such as can be grasped in the hand] of rice; for each *chō* the tax is twenty-two sheaves of rice. On mountains or in valleys where the land is precipitous, or in remote places where the population is scanty, such arrangements are to be made as may be convenient.

"IV. The old taxes and forced labor are abolished, and a system of commuted taxes instituted. These shall consist of fine silks, coarse silks, raw silk, and floss silk, all in accordance with what is produced in the locality. For each *chō* of rice land the rate is one rod[45] of fine silk, or for four *chō* one piece forty feet in length by two and a half feet in width. For coarse silk the rate is two rods [per *chō*], or one piece for every two *chō* of the same length and width as the fine silk. For cloth the rate is four rods of the same dimensions as the fine and coarse silk, i.e., one *tan*[46] for each *chō*. [No rates of weight are anywhere given for silk or floss silk.] Let there be levied separately a commuted house tax. All houses shall pay each one rod and two feet of cloth. The extra articles of this tax, as well as salt and offerings, will depend on what is produced in the locality. For horses for the public service, let every hundred houses contribute one horse of medium quality. Or if the horse is of superior quality, let one be contributed by every two hundred houses. If the horses have to be purchased, the price shall be made up by a payment from each house of one rod and two feet of cloth. As to weapons, each person shall contribute a sword, armor, bow and arrows, a flag and a drum. For coolies, the old system, by which one coolie was provided by every thirty houses, is altered, and one coolie is to be furnished from every fifty houses (one is for employment as a menial servant) for allotment to the various functionaries. Fifty houses shall be allotted to provide rations for one coolie, and one house shall contribute two rods and two feet of cloth and five *masu*[47] of rice in lieu of service." [pp. 206–209]

. . .

Autumn, 8th month, 14th day. An edict was issued saying:

"Going back to the origin of things, We find that it is Heaven and Earth with the male and female principles of nature,[48] which guard the four seasons from mutual confusion. We find, moreover, that it is this Heaven and Earth[49] which produces the ten thousand things. Among these ten thousand things man

---

44. Allowing five feet to the pace, this would make the *tan* nine thousand square feet.
45. Ten feet.
46. There are two *tan* to the *hiki* or piece, which now measures about 21.5 yards.
47. Or *shō* = 109 cubic inches.
48. Yin and yang.
49. That is, Nature.

is the most miraculously gifted. Among the most miraculously gifted beings, the sage takes the position of ruler. Therefore the sage-rulers, viz. the emperors, take Heaven as their exemplar in ruling the world and never for a moment dismiss from their breasts the thought of how men shall gain their fit place.

"Now as to the names of the early princes, the imperial chieftains, deity chieftains, court chieftains, and local chieftains have divided their various hereditary corporations[50] and allotted them severally to their various titles (or surnames). They afterwards took the various hereditary corporations of the people, and made them reside in the provinces and districts, one mixed up with another. The consequence has been to make father and child to bear different surnames, and brothers to be reckoned of distinct families, while husbands and wives have names different from one another. One family is divided into five or split up into six, and both court and country are therefore filled with contentious suits. No settlement has been come to, and the mutual confusion grows worse and worse. Let the various hereditary corporations therefore, beginning with those of the reigning emperor and including those in the possession of the imperial and deity chieftains, etc., be, without exception, abolished, and let them become subjects of the state. Those who have become court chieftains by borrowing the names of princes and those who have become imperial or deity chieftains on the strength of the names of ancestors, may not fully apprehend our purport and might think, if they heard this announcement without warning, that the names borrowed by their ancestors would become extinct. We therefore make this announcement beforehand, so that they may understand what are our intentions." [pp. 223–224]

. . .

"Let the local governors who are now being dispatched, and also the local chieftains of the same provinces, give ear to what we say. In regard to the method of administration notified last year to the Court Assembly, let the previous arrangement be followed, and let the rice lands which are received and measured be granted equally to the people, without distinction of persons. In granting rice lands the peasants' houses should adjoin the land. Those whose houses lie near the lands must therefore have the preference. In this sense receive our injunctions.

"In regard to commuted taxes,[51] they should be collected from males [only].

"Laborers should be supplied at the rate of one for every fifty houses. The boundaries of the provinces should be examined and a description or map prepared, which should be brought here and produced for our inspection. The names of the provinces and districts will be settled when you come.

---

50. Instituted in the commemoration of princes and bearing their names, or names intended to recall their memory.

51. Of things other than rice.

"With respect to the places where embankments are to be constructed, or canals dug, and the extent of rice land to be brought under cultivation, in the various provinces, uniform provision will be made for causing such work to be executed.

"Give ear to and understand these injunctions." [pp. 225–226]

[Aston, *Nihongi*, II, pp. 200–226]

THE WHITE PHEASANT

Just as in the years preceding the Great Reform, many calamities and bad omens are recorded in the *Nihongi* to justify a change of rule, so in later years, auspicious events are recorded to show that Heaven favored the new regime. The greatest stir at court was over the discovery of a white pheasant, a sign interpreted with reference to Chinese legend as if this were the authentic heritage of Japan itself. The episode is thus an apt illustration of the Han view of politics and the writing of history.

Hakuchi era, 1st year [650], 2nd month, 9th day. Shikofu, deity chieftain of Kusakabe, governor of the province of Anato, presented to the emperor a white pheasant, saying: "Nihe, a relation of Obito, the local chieftain, caught it on the ninth day of the first month on Mount Onoyama." Upon this inquiry was made of the lords of Paekche, who said: "In the eleventh year of Yongping,[52] in the reign of Mingdi of the Later Han dynasty, white pheasants were seen in a certain place." Further, inquiry was made of the Buddhist monks, who answered and said: "With our ears we have not heard, nor with our eyes have we seen such. May it please Your Majesty to order a general amnesty; and so give joy to the hearts of the people."

. . .

15th day. The array of guards at court was like that on the occasion of a New Year's reception. The great ministers of the right and left and all the functionaries formed four lines outside of the purple gate. . . . The Prince Imperial . . . made repeated obeisances and caused the Great Minister Kose to offer a congratulatory address, saying: "The ministers and functionaries offer their congratulations. Inasmuch as Your Majesty governs the empire with serene virtue, there is here a white pheasant, produced in the western region. This is a sign that Your Majesty will continue for a thousand autumns and ten thousand years peacefully to govern the Great Eight Islands of the four quarters. It is the prayer of the ministers, functionaries, and people that they may serve Your Majesty with the utmost zeal and fidelity."

---

52. 68 C.E.

Having finished this congratulatory speech, he made repeated obeisances. The emperor said:

"When a sage ruler appears in the world and rules the empire, Heaven is responsive to him, and manifests favorable omens. In ancient times, during the reign of Chengwang of the Zhou dynasty, a ruler of the Western land,[53] and again in the time of Mingdi of the Han dynasty, white pheasants were seen. In this our land of Japan, during the reign of the Emperor Homuda,[54] a white crow made its nest in the palace. In the time of the Emperor Ō-sazaki,[55] a dragon-horse appeared in the West.[56] This shows that from ancient times until now, there have been many cases of auspicious omens appearing in response to virtuous rulers. What we call phoenixes, unicorns, white pheasants, white crows, and such like birds and beasts, even including herbs and trees, in short all things having the property of significant response, are favorable omens and auspicious signs produced by Heaven and Earth. Now that wise and enlightened sovereigns should obtain such auspicious omens is meet and proper. But why should we, who are so empty and shallow, have this good fortune? It is no doubt wholly due to our assistants, the ministers, imperial chieftains, deity chieftains, court chieftains, and local chieftains, each of whom, with the utmost loyalty, conforms to the regulations that are made. For this reason, let all, from the ministers down to the functionaries, with pure hearts reverence the gods of Heaven and Earth, and one and all accepting the glad omen, making the empire to flourish."

Again he commanded, saying:

"The provinces and districts in the four quarters having been placed in our charge by Heaven, We exercise supreme rule over the empire. Now in the province of Anato, ruled over by our divine ancestors, this auspicious omen has appeared. For this reason we proclaim a general amnesty throughout the empire and begin a new year-period, to be called White Pheasant. Moreover we prohibit the flying of falcons within the limits of the province of Anato."

[Aston, *Nihongi*, II, pp. 236–239]

THE CHINESE MODEL OF RULERSHIP

Three Chinese political texts were particularly influential in the state-building process during the Nara and early Heian periods: the *Plan for the Emperor* (*Difan*) written by the Tang emperor Taizong in 648; the *Minister's Path* (*Chen-*

---

53. China.

54. Emperor Ōjin.

55. Emperor Nintoku.

56. The dragon horse has wings on its head and can cross water without sinking. It appears when an illustrious sovereign is on the throne.

gui), a model for the minister attributed to Empress Wu in the late seventh century; and the *Major Acts of Government in the Zhenguan Reign*, an idealized account of Taizong's reign by the historian Wu Jing written in 709–712.

The *Plan* was written by Tang Taizong in his last years to sum up his political legacy for his successor, Tang Gaozong. Much of the preface and postface is self-justifying, emphasizing the boldness, determination, and prudence needed to master the historical situation and unify the empire, with the passages deleted here not particularly relevant to those simply inheriting the throne rather than having to win it. Instead, emphasized in the following excerpts are more general principles of rulership, expressed by a very practical man who was also well read in Chinese historical lore and had a strong sense of the continuing relevance of the past—especially the example of the Han dynasty and its ideology.

TAIZONG: *PLAN FOR AN EMPEROR* (*DIFAN*)

The "Preface" Says

We have heard that the great virtue of [Heaven and Earth] is to bestow life, while the supreme treasure for the holy sage is to occupy the [imperial] position.[57] To differentiate high and low [among the living beings] the categories of prince and subject were set up, as a means by which the common people might be comforted and reared, and the multitudes might be molded as on a potter's wheel.[58] This position is not [solely] to be gained by a ruler's being capable of understanding, capable of wisdom, or being equally able in civil and military affairs. "He rules by following the decree of August Heaven."[59] "The determinative appointment of Heaven rests on his person."[60] How is it possible for [a ruler] simply to usurp control of the holy plan,[61] or without authority to preside over the sacred regalia? . . .

Section One: The Body of the Sovereign

The people are the origin of the state. The state is the foundation of the sovereign. The body [substance] of the lord of men should be like the great holy peaks, lofty and towering and unmovable. It should be like sun and moon, constant in their brilliance, and illuminating all alike.

---

57. Wilhelm and Baynes, trans., *The I Ching*, p. 328.

58. The potter working his clay is a common metaphor for the ruler transforming and perfecting his people.

59. Classic of Documents, "Dayumo"; Legge, *The Chinese Classics*, p. 54.

60. Ibid., p. 61.

61. Refers to the "River Plan" (Hotu), which the sage-ruler Yao received at the Cuigui River, written in red on the back of a turtle.

He is the one to whom the myriad people look up, to whom the entire empire turns. His will should be broad and magnanimous, sufficient to bind them together. His heart should be impartial and just, sufficient for him to make forceful decisions. Without awesome power, he will have no means to effect the most distant regions: without benign liberality he will have no means to cherish his people. He must comfort the nine grades of his kinsfolk by humanity.[62] He must bind his great ministers to him by the rites.[63] In serving his ancestors, he must bear in mind his filial obligations; in occupying his position [as ruler] he must remember to be reverent. He must repress his own [personal interests] and toil diligently, so as to put into practice virtue and rightness.

Such then is the body of the sovereign.

Section Two: Establishing One's Kinsmen

The limits of the empire[64] are broad and far extended. The emperor's most precious endowment is his position of supreme power. The far-extended empire cannot be controlled by the will of one man alone: thus the emperor must control it together with others. The position of supreme power cannot be occupied by [the emperor] alone: thus he must maintain it together with others. For this reason he should enlist his relatives "as a fence and protection" for his state. Both in tranquillity and peril they will all join their strength together: in times of prosperity and decay alike they will be of one heart. Distant and near will support one another, both close and remote kin will be employed. "The road to territorial aggrandizement will be blocked; disobedience to the ruler's commands will not arise." . . .

Assistance in the task of rectifying the state must wait upon loyal and good [ministers]. If in the employment [of officials] the emperor obtains the appropriate men, then the empire will rule itself. . . . Thus, the enlightened ruler "seeks men of eminence suitable for office on every side," inquires broadly for distinguished and talented men, "sets forth [suitable worthies] from among the poor and mean." Do not fail to employ anyone because he is of inferior status: do not fail to honor anyone because he is in disgrace. . . .

Section Four: Carefully Examine Candidates for Offices

The establishment of offices and the demarcation of their duties are the means whereby one expounds moral transformation and propagates good customs. . . .

---

62. Documents, "Yaodian"; Legge, *The Chinese Classics*, p. 17.

63. *Analects* 3:19; Legge, *The Chinese Classics*, p. 161.

64. The six bounds (*liuhe*) are Heaven, Earth, and the four cardinal points. It means "the universe over which the emperor reigns."

From the wise he takes their counsel; from the foolish he takes their strength; from the valiant he takes their awesome majesty; from the cowardly he takes their prudence. Without distinction, every man alike, whether he is wise [or foolish], valiant or cowardly, can be employed. . . .

Now the knowledge of men is in some cases short, in some cases long, their capabilities are in some cases great and in others slender. For some men, being responsible for a hundred items of business is still too few; for others, to control a single matter is too many. There are men of light talents, who may not be entrusted with weighty employments. There are those of inferior wisdom, who may not be entrusted with great tasks. If [the ruler] selects his subjects and grants them offices, and the subjects estimate themselves and accept their duties, then he will depute employments [the right men] and hold the incumbents responsible for completing their tasks. Without undue effort, government will be transformed. This is the correct pattern for setting up officials.

These two principles ["Seeking Sage-Worthies" and "Carefully Examining Officials"] are the source of the distinction between good government and disorder. In establishing the state and controlling the people, [officials] provide the ruler's arms and legs, by means of which he brings together his strength. To spread good behavior and lead people to good customs, the ruler should await enlightened sages, and then commit his heart to them. The lord of men rules over his inferiors, unifies the supreme powers, controls the seasons. Yet if he wishes to exert his inch-square heart alone in order to embrace together all men within the nine provinces, unless he can depend upon the strength of a multitude [of others], how can he succeed in his task?

He must clearly understand the duties of officials, carefully examine the worthy, select the talented, allocate stipends. If he gets the right men, then customs and behavior will be transformed and will spread everywhere. But if he loses their employment, then the proper instruction of the people will be lost, and the people injured. . . .

Section Five: Accepting Remonstrance

Now the king occupies the highest place, and oversees his government from the depths of his seclusion (in the palace). This impairs his clearly hearing [about events], and stops him from clearly seeing [what is happening]. He is afraid that, if there are faults committed, he will not hear of them, and frightened that, if there are deficiencies in government, nobody will repair them. For this reason the petitioner's drum (*tao*) was set out, and the complainants' tree planted. He should give careful thought both to the policies that are accepted and to those that are declined, and will listen to proposals carefully with an open mind (that is, with no preconceptions): this is the way in which he should stand and await loyal and just counsel.

Whatever is said that is right, even though it comes from servants or slaves, grass cutters and firewood gatherers, still may not be rejected; while anything that is said that is wrong, even if it comes from princes or marquises, great ministers or chancellors, may certainly not be tolerated. Counsel that is worthy of attention [should be looked at] without criticizing [its authors] over their precise details; policies that are fit for use should be adopted without demanding eloquence of style from their authors. . . .

For this reason, the loyal will express what is in their hearts to the last drop, and the wise will present their policies in their entirety. Ministers will not block off the true situation from [the ruler] above; and the prince will be able to spread his light everywhere over [his subjects] below. . . .

Note: *The sections deleted here deal with Flatterers, Guarding against Excess, Frugality, Rewards and Punishments, Agriculture, and War.*[65]

Section Twelve: Honoring Learning

"After victory has been obtained, music should be performed: when government has been established, the rites should be set up.[66] The rise of the rites and music takes learning as its basis. To broaden customs and to guide common practices, nothing excels written literature (*wen*). To propagate instruction and teach the people, nothing is better than study.[67] By following written culture one makes the Way resplendent; by making use of study one can make oneself glorious. Unless you have looked down into a deep ravine you cannot know the thickness of the earth.[68] If you have not roamed around in literature, you will not recognize the well-springs of wisdom." . . .

[Postface]

These twelve matters provide the grand outline for an emperor or king. His safety and peril, success or destruction, all depend on these things! The ancients had a saying, "It is not that knowing is difficult, only that putting it into practice is not easy."[69] Putting it into practice can be achieved with hard effort, but it is only bringing it to a conclusion that is truly difficult. For this reason, even violent and misgoverning rulers do not have a clear understanding of only the paths of evil. Can saintly and wise lords only be seen following the path of

---

65. For a complete, annotated translation, see Twitchett, "How to Be an Emperor."
66. *Liji* 17, "Yueji," Legge, vol. 2, pp. 101–102.
67. *Liji* 16, "Xueji," Legge, vol. 2, p. 82.
68. *Xunzi* 1:2, Quanxue; Knoblock, trans., *Xunzi* 1, pp. 135–136.
69. Legge, "Yueming," *The Chinese Classics* 2, p. 258.

goodness? This is truly because the great Way is distant and hard to follow, while the path of evil is close at hand and easy to tread upon. Inferior men all submissively follow the easy option, and are unable to make the effort to follow the difficult path. As a result misfortune and disaster come upon them. The true gentleman makes great exertions to keep himself on the difficult path, and is unable to run away [from the trouble this involves] and take up the easy option. As a result good fortune and felicities flow to him. Hence we know that "misfortune and good fortune have no particular gate by which they must enter. Each man calls in the one or the other for himself."[70] If you wish to show regret for wrongs you have committed in the past, simply be careful about faults you may commit in the future. . . .

You yourself have not yet the slightest positive achievement; you are only following on the foundation (laid by your grandfather and father) and inheriting their felicities. If you venerate the good so as to broaden your virtue, then your reign will be a great one, and you yourself will enjoy peace. But if you give rein to your feelings so as to indulge in wrong-doing, then your reign will end in collapse and you yourself will perish.

Moreover, that success comes slowly whereas defeat can come rapidly is at the very foundation of the state. That loss is easy, and gain difficult, is part of the position of Son of Heaven. How can you not regret this! How can you not take great care!

[Adapted from Twitchett, "How to Be an Emperor," pp. 50–92; DT]

THE COMMENTARY ON THE LEGAL CODE (RYŌ NO GIGE)

One of the principal Chinese influences on the thought of early Japan was the legal codes of Tang China. As early as the reign of Emperor Tenchi (668–671), a Japanese code appears to have been compiled, but almost nothing of it remains. The Taihō Code of 701–702, however, continued to be the basic law of Japan until after the Meiji Restoration of 1868. This code directly adopted many Chinese institutions in spite of their unsuitability for the far less developed society of Japan, and an elaborate bureaucracy was organized based on the merit system. But the Taihō Code was not a mere copy of Tang precedents, as new provisions were made for the Shinto priesthood and other peculiarly Japanese institutions.

The laws themselves came to assume an even greater importance for the Japanese than they did for the Chinese and occupied a central place in Japanese thinking for many centuries. The commentary on the legal code of 834 was a successful attempt to interpret the laws and show their significance for Japanese society.

---

70. Legge, *Zuozhuan, The Chinese Classics,* Hsiang 23, p. 502.

MEMORIAL ON THE SUBMISSION OF THE COMMENTARY
ON THE LEGAL CODE

Your subjects, Natsuno[71] and others, report: the study of the successive rulers of old and the perusal of early writings show that whenever a sovereign assuming the succession mounted the throne, took his position facing south,[72] and declared himself emperor, decrees were invariably announced and the law proclaimed as the warp and woof of the government of the country. Rites and punishments were also established to serve as a bulwark in the protection of the dynasty. Although, just as dragons and phoenixes differ in their appearance, some rulers favored literary pursuits and others the simple virtues, they all arrived by different roads at the same end of instructing the common people and protecting them.

Your subjects prostrate themselves and state as their considered opinion: Your Majesty, whose way shines to the four quarters and whose virtue surpasses that of all kings, sits impassively in marble halls, a model to the world. Wherever in your domains human society exists, rites and music are in honor; and as far as your powerful influence extends, all men, civilized and barbarian alike, show joyful appreciation. Now Your Majesty, who rises so early he dresses in darkness, lest the conduct of government go amiss, and who neglects eating until it is late because of his concern for the people's happiness, has issued an edict decreeing that experts in law be found. It was your consideration that the interpretations of earlier scholars were at times contradictory; the shallow observations tended to get mixed with the profound; and their merits were difficult to judge.

Your subjects cannot approach Zhang Cang in scholarship or Chen Chong in achievements.[73] Mediocre of talent as we are, how great was our honor in accepting your appointment! We have attempted to revise and correct the legal writings, now adding and now deleting. Whenever there were problems which we could not solve, or ambiguities which could not be cleared up, we always looked up to Your Majesty's august rulings for our authority. New times require new laws, which are in the spirit of those of ancient times, but suited to the present. Indeed, these laws will change the ways of thought of the people, and will also serve as a guide for all rulers. The compilation is in ten volumes and is entitled the *Commentary on the Legal Code*. Five years elapsed before the fair copy could be completed and respectfully submitted.

---

71. Kiyohara no Natsuno (782–837).

72. In the yin-yang cosmology, the ruler's place was in the north, facing south. He was likened to the North Star, to which all the other stars "bow."

73. Zhang Cang (d. 161 B.C.E.) and Chen Chong (d. 107 C.E.) were noted statesmen and lawgivers of the Han dynasty.

Your subjects, Natsuno and others, bow their heads and, with awe and trepidation, offer these words. [January 28, 834].

[From the *Kokushi taikei*, XXII, pp. 348–350]

REGULATIONS FOR FITNESS REPORTS

A merit system of recruitment and promotion was the heart of the imperial bureaucracy in China, and in the following, the Japanese attempt to duplicate it. Eventually, their inability to overcome by these means the strong native tradition of hereditary rank and officeholding completely vitiated the civil service system and, with it, the whole bureaucratic structure.

Fitness reports must be submitted annually by the chief of every department for all civil and military officers under his command in the court or in the provinces. The merits, demerits, conduct, and abilities of all persons for whom reports are made should be recorded in detail so that they may be consulted in classifying the officers into nine grades of merit. The reports must be completed by the thirtieth day of the eighth moon. Reports on officers stationed in the capital or the provinces of the Inner Circuit should be submitted to the Great Council of State by the first day of the tenth moon; reports for officers in other provinces should be submitted not later than the first day of the eleventh moon through the imperial inspectors. Acts of merit or demerit performed after the submission of reports should be entered in the records of the following year. In case a department is without a chief, the fitness reports should be made by a vice chief. . . .

Chiefs of department submitting fitness reports must state only the facts with no interpolations of either favorable or unfavorable material. If a false report results in an unwarranted promotion or demotion or if an officer's actual fitness is concealed so that his rank will be raised or lowered, the reporting officer responsible shall be demoted in accordance with the seriousness of his error. An imperial inspector who promotes or demotes an officer in disregard of his record shall similarly be held responsible.

Merits:
1. When an officer has a reputation for virtue and a sense of duty, it is to be counted as a merit.
2. When an officer's honesty and conscientiousness are evident, they are to be counted as merits.
3. When an officer's devotion to public good and justice arouses praise, it is to be counted as a merit.

4. When an officer performs faithful and diligent service, it is to be counted as a merit.

Articles of Excellence:

To carry out the festivals and ceremonies of the deities of Heaven and Earth in exact compliance with established procedure is to be counted the excellence of a Shinto official.

To address memorials in favor of that which is advantageous to the state and against that which is harmful and to discuss government business in accordance with reason are to be counted the excellence of a major counselor.

To act in strict accord with instructions received and to be clear and fluent of speech are to be counted the excellence of a minor counselor.

To handle general state business and to dispose of it without delay are to be counted the excellence of a controller.

To wait in attendance on the emperor and transmit memorials to him and to be prompt in the execution of his duties are to be counted the excellence of an officer of the Ministry of Central Affairs.

To evaluate men and to select all those of ability and talent are to be counted the excellence of an officer of the Ministry of Rites.

To hold monks and nuns to the teachings of Buddha and to keep registered subjects under control are to be counted the excellence of an officer of the Ministry of Civil Administration.

To maintain order among the population and to ensure abundant supplies in the storehouses are to be counted the excellence of an officer of the Ministry of the Interior.

To select military officers and to prepare munitions of war are to be counted the excellence of an officer of the Ministry of Military Affairs.

To pass judgments without delay and to give rewards or exact punishments justly are to be counted the excellence of an officer of the Ministry of Justice.

To be scrupulous in the care of deposits and to be well informed of expenditures and receipts are to be counted the excellence of an officer of the Ministry of the Treasury.

To be competent in furnishing provisions and to expedite the management of the various departments of the palace are to be counted the excellence of an officer of the Ministry of the Imperial Household.

To be energetic in investigations and competent in the arraignment of suspects is to be counted the excellence of a censor.

To promote good manners and morals and to suppress robbery and banditry are to be counted the excellence of an officer of the capital.

To prepare the imperial meals and to observe faultless cleanliness are to be counted the excellence of a commissioner of food.

To maintain rigid discipline and constant vigilance is to be counted the excellence of a guards officer.

To ensure that music is well harmonized and does not fall into discord is to be counted the excellence of an officer of the Bureau of Music.

To keep order among monks and nuns and to see to it that aliens are lodged in suitable quarters are to be counted the excellence of an officer of the Bureau of Buddhism and Aliens.

To budget court expenditures and to be accurate in accounting are to be counted the excellence of an officer of the Bureau of Statistics.

To be scrupulous in the care of storehouses and to be well informed about incoming and outgoing shipments are to be counted the excellence of an officer of the Bureau of Tax Collection.

To feed, train, and stable horses and to have grooms available are to be counted the excellence of an officer of the Bureau of Horses.

To dry in the sun or air stores with care and to be well informed about incoming and outgoing shipments are to be counted the excellence of an officer of the Bureau of Military Storehouses.

To serve in constant attendance at court and to repair omissions and supplement deficiencies are to be counted the excellence of a chamberlain.

To engage in unremitting supervision and to be accurately informed about all incoming and outgoing property are to be counted the excellence of an inspector official.

To perform night watch in the palace and to behave in perfect conformity to etiquette are to be counted the excellence of a lord-in-waiting.

To regulate official business and to see to it that office hours are properly observed are to be counted the excellence of all officers of the secondary rank and above.

To promote the pure and to remove evildoers and to ensure that praise or censure is properly given are to be counted the excellence of a commissioner of personnel.

To carry out examinations in a thorough and detailed manner and to be familiar with all types of affairs are to be counted the excellence of a judge.

To engage unremittingly in public service and to perform one's work without oversights are to be counted the excellence of all officers.

To be assiduous in keeping records and to examine into failings without glossing over them are to be counted the excellence of a clerk.

To keep detailed records in model order and to excel both in language and in reasoning are to be counted the excellence of a historian.

To be clear in the recording of facts and to communicate successfully imperial orders are to be counted the excellence of a palace scribe.

To be methodical in instruction and to fit students for their work are to be counted the excellence of a learned scholar.

To be effective in yin-yang divination, astronomy, medicine, and fortune-telling is to be counted the excellence of a diviner.

To observe the motions of the celestial bodies and to be accurate in the calculation of their movements are accounted the excellence of a scholar of the calendar.

To supervise markets and shops and to prevent cheating and other forms of deception are accounted the excellence of a markets officer.

To investigate the facts of a case and to reveal their circumstances are accounted the excellence of a constable.

To perform state ceremonies and to maintain suitable military preparation are accounted the excellence of the governor-general of Kyūshū.

To be strict in the administration of all business and to insist on the honesty of his subordinates are accounted the excellence of a provincial governor.

To be impartial in his dealings with local people and accomplished in his official duties are accounted the excellence of an assistant governor.

To keep the coast guard in fighting trim and to have munitions ready for an emergency are accounted the excellence of the coast guards officer.

To be brief in his questions and not to delay travelers unnecessarily is accounted the excellence of a barrier keeper.

An officer who possesses four merits in addition to the excellence suited to his post is to be classified superior, first class.

An officer who possesses three merits in addition to his excellence or who possesses four merits without his excellence, is to be classified superior, second class.

An officer who possesses two merits in addition to his excellence or who possesses three merits without his excellence, is to be classified superior, third class.

An officer who possesses one merit in addition to his excellence or who possesses two merits without his excellence, is to be classified medium, first class.

An officer who possesses his excellence but no merits or who possesses one merit without his excellence, is to be classified medium, second class.

An officer who has a crude competence in his position but possesses neither a merit nor his excellence is to be classified medium, third class.

An officer who indulges in his own likes and dislikes and who is unreasonable in his judgments is to be classified inferior, first class.

An officer who acts against the public interest for personal reasons and fails in his official duties is to be classified inferior, second class.

An officer who flatters and lies or who appears avaricious and dishonest is to be classified inferior, third class.

Special consideration should be given when an officer's record is being reviewed whether he possesses praiseworthy characteristics not covered under the list of merits or excellences or whether, if he is guilty of some offense, there are not extenuating circumstances or whether, if he is technically guiltless, he should nevertheless be condemned.

[From the *Kokushi taikei*, XXII, pp. 149–156]

NEW COMPILATION OF THE REGISTER OF FAMILIES

The importance of genealogy in determining claims to sovereignty was demonstrated by the *Records of Ancient Matters* (712 C.E.). The Japanese, who thus stressed the divine descent of the imperial family, were confirmed in this by the Han view of the Mandate of Heaven as conferred not on individuals but on dynasties, which themselves had been provided with genealogies going back to the sage-kings. However, the genre of genealogy, like most forms of early written literature, came from China, in which during the late Six Dynasties period and into the Tang, membership in well-established aristocratic descent groups was an important determinant of social status, marriage alliances, and eligibility for office. For his part, the founder of the Tang dynasty, trying to curb the power of the old aristocracy and strengthen central control, had ordered the compilation of a comprehensive register of genealogies that would define and limit the powers of the old elite. Now, as a similar state-building effort was mounted in Japan and the ruling house attempted, with difficulty, to assert its dominion over the old clans, it too felt the need to order and control genealogical claims. The contents of the following preface recount successive attempts by different emperors to assert this control—reasserted here in *The New Compilation of the Register of Families* (*Shinsen shōji roku*, 815) of the early Heian period.

In the *Register of Families*, the names are divided into three classes: "All descendants of heavenly and earthly deities are designated as the Divine Group; all branches of the families of Emperors and royal princes are called the Imperial Group; and families from China and Korea are called the Alien Group." It may seem surprising that the "descendants of heavenly and earthly deities" (who must have included a good part of the Japanese population) should have been mentioned before the imperial family. However, since these deities and their protégés had ruled over much of Japan before the rise of the imperial house, their early pride of place could not be denied.

The influx of Korean and Chinese immigrants during the Nara period and earlier had, in some respects, presented a challenge to the Japanese, for the immigrants were clearly superior to the Japanese in their knowledge of the techniques of civilization. The advantage that the Japanese claimed was their descent from the gods, and to this heritage they jealously clung.

PREFACE IN THE FORM OF A MEMORIAL TO EMPEROR SAGA

They say that the Divine Dynasty had its inception when the Grandson of Heaven descended to the land of So[74] and extended his influence in the West,[75]

---

74. An ancient name for the southern part of the island of Kyushu and the location of Mount Takachiho where Ninigi, the Grandson of Heaven, made his descent.

75. That is, in Kyushu.

but no written records are preserved of these events. In the years when Jinmu assumed command of the state and undertook his campaign to the east, conditions grew steadily more confused, and some tribal leaders rose in revolt. When, however, the Heaven-sent sword appeared and the Golden Kite flew to earth,[76] the chieftains surrendered in great numbers and the rebels vanished like mist. Jinmu, accepting the mandate of Heaven, erected a palace in the central province and administered justice. Peace reigned throughout the country. Land was allotted to men who were deemed virtuous in accordance with their merits. Heads of clans were granted such titles as local chieftain [kuni-no-miyatsuko] and district chieftain [agata-nushi] for the first time.

Suinin cultivated good fortune by his ever-renewed benevolent favors. Through such acts the Golden Mean was attained. [At this time] clans and families were gradually distinguished one from the other. Moreover, Imna came under our influence and Silla brought tribute. Later, barbarians from other countries, in due reverence for his virtue, all wished to come to Japan. Out of solicitude for these aliens, he bestowed family names on them. This was an outstanding feature of the time.

During the reign of Ingyō,[77] however, family relationships were in great confusion. An edict was accordingly issued, ordering that oaths be tested by the trial of boiling water. Those whose oaths were true remained unscathed, while the perjurers were harmed. From this time onwards the clans and families were established and there were no impostors. Rivers ran in their proper courses.

While Kōgyoku held the Regalia,[78] however, the provincial records were all burned, and the young and defenseless had no means of proving their antecedents. The designing and the strong redoubled their false claims. Then, when the Emperor Tenchi was heir apparent, Eseki, an archivist of the Funa family, presented to the court the charred remains of the records. In the year of metal and the horse (670 C.E.) the family registers were re-compiled and the relationships of clans and families were all clarified. From this time on revisions were always made by succeeding sovereigns from time to time.

During the Tempyō Shōro era (749–757), by special favor of the court, all aliens who had made application were granted family names. Since the same surnames were given to the immigrants as Japanese families possessed, uncertainty arose as to which families were of alien and which of native origin. There were commoners everywhere who pretended to be the scions of the high and the mighty, and immigrant aliens from the Korean kingdoms claimed to be the descendants of the Japanese deities. As time passed and people changed scarcely anyone was left who knew the facts.

---

76. Signs confirming Jinmu's divine right to imperial dominion (see Aston, *Nihongi*, I, pp. 115, 126).

77. Traditional dates: 411–453 C.E..

78. 642–645 C.E..

During the latter part of the Tempyō Hōji era (757–765) controversies about these matters grew all the more numerous. A number of eminent scholars were thereafter summoned to compile a register of families. Before their work was half completed, however, the government became involved in certain difficulties. The scholars were disbanded and the compilation was not resumed. . . .

Our present sovereign,[79] of glorious fame, desired that the work be resumed at the point where it was abandoned. . . . We, his loyal subjects, in obedience to his edicts, have performed our task with reverence and assiduity. We have collected all the information so as to be able to sift the gold from the pebbles. We have cleared the old records of confusion and have condensed into this new work the essential facts contained in them. New genealogies have been purged of fictitious matter and checked with the old records. The concision and simplicity of this work are such that its meaning will be apparent as the palm of one's hand. We have searched out the old and new, from the time of the Emperor Jinmu to the Kōnin era (811–824) to the best of our abilities. The names of 1,182 families are included in this work, which is in thirty volumes. It is entitled the "New Compilation of the Register of Families." It is not intended for pleasure reading, and the style is far from polished. Since, however, it is concerned with the key to human relationships, it is an essential instrument in the hands of the nation.

[*Kōgaku sōsho*, IV, pp. 123–124]

PREFACE TO THE *KAIFŪSŌ*

The *Kaifūsō*— "Fond Recollections of Poetry"—is the first anthology of poetry in Chinese written by Japanese. It was compiled in 751 C.E. but includes verses dating back some seventy-five years, to the reign of Emperor Tenchi. The *Kaifūsō* is today chiefly of historical interest. It contains some of the earliest attempts by Japanese writers (including emperors and princes) to compose in literary Chinese and therefore often gives more the effect of copybook exercises than true poetry. Even when the subject of a poem is Japanese—such as a visit to Yoshino River—the writer's main effort appears to be directed toward including as many allusions as possible to Chinese literature and history.

The preface to the *Kaifūsō* is, in addition, an example of Chinese parallel prose. The style is rather clumsily handled by the unknown compiler, who is sometimes driven to desperate measures to maintain a parallel. Almost every sentence is jammed with allusions, some of them now extremely difficult to puzzle out. But however imperfect the style and technique of this preface are, it is important because it clearly shows how great the prestige of Chinese literature (and thought) was even during this early period.

---

79. Saga (809–823).

From what I have heard of ancient practices and seen of the records of long ago, in the age of the divine descent from Heaven on the mountain of So and in the time when the country was founded at Kashiwabara, Heaven's work was at its bare inception, and human culture was yet to flourish. When the Empress Jingū led the expedition over the water and the Emperor Ōjin mounted the throne, Paekche brought homage to the court and revealed the dragon-writing. Koguryŏ presented memorials inscribed with crow writing and bird writing. It was Wani who first brought learning to Karushima; Shinji later spread his teachings in the field of translation. He caused the people to become imbued with the breeze from the riversides dear to Confucius and Mencius and made them direct their steps towards the doctrines of Qi and Lu.[80] With Prince Shōtoku the ranks of honor were established; the offices of government were demarcated; and court rites and ceremonies were for the first time regulated. However, because of the exclusive devotion shown to Buddhism, there was no time for literature. But when the former emperor Ōmi[81] received Heaven's mandate, he vastly expanded the imperial achievements and widely extended the sovereign's counsels. His virtue reached to heaven and earth; his merit shone through the universe like sunlight. Thus did he long meditate: "To regulate customs and bring culture to the people, nothing is more valuable than literature; to cultivate virtues and make oneself resplendent in them, what could come before learning?" Therefore he founded schools and sought persons of flourishing talent. He determined the Five Rites and fixed the Hundred Regulations. The principles of government, the laws, and the rules of state were promulgated far and wide, as never before in history. Then the Three Classes enjoyed peace and glory; within the Four Seas reigned prosperity and wealth. The great dignitaries had surcease from their labors; the palace galleries knew much leisure. At times the emperor summoned men of letters; often great banquets were held. On these occasions the imperial brush let fall prose; the courtiers offered their eulogies in verse. Many more than a hundred were the pieces of chiseled prose and exquisite calligraphy. But with the passage of time, disorders reduced all these writings to ashes. How heartrending it is to think of the destruction!

In later times men of letters occasionally appeared. A prince, a dragon apparent, made cranes soar in the clouds with his brush; a phoenix-like emperor floated his moonlit boat on misty waters. Ōkami, the councillor of state, lamented his graying hair and demonstrated the flourishing fruits of his art during the last emperor's reign; Fujiwara, the grand minister, celebrated the imperial rule and caused his glorious voice to echo through later times.

My minor position at the court has permitted me the leisure to let my fancy wander in the garden of letters and to read the works left by the men of former

---

80. Native states of Mencius and Confucius.
81. Emperor Tenchi.

days. When I recall now those sports with the moon and poetry, how blurred are my remembrances—yet, the words left by old brushes remain. As I go over the titles of the poems my thoughts are carried far away, and the tears flow without my realizing it. As I lift the lovely compositions, my mind searches the distant past, and I long for those voices which are now stilled.

Thus it has come about that I have collected the scraps left in the wall at Lu and assembled the fragments remaining in the ashes left by Qin,[82] beginning with the long-ago reign at Ōmi and coming down to the court of Nara. Altogether I have included 120 pieces, enough to make a volume. I have listed in detail the names, court ranks, and origins of the sixty-four authors. Since my reason for making this anthology was to keep from oblivion the poetry of the great men of former days, I think it is proper to call the collection *Kaifū*—"Fond Reminiscences."

It is the eleventh moon of the third year of Tempyō Shōhō [751], and the stars are at the juncture of metal and hare.

[(Shinsen) *Meika shishū*, pp. 499–500]

---

82. Likening himself to the Han dynasty scholars who rediscovered and preserved the Confucian texts.

Chapter 5

NARA BUDDHISM

In the tenth month of 552 C.E., the king of Paekche sent to Japan an envoy with presents of an image of Buddha and sacred writings, apparently hoping thereby to ingratiate himself with the Japanese court so as to win their military support. He also sent a memorial lauding Buddhism:

> This doctrine is among all doctrines the most excellent, but it is hard to explain and hard to comprehend. Even the Duke of Zhou and Confucius could not attain a knowledge of it. This doctrine can create religious merit and retribution without measure and without bounds, and so lead on to a full appreciation of the highest wisdom. Imagine a man in possession of treasures to his heart's content, so that he might satisfy all his wishes in proportion as he used them. Thus it is with the treasure of this wonderful doctrine. Every prayer is fulfilled and naught is wanting. Moreover, from distant India it has extended hither to Korea, where there are none who do not receive it with reverence as it is preached to them.[1]

We are told that Emperor Kinmei was so delighted with these tidings that he leaped for joy. The head of the Soga clan, no less affected, urged that Japan

---

1. Aston, *Nihongi*, II, p. 66.

follow the lead of all other civilized nations in adopting the new religion. More conservative elements at the court objected, however, saying that the worship of foreign deities could not help but incense the national gods. Soga was presented with the image and allowed to worship it, but shortly afterward, when a pestilence broke out, Shinto adherents persuaded the emperor that it was a manifestation of the gods' wrath. The image of Buddha was thrown into a moat, and the temple built by the Soga family was razed.

Nothing much more was heard of Buddhism until 584, when another member of the Soga clan was given two Buddhist images that had come from Korea. He erected a temple to enshrine them and had three girls ordained as nuns by a Korean monk living in Japan. This, we are informed by the *Chronicles of Japan*, marked the real beginning of Buddhism in the country. It was not long, however, before another plague caused the Shinto factions to throw the holy images into the moat and to defrock the nuns. When these rigorous measures failed to halt the spread of the disease, the emperor finally agreed to allow the Soga family to worship Buddhism as it chose, and the nuns were given back their robes.

Within a few years of the second start of Buddhism in Japan, a number of learned Korean monks began to arrive. Among their most eager disciples was Prince Shōtoku. Most of the emperors and empresses in the next century became Buddhists; and the subsequent Nara period (709–784) in some ways marks a high point of early Buddhism in Japan.

It is not difficult to understand the success of the new religion. At the time of its introduction to Japan, Buddhism was nearly a thousand years old and, as the first world religion, had marched triumphantly to the east and west, raising temples and monasteries and filling grottoes and caves with an amazing profusion of art. It had become a well-organized and tested faith constituted under its Three Treasures — Buddha, the Law (dharma), and the monastic orders (sangha). It possessed a highly developed and decorated pantheon as its objects of worship, a tremendous accumulation of literature called the Tripiṭaka, and religious orders dedicated to the propagation of its teachings by oaths of celibacy, sobriety, and poverty.

In this connection, we should stress that the importance of Buddhist missionary activity in Japan went far beyond propagation of the faith alone. Chinese and Korean monks, carried across stormy seas by religious zeal, at the same time served as the carriers of superior Chinese culture. They were no doubt well aware that identification or association with this high culture lent them great prestige in the eyes of admiring Japanese, but whether or not they chose to capitalize on this, it would in any case have been impossible to disengage this new religion from its cultural embodiment in China and Korea, the lands of its adoption. To establish the new faith in Japan thus required the transplanting of essential articles — images, vestments, books, ritual devices — as well as ideas. The Japanese apprenticeship in the study of Chinese writing was undoubtedly served in the copying by hand of large numbers of Buddhist sūtras, distributed by imperial order to the various temples and monasteries. Furthermore, to erect temples and monasteries, carpenters and artisans had to be brought over along with missionary monks, as illustrated by an entry in the *Chronicles of Japan* (*Nihongi*) for the reign of Sujun (ca. 588):

> This year the land of Paekche sent envoys, and along with them the Buddhist monk Hyejong [and others] with a present of Buddhist relics. The land of Paekche sent the Buddhist ecclesiastics Susin [and others] with tribute and also with a present of Buddhist relics, the Buddhist monk Nyōng-chyo, the ascetics Yongwi [and others], the temple carpenters Taeryangmidae and Mungagoja, a man learned in the art of making braziers and chargers . . . men learned in pottery . . . and a painter named Poega.[2]

It is apparent, too, that Buddhist monks were vessels for the transmission of branches of learning that had no direct connection with religious doctrine or institutions yet that they evidently regarded as being in no way incompatible with the former. Thus during the tenth year of Suiko (602), it is recorded:

> A Paekche monk named Kwallŭk arrived and presented by way of tribute books of calendar-making, of astronomy and of geomancy, and also books on the art of invisibility and magic. At this time three or four pupils were selected and made to study under Kwallŭk. Ōchin, the ancestor of the scribes of Yako, studied the art of calendar-making. Kōsō, Otomo no Suguri, studied astronomy and the art of invisibility. Hinamitatsu, the Imperial Chieftain of Yamashiro, studied magic. They all studied so far as to perfect themselves in these arts.[3]

In the forms it took, Nara Buddhism was an extension of that of Tang China and Silla. For example, it is in the Nara period that we first hear of Buddhist sects in Japan, and it is customary to speak of the "six schools" then introduced from China. Some of them, particularly the two Hīnayāna sects, appear never to have been independent, having served primarily as forms of religious discipline for monks. The three main philosophical features of Nara Buddhism were the dialectics of negation (the Sanron or "Three-Treatises" sect, associated with the great Indian scholar Nāgārjuna and transmitted by Kumārajīva), the doctrine of the attainment of enlightenment through the powers of the mind (the Hossō or "Dharma-Character" sect, associated with Vasubandhu and Xuan-

---

2. Ibid., p. 117.
3. Ibid., p. 126.

zang), and the metaphysics of the harmonious whole (taught by the Kegon or "Flower Garland" sect). The metaphysics of Kegon had been worked out and elaborated by gifted philosophers in China and Korea and was known by the time of its introduction to Japan as a philosophy so intricate and complex that it could never be realized in actual practice. It was not until the revival of Nara Buddhism during the early Kamakura period that practitioners like Myōe Shōnin (1173–1232) successfully took up the challenge of transforming the Kegon metaphysics of the interrelatedness of all things into a religion that could be practiced by lay persons as well as monks.

The sixth sect (the Ritsu or Precepts school) was based on the rules of discipline governing the lives of monks and nuns. A person could be initiated into this discipline (called "receiving the precepts") only by a qualified master of the precepts, and in 754 the intrepid Chinese priest Jianzhen (Ganjin) finally arrived in Nara after five earlier attempts that had ended in shipwrecks. With his legitimate transmission of the precepts to Japan and the establishment of the ordination platform at Tōdaiji, Buddhists could finally be ordained as authentic clergy. As it is with most rules, however, the precepts became a legalistic matter of formal obedience rather than the principles by which a Buddhist lived and sought enlightenment. Like the metaphysics of Kegon, the precepts in time became watered down and had to be infused with new life and philosophical meaning in the Kamakura period by monks like Myōe and Gedatsu Shōnin (1155–1213).

Common to these seemingly disparate views was the basic Buddhist doctrine of impermanence, of non-ego (the absence of any enduring, substantial self), and of the need for liberation from illusion and suffering by the attainment of Nirvana or Buddhahood. Buddhism insisted on the need to free oneself from relying on externals so changeable that they can only deceive. Therefore, these must be negated exhaustively until all the usual distinctions of becoming, which arise from incomplete knowledge, are denied and perfect knowledge can be attained. Such was the teaching of Nāgārjuna. For the followers of the Hossō sect, the school of the great Chinese pilgrim Xuanzang, the outer world did not exist at all but was a creation of the mind. How could someone turn to the motions of the stars for guidance when they were illusory and without permanent reality? Even in the Kegon school, which preached a cosmological harmony governed by Lochana Buddha—who sits on a lotus throne of a thousand petals, each of which is a universe containing millions of worlds like ours—it is the mutable nature of this system and not its permanence (like the Confucian Heaven) that is emphasized. Within the great harmony of the Kegon (or Flower Garland), all beings are related and capable of mutual interaction until they attain a fundamental communion with Buddha and, through him, with all other beings.

We do not know how much of these abstruse doctrines was understood by Japanese Buddhists of the Nara period, but expressions of religious fervor generally assumed a tangible form. The court's patronage of Buddhism led to the building of Nara's magnificent temples and monasteries, some of which still survive. Certain court ceremonies such as the open confession of sins (*keka*) show how the strong desire to lead a religious life permeated ruling circles. Buddhist influence led also to the making of highways and bridges, to the use of irrigation, and to the exploration of distant parts of the country by itinerant monks (who drew the earliest Japanese maps). Even such features of Japanese life as the public bath and cremation also date from the Buddhist inspiration of this time.

For the small number of monks and scholars of the Nara period who were well versed in Buddhist literature, four sūtras were of special importance: the Sūtra of Past and Present, Cause and Effect; the Sūtra of the Golden Light; the Sūtra of the Humane Kings; and the Kegon, or Flower Garland Sūtra. The first of these sūtras is a biography of Buddha that declares his extraordinary attainments to have been the cumulative merit of his meritorious deeds from the infinitely distant past to the present. This concept contrasts with the Han Confucian doctrine of kingly rule based on moral virtue in conformity with the Way of Heaven, or the theory of the *Record of Ancient Matters* (*Kojiki*), where we find genealogy to be essential to the legitimation of rulership.

The ruler's responsibilities—and indeed the entire question of the relationship between the state and Buddhism—were discussed most completely in the Sūtra of the Golden Light. This major work of Buddhist literature played a more important role than any other text in establishing Buddhism as the state religion of Japan, and its influence continued undiminished for centuries. It opens with an eloquent proclamation of the eternity of Buddha's life and declares that he exists not only as a historical figure with a human form but also in the cosmos as the ultimate law or Truth, and in the life hereafter as the savior possessed of an all-embracing love. Since Buddha is omnipresent, everything that exists is subject to his eternal vigilance of boundless compassion. The sūtra declares further that the gates of the paradise of the Lotus where Buddha dwells are always open to all of humanity, for anyone can become a Buddha. The methods the sūtra especially recommends for bringing about this change for the better are expiation and self-sacrifice, and accordingly, the climax of the entire narration is the parable of Buddha giving himself up to feed a hungry tiger.

The central theme of the sūtra is the life of wisdom—*prajñā*, which distinguishes good from evil and right from wrong. Everyone, from the king to his lowliest subject, must obey the dictates of the inner light of reason. The religious life starts with an awareness of one's sins and the need to atone for them. It is wisdom that enables people to surmount their failings, and the highest expression of the triumph of wisdom is an act of self-sacrifice. Wisdom is also associated with healing; Buddha is supremely possessed of wisdom and is the great healer as well. It was this aspect of Buddha that appealed most to Japanese of the Nara period, as witnessed by the predominant role of Yakushi, the Healing Bodhisattva, in both temples specifically dedicated to him and in most centers of worship. The Sūtra of the Golden Light contains a chapter entirely devoted to medicine and healing, illustrating the close connection between religious belief and medicine. (Buddhist monks introduced many medicines from China during the Nara period.)

The political aspects of the sūtra are most clearly stated in the chapter on kingly law (Ōbōshō-ron), which declares that government and religion are united by the Buddhist Law (or dharma). The law of men must be universal but not final, always subject to change, with peace as its ultimate end. Any king who violates the Law will be punished, but as long as he is faithful to it, Buddha will see to it that he enjoys immeasurable blessings. Japanese monarchs during the Nara period held this sūtra in such reverence that they attempted to make it an instrument of state ideology. Copies of the sūtra were distributed in all the provinces in 741 C.E. by order of Emperor Shōmu, one of Japan's most devout rulers. At about the same time, Shōmu ordered each province to build a seven-story pagoda and to establish a Guardian Temple of the Province and an Atonement Nunnery of the Province.

Shōmu also was responsible for building the Great Image of Lochana Buddha, the most famous monument of the Nara period. Just as Lochana Buddha is the central figure of the cosmogony of the Kegon Sūtra, the Great Image and its temple were intended as the center of the provincial temples and nunneries. The Kegon Sūtra is said to have been the teaching delivered by Buddha immediately after attaining enlightenment, when he made no attempt to simplify the complexities of his doctrines for the benefit of the less capable. Its difficulty kept it from attaining the popularity of the Sūtra of the Golden Light, but its importance is evident from the efforts devoted to completing the Great Image (more than fifty feet high). In 749, when gold was discovered in Japan for the first time, it was regarded as an auspicious sign for completion of the monument. Emperor Shōmu declared:

This is the Word of the Sovereign who is the Servant of the Three Treasures, that he humbly speaks before the Image of Lochana.

In this land of Yamato since the beginning of Heaven and Earth, Gold, though it has been brought as an offering from other countries, was thought not to exist. But in the East of the land which We rule . . . Gold has been found.

Hearing this We were astonished and rejoiced, and feeling that this is a Gift bestowed upon Us by the love and blessing of Lochana Buddha, We have received it with reverence and humbly accepted it, and have brought with Us all Our officials to worship and give thanks.

This We say reverently, reverently, in the Great Presence of the Three Treasures whose name is to be spoken with awe.[4]

We cannot help but be struck by the humility of the terms that Shōmu uses. For him to claim to be a "servant" of the Three Treasures marks an astonishing departure from the previously held ideas of kingship in Japan. There seemingly remained only one more step to be taken to make Japan into a true Buddha land: to have a sovereign who was ordained as a minister to Buddha's Law so that the country could be governed in perfect consonance with these teachings. And during the reign of Shōmu's daughter, rule was nearly transferred to a Buddhist monk.

In 764 C.E., Empress Kōtoku, who had previously abdicated to enter the religious life, suddenly decided to resume her rule despite the Buddhist vows she had taken. Adopting a new reign title, Shōtoku, she appointed Dōkyō, a master of the Hossō sect, to be her chief minister. Dōkyō steadily rose in power. In 766 he was appointed "king of the law" (hōō), and several years later the empress, acting on a false oracle, was on the point of abdicating the throne in his favor. However, powerful conservative forces at the court blocked this move, and Japan never again came so close to becoming a Buddha land. Empress Shōtoku died in 770; Dōkyō was disgraced; and later new rulers turned from Nara to Kyoto, where new forms of Buddhism were to dominate the scene.

THE SŪTRA OF THE GOLDEN LIGHT

The full title of this work, Sūtra of the Sovereign Kings of the Golden Light Ray (Konkō myō saishō ōgyō), refers to the Deva Kings who came to pay homage to the Buddha. The sūtra is credited with inspiring the first temple built by the court, the Shitennōji (or Temple of the Four Deva Kings). When Tenmu seized the throne in 672, this sūtra appears to have influenced his decision to promote Buddhism in the interest of the new regime. His predecessor, Tenchi (Tenji), had been clearly associated with the Confucian political order, and as we have seen, Tenchi's assumption of power was justified by numerous portents indicating that he had received the Mandate of Heaven. Tenmu found a similar justification in the Golden Light Sūtra, which set forth a doctrine of kingship based on merit—merit achieved in former existences and through the wholehearted support of Buddhism. It thus strongly implied that kings rule by a kind of "divine right" not based on any hereditary claim but, rather, on the ruler's religious merit. In Tenmu's case, his realm would enjoy peace and harmony from the beneficial influence of Buddhist teachings on public morality, and even the cosmic order would respond to his virtue and bestow blessings on him and his people. Here, then, is a Buddhist claim to religious legitimacy overriding any customary right

---

4. Sansom, "The Imperial Edicts in the Shoku-Nihongi," p. 26.

of dynastic inheritance. It is no wonder that Tenmu held this sūtra in particular honor and fostered the growth of Buddhism by ordering every family to have a Buddhist shrine in its house.

THE PROTECTION OF THE COUNTRY BY THE FOUR DEVA KINGS

Then the Four Deva Kings, their right shoulders bared from their robes in respect, arose from their seats and, with their right knees touching the ground and their palms joined in humility, thus addressed Buddha:

"Most Revered One! When, in some future time, this Sūtra of the Golden Light is transmitted to every part of a kingdom—to its cities, towns, and villages, its mountains, forests, and fields—if the king of the land listens with his whole heart to these writings, praises them, and makes offerings on their behalf, and if moreover he supplies this sūtra to the four classes of believers, protects them, and keeps them from all harm, we Deva Kings, in recognition of his deeds, will protect the king and his people, give them peace and freedom from suffering, prolong their lives, and fill them with glory. Most Revered One! If when the king sees that the four classes of believers receive the sūtra, he respects and protects them as he would his own parents, we Four Kings will so protect him always that whatever he wishes will come about, and all sentient beings will respect him." . . .

Then Buddha declared to the Four Deva Kings:

"Fitting is it indeed that you Four Kings should thus defend the holy writings. In the past I practiced bitter austerities of every kind for 100,000 kalpas [eons]. Then, when I attained supreme enlightenment and realized in myself universal wisdom, I taught this law. If a king upholds this sūtra and makes offerings in its behalf, I will purify him of suffering and illness and bring him peace of mind. I will protect his cities, towns, and villages and scatter his enemies. I will make all strife among the rulers of men to cease forever.

"Know ye, Deva Kings, that the 84,000 rulers of the 84,000 cities, towns, and villages of the world shall each enjoy happiness of every sort in his own land; that they shall all possess freedom of action and obtain all manner of precious things in abundance; that they shall never again invade each other's territories; that they shall receive recompense in accordance with their deeds of previous existences; that they shall no longer yield to the evil desire of taking the lands of others; that they shall learn that the smaller their desires the greater the blessing; and that they shall emancipate themselves from the suffering of warfare and bondage. The people of their lands shall be joyous, and upper and lower classes will blend as smoothly as milk and water. They shall appreciate each other's feelings, join happily in diversions together, and, with all compassion and modesty, increase the sources of goodness.

"In this way the nations of the world shall live in peace and prosperity, the peoples shall flourish, the earth shall be fertile, the climate temperate, and the seasons shall follow in the proper order. The sun, moon, and the constellations of stars shall continue their regular progress unhindered. The wind and rain shall come in good season. All treasures shall be abundant. No meanness shall be found in human hearts, but all shall practice almsgiving and cultivate the ten good works. When the end of life comes, many shall be born in Heaven and increase the celestial multitudes."

[Tsuji, *Nihon bukkyō shi*, jōsei-hen, pp. 194–195]

THE FLOWER GARLAND SCHOOL

In seventh-century China and the Korean state of Silla, the teachings of the Flower Garland (J: Kegon) school of Mahāyāna Buddhism was a religious accompaniment to the state-building process, and in eighth-century Nara-period Japan, it served the same function. It preached a universal spiritual communion in accordance with the doctrine of interdependent existence and interdependent salvation as the basis for a universal state that would also be a Buddha land or state.

THE FLOWER GARLAND SŪTRA

The basic scripture of the Flower Garland school is the Flower Garland Sūtra (Kegon-kyō), a lengthy work describing an enormously grand vision of the universe. The language of the sūtra is so mythic and extravagant that it has acquired a reputation for being abstruse and almost impossible to comprehend. Widely regarded in the Mahāyāna tradition as being the first sermon preached by the Buddha, revealing the full content of his enlightenment, this sūtra was said to be too profound and lofty for most humans to understand. Therefore, after making concessions to human limitations, the Buddha preached other sūtras that were easier to grasp.

The Flower Garland Sūtra teaches tenets similar to those developed in other schools and contributes to a doctrinal common ground for Mahāyāna Buddhism in general. The terms "interdependence," "interpenetration," "simultaneous co-arising," and "nonduality" express this basic notion that the diverse elements of the universe are interdependent and interrelated. This is not to say that everything is identical, however; rather, the Kegon vision affirms diversity and attempts to explain the inherent and simultaneous interrelatedness of each thing with all things and all things with each thing, without the loss of individual identities.

The patriarchs of the school in China often enjoyed their rulers' patronage. Dushun (557–640), the school's founder, was held in high esteem by Emperor Wen (r. 589–605) of the Sui dynasty, and Fazang (643–712), the third patriarch and great systematizer of Kegon (Ch: Huayan) teachings, was honored several times by Empress Wu (r. 684–704) of the Tang,[5] who supported a new Chinese translation of the Flower Garland Sūtra by Śikṣānanda and was acclaimed by Huayan monks as an incarnation of the bodhisattva Maitreya.

THE FLOWER GARLAND SŪTRA: THE TOWER OF VAIROCHANA

The last section of the sūtra tells of the pilgrimage of Sudhana, a youth who visits various people, each of whom teaches him something about the Flower Garland universe. Maitreya welcomed Sudhana by showing him the great tower of Vairochana, the central Buddha of the sūtra. The tower was a place in which the interrelatedness of the universe could be seen and is described in the following excerpt taken from Śikṣānanda's translation.

In the Kegon view, a Buddhist state (*bukkoku*) would be one that supported this universal spiritual communion. However, as a universal principle underlying a universal state—the mutual fusion and permeability of all things—even while acting as a solvent of all local loyalties and cultural particularism, it also left questions as to the solid ground on which one might erect any social or political structure or ethic. In effect, this left room for the persistence of strong indigenous customs, thus enabling egalitarian spirituality to coexist with political and social hierarchy.

This is the place where all the buddhas live peacefully. This is the dwelling place where a single eon permeates all eons and all eons permeate one eon without loss of any of their own characteristics. This is the dwelling place where one land permeates all lands and all lands permeate one land without loss of any of their own characteristics. This is the dwelling place where one sentient being permeates all sentient beings and all sentient beings permeate one sentient being without loss of any of their own characteristics. This is the dwelling place where one buddha permeates all buddhas and all buddhas permeate one buddha without loss of their own characteristics. This is the dwelling place where in a single moment of thought everything about the past, present, and future can be known. This is the dwelling place where in a single moment of thought one can travel to all countries. This is the dwelling place where all sentient beings manifest all of their prior lives. This is the dwelling place of concern for the benefit of everyone in the world. This is the dwelling place of those who can go everywhere. This is the dwelling place of those who are detached from the world and yet constantly remain there to teach other people.

[*Kegonkyō*, TD 10, no. 279:423; GT]

---

5. Actually, Empress Wu assumed the title of emperor, the only woman in Chinese history to have done so, and adopted the dynastic name of Zhou, rather than Tang, during her period of personal ascendancy.

THE BUDDHA KINGDOM OF THE FLOWER GARLAND

A common refrain in Kegon Buddhism is the claim that the perfect realm of the Buddha (*ri*) is interfused with the ordinary world (*ji*) without obstruction (*muge*) and that earthly rulers should manifest this universal harmony and order by "turning the wheel of the dharma" throughout the land. With its vivid descriptions of this unity of all parts within a whole, the Flower Garland Sūtra articulated a spiritual ideal that easily resonated with political objectives for unification and stability. In other East Asian countries as well, the Kegon ideal of harmony inspired the building of the Bulguk-sa (Temple of the Kingdom of the Buddha), which commemorated the unified rule of the Korean kingdom of Silla, and the establishment of the Great Temple of the East (Tōdaiji) in Nara, which exemplified Emperor Shōmu's (r. 724–49) vision of centralized rule in Japan.

Chapter on the Exquisite Adornments of the Rulers of the World

All of the kingdoms in the ten directions
Will become purified and beautiful in a single moment
When rulers turn the wheel of the dharma
With the wondrous sounds of their voices
Reaching everywhere throughout their lands
With no place untouched.

The world of the Buddha is without bounds,
And his dharma realm inundates everything in an instant.
In every speck of dust the Buddha establishes a place of practice,
Where he enlightens every being and displays spiritual wonders.
The World Honored One practiced all spiritual disciplines
While coursing through a past of a hundred thousand eons,
Adorning all of the lands of the buddhas,
And manifesting himself without obstruction, as if in empty space.

The Buddha's divine powers are unbounded,
Filling endless eons;
No one would tire of constantly watching him
Even for countless ages.

You should observe the realms of the Buddha's power
Purifying and adorning all of the countries in the ten directions.
In all these places he manifests himself in myriad forms,
Never the same from moment to moment.

Observe the Buddha for a hundred thousand countless eons,
But you will not discern a single hair on his body,
For through the unhindered use of skillful means
It is his radiance that shines on inconceivably numerous worlds.

In past ages the Buddha was in the world
Serving in a boundless ocean of all the buddhas.
All beings therefore came to make offerings to the World-Honored One,
Just as rivers flow to the sea.

The Buddha appears everywhere in the ten directions,
And in the countless lands of every speck of dust
Wherein are infinite realities
The Buddha abides in all, infinitely unbounded.

The Buddha in the past cultivated an ocean
Of unbounded compassion for sentient beings,
Whom he instructed and purified
As they entered life and death.

The Buddha lives in the dharma realm complex of truth
Free of forms, signs, and all defilements.
When people contemplate and see his many different bodies.
All their troubles and sufferings disappear.

[*Kegonkyō*, TD 10, no. 279:22; GT]

STATE SPONSORSHIP AND CONTROL OF BUDDHISM

Buddhism's early claim to exist beyond the authority of the state, as asserted by Huiyuan in fifth-century China, was radically transformed in the Tang period when it became an institutional arm of the state. The office of the "superintendent of the Buddhist clergy (*sangha*)," which first appeared under the Northern Wei in the mid-fifth century, marked the inception of this transformation. The superintendent headed a bureaucracy staffed by lay officials or nominal "monks" charged with overseeing monastic affairs. He was not the head of an autonomous religious organization but, rather, an appointee of the emperor and given tonsure by the emperor's hand.

The religious rationale for this government-run Buddhism in China was supplied by the first superintendent, Faguo, who justified the monks' service to the government by directly identifying the emperor as the Buddha. In contrast to Huiyuan's rigorous defense of clerical independence, Faguo said that "Taizu is enlightened and loves the Way. He is in his very person the Thus-Come One. Monks (*shramanas*) must and should pay him all homage. . . . He who propagates the teaching of the Buddha is the lord of men. I am not doing obeisance to the Emperor, I am merely worshiping the Buddha."[6] A somewhat less accommodating view is put forward in the following commentary on the Perfect Wisdom Sūtra for Humane Kings Who Wish to Protect Their States (known in Japan as the Ninnōkyō).

THE HUMANE KING AS PROTECTOR OF BUDDHISM

As an alternative to Buddhism's serving the state, the Sūtra of the Humane King proposes that the state and Buddhism serve each other. Using the vocabulary of Chinese monarchy, the scripture asserts that "humane" or "benevolent" kings (*renwang*) practice "outer protection" (*waihu*) and that this protection involves the patronage of an independent clergy who practice the "inner protection" (*neihu*) of the bodhisattva virtue of "forbearance" (*ren*). The pun on the term *ren*[7] is the basis of the scripture and the starting point of all its commentaries. Thus, according to the early-seventh-century *Commentary on the Sūtra of the Humane King*, the ruler who protects Buddhism thereby protects the state.

Because the humane king (*renwang*) explicates the Teaching and disseminates virtue here below, he is called "humane." Because he has transformed himself, he is called "king." The humane king's ability is to protect (*hu*). What is protected is the state. This is possible because the humane king uses the Teaching to order the state. Now if we consider the Highest Perfect Wisdom (*Prajñāpāramitā*), its ability is to protect. The humane king is he who is protected. Because he uses the Highest Perfect Wisdom, the humane king is tranquil and hidden. Thus, if he uses his ability to propagate the Teaching, the king is able to protect [the state], and it is the Highest Perfect Wisdom which is the [method of] protection. Moreover, one who is humane is forbearing [*renzhe ren ye*].[8] Hearing of good he is not overjoyed; hearing of bad he is not angry. Because he is

---

6. Hurvitz, *Wei Shou*, p. 53.

7. *Ren*, meaning "humaneness," and *ren*, meaning "forbearance," are homophones, but the words are written with different Chinese characters.

8. A punning inversion of *Mencius* 7B:16, "To be humane (*ren*) is what it means to be human (*ren*)," recalling also Confucius' pun on "humaneness" (*ren*) and "forbearance" (*ren*) in *Analects* 12:3.

able to hold to forbearance in good and bad, therefore he is called forbearing (*ren*).

[TD 33, no. 1705:253; CO]

Here the scripture's adroit use of language to reorder the relationship between religion and the state is coupled with Mahāyāna teachings of Perfect Wisdom. This eighth-century recension of the text by Amoghavajra, a leading monk at the Tang court, further accentuates these teachings through the addition of such passages as the following based on the dialectics of negation.

At that time the World-honored One said to King Prasenajit, "By what signs do you contemplate the Thus-Come One?" King Prasenajit answered, "I contemplate his body's real signs; [I] contemplate the Buddha thus: without boundaries in front, behind, and in the middle; not residing in the three times and not transcending the three times; not residing in the five aggregates, not transcending the five aggregates; not abiding in the four great elements and not transcending the four great elements; not abiding in the six abodes of sensation and not transcending the six abodes of sensation; not residing in the three realms and not transcending the three realms; residing in no direction, transcending no direction; [neither] illumination [nor] ignorance, and so on. Not one, not different; not this, not that; not pure, not foul; not existent nor nonexistent; without signs of self or signs of another; without name, without signs; without strength, without weakness; without demonstration, without exposition; not magnanimous, not stingy; not prohibited, not transgressed; not forbearing, not hateful; not forward, not remiss; not fixed, not in disarray; not wise, not stupid; not coming, not going; not entering, not leaving; not a field of blessings, not a field of misfortune; without sign, without the lack of sign; not gathering, not dispersing; not great, not small; not seen, not heard; not perceived, not known. The mind, activities, and senses are extinguished, and the path of speech is cut off. It is identical with the edge of reality and equal to the [real] nature of things. I use these signs to contemplate the Thus-Come One."

[TD 8, no. 246:836; CO]

In the preceding passage, the "unboundedness" of the Buddha's body and the principle of universal emptiness in the Prajñāpāramitā (expressed in the negation of all determinate views) can also be understood in the more affirmative terms of the Kegon philosophy, that is, the universal tolerance and mutual nonobstruction of all things (expressed as "nothing precludes or bars anything else," jiji muge, or, politically, "any expedient means may be made to serve the purposes of Buddhism." Both formulations underlay the practice of Amogavajra's Esoteric Buddhism or Mystical Teaching, which was predicated on a view similar to Huayan's "True Emptiness [allows for] Mysterious or Wondrous Man-

ifestations (shinkū myōyū)." Thus mystic rites and incantations could play a part in Buddhism's consecrating and legitimizing of imperial rule.

BUDDHISM AND THE STATE IN NARA JAPAN

PROCLAMATION OF THE EMPEROR SHŌMU ON THE ERECTION OF THE GREAT BUDDHA IMAGE

Having respectfully succeeded to the throne through no virtue of our own, out of a constant solicitude for all men, We have been ever intent on aiding them to reach the shore of the Buddha land. Already even the distant seacoasts of this land have been made to feel the influence of our benevolence and regard for others, and yet not everywhere in this land do men enjoy the grace of Buddha's law. Our fervent desire is that under the aegis of the Three Treasures, the benefits of peace may be brought to all in heaven and earth, even animals and plants sharing in its fruits, for all time to come.

Therefore on the fifteenth day of the tenth month of the fifteenth year of the Tempyō reign [743], which is the year of the goat and water junior,[9] We take this occasion to proclaim our great vow of erecting an image of Lochana Buddha in gold and copper. We wish to make the utmost use of the nation's resources of metal in the casting of this image, and also to level off the high hill on which the great edifice is to be raised, so that the entire land may be joined with us in the fellowship of Buddhism and enjoy in common the advantages which this undertaking affords to the attainment of Buddhahood.

It is we who possess the wealth of the land; it is we who possess all power in the land. With this wealth and power at our command, we have resolved to create this venerable object of worship. The task would appear to be an easy one, and yet a lack of sufficient forethought on our part might result in the people's being put to great trouble in vain, for the Buddha's heart would never be touched if, in the process, calumny and bitterness were provoked which led unwittingly to crime and sin.

Therefore all who join in the fellowship of this undertaking must be sincerely pious in order to obtain its great blessings, and they must daily pay homage to Lochana Buddha, so that with constant devotion each may proceed to the creation of Lochana Buddha.[10] If there are some desirous of helping in the

---

9. Year designation according to the Chinese sexagenary cycle (see chapter 4).

10. Although it might seem impious to think that the Cosmic Buddha himself could be so created, in the Kegon philosophy the particular and the universal are one and inseparable, so that an image properly conceived with a devout realization of the Buddha's true nature might stand for the Buddha himself.

construction of this image, though they have no more to offer than a twig or handful of dirt, they should be permitted to do so. The provincial and county authorities are not to disturb and harass the people by making arbitrary demands on them in the name of this project. This is to be proclaimed far and wide so that all may understand our intentions in this matter.

[From *Shoku Nihongi*, in *Rikkokushi*, III, pp. 320–321]

THE BODHISATTVA GYŌGI

Gyōgi [670?–749], a major figure in the Buddhism of the Nara period, gained great renown as a popular teacher and practitioner of good works—establishing hospitals, orphanages, old people's homes, rest houses, and the like and performing public works such as the construction of bridges, harbors, and canals for navigation and irrigation. At these sites, he established practice halls (*dōjō*) that also served as seminaries for those serving on these projects. Although early on, the court looked askance at Gyōgi's unconventional and unauthorized activities, in time, as he became popularly revered as a bodhisattva incarnate, the court sought to appropriate his popularity and prestige for itself, at which point Emperor Shōmu conferred on him high ecclesiastical rank (*daisōjō*) in recognition of his standing among the people.

The following is taken from a collection of hagiographical writings compiled by the Tendai monk Chingen around 1040, containing miracle stories ostensibly connected with the Lotus Sūtra. It shows how a charismatic figure like Gyōgi quickly became the stuff of legend and how the popularization of Buddhism attended the state-building process in the Nara period.

Bodhisattva Gyōgi was a man from the Ōtori District of Izumi Province. Koshi was his secular clan name.

When born, he was wrapped in a caul. His parents placed him on a tree branch as a method of decontaminating him. After one night, the parents found that their baby was out of the skin and already spoke well. They took him home and reared him.

When still a boy, Gyōgi used to praise the Law together with the neighborhood children. As time passed, Gyōgi had several followers, including young cowherds who attended Gyōgi and ignored their cows and horses. When the masters of these cowherds needed them, they sent people to fetch the boys. But those who were sent for the boys, including men and women, the young and the old, listened to Gyōgi preach and stayed with him, forgetting to ask the cowherds about the cattle. So finally Gyōgi would climb to a high place and call out to gather the cattle. The scattered cows and horses gathered near Gyōgi and each master took his cattle home by himself.

Later Gyōgi took the tonsure and became a monk of Yakushiji Temple. He read the commentaries including the *Yugayuishikiron*[11] and perceived the deep significance in these writings.

Gyōgi traveled widely in cities and in rural areas, cultivating the people. Nearly one thousand people followed him, wishing to be taught. . . .

Gyōgi visited various dangerous and yet important places. He constructed bridges and roads. He investigated the irrigation and cultivation of rice fields and he dug ponds for reservoirs and built dikes. Those who heard of his projects all gathered and helped him. So the construction was finished in a short time. Since then, farmers and peasants have greatly benefited.

Gyōgi built as many as forty-nine halls[12] in the area near the capital including Yamato, Kawachi, Yamashiro, Izumi and Settsu and built more in other provinces.

Once while on his way home after traveling in various provinces practicing the Way, Gyōgi saw some villagers including adults and children gathered around a pond, catching fish and eating them. As Gyōgi passed by, one of the youngsters playfully urged Gyōgi to eat some of the cut-up raw fish. As Gyōgi put the morsels into his mouth and spat them out, the fish meat became small fish. Those who watched marveled greatly.

Emperor Shōmu respected Gyōgi and granted him the rank of Grand Abbot.[13] Chikō,[14] another eminent monk of that time, felt jealous of Gyōgi, and thought, "I am a learned Grand Abbot while Gyōgi is a mere monk without much learning. Why does the emperor appreciate him so much more and ignore me?" Holding a strong grudge against the emperor and Gyōgi, Chikō retired into a mountain and soon died there. According to his wishes, Chikō's body was not immediately buried but was left as it was.

Ten days later, Chikō revived and said to his disciples, "Messengers from King Yama's palace pursued me. As we ran, we saw a beautiful golden edifice glittering with radiance. I asked the messengers whose palace it was. The messengers replied that it was the place where Bodhisattva Gyōgi was born. As we proceeded further, we saw fire and smoke ahead. When I asked the messengers, they said that the fire and smoke were from the hell where I was going. Soon we arrived there.

King Yama told me in a roaring voice that I was brought down to hell to be punished for my evil and jealous feelings toward Gyōgi in the country of Japan. Soon I was made to hold a hot copper pole and my flesh and bones burned and festered. After I atoned for my sins, I was released."

---

11. A major text of the Dharma Character (Hossō) school translated by Xuanzang.

12. Temple construction was restricted in the Nara period, so village temples, which did not conform to government restrictions, were called *dōjō*, "practice halls."

13. Grand abbot or superintendent.

14. An eminent scholarly monk of the Nara period who studied the Three Treatise (Sanron) Teachings, belonged to the Gangōji Temple, and left numerous commentaries on the sūtras.

Now that Chikō had revived, he wished to apologize to Gyōgi. At that time, Gyōgi was engaged in constructing a bridge spanning Naniwa Bay in Tsu Province. When Gyōgi saw Chikō at a distance, he smiled at him. Chikō prostrated himself before Gyōgi and tearfully begged his pardon.

When the emperor built the Tōdaiji Temple,[15] he ordered Gyōgi to offer a dedication service for the temple as lecturer. Gyōgi replied that he would not be able to serve as a lecturer at such a great meeting, but that a holy man from a foreign country would come to offer the service.

When the day arrived, Gyōgi said that they should welcome the holy man. With an imperial order, Gyōgi led ninety-nine priests and the officials from three offices including those for aristocrats, for priests and nuns, and for music. He went to the port of Naniwa and waited there with music.

Holding a set of *argha*[16] (Buddhist utensils for offerings), with arranged flowers and burning incense, Gyōgi took the hundredth place among the priests and boarded a boat. . . .

After a while . . . they saw a small boat approaching. As it arrived at the shore, an Indian stepped on the beach. Seeing this, Gyōgi raised a hand, smiled at the Indian priest, and recited a poem,

> The truth of the words
> Vowed before Shākyamuni
> At Vulture Peak
> Did not die and
> We have met again.

The holy man from the foreign country responded by reciting his poem,

> As promised to each other
> At Kapilavastu,
> I can now see
> The face of Mañjushrī.

Gyōgi said to the monks and laymen in his presence that the holy man was Bodhisena, a monk from South India. The people gathered at the place now knew that Gyōgi was an incarnation of Mañjushrī. There is no more space to itemize other miraculous happenings.

Gyōgi, at the age of eighty, passed away on the fourth day of the second month of the first year of Tenpyōshōhō (749).

[Trans. adapted from Dykstra, *Miraculous Tales*, pp. 27–29]

---

15. The Indian Bodhisena (704–760) came to Japan in 736 and, on Gyōgi's recommendation, presided at the Eye-Opening Ceremony of the Great Buddha of the Tōdaiji Temple in 752.

16. A set of special containers are used for the *aka* or the water offered to the Buddha.

REGULATION OF THE BUDDHIST ORDERS
BY THE COURT

Not all those who embraced Buddhism, "left the world," and joined monastic orders did so with a full realization of what would be required of them in the religious life. Consequently, it was not long after the first establishment of monasteries and nunneries in Japan that charges were made of flagrant violations of Buddhist vows in regard to the taking of life, sexual incontinence, and drunkenness. Since the throne had taken a prominent part in establishing Buddhist institutions, it was expected that the court would likewise assert its control over them, as indicated by the measures taken by Suiko as early as 623 C.E. Such external controls proved largely ineffective, however, for serious violations were common throughout the seventh and eighth centuries, and it remained for reformers such as Ganjin and Saichō (see chapter 6) to attempt to tighten discipline from within.

31st year [623], Spring, 4th month, 3rd day. There was a Buddhist monk who took an axe and smote therewith his paternal grandfather. Now the empress, hearing of this, sent for the Great Imperial Chieftain Soga, and gave command, saying: "The man who has entered religion should be devoted to the Three Treasures and should cherish devoutly the prohibitions of the Buddhist Law. How can he without compunction be readily guilty of crime? We now hear that there is a monk who has struck his grandfather. Therefore, let all the monks and nuns of the various temples be assembled, and investigation made. Let severe punishment be inflicted on any who are convicted of offenses." Hereupon the monks and nuns were all assembled, and an examination held. The wicked monks and nuns were all about to be punished, when Kwallŭk, a Buddhist monk of Paekche, presented a memorial, as follows: "The Law of Buddha came from the Western country to Han.[17] Three hundred years later it was handed on to Paekche, since which time barely one hundred years had elapsed, when our king, hearing that the emperor of Nippon was a wise man, sent him tribute of an image of Buddha and of Buddhist sūtras. Since that time, less than one hundred years have passed, and consequently the monks and nuns have not yet learned the Buddhist laws and readily commit wickedness. On this account all the monks and nuns are afraid and do not know what to do. I humbly pray that with the exception of the wicked [monk who struck his grandfather], all the other monks and nuns be pardoned and not punished. That would be a work of great merit."

Accordingly the empress granted [his petition].

---

17. The Chinese dynasty of that name.

13th day. A decree was made as follows: "If even the monks continue to offend against the Law, wherewithal shall the laymen be admonished? Therefore from this time forward we appoint a Sōjō and a Sōzu for the superintendence of the monks and nuns."

Autumn, 9th month, 3rd day. There was an inspection of the temples and of the monks and nuns, and an accurate record made of the circumstances of the building of the temples, and also of the circumstances under which the monks and nuns embraced religion, with the year, month, and day of their taking orders. There were at this time 46 temples, 816 monks, and 569 nuns—in all, 1,385 persons.

32nd year [624], Spring, 1st month, 7th day. The king of Koryŏ sent tribute of a Buddhist monk, named Hyegwan. He was appointed Sōjō [superintendent of monks and nuns].[18]

[Adapted from Aston, *Nihongi*, II, pp. 1522–1554]

EDICTS OF THE EMPRESS SHŌTOKU CONCERNING DŌKYŌ

These edicts, one making the priest Dōkyō the chief minister of the court and the other naming him the king of the Law, preceded Empress Shōtoku's attempt to abdicate the imperial throne in his favor.

EDICT OF OCTOBER 19, 764

It has been represented to us, in view of the master's constant attendance on us, that he has ambitions of rising to high office like his ancestors before him, and we have been petitioned to dismiss him from our court. However, We have observed his conduct and found it to be immaculate. Out of a desire to transmit and promote Buddha's Law, he has extended to us his guidance and protection. How could we lightly dismiss such a teacher?

Although our head has been shaven and we wear Buddhist robes, we feel obliged to conduct the government of the nation. As Buddha declared in the [Bommō, Brahmajāla] Sūtra, "Kings, ye who take up thrones, receive the ordination of the bodhisattvas!" These words prove that there can be no objection even for one who has taken holy orders in administering the government. We deem it proper therefore, since the reigning monarch is ordained, that the chief minister should also be an ordained monk. Hearken, all ye people, to our words:

---

18. The Japanese were still such novices in Buddhism that Korean monks were generally selected as religious authorities.

We confer on the Master Dōkyō the title of chief minister and master, though the title is not of his seeking. [pp. 93–94]

EDICT OF NOVEMBER 26, 766

We do affirm in this edict our belief that when the Law of Buddha, the Supreme One, is worshiped and revered with perfect sincerity of heart, he is certain to vouchsafe some unusual sign. The sacred bone of the Tathāgata which has now been manifested, of perfect shape and unusually large, is brighter and more beautiful of color than ever we have seen; the mind cannot encompass its splendor. Thus it is that night and day alike we pay it humble reverence with our unwavering attention. Indeed, it appears to us that when the Transformation Body of the Buddha extends its guidance to salvation in accordance with circumstances, his compassionate aid is manifested with no delay. Nevertheless, the Law depends on men for the continuation and spread of its prosperity. Thus, it has been due to acts of leadership and guidance in consonance with the Law performed by our chief minister and master, who stands at the head of all priests, that this rare and holy Sign has been vouchsafed us. How could so holy and joyous a thing delight us alone? Hearken, all ye people, to your sovereign's will: We bestow on our teacher, the chief minister, the title of king of the Law.[19] We declare again that such worldly titles have never been of his seeking; his mind is set, with no other aspiration, on performing the acts of a bodhisattva and leading all men to salvation. Hearken, all ye people, to your sovereign's will: We confer this position on him as an act of reverence and gratitude. [pp. 140–141]

[From Shoku Nihongi, in Rikkokushi, VI, pp. 93–141]

THE MERGER OF BUDDHIST AND SHINTO DEITIES

It is difficult to trace the early stages of the important process by which Buddhism was made compatible with Shinto and thus became more easily acceptable to the Japanese. The first clear indication of this appears in the middle of the Nara period—more than two hundred years after the official introduction of Buddhism to Japan—in a biography of Fujiwara Muchimaro. The author was obviously a Buddhist himself, and he portrayed a Shinto deity seeking refuge in the power of Buddhism. The mutual relationship of Buddhism with Shinto later developed in complex ways and by the Kamakura period resulted in detailed explanations of the Shinto gods as the concrete manifestations of Buddhist deities. This Buddhist argument was widely accepted and contrib-

---

19. Sometimes translated as "pope."

uted significantly to the doctrinal, ritual, and institutional blending of both religions. Muchimaro's biography marks the textual beginning of this merger and tells how a Shinto deity, still in command of its own powers, made a spiritual request that had an institutional answer.

In the year 715, Fujiwara Muchimaro had a dream in which a strange man appeared and said, "Since you revere the teachings of the Buddha, please build a temple for my sake. I beg of you to fulfill my request and save me, for my past karma has caused me to be a Shinto deity for a long time. Now I place my trust in the way of the Buddha, and I wish to perform meritorious acts for my happiness. Thus far, I have not been able to obtain the proper causes and conditions for this, and therefore I have come to speak with you."

Muchimaro was suspicious and thought that the man might be the Kibi deity. He wanted to say something in reply but found himself unable to speak. Then he woke up from his dream. He offered a prayer, saying, "The ways of the gods and men are different. What is obvious to the one is obscure for the other. Who was that strange man appearing in my dream last night? If he should prove himself to be a deity by showing me a sign, then I shall surely build a temple for him." At that point, the deity picked up a monk named Kume Katsuashi and placed him at the very top of a tall tree. That, he said, was the sign. Muchimaro then realized the truth and built a temple, which is now a part of a Buddhist-Shinto shrine complex in Echizen Province.

[Tsuji, Bukkyō shi, 1, p. 440; GT]

PART II

Mahāyāna Universalism and the Sense of Hierarchy

The name Heian means "peace and tranquillity" and was originally given to the imperial capital, Kyoto, which remained the actual seat of ruling power throughout this period (late eighth to late twelfth centuries C.E.). During its earlier years at least, the period lived up to its name. After removal of the court to Kyoto in 794, the struggles for power around the throne that had marked the Nara period diminished in intensity, and there was no recrudescence of the drastic reforms attempted earlier to remake Japan on the Chinese model. Not that complete success had been achieved in unifying Japan and centralizing its administration—on the contrary, control of the so-called provinces, tenuous even at the start, was in the ninth and tenth centuries almost entirely lost to great families who made a mockery of the land and tax system imported from Tang China. And if there was a greater stability and continuity of power at the court itself, this too was gained not through a strengthening of the bureaucratic structure or civil service but through the complete triumph of the hereditary principle and the concentration of power in a single family, the Fujiwara. Such peace as the Heian period enjoyed, then, was due to the skill of the Fujiwara in managing their own interests and those of the imperial house (not without some intrafamily contention) so as to preserve their dominance even in the new circumstances. That the diffusion of power from the court was a long and gradual process, during which the imperial capital remained the unrivaled center of national life, due also to the great weight of tradition and to the enormous prestige of the capital in cultural affairs. Indeed, Kyoto's position as the cynosure of civilization was even further enhanced during this period by the military weakness of China from the eighth to twelfth centuries, to which the Japanese looked less and less often as a final authority in all matters. In religion, it is true, the two great movements inaugurated in the early eighth century, the Tendai Buddhism introduced by Saichō and the Esoteric Buddhism ably propagated by Kūkai, were imports from China significantly adapted by their Japanese proponents. Nevertheless, their progress was advanced by close association with the court, and their characteristic forms of expression increasingly reflected the court's prevailing attitudes and manner of life. Thus, although both these forms of Buddhism were egalitarian in theory—that is, as outgrowths of the Mahāyāna teaching, they stressed that all men had the potential for Buddhahood—in the Japanese setting, their activities were strongly conditioned by the aristocratic nature of court society. Again, despite the universalistic claims of the Mahāyāna as revealed in Tendai and Shingon eclecticism—their readiness to grant a place for all religious teachings and all forms of religious practice in a comprehensive view of Truth—there was a noticeable tendency to stress the hierarchic order of these forms of religious consciousness in the ascent to Truth. Thus, even though Tendai and Shingon Buddhism contained the seeds later sown abroad by the popular religious movements of the medieval period, in the Heian period itself the dissemination process was somewhat delayed.

Meanwhile, however, the Heian court attained great heights of cultural achievement. Increasingly, the Japanese asserted their independence of Chinese forms in literature and art and developed a native script better suited to the expression of their own language. The great monuments of this period of cultural efflorescence are the famous *Tale of Genji* by Lady Murasaki and the *Pillow Book* by Sei Shōnagon mirroring the court life of the time and the aesthetic preoccupations of the Heian aristocrats, as well as the great imperial collections of native poetry and the magnificent scroll paintings of this period. In them we find elegant expressions of the Heian passion for aesthetic refinement and the first clear intimations of the classic canons of Japanese taste, which inspired and guided the later development of a distinctive and highly distinguished artistic tradition.

Chapter 6

SAICHŌ AND MOUNT HIEI

One day in the seventh moon of 788, a young monk made his way up the side of Mount Hiei repeating this song of prayer he had composed:

> O Buddhas
> Of unexcelled complete enlightenment
> Bestow your invisible aid
> Upon this hut I open
> On the mountain top.[1]

The monk was Saichō (767–822), and the little temple he founded developed into a center of learning and culture for the entire nation until, by order of a ruthless military leader, the complex of three thousand temple buildings on Mount Hiei was razed in 1571. Saichō's temple would almost certainly never have attained such a remarkable position had it not been for the decision of Emperor Kanmu [r. 781–806] to move the capital away from Nara, the stronghold of the established sects of Buddhism. Kanmu was a Confucian by training and, as such, was opposed to the encroachment into political power by the Buddhist clergy. The attempt to establish Dōkyō as the ruler of Japan repre-

---

1. *Dengyō Daishi zenshū*, IV, p. 756 (1912 ed.).

sented the closest the monks came to success in creating a "Buddha land," but even when this failed, they were by no means reduced to a purely religious status. It was in order to restore to the sovereign his full prerogatives that Kanmu determined to move the seat of government. In this decision he had the support of the Fujiwara and certain important families traditionally opposed to Buddhism, as well as that of the descendants of such Chinese immigrant families as the Hata, who are credited with having introduced sericulture to Japan. Saichō himself was of Chinese descent. Another outstanding figure of the period, General Sakanoue no Tamuramaro, who extended the imperial domains to the northern end of the main island of Japan, was of Korean descent.

Although Kanmu's dislike of the monks' secular ambitions and his impatience with their interminable wrangling had made him somewhat distrustful of them, he realized that he needed Buddhist support for the reforms he intended to effect. These included steps to enforce Buddhist discipline, to secularize those monks and nuns who violated the laws of celibacy, to limit the economic activities and acquisition of land by temples and monasteries, and to tighten the restrictions on the establishment or maintenance of private temples outside the authorized system of provincial monasteries and nunneries. Saichō suited Kanmu's purposes. He had originally left Nara because of his dissatisfaction with the worldliness and, he believed, the decadence of the monks there. He became convinced that only in an entirely different environment could a true moral purge and ethical awakening take place. When he first established his little temple, the area around Mount Hiei was mainly uncultivated marshland, but six years later, in 794, it was chosen as the site of the capital. Saichō may have been instrumental in adopting this site, but in any case, once the capital had been moved there, he enjoyed the patronage of Emperor Kanmu. Saichō was sent to China in 804, chiefly to gain spiritual sanction for the new Buddhist foundation on Mount Hiei. China was considered the "fatherland" of Japanese Buddhism, and without some Chinese credentials, Saichō's monastery would have no standing alongside those of the powerful sects in Nara.

Saichō did not originally intend to found a new sect but, rather, an ecumenical center for the combined study of the teachings separately established in Nara. When Saichō's first temple opened, the Healing Buddha was enshrined there, just as it was in so many of the Nara temples. Moreover Saichō's initial inclinations, no doubt in reaction to the intense sectarian rivalries in Nara, were to try to reconcile competing claims in an eclectic, ecumenical movement. In his early religious training, Saichō had learned about Zhiyi's commentaries on the Lotus Sūtra that had been brought to Japan by Ganjin, a disciplinary master invited from Tang China to help reform Nara Buddhism. Zhiyi's comprehensive synthesis of Mahāyāna Buddhist doctrine and practice — a religious accompaniment to the unification process in late-sixth-century China — also fitted Emperor Kanmu's efforts to build the new capital of Heian (Kyoto) and strengthen the state's control over many aspects of Japanese life, including religious institutions.

Thus when Saichō was designated by the court to visit China and learn the latest developments in Tang Buddhism, he made an effort to acquaint himself with several current trends, receiving initiation in forms of Esoteric Buddhism and Zen as well as Zhiyi's Tendai (Ch: Tiantai) teachings and practices then undergoing something of a revival in late-eighth- and early-ninth-century China. In the short year of his stay, however, Saichō devoted his attention mostly to Zhiyi's grand synthesis of Exoteric[2] Buddhism in scripture, philosophy, and meditation and less to the other two schools, which emphasized practice. By contrast, Kūkai, who accompanied Saichō on this mission, went on to the Tang capital and, during a much longer stay, acquired a greater mastery of Esoteric texts, mandalas, and practices.

On his return to Japan, Saichō was authorized to conduct a training program at his center on Mount Hiei, which was dedicated to the "One Way" (of the Mahāyāna) and the Tendai form of meditative praxis known as the "calming" (lit., "cessation") and "contemplation" (*shikan*). Thus Saichō's initial aim was clearly to promote the Tendai Lotus school, as it was known, but not to the exclusion of other schools. His program of study included the Esoteric discipline identified with the Vairochana Sūtra, as well as the study of Confucian Classics, and the students authorized to participate in the program included representatives of the Nara sects in an ecumenical company.

If, however, Saichō's hope was to promote an inclusive religious movement in keeping with Zhiyi's own synthetic philosophy and Kanmu's aim to overcome the divisive rivalries of the Nara temples, events turned in an opposite direction. Cooperation with other sects failed, and Saichō was compelled to press his own primary aims in a more single-minded way, almost, one might say, as a loner.

One of Saichō's disappointments was the deterioration of his relationship with Kūkai, whose superior knowledge of Esoteric rituals he had hoped to use. Saichō's dedication to Mahāyāna universalism and the cause of the One Way manifested a genuine desire to improve his knowledge and understanding of Buddha's Law, regardless of whether or not the material he studied formed part of the Tendai teachings. He stated as his principle:

A devout believer in Buddha's Law who is also a wise man is truly obliged to point out to his students any false doctrines, even though they are principles of his own sect. He must not lead the students astray. If, on the other hand, he finds a correct doctrine, even though it is a principle of

---

2. That is, doctrines openly stated in rational, discursive terms rather than profound mysteries only hinted at or pointed to by subtle signs, symbols, and gestures (Esoteric Buddhism).

another sect, he should adopt and transmit it. This is the duty of a wise person. If a man maintains his partisan spirit even when his teachings are false; conceals his own errors and seeks to expose those of other people; persists in his own false views and destroys the right views of others — what could be more stupid than that? From this time forward, monks in charge of instruction in the Law must desist from such practices.[3]

Saichō was much impressed with the splendid Esoteric rituals, and senior though he was to Kūkai, he humbly requested and received from him initiation into one of the most important of these rites. Also, he frequently borrowed texts from Kūkai's extensive library. Saichō even sent Taihan, one of his favorite disciples, to study with Kūkai. But these deferential relations only glossed over important differences in the interpretation of how Esoteric Buddhism was related to the Lotus, since Saichō believed in the essential harmony of the two, whereas Kūkai asserted the former's superiority over the latter. Relations between Saichō and Kūkai came to an abrupt end when Kūkai, writing on Taihan's behalf, refused Saichō's request that Taihan return to Mount Hiei. Then, when Saichō asked to borrow a certain Esoteric sūtra, Kūkai this time replied that if he wished to study the Truth, it was everywhere apparent in the cosmos, but if he wished to learn about Esoteric Buddhism, he would have to become a regular student. The tone of Kūkai's letter was condescending, and we cannot be surprised that Saichō was offended by it.

At the same time, Saichō's relations with the Nara temples worsened. Like Kanmu, he had hoped not to alienate the established sects but found himself increasingly embroiled with them (especially the dominant Hossō sect) over his proposals on behalf of the Tendai Lotus teaching and Zhiyi's system of practice as the culmination of the Mahāyāna. Defending himself from these criticisms, Saichō argued that with the exception of the Kegon, the Nara schools had derived authority for their doctrines from secondary sources—the commentaries—instead of from the sūtras themselves. Saichō denounced this feature of Nara Buddhism in pointing out the superiority of the Lotus's teachings based (as he supposed) on Buddha's own words.

Saichō referred often to the "Two Vehicles" of Nara Buddhism. By this he meant Hīnayāna and what may be called Quasi-Mahāyāna, the latter referring to such schools as the Hossō and Sanron. Against these doctrines Saichō upheld the "One Vehicle" of the true Mahāyāna. The emphasis on "oneness" took various forms. Most important, it meant universality, in contrast, say, to the Hossō sect, which had evolved as a somewhat exclusive religion, with certain persons seen as precluded by their inborn shortcomings from attaining Buddhist

---

3. *Dengyō Daishi zenshū* I, p. 447 (1912 ed.).

perfection, whereas Tendai Buddhism preached enlightenment for all. Saichō declared that all men had in them the possibility of gaining enlightenment:

> In the lotus-flower is implicit its emergence from the water. If it does not emerge, its blossoms will not open; in the emergence is implicit the blossoming. If the water is three feet deep, the stalk of the flower will be four or five feet; if the water is seven or eight feet deep, the stalk will be over ten feet tall. That is what is implied by the emergence from the water. The greater the amount of water, the taller the stalk will grow; the potential growth is limitless. Now, all human beings have the lotus of Buddhahood within them. It will rise above the mire and foul water of the Hīnayāna and Quasi-Mahāyāna, and then through the stage of the bodhisattvas to open, leaves and blossoms together, in full glory.[4]

The strong language that Saichō uses here in his characterization of the Nara schools as Hīnayāna is not out of keeping with the Lotus's stigmatizing of those who refuse to accept Shākyamuni's final revelation, but it contrasts with Saichō's own initial efforts at reconciling and harmonizing the different schools.

Among the contentious issues was Saichō's relaxation of the traditional disciplinary rules or precepts that the Nara monks accepted when they were inducted into the full Hīnayāna ordination. Hiei monks were allowed to take a simpler set of Mahāyāna or Bodhisattva vows less tied to the traditional monastic discipline and more adapted to the life of a lay bodhisattva. The latter "precepts" (actually more like injunctions) featured ten major and forty-eight minor rules of conduct, simpler and more general than the exacting 250 rules of the earlier monastic regimen directed toward strict disciplinary observance and meditative praxis. Ganjin's reform movement in the Nara period reinforced this strict discipline, but Saichō's featured a more generalized ethic, as found in the *Fanwang jing* (J:. *Bonmō kyō*), a Chinese text purporting to be the words of the Buddha in India. This text had come to be widely accepted in China, though disagreement remained over whether the *Fanwang* precepts alone were sufficient for the ordination of monks. Despite uncertainty over its authorship, Saichō believed that the *Fanwang* precepts were more in keeping with the Lotus's teaching of the universality of the Buddha nature and the accessibility of salvation for all, whereas the so-called Hīnayāna path—assuming that Nirvana was more difficult to attain and, practically speaking, achievable in this life only by a few—insisted on the need for monks to make a more rigorous and protracted effort to fulfill the traditional Noble Eightfold Path.

More was involved here, however, than simply issues of discipline. In op-

---

4. Ibid., p. 436.

posing Saichō, the Nara temples were not only defending their vested interests—including a monopoly of the ordination process as established in the old capital, as well as their key role in the system of state superintendence over Buddhist institutions—but were also standing firm for what they believed to be authentic Buddhist tradition. Saichō found himself at odds with them on both counts.

Although the court-approved system of accredited students registered at Mount Hiei provided for a substantial representation of monks from the Nara denominations, records kept by Saichō himself indicate that many of them were not in residence on Mount Hiei but had drifted away, several back to their home temples, no doubt because they were more concerned with their own ordination and certification in Nara than with satisfying Saichō's curriculum.

Disappointed at this outcome but still undeterred, Saichō asked Kanmu's successor, Emperor Heizei, to approve a new set of regulations for Mount Hiei that would sequester the students on the mountain for a full twelve years. These regulations would also provide for an ordination platform to be established there that would free the monks from being held hostage to Nara and liberate Saichō's Enryakuji Temple from supervision by the Nara monks. Saichō's ordination, called the "Bodhisattva or Mahāyāna ordination," was based on the simpler rules of the *Fanwang jing*, which, being more generally adaptable to the roles of the Bodhisattva, also would serve his aim of training monks for service to state and society.

Thus on the one hand, Saichō's new regimen was more relaxed in relation to the earlier, more numerous and detailed disciplinary rules identified with the so-called Hīnayāna ("narrow or smaller vehicle"), but on the other hand, it imposed a new strictness insofar as it emphasized seclusion on the mountain to concentrate on an intensive program of study, known as the "Buddhist discipline (or regulations) of the mountain school" (*sanga buppō* or *sanga shiki*). In this way the demands of the training became associated not with the old *vinaya* but with the rigors of life for those identified as "monks confined to the mountain" (*rōzan bikku*) engaged in "mountain training and mountain learning" (*sanshū, sangaku*).

Yet for all this confinement and constraint, Saichō's program reflected his attempt to prepare the Bodhisattva monks for broad service to society. In this respect, the program incorporated some of the public, charitable activities earlier associated with Gyōgi (see chapter 5) in Shōmu's time and also the secular roles traditionally identified with the Confucian "noble person" (Ch: *junzi*, J: *kunshi*). This breadth of scope and balance of learning was represented by the three roles that Saichō had in mind for his monks: those who were gifted in both speech and action, who would be called "treasures of the nation" (*kokuhō*) and would be kept at the mountain headquarters to serve as religious leaders; those gifted in speech but perhaps not in action, who would be "teachers of the nation" (*kokushi*) who would spread the teaching in the country at large; and those primarily adept at practical activities who would be known as "of service to the nation" (*kokuyō*), performing useful public works in construction, engineering, and charitable projects.

At the height of the state-building phase in early Japan, the word rendered here as "nation" had strong connotations of the dynastic state, and Saichō thought of his efforts as serving the aim of mutual support and protection between Buddhism and the imperial state, known as "Buddhism protective of the state" (*gokoku bukkyō*). Indeed, his monastic establishment—standing as a moral and spiritual bastion to the northeast of the capital (as protection against evil spirits from that direction)—was known as the "Protector of the Nation" (*Chingo kokka*). Hence Saichō, both dependent on Kanmu's support and intensely devoted to him, emphasized loyalty to the ruler and also, in his emphasis on service to the people and on making religious salvation more accessible to them, gave a certain populist, if not nationalist, tone to his concept of the state or nation (*koku*). In an age often obsessed with the pessimistic view that Buddhism had entered a state of decline (in the latter degenerate stage of the Law, *mappō*), Saichō seemed almost optimistic with regard to the Japanese people's capacity for fulfilling the Lotus's promise of universal salvation.

Saichō's last years were difficult ones personally. When his political fortunes were reversed after the death of his great patron Kanmu in 806, Saichō's petition to establish an independent ordination platform for his Bodhisattva monks and to be free of the state superintendency dominated by the Nara sects was strongly opposed by the latter, which held steadfastly to traditional Buddhist practices. Accusations between Nara and Mount Hiei became more and more acrimonious.

Thus, contrary to Saichō's original, rather generous, ecumenical impulses in the context of continuing sectarian rivalry, even his efforts to project and implement a vision of the Greater Vehicle as a broad-based religious movement were beset by sectarian defensiveness and a siege mentality. It was only after Saichō's death in 822, following years of unremitting and unrewarding struggle, that the court gave its belated approval, as a kind of posthumous tribute, to his proposals for an independent center at Mount Hiei.

The groundwork done and the broad religious base established by Saichō for this mountain monastery proved remarkably durable. The Tendai Lotus school and his Enryakuji Temple continued to serve as a major headquarters of Japanese Buddhism and as a fountainhead for many of the most vital religious currents of succeeding ages.

THE TENDAI LOTUS TEACHING

Although its basic scripture is the Lotus of the Wondrous Law (Saddharmapundarīka Sūtra), a work from north India or Central Asia, the Tendai school was founded on its interpretation by the great Chinese monk Zhiyi (538–597), who is identified with the Tiantai (J: Tendai) (Heavenly Terrace) Mountain of Eastern Zhejiang Province where Zhiyi taught.

For this Grand Master of the Tendai (Zhiyi), the Lotus, one of the most popular Mahāyāna sūtras, was primarily a guide to religious salvation through practice, to which Zhiyi added a systematic philosophical commentary while also giving special attention to the methods of religious practice embodied in the Lotus. His deliberations were recorded by his pupil Guanding and have come down to us as the "Three Great Works" of the school, namely, the *Words and Phrases of the Lotus* (Ch: *Fahua wenju*, J: *Hokke monku*), the *Profound Meaning of the Lotus* (Ch: *Fahua xuanyi*, J: *Hokke gengi*), and the *Great Cessation and Contemplation* (Ch: *Mohe zhiguan*, J: *Maka shikan*).

In Zhiyi's time, Buddhist thought in South China was distinctly philosophical in character, while in the north Buddhists were developing a religion of faith and practice. Himself a product of the Southern Chinese gentry but with a northerner, Huisi (514–577), as his teacher, Zhiyi came to the conclusion that the contemplative and philosophical approaches to religion were like the two wings of a bird. Consequently, the Tendai school is characterized by both a strong philosophical content and an even stronger emphasis on meditative practice.

The Tendai doctrine centers on the principle of the Perfectly Harmonious Threefold Truth. This means that (1) all things or dharmas are empty because they are produced by a combination of causes and conditions and therefore are insubstantial, without any self-nature, but that (2) they do have a transient or provisional existence, and that (3) being both Empty and Provisional is the nature of all phenomena and to recognize this, without holding to the extremes of either permanence or extinction, is the Mean. These three—Emptiness, Transiency, and the Mean—implicate one another so that tentative or provisional reality implies Emptiness, and in that light its reality ceases to be provisional, the conditional thus being correlated with the unconditional.

Furthermore, the world of Provisional Truth may be categorized in terms of different existences and their corresponding states of consciousness—those of the Buddhas, bodhisattvas, *pratyeka*-buddhas ("private" buddhas or buddhas-for-themselves), *shrāvakas* ("voice-hearers" or direct disciples of Buddha), heavenly beings, titans, human beings, hungry ghosts, beasts, and hell dwellers. Each of these may share the characteristics of the others, thus making one hundred realms, and each of these in turn may be characterized by ten thusnesses or such-likenesses through which the true state is manifested in phenomena, namely, such-like causes, such-like conditions, such-like effects, such-like retributions, and such-like beginning-and-end-ultimately alike. This makes one thousand realms or categories of existence. In turn, each realm consists of the three divisions (of individuals, societies, and the attributes that constitute dharmas), thus making a total of three thousand realms of existence, representing experienced reality in all its diversity, for which there is a corresponding diversity and an expedient means to the achievement of Buddhahood.

The realms of consciousness are so interwoven and interpenetrated that they may be considered microcosmically as "immanent in a single instant of thought." This does not mean that they are produced by the thought of man or Buddha, as taught in some Mahāyāna schools, but rather that in every thought-moment, all the possible worlds are involved or implicated. On this basis the school aims to achieve a liberating wisdom through the cessation of attachments and the contemplation of qualified reality as a means of perceiving the ultimate truth embodied in such a thought-moment. In short, this teaching is crystallized in the celebrated saying that "every form or fragrance is none other than the Middle Path." Every phenomenon or dharma is thus seen as an embodiment of the real essence of the Ultimate Emptiness, or True Thusness. Since all beings possess the Buddha nature, they can attain this realization by an insight that goes beyond all ordinary perception, conception, and reasoning—hence an insight spoken of as "wondrous" and "sublime."

The school claims that the Lotus is the most complete of all the Buddha's teachings and for this purpose it classifies his teachings into five periods. The first four, represented by the literature of various schools, are regarded as provisional or tentative, having a qualified value as leading up to the Lotus but no more. Thus a qualified truth is seen in the teachings of other schools, but only insofar as they are recognized as partial and preparatory and see their own fulfillment in the final synthesis of the Great Vehicle which replaces the Three Vehicles[5] of lesser scope and capacity. In its all-inclusiveness, then, the Tendai Lotus teaching points again to the doctrine of universal salvation, the outstanding characteristic of the Mahāyāna movement.

GUANDING: ON THE FIVE PERIODS OF THE BUDDHA'S TEACHING

The following excerpts from the writings of Zhiyi, his teacher Huisi, and his disciple Guanding illustrate two main themes keynoted by Saichō in his choice of the title (*Ichijō shikan in*) for the religious center on Mount Hiei: the "One Vehicle of the Mahāyāna" as revealed in the Lotus, and the method of "calming" (lit., "cessation") and "contemplation" as the method of meditation leading to the attainment of Buddhahood. The following explains, in both philosophical terms and the religious par-

---

5. Those of the *pratyeka*-buddhas who attain their personal enlightenment by their own exertions, the *shrāvakas* who attain their own salvation by hearing the Buddha's teaching, and the bodhisattvas who postpone their translation into final Nirvāna for the sake of helping all beings to be saved.

allels of the Lotus, how the Buddha prepared his followers for the full revelation of the Mahāyāna.

During the late Northern and Southern Dynasties period (317–589), the practice of "classification of the teachings" (Ch: *panjiao*, J: *hangyō*) became the principal means by which Buddhist exegetes sought to deal with the overwhelming diversity of scriptures and teachings that poured into China between the second and sixth centuries. Motivated by the desire to explain the comprehensive design of the Buddha's preachings as well as the most effective path to salvation, this classification of the teachings played a seminal role in reshaping Indian modes of Buddhist thought and practice into a distinctive Sinitic Buddhist tradition.

The next selection is an outline of the five periods or flavors—the core of the Tendai scheme of doctrinal classification. It is taken from the *Guanxinlun shu*, a commentary on Zhiyi's short *Treatise on the Contemplation of the Mind (Guanxin lun)* compiled by his disciple Guanding. This system, derived from the Nirvāna Sūtra but supported by parables from the Lotus, organizes the Buddha's preaching career into five basic periods, which unfold one upon the other, leading the Buddha's assembly of followers progressively to the highest and purest expression of the Buddha's vision. That vision is the unadulterated preaching of the final revelation in the Lotus Sūtra, in which the Buddha reveals both his pedagogic strategy and the ultimate purpose of his teaching career.

Note that throughout his discussion of the five periods, Guanding refers repeatedly to the parable of the impoverished son in the Lotus Sūtra (see SCT I, 450) and to a classification of the Four Teachings used in guiding beings of different spiritual capacities, namely, (1) the "Tripiṭaka teaching," attracting them to the attainment of arhathood and extinction in nirvāna; (2) the "shared teaching," involving an elementary and one-sided understanding of Emptiness; (3) the "separate teaching," aimed at reaching Buddhahood by intermediate stages involving both the empty and the provisional; and (4) the "perfect or rounded teaching," as the direct and full realization of the Middle Truth or Mean, embracing all polarities of empty and provisional, nirvāna and samsāra, and so on.

When the Buddha first attained the Way on the bodhi seat of perfect quiescence, he conceived the desire to test [beings of the transmigratory world] with the [perfect] Dharma of the Great [Vehicle].[6] However, animate beings did not have the capacity [for it] and were unreceptive to training by the Great [Vehicle]. Hence, in the chapter on Faith and Understanding [of the Lotus Sūtra], [the Buddha] illustrates [this situation] by saying, "The rich old man, seated on his lion throne, spied his [long lost] son and recognized him immediately.

---

6. That is, the teaching of the Flower Garland Sūtra (the Huayanjing or Avatamsaka Sūtra), which the Buddha allegedly preached on the bodhi seat during the first three weeks after his enlightenment.

Thereupon he dispatched a bystander to go after the son as quickly as possible and bring him back. At that time the messenger raced swiftly after the son and laid hold of him. . . . The impoverished son, alarmed and fearful, cried out in an angry voice, 'I have done nothing wrong! Why am I being seized?' But the messenger held on to him more tightly than ever and forcibly dragged him back." . . .

In the Expedient Means chapter of the Lotus Sūtra [the Buddha says], "If I were to force my teaching on sentient beings, they would persecute the dharma and thereby fall into evil destinies of rebirth." Thus he says, "I would rather speedily enter nirvāna and not preach the dharma." This, then, is the [meaning of the simile that] likens everything that the Buddha produced to the [tasteless] *flavor of plain milk*.[7] Calling to mind the powers of expediency employed by Buddhas of the past, the Buddha thought to himself, "I now will do as they have done and bring sentient beings to salvation through expedient devices."[8] Thereupon he set off for Varanasi, where he preached the doctrine of the arising and cessation [of samsāra] and the elimination of the four bases of delusion. It is with this idea in mind that [the Faith and Understanding chapter of the Lotus Sūtra] says, "[The rich father] dispatched two more attendants to pursue his son and bring him back." For "twenty years" [the son, unaware of his heritage, labored to] expel the excrement of the intellectual and affective delusions. This [period] corresponds to the transformation of raw milk into *cream*, which represents the shift from the ordinary unenlightened state to the sainthood [of the Hīnayāna].

Next comes the [period when the Buddha] preached the expanded or *vaipulya* [discourses], drawing on the expedient devices of the three [tripiṭaka, shared and separate] teachings to advocate [eventual] submission to the perfect [teaching]. Thus, in the Vimalakīrti [Sūtra], the two separate and perfect teachings are used to humble the ten great [arhat] disciples [of the Buddha], and the perfect [teaching] is employed to repudiate the approach that progresses through distinct [stages] and is adhered to by bodhisattvas of one-sided practice. In this way they are led gradually to submit [to the perfect teaching].

Previously, people responded to the Buddha's expounding of the Great [Vehicle] with revilement and disbelief, making it impossible for [the Buddha] even to preach it. At this juncture, when persons who had already obtained the saintly path of the two vehicles heard him preach the Great [Vehicle], they harmed themselves and destroyed their karmic propensity [for the Mahāyāna by slandering it]. Thus, with a voice that reverberated through the great chiliocosm, [the Buddha] praised the wondrous dharma [of the Mahāyāna] as some-

---

7. That is, ordinary sentient beings derived no benefit from the Buddha's initial preaching of the perfect middle truth of the Mahāyāna, responding to it as though "deaf and dumb."

8. From the Expedient Means chapter of *The Lotus Sutrūa*, trans. Watson, p. 44.

thing difficult to conceive. [Consequently,] even those who had not yet achieved enlightenment no longer gave rise to disparagement. With this idea in mind, [the Faith and Understanding chapter of the Lotus] states, "By the end of this time the son felt that he was understood and trusted, and he could come and go at ease, but he still lived in the crude hut as before." Moreover, "He could not cease thinking of himself as mean and lowly." This represents the transformation of cream into *butter curds*, which corresponds to the preaching of the *vaipulya* or expanded teaching that followed in the wake of the tripiṭaka teaching.

Next comes [the period in which the Buddha] preached the Wisdom (Prajñā) Sūtras. The Buddha expounded the Perfection of Wisdom (Prajñā-pāramitā) Sūtras for the bodhisattvas, drawing on the expedients of the two shared and separate teachings in an effort to advocate [eventual] submission to the perfect [teaching]. The Belief and Understanding chapter [of the Lotus] says, "The father perceived that his son was bit by bit becoming more self-assured and magnanimous in outlook," and "he ordered him to take over the family affairs." Hence it says in the verses [of the same chapter] that "the Buddha charged us to preach the *pāramitā* on behalf of the bodhisattvas," and yet "we never thought of appropriating for ourselves even a single meal." This represents the transformation of raw butter curds into *butter*. It corresponds to the preaching of the Wisdom [Sūtras] that came after the expanded (*vaipulya*) [period].

After the Wisdom [period] comes the preaching of the perfect teaching of the Lotus Sūtra. In the [Expedient Means chapter of the Lotus] Sūtra [the Buddha] says, "I will straightaway cast aside [all] expedients and preach only the unexcelled way." This [refers to] none other than the expounding of the present contemplation of the perfect [teaching], in which one contemplates the mind of a single instant of thought as being identical with the Thus-Come One's jeweled trove of the middle way and the Buddha's wisdom of permanence, pleasure, selfhood, and purity. Thus, the [Expedient Means chapter of the Lotus] Sūtra says, "I will straightaway cast aside [all] expedients and preach only the unexcelled way." This [refers to] none other than the expounding of the present contemplation of the perfect [teaching], in which one contemplates the mind of a single instant of thought as being identical with the Thus-Come One's jeweled trove of the middle way and the Buddha's wisdom of permanence, pleasure, selfhood, and purity. Thus the [Expedient Means chapter of the Lotus] Sūtra says, "[A Buddha] comes forth into the world for one great reason alone." The Buddha replies, "[It is] to cause sentient beings to open the door to Buddha Wisdom," as well as to reveal, awaken to, and enter [this wisdom]. With this idea in mind, it says in the chapter on Belief and Understanding, "The father, realizing that his end was approaching, gathered his relatives and said, "I am your father; you are my son. All of my wealth and property I entrust to you."" [This corresponds to the transformation of melted butter into the finest *essence of ghee*], which represents the preaching of the prefect teaching of the Lotus [Sūtra] that comes in the wake of the Wisdom [Sūtras].

Thus one should realize that the other three teachings are all expedients for this marvelous contemplation of the perfect teaching, [devised for the purpose of] subduing and readying people to receive this wondrous contemplation. Also one should know that the perfect contemplation is both arcane and wondrous. How could the three other teachings possibly compare with it?

[*Guanxin lun shu*, TD 46, no. 1921:599–600; DS]

HUISI: THE METHOD OF CALMING AND CONTEMPLATION IN THE MAHĀYĀNA

In the following, Huisi explains how by the method of calming (lit., "cessation or stopping") one puts an end to discriminating thoughts and attains the unity of the Pure Mind. This method corresponds to the truth of Emptiness. At the same time, by means of "contemplation," one recognizes or observes the provisional, conditional reality of all phenomena in the *samsāra* world of ordinary experience. This corresponds to the truth of Tentativeness. The ultimate reality attained by the Middle Path (the truth of the Mean in the threefold conception) embraces and harmonizes the other two as at once both conditional and unconditional, through an insight that is transrational and not definable in words.

QUESTION: Why is [the Mind] called True Thusness?
ANSWER: All dharmas depend on this Mind for their being and take Mind as their substance. Viewed in this way, all dharmas are illusory and imaginary and their being is really nonbeing. Contrasted with these unreal dharmas, the Mind is called True (Real).

Furthermore, although the dharmas have no real being because they are caused by illusion and imagination, they have the appearance of arising and ceasing. . . . Because of the power, from time immemorial, of ignorance and imagination to influence it, the substance of the mind is affected by this influence and manifests itself. These unreal appearances have no substance; they are but the Pure Mind. Hence it is said that [substance and appearance] are not different. . . .

The substance of the Pure Mind does not have the character of distinction between the two [purity and being defiled]; all is everywhere the same and undifferentiated. It is only because of the illusory manifestations caused by the power of influence that differences appear.

But these illusory appearances are created and annihilated, whereas the substance of the Pure Mind is eternal, without coming into or going out of existence, and endures forever without change. Hence it is said that [substance and appearance] are not one [and the same]. [p. 645]

The substance of the Store is everywhere the same and undifferentiated and in fact has no character of differentiation. In this respect it is the Tathāgata-Store of Emptiness. However, because this substance of the Tathāgata-Store also has mysterious functions, it possesses all dharma natures to the fullest extent, including their differentiations. In this respect, it is the Tathāgata-Store of Non-Emptiness, that is, the difference in the realm of no-difference.

By cessation is meant to realize that all dharmas originally have no self-nature of their own, are never created or annihilated by themselves, but come into being because they are caused by illusion and imagination and exist without real existence. In those created dharmas, their existence is really nonexistence. They are only the One Mind, whose substance admits of no differentiation. Those who hold this view can stop the flow of false ideas. This is called cessation (or calming).

By contemplation is meant that although we know that [things] are originally not created and at present not annihilated, nevertheless they were caused to arise out of the Mind's nature and hence are not without a worldly function of an illusory and imaginative nature. They are like illusions and dreams; they [seem to] exist but really do not. This is therefore contemplation (insight).

As to the function of cessation and contemplation (insight): it means that because of the accomplishment of calming ["cessation"], the Pure Mind is merged through Principle with the Nature which is without duality and is harmoniously united with all beings as a body of one single character. Thereupon the Three Treasures [the Buddha, the Law, and the Order] are combined without being three, and the Two Levels of Truth are fused without being two. How calm, still, and pure! How deep, stable, and quiet! How pure and clear the inner silence! It functions without the appearance of functioning and acts without the appearance of acting. It is so because all dharmas are originally the same everywhere without differentiation, and the nature of the Mind is but dharma. That is the substance of the most profound Dharma Nature.

It also means that because of the accomplishment of contemplation (insight), the substance of the Pure Mind, and the functioning of the objective world are manifested without obstacle, spontaneously producing the capabilities of all pure and impure things. . . . Again, owing to the accomplishment of calming, one's mind is the same everywhere, and one no longer dwells within the cycle of life and death; yet owing to the accomplishment of contemplation (insight), one's attitudes and functions are the results of causation and one does not enter nirvāna. Moreover, owing to the accomplishment of calming, one dwells in the great nirvāna, and yet owing to the attainment of insight, one remains in the realm of life and death.

[*Dacheng zhiguan famen*, in TD 46, no. 1924:642–661; LH]

ZHIYI: CALMING AND CONTEMPLATION

The *Mohe zhiguan*, from which the following portion is quoted, is a manual of religious practice, specifically of the methods of gaining religious insight. Zhiyi then goes on to explain in great detail (not reproduced here) the method of the Great Calming and Contemplation, using the conceptual language of the "suchlikeness" (provisional truth) to provide a guide for the attainment of the state of *samādhi* (a trance state of supreme wisdom and bliss) which is concomitant with the attainment of nirvāna and Buddhahood.

The name "ten dharma spheres" applies in each case to the aggregates, objects of perception, and spheres. . . .

Now one Mind comprises ten dharma spheres, but each dharma sphere also potentially contains ten dharma-spheres, giving a hundred dharma spheres. One sphere comprises thirty kinds of worlds, hence a hundred dharma spheres comprise three thousand kinds of worlds. These three thousand are contained in a fleeting moment of thought. Where there is no Mind [consciousness], that is the end of the matter; if Mind comes into being to the slightest degree whatsoever, it immediately contains the three thousand. One may say neither that the one Mind is prior and all dharmas posterior nor that dharmas are prior and the one Mind posterior. For example, the eight characters [of matter][9] change things. If the thing were prior to the characters, the thing would undergo no change. If the characters were prior to the thing, it would also undergo no change. Thus neither priority nor posteriority is possible. One can only discuss the thing in terms of its changing characters or the characters in terms of the changing thing. Now the Mind is also thus. If one derives all dharmas from the one Mind, this is a vertical relationship. If the Mind all at once contains all dharmas, this is a horizontal relationship. Neither vertical nor horizontal will do. All one can say is that the Mind is all dharmas and that all dharmas are the Mind. Therefore the relationship is neither vertical nor horizontal, neither the same nor different. It is obscure, subtle, and profound in the extreme. Knowledge cannot know it, nor can words speak it. Herein lies the reason for its being called "the realm of the inconceivable."

[*Mohe zhiguan*, TD 46, no. 1911:52, 54; LH]

---

9. The primary and secondary characteristics of coming into being, abiding, changing, and perishing (an Abhidharma doctrine).

SAICHŌ: VOW OF UNINTERRUPTED STUDY OF THE LOTUS SŪTRA

This vow taken by monks on Mount Hiei expresses Saichō's (and their own) commitment to the Lotus teaching as expounded by Zhiyi and practiced according to his prescriptions for the calming and contemplation discipline. It also invokes the Imperial authority of Kanmu as the great patron and supporter of Saichō's project and, by its reference to the Golden Light Sūtra, reaffirms the monastery's role as protector of the state.

The disciple of Buddha and student of the One Vehicle [name and court rank to be filled in] this day respectfully affirms before the Three Treasures that the saintly Emperor Kanmu, on behalf of Japan and as a manifestation of his unconditional compassion, established the Lotus sect and had the Lotus Sūtra, its commentary, and the essays on "Calming and Contemplation" copied and bound together with hundreds of other volumes and installed them in the seven great temples. Constantly did he promote the Single and Only Vehicle, and he united all the people so that they might ride together in the ox cart of Mahāyāna[10] to the ultimate destination, enlightenment. Every year assemblies[11] on the Golden Light Sūtra were held to protect the state. He selected twelve students and established a seminary on top of Mount Hiei where the Tripiṭaka, the ritual implements, and the sacred images were enshrined. These treasures he considered the guardian of the Law and its champion during the great night of ignorance.

It is for this reason that on the fifteenth day of the second moon of 809, Saichō, with a few members of the same faith, established the uninterrupted study of the sūtra of the Lotus of the Wondrous Law.

I vow that, as long as heaven endures and earth lasts, to the most distant term of the future, this study will continue without the intermission of a single day, at the rate of one volume every two days. Thus the doctrine of universal enlightenment will be preserved forever and spread throughout Japan to the farthest confines. May all attain Buddhahood!

[Dengyō Daishi zenshū IV, 749 (1912 ed.)]

---

10. The three vehicles are described in the Lotus Sūtra; of them the oxcart stands for Mahāyāna.

11. These assemblies, often called *gosaie* ("imperial vegetarian entertainments" of monks), were held during the first moon of the Imperial Palace from 802, when Kanmu founded them, until 1467 (see De Visser, *Ancient Buddhism in Japan*, pp. 471–479). The text studied was the Golden Light Sūtra.

SAICHŌ: EXPLAINING THE PRECEPTS

The rather long essay of this title, of which an excerpt is given here, was written and presented to Emperor Saga in 819. It was intended as an answer to the attacks on Saichō and the Tendai teachings by the Nara monks and to assert the need for a true Mahāyāna ordination hall, independent of the Nara ones that were based, as Saichō avers, on a negative Hīnayāna concept of the discipline. Saichō also inveighs against the oppression of the Nara superintendents who still adhered to the narrow view of religion repudiated by the Buddha in the Lotus Sūtra.

I now initiate the discipline of the One Vehicle in order to profit and delight all sentient beings; this essay has been written to initiate the discipline of universality. I offer my prayers to the everlasting Three Treasures to extend their invisible and visible protection so that the discipline will be transmitted unhampered and unharmed, protecting the nation for all time to come. May all sentient beings who lead worldly or spiritual lives ward off what is wrong, put an end to all evil, and protect the seed of Buddhahood; may they awaken to the universal nature of things and partake of spiritual joy in the land of tranquil light.

I have heard that a gentleman of the laity should not pride himself on his superiority—how much less should I, a monk, discuss the failings of others? If, however, I followed such a philosophy and kept silent, the discipline of universality might perish. If, on the other hand, I were to speak out boldly, as is the fashion nowadays, there would be a never-ending controversy. I have therefore compiled this essay elucidating the discipline. I submit it to the emperor.[12]

His Majesty the emperor is equal to the sun and the moon in enlightenment, and his virtue does not differ from that of heaven and earth. His administration is in accord with the five human relationships,[13] and his religious faith is based on the teachings of Buddha. Nothing falls outside the scope of his great benevolence; there is no wise statesman but serves the court. The Buddha sun shines brightly again, and the Way of inner realization flourishes. Now is the moment for the Mahāyāna discipline of the Perfect Doctrine to be proclaimed and promoted; it is the day when the temple should be erected. I have therefore cited the texts which describe the three kinds of temples[14] in making my request for a Mahāyāna Hall where [the image of] Mañjushrī may be installed and bodhisattva monks be trained. When a white ox cart is granted, the three other

---

12. Emperor Saga, reigned from 809 to 823.
13. Of Confucianism.
14. Mahāyāna, Hīnayāna, and combined Mahāyāna-Hīnayāna.

vehicles are unnecessary.[15] When a positive teaching has been found, why should we use the negativism of others?[16] The Lotus Sūtra says, "Choose the straight way and cast aside expediencies; preach the peerless doctrine." It also says, "What we should practice now is Buddha's wisdom alone."

At present the six supervisors[17] wield so much power as to suppress the Buddha's discipline. The hordes of monks have vociferously been demanding that I debate with them; in three hundred ways have they slashed my heart. How then can I remain silent? Instead of speech, however, I have used my brush to express the barest fraction of my thoughts.

[*Dengyō Daishi zenshū*, IV, 749 (1912 ed.)]

THE MAHĀYĀNA PRECEPTS IN ADMONITIONS OF THE FANWANG SŪTRA

Saichō early espoused the simpler and more general rules set forth in the Chinese text of the Fanwang Sūtra (J: Bonmō kyō), which purported to speak for the Buddha (i.e., to have the status of a sūtra) but actually represented a more common denominator adapted to the life of both lay and monastic practitioners of the Mahāyāna vehicle and more open to Chinese customary practices. Though still in the form of injunctions and prohibitions, it served as a more general Mahāyāna ethic applicable to both lay and monastic life. For Saichō, this was primary, and whether one also took the more detailed vows and practices of the *vinaya* rule was optional for the fewer number who chose to keep to the more traditional monastic discipline.

Note in these Admonitions the strong invocation of filial piety as a basis for Buddhist discipline. This adaptation to the more life-affirming, family orientation of Confucianism contrasts with the earlier characterization of the Buddhist religious vocation as "leaving the family" (Ch: *chujia*, J: *shukke*). As a major concession to Chinese values, this new view of Buddhism as fulfilling the ends of filial piety became a marked feature of East Asian Buddhism in general. Because of this more positive emphasis, too, what were originally disciplinary strictures or injunctions came to be understood more as simple "precepts."

At that time, the Buddha Shākyamuni, seated under the Bo tree after having attained supreme enlightenment, first set up the Precepts (Pratimoksa): to be filial to one's parents, teacher(s), members of the Buddhist community, and the Three Treasures. Filial obedience is the way by which one attains the Way. . . .

---

15. The white ox was frequently used as a symbol for Mahāyāna. The other three vehicles were the means of enlightenment expounded by the Hīnayāna and Quasi-Mahāyāna sects.

16. Saichō considered that the Hīnayāna desire to achieve Nirvāna as the extinction of the self was as negative as "getting rid of excrement," the image he uses here.

17. Each of the six sects of the Nara period had its own "supervisor" or nominal head.

At the time, trillions of participants in the assembly, including all the bo-dhisattvas, eighteen Brahmin kings, the kings of the six heavens in the realm of desires, and sixteen great kings, etc. all joined their palms in front of their chest and listened to the Buddha reciting the Mahāyāna Admonitions to all the Buddhas.

The Buddha told all the bodhisattvas: I now recite by myself every fortnight, the Admonitions of the Law. All of you bodhisattvas—bodhisattvas who have just aspired [for supreme enlightenment]—should also recite them; bodhisatt-vas who are in the ten stages of directional decision, the ten stages of the well-nourished heart, [and] the ten stages of "diamond heart" and bodhisattvas who are in the ten stages before attaining Buddhahood should also recite them. This is why the light of the Admonitions issues forth from my mouth. . . .

All sons of the Buddha, listen carefully: those who wish to receive the Ad-monitions, be they kings, princes, ministers, prime ministers, monks, nuns, eighteen Brahmin kings, the six kings of heaven's realm of desire, or sixteen great kings, commoners, . . . male prostitutes, female prostitutes, male servants and female servants, the eight classes of supernatural beings, guardians, animals, even illusory beings, as long as they understand the language of the master [who gives the Admonitions], they are all able to receive the Admonitions and thereby be called "most pure ones."

The Buddha proclaimed to all the sons of the Buddha, saying: "There are ten major precepts. Anyone who has received the Bodhisattva Admonitions and yet does not recite them, is not a bodhisattva, nor is one the seed of a Buddha. I also recite them. All the [past] bodhisattvas have learned, all the [future] bodhisattvas will learn, and all the [present] bodhisattvas are learning them. Now that I have explained briefly the nature of the Bodhisattva Precepts, you should learn them and follow them with respect."

1. The Buddha said: sons of the Buddha, in the case of killing or urging others to kill; killing for expediency or condoning others who kill; or rejoicing at seeing others kill, or killing by means of a spell—whatever the causes of killing, the condition of killing, the method of killing, or the action of killing—killing of any living being should not be done intentionally. A bodhisattva should always give rise to a heart of compassion, a heart of filial piety, using all expedient means to save all sentient beings. If, on the contrary, one kills living beings as one pleases, one commits an unpardonable offense for a bodhisattva.

2. In the case of a son of the Buddha stealing, urging others to steal, stealing for expediency, or stealing by means of spells—whatever the cause of stealing, the condition of stealing, the method of stealing, and the action of stealing—even things owned by gods and spirits—and whatever the goods—even a needle or blade of grass—there should be no intentional stealing. A bodhisattva should give rise to the heart of filial piety of the buddha nature, a heart of compassion, always helping all people to achieve felicity and happiness. If, on the contrary,

one goes so far as to steal the property of others, one commits a most unpardonable offense for a bodhisattva.

3. In the case of a son of the Buddha committing fornication, urging others to commit fornication, or committing fornication with any woman—there should no intentional fornication, no matter what the cause, condition, method, or act of fornication, whether with female animals, female deities, or female spirits or any such sexual misconduct. A bodhisattva should give rise to the heart of filial piety, bring all sentient beings to salvation, and offer them pure truth. If, on the contrary, one commits any kind of fornication, whether with animals, one's own mother, sisters, and relatives, showing no compassion or restraint, one commits an unpardonable offense for a bodhisattva.

4. In the case of a son of the Buddha lying, urging others to lie, or lying for expediency—whatever the cause . . . condition . . . method . . . or the act of lying—even if one says one sees something without actually seeing it or says one did not see something when one has seen it—a bodhisattva should always give rise to correct speech and [help] all sentient beings to give rise to correct speech and correct views. If, on the contrary, one prompts sentient beings to evil speech or evil views, one commits a most unpardonable offense for a bodhisattva.

5. In the case of a son of the Buddha dealing in alcoholic liquors or urging others to deal in them—whatever the cause . . . the condition . . . the method . . . or the act of dealing in alcohol—one should do nothing of that kind. Alcoholic liquors are a cause and condition that gives rise to wrongdoing, whereas a bodhisattva should give rise to the clear and thorough wisdom of all sentient beings. If, on the contrary, one causes confusion in the minds and hearts of all sentient beings, one commits an unpardonable offense for a bodhisattva.

6. In the case of a son of the Buddha criticizing the transgressions of a bodhisattva who has renounced the world, a bodhisattva who is a householder, a bhikshu monk or bhikshuni nun, or of something urging others to criticize such people—whatever the cause . . . condition . . . method . . . or act of criticizing—or when a bodhisattva hears an evil person of a non-Buddhist sect or an evil person who is either a Shrāvaka or a Pratyeka buddha criticizing any Buddhist's violations of law or discipline, if, instead of motivating such an evil person to adopt a positive Mahāyāna mind, the bodhisattva rather lends himself to such criticism, it is a transgression of the Buddha's law and a most unpardonable offense.

7. In the case of a son of the Buddha himself praising or blaming others or telling others to do so—whatever the cause . . . the condition . . . the method . . . or act of blaming—whereas the bodhisattva should take upon himself the blame or shame that attaches to all other living beings, whether for evil deeds to oneself or great deeds of others, if instead he praises his own merits and

conceals others' good deeds or lets others take the blame, it is a most unpardonable offense for a bodhisattva.

Similar formulations are given for three other offenses—stinginess, anger, and slander against the Three Treasures—which, with the preceding items, make up the ten major vices. These are then followed by a detailing of forty-eight minor violations or vices to be avoided by the bodhisattva, such as disrespect to one's master, drinking liquor, eating meat, and eating five forbidden kinds of onions.

[*Fanwang jing*, TD 24, no. 1484, 24:1004a–5a; CHD]

REGULATIONS FOR STUDENTS OF THE MOUNTAIN SCHOOL IN SIX ARTICLES I

Saichō's new regulations set forth his threefold conception of the vocation of bodhisattva monks who will both propagate the Mahāyāna teaching and engage in socially beneficial activities. These rules are intended specifically for monks authorized to pursue the Tendai Lotus teaching, but in addition to this exoteric (public) doctrine, they are to be versed in some esoteric mysteries, as well as with the standard texts associated with "Buddhism as the protector of the state." This broad program is to occupy them during their twelve-year confinement on the mountains, whose rigors supplant the strict observance of *vinaya* discipline

The original version of these regulations, drawn up in 818, is in three sections, of which the first two are translated here. The first two paragraphs are often cited at Mount Hiei as a kind of charter for the school.

What is the treasure of the nation? The religious nature is a treasure, and he who possesses this nature is the treasure of the nation. That is why it was said of old that ten pearls big as pigeon's eggs do not constitute the treasure of a nation, but only when a person casts his light over a part of the country can one speak of a treasure of the nation. A philosopher of old[18] once said that he who is capable in action but not in speech should be of service to the nation; but he who is capable both in action and speech is the treasure of the nation. Apart from these three groups, there are those who are capable neither of speech nor action: these are the betrayers[19] of the nation.

---

18. Mouzi, a late Han philosopher, who attempted to synthesize Buddhism, Confucianism, and Taoism, according to Buddhism, which had the highest position. (Saichō quotes from *Mouzi*, p. 13b, *Bing-jin-guan cong-shu* ed.)

19. This word seems far too strong for the offense, and it may be a corruption in the text in which Mouzi calls these people "mean" (or "lowly").

Buddhists who possess the religious nature are called in the west bodhisatt-vas; in the east they are known as superior men.[20] They hold themselves responsible for all bad things while they credit others with all good things. Forgetful of themselves, they benefit others. This represents the summit of compassion.

Among Buddha's followers there are two kinds of monks, Hīnayāna and Mahāyāna; Buddhists possessing a religious nature belong to the later persuasion. However, in our eastern land only Hīnayāna is revered[21] and not the Mahāyāna. The Great Teaching is not yet spread; great men have not been able to rise. I fervently pray that in accordance with the wishes of the Emperor,[22] all Tendai students annually appointed will be trained in the Mahāyāna doctrines and become bodhisattva monks.[23]

Regulations for the Two Students Annually Appointed by the Court

1. All annually appointed Tendai Lotus students, from this year 818 to all eternity, shall be of the Mahāyāna persuasion. They shall be granted Buddhist names without, however, having their own family names removed from the register. They shall be initiated into the Perfect Ten Good Precepts of Tendai when they become novices and, when they are ordained government seals will be requested for their certificates.

2. All Mahāyāna students, immediately after their ordination, shall be administered the vows of Sons of Buddha and thus become bodhisattva monks. A government seal will be requested for the certificates of oaths. Those who take the Precepts will be required to remain on Mount Hiei for twelve years without ever leaving the monastery. They shall study both disciplines.

3. All monks studying the Calming and Contemplation (*shikan*) discipline shall be required every day of the year to engage in constant study and discussion of the *Lotus, Golden Light, Sūtra of the Humane Kings, Protector,* and other Mahāyāna sūtras for safeguarding the nation.[24]

4. All monks who study the Vairochana discipline shall be required every day of the year to recite the True Words (*mantra*) of the Vairochana, the Pea-

---

20. Or "gentlemen"—the name given by Confucius to people who followed his code.
21. Even though Nara Buddhism was predominantly Mahāyāna, Saichō deprecated its continued adherence to vestiges of the so-called Hīnayāna.
22. Emperor Kanmu issued this order shortly before his death in 806.
23. That is, Mahāyāna monks, for the bodhisattva was held up by Mahāyāna Buddhism as the ideal to be followed.
24. Japanese names for the sūtras: *Hokkekyō, Konkōkyō, Ninnōkyō,* and *Shugokyō.*

cock, the Rope [of salvation], the Wise King, and other sūtras for safeguarding the nation.[25]

5. Students of both disciplines shall be appointed to positions in keeping with their achievements after twelve years' training and study. Those who are capable in both action and speech shall remain permanently on the mountain as leaders of the order: these are the treasures of the nation. Those who are capable in speech but not in action shall be teachers of the nation, and those capable in action but not in speech shall be of service to the nation.

6. Teachers and functionaries of the nation shall be appointed with official licenses as transmitters of doctrine and national lecturers. The national lecturers shall be paid during their tenure of office the expenses of the annual summer retreat and provided with their robes. Funds for these expenses shall be deposited in the provincial offices where they will be supervised jointly by provincial and district governors.

They shall also serve in undertakings which benefit the nation and the people, such as the repair of ponds and canals, the reclamation of uncultivated land, the reparation of landslides, the construction of bridges and ships, the planting of trees and ramie[26] bushes, the sowing of hemp and grasses, and the digging of wells and irrigation ditches. They shall also study the sūtras and cultivate their minds but shall not engage in private agriculture or trading.

If these provisions are followed, men possessing the religious nature will spring up one after another throughout the country, and the Way of the Superior Man shall never die.

Overcome by profound awe, I offer these articles of Tendai and respectfully request the imperial assent.

Saichō, the Monk who formerly sought the Law in China [June 19, 818].

[*Dengyō Daishi zenshū* I, pp. 11–13 (1989 ed.)]

REGULATIONS FOR STUDENTS OF THE MOUNTAIN SCHOOL II

The following regulations provide more specific provisions governing the life of the monastery and the content of the curriculum. Scripture studies have priority over meditative practice during the first six years, but the order is reversed in the last six. Confucian classics constitute one-third of the monks' textual studies, as if to acknowledge that a public philosophy and political ethos are not provided by the sūtras avowing loyalty to the state and that the latter needs to be supplemented if substantive service to the state and society is to be realized. Details are lacking, however, on the classics to be read or on how strictly the regulations were followed.

---

25. Japanese names for the sūtras: Dainichi-kyō, Kujaku-kyō, Fukū Kensaku Kannon-gyō, and Ichiji Chōrinnō-gyō. These represent the Esoteric discipline.

26. A plant whose fibers are similar to those of hemp in their properties and uses.

1. Twelve regular students of the Tendai sect will be appointed for terms of six years each. Each year as two places fall vacant, they are to be replaced by two new students.

The method of examining students will be as follows. All Tendai teachers will assemble in the Seminary Hall and there examine candidates on their recitations of the Lotus and Golden Light Sūtras. When a student passes the examinations, his family name and the date of the examination will be reported to the government.

Students who have completed six years of study will be examined in the above manner. Students who fail to complete the course will not be examined. If any students withdraw, their names, together with those of the candidates for their places, should be reported to the government.

2. Regular students must provide their own clothing and board. Students who possess the proper mental ability and whose conduct is excellent but who cannot provide their own clothing and board shall be furnished by the monastery with a document authorizing them to seek alms throughout the county for their expenses.

3. If a regular student's character does not accord with the monastic discipline and he does not obey the regulations, a report will be made to the government requesting his replacement in accordance with the regulations.

4. Regular students are required to receive the Mahāyāna initiation during the year of their ordination. After the ceremony, they shall remain for twelve years within the gates of the monastery engaged in study and practice. During the first six years, the study of the sūtras under a master will be their major occupation, with meditation and the observance of discipline their secondary pursuits. Two-thirds of their time will be devoted to Buddhism and the remaining third to the Chinese classics. An extensive study of the sūtras will be their duty, and teaching others about Buddhism, their work. During the second six years in residence, meditation and the observance of discipline will be their chief occupation, and the study of the sūtras their secondary pursuit. In the practice of Calming and Contemplation (*shikan*) students will be required to observe the four forms of meditation and in the esoteric practice will be required to recite the three sūtras.[27]

5. The names of Tendai students at the Ichijō Shikan Monastery[28] on Mount Hiei, whether students with annual grants or privately enrolled, should not be removed from the rolls of temples with which they were originally affiliated. For the purposes of receiving provisions, they should nevertheless be assigned

---

27. The three basic sūtras of Esoteric Buddhism: the Dainichi-kyō, the Kongōchō-gyō, and the Soshichi-kyō.

28. The temple's name may be translated literally as "of the one Vehicle for Calming and Contemplation."

to one of the wealthy temples in Ōmi.[29] In keeping with Mahāyāna practice, alms will be sought throughout the country to provide them with summer and winter robes. With the material needs of their bodies thus taken care of, they will be able to continue their studies without interruption. Once admitted to the monastery, it will be a fast rule for these students that a thatched hut will serve as their quarters and bamboo leaves as their seats.[30] They will value but slightly their own lives, reverencing the Law. They will strive to perpetuate the Law eternally and to safeguard the nation.

6. If ordained monks who belong to other sects and are not recipients of annual appointments wish of their own free will to spend twelve years on the mountain in order to study the two courses [of study or practice], their original temple affiliation and the name of their master, together with documents from this monastery, must be deposited in the government office. When they have completed twelve years of study, they will be granted the title of master of the Law as in the case of the annual appointees of the Tendai sect. If they should fail to live up to the regulations, they are to be returned to the temple with which they were originally affiliated.

7. The request will be made that the court bestow the title of great master of the Law on students who have remained twelve years on the mountain and have studied and observed the disciplines in strict adherence to the regulations. The request will be made that the court bestow the title master of the Law on students who, although they may not be accomplished in their studies, have spent twelve years on the mountain without ever having left it.

If any members of the sect fail to observe the regulations and do not remain on the mountain or if, in spite of their having remained on the mountain, they have been guilty of numerous infractions of the Law or have failed to remain the full period, they will be removed permanently from the official register of the Tendai sect and returned to the temple with which they were originally affiliated.

8. Two lay attendants will be appointed to this Tendai monastery to supervise it alternately and to keep out robbers, liquor, and women. Thus the Buddhist Law will be upheld and the nation safeguarded.

The above eight articles are for the maintenance of the Buddhist Law and the benefit of the nation. They should serve the way of goodness.

The imperial assent is respectfully requested.

Saichō, the Monk who formerly sought the Law in China [September 30, 818].

> [*Dengyō Daishi zenshū* I, pp. 13–16 (1989 ed.)]

---

29. The region near Lake Biwa, where many rich immigrants, often of Chinese extraction, were domiciled.

30. That is, they will lead a life of poverty.

SUBSEQUENT HISTORY OF TENDAI AND MOUNT HIEI

At the time of Saichō's death, the Tendai school consisted of only a few underfunded monks on Mount Hiei, a site that must have seemed cold and inhospitable compared with life in the monasteries of Nara and Kyoto. Saichō's attempts to master Esoteric Buddhism had been eclipsed by those of Kūkai's Shingon school, so much so that some of Saichō's students attempted to study with Kūkai even after relations between Saichō and Kūkai had worsened. Despite these inauspicious beginnings, within 150 years the Tendai institution on Mount Hiei became the most powerful religious institution in Japan. Some of the reasons for its success are surveyed next. The Japanese nobility were much more interested in Esoteric Buddhism than in the details of Chinese Tiantai doctrine or in complex systems of meditation. Whereas Kūkai had given the Shingon school a system of Esoteric doctrine that would seem to require little modification for several centuries, the Tendai school's incomplete system demanded additions. As a result, Ennin (794–864) and Enchin (814–891) traveled to China to bring back supplementary teachings and rituals. Tendai Esoteric teachings were then systematized by Annen (841–897?). The result was a body of Esoteric ritual and doctrine that rivaled and even surpassed that of the Shingon school.

By the tenth century, Tendai monks had forged close ties with factions of the nobility by performing rituals, often Esoteric, that were designed to help the lay patrons prosper and defeat their enemies. The purposes of Esoteric rituals performed by Ryōgen (912–985), the cleric who helped make Tendai power prominent in medieval Japan, serve as a good example. These rituals were directed at ensuring the repose of the regent Fujiwara no Tadahira (880–949), ensuring that Tadahira's son Morosuke (908–960) would succeed in his plans to control the throne, protect Morosuke's wives in childbirth as they gave birth to future emperors, and then protect those emperors against the angry ghosts of Morosuke's competitors, as well as healing various illnesses and bringing good fortune. In return for their services, the Tendai establishment received land in the form of manors (*shōen*). In addition, some of the younger sons of the nobility became monks so that they could oversee the manors and rituals, thereby cementing the ties between the monastic factions and their secular patrons.

The Tendai school's success was also assured by the development of an impressive system for educating monks. Young monks were taught to read scriptures and then tested in a series of examinations that began at the local level and ended at the monasteries on Mount Hiei. The examinations often consisted of a question drawn at random. The student was then required to recite the relevant passages from scripture concerning the topic, discuss and reconcile passages that seemed to be contradictory, and then sum up his argument. Specially chosen older monks questioned him as he went through the process. A monk who successfully completed these would be a skilled lecturer and intellectually agile enough to compete with Tendai rivals, particularly the Hossō monks. The process of taking passages out of context sometimes gave Tendai scholars the freedom to develop doctrinal positions remote from those of their Chinese Tiantai antecedents.

A severe persecution of Chinese Buddhism in 845 had resulted in the loss of most Tiantai texts on the Chinese mainland. Accordingly, Japanese Tendai monks rarely consulted their Chinese counterparts about Tiantai doctrine and instead developed teachings in their own ways. When Japanese nobles became monks, they often maintained control over the lands they brought to the school, and so only certain monks could be appointed as high-ranking monastic officials in many Tendai temples. This system of favoritism, along with the alliances between certain temples and certain cliques of nobles, increased the factionalism within the school. By the early eleventh century, monks from Enchin's lineage were being expelled from the main complex on Mount Hiei by monks from Ennin's lineage and retreated to Onjōji near Lake Biwa. In the ensuing centuries, the monks from the two factions fought, sometimes burning each other's monasteries and killing each other.

One of the main components of Tendai doctrine during the middle ages was called *hongaku*, translated by such terms as "primordial" and "original enlightenment." This teaching, derived from Mahāyāna teachings on the Buddha nature, maintained that people already were enlightened but had lost sight of this truth. This insight was interpreted in a variety of ways. In its most extreme form, monks might argue that people, just as they were, were already Buddhas. Thus little or no religious practice was required. But the same teachings also could be interpreted as requiring a variety of degrees of religious practice. *Hongaku* teachings were often given verbally in secret transmissions that strengthened lineages.

Although the medieval Tendai school was often criticized for its involvement in politics, some Tendai monks were noted for their desire to withdraw from society. Ryōgen's student Genshin (942–1017) is typical of a number of Tendai monks who refused to become involved in politics. His work, *Essentials of Rebirth*, played a major role in popularizing Pure Land Buddhism in Japan. Shōshin (1136–1220 or 1131–1215) was famous for his classical learning, criticisms of *hongaku* interpretations, and attempts to promote the classical Chinese Tiantai works by Zhiyi. Although most of the Tendai school did not return to the Chinese interpretation of Zhiyi's texts, the return to the study of those texts remains a potent force in the modern Tendai school. Still other monks called for renewed emphasis on the disciplinary precepts. Among them were Shunjō (1166–1227), who traveled to China to bring back traditional "Hīnayāna" ordinations, and Kōen (1263–1317), who attempted to revive Saichō's system of being in retreat on Mount Hiei for twelve years and strictly observing the precepts. Such a wide range of teachings, practices, and interpretations indicates the Tendai school's success in creating a broad synthesis under the rubric of the Lotus Sūtra's teaching of the One-Vehicle.

The Tendai school's power came to an end when Oda Nobunaga burned down the Tendai establishment on Mount Hiei in 1571. However, the Tendai prelate Tenkai (1536–1643) managed to revive the Tendai's fortunes somewhat by establishing a mausoleum for Tokugawa Ieyasu at Nikkō. Today the Tendai school is one of the smaller Buddhist schools, although it still controls many historically significant temples.

Chapter 7

KŪKAI AND ESOTERIC BUDDHISM

Outstanding among the Buddhist leaders of the Heian period was Kūkai (774–835), a man whose genius has well been described: "His memory lives all over the country, his name is a household word in the remotest places, not only as a saint, but as a preacher, a scholar, a poet, a sculptor, a painter, an inventor, an explorer, and—sure passport to fame—a great calligrapher."[1] Indeed, his reputation was so great that Shingon Buddhism, the sect of Buddhism that he founded, is centered as much on the worship of Kūkai the saint as it is on the teachings of Esoteric Buddhism, the larger tradition to which Shingon belongs. From the ninth century to this day, faithful Shingon believers have revered Kūkai as a living savior who still sits in eternal meditation on Mount Kōya ready to respond to those who call on him for help. The divinization of Kūkai is the product of an imagination inspired by faith, and it is also based on the memory of a real person of extraordinary accomplishments.

Kūkai came from one of Japan's great aristocratic families. As a boy, he showed exceptional ability in his studies, and at the age of fifteen, he was taken by his uncle, a Confucian scholar and imperial tutor, to the capital for further education. In 791 the eighteen-year-old Kūkai entered the Confucian college that had been established to train young men to serve in official government

1. Sansom, *Japan, a Short Cultural History,* p. 230.

positions, and there he read widely in the Confucian classics. By this time, his family's political fortunes had waned, and his relatives expected him to use his talents and training to help restore their position. But Kūkai abruptly withdrew from college and left the capital to become a wandering mendicant in the forests.

The reasons for this sudden change are given in the preface to his first major work, *Indications of the Goals of the Three Teachings*, which he wrote in 797 at the age of twenty-four. He describes his meeting a Buddhist monk while he was a student at the university and learning a mantra for increasing his memory and understanding of Buddhist scriptures. "Believing what the Buddha says to be true," Kūkai threw himself into this practice in the mountains and by the seashore and had such a deeply moving experience that he decided to enter the Buddhist order against his family's wishes. In arguing for the superiority of Buddhism over Confucianism and Taoism, Kūkai wrote the *Indications* to justify his decision to take up the religious life and to explain why such a seemingly rash action was not really at odds with loyalty, filial piety, and morality.

Having discovered a copy of the Mahāvairocana Sūtra, one of the basic scriptures of Esoteric Buddhism, Kūkai was determined to learn more of its teachings and rituals. A rare opportunity was afforded him when he was selected to accompany an official diplomatic mission to China in 804. The ship on which he was traveling with the ambassador of the mission ran into severe weather and drifted far to the south, landing near the city of Fuzhou. Another ship carried the vice ambassador and the monk Saichō, the founder of Tendai Buddhism in Japan, and managed to arrive at Mingzhou to the south of the Yangtze River. Unlike Saichō, who studied different forms of Buddhism for less than a year before returning to Japan, Kūkai traveled far inland to the capital of Changan, where he stayed for two and a half years studying Sanskrit and Esoteric Buddhism with Indian and Chinese masters at the Ximing Temple, one of the major centers of Buddhist studies.

The international character of Buddhism was very much in evidence in Changan, one of the world's great cities at that time. Chinese, Japanese, Korean, and Southeast Asian students studied with learned teachers from India, Central Asia, and China and joined together to translate Sanskrit and Central Asian texts into Chinese. They also wrote commentaries, compiled dictionaries and concordances, wrote language textbooks, discussed doctrinal issues, debated sectarian differences, and engaged in the life of practice and rituals. Kūkai thrived in this rich atmosphere of learning and concentrated on studying Sanskrit with an Indian teacher and Esoteric Buddhism under the tutelage of Huiguo (746–805), the Chinese heir to the Esoteric tradition developed by Indian and Central Asian masters. He returned to Japan as the eighth—and first Japanese—patriarch of the Shingon school.

As used to describe the kind of Buddhism Kūkai learned in China, the term Esoteric has several meanings. In terms of *practice*, Esoteric Buddhism is characterized by—though it has no monopoly over—the use of *mantras* (formulaic chants), *mandalas* (diagrams of deities and the ritual universe), *mudras* (ritual hand gestures), and graphic forms of meditation that use the sensory faculties to allow the practitioner to be immersed in the world of the buddhas and bodhisattvas. In a strict *sectarian* sense, Esoteric Buddhism is identified primarily with the Shingon school, although it later included Tendai (technically a form of Exoteric Buddhism) after Saichō's successors adopted Shingon ideas and practices. In its style of *transmission*, Esoteric Buddhism is thought of as abstruse and secret and therefore can be passed on from a master only to qualified and worthy disciples who will maintain the confidentiality of the knowledge they receive. Kūkai related how Huiguo waited almost until his death before he found in his Japanese student an adequate receptacle of knowledge.

Shingon Buddhism was readily received by Heian aristocrats and later by commoners as well. The basis of its appeal lay in its bold reinterpretation of the basic Mahāyāna idea that the ordinary world is identical with the world of the buddhas. While Kūkai still affirmed that the world of the buddhas resists articulation and expression, he was optimistic in championing the teachings and rituals of Esoteric Buddhism as a means for overcoming that resistance. For instance, whereas in Exoteric teachings the dharma body (*dharmakaya*) of the Buddha was said to be beyond the reach of words and ideas, Kūkai asserted that the Dharmakaya Buddha preaches, has form, and therefore can be expressed in words and objects. In a society that valued literature and art so highly, Heian aristocrats found Shingon Buddhism aesthetically accessible. Kūkai brought back a trove of texts and ritual objects, and in his memorial to the emperor which lists and explains each item, he wrote:

> The law [dharma] has no speech, but without speech it cannot be expressed. Eternal truth [*tathatā*] transcends color, but only by means of color can it be understood. Mistakes will be made in the effort to point at the truth, for there is no clearly defined method of teaching, but even when art does not excite admiration by its unusual quality, it is a treasure which protects the country and benefits the people.
>
> In truth, the Esoteric doctrines are so profound as to defy their enunciation in writing. With the help of painting, however, their obscurities can be understood. The various attitudes and mudras of the holy images all have their source in Buddha's love, and one may attain Buddhahood at sight of them. Thus the secrets of the sutras and commentaries can be depicted in art, and the essential truths of the Esoteric teaching are all set forth therein. Neither teachers nor students can dispense with it. Art is what reveals to us the state of perfection.[2] Shingon painting and sculp-

---

2. From Kūkai's *Memorial on the Presentation of the List of Newly Imported Sutras*, quoted in Moriyama, ed., *Kōbō Daishi den*, p. 249.

ture utilize rich colors and elaborate motifs, all of which are filled with symbolic meanings communicated through the forms themselves and can be discussed with extensive elaboration.

Probably the Shingon school's most important use of painting was in the two mandalas, representations of the cosmos under the two aspects of potential entity and dynamic manifestations. The indestructible potential aspect of the cosmos is depicted in the Diamond (Vajra) Mandala. In the center, Mahāvairocana Buddha is shown in contemplation, seated on a white lotus and encircled by a white halo. Around him are various buddhas and sacred implements. The dynamic aspect of the cosmos is depicted in the Womb (Garbha) Mandala, "wherein the manifold groups of deities and other beings are arrayed according to the kinds of the powers and intentions they embody. In the center there is a red lotus flower, with its seed-pod and eight petals, which symbolizes the heart of the universe."[3] Mahāvairocana Buddha is seated on the seedpod of the lotus, and the petals are occupied by other buddhas.

The mandalas were used to represent the life and being of Mahāvairocana Buddha and also served to evoke mysterious powers, much in the way that the mudras were performed. One important ceremony in which the mandalas figured was that in which an acolyte was required to throw a flower on the mandalas. The Buddha on which his flower alighted was the one he was to worship and emulate particularly. It is recorded that Kūkai's flower fell on Mahāvairocana Buddha in both the Diamond and Womb Mandalas. His master was amazed at this divine indication of the great destiny in store for the young Japanese.

The special relationship between Kūkai and Mahāvairocana is symbolic of the central Shingon teaching of the Three Mysteries of the body, mouth, and mind by which even ordinary people can gain intimacy with the world of the Buddha. Through the use of mudras, which are prescribed gestures formed with the hands, a kind of ritual sign language is made possible by which one can both communicate with Mahāvairochana Buddha, the dharmakaya who speaks, and also be bodily identified with this central figure of the Shingon pantheon. With one's mouth, mantras can be recited, and in the proper ritual context, verbal communication and identity can be established. The mind is the means of meditation, and through it, one can think right thoughts and visualize the buddhas and the worlds they live in. Human faculties are thus capable of understanding and experiencing a good part, if not the entirety, of what it means to be enlightened, and it is this optimistic affirmation of the ability to become a buddha in this bodily existence that found ready appeal. Later in the Kamakura period, doubts about and a loss of confidence in this

---

3. Anesaki, *History of Japanese Religion*, pp. 126–127.

claim gave rise to Pure Land Buddhist movements that proposed rebirth in the Pure Land as an alternative to achieving enlightenment.

Despite its inherent appeal, the Shingon Buddhism of Kūkai still represented a new sect and thus posed an institutional challenge to the Buddhism established in Nara. Saichō's Tendai Buddhism also faced the same difficulty of gaining acceptance, but unlike Saichō, who chose to oppose the Nara establishment and press for the independent right to ordain his own priests, Kūkai adopted a cooperative approach. He established good relations with major Buddhist leaders and even gained ecclesiastical appointments to important temples. These appointments were made by the government, and throughout his life after his return from China, he held a variety of positions in temples other than those of his own Shingon sect. In 810, for instance, Kūkai was made the administrative head of Tōdaiji, the most important institution of the Nara establishment, and in 827 he held the government post of senior director of monastic officials (*daisōzu*).

Kūkai held these and other positions all the while he worked to establish his own Shingon institution. In 816, at the age of forty-three, he received permission from the court to build a monastic center on Mount Kōya, a site he selected in the remote mountains far to the south of Nara and even farther from the new capital in Kyoto. He chose this location precisely because of its remoteness, believing that natural wilderness was most conducive to religious discipline and practice. Since his official duties kept him away from Mount Kōya most of the time, his disciples assumed the responsibility of developing the monastery as the headquarters of his growing sect. After Kūkai died on Mount Kōya at the age of sixty-two in 835, they propagated the legend that he really did not die but was still alive sitting in eternal meditation in his mausoleum. Mount Kōya is still the destination of many pilgrims who worship him as a living savior and call him by his posthumous name, Kōbō Daishi, the Great Master of the Extensive Dharma.

INDICATIONS OF THE GOALS OF THE THREE TEACHINGS
(*SANGŌ SHĪKI*)

In the *Indications*, the earliest of his writings, Kūkai evaluates Confucianism, Daoism, and Buddhism and concludes that Buddhism is the most profound of the three religions. In his preface, he makes it clear that the superiority of Buddhism justifies his entry into its priesthood.

The work consists of four parts: the preface; the speeches of Kimō (Tortoise Hare), who represents Confucianism; of Kyobu (Nothingness), who speaks for Daoism; and of Kamei-kotsuji (Mendicant X), who makes the case for the superiority of Buddhism and whose identity with Kūkai himself is suggested at one point. A concluding poem summarizes the essence of the three teachings and indicates Kūkai's determination to abandon his effort to become a state official.

The discussion is developed in a dramatic way. At the home of their host, Tokaku (Hare's Horn), the Confucian Kimō is asked to admonish a delinquent youth known as Shitsugakōshi (Leech's Tusk), who represents Kūkai's own dissolute nephew. After the Confucian reproves the young man and lectures him about the excellence of the Confucian virtues of filial piety and loyalty, the Daoist scoffs at his teaching and explains the superiority of the Daoist way of standing apart from the world and becoming an immortal. Finally, the Buddhist mendicant criticizes the Confucian for promoting his own standing in the world and the Daoist for seeking longevity. The superior alternative, he argues, is Buddhism, which does not reject loyalty and filial piety but adds to those virtues the teaching of moral retribution, the principle of unity, freedom from discrimination, detachment from fame and profit, and the joys of tranquillity. Overwhelmed by this argument, the Confucian and the Daoist convert to Buddhism.

The following are excerpts from the preface and the mendicant's speech in which Kūkai explains some of the basic tenets of Buddhism in response to his hearers' request upon their conversion.

Preface

My relatives and teachers opposed my entering the priesthood, saying that by doing so I would be unable to fulfill the Five Cardinal Virtues[4] or accomplish the duties of loyalty and filial piety. I thought then: living beings are not of the same nature; there are birds which fly high in the sky and fish which sink low in the water. To guide different types of people, there are three teachings: Buddhism, Daoism, and Confucianism. Although their profoundness varies, they are still the teachings of the sages. If an individual chooses one, he does not necessarily repudiate loyalty and filial piety by doing so.

Now I have a nephew who is depraved and indulges in hunting, wine, and women and whose usual way of life consists of gambling and dissipation. It is obvious that an unfavorable environment has caused him to lead this kind of life. What has induced me to write [this story] are the opposition of my relatives [to my becoming a Buddhist] and the behavior of this nephew.

The Mendicant's Speech

The mendicant replied [to his nephew]: "Indeed it is fortunate that you have repented before you went too far. Now I will tell you of the origins of suffering

---

4. The Five Confucian Virtues: humaneness, rightness, ritual decorum, wisdom, and trustworthiness.

in this life of transmigration and of the bliss of nirvana. On these points the duke of Zhou and Confucius did not speak, nor did Lao Zi and Zhuang Zi preach. Even the followers of Hīnayāna do not know about the attainment of bliss. Only the bodhisattvas who are destined to be Buddhas in the next stage can obtain and enjoy it. Listen well. I will summarize the essential points and show them to you."

Kimō and the others came down from their seats and said: "Yes, we will compose ourselves and listen to you attentively."

The mendicant opened his innermost heart, and with flowing eloquence narrated the essence in a rhyme prose entitled "The Ocean of Transmigration" and, in addition, showed them how to attain great enlightenment:

The ocean of transmigration is limitless, surrounding the furthermost limits of the triple world. It is without end, encompassing all the four continents. It gives breath to all and regulates all. By emptying its enormous stomach, it absorbs many rivers; with its huge mouth, it sucks in many lakes and ponds. Huge waves strike incessantly with relentless force against the hills, and billows roar constantly against the capes. The sound of stones crushing against each other in the sea rumbles day and night like thunder. Within its waters grotesque objects are produced, monstrous creatures grow, and strange beings abound.

Among them are scaly fishes filled with hatred, stupidity, and extreme greed. Their heads and tails are endlessly long, and they seek constantly after food, with their fins raised, tails striking, and their mouths open. When they swallow a billow, the boat of nongreed is smashed, and its sail vanishes from sight. When they spew forth spray, the rudder of the boat of compassion is broken, and all the people on it are killed. Swimming and diving haphazardly, they are filled with avarice and dishonesty. Their greed being as deep as a valley, they fail to consider the inevitable later harm. Like mice or silkworms, they gnaw at everything, having no sympathy or regard for others. They forget completely the retribution that will afflict them for endless eons in the future; they look forward only to acquiring honor and prosperity while alive.

. . .

Therefore, the small boat bearing the Five Precepts[5] must be made to float to the shore where the demons abide, and the wagon carrying the Ten Precepts[6] must be drawn to the regions where the devils dwell. Unless

---

5. Not killing, not stealing, not committing adultery, not telling lies, and not drinking intoxicating beverages.

6. These are the basic vows not to kill, steal, commit adultery, lie, use exaggerated speech, slander, equivocate, cover, give way to anger, and hold biased views.

a man gives rise to the excellent aspiration to attain enlightenment in the evening and seek after the result of enlightenment in the morning, he cannot approach the grand Dharmakaya[7] and break through the vast ocean of transmigration. Borne on the raft of the Six Paramitas,[8] he should cross to the other side. He should cross the waves of passion on the ship of the Noble Eightfold Path,[9] using the mast of effort and the sail of meditation, with the armor of patience for protection from thieves, and the sword of wisdom for defense against enemies. Whipping the horse of the Seven Means[10] to attain enlightenment, he should gallop away from the ocean of transmigration and transcend the clamorous dust-filled world. Then as a token of predicted future enlightenment, he will receive the gem hidden in the topknot of the Universal Monarch, as did Shāriputra and the Nāga girl, who offered her necklace to the Buddha.[11] Soon he will pass through the ten stages of attaining enlightenment. The stages may be many, but the required disciplines are not difficult to fulfill. Meanwhile, he will overcome all obstacles and attain Suchness (*tathatā*) and, upon reaching enlightenment, will be called the Lord, the Buddha. Then he will abide in the principle of unity with his mind freed from discriminations; by virtue of his wisdom shining like four mirrors,[12] he will be detached from both the abuse and the praise of the world. Transcending the phenomenal world, he will be immutable. Knowing neither increase nor decrease, he will be tranquil and serene, rising above the three divisions of time.[13] How magnificent and splendid will he be! Not even the Yellow Emperor, the sage king Yao, and Fu Xi will be worthy of tending his footgear, nor will the Universal Monarch, Indra, Brahmā, and the rest be worthy to serve as his footmen. No matter how much abuse the devils and heretics may heap on him, it will be in vain, and no matter how much praise the disciples of the Buddha and those who have attained enlightenment by themselves may offer him, it will still be inadequate.

. . .

---

7. The Ultimate Reality, the unconditioned Absolute, personified.

8. Charity, morality, patience, effort, meditation, and wisdom.

9. The path by which one can approach final deliverance: right views, right thinking, right speech, right action, right livelihood, right effort, right mindfulness, and right concentration.

10. Contemplation, choosing the correct doctrine, effort, joy, repose, samādhi, and equanimity.

11. Predictions that Shāriputra and the Nāga (serpent) girl would be future Buddhas appear in the Lotus Sūtra. After the Nāga girl had offered the Buddha a priceless necklace, she was transformed into a man and later attained Buddhahood (TD 9, p. 35c).

12. In *The Awakening of Faith*, the characteristics of enlightenment are discussed with analogies to four types of mirror. See Hakeda, trans., *The Awakening of Faith*, pp. 42–43.

13. Past, present, and future.

"Though what I have said is but the smallest part of the teachings of my master the Buddha, now it should be evident to you that the petty seeking for longevity of Daoism and that dusty breeze of the secular world, Confucianism, are not worthy of comparison. They are not worthy to be spoken of in the same breath with Buddhism."

Kimō and the others were, while listening, at times frightened, ashamed, sorrowful, or filled with laughter. Along with the development of the story, they changed their expressions, sometimes they dropped their heads, and then again they lifted their faces. Finally they said approvingly:

"We are fortunate to have met this great authority and to have learned the supreme teaching which transcends the mundane world. We had not heard this doctrine before, and perhaps we would not again have had the opportunity to listen to it. If we had not met you, we would still be occupied in greedy activities and would have fallen into hell, the world of ghosts, or the world of beasts. Your instructions have made us feel much relieved in both body and mind. We feel that we are awakened, like worms stirred by thunder in the spring after the long sleep of winter or like the ice in the shade that starts to melt when the sun rises. How superficial the teachings of Confucius and Laozi are! From now on we will observe faithfully your teaching with our whole beings—by writing it on the paper of our skins, with pens of bone, ink of blood, and the inkstone of the skull. Thus your teaching will be the boat and the wagon by which we may cross over the ocean of transmigration."

The mendicant said: "Please go back to your seats. I will compose a poem of ten rhymes clarifying the three teachings; recite it instead of singing popular songs." Then he made this poem:

The light of the sun and moon breaks through darkness,
And the three teachings illumine ignorance.
Nature and desire vary from person to person,
Treatment differs with each physician.
Human duties were preached by Confucius;
On learning them one becomes a high government official.
Laozi taught the creation by yin and yang;
On receiving his instructions one can observe the world from the tower of a
    Daoist temple.
Most significant and profound is the teaching of the ultimate path of
    Mahāyāna.
It teaches the salvation of oneself and of others;
It does not exclude even animals or birds.
The flowers in the spring fall beneath the branches;
Dew in autumn vanishes before the withered grass.
Flowing water can never be stopped;
Whirling winds howl constantly.

The world of senses is a sea in which one well may drown;
Eternity, Bliss, the Self, and Purity are the summits on which we ultimately
    belong.
I know the fetters that bind me in the triple world;
Why should I not give up the thought of serving the court?

[Adapted from Hakeda, trans., *Kūkai: Major Works*, pp. 134–139]

KŪKAI AND HIS MASTER

This and the following passage are taken from A *Memorial Presenting a List of Newly Imported Sutras and Other Items*, which Kūkai wrote to the emperor upon his return from studying in China. In addition to listing the many religious articles that he brought back with him, Kūkai reports on the results of his studies and extols the doctrines into which he was initiated. Among the points that he especially emphasizes are (1) his personal success in gaining acceptance by the greatest Buddhist teacher of the day in China; (2) the authenticity of this teaching in a direct line of succession from the Buddha; (3) the great favor in which this teaching was held by the recent emperors of the Tang dynasty, to the extent that it represented the best and most influential doctrine current in the Chinese capital; and (4) the fact that this teaching offers the easiest and quickest means of obtaining Buddhahood, probably an important recommendation for it in the eyes of a busy monarch.

ENCOUNTER WITH HUIGUO

During the sixth month of Enryaku 23 (804), I, Kūkai, sailed for China aboard Ship One in the party of Lord Fujiwara, envoy to the Tang court. By the eighth month we reached the coast of Fujian and by the end of the twelfth month arrived at Changan, where we lodged at the official guest residence. The envoy and his retinue started home for Japan on the eleventh day of the third month, Enryaku 24 (805), but in obedience to an imperial edict, I alone remained behind in the Ximing Temple where our Eichū (d. 816)[14] formerly had resided.

One day, while calling on the eminent Buddhist teachers of the capital, I happened to meet the abbot of the East Pagoda Hall of the Qinglong Temple, whose Buddhist name was the Acharya Huiguo. This great priest was the disciple chosen to transmit the dharma from the Tripiṭaka Master of Broad Wisdom [Bukung] of the Daxingshan Temple. His virtue aroused the reverence of his age; his teachings were lofty enough to guide emperors. Three sovereigns who revered him were initiated by receiving *abhiṣeka* consecration. The four

---

14. A Japanese monk who studied in China before Kūkai.

classes of believers looked up to him for instruction in the Esoteric Buddhist teachings.

I called on the abbot in the company of five or six monks from the Ximing Temple. As soon as he saw me, he smiled with pleasure and joyfully said, "I knew that you would come! I have waited for such a long time. What pleasure it gives me to look upon you today at last! My life is drawing to an end, and until you came, there was no one to whom I could transmit the teachings. Go without delay to the altar of *abhiṣeka* with incense and a flower." I returned to the temple where I had been staying and got the things which were necessary for the ceremony. It was early in the sixth month then that I entered the altar of *abhiṣeka* for primary initiation. I stood before the Matrix Mandala and cast my flower in the prescribed manner. By chance it fell on the Body of Mahā-vairocana Tathāgata in the center. The master exclaimed in delight, "How amazing! How perfectly amazing!" He repeated this three or four times in joy and wonder. I was then given the fivefold *abhiṣeka* and received instruction in the grace (*kaji*) of the Three Mysteries. Next I was taught the Sanskrit formulas and ritual manuals for the Matrix Realm and learned the yogic practices which use various sacred objects of concentration to gain transcendental insight.

Early in the seventh month I stood before the Diamond Mandala, and I was given once more the fivefold *abhiṣeka*. When I cast my flower it again fell on Mahāvairocana, and the abbot marveled as he had before. Also, early in the following month I received the *abhiṣeka* for the ordination into the mastership of the transmission of the dharma. On this day I provided a feast for five hundred monks and made wide offerings to the four classes of believers. The dignitaries of the Qinglong Temple, Daxingshan Temple, and others all attended the feast, and everyone was delighted for my sake.

Then I received instruction in the mantras and mudras of the five divisions of the Vajraśekhara Sūtra and spent some time learning Sanskrit and the Sanskrit hymns. The abbot informed me that the Esoteric Buddhist scriptures are so abstruse that their meaning cannot be conveyed except through art. For this reason, he ordered the court artist Li Zhen and about a dozen other painters to execute ten scrolls of the Matrix and Diamond Mandalas and assembled more than twenty people to make copies of the Vajraśekhara Sūtra and other important Esoteric Buddhist scriptures. He also ordered the bronzesmith Zhao Wu to cast fifteen ritual implements. These orders for the painting of religious images and the copying of the sūtras were issued at various times.

One day the abbot told me: "Long ago, when I was still young, I met the great Tripiṭaka master [Bukung]. From the first moment he saw me he treated me like his son, and on his visit to the court and his return to the temple, I was as inseparable from him as his shadow. He confided to me, 'You will be the receptacle of the Esoteric Buddhist teachings. Do your best! Do your best!' I was then initiated into the teachings of both the Matrix and the Diamond and into the secret mudras as well. The rest of his disciples, monks and laity alike, studied just one of the two great teachings [Diamond and Matrix] or a yogic practice on one sacred object of concentration with the use of one mudra, but not all of them as I did. How deeply I am indebted to him I shall never be able to express.

"Now my existence on earth approaches its term, and I cannot long remain. I urge you, therefore, to take the mandalas of both realms and the hundred volumes of the teachings of the Diamond Vehicle, together with the ritual implements and these objects which were left to me by my master. Return to your country and propagate the teachings there.

"When you first arrived, I feared I did not have enough time left to teach you everything, but now I have completed teaching you, and the work of copying the sūtras and making the images has also been finished. Hasten back to your country, offer these things to the court, and spread the teachings throughout your country to increase the happiness of the people. Then the land will know peace, and people everywhere will be content. In that way you will return thanks to the Buddha and to your teacher. That is also the way to show your devotion to your country and to your family. My disciple Yi-ming will carry on the teachings here. Your task is to transmit them to the Eastern Land. Do your best! Do your best!" These were his final instructions to me, kind and patient as always. On the night of the full moon, in the twelfth month of the past year, he purified himself in a ritual bath, and lying on his right side and making the mudra of Mahāvairocana, he breathed his last.

That night, while I sat in meditation in the hall, the abbot appeared to me in his usual form and said, "You and I have long been pledged to propagate the Esoteric Buddhist teachings. If I am reborn in Japan, this time I shall be your disciple."

I have not gone into the details of all that he said but have given the general import of the acharya's instructions.

[Adapted from Hakeda, trans., *Kūkai: Major Works*, pp. 146–149]

The Transmission of Esoteric Buddhism

The sea of dharma is of one flavor but has deep and shallow aspects in accordance with the capacity of the believer. Five Vehicles[15] can be distinguished, sudden and gradual according to the vessel. Among the teachings of sudden enlightenment, some are Exoteric and some, Esoteric. In Esoteric Buddhism itself, some aspects represent the source, others, the tributary. The teachers of the dharma of former times swam in the waters of the tributary and hung on

---

15. Vehicle (*yāna*) means the teachings that carry sentient beings to their respective goals. There are vehicles for common men, celestial beings, sravakas, pratyeka-buddhas, and bodhisattvas.

to the leaves, but the teaching transmitted to me now uproots the stump which blocks the source and penetrates it through and through. Why?

In ancient times Vajrasattva personally received the teaching from Mahā-vairocana. Several centuries later it was transmitted to the Bodhisattva Nāgār-juna, who transmitted it to the Acharya Vajrabodhi (670–741), the Tripiṭaka master, who for the first time taught the fivefold Esoteric Buddhist doctrine[16] in China during the Kaiyuan era (713–741). Although the emperor himself revered the doctrine, Vajrabodhi could not spread it widely. Only through my spiritual grandfather [Bukung], the Acharya of Broad Wisdom, did it become popular. Bukung first received the transmission from Vajrabodhi, the Tripiṭaka master, and moreover visited the Acharya Nāgabodhi in southern India and acquired completely the Vajraśekhara Sūtra comprising eighteen divisions. Af-ter having studied thoroughly the Esoteric Buddhist teachings consisting of the doctrines of the Matrix, etc., he returned to China during the Tianbao era (742–756). At this time Emperor Xuanzong first received *abhiṣeka* from him; the emperor revered him as his teacher. Since then Emperors Suzong (r. 756–762) and Daizong (r. 763–779) have received the Dharma. The Shenlong Monastery was built within the imperial palace, and everywhere in the capital the altars for *abhiṣeka* were set up. The emperor and the government officials went to the altars to receive *abhiṣeka*; the four classes of believers and the populace reverently learned the Esoteric Buddhist teachings. This was the period when the Esoteric Buddhist school began to flourish, and from this time on the prac-tice of *abhiṣeka* was widely adopted.

According to Exoteric Buddhist doctrines, one must spend three eons to attain enlightenment, but according to the Esoteric doctrines, one can expect sixteen great spiritual rebirths [within this life].[17] In speed and in excellence, the two doctrines differ as much as one endowed with supernatural power differs from a lame donkey.

[Adapted from Hakeda, trans., *Kūkai: Major Works*, pp. 143–144]

ENLIGHTENMENT IN THIS BODILY EXISTENCE

Throughout the history of Buddhism, the central debate regarding enlightenment has been whether it can be realized in this existence or only after many lifetimes. Kūkai's position, which is characteristic of Esoteric Buddhism as a whole, is that it can be

---

16. The fivefold Esoteric Buddhist doctrine means the teachings given in the Vajraśekhara Sūtra in which the buddhas, bodhisattvas, and others are classified under the five divisions — Buddha, Vajra, Ratna (jewel), padma (lotus), and karma (action). Vajrabodhi, who came from India to China in 720, first introduced the Esoteric Buddhist teachings belonging to the Diamond Realm.

17. To experience the samādhi of sixteen Bodhisattvas in the mandala of the Diamond Realm.

realized immediately, and he wrote a treatise, *Attaining Buddhahood in This Bodily Existence* (*Sokushin jōbutsu gi*), to explain and prove his point. After establishing that the idea is attested to in the scriptures, Kūkai presses his point forward with some standard Mahāyāna ideas such as harmony and the notion of the interpenetration of things with all other things, which is exemplified in the image of Indra's Net. He also uses Esoteric Buddhist ideas, in particular the teaching of the Three Mysteries and *kaji*, or grace. It is important to note—as Kūkai himself reiterates—that these ideas are to be experienced in meditation and ritual practice, for it is only in this context that the practitioner's three mysteries of body, mouth, and mind will be interfused with the Three Mysteries of Mahāvairocana. A similar harmony can be reached in the experience of *kaji*, which is linked with the practice of prayer. *Ka* is the bestowal or adding of grace by Mahāvairocana, and *ji* is the receiving and retaining of it by the practitioner. The idea of enlightenment in this existence was continually debated by those who accepted it as a practical goal and those who rejected it as an impossibility, and as such, it exerted an enormous influence on Buddhist thought in Japan.

QUESTION: In sūtras and shastras it is explained that after three eons, one can attain enlightenment. Is there evidence for the assertion that one can attain enlightenment in this very existence?

ANSWER: The Tathāgata has explained it in the Esoteric Buddhist texts.

QUESTION: How is it explained?

ANSWER: It is said in the Vajraśekhara Sūtra that "he who practices this samadhi can immediately realize the enlightenment of the Buddha." Also: "If the sentient beings who have come across this teaching practice it diligently four times day and night, they will realize the stage of joy in this life and perfect enlightenment in their subsequent sixteen lives."

REMARKS: "This teaching" in the foregoing quotation refers to the king of teachings, the teaching of samādhi realized by the Dharmakaya Buddha himself. "The stage of joy" is not the first stage of Bodhisattvahood as defined in the Exoteric Buddhist teachings but the first stage of Buddhahood of our Buddha Vehicle, the details of which are explained in the chapter discussing stages.[18] By "sixteen lives" is meant that one is to realize the attainments of the sixteen great Bodhisattvas,[19] the details of which are also explained in the chapter discussing the stages. Again it is said: "If a man disciplines himself according to this

---

18. Kūkai seems to be referring to the discussion of the ten stages of the development of the religious mind in the first chapter of the Mahāvairocana Sūtra (see p. 23).

19. Kūkai interprets "sixteen lives" as realizing the samādhi of the sixteen Bodhisattvas surrounding the Four Buddhas in the inner circle of the Diamond Mandala, not as repeating the cycle of birth and death sixteen times.

superior doctrine, he will be able to attain in this life unsurpassed enlightenment." Furthermore: "It should be known that he himself turns into the Diamond Realm; since he becomes identical with the Diamond, he is firm and indestructible. An awareness will emerge that he is of the Diamond Body." The Mahāvairocana Sūtra states: "Without forsaking his body, he obtains supernatural power, wanders on the ground of great space, and perfects the Mystery of Body." Also: "If he wishes to gain the perfection of religious discipline in his lifetime, he must select a certain method of meditation that suits his inclinations and concentrate on it. For this, he must personally receive instruction in mantra recitation from an authentic master. If he observes the mantras and masters yoga, he will gain perfection."

. . .

QUESTION: How do you analyze the meaning of the words [attaining enlightenment in this bodily existence] given in these sūtras and shastras?

A summary in verse:

The Six Great Elements are interfused and are in a state of eternal harmony;
The Four Mandalas are inseparably related to one another:
When the grace of the Three Mysteries is retained,
[our inborn three mysteries will] quickly be manifested.
Infinitely interrelated like the meshes of Indra's net are what
    we call existences.

There is the One who is naturally equipped with all-embracing wisdom.
More numerous than particles of sand are those who have the King of
    Mind and the consciousnesses;
Each of them is endowed with the Fivefold Wisdom, with infinite wisdom.
All beings can truly attain enlightenment because of the force of mirrorlike
    wisdom.

. . .

    These Esoteric Buddhist texts explain the methods of the samādhi of swift effect and suprarational action. If there is a man who wholeheartedly disciplines himself day and night according to the prescribed methods of discipline, he will obtain in his corporeal existence the Five Supernatural Powers.[20] And if he keeps training himself, he will, without abandoning his body, advance to the stage of the Buddha. The details are as explained in the sūtras. For this reason it is said, "When the grace of the Three Mysteries is retained, [our inborn three

---

20. Supernatural action, vision, hearing, ability to read the minds of others, and knowledge of former states of existences.

mysteries will] quickly be manifested." The expression "the grace . . . is retained (*kaji*)" indicates great compassion on the part of the Tathāgata and faith (*shinjin*) on the part of sentient beings. The compassion of the Buddha pouring forth on the heart of sentient beings, like the rays of the sun on water, is called *ka* [adding], and the heart of sentient beings which keeps hold of the compassion of the Buddha, as water retains the rays of the sun, is called *ji* [retaining]. If the devotee understands this principle thoroughly and devotes himself to the practice of samādhi, his three mysteries will be united with the Three Mysteries, and therefore in his present existence, he will quickly manifest his inherent three mysteries. This is the meaning of the words, "[our inborn three mysteries will] quickly be manifested."

"Infinitely interrelated like the meshes of Indra's net are what we call existences." This line explains in simile the state of perfect interfusion and interpenetration of the infinite Three Mysteries of the manifestations [of Mahāvairochana]. Existence is my existence, the existences of the Buddhas, and the existences of all sentient beings. Also designated by this word is the Mahāvairocana Buddha in Four Forms, which represent his absolute state, his state of bliss, his manifesting bodies, and his emanating bodies. The three kinds of symbol—letters, signs, and images—are also included in this category. All of these existences are interrelated horizontally and vertically without end, like images in mirrors, or like the rays of lamps. This existence is in that one, and that one is in this. The Existence of the Buddha [Mahāvairocana] is the existences of the sentient beings and vice versa. They are not identical but are nevertheless identical; they are not different but are nevertheless different.

[Adapted from Hakeda, trans., *Kūkai: Major Works*, pp. 225–232]

THE TEN STAGES OF RELIGIOUS CONSCIOUSNESS

The realization of the nondual identity between Mahāvairocana and all forms of existence represents the highest level of consciousness that is not immediately apparent. This insight is attained by making progress through levels of understanding, which can be associated with the teachings of various religions and schools. The immediate occasion for Kūkai's *Ten Stages of Religious Consciousness*, in which Shingon is treated as a separate philosophy, was a decree issued in 830 by Emperor Junna ordering the six existing Buddhist sects to submit in writing the essentials of their beliefs. Of the works submitted at this time, Kūkai's *Ten Stages* was by far the most important in both quality and magnitude. Each of its ten chapters presents a successive stage upward of religious consciousness. The work was written entirely in Chinese, not merely good Chinese for a Japanese writer, but with an ornate poetical style somewhat reminiscent of Pope's attempt in his *Essay on Man* to present philosophical ideas in rhymed couplets. The following is Kūkai's own summary of his long and detailed essay on the ten stages.

RECAPITULATION OF THE TEN STAGES OF RELIGIOUS CONSCIOUSNESS

1. The mind animal-like and goatish in its desires.

    The ordinary man in his madness realizes not his faults.

    He thinks but of his lusts and hungers like a butting goat.

2. The mind ignorant and infantile yet abstemious.

    Influenced by external causes, the mind awakens to temperance in eating.

    The will to do kindnesses sprouts, like a seed in good soil. [Confucianism.]

3. The mind infantile and without fears.

    The non-Buddhist hopes for rebirth in heaven, there for a while to know peace.

    He is like an infant, like a calf that follows its mother. [Brahmanism or popular Daoism.]

4. The mind recognizing only the objects perceived, not the ego.

    The mind understands only that there are Elements, the ego it completely denies.

    The Tripiṭaka of the Goat Cart is summed up by this verse [Shrāvaka vehicle of Hīnayāna Buddhism].

5. The mind freed from the causes and seeds of karma.

    Having mastered the twelve-divisioned cycle of causation and beginning, the mind extirpates the seeds of blindness.

    When karma birth has been ended, the ineffable fruits of nirvana are won. [Pratyeka Buddha vehicle of Hīnayāna Buddhism]

6. The Mahāyāna mind bringing about the salvation of others.

    When compassion is aroused without condition, the Great Compassion first appears.

    It views distinctions between "you" and "me" as imaginary; recognizing only consciousness, it denies the external world [the Hossō school].

7. The mind aware of the negation of birth.

    Through eightfold negations, foolishness is ended; with one thought the truth of absolute Voidness becomes apparent.

    The mind becomes empty and still; it knows peace and happiness that cannot be defined [the Sanron school].

8. The mind which follows the one way of Truth.

    The universe is by nature pure; in it knowledge and its objects fuse together.

    He who knows this state of reality has a cosmic mind [the Tendai school].

9. The mind completely lacking characteristics of its own.

    Water lacks a nature of its own; when met by winds, it becomes waves.

    The universe has no determined form but, at the slightest stimulus, immediately moves forward [the Kegon school].

10. The mind filled with the mystic splendor of the cosmic Buddha.

When the medicine of Exoteric teachings has cleared away the dust, the True Words open the Treasury.

When the secret treasures are suddenly displayed, all virtues are apparent [the Shingon school].

[From *Kōbō Daishi zenshū*, I, p. 420; adapted from Hakeda, trans., *Kūkai: Major Works*, pp. 163–164]

A SCHOOL OF ARTS AND SCIENCES

Kūkai's proposal to establish a "school of arts and sciences (*shūgei shūchi-in*)" reveals two important tendencies in his thought. First is the universalistic and egalitarian character of Mahāyāna Buddhism. Citing the teachings of the Lotus Sūtra, which stress the essential oneness of all being, Kūkai asks support for a school that would be open to all, regardless of social status or economic means. The second reflects Kūkai's catholic outlook, affirming the value of both religious and secular studies and also of combining the Three Teachings (Confucianism, Daoism, and Buddhism) in the school's curriculum.

Generally, in Japan as in China, religious and secular studies represented two separate ways of life. Recall that Saichō wished his monks to combine a religious and secular vocation, but classical Confucian studies had a very subordinate role in the training of Mount Hiei's monks, for whom he conceived social action and public service in very practical terms.

In Kūkai's time, secular education was closely linked to official recruitment and training and largely restricted to the ruling classes. Though ostensibly Confucian, it failed to measure up to Confucius's ideals of brotherhood, as Kūkai points out. Indeed, the aristocratic character of Japanese society strongly resisted the potentially egalitarian elements in Buddhism and Confucianism. In this case, even though a Fujiwara nobleman donated an attractive site for the school, Kūkai had difficulty obtaining continuing support for his work, and the school was forced to close ten years after his death, in 845. In recent times, however, it has been revived and is now an active four-year college supported by the Shingon sect.

Having dedicated myself to the salvation of all beings, and hoping to establish a school for the study of the Three Teachings [Buddhism, Confucianism, and Daoism], I asked Lord Fujiwara for the donation of his residence. Without even exchanging a formal document of agreement, he immediately offered me the house, which may well be worth one thousand gold pieces, for the sake of accumulating merit toward his enlightenment.

Thus, I obtained this superb site, as lovely as the park of Jeta,[21] without having to spend any money. My long cherished desire was at once fulfilled. I have given it the name of School of Arts and Sciences and made up a tentative program as follows:

The Nine Schools[22] and Six Arts[23] are the boats and bridges that save the world; the Ten Baskets[24] and the Five Sciences,[25] are the treasures that benefit people. The Tathāgatas of the past have studied them, those of the present are now studying them, and those of the future will also, thereby attaining great enlightenment. Bodhisattvas of the ten directions have studied them all and realized the all-pervading wisdom. Unless one resorts to these studies, one cannot gain the essentials of how to establish oneself in the world, cannot learn the principles of governing the country, and cannot attain nirvana on the other shore, terminating the transmigratory life on this shore.

Emperors have built state temples; their subjects have constructed private temples; in this way they have made efforts to spread the Way [Buddhism]. But those who wear robes in the temples study Buddhist scriptures, while scholars and students at the government college study non-Buddhist texts. Thus they are all stuck when it comes to books representing the Three Teachings and Five Sciences [as a whole]. Now I shall build a school of arts and sciences, offering instruction in the Three Teachings, and invite capable persons to join. With the aid of these teachings, which can be compared to the sun [Buddhism], the moon [Daoism], and the stars [Confucianism], my sincere desire is to enlighten those who are wandering in the dark down the wrong path, and lead them to the garden of enlightenment mounted on the Five Vehicles. . . .

It may be objected, however: "The government maintains a state college where the arts and sciences are encouraged and taught. What good is a mosquito's cry [a private school] compared to rumbling thunder [a government school]?"

My reply is: "In the capital of China, a school is set up in each ward to teach the young boys. In each prefecture a school is maintained in order widely to educate promising young students. Because of this, the capital is filled with talented young men and the nation is crowded with masters of the arts. In the

---

21. The park where Shākyamuni had his monastery and taught. It is said that the rich man Anāthapindika bought the park from Prince Jeta, paying him the sum of gold pieces needed to cover the surface of the land, and offered the park to the Buddha.

22. The nine schools of philosophy: Confucian, Daoist, Yin-yang, Legalist, Logic ("Names"), Mo-ist, Horizontal and Vertical Alliances, Unclassified Teachings, and Agriculture.

23. Rites, music, archery, charioteering, writing, and mathematics.

24. The classification of all teachings into ten categories in Buddhism. "Basket" signifies a container of the scriptures.

25. The five subjects of study in Buddhism: grammar, logic, medicine, arts, and Buddhism.

capital of our country, however, there is only one government college and no local schools. As a result, sons of the poor have no opportunity to seek knowledge. Those who like to study but live a great distance from the college encounter great difficulty traveling to and fro. Would it not be good, then, to establish this school to assist the uneducated?" . . .

Although I am not of much ability, I am determined to pursue the plan under way; I will not give up this task, no matter how difficult it may be. Thus I may requite my vast obligations to the emperors, my parents, the people, and the Three Treasures and also make this a means of realizing Ultimate Truth, achieving the Highest Wisdom, and winning final deliverance.

REGULATIONS FOR INVITING THE INSTRUCTORS

Confucius said in the *Analects*: "It is best to live in a community where the spirit of humaneness prevails. Unless one dwells in its midst, how can he attain true knowledge?"

[IV,1] He also said: "One should study the [six] arts." It is stated in the [Mahāvairochana] Sūtra: "By the time one has become an authentic master, one should have studied the various arts and sciences." A commentary [to the Dasabhhūmika] also says: "In order to attain enlightenment, a bodhisattva studies the five sciences." Therefore, Sudhana visited a hundred and ten cities to seek the teachings of fifty-[three] teachers;[26] the Bodhisattva "Always Crying" went throughout the city in his search for wisdom; both sought seriously for the profound dharma. . . .

Even if one finds a suitable place, there will be no way of getting an understanding without teachers. Therefore, first of all, teachers should be invited. Of these there should be two kinds: those who teach the Way and those who teach secular subjects. The teachers of the Way must teach the Buddhist scriptures, and the secular teachers must set forth the non-Buddhist texts. That religious and secular teachings should not be separated is the noble saying of my teacher.

A. INSTRUCTION BY TEACHERS OF THE WAY

To teach both Exoteric and Esoteric Buddhism is the pleasure of the clergy. Should there be students who want to study non-Buddhist texts alongside Buddhism, let the secular teachers take care of them. For those who want to study Buddhist scriptures and commentaries, the clergy should spare no efforts, abid-

---

26. This story appears in the Gandavyūha Sūtra.

ing by the Four States of Mind[27] and the Four All-Embracing Virtues.[28] Without discriminating between noble and low-born, the clergy should offer instruction in Buddhism as appropriate to all students.

B. INSTRUCTION BY SECULAR DOCTORS

The secular doctors should be well versed in one part of each of the following subjects: The Nine Classics,[29] the Nine Schools,[30] the Three Profound Texts,[31] the Three Histories,[32] the Seven Outlines,[33] and the Histories of the Seven Dynasties.[34] Through one text in each of these subjects, they should be able to instruct the students in poetry, metrical prose, pronunciation, reading, punctuation, and interpretation. . . .

Should there be religious who desire to study non-Buddhist subjects, the secular doctors should teach them according to their needs. If young, uneducated children wish to learn how to read and write, genuine teachers should instruct them in a spirit of deep compassion, filial piety, and loyalty. Whether the students are high-born or low, rich or poor, they should receive appropriate instruction, and their teachers should be unremitting in admonishing them. "The beings in the three worlds are my children" roars the Buddha [in the Lotus Sūtra]. And there is the beautiful saying of Confucius: [in *Analects*, VII, 5] "All within the four seas are brothers." Do honor to them!

C. MEALS FOR BOTH TEACHERS AND STUDENTS

"Man is not a hanging gourd [fed by the vine]" said Confucius. That man lives on food is what Shākyamuni taught. If one wants to propagate the Way, one must necessarily feed those who follow it. Whether they be religious or laymen,

---

27. The Four Brahma Vihāras—positive loving kindness, compassion, joy, and indifference.

28. In order to lead others to love and receive the truth of Buddhism, one must (1) give them what they like, (2) speak affectionate words to them, (3) practice conduct profitable to them, and (4) cooperate with and adapt oneself to them.

29. The *Classic of Changes*, the *Classic of Odes*, the *Classic of History*, the *Record of Rites*, the *Classic of Ceremonials*, the *Rites of Zhou*, the *Zuo Zhuan*, the *Gong-yang Zhuan*, and the *Gu-liang Zhuan*.

30. Compare Kūkai's *Memorial on the Presentation of the List of Newly Imported Sutras*, quoted in Moriyama, ed., *Kōbō Daishi den*, p. 249.

31. The *Classic of Changes*, *Dao-de jing*, and *Zhuang Zi*.

32. The *Historical Records of Sima Qian*, the *History of Former Han* and the *History of Later Han*.

33. Outlines of compilations made of the six arts; the schools of philosophy; poetry and metrical prose; military science; divination; and technical, medical, and agricultural subjects.

34. The histories of Song, Southern Qi, Liang, Chen, Wei, Northern Qi, and Zhou.

teacher or student, any who want to study should be provided with free meals. I am a poor monk, however, and am unable to bear the expenses of the school. For the time being, I shall somehow provide the means, but should there be anyone who cares to render a service to the nation or who wishes to escape from illusions and realize enlightenment, let him give a donation, no matter how small the amount may be, to help me fulfill my aspirations. May we, then, ride together on the vehicle of Buddhism to benefit the people of later generations.

Written by Kūkai on the Fifteenth Day of the Twelfth Month, the Fifth Year of Tenchō (828).

[From *Kōbō Daishi zenshū*, III, pp. 535–539]

Chapter 8

THE SPREAD OF ESOTERIC BUDDHISM

Students of the history of Japanese Buddhism may get the impression that the various schools were not only succeeded but also superseded by other sects as the religion developed. They may thus suppose that the schools of the Nara period gave way to Tendai and Shingon Buddhism, which in turn were replaced by one after another of the popular sects of the medieval period. Instead of following a regular sequence of rise, flourishing, decline, and extinction, however, most of the sects continued to exist long after their periods of glory and within their general patterns of growth, and were sometimes capable of unexpected revivals. This was certainly true of the Nara sects, some of which not only preserved their identity throughout the Heian and medieval periods but still exist today. Similarly, Esoteric Buddhism—by which is meant here both Tendai and Shingon—continued to be influential long after Kūkai's time. Esoteric Buddhism set the predominant tone of religious life in the Heian period, and its influence extended to all the other schools. Even the popular sects that turned away from its emphasis on ritual drew much of their inspiration from ideas and practices from the vast storehouse of Esoteric Buddhism. Its syncretism readily combined with other beliefs, whether the Buddhism of other sects, Shinto, or even disparate teachings like yin-yang. And a place for some new god could always be found in its spacious pantheon.

When, however, the hundreds of deities who populated the mandalas proved too much even for the polytheistic Japanese, their number was gradually reduced to thirteen preferred objects of worship: Fudō, Shaka, Monju, Fugen, Jizō, Miroku, Yakushi, Kannon, Seishi, Amida, Ashiku, Dainichi, and Kokūzō. Of these thirteen, the most exalted were considered to be Dainichi (Vairochana), Ashiku (Akshobhya), Amida (Amitābha), Miroku (Maitreya), and Shaka (Shākyamuni). Dainichi occupied the center of Esoteric Buddhism's pantheon. To the east of him sat Ashiku, the source of life, and, to the west, Amida, the dispenser of infinite love. Miroku, the Buddha of the future, and Shaka, the historical Buddha, completed this group of Tathāgatas.

Each of the thirteen deities had claims to the worshipers' attention, but by the late Heian period, three of them came to occupy a special place in the religious life of Japan: Kannon (Avalokiteshvara), one of the Bodhisattva attendants of Amida, who came to be worshiped as a goddess of mercy (although a male deity in India); Fudō (Achala), a fierce god apparently of Indian origin, although neither a Buddha nor a Bodhisattva; and Jizō (Ch: Dicang), whose cult took many forms identified with compassion and redemption. Statues of Kannon were erected at thirty-three sites of remarkable beauty in Japan, and pilgrimages to the different shrines were popular with all classes, from the imperial family downward. The famous temple of the "33,333 Kannons," in Kyoto, each with a "thousand hands" for dispensing mercy, was built in the twelfth century and serves as an indication of the great popularity of this deity during the late Heian period. In contrast to the merciful Kannon, Fudō was represented as a "terrible figure, livid in color and of a ferocious expression. He is surrounded by flames and carries a sword and a rope to smite and bind evil. He is generally explained as typifying the fierce aspect assumed by Vairochana when resenting wrong doing."[1] If Kannon represented the female (or Garbha mandala), Fudō stood for the male (or *vajra*) and, as such, was popular with the rising warrior class, who—as the guardians of the state in the face of disorder—may have likened themselves to the powerful Fudō. Accordingly, the cult of Fudō spread to regions where nature presented its severest face—rocky crags and seashores. Illustrations of Jizō's widespread cult are given in the following reading.

Probably the most important event in the history of Esoteric Buddhism after the death of Kūkai (who established the teachings in Japan) was its triumph on Mount Hiei, the stronghold of Tendai. Saichō himself had studied Esoteric learning with Kūkai, but it remained for his disciple and successor Ennin (794–864) to found Tendai esotericism (Taimitsu). Ennin had led a rather colorless life as a priest and teacher and was already in his forties when he was sent to China for study in 838. At first unable to obtain the necessary authorization to visit either Wutai or Tiantai shan, the two most important Buddhist centers,

---

1. Eliot, *Japanese Buddhism*, pp. 348–349.

Ennin managed with great difficulty to be set ashore on the Chinese coast and was later fortunate enough to meet a general who secured permission for him to visit Wutai shan and other holy sites. Ennin finally returned to Japan in 857 after extensive study with the masters of each of the Tendai disciplines. Upon his return to Mount Hiei, he organized study of the two mandalas, instituted Esoteric initiation, and promoted other branches of Esoteric learning. Ennin also introduced to Japan the invocation of Amida Buddha's name (*nembutsu*), which he had heard at Wutai shan, and had a special hall built for this purpose. For some people, the *nembutsu* became an all-sufficient means of gaining salvation, but for Ennin it was only one among many means of achieving Buddhahood.

Common to both Tendai and Shingon esotericism was the idea that all people could attain Buddhahood in this very life and body through the infinite variety of means and practices represented symbolically in the different forms of the mandala. These could range from the simplest forms of religious practice to the most sophisticated—from the rugged practices and severe austerities of mountain religion to the highly cultivated arts of court society. In this respect, the mysteries of the Esoteric religion, seen as emerging from the timeless bliss of the law body of the Buddha, could take any number of forms, including the secret transmission from master to monk, the aesthetic refinements that induced an emotional rapture among courtiers and court ladies alike, or the mantras, hand signs (*mudras*), and incantations that, for the ordinary believer, were a palpable expression of numinous mysteries.

In affirming this universality of means and ends, the esoteric teachings spoke of a simple gate to salvation that was the equivalent of all other gates, *ichimon fumon*, with a gate open to everyone corresponding to one's own personal makeup or level of religious consciousness, but all leading to Buddhahood. Through this gate, one entered into the reality of the Cosmic Buddha and the Buddha entered into oneself by a process of reciprocal response and interpenetration as the grace and power of the Buddha was "added" to one's own effort (*kaji*). In this way, Esoteric Buddhism could appeal to both the most refined sensibilities and the simplest or even crudest emotions. Functioning as both a court religion and a popular cult, it could exemplify the universalism of Mahāyāna salvation as well as the particularisms of an aristocratic, hierarchical society. What it did not attempt to provide or define was a universal political code, or a social ethic— no doubt reflecting the ambivalence of Kegon philosophy in these matters (see chapter 5). The Kegon philosophy tended to turn to Confucianism, as Saichō and Kūkai had done, and as the Shingon monk Mongaku would do in a letter to the shogun included in the following readings.

Nevertheless, in the infinite variety of its adaptive means, Esotericism served as the dynamic source of new religious practices and movements that emerged in the medieval period, responding to conditions greatly changed from the relative peace and stability of the Heian period. The competitions and, indeed, conflict that often ensued in the darker, more dangerous medieval age, however, already had their antecedents in the rivalry among Mount Hiei and other religious centers in the late Heian period.

The very establishment of Tendai esotericism had marked a new phase in the relations between Tendai and Shingon. The Tendai monks had never forgiven Kūkai for placing Tendai below Kegon in his *Ten Stages*, and for a long time they had sought some way of emerging from under the domination of Shingon. With the development of Tendai esotericism, it was believed on Mount Hiei that Shingon's claim to stand at the head of the Ten Stages in unique splendor had at last been rendered untenable. The two schools of esoteric teaching had many points in common but at least one basic difference: Shingon had originated in China as the esoteric teachings of the Kegon school and held as its central tenet the superiority of Esoteric over Exoteric Buddhism. Tendai esotericism, however, originated in China as the esoteric discipline of Tendai itself, which taught that the exoteric and esoteric teachings were one.

The contest between Tendai and Shingon for recognition as the center of esotericism resulted in victory for the Hiei monks. Their success was due partially to the failure of Shingon to produce great leaders in the generations after Kūkai and partially to the advantage that geographical proximity to the capital gave to Hiei over the more distant Kōya. But the split in the ranks of Tendai esotericism caused by the founding of the Miidera school prevented the Mount Hiei monks from taking full advantage of the supremacy they gained over Shingon and led to some of the least attractive episodes in the history of Japanese Buddhism.

Miidera was a temple founded in 674 by the shores of Lake Biwa. It was associated with the Ōtomo family, and with the decline in the family's fortunes, the temple fell into ruins. Enchin (814–891), a nephew of Kūkai, opened a center of study at the Miidera shortly after his return to Japan in 858 from six years of study in China of the Tendai and esoteric teachings. In 864 the temple was attached to the Enryakuji on Mount Hiei. Enchin's appointment in 868 as abbot of the Enryakuji made him the most important figure in Tendai Buddhism, and his strong personality earned for him devoted followers and bitter enemies. Enchin's immediate successors to the abbacy of the Enryakuji were of his school, but they were followed by a line of men who were identified with Ennin. When in 933 the emperor unexpectedly appointed a follower of Enchin's as abbot, the Ennin faction rebelled against him, and as a result the followers of Enchin marched from Mount Hiei to the Miidera, where they formed an almost entirely independent school. Violent disputes frequently broke out between the two branches of Tendai esotericism. In 1039, for example, the appointment of a Miidera man resulted in a demonstration by three thousand Hiei monks before the house of the regent in Kyoto, thereby compelling the deposition of the unwanted abbot. This violence peaked in 1081 when Hiei monks burst into the confines of the Miidera and set it afire, destroying most of the buildings. They returned three months later to finish the job. During the next three centuries, the Miidera Temple was burned seven times, usually by the Hiei monks, and reconstructed each time by Enchin's determined followers.

The rise of "warrior-monks" was a prominent feature of the late Heian period and medieval Buddhism. Their lawlessness grew during the reigns of Emperor Shirakawa (1082–1086) and his immediate successors. Whenever the monks had a demand, they would march in force on the capital, bearing with them the palanquins of the Shinto god Sannō, the guardian deity of Mount Hiei. The first such descent took place in 1095, and in almost every one of the next thirty or forty years, either the Tendai warrior-monks or those of the Hossō sect from the Kōfukuji in Nara, brandishing the sacred tree of the Kasuga (Shinto) Shrine, stormed into the capital. Frequent battles between the Tendai and the Hossō monks disturbed the peace in the capital for about a century starting with Shirakawa's reign. In 1165, the Hiei monks burned the Kiyomizudera, the stronghold of the Hossō sect in Kyoto, and the Hossō monks attempted unsuccessfully to burn the Enryakuji.

Beset by such internecine warfare, Esoteric Buddhism also had to struggle against a tendency for the impressive rituals associated with the Three Mysteries to degenerate into mere superstition. The spells recited to prolong life were typical of this trend in the late Heian period. Texts of these spells had been brought to Japan from China by Kūkai, Ennin, and Enchin, but the earliest mention of the performance of the secret rituals accompanying them dates from 1075, during Shirakawa's reign, when the abbot of the Enryakuji performed the ceremony. It was performed again in 1080 in the imperial palace. This ritual was carried out in exact conformity to the texts, which prescribed that before the presiding monk could perform the spell, he had to bathe with perfumed water, don newly purified clothes, receive the Eight Commandments, and eat a meal of plain rice, honey, and milk. The actual ceremony required twenty-one small platforms built on top of a large platform, and different types of rare incense and flowers to accompany each part of the prayers.

As time went on, various heresies gained currency that tended to discredit Esoteric Buddhism. The most notorious was the so-called Tachikawa school, founded in the early twelfth century by a Shingon believer with the aid of a yin-yang teacher whom he met while in exile. They evolved a doctrine teaching that "the Way of man and woman, yin and yang, is the secret of becoming a Buddha in this life. No other way exists but this one to attain Buddhahood and gain the Way."[2] As authority for this statement, the Vajra and Garbha Mandalas were declared to be symbols of the male and female principles, and other elaborate yin-yang correspondences were drawn as well. The Tachikawa school appears to have indulged in the sexual rites practiced by the somewhat similar Shāktist sects of Tibet. In 1335, as the result of a memorial submitted by the Mount Kōya monks against the Tachikawa school, its leader was exiled and books expounding its principles were ordered to be burned. Traces of its doctrines still survive, however, in existing Buddhist sects.

PRAYER OF THE RETIRED EMPEROR SHIRAKAWA ON OFFERING THE TRIPIṬAKA TO HACHIMAN

In November 1128, the retired Emperor Shirakawa—father, grandfather, and great-grandfather of emperors reigning in his own lifetime—offered his prayer to the god Hachiman for ten more years of life. On this occasion, he presented a copy of the Tripiṭaka to be read without interruption by six priests, and in his prayer, the emperor enumerated other acts of piety already performed. These reflect the Esoteric Buddhism then prevalent at court, especially in its iconographic forms. The syncretic tendencies of Esoteric Buddhism also are apparent in its association with notions concerning immortality and longevity, which are typical of popular Daoism. These same tendencies account for making such an offering to Hachiman. It may seem curious that the Shinto god Hachiman was favored with a copy of the Buddhist scriptures, but in the ages of Combined Faith, Hachiman was worshiped as a great bodhisattva, and such a gift seemed wholly appropriate. Despite the fervent prayers made to him, however, Shirakawa died the following year.

The practice of a sovereign's abdicating and becoming a Buddhist monk while continuing to rule in the name of a boy emperor was inaugurated by Emperor Uda (r. 889–897) and became an established institution with Shirakawa. Not only a devout Buddhist but also an astute politician, Shirakawa saw the advantages of governing from behind the scenes with the title "Emperor of the [Buddhist] Law (hōō)." This represents a fusion of the tennō concept with the title King of the Law (hōō) once accorded the monk Dōkyō, who in the Nara period was thwarted in his attempt to become emperor. With the emperors themselves becoming monks, power could hide behind a religious screen without clear public accountability.

Shirakawa's prayer was actually written by a courtier, Fujiwara no Atsumitsu (1062–1144). It is in balanced prose, the ornate Chinese style that Kūkai had popularized in Japan.

---

2. Statement in the *Hōkyōsho*, an anti-Tachikawa work that is one of our chief sources of information about the school.

This copy of the Tripiṭaka, transcribed by imperial order, is composed as follows:

Mahāyāna sūtras	2,395 volumes
Hīnayāna sūtras	618 volumes
Mahāyāna vinayas	55 volumes
Hīnayāna vinayas	441 volumes
Mahāyāna shāstras	515 volumes
Hīnayāna shāstras	695 volumes
Biographies of the Bodhisattvas and Arhats	593 volumes
Total	5,312 volumes

The above enumerated sūtras, vinayas, shāstras, and biographies are respectfully offered to the Hachiman Temple at Iwashimizu, to be used for lectures and sermons.

I recall that when I was still young and inexperienced, the former sovereign transmitted to me the imperial rank. Grave though the responsibility was, I remained ignorant of the ways of administration. When I received the documents and records of the domains within the four seas, I felt as though I stood before a profound abyss, and when I tried to control the multifarious activities of government, it was like driving a team of horses with rotting reins. How, I wondered, could I devise a good plan so that I might rule my land in peace? I placed my faith in the spirits of my ancestors and relied on the powers of the gods of Heaven and Earth.

Soon after my assumption of the imperial rank, in the year 1074, I paid homage at the palace of the Bodhisattva Hachiman. Since that time, I have arranged an imperial visit every year in the third moon. In the morning, when the petals of the palace cherry blossoms are wet with dew, I leave the purple gate in my palanquin; in the evening, when the mountain nightingales are singing in the mist, I stand in worship by the fence of the shrine while voices and flutes harmoniously blend. This has become an established practice, although unknown in former times.

More than forty years have passed since my abdication. Often have I urged my carriage forward through stormy winds in the pine-clad hills; many times have I offered my devotion on the steps of the shrine in the woods. I have made this pilgrimage twenty-five times. During this period I have built a pagoda at the Usa Shrine to help establish the prestige of the sacred precincts. I have had the Great Wisdom Sūtra copied in gold to extol the bliss of the temporal and real Law. It would be hard to recall all the treasures that have been offered, the lectures on the holy writings that have been sponsored, and the devotion expressed by my pilgrimages of thanks. During all this time, whenever I have stood in thought by the window, my mind has been drawn to the moon[3] of

---

3. In Buddhist writings, the moon is often used as a symbol of wisdom.

clear insight, and whenever I have sat in meditation, my graying brows have been knitted in concentration.

My descendants, always increasing in numbers, have succeeded one after another to the imperial rank,[4] and each one has enjoyed a long reign devoted to solicitude for the people. That now, despite my advanced age, I am able to help my lord, the boy sovereign, is indeed a sign that I have obtained the grace of Heaven and the favor of the gods. For me to have witnessed my great-grand-son receive the prognostications for his reign[5] shows that I have attained an age approaching a rarity.

"It is not the millet which has a piercing fragrance; it is bright virtue."[6] Buddha's teachings, not bright gems, are what is precious. All the true teachings we possess are those preached by the peerless Shākyamuni during his lifetime. At his birth he stood on the lotus, and the air of the Lumbinī Grove first was replete with his fragrance.[7] In his wanderings he saw the Tree, and the moon of enlightenment attained its fullness. On high mountains and level fields alike, the sun of mercy shone everywhere. In the Deer Park and on Vulture Peak, the fructifying rain of the Law fell in abundance. The Greater and Lesser Vehicles ran abreast, and the Basic and the Complete Schools[8] both opened their gates. The teachings traveled ten thousand leagues over the boundless seas, above the high-tossing billows, to be transmitted at last from those distant lands to our imperial realm. Here sovereigns and subjects all have offered devout reverence; the high and the mighty have vied with each other in acts of piety. The prosperity of the land has no other source but this.

Therefore, I have had several copies of the sūtras, vinayas, and shāstras made on behalf of the Three Bodies of the Buddha, in order to promote the Surpassing Cause of enlightenment and to bring about the perfect and ultimate Enlightenment of the Buddha. . . .

---

4. Shirakawa reigned from 1072 to 1086 and abdicated in favor of his seven-year-old son Horikawa, who reigned from 1086 to 1107. On Horikawa's death, his four-year-old son Toba (Shirakawa's grandson) succeeded him and reigned from 1107 to 1123, abdicating in favor of his four-year-old son Sutoku (Shirakawa's great-grandson). In 1128, the year of this document, Shirakawa was seventy-five years old; his son was dead; his grandson Toba was twenty-five years old; and his great-grandson Sutoku was nine years old.

5. Prepared at the beginning of an emperor's reign by specialists in the Chinese art of prognostication.

6. A quotation from the *Classic of History*. See Legge, *The Chinese Classics, Shoo-King*, pt. V, bk. XXI, p. 2.

7. Important episodes in the life of the historical Buddha are given here: his birth in the Lumbinī Grove, his attainment of enlightenment under the bodhi tree, his first sermon at the deer park in Benares, and his teaching to the ascetics of Vulture Peak.

8. The two vehicles and two schools refer to Mahāyāna and Hīnayāna.

At this point we have omitted the details of other donations by Emperor Shirakawa, including temples, statues, and the copying of the Tripiṭaka.

Of the six fundamental disciplines, the observance of the commandments is considered the most important; of the ten commandments, the prohibition on the taking of life is the prime one. All living creatures are our dear friends; successive generations are of one flesh and blood. There is no end to the turning of the Wheel and no escape from the torments of hell. There is no one source of life, but fish, insects, birds, and beasts are variously born from transformation, moisture, eggs, and the womb.[9] However tiny a creature may be, it clings to life as though it were more important than Mount Tai. . . . When word reached me that various provinces offered a tribute of fish, in accordance with regulations, I forbade this practice completely. Eleven provinces halted their offerings of regional maritime produce; the people left off their tribute. As time went on, fish could dart about without fear. In addition, 9,823 fine-meshed fishing-nets were burned, and in more than 45,300 places, hunters' trails were covered. Those who violated the edicts were severely punished.

The virtue of sparing life comes from the fact that it arouses divine retribution. Brahmā, sitting in his lofty palace in Heaven, scrutinizes the minds of men and clearly knows their thoughts. Shakra, dallying in his pleasure garden, turns his compassionate glance and illuminates all actions. He who accomplishes an act of mercy will have a prayer accomplished; he who increases the happiness of others will have his span of life increased. . . . When I consider my own life and attempt to calculate how long it will last, I realize that if I pray to live 120 years, there are but rare precedents for such a great age. If I hope for eighty years, not much remains of my old age. The most I desire is to prolong my life ten years more. Then, as progenitor of three successive sovereigns, I shall be without peer in the world, and as the senior by six years of Shākyamuni,[10] I shall have all I desire in this mortal world. If the Great Bodhisattva Hachiman extends his divine protection, the gods will answer my great prayer; if the Tathāgatas of the ten directions[11] vouchsafe their aid, my life will be strong as the Diamond. I shall then be able to attain enlightenment, and I shall certainly be born in the paradise of peace and purity. The moral force of good actions brings neighbors;[12] their merit has no bounds. This one good action

---

9. The four modes of birth: (1) birth from the womb as animals, (2) birth from the egg as birds, (3) birth from moisture as fish and insects, (4) sudden birth without any apparent cause as bodhisattvas.

10. By Japanese reckoning, Shirakawa was seventy-six years old. Since Shākyamuni is said to have died at the age of eighty, if Shirakawa had lived ten more years, he would have been six years older than Shākyamuni was when he died.

11. The eight points of the compass plus up and down.

12. A quotation from the *Analects*, IV, 25: "The Master said: Moral force never dwells in solitude; it will always bring neighbors."

will reach alike the reigning emperor, the retired emperor, the empress dowager, the empress, the princes and the princesses, and they will enjoy great longevity. The nation will boast a reign of peace and harmony; all people will be at liberty to enjoy their pleasures. Thus may all, from the pillars of Heaven above, to the circle of the wind below,[13] taste the savor of the Law and sojourn in the garden of enlightenment. [November 17, 1128]

[From Tsuji, *Nihon bukkyō shi*, jōsei hen, pp. 728–733]

MIRACLE TALES OF THE BODHISATTVA JIZŌ

Jizō was already a popular earth goddess in India and a bodhisattva figure in China before entering the pantheon of Japanese Esoteric Buddhism as it became incorporated into the amorphous and readily permeable conception of divinity in various Shinto cults, themselves highly fluid and miscible. In Japan, Jizō was often portrayed as a savior or god of mercy, associated with acts of repentance. In this respect, his cult functioned in ways similar to that of the Bodhisattva Kannon. Like the latter, Jizō was much involved with the popularization of the Lotus Sūtra and with the cult of Amida and the Pure Land. His versatility is shown by his popularity among warriors and women and by his identification as a special protector of children — in which function he often appeared as a child.

The following two stories appeared in a collection of popular tales, *Miracles of the Bodhisattva Jizō (Jizō Bosatsu reigen ki)*, attributed to the monk Jitsuei (early eleventh century) of the Miidera, a major center of Tendai esotericism not far from its rival, Enryakuji, on Mount Hiei.

HOW MOCHIKATA RECEIVED A MIRACULOUS REVELATION

A warrior called Musashinosuke Mochikata lived in the household of a former governor of Owari. As a warrior Mochikata naturally appreciated the martial arts, but at the same time he engaged in unvirtuous deeds; nevertheless he still placed his trust in Jizō. On the eighteenth and twenty-fourth days of every month he abstained from *sake*, meat, and women. He observed this abstinence, singlemindedly thought of Jizō, and devoted himself to religious services. He continuously recited the name of Jizō even when giving vent to abuse and danger. He tried to repay the care his mother had taken of him in childhood by devoting himself to the way of the Ikkō followers and by giving away his wealth and property.

A *hijiri* ascetic named Chūjitsu constantly relied on Jizō and never ceased reciting his name. One night he dreamed that he met a golden Jizō who said

---

13. The lowest circle of the world in the Buddhist cosmogony was that of the wind.

to him, "At dawn tomorrow I will meet you again at Tō-in to the east of Rokkaku. The person whom you will meet there will be no one else but me." Just as Jizō said this, Chūjitsu woke up.

So at dawn Chūjitsu went there as instructed and saw Mochikata. He hurried up to him, bowed, and worshiped him. Mochikata felt that this was strange and asked Chūjitsu why he did this. Chūjitsu described in detail the marvelous dream of the previous night.

Mochikata thought, "In spite of my deluded mind, this dream is probably because I have concentrated on Jizō during these days. I am truly grateful that I have had this meeting on such a significant occasion." Deeply moved, he said to Chūjitsu, "I am a lowly and vulgar man who does not deserve worship. However, since a person's merciful mind is the same as that of the Buddha, we should not despise anyone and regard his mind as lowly. Your dream was probably due to my constant devotion to Bodhisattva Jizō. To practice filial piety toward my mother, I have been reciting Jizō's name and observing abstinence. These good deeds may sound small and insignificant, but they must have touched the heart of the Buddha.

"As the vow of the Bodhisattva Jizō says, 'If a man obeys his mother's instructions, he will occupy the same body with Jizō.' My merciful mind and filial piety are the same as those of Jizō—they are no different. If a man has a deeply sincere mind, he will move and finally communicate with the divine mind. Such a mind is regarded as the same as that of Jizō. Since mind and body are the same, my body is that of Jizō. But alas, I am still arrogant and insufficient in faith and practice. I will abandon my worldly life and harken to Jizō's vow."

[Dykstra, *Jizō*, p. 192]

ABOUT THE "MALT JIZŌ" OF KANUKI IN SURUGA

Long ago there was a woman who lived near Kanuki in Suruga. She was very poor and had no savings at all, and since she had no support she occasionally visited shrines and temples. While listening to the sacred words in the shrines and the sermons in the temples, she learned that Bodhisattva Jizō excelled other Buddhas, and that if a person merely thought about Jizō, his greatest desire would be instantly realized and he would become a Buddha in the future. Ever since that time the woman had deeply trusted in Jizō and had never neglected him.

The woman had a deep sense of filial obligation and she felt constantly distressed because she had no means of fulfilling her duty. With much sadness she thought to herself, "I am getting older, and how many years are now left to me? The anniversary of my mother's death will come soon and I do not know what to do."

She then decided to go to an acquaintance, borrow some rice, make some *sake* out of it, sell it, and with the profit therefrom she could arrange for a small memorial service. Reciting the name of Jizō, she went to the acquaintance to borrow the rice.

The owner of the rice said to her, "Do you have any collateral if you can't pay back the rice?" She replied, "Since I am doing this for the sake of my mother, I do not mind how much I have to suffer in repaying the loan. I myself will be the collateral."

The man was impressed by her sincerity and said to her, "Why don't you sell *sake* then?" and agreed to loan her three hundred pieces of copper at fifty percent interest.

"How kind of you," the woman said as she pressed her palms together in prayer and recited the name Jizō. . . .

The woman thought that this was solely due to the mercy of Jizō, and so she placed the loaned money in front of her wooden statue of Jizō which she worshiped daily. She said to the Jizō, "Using this money as capital, I will make some *sake*, obtain a small profit, and then use it to console my late mother's soul. Please help me to fulfill my filial duty." . . .

So the woman made *sake* and sold it. She was most successful, for since her *sake* tasted better, buyers gathered at her gate as though it were a marketplace. And so she eventually made a considerable profit. She then thought to herself, "At the very outset I had no idea of making a large profit and decided to sell the *sake* for a small profit." She then returned the three hundred copper pieces along with the interest. . . .

Many days passed and the woman continued to sell her *sake* at a low profit. Her customers told her, "We just can't do without your *sake*." So as a result, she was able to make a lot of money and her business was immensely successful.

One day the woman heard that a close friend in Numazu was critically ill and she thought, "Since the place is nearby, I will go over and see her and return quickly." Being a widow, the woman was especially careful about being away from home. She shut the brushwood-fence door and the braided doors four times to make quite sure that they were secure, and then she left and hurried off to her friend.

While she was chatting with her friend about the old days, it suddenly began to rain. As the rain became so torrential that it even made holes in rocks, the woman thought that it would be better to wait for it to stop before returning home. But the rain continued and finally a flood washed away a bridge, thus making it impossible for her to get home. The woman worried to herself,

"I may have to stay here indefinitely. All my work now seems to have been in vain, despite all my plans to save my mother by making a small profit from the rich owner's loan. This flood will spoil all the *sake* I have made and I will lose my customers. O Bodhisattva Jizō, what a shame that I have failed to attain my purpose! Surely it must have been a demon's trick to make me think of coming here!" In this way the woman lamented in a pitiful manner.

On the third day the rain finally stopped and the river fell. The woman asked for help, crossed the river by boat, and finally reached home. She was pleased to see that the fastened brushwood door was still shut and seemed to be just as she had left it. She took the lid off the *sake* jar, wondering how much had been spoiled—but not a single drop of *sake* was left!

The woman was greatly astonished and looked about, thinking that the *sake* might have leaked out. She then noticed strained lees heaped up beside the jar, and when she carefully examined them she found three *kan* and thirty copper pieces.

So she made inquiries among her neighbors and they told her, "We heard that you had asked someone to sell the *sake*, since you could not return home for the last few days on account of the flood. We saw a person of noble appearance with a blue hat selling *sake* at your place. Since his *sake* tasted better than yours and he served his customers courteously, many people heard about it and came and bought his *sake*."

The woman was very pleased and said, "I can't believe it!" But a neighbor continued, "Ask people and listen carefully to what they tell you. A sick man on his deathbed in this neighborhood drank the *sake*—and he suddenly recovered and has been walking around without difficulty since this morning. My own husband had been ill in bed for the past hundred days, but he regained his strength through drinking this *sake*. So you can see, it can't have been a trick."

"I wonder who sold the *sake*?" the woman thought. "I will inform my Buddha and thank him." So she washed her hands, purified herself, and went on to the Jizō statue which she had worshiped for so long. She prayed to him, "Merciful Jizō, thanks to your aid I can now undertake my filial responsibility to my late mother."

She then opened the doors of her Jizō's portable shrine. What a surprise! Instead of a string of beads, the Jizō statue was graciously holding some malt in his hand. Now the woman understood that the bodhisattva had sympathized with her in her poverty and had manifested his mercy by responding to her desperate petition. This was indeed a most unusual happening in this degenerate age. . . .

This was truly unusual. Since divine power operates in mysterious ways, it can never pervert the truth. This means that the Buddha appears only in the mind of faith. If a person has doubts, how can a Buddha manifest himself? But if a person has a strong and firm faith, a Buddha will most certainly appear.

People called him the "Malt Jizō" of Kanuki in Suruga, and he exists to this very day. Those who have placed their trust in this Jizō have never failed to obtain their requests. It is said that Jizō's vows to save sentient beings surpass those of other bodhisattvas.

[Dykstra, *Jizō*, pp. 197–200]

SEX AND BUDDHAHOOD — A SHINGON HERESY

SELECTIONS FROM *THE PRECIOUS MIRROR* (HŌKYŌSHŌ)

This short work written by the Shingon monk Yūkai (1345–1416) is of interest in tracing certain developments in the later history of Esoteric Buddhism. In its emphasis on the pedigree of the Shingon teachings, it was no more than echoing Kūkai's words of six hundred years before, but in the meantime the orthodox tradition suffered greatly from the numerous heresies that developed out of the religion's Tantric aspects. In the excerpts given here, Yūkai attacks one of the most notorious heresies, the so-called Tachikawa school, and in other parts of his essay, he mentions that Shingon's name had been lent to magical arts that bore little relation to the doctrines taught by Kūkai, including the art of discovering buried treasure and the art of flying about at will. Even the most outlandish heresy was capable of producing scriptural evidence for the validity of its view, for the Buddhist canon as transmitted to Japan contained an incredible variety of texts, some of them little more than formulas for magical rites. The Tachikawa school was almost extinct by Yūkai's day, as he himself states, but other bizarre heresies continued to dominate Esoteric Buddhism.

Shingon Esotericism is the secret doctrine taught by Vairochana, the King of Enlightenment, and transmitted by the Eight Founders. It is called the Supreme Highest Vehicle of the Buddha and bears the title of the Realm Surpassing All Sects. Indeed, only through this teaching can one exterminate the extremely heavy burdens of karma or save the living creatures difficult of conversion or quickly realize the Buddhist knowledge. That is why in ancient times eight wise philosophers who went to China to seek the Law received instruction in Shingon. The Eastern Temple [Shingon] had five transmitters of the teachings: Kūkai, Shūei, Eun, Engyō, and Jōgyō.[14] The other school [Tendai] had three transmitters: Saichō, Ennin, and Enchin. . . . Among the teachings received from China, those obtained by Kūkai are the senior ones because they were passed down from one heir to the traditions to the next, from the Great Founder Vairochana to Huiguo, the abbot of the Green Dragon Temple in China. I cannot enter into details here, but although Huiguo transmitted the Law to many people . . . only Kūkai and Yiming were instructed in the two mandalas, and Yiming was not fully instructed. He died without transmitting the Law to anyone. Only Kūkai was the true heir of Huiguo. . . . Kūkai in turn transmitted the teachings to many disciples. [Genealogical tables are omitted.]

Someone asked, "It is indeed true that the Shingon teachings are the highest

---

14. Shūei (808–884), Eun (798–869), Engyō (799–852), and Jōgyō (d. 866) — together with the more famous Kūkai — Saichō, Ennin, and Enchin are often spoken of as the eight monks who sought the Law in China.

of all the schools and are the direct road for attaining Buddhahood. However, in late years the false and the true have become confused. To enter a false path and to violate the true way of becoming a Buddha is like saying East is West, and the point of view becomes topsy-turvy. How then can one attain the goal of becoming a Buddha? I crave your instruction on this matter."

I replied, "It is difficult to distinguish jade and stone; it is easy to be misled by worthless things and difficult to establish the difference between the false and the true. For example, among the disciples of the Daigo-Sambō-in, there was a man called the *ajari* Ninkan. On account of some crime of which he was found guilty, he was exiled to the province of Izu, and there he earned his living by teaching Shingon to married laity and to meat-eating, defiled people, whom he made his disciples. A yin-yang teacher from a place called Tachikawa in the province of Musashi studied Shingon with Ninkan and combined it with his yin-yang doctrines. The false and the true were thus confounded; the inner and the outer learning were indiscriminately mixed. He called it the Tachikawa school and expounded it as a branch of Shingon. This was the origin of the heresy . . . .

The principle of this sect was to consider the way of men and women, yin and yang, to be the secret art of obtaining Buddhahood in this flesh and the only means of obtaining Buddhahood and gaining the Way. They made outrageous assertions that the Buddha had previously taught their doctrines, a diabolic invention deserving of eternal punishment in hell. Ignorant people, not realizing this, upheld it as the most profound and secret Law. How can one say that they possessed true views and genuine knowledge? The Shūrangama Sūtra declares, "Those who secretly desire to perform acts of greed and lust are fond of saying that the eyes, ears, nose and tongue are all 'pure land' and that the male and female organs are the true places of perfect knowledge [bodhi] and nirvāna. The ignorant people believe these foul words. They are to be called poisoners, hinderers, and demons. When they die, they become devils who afflict and unsettle people in this world, causing them to become confused and unwittingly to fall into the hell of eternal punishment." How can people belonging to that hell be called Shingon believers? . . .

This Tachikawa school later spread to the province of Etchū. In successive generations, two teachers, Kakumei and Kakuin, lived on Mount Kōya [and taught Tachikawa doctrine there]. At this time, many secret manuals and texts of this heretical school were in circulation, often called "oral transmission of the secrets of esoteric doctrine." To this day, there are ignorant people who study such works and believe them to possess the loftiest thoughts. In truth, they are neither exoteric nor esoteric but merely so many stones wrapped in jade. . . . Many people studied these teachings, but they did not meet with divine favor, and for the most part, both the teachings and the men have perished. A few are left, but I do not know how many.

[From TD 77, no. 2456:847–849]

PRAYERS FOR THE SHOGUN

This letter was written to Shogun Yoriie by the Shingon monk Mongaku, who had been a close adviser of Yoriie's father, Minamoto Yoritomo. In refusing to offer prayers for the shogun, Mongaku does not hesitate to scold him for his failings as a ruler. The forthrightness and independence of mind displayed by this monk of the more formalistic Shingon sect show that these were qualities characteristic of Kamakura Buddhism in general—and not just of figures like Dōgen and Nichiren. This letter is a fine illustration of both the abuse of esoteric practices by those with little understanding of them, and the reaffirmation of true religion by persons like Mongaku.

LETTER OF THE MONK MONGAKU TO SHOGUN YORIIE A.D.1200

I respectfully acknowledge your second letter. I sent you an answer before, but since you have written me again, I am replying again in the same tenor. While reading your letter, I repeatedly felt that I was listening to a message from the late shogun and I was deeply moved.

[You ask me] to offer prayers—and I remember with gratitude beyond expression that the late shogun rebuilt the East Temple[15] and made possible through his generosity the reestablishment of the Takao monastery. Through these merits, he will be saved in the life hereafter. It is also due only to his generosity that I, Mongaku, have been able to do something for Buddhism and accomplish something for the good of man. I therefore have remained ever grateful for his generosity and happy beyond words. Even before you asked me to offer prayers, it was always my fervent desire that you should enjoy peace and security.

[May I say], however, that prayer takes effect only for those who practice virtue and who love the good. In the dwellings of those who offend, prayer is of no avail. By offenders, I mean those who destroy life without proper cause and those who live a life of pleasure and indulge themselves with liquor, women, and wealth, ignoring the grief of others and disregarding the well-being of the nation. When men are virtuous and good, on the other hand, it means that they reverence both the law of Buddha and the law of the state and are ever concerned with the welfare of the people. In short, it means that they must have character such as is expected of a parent by all people, even the lowliest man or woman—peasants and those in all walks of life.

When a man who has no concern for these things or who is ruthless and offensive or who has only selfish motives orders a monk or other spiritual in-

---

15. Tōji in the original text, but it must refer to the Tōdaiji in Nara, which Yoriie's father, Yoritomo, helped rebuild in 1190.

termediary to offer prayers, there may be those who will reply with favorable works because the order comes from a lofty source. But if the petitioner is not a good man, he must not only expect that there will be no answer to his prayers, but he must expect that he may be worse off than before.

Therefore, if you must have prayers offered, Your Highness should command only those monks or astrologers who are not dishonest or subservient but are straightforward. Your Highness should tell them your misdemeanors and try at all times to make amends. This Your Highness should by all means do. If your actions are not good and you tell others to pray for you, you are really putting yourself in a precarious situation.

Your Highness is the shogun of Japan. He who is asked to pray for you should be a man of great mind and great integrity. A person of steadfast virtue and lofty disdain of flattery but yet of compassionate heart must be selected to be the master of your prayers.

When it is a question of offering prayer as a sovereign as well as an individual, the first object of prayer should be the whole country and the whole people. How one may pray depends upon one's position in life. He whose influence does not affect the nation may offer prayers for his own benefit. But in these days, the rulers as well as the ruled offer up prayers on their own account. Such prayers have no effect, for they are not in accord with the invisible mind of Buddha and are in discord with the transparent light of Heaven. I beg Your Highness, and must repeat it again and again, that you deem it your duty to merit the confidence of all, so that with you as shogun in Kamakura, complaints of injustice will nowhere be heard and unreason will nowhere prevail.

If Your Highness acts in that way, you [will] have no need for prayers for yourself. [The goddess of] the Great Shrine of Ise, the Bodhisattva Hachiman, [the deities of] Kamo and Kasuga will all be pleased; and all Buddhas, sages, gods, and goddesses, without exception, will extend their hands to safeguard you.

Even before Buddhism came into existence, there were in India and in China, as well as in Japan, wise kings and sage rulers under whom all the land was prosperous and all the people lived a happy life. The sovereigns, long of life, were like father and mother to the people. The Five Emperors and the Three Sovereigns, among whom were Yao and Shun, were rulers who came before the time of Buddha. Your Highness is more fortunate [than they] in that you are acquainted with the Three Treasures of Buddhism which those others could not know. Your Highness, therefore, should put your mind on the life hereafter. You should endeavor to get away from this "house of fire" of the three existences and, rising above the troubles of repeated transmigration, attain to Buddhahood. Such should be the first prayer of the ruler as well as of the ruled.

. . .

In these days, however, all religious works and rituals sponsored by the great are merely for the eye and are only an expense to the country and a burden to the people. Buddha and the deities do not accept them at all. Those who pray should know that Buddha and the deities accept only virtue and faith; material treasures have no appeal for them.

It is with this in mind that Your Highness, at the head of your warriors, should guard the emperor and become the mainstay of the whole nation. If you go astray in any way or have evil in your heart, you will prove to be only an enemy of the country. Its downfall will be the logical result. . . .

If Your Highness does not conduct yourself well, all men throughout the land will come to believe that you are not a good man. Then mountain bandits, sea marauders, highwaymen, and thieves will abound and in the end will bring ruin to your regime. . . . Then Your Highness, not realizing that all this is your own fault but believing it to be the work of criminals will merely go on arresting men, punishing them, imprisoning them, and cutting off their heads or their limbs to the detriment of the country. It is necessary to think of the retribution waiting in the life to come.

When your Highness once realizes that these crimes are not always the offenses of others but are due to your own recklessness and when you are sincerely convinced of it, if you ask any learned man how best to govern, the answer will be simple—as simple as shooting at a target, as the saying goes. As long as your Highness knows how to rule yourself, there is no need for regulations about this or that, no need for prohibitions, orders, or proclamations, because the people will be submissive and obedient. Then the land will naturally be at peace and well ordered. . . .

The late shogun always thought Mongaku to be a man of tough fiber and straightforward speech. I have never been in the personal service of Your Highness; it must have been offensive to Your Highness for me to write to you in the way I do. For this I beg your forgiveness. However, it has seemed to me that Your Highness is too much addicted to pleasures and has no regard for the complaints or the sufferings of the people. I thought this so deplorable that I told the late shogun confidentially that you should be sent away somewhere into exile—that such a course would be a real act of love toward you. . . .

Because I am frank and outspoken, I am certain that your Highness hates me. That I do not mind. I have written you thus only because I desire you to be good, and more than that, to grow in virtue.

A learned scholar quotes a text to the effect that a good word spoken for the sake of the ruler and the people is more valuable than hundreds and thousands of gold offerings. To this the ancient sage-kings bore testimony. Therefore do not fail to listen to those who tell you your shortcomings. If Your Highness tries to keep the nation in order without being mindful of your own faults, you will be like a man who expects to get rid of illness without taking medicine.

There are men of loyalty and faithfulness from whom you can learn your shortcomings, who do not change their colors in the service of Her Highness your mother. Let them speak to you in secret, not in public. Listen to them directly; do not heed the lip service of monks. If they speak ill of you, you will be apt to become angry; but you must practice patience. Cure by fire is painful, but it is only through endurance that illness can be cured.

There are none more despicable than those who change their colors. There are none more loyal than those who tell you your faults. I pray Your Highness to remember this. Even if a man is agreeable and likable, beware of him if he is a cheat. But if there be one whom you dislike and do not wish to see, give him his due if he be of sterling character. The art of government, it seems to me, lies in nothing more nor less than in this awareness of true character.

I cannot thank Your Highness enough for the two letters with which you have honored me. This is my answer, written with all reverence and respect.

Tenth day of the first month of the second year of Shōji [1200].

[From *Kokushi taikei*, XXXIII, *Azuma Kagami*, pp. 579–584]

ANNEN: MAXIMS FOR THE YOUNG (DŌJIKYŌ)

Annen (841–889) was a major figure in the promotion of Tendai esotericism at Mount Hiei after Saichō's time. "Esoteric," which basically means "mysterious," can be understood as "secret" or even "exclusive" in a particularistic sense but in its more universalistic aspect can represent the wondrous workings of the Three Mysteries (body, speech, and mind) in all humankind. It is in this sense that Annen's "Maxims for the Young" should be taken as an accommodation of Mahāyāna's adaptive means to the common person, often in a quite conventional and prosaic manner.

Many of these instructions for the young are drawn from the Chinese, and especially Confucian, canonical literature, syncretized with Indian and Buddhist views. Indeed, they often seem to express a proverbial wisdom or etiquette common to many cultures. But Annen makes it clear that Buddhism represents the highest wisdom, that worship of the native Japanese gods comes next in the hierarchy of values, and that Confucian morality stands on a lower level. Similarly, although filial piety is encouraged, loyalty to parents and lay teachers cannot compare with that to religious teachers, whose redemptive function goes far beyond this life. Given the religious goal toward which these instructions lead, it may not be surprising that instead of providing a guide for schooling or systematic education, the following excerpts often refer to matters of adult life and society that the young might find relevant only later in life.

In the presence of a superior, do not suddenly stand up.
If you meet [such a person] on the road, kneel and then pass on.
Should he summon you, comply respectfully
with hands clasped to your breast, face him directly.
Speak only if spoken to; if he addresses you, listen attentively.

Make threefold obeisance to the Three Treasures [of Buddhism],
twofold obeisance to the [Shinto] gods.

In the presence of others, bow once
But show the highest respect to your teacher or lord.

When passing a graveyard, be reverent;
When passing a [Shinto] shrine, descend [from horse or carriage],
In front of a [Buddhist] temple or pagoda, do nothing to defile it [such as
    defecation or urination].
When the writings of the [Confucian] sages are being read, do nothing
    indecorous.

In all human relations there are appropriate forms of ritual respect
At court there must be laws and regulations;
If men [in authority] contravene ritual respect, transgressions will follow
    among the masses.

In dealing with the people, say no more than is needed;
your business done, move on quickly.
In the conduct of business, let there be no breach of trust;
In your speech, keep to your word.

When words are many, they are worth little . . .
The man who is bold inevitably falls into danger . . .
The guileless man commits no transgressions . . .

The walls have ears; keep to yourself whatever might be taken in slander.
Even the heavens have eyes; commit no wrongdoing even in secret . . .
A three-inch tongue can do untold harm to a five-foot body;
The mouth is the gate of much misfortune; the tongue is the root of many
    mishaps . . .

Natural disasters can be averted; from disasters of one's own making, there is
    no escape.
Pile up good deeds and a house will have no end of blessings;
Indulge in evil deeds and it will have no end of calamities.

Good deeds done in secret/are bound to reap rewards in the open.
Good conduct performed unseen/will make one's good name shine . . . . . .

Hearts, like faces, differ from one another; like water, they take the shape of
    the container.
Do not try to bend another man's bow or ride another's horse.

Seeing the cart ahead overturned should be a warning to the cart behind.
Not to forget what happened before is to learn a lesson for the future . . .

When the gods punish fools, it is not to slay but to chasten them,
A teacher strikes the student not from malice but for the student's own
  improvement.

Birth confers no honor on one; it is the practice of self-cultivation that
  endows one with wisdom and virtue.
The man of worth may not enjoy riches; the one who is rich may not be
  worthy of honor.
If one, though rich, still has many desires, he may be called poor.
If one, though poor, is contented, he may be called rich.

A teacher who fails to admonish his disciple, may be called a breaker of the
  commandments.
A teacher who admonishes his disciple may be called an upholder of the
  commandments.

When one keeps a bad disciple, both teacher and disciple will fall into Hell;
When one nourishes a good disciple, both teacher and disciple will attain
  Buddhahood. . . .

Leaving one's kin and cleaving to a strange teacher, one may achieve [the
  three forms of Buddhist learning]: Discipline, Concentration, and
  Compassion.
Even though one may be dull by nature, one can surely attain the learning of
  Buddhahood.

One character learned each day amounts to 360 in a year.
Each character learned is worth a thousand pieces of gold.
One stroke of the brush may save many lives.

One should not neglect a teacher who has taught you even for the length of
  one day; how much less a teacher who has taught you for years.

To a Buddhist teacher, you are indebted for three generations (past, present,
  and future, that is, for all time).
To a parent you are only indebted for one lifetime . . .
A disciple must walk seven feet behind his teacher, and not tread on his
  shadow. . . .

On a winter's night, dressed lightly, endure the cold as you recite the whole
  night through;
On a summer day with little to eat, repel hunger as you persist in learning till
  the day is done. . . .

Great though the vices of the wise man be, he will not fall into Hell;
Slight though the vices of the foolish man be, he will assuredly fall into Hell.
The fool clings to sorrow like a prisoner clasped in jail.
The wise man ever enjoys happiness, like one resplendent with Heaven's
    light. . . .

Each morning in the hills and fields, one kills other creatures to feed one's
    own;
Each night in the rivers and seas, one fishes to support one's life;
To support life day and night, day and night one creates evil karma.
To satisfy one's tastes for the span of a day, one falls into Hell for eons. . . .

The cycle of birth and death is unceasing; seek nirvana now.
The life of the body is impure, befouled by the passions; seek enlightenment
    straight away.
Even in the halls of Indra's palace, there is the grief of unceasing change.
Even in Brahmā's heaven, the pain of fire and sword awaits.

Compassion shown to one person is worth a sea of merit;
What is done for many but with selfish intent gains only a poppy seed's
    reward. . . .
Piling up sand to make a stupa will earn a golden body,
An offering of flowers to the Buddha will merit a lotus seat. . . .

For the guidance of the young, I have explained the doctrine of retribution.
What is drawn from the Inner and Outer [Buddhist and Confucian] canons,
    let no reader
despise or ridicule.

[*Annen Oshō no kenkyū*, pp. 2–32; dB]

Chapter 9

THE VOCABULARY OF JAPANESE AESTHETICS I

It is surprising how often we find the same few terms used to express the preferences or ideals of Japanese creative artists throughout the ages, indeed, so often that we can identify them as a special "vocabulary of Japanese aesthetics." Such terms varied in meaning with the times and the individual critics, as is to be expected of words employed for well over a thousand years in some cases. Some knowledge of this vocabulary may therefore serve as a key to Japanese canons of taste in literature and the other arts.

The most famous of these words, and one that has had whole volumes of serious research devoted to it, is *aware*. In old texts, we find it first used as an exclamation of surprise or delight, a person's natural reaction to what an early Western critic of Japanese literature called the "ahness" of things, but gradually it came to be used adjectivally, usually to mean "pleasant" or "interesting." One scholar who analyzed the uses of *aware* in the *Man'yōshū*, the great eighth-century collection of poetry, discovered that an *aware* emotion was most often evoked by poets on hearing the melancholy calls of birds and beasts. An inscription from the year 763 contains the word *aware* to describe the writer's emotions on seeing the spring rain. Gradually, therefore, *aware* came to be tinged with sadness. By the time of *The Tale of Genji*, only the lower classes (or the upper classes in moments of great stress) used the word *aware* as a simple exclamation; elsewhere, it expressed a gentle sorrow, adding to a sentence not so much a meaning as a color or a perfume. It bespoke the sensitive poet's awareness of a sight or a sound, its beauty and its perishability. With the steady heightening of the poets' sensitivity to the world around them, it was probably inevitable that the tone of sadness would deepen.

The famous eighteenth-century critic of Japanese literature Motoori Norinaga (1730–1801) once characterized *The Tale of Genji* as a novel of *mono no aware*, a phrase that has sometimes been translated as "the sadness of things." Motoori, however, seems to have meant something closer to a "sensitivity to things"—a sensitivity to the fall of a flower or to an unwept tear.

Some of the early works of criticism use the word *aware* so often as to make it almost the exclusive criterion of merit. In a work written around 1200, for example, we find this discussion of *The Tale of Genji*:

> Someone asked, "Which chapter is the best and creates the most profound impression?"
>
> No chapter is superior to *Kiritsubo*. From the opening words, "At the Court of an Emperor (he lived it matters not when)" to the final description of Genji's initiation to manhood, the whole chapter is filled with a moving (*aware*) pathos which colors the language, the circumstances portrayed, and everything else. In *The Broom-Tree* the discussion on a rainy night of the appraisal of women contains many praiseworthy things. The chapter *Yūgao* is permeated with a moving (*aware*) sadness. *The Festival of Red Leaves* and *The Flower-Feast* are unforgettable chapters, each possessed of its own charm (*en*) and interest. *Aoi* is an extremely moving (*aware*) and absorbing chapter. The chapter *Kashiwagi* contains the scene of the departure for Ise, which is at once charming (*en*) and magnificent. The scene when, after the death of the Emperor, Fujitsubo takes vows as a nun is moving (*aware*). *Exile at Suma* is a moving (*aware*) and powerful chapter. The descriptions of Genji leaving the capital for Suma and of his life in distant exile are extremely moving (*aware*).[1]

As this excerpt shows, the word *aware* was used to describe almost every chapter considered to be of unusual beauty, and in each case the meaning, though vague, was associated with deep emotions and not a mere exclamation, as in early times. But *aware* had not yet darkened to its modern meaning of "wretched," which represents perhaps the final evolution in its long history.

In the same excerpt, one other word appears several times—*en*, which may be translated as "charming." Its use as a term of praise indicates that not only the melancholy but also the colorful surface of *Genji* was appreciated. Indeed, if we look at the superb horizontal scroll illustrating the novel—which is

---

1. *Mumyō sōshi*, pp. 17–18.

roughly contemporary with this criticism—we are struck far more by its exquisite charm than by the sadness of the scenes (although, of course, the two conceptions are not mutually exclusive). *En* evokes the visual beauty in which much of the literature of the time was clothed.

A term of cheerful aesthetic criticism is *okashi*, a word we find in many Heian works, particularly in the celebrated *Pillow Book*. *Okashi* seems originally to have meant something that brought a smile to the face, of either delight or amusement. It was not applied to the serious or sad things of life except ironically, and thus as one Japanese critic pointed out, its making light of the tragic was just the opposite of *aware*, which sought to impart to the otherwise meaningless cries of a bird or the fall of a flower a profound and moving meaning.

Both *aware* and *okashi*—the former best represented by Murasaki Shikibu, who saw the *aware* nature of a leaf caught in the wind, the latter by Sei Shōnagon, whose witty essays are dotted with the word *okashi*—are standards typical of an aristocratic society of great refinement. That aristocrats of the Heian period were aware of the special nature of their society is attested to by one other word of their aesthetic vocabulary—*miyabi*, literally "courtliness" but in general "refinement." The court was a small island of refinement and sophistication in a country otherwise marked by ignorance and uncourtliness, so it is not surprising that people at court tended to think with horror of the world outside the capital. "Courtliness" here meant not only the appropriate decorum for lords and ladies at the palace but also the Japanese reflection of the culture that had originally come from China.

Miyabi was perhaps the most inclusive term for describing the aesthetics of the Heian period. It was applied mainly to the quiet pleasures that, supposedly at least, could be savored only by the aristocrat whose tastes had been educated to them—a spray of plum blossoms, the elusive perfume of a rare wood, the delicate blending of colors in a robe. In lovemaking, too, the "refined" tastes of the court were revealed. A man might first be attracted to a woman by catching a glimpse of her sleeve, carelessly but elegantly draped from a carriage window, or by seeing a note in her calligraphy, or by hearing her play a lute one night in the dark. Later, the lovers would exchange letters and poems, often attached to a spray of the flower suitable for the season. Such love affairs are most perfectly portrayed in *The Tale of Genji* and, even if somewhat idealized in that novel, suggest to what lengths a feeling for "refinement" could govern the lives of those at court. Perhaps nowhere is this insistence on the refinement of taste more clearly revealed than in the passage known as the Grading of Quality,[2] in

---

2. *Shina no sadame*—literally, "the determination of grade or rank," or what today might be called "rank ordering."

which Prince Genji and his sophisticated companions discuss the relative virtues of the women they have known. In love, no less than in art, the same aristocratic hierarchy of values, the same subtlety of discrimination, prevailed as in social relations. Indeed, it was in just such a society as this that so much importance was attached—even in religious matters and contrary to the equalitarian trend of Mahāyāna Buddhism—to the ascending hierarchy or gradations of religious consciousness.

The influence of *miyabi* was not wholly beneficial, though. By refining and polishing the cruder emotions found in the *Man'yōshū*, it also severely limited the range of Japanese poetry and art. *Miyabi* led poets to shun the crude, the rustic, and the unseemly, but in so doing, it tended to remove or dilute real feeling. Today, when reading much of this later Japanese poetry, we cannot help wishing at times that the poet would break away from the oft-sung themes of the moon, the cries of birds, and the fall of cherry blossoms and treat instead harsher and more compelling subjects.

In a sense, *miyabi* was a negation of the simple virtues, the plain sincerity (*makoto*) that *Man'yōshū* poets had possessed and that poets many centuries later rediscovered. "Refinement" gave to the courtiers a justification for their own way of living and at the same time a contempt for the noncourtly similar to the attitude that has given the English words "peasant-like," "boorish," and "countrified" their uncomplimentary meanings. But in a curious way, this specifically aristocratic standard was transmitted to the military classes when they rose to power and later to the common people and even the peasantry, so that today much of what "refinement" represented is part of the common heritage of all Japanese. The hackneyed imagery of Heian poetry—the falling of the cherry blossoms, the reddening of the autumn leaves, and the rest—has become very much a part of even the least aesthetic of Japanese. Steel mills dismiss their employees for the day to enable them to admire the cherry blossoms (and drink *sake* under them), and the hardest-headed businessman does not begrudge an afternoon off spent at Takao when the maples are their most brilliantly colored. This love of conventionally admired sights of nature is genuine, not a pose, and it extends to all classes. The annually renewed excitement over cherry blossoms or reddening maples or first snow is an important element of the Japanese year. A letter that failed to open with mention of these sights of nature would strike the recipient as being curiously insensitive. The peoples of other countries are certainly not indifferent to the beauty brought by the seasons, but nothing can compare elsewhere with the love of beauty that has played so prominent a role in Japanese life and history since early times. *Aware* and *okashi* are no longer used in the present-day vocabulary of aesthetic criticism, but the *miyabi* spirit of refined sensibility is still apparent in literature and also Japanese craftwork—ceramics, lacquerware, and other arts—which have influenced artistic production throughout the world.

MURASAKI SHIKIBU: ON THE ART OF FICTION

The Tale of Genji has been read and commented on ever since it was first written, almost a thousand years ago, and many theories have been advanced regarding what the author Murasaki Shikibu was trying to express in her novel. In the following excerpt from *The Tale of Genji*, we find what is perhaps the best answer to this question. It seems likely that here, in one of the earliest and most famous examples of Japanese criticism, Murasaki was stating her own views of the novel's function.

This year the rainy season was more severe than usual. Day after day the rains came down without a let-up, and time hung heavily on the hands of the ladies in Prince Genji's household. As a distraction they had recourse to illustrated romances.

Lady Akashi was proficient in this art and had several such works prepared for her daughter, the little Princess. The greatest enthusiast, however, was Tamakazura, who now spent all day reading and copying romances. Many of her young ladies-in-waiting also took an interest and had accumulated a fascinating collection of stories, some from real life, some fictitious. . . .

One day when Genji came into Tamakazura's rooms he noticed several illustrated romances scattered about the place. "Really," he said with a smile, "you women are incorrigible. Sometimes I wonder whether you haven't been born into this world just so that you can be deceived by people. Look at these books! There probably isn't an ounce of truth in the lot of them—and you know that as well as I do. Yet here you are, utterly fascinated and taken in by all their fabrications, avidly copying down each word—and, I may add, quite unaware that it is a sultry day in the middle of the rainy season and that your hair is in the most frightful mess."

Genji paused for a while. "But then," he continued, "if it weren't for old romances like this, how on earth would you get through these long tedious days when time moves so slowly? And besides, I realize that many of these works, full of fabrications though they are, do succeed in evoking the emotion of things in a most realistic way. One event follows plausibly on another, and in the end we cannot help being moved by the story, even though we know what foolishness it all really is. Thus, when we read about the ordeals of some delightful princess in a romance, we may find ourselves actually entering into the poor girl's feelings.

"Again, the author may so dazzle us with the brilliance of his writing that we forget about our initial incredulity. Later on, when we think back calmly on the story, we may be annoyed that we should have swallowed its absurdities. But at first hearing we only notice how fascinating it all is.

"Of late I have occasionally stopped to listen while our young Princess' ladies are reading aloud to her, and I have been much impressed by what good authors we have. Perhaps the reason they write so well is simply that they are used to telling lies, but I expect there is more to it than that."

"I rather imagine," said Tamakazura, pushing away her inkstone, "that it is only those who are themselves in the habit of being deceitful who have to delve like that into the writer's possible motives. Honest people accept what they read as completely true.

"Yes," said Genji, "it was rather churlish of me to speak badly about these books as I did just now. For the fact is that works of fiction set down things that have happened in this world ever since the days of the gods. Writings like *The Chronicles of Japan* really give only one side of the picture, whereas these romances must be full of just the right sort of details."

He smiled and continued, "The author certainly does not write about specific people, recording all the actual circumstances of their lives. Rather it is a matter of his being so moved by things, both good and bad, which he has heard and seen happening to men and women that he cannot keep it all to himself but wants to commit it to writing and make it known to other people—even to those of later generations. This, I feel sure, is the origin of fiction.

"Sometimes the author will want to write favorably about people, and then he will select all the good qualities he can think of; at other times, when he wants to give a fuller description of human nature, he introduces all sorts of strange and wicked things into his book. But in every case the things he writes about will belong to this actual world of ours.

"Chinese story-tellers differ from our own, both in their learning and in the way they write. Even in Japan, literature has changed greatly since earlier times. And then, of course, there is a large gap between serious and superficial works. To dismiss all these types of fiction as so much falsehood is surely to miss the point. For even in the Law that the Buddha in his great mercy bequeathed to us there are parts known as Accommodated Truths (Expedient Means). As a result we find certain seeming inconsistencies, especially in the Vaipulya sutras, which no doubt give rise to doubts in the minds of the unenlightened. Yet in the last analysis these Accommodated Truths tend to the same aim as all the rest of the sutras. The difference between Buddhahood and Earthly Lust as described in the scriptures is precisely the same as that between the good and the bad qualities of fictitious characters.[3] So, when we regard these works of fiction in the proper light, we find that they contain nothing superfluous."

Thus did Genji show that romances could serve a most useful purpose.

[Morris, *The World of the Shining Prince*, pp. 308–310]

---

3. In Genji's analogy, the deception in fiction corresponds to the Accommodated Truth (*hōben*) in the scriptures: both represent departures from the truth, but both serve good purposes. Hence, the good and the bad in fiction correspond to Buddhahood (*bodai*) and earthly lust (*bonnō*), which are co-implicated in enlightenment (*bonnō soku bodai*).

FUJIWARA TEIKA: INTRODUCTION TO THE *GUIDE TO THE COMPOSITION OF POETRY*

Fujiwara Teika (1162–1241) was more responsible than any other individual for the formation of Japanese literary taste. Attempting in the early medieval period to preserve the best of the classical tradition, he defined for all time the classic canons of Japanese verse. His judgments influenced not only writers who consulted his books of poetry and criticism but also, indirectly, the entire nation. The *Hundred Poets, a Poem Each* (*Hyakunin isshū*), which Teika is generally believed to have compiled, is the most popular anthology of Japanese verse, and almost every Japanese knows its contents by heart, largely through a game based on them. Teika also helped give direction to later trends in Japanese poetry by his selection of the works to be included in the *New Collection* (1205), the last of the great anthologies and the most influential. Finally, all the principal works of Heian literature extant today were edited by Teika, and our picture of that glorious period of Japanese literature has thus been conditioned by his taste.

In the field of literary criticism, Teika's *Guide to the Composition of Poetry* has long been considered an authoritative statement of the ideals of Japanese poetry. It is brief to the point of sometimes being cryptic; later writers have expanded it to seventy times its original length in an attempt to elucidate Teika's meanings. Perhaps the most striking feature of this little essay is its insistence on using the language of former poets. To the degree that this counsel was followed—the *Guide* became in fact a set of golden rules for later court poets—the result tended to be sterile poetry. Any new conceit or turn of phrase was considered to be a sufficiently original contribution, even though a poem differed very little from earlier ones, and the use of outmoded clichés robbed the poetry of even the vitality that fresh language can impart.

In the expression of the emotions, originality merits the first consideration. (That is, one should look for sentiments unsung by others and sing them.) The words used, however, should be old ones. (The vocabulary should be restricted to words used by the masters of the Three Anthologies:[4] the same words are proper for all poets, whether ancient or modern.)

The style should imitate the great poems of the masters of former times. One must discard every last phrase of the sentiments and expressions written by men of recent times. (Expressions which appear in the poetry of the last seventy or eighty years must be avoided at all cost.)

It has become a popular practice to borrow many of the same expressions that appear in the poetry of former masters for use in making new poems. It is,

---

4. The *Kokinshū* (905), the *Gosenshū* (951), and the *Shūi Wakashū* (ca. 1005–1008)—three anthologies of poetry compiled by imperial order.

however, rather excessive to borrow as many as three of the five lines[5] and betrays a lack of originality. Three or four words over two lines are permissible, but it is simply too exasperating if in the remaining lines the same imagery as in the original poem is used. . . .[6]

One should impregnate one's mind with a constant study of the forms of expression of ancient poetry. The *Kokinshū*, the *Tales of Ise*,[7] the *Gosen*, and the *Shūi* are truly deserving of study. One should especially concentrate on the outstanding poems in the collection of the Thirty-Six Poets (e.g., those of Hitomaro, Tsurayuki, Tadamine, Ise, and Komachi). The first and second books of Bo Juyi's *Collected Works*[8] should be gone over constantly; although he was not a master of Japanese poetry, his works are remarkable for their descriptions of the time and for their portrayal of the splendors and decline of his age.

There are no teachers of Japanese poetry. But they who take the old poems as their teachers, steep their minds in the old style and learn their words from the masters of former time—who of them will fail to write poetry?

[*Eika taigai*, in Hisamatsu, *Chūsei karon shū*, pp. 188–189]

---

5. The *waka* is written in five lines of 5, 7, 5, 7, and 7 syllables, respectively. This is the standard Japanese verse form.

6. Some examples of phrases often occurring in poetry have been omitted in this translation.

7. A tenth-century work consisting of 125 episodes, most of them relating to the great lover Ariwara no Narihira. Each of these episodes contains one or more poems. For the other works mentioned in this sentence, see the *Kokinshū*, the *Gesenshū*, and the *Shūi Wakashū*.

8. Bo Juyi (772–846) is the most widely read Chinese poet in Japan, partially at least because he is the simplest to understand. During the Heian period, his writings were so popular that the word *Works* itself, with no other qualification, meant Po's collected poetry and prose.

PART III

The Medieval Age: Despair, Deliverance, and Destiny

The term "medieval Japan" represents only a general phase in the continuing process of historical evolution. For the sake of convenience, we may consider it to embrace the late twelfth through the late sixteenth centuries, including those periods identified politically with the shogunates of the Kamakura and Muromachi periods. Actually, the characteristic feudal institutions of medieval Japan had their roots in the Heian period. The warrior or samurai class that dominated both the medieval and the early modern ages, for example, began its rise in the provinces from about the late ninth century; and the system of land tenure that characterized the medieval age, the *shōen* or private estate system, had its origins in the Nara period in the eighth century. But it was only in the twelfth century that the power of these feudal tendencies was fully manifested in the bloody struggles for military ascendancy between the Taira and the Minamoto clans, climaxed by the establishment of a military government in Kamakura, which effectively limited rule by the old Kyoto court. Thereafter, in one form or another, under one family or another, military government endured until the late nineteenth century. What especially distinguishes the medieval period is the prevailing disintegration and instability compared with the "peace and tranquillity" with which the earlier Heian period had been identified, and the stable rule of the Tokugawa, who brought unity and relative peace to Japan at the end of the sixteenth century. Medieval Japan began and ended in protracted feudal warfare. Thus, despite our natural tendency to think of historical periods in terms of political unities or continuities like the Kamakura and Muromachi regimes, it is, rather, disunity and violent change that give this period its distinctive character.

Medieval literature sharply reflects the sudden transition that Japan underwent in the eleventh and twelfth centuries. Whether in the first romantic tales of the epic wars that loosed this fury over the land or in the more contemplative and still highly refined art of the Nō that flourished during the fourteenth century, there is an intense awareness of the tragedy of life. In religion, too, we see a deepening of that pessimism toward the world that had always pervaded Buddhism.

Intellectually and emotionally, the tone of the medieval age was set by the Mahāyāna Buddhist belief in *mappō* or the "end of the Law." According to this belief, the world would pass through three ages from the time of Gautama Buddha, in around 500 B.C.E., an age of the flourishing of the Buddhist Law; an age of the decline of the Law; and, finally, the age of *mappō*, the "end of the Law." The Japanese calculated the first age to last one thousand years and the second, five hundred years. They believed that the first age, the age of the flourishing of the Law, ended in 552, the year the *Chronicles of Japan* gives for the introduction of Buddhism to Japan from Korea, and that the second age, the age of the decline of the Law, would yield to the age of *mappō* a half millennium later, in 1052.

Changes in both the capital and the provinces of Japan in the late eleventh century convinced many at the time, especially courtiers, that the age of *mappō* had indeed begun. The Fujiwara regents, politically supreme at court for two centuries and by this time regarded as second only to the emperors as custodians of traditional court authority and order, were increasingly challenged for their conduct of government by retired emperors (*in*) and others; and warrior chieftains, including those of the Minamoto (or Genji) and Taira (or Heike) clans, began establishing regional military hegemonies that threatened the authority of the court's provincial officialdom. A century later, in a series of armed conflicts from 1156 until 1185, when the military under the Minamoto founded Japan's first warrior government, the Kamakura shogunate (1185–1333), and ushered in the medieval age, the rise of warriors to power was seen as an inevitable result of the workings of *mappō*. Thus the priest historian Jien, writing in *Gukanshō* about the final Minamoto victory over the Taira at the naval battle of Dannoura in 1185, in which the child emperor Antoku drowned and one of the three objects of the Imperial Regalia, the sword, was also lost to sea, observed: "[Since] soldiers have emerged for the purpose of protecting the sovereign, the Imperial Sword turned its protective function over to soldiers and disappeared into the sea."[1] In the age of *mappō*, Jien informs us, emperors could no longer

---

1. Brown and Ishida, trans., *The Future and the Past*, p. 144.

rely on the traditional sources of protection of the state, symbolized by the Imperial Sword, but were obligated to accept the guardianship of members of the newly ascendant warrior class.

In medieval literature, *mappō* thought gave rise to a heightened sensitivity to that most fundamental of Buddhist principles, the impermanance (*mujō*) of all things. Manifested in various forms, impermanance became the theme of much of the age's prose and poetry. Expressions of this can be found, for example, in the opening lines of two of the best-known prose works of the early medieval age, *An Account of My Hut* (*Hōjōki*) and *The Tale of the Heike* (*Heike monogatari*):

> The flow of the river is ceaseless and its water is never the same. The bubbles that float in the pools, now vanishing, now forming, are not of long duration: so in the world are man and his dwellings. It might be imagined that the houses, great and small, which vie roof against proud roof in the capital remain unchanged from one generation to the next, but when we examine whether this is true, how few are the houses that were there of old (*An Account of My Hut*).[2]

and

> The sound of the bell of the Gion Temple tolls of the impermanance of all things, and the hue of the Sala tree's blossoms reveals the truth that those who flourish must fade. The proud ones do not last forever, but are like the dream of a spring night. Even the mighty will perish, just like dust before the wind (*The Tale of the Heike*).[3]

The Tale of the Heike is the finest product of a genre of literature known as "war tales" (*gunki mono*) that first appeared with the emergence of the warrior class itself in the mid-Heian period and reached its highest flourishing in the Kamakura and early Muromachi periods. Suffused with a darkly pessimistic and fatalistic sense of decline and disaster, the *Heike* is at the same time a celebration of warriors and their way of life. In contrast to the still atmosphere, the gentle sophistication, and the refinement of life expressed in Heian courtly writing, the *Heike* and other war tales depict a world of turbulence, danger, and brutality that inspired in some a new sense of realism and bold adventure but that produced in others, especially those identified with the old regime or imbued with the old culture, a sense of shock and impending doom, often coupled with a nostalgic yearning for the past.

---

2. Keene, *Anthology of Japanese Literature*, p. 197.
3. Quoted in Varley, *Warriors of Japan*, p. 85.

Yearning for the past became a powerful sentiment for many during medieval times. In particular, people looked back to what they regarded as the "golden age" of the mid-Heian period, when the Fujiwara were at the height of their power and such classics of courtly literature as *Kokinshū*, *The Tales of Ise*, and *The Tale of Genji* were either compiled or written. Although the theme of nostalgic yearning can be found in much medieval writing, it was probably most movingly and profoundly depicted in the plays of the Nō theater, which was created in the late fourteenth and early fifteenth centuries. By means especially of the "ghostly dream" play, Zeami and other playwrights of the Nō were able to evoke with haunting intensity the ghosts or spirits of both real people and fictional characters (e.g., the Shining Genji) from the past.

Yet in religion, as in Japanese society as a whole, on the threshold of death appeared new life. If the collapse of the old order brought new blood and more vigorous leaders on the scene and if the eclipse of the aristocratic Kyoto court signified a greater participation by the provinces in the national life, so too in these circumstances the new forms of religion arose from the old, responding to the needs of the country as a whole. Thus, for example, the sense of despair, of the inability to rise above the evils of the times, was met by a powerful movement offering salvation through faith alone, which brought the hope of new life and light to thousands of Japanese untouched by the older forms of Buddhism. The cult of Amida, who shared the bliss of his Pure Land with those who put their trust in him, is the best example of this tendency. The teaching of Nichiren, too, emphasizes faith in the Lotus Sūtra as the key to salvation, and it was a notable trait of both these movements that their leaders sought converts among the humblest folk in the farthest reaches of Japan, especially in the near wilderness of the north.

This process of popularization was in one sense a direct and natural development of the practices encouraged by Esoteric Buddhism as an adaptation to different religious situations and mentalities. What differentiates the new forms from the old is the marked simplification for ease of practice, during which several of the new movements emphasized exclusive devotion to one object of worship and concentration on one form of practice.

The invocation of Amida had been one of many esoteric practices available in the Heian period, and the Lotus Sūtra so intently invoked by Nichiren had offered many objects of worship and an unlimited number of adaptive means for attaining Buddhahood. In this sense, both the exoteric and esoteric forms of Heian Buddhism were universalistic, embracing any and all gates (*ichimon fumon*). By contrast, the new movements of the Kamakura period were selective and exclusive. They stressed only one form of religion as correct and orthodox. Tending to be intolerant of competing schools, they became increasingly partisan and sectarian. Indeed, such exclusionism was manifested also in Shinto, as the easy accommodationism of Dual Shinto was challenged by the more sectarian form of the "one and only" (*yui-itsu*) Prime Shinto. Exceptions to this trend remained, of course, among those who held nostalgically to the older, more generous ideal, but as conservatives conducting a rear guard defense of an irretrievable past, they tended to be less popular and dynamic.

In this way, parallel to the political process by which the attempted establishment of a universal state in the Nara and early Heian periods yielded to a phase marked by the increasing dispersion, decentralization, and privatization of power in the medieval age, religion moved from the universal—understood as catholic, all-embracing, and inclusive—to a common ground that was paradoxically more particularistic and partisan, inspired more by personal faith than committed to any public philosophy. In Zen Buddhism, which insisted on individual effort rather than a reliance on faith in something external, we find evidences of both tendencies. Aristocratic though it was in spirit and intimately associated with the most sophisticated arts of the Ashikaga period, Zen not only embodied the vigorous simplicity of this age but also, in the most concrete and practical manner, raised to a new artistic dignity the humblest activities of the Japanese household: the preparing of tea, the arranging of flowers, the designing of house and garden, and many other everyday pursuits of the medieval Japanese.

From this process emerged, for example, the rules for the tea ceremony, which were derived from Zen monastic rules; the ceremony's setting, the tea room, which was modeled on a type of room found in Zen temples; and many of the articles used for preparing and serving the tea and for decoration during a ceremony, including ceramicware, lacquerware, and ink painting, which were brought from China primarily by Zen monks. In this way, the spirit of the tea ceremony became increasingly that of Zen, as expressed in the saying "tea and Zen have the same flavor (*cha-Zen ichimi*)."

Thus while making a place for itself in the new society, religion contributed to the development of a new and more broadly based culture. To call this trend "democratic" would be going too far, though, since it was not attended by any significant increase in people's political freedom or activity as a whole. Nevertheless, the spread of popular religions no doubt contributed to a general uplift of the people and a sense of unity transcending class distinctions. At the same time, we already have in the medieval period—from Nichiren and from the exponent of nationalism linked to Shinto traditions, Kitabatake Chikafusa—intimations of a special destiny reserved for the Japanese people, an idea that gained potency in the next age.

Another important development of the medieval age was the renewal of trade with and cultural borrowing from China. The last Japanese mission to the Tang dynasty had been dispatched by the Heian court in 838. Thereafter, official (court) contact with China ceased for nearly three centuries. In the mid-twelfth century, as the warrior house of Taira rose to prominence in the service of retired emperors and secured extensive estate holdings in the western provinces, it began sending ships abroad and even opened a quasi-official trading relationship with the Southern Song. This Taira initiative marked the start of a new period of trade with and borrowing from China that lasted through the medieval age. Only during the Mongol invasions and their aftermath in the late thirteenth and early fourteenth centuries were this trade and borrowing seriously interrupted. In the early fifteenth century, the third Ashikaga shogun, Yoshimitsu, institutionalized ties with China by establishing a tributary relationship, even though by doing so he contravened an almost millennium-old policy of avoiding status inferiority vis-à-vis China in international relations. Among the things that the Japanese imported from China during the medieval centuries were printed books (brought over in quantity to form the nuclei of medieval Japan's libraries), including the texts of Neo-Confucianism, which became the basis for a new intellectual movement in the succeeding period.

Chapter 10

AMIDA, THE PURE LAND, AND THE RESPONSE OF
THE OLD BUDDHISM TO THE NEW

By the end of the Heian period in the twelfth century, Buddhism was firmly established in the institutions and teachings of the Nara schools and Esoteric Buddhism, which by that time included both Tendai and Shingon. Taken as a whole, this Buddhist establishment was richly diverse, and even though each sect could claim to have its own unique characteristics, together they also had much in common. One of these common elements was the belief in gaining rebirth in one of the many Pure Lands that were part of the Buddhist cosmology. Each Pure Land was presided over by a buddha or bodhisattva and represented a perfect existence for those fortunate enough to be reborn there rather than in some lower level of transmigration. Rebirth in a Pure Land was as much desired as descent into one of many hells was feared.

Whether one was to be reborn in a Pure Land or in hell depended on one's karmic record, and accumulating merit through good works was thus of critical importance. This could be accomplished through actions ranging from ordinary moral behavior to ritual performances such as chanting sūtras, copying sūtras, sponsoring rituals, or giving alms. Popular among lay persons because of its simplicity was recitation of the name of Amida Buddha, who presided over a Pure Land known as the Western Paradise. The chant was the repetition of the phrase *namu Amida Butsu*, which simply means "praise be to Amida Buddha." Popular in China as well, this practice was known as the *nembutsu*, a term that originally meant meditating on Amida but later was understood primarily as reciting his name. Promoted by all schools of Buddhism, especially Tendai, the *nembutsu* was thought to be more efficacious with greater numbers of recitations, and exaggerated accounts tell of pious lay persons seeking maximum merit reciting the *nembutsu* up to a million times a day. With enough merit accumulated, one could be assured of being reborn in Amida's Pure Land; the only final condition needing to be fulfilled was death.

Even though the final reward of rebirth in paradise would come only after death, this objective was much easier to hold to than was the ideal goal of enlightenment or, as Kūkai put it, becoming a buddha in this existence. Becoming a buddha required serious practice and meditation informed by complex doctrines difficult to master. Chinese Pure Land Buddhists had already distinguished between the difficult path of the sages seeking enlightenment and the easy path of the Pure Land believers seeking rebirth in paradise. In noting the contrast between the easy and difficult paths, however, the Chinese masters did not see them as mutually exclusive or entirely contradictory: the recitation of the *nembutsu* was an excellent aid to meditation, not a rejection of it. Pure Land thought also emphasized reliance on the saving power of the Buddha rather than on individual effort, but as has already been seen in Kūkai's explanation of *kaji* (divine grace humanly received), the relationship between the two is complementary rather than contradictory.

This traditional understanding of Pure Land Buddhism had effective proponents such as Kūya (903–972), Genshin (942–1017), and Ryōnin (1072–1132), all monks of the Tendai school. Stressing the simplicity of reciting the *nembutsu*, Kūya propagated it in the streets and marketplaces. Dancing through the city streets with a tinkling bell hanging from his neck, Kūya called out the name of Amida and sang simple ditties of his own composition, such as

Hito tabi mo	He never fails
Namu Amida bu to	To reach the Lotus Land of Bliss
Yū hito no	Who calls,
Hasu utena ni	If only once,
Noboranu wa nashi.	The name of Amida.

And

Gokuraku wa	A far, far distant land
Harukeki hodo to	Is Paradise,
Kikishi kado	I've heard them say;
Tsutomete itaru	But those who want to go
Tokoro narikeri.	Can reach there in a day.

In the marketplaces, all kinds of people joined Kūya in his dance and sang out the invocation to Amida, *namu Amida Butsu*. Then, when a great epidemic struck the capital, Kūya proposed that these same people join him in building an image of Amida in a public square, saying that common folk could equal the achievement of their rulers, who had built the Great Buddha of Nara, if they cared to try. In country districts, he built bridges and dug wells for the people where these were needed, and to show that no one was to be excluded from the blessings of Paradise, he traveled into regions inhabited by the Ainu and, for the first time, brought to many of them the evangel of Buddhism.

Just as Kūya came to be called "the saint of the streets" for his dancing, so another Tendai monk, Ryōnin (1072–1132), later became known for his propagation of the *nembutsu* through popular songs. Ryōnin's great success in this medium reflected his own vocal talents and his mastery of traditional liturgical music. At the same time, his advocacy of the *nembutsu* chant reflected the influence on him of Tendai and Kegon doctrine. From the former philosophy, he drew the idea that "one act is all acts, and all acts are one act." From the Flower Wreath (Kegon) Sūtra, he took the doctrine of the interrelation and interdependence of all things: "one man is all men, and all men are one man." Joining these to faith in Amida, Ryōnin produced the "circulating *nembutsu*" or "*nembutsu* in communion" (*yūzū nembutsu*). That is, if one person calls the name of Amida, it will benefit all persons; one person may share in the invocations of all others. Spreading this simple but all-embracing idea in a musical form, Ryōnin became an evangelist on a vast scale. Among his early converts were court ladies, and Emperor Toba was so deeply impressed that he gave Ryōnin a bell made from one of his own mirrors. With this, Ryōnin traveled the length and breadth of the land, inviting everyone to join him in the "circulating *nembutsu*" and asking them to sign their names in a roster of participants. According to tradition, the entries accumulated during a lifetime of evangelizing added up to the modest figure of 3,282.

In the early thirteenth century, shortly after the founding of the Kamakura shogunate, there appeared a Tendai monk, Hōnen, who rejected traditional Pure Land Buddhism in favor of a bold, new interpretation that became the basis of his new school of Pure Land Buddhism (Jōdo-shū). Although Hōnen (1133–1212) was a learned monk trained at Mount Hiei, because this was a time at which it was widely believed that Buddhist teaching and practice had entered an age of decline (*mappō*), he no longer thought that full enlightenment was a practical possibility, and he explicitly rejected even the aspiration toward enlightenment (*bodaishin*), which had long been regarded as the essential first step toward Buddhist liberation. Hōnen's rejection of traditional practice was sweeping, and he declared that except for the *nembutsu*, all other practices were useless.

Hōnen was keenly aware of how radical his teaching was and therefore kept it a closely guarded secret. Publicly, he presented himself as a traditional monk; privately, he had concluded that traditional Buddhism was no longer valid for the conditions of his time. For more than twenty years, he led this double life until finally in 1198, he committed his thoughts to writing. The result was *Choosing the Recitation of the Buddha's Name According to the Original Vow* (*Senchaku hongan nembutsu shū*), a book that he insisted on circulating only within his small band of disciples. Although word of it leaked out, causing a group of traditional monks to petition the imperial court to ban his teachings, *Choosing the Original Vow* was for the most part kept a secret and did not become widely available until 1212, the year that Hōnen died.

The publication of *Choosing the Original Vow* caused a great uproar. Hōnen's secret was now in the public domain for all to read, and many were surprised to learn that the monk whom they thought quite traditional was really quite radical. Hōnen's teaching was indeed revolutionary, and *Choosing the Original Vow* states his manifesto in no uncertain terms: throw out all traditional practices except for one, the recitation of the name of Amida Buddha. With a clear awareness of the long history of Buddhism, Hōnen argued that the historical Buddha was long gone and that his enlightenment was impossible to attain. In such a situation, it was useless to meditate, to follow the monastic rules, to chant the sūtras, to make images and statues, and to make a vow to become enlightened. Only one practice was effective in these terrible times, and that was reciting the name of Amida: "praise be to Amida Buddha."

Hōnen's argument is quite simple, but his rhetoric is complex and subtle. Since innovation in a religious tradition that valued transmission of past truths was an invitation to the charge of heresy, Hōnen had to show that his new interpretation really was an old doctrine, that is, that it had already been articulated by past masters. The problem, of course, was that Hōnen's message was in fact new and thus could not be found in the writings of earlier teachers. How, then, was he to collect passages from previous writers and make them support his teaching? He did this by taking passages maintaining that the recitation of Amida's name was the *best* practice and arguing that this meant it was the *only* practice. If something is the best of the lot, then why not throw out the rest? There was a certain persuasiveness to his argument, and many people accepted his claim that the exclusive practice of reciting Amida's name had the sanction of past tradition.

Hōnen's argument did not pass without vigorous debate, however. His most vociferous critic was Myōe (1173–1232), a monk whose thought and practice crossed sectarian boundaries. Myōe attacked *Choosing the Original Vow* by writing *Smashing the Evil Chariot* (*Zaijarin*), in which he charged Hōnen with betraying the Pure Land tradition itself and also with no longer being a Buddhist. As a traditional Buddhist committed to a wide variety of religious disciplines, Myōe was shocked to read in *Choosing the Original Vow* of Hōnen's rejection of all practices except for the recitation of Amida's name. Against Hōnen's claim that traditional practices were taught in order to be discarded, Myōe contended that instead, these practices, especially the vow to attain enlightenment, were an integral part of practices for rebirth into the Pure Land, of which recitation was but one method. Against Hōnen's advocacy of the exclusive *nembutsu*, Myōe defended a pluralism of practices.

Although he was conservative, Myōe also saw the need to create simpler forms of practice. His own innovation was a simple chant, much like the *nembutsu*, that sang the praises of the Three Treasures (the Buddha, the dharma, and the sangha) and the aspiration toward enlightenment. Simplification, he was convinced, need not require rejecting traditional practices and, in fact, should be centered on them. Because other monks from the older sects were likewise active in the revival of traditional Buddhism, we should not let the remarkable developments in Pure Land, Nichiren, and Zen thought and practice obscure the activities and achievements of the Tendai, Shingon, and Nara schools. As a sect, Shingon, for instance, underwent its greatest expansion during the Kamakura period and was far from being effete or eclipsed by newer movements. Just as historians now recognize that court and bakufu, aristocrats and warriors, and Kyoto and Kamakura were equally influential in political circles, we should remember that many monks from the old establishment were just as active as the founders of new schools. In addition to Myōe, who worked to revive Kegon, the Tendai monk Jien (1155–1225) wrote the *Gukanshō*, an innovative history of Japan; the Hossō school's Jōkei (1155–1213) revived the disciplinary precepts; the Shingon monk Kakukai (1142–1223) argued that the Pure Land could be realized in this life; and another Shingon monk, Eizon (1201–1290), simplified the precepts for lay persons and carried out many social welfare projects.

As radical as Hōnen was in his innovations, it was Shinran (1173–1262) and Ippen (1239–1289), two of his spiritual descendants, who pushed the issue of simplicity even beyond Hōnen's position. Although they never disputed Hōnen's teachings openly, their interpretations differed from his understanding of the *nembutsu* as a means to rebirth that required human initiative and effort. While studying at Mount Hiei as a young monk, Shinran underwent a spiritual crisis in which he came to doubt the efficacy of his own efforts to gain perfection. Morality was of limited effect, as were ritual actions; nothing, it seemed, could eradicate the deep-seated imperfection of being human. When Shinran left Mount Hiei and the path of the sages, he turned to Hōnen's new teaching of the exclusive *nembutsu*, but he came to see that even chanting Amida's name was a matter of individual effort and therefore of limited effect in gaining full salvation. His dilemma was resolved when he realized that salvation was not won through human effort but was granted by Amida Buddha, the compassionate one who vowed to save all people, regardless of their moral standing or religious achievements. By rejecting all practices performed through one's own effort (*jiriki*), Shinran went even further than his teacher by suggesting that chanting the *nembutsu* should not result from deliberative effort but from the saving action granted by Amida. Monastic discipline and other religious rituals were no longer necessary, and while in exile with Hōnen, who had been banished to the northern province of Echigo for his heterodox teaching, Shinran openly married a woman and later had children by her. "If even good people can be reborn in the Pure Land," he said, "how much more the wicked man."

Despite his sweeping rejection of human effort, Shinran still retained the religious virtue of faith (*shinjin*). Instead of enlightenment, and even more than rebirth in the Pure Land, the objective in Shinran's religion was to have faith in Amida's power and compassion to save one despite oneself. The ideal believer was not characterized by doctrinal learning or religious discipline but by complete trust in Amida's vow. Although Shinran understood that his ideal of pure faith was actually more difficult to hold to than it would be to perform some kind of practice, it still was a goal easily understood and propagated. In his own lifetime, Shinran did not attempt to organize a new sect, but he did establish numerous religious communities bound together by loyalty to him and his teachings.

Ippen studied in Kyoto under one of Hōnen's leading disciples and later returned to his home in Shikoku, where he married and carried out his duties as both a monk and a head of a household. In 1263, at the age of twenty-five, he came to doubt the spiritual quality of his householder's life and, thinking that he should go to the mountains to practice asceticism, set out on a pilgrimage that took him to Zenkōji, a popular destination for pilgrims in what is now Nagano City. He returned home still imbued with the idea of becoming a recluse and thereafter set out on several more pilgrimages, mostly to mountainous areas. During his travels, he devised a means of propagating the *nembutsu* by asking people to recite the *nembutsu* just "once" (*ippen*) and, when they did so, giving them a *fuda*, a paper talisman on which was written the Chinese characters for "na-mu A-mi-da Butsu." Like Ryōnin before him, Ippen sought to propagate the *nembutsu* to as many people as possible, and the names in his registry numbered several hundred thousand.

The talismans distributed by Ippen signified assurance that the recipient was sure to be born in the Pure Land. Ippen's standard appeal was to ask each person to accept the talisman, awaken one moment of faith, and utter the *nembutsu*. While at the Kumano Shrine on one of his many travels, Ippen made his appeal to a monk, but the monk surprised Ippen by refusing the offer on the grounds that he did not feel the arising of faith. Ippen insisted that the monk accept the talisman even if he lacked faith, and the monk obliged, but Ippen wondered whether what he had done was effective and legitimate. That night, the Kumano deity appeared to him and told him that rebirth was not determined by his act of propagation or the faith of the recipients but by the decisive power of Amida. Thereafter, Ippen distributed his talismans without regard for whether people had faith. Ippen thus represents the furthest point of development among the Pure Land innovators: Hōnen rejected all practices but the *nembutsu*; Shinran rejected the *nembutsu* of self-power but retained the importance of faith in Amida's other-power; and Ippen, in a supreme act of faith, dispensed with faith as a spiritual requirement. During the last days of his life, Ippen burned the sūtras that he possessed and declared that all of the Buddha's teachings were epitomized in the *nembutsu*.

The tendency to reduce Pure Land Buddhism to its barest essentials challenged those who tried to institutionalize paths that rejected organized rituals and practices. Ippen's heirs successfully developed his Time (Ji) sect of Pure Land Buddhism through a strict system of loyalty to the head of the school, who was regarded as the incarnation of Amida and therefore could grant—or deny—salvation. As Amida, he also was the object of faith and gratitude. Of Shinran's lineal descendants who organized the True Pure Land Sect (Jōdo Shinshū), the most important was Rennyo (1415–1499), who, in an age torn by conflicting feudal loyalties, attracted adherents with his clear explanation of Shinran's teachings, specific rules to live by, and loyalty. Shinran had urged his followers to make every act an act of thanksgiving to Amida, and now this sense of obligation was redirected to Shinran's heirs, who were not, however, seen as incarnations of Amida.

Blessed with the charisma of a good preacher and effective leader, Rennyo also won the respect and allegiance of many for his common touch characterized by a personal openness and skill at explaining things clearly. His teaching emphasized an egalitarianism that recognized no fundamental difference between men and women, young and old, upper and lower classes, and good and evil. Even hunters and fishermen, who, according to Genshin's *Essentials of Salvation*, were condemned to hell for taking life, were saved by Amida's universal compassion. Rennyo held true to Shinran's teaching that reciting the *nembutsu* was not a means for gaining salvation and emphasized that it was an expression of gratitude for the salvation already granted by Amida despite one's faults and through no merit of one's own. But unlike Hōnen and Shinran, who felt that the *nembutsu* and faith were exclusively sufficient, Rennyo's reliance on Amida's broadly applicable compassion allowed him to tolerate social and religious conventions that his predecessors did not think necessary. *Rennyo's Rules* codified this tolerance and simplicity for his followers and laid a practical foundation for what is today the largest institutional system of temples in Japan.

TRADITIONAL PURE LAND BUDDHISM

GENSHIN: *THE ESSENTIALS OF SALVATION*

A monk of the Tendai school, Genshin promoted the practice of the *nembutsu* as an appropriate means for those who are not learned or wise enough to gain rebirth in the Pure Land. His *Essentials of Salvation* (*Ōjōyōshū*) became popular for its graphic descriptions of the glories of the Pure Land and the torments of hell. The following excerpts are from the initial chapters in the first two divisions of the ten cited by the author. The scriptural authorities cited by Genshin are deleted from the text.

The teaching and practice which leads to birth in Paradise is the most important thing in this impure world during these degenerate times.[1] Monks and laymen, men of high or low station, who will not turn to it? But the literature of the exoteric and the esoteric teachings of Buddha are not one in text, and the practices of one's work in this life in its ritualistic and philosophic aspects are many. These are not difficult for men of keen wisdom and great diligence, but how can a stupid person such as I achieve this knowledge? Because of this I have chosen the one gate of the *nembutsu* to salvation. I have made selections from the important sūtras and shāstras and have set them forth so that they may be readily understood and their disciplines easily practiced. In all there are ten divisions, divided into three volumes. The first is the corrupt life which one must shun, the second is the Pure Land for which one should seek, the third is the proof of the existence of the Pure Land, the fourth is the correct practice of *nembutsu*, the fifth is the helpful means of practicing the *nembutsu*, the sixth is the practice of *nembutsu* on special occasions, the seventh is the benefit resulting from *nembutsu*, the eighth is the proof of the benefit accruing from *nembutsu* alone, the ninth is the conduct leading to birth in Paradise, and the tenth comprises questions and answers to selected problems. These I place to the right of where I sit lest I forget them.

The first division, the corrupt land which one must shun, comprises the three realms[2] in which there is no peace. Now, in order to make clear the external appearances of this land, it is divided into seven parts: (1) hell; (2) hungry demons; (3) beasts; (4) fighting demons; (5) man; (6) Deva; and (7) a conclusion. The first of these, hell, is further divided into eight parts: (1) the hell of repeated misery; (2) the hell of the black chains; (3) the hell of mass suffering; (4) the hell of wailing; (5) the hell of great wailing; (6) the hell of searing heat; (7) the hell of great searing heat, and (8) the hell of incessant suffering.

The hell of repeated misery is one thousand *yojanas*[3] beneath the Southern Continent[4] and is ten thousand *yojanas* in length and breadth. Sinners here are always possessed of the desire to do each other harm. Should they by chance

---

1. A reference to *mappō*, the last of the three periods of Buddhist Law, that of degeneration and destruction of the Law that extends for countless years. The first period, *shōbō*, the period of the true Law, lasted for one thousand years. The second period, *zōbō*, the period of the simulated doctrine, endured for five hundred years.

2. Past, present, and future.

3. The distance that an army can march in one day.

4. India and adjoining regions.

see each other, they behave as does the hunter when he encounters a deer. With iron claws they slash each other's bodies until blood and flesh are dissipated and the bones alone remain. Or else the hell-wardens, taking in their hands iron sticks and poles, beat the sinners' bodies from head to foot until they are pulverized like grains of sand. Or else, with a sword of awful sharpness, they cut their victims' bodies in regular pieces as the kitchen worker slices the flesh of fish. And then a cool wind arises, and blowing, returns the sinners to the same state in which they were at the outset. Thereupon they immediately arise and undergo torment identical to that which they had previously suffered. Elsewhere it is said that a voice from the sky above calls to the sentient beings to revive and return to their original state. And again, it is said that the hell-wardens beat upon the ground with iron pitchforks calling upon the sinners to revive. I cannot tell in detail of the other sufferings similar to those already told. . . .

Fifty years of human life is equivalent to one day and night in the realm of the Four Deva Kings,[5] and there life lasts five hundred years. The life in the realm of the Four Deva Kings is the equivalent of one day and night in this hell, and here life lasts five hundred years. People who have taken the life of a living creature fall into this hell. . . .

Outside the four gates of this hell are sixteen separate places which are associated with this hell. The first is called the place of excrement. Here, it is said, there is intensely hot dung of the bitterest of taste, filled with maggots with snouts of indestructible hardness. The sinner here eats of the dung and all the assembled maggots swarm at once for food. They destroy the sinner's skin, devour his flesh and suck the marrow from his bones. People who at one time in the past killed birds or deer fall into this hell. Second is the place of the turning sword. It is said that iron walls ten yojanas in height surround it and that a terrible and intense fire constantly burns within. The fire possessed by man is like snow when compared to this. With the least of physical contact, the body is broken into pieces the size of mustard-seeds. Hot iron pours from above like a heavy rainfall, and in addition, there is a forest of swords, with blades of exceptional keenness, and these swords, too, fall like rain. The multitude of agonies is in such variety that it cannot be borne. Into this place fall those who have killed a living being with concupiscence. Third is the place of the burning vat. It is said that the sinner is seized and placed in an iron vat, and boiled as one would cook beans. Those who in the past have taken the life of a living creature, cooked it, and eaten of it fall into this hell. Fourth is the place of many agonies. In this hell there are a trillion different numberless tortures which cannot be explained in detail. Those who at some time in the past bound men with rope, beat men with sticks, drove men and forced them to make long journeys, threw men down steep places, tortured men with smoke, frightened

---

5. The lowest of the six heavens in the world of desire.

small children, and in many other ways brought suffering to their fellow man fall into this hell. Fifth is the place of darkness. It is said that here is pitch blackness that burns constantly with a dark flame. A powerful and intense wind blows against the adamantine mountains, causing them to grind against each other and to destroy each other, so that the bodies of the sinners in between are broken into fragments like grains of sand. Then a hot wind arises which cuts like a sharply honed sword. To this place fall those who have covered the mouths and noses of sheep or who have placed turtles between two tiles and crushed them to death. Sixth is the place of joylessness. Here, it is said, is a great fire which burns intensely night and day. Birds, dogs, and foxes with flaming beaks whose intensely evil cries cause the sinner to feel the greatest of fear come constantly to eat of the sinner, whose bones and flesh lie in great confusion. Hard-snouted maggots course about inside the bone and eat of the marrow. Those who once blew on shells, beat drums, made frightening sounds, or killed birds and animals fall to this hell. Seventh is the place of extreme agony. It is located beneath a precipitous cliff where a fire of iron burns continuously. People who once killed living creatures in a fit of debauchery descend to this hell.

The second division is the Pure Land towards which one must aspire. The rewards of Paradise are of endless merit. Should one speak of them for a hundred *kalpas* or even for a thousand *kalpas*, one would not finish describing them; should one count them or give examples of them, there would still be no way to know of them. At present, ten pleasures in praise of the Pure Land will be explained, and they are as but a single hair floating upon the great sea.

First is the pleasure of being welcomed by many saints. Second is the pleasure of the first opening of the lotus.[6] Third is the pleasure of obtaining in one's own body the ubiquitous supernatural powers of a Buddha. Fourth is the pleasure of the realm of the five wonders. Fifth is the pleasure of everlasting enjoyment. Sixth is the pleasure of influencing others and introducing them to Buddhism. Seventh is the pleasure of assembling with the holy family. Eighth is the pleasure of beholding the Buddha and hearing the Law. Ninth is the pleasure of serving the Buddha according to the dictates of one' own heart. Tenth is the pleasure of progressing in the way of Buddhahood. . . .

[Among these] first is the pleasure of being welcomed by many saints. Generally when an evil man's life comes to an end, the elements of wind and fire leave first, and as they control movement and heat, great suffering is felt. When a good man dies, earth and water depart first, and as they leave gently, they cause no pain. How much less painful then must be the death of a man who has accumulated merit through *nembutsu*! The man who carries this teaching firmly in his mind for a long time feels a great rejoicing arise within him at the

---

6. The pleasure of being first born in this land.

approach of death. Because of his great vow, Amida Nyorai, accompanied by many bodhisattvas and hundreds of thousands of monks, appears before the dying man's eyes, exuding a great light of radiant brilliance. And at this time the great compassionate Kanzeon,[7] extending hands adorned with the hundred blessings and offering a jeweled lotus throne, appears before the faithful. The Bodhisattva Seishi and his retinue of numberless saints chant hymns and at the same time extend their hands and accept him among them. At this time the faithful one, seeing these wonders before his eyes, feels rejoicing within his heart and feels at peace as though he were entering upon meditation. Let us know then, that at the moment that death comes, though it be in a hut of grass, the faithful one finds himself seated upon a lotus throne. Following behind Amida Buddha amid the throng of bodhisattvas, in a moment's time he achieves birth in the Western Paradise. . . .

Second is the pleasure of the first opening of the lotus. After the believer is born into this land and when he experiences the pleasures of the first opening of the lotus, his joy becomes a hundred times greater than before. It is comparable to a blind man gaining sight for the first time, or to entering a royal palace directly after leaving some rural region. Looking at his own body, he sees it become purplish gold in color. He is gowned naturally in jeweled garments. Rings, bracelets, a crown of jewels, and other ornaments in countless profusion adorn his body. And when he looks upon the light radiating from the Buddha, he obtains pure vision, and because of his experiences in former lives, he hears the sounds of all things. And no matter what color he may see or what sound he may hear, it is a thing to marvel at. Such is the ornamentation of space above that the eye becomes lost in the traces of clouds. The melody of the wheel of the wonderful Law as it turns flows throughout this land of jeweled sound. Palaces, halls, forests, and ponds shine and glitter everywhere. Flocks of wild ducks, geese, and mandarin ducks fly about in the distance and near at hand. One may see multitudes from all the worlds being born into this land like sudden showers of rain. And one may see a throng of saints, numerous as the grains of sand in the Ganges, arriving from the many Buddha lands. There are some who climb within the palaces and look about in all directions. There are those who, mounted upon temples, dwell in space. Then again there are some who, living in the sky, recite the sutra and explain the Law. And again there are some who, dwelling in space, sit in meditation. Upon the ground and amid the forests there are others engaged in the same activities. And all about there are those who cross and bathe in the streams and those who walk among the palaces singing and scattering flowers and chanting the praises of the Tath-āgata. In this way the numberless celestial beings and saints pursue their own pleasures as they themselves desire. How indeed can one tell in detail of the

---

7. More commonly Kannon.

throng of incarnate Buddhas and bodhisattvas which fills this land like clouds of incense and flowers!

[From Yampolsky, *The Essentials of Salvation*, pp. 10–16, 90–94]

INNOVATORS OF THE NEW PURE LAND BUDDHISM

HŌNEN: *CHOOSING THE ORIGINAL VOW FOR THE RECITATION OF THE BUDDHA'S NAME (SENCHAKU HONGAN NEMBUTSU SHŪ)*

The following is an excerpt from chapter 4 of *Choosing the Original Vow*, which begins with a quotation from the Sūtra of Infinite Life that establishes three classes of people who will be reborn into the Pure Land by reciting the name of Amida. In addition to reciting Amida's name, all people, no matter what their class, should also perform other practices: renouncing the householder's life, casting off desires, making a vow to become enlightened, cultivating virtue, carving images, building temples, listening to sermons, and so forth. The sūtra thus seems to be contradicting Hōnen's call to reject these practices, and it is this issue that he addresses in a question-and-answer discussion defending his argument for throwing them out.

QUESTION: In the scriptural passage concerning the superior class of persons to be reborn in the Pure Land, there are other practices, such as rejecting the householder's life and casting off desires, which are mentioned besides the recitation of Amida's name. The passage concerning the mediocre class mentions the practices of building temples and carving statues. In the passage concerning the inferior class, the practice of making a vow to become enlightened is mentioned. Why, then, do you say that rebirth in the Pure Land is to be attained only through the recitation of Amida's name?

ANSWER: In his *Gateway to Meditating on the Teaching*, the Chinese Master Shandao says, "The first part of the last section of the Sūtra of Infinite Life says that all people have dissimilar capacities that can be classified into superior, mediocre, and inferior classes. In accordance with their capacities, the Buddha taught them to concentrate on reciting the name of the Buddha of Infinite Life. When those people are about to die, the Buddha will come with his holy retinue, greet them himself, and cause each and every one of them to be reborn in the Pure Land." It is in accordance with the meaning of Shandao's interpretation that I say that the three classes of people will all be reborn in the Pure Land by reciting the name of Amida.

QUESTION: This explanation still does not answer the above problem.

Why do you discard the other practices and speak only of reciting
Amida's name?

ANSWER: There are three ways of understanding this: (1) all of the other
practices were explained so that they could be discarded in favor of
reciting Amida's name; (2) all of the other practices were explained in
order to assist the practice of reciting Amida's name; and (3) all of the
other practices were explained in order to establish each of the three
classes of people according to the two approaches of reciting Amida's
name on the one hand and of all the other practices on the other.

1. When I say in the first case that the other practices were explained so that
they could be rejected in favor of reciting Amida's name, I am following the
interpretation of Shandao in the second volume of his *Commentary to the Sūtra
on Meditation*: "Although the benefits of both meditation and moral actions
have been taught since ancient times, the intention of the Buddha according
to his original vow was to make people recite the name of Amida Buddha with
single-minded devotion." Let me explain this further. Although the other practices such as making a vow to become enlightened were explained for the
superior class of people, the intention of the Buddha in accordance with his
previously mentioned original vow was simply to make all people concentrate
on reciting the name of Amida Buddha. There are no other practices in the
original vow. All three classes of people together rely on the original vow, and
therefore they call on the Buddha of Infinite Life with single-minded devotion.

"Single-minded" is a word used in contradistinction to double-minded and
triple-minded. This is much like, for example, the three kinds of temples in
India. In the first type of temple, there is only the single-minded practice of the
Great Vehicle (Mahāyāna); the Buddhism of the Small Vehicle (Hīnayāna) is
not taught there. In the second kind of temple, there is only the single-minded
practice of the Small Vehicle, and they do not study the teachings of the Great
Vehicle there. The third type of temple has the Great and the Small Vehicles;
and since both types of Buddhism are studied there, they are called temples for
joint practices. You should take note that in the Great Vehicle and the Small
Vehicle temples, the word "single-minded" is used, but in the temples for joint
practices the word "single-minded" is absent.

This is the same manner in which "single-minded" is used in the sūtra. If
we add the other practices to the recitation of Amida's name, it would no longer
be single-minded, and following the example of the temples, we would have to
refer to it as a joint practice. It is clear, then, from the reference to it as a single-
minded recitation that we cannot add to it the other practices. These other
practices were explained in the beginning, but in the end there is only the
single-minded devotion of recitation. Clearly, we know that since all other prac-

tices are to be discarded and only the recitation of Amida's name is to be used, it is called the single-minded practice. If this were not the case, then perhaps the word "single-minded" should be erased from the sūtra.

2. When I say in the second case that all of the other practices were explained to assist the practice of reciting Amida's name, I mean it in two ways. First, the recitation of Amida's name is assisted by the good works that are complementary, and second, it is assisted by the good works that are different from recitation.

In the first sense of what I mean, the complementary practices that assist the single practice of reciting Amida's name are given by Master Shandao in his *Commentary to the Sūtra on Meditation* as the five kinds of supplementary practices. They are explained in detail within the two categories of correct and miscellaneous practices.

In discussing the different practices that assist recitation, we must first establish that in consideration of the two categories of primary and supplementary practices for the superior class of people, calling on the Buddha of Infinite Life with single-minded devotion is the correct practice and is that which is assisted. Leaving home, renouncing desires, becoming a disciple, and making a vow to attain enlightenment are supplementary practices and are that which assist. This is to say that in the practices for rebirth in the Pure Land, the recitation of Amida's name is primary. Therefore, leaving home, renouncing desires, becoming a disciple, and making a vow to attain enlightenment are all for the sake of engaging in the recitation of Amida's name single-mindedly. These practices of leaving home, making a vow, and so forth all indicate the first point of departure toward the recitation of Amida's name. The recitation of Amida's name is a long-term practice by which one does not go backward. How can it be hindered?

For the mediocre people, there are the practices of building temples, carving images, hanging banners, lighting lamps, scattering flowers, offering incense, and so forth. These assist the practice of reciting Amida's name. This is the understanding we see in the *Essentials of Salvation*, written by the monk Genshin, who speaks of selecting a proper place, furnishing it with ritual implements, and so forth as methods for assisting recitation. Those of inferior capacities can make vows to attain enlightenment or recite the name of Amida. The meaning of what is primary and what is supplementary should be understood as discussed previously.

3. When I say in the third case that all of the other practices were explained in order to establish each of the three classes of people according to the two approaches of reciting Amida's name, on the one hand, and of all the other practices, on the other, I first of all mean that the establishment of the three classes of people according to the practice of reciting Amida's name indicates

that everyone in the three classes is called upon to recite together the name of the Buddha of Infinite Life with single-minded devotion. This is the establishment of the three classes in accordance with the practice of reciting Amida's name. Therefore in the "Scriptural Support for the Recitation of Amida's Name" chapter in the *Essentials of Salvation*, Genshin says, "Although there is a range of differences from the deep to the shallow in the actions of the three classes of people as explained in the Sūtra of Infinite Life, they all share in common the calling upon the Buddha of Infinite Life with single-minded devotion."

The establishment of the three classes according to all of the other practices refers to practices such as making a vow to attain enlightenment that are common to all three classes. This is the establishment of the three classes according to all of the other practices. Therefore in the chapter on "Rebirth Through All of the Other Practices" in the *Essentials of Salvation*, Genshin says, "As explained in the Sūtra of Infinite Life, the three classes of people do not go beyond this."

Although these three classes are not the same, they share in common the single-minded recitation of Amida's name. In the first case, all of the other practices were explained for the sake of rejecting and establishing. In other words, all of the other practices were explained in order to be rejected so that the recitation of Amida's name could be established. In the second case, all of the other practices were explained for the sake of distinguishing between the primary and the supplementary. In other words, all of the other practices were explained as supplementary practices that would aid the primary practice of reciting Amida's name. In the third case, the other practices were explained so that the central and the peripheral could be distinguished. In other words, the two approaches of recitation, on the one hand, and all of the other practices, on the other, were explained, but recitation is central while the other practices are peripheral. Therefore all three classes of people share in common the practice of reciting the name of Amida.

It is difficult to ascertain which of these three cases takes precedence over the others. I appeal to all scholars who are inclined to accept or reject. If we follow Shandao, we would have to say that the first case takes precedence.

[Ishii Kyōdō, ed., *Shōwa shinshū Hōnen Shōnin zenshū*, pp. 322–323; GT]

THE ONE-PAGE TESTAMENT

Written by Hōnen, two days before he died, for a disciple who asked that he "write me something with your own hand that you think will be good for me, so that I may keep it as a memento." After Hōnen's death, this note was honored as his final testament and as a complete credo for the faithful.

The method of final salvation that I have propounded is neither a sort of meditation, such as has been practiced by many scholars in China and Japan, nor is it a repetition of the Buddha's name by those who have studied and understood the deep meaning of it. It is nothing but the mere repetition of the "*Namu Amida Butsu*," without a doubt of His mercy, whereby one may be born into the Land of Perfect Bliss. The mere repetition with firm faith includes all the practical details, such as the three-fold preparation of mind and the four practical rules. If I as an individual had any doctrine more profound than this, I should miss the mercy of the two Honorable Ones, Amida and Shāka, and be left out of the Vow of the Amida Buddha. Those who believe this, though they clearly understand all the teachings Shāka taught throughout his whole life, should behave themselves like simple-minded folk, who know not a single letter, or like ignorant nuns or monks whose faith is implicitly simple. Thus without pedantic airs, they should fervently practice the repetition of the name of Amida, and that alone.

[From Coates and Ishizuka, *Honen*, pp. 728–729]

THE LAMENTATION AND SELF-REFLECTION OF GUTOKU SHINRAN

Keenly aware of the personal flaws that make it impossible to save himself through the accumulation of merit, Shinran called himself Gutoku, the "Foolish Bald-headed One." This self-awareness of imperfection is at the heart of Shinran's religion of salvation by Amida's compassionate vow, and is understood to be part of the human condition shared by monks and commoners alike, who are criticized by Shinran not only for their moral failings but for worshipping Shinto deities as well.

Although I have entered the Pure Land path,
I remain incapable of true and genuine thoughts and feelings.
My very existence is pervaded by vanity and falsehood;
There is nothing at all of any purity of mind.

Towards others we each may seek to conduct ourselves
With the appearance of wisdom, virtue, and steadfastness,
But within us desire, rage, and deviousness are rife,
So that deceit in myriad forms permeates our existence.

We cannot put a stop to our evil nature;
Our own minds are like vipers and scorpions.
Even the good we may do is poisoned;
As practice, it must be called hollow and vain.

Being unrepentant and lacking in shame,
I have no mind of truth and sincerity.
And yet, because the Name has been given by Amida Buddha,
The universe is suffused with its virtues.

As one lacking even small love and small compassion,
I give not a thought to the good of others.
If not for the ship of Amida's Vow,
How could such a person cross beyond this ocean of pain?

With minds of malicious deceit, minds like vipers and scorpions,
There is no accomplishing good acts through self-power.
Unless we entrust ourselves to Amida's giving of virtue,
We will die having never known true shame or repentance.

As a sign of the deepening of the five defilements,
All the monks and laity of our times
In externals, display the manner of Buddhists,
While in their hearts, they embrace non-Buddhist teachings.

. . . .

Deeply saddening is it that in these times
Both the monks and laity in Japan,
While seeking to conform with Buddhist manner and deportment,
Worship gods and spirits of the heavens and earth.

[Translated by Dennis Hirota from *Shōzōmatsu wasan* in *Shinshû shōgyō zensho*,
vol. 2 (Kyoto: Ōyagi Kōbundō, 1941), pp. 527–529]

SHINRAN: A RECORD IN LAMENT OF DIVERGENCIES (*TANNISHŌ*)

This collection of sayings by Shinran is attributed to his disciple Yuienbō, who was concerned about the confusion and divergent understandings developing among Shinran's followers. Stating that rebirth in the Pure Land takes place "immediately" at the moment of faith in Amida's vow rather than after death, Shinran reiterates the possibility of salvation in this life for the evil as well as the good.

"Saved by the inconceivable working of Amida's Vow, I shall realize birth in the Pure Land": the moment you entrust yourself thus to the Vow, so that the mind set upon saying the Name (*nembutsu*) arises within you, you are brought to share in the benefit of being grasped by Amida, never to be abandoned.

Know that the Primal Vow of Amida makes no distinction between people young or old, good or evil; only the entrusting of yourself to it is essential. For it was made to save the person whose karmic evil is deep-rooted and whose blind passions abound.

Thus, entrusting yourself to the Primal Vow requires no performance for good, for no act can hold greater virtue than saying the Name. Nor is there need to despair of the evil you commit, for no act is so evil that it obstructs the working of Amida's Primal Vow.

Thus were his words. . . .

> Even a good person can attain birth in the Pure Land,
> so it goes without saying that an evil person will.

Though such is the truth, people commonly say, "Even an evil person attains birth, so naturally a good person will." This statement may seem well founded at first, but it runs counter to the meaning of the Other established through the Primal Vow. This is because a person who relies on the good that he does through self-power fails to entrust himself wholeheartedly to Other Power and therefore is not in accord with Amida's Primal Vow, but when he abandons his attachment to self-power and entrusts himself totally to Other Power, he will realize birth in the Pure land.

It is impossible for us, filled as we are with blind passions, to free ourselves from birth and death through any practice whatever. Sorrowing at this, Amida made the Vow, the essential intent of which is the attainment of Buddhahood by the person who is evil. Hence the evil person who entrusts himself to Other Power is precisely the one who possesses the true cause for birth.

Accordingly he said, "Even the virtuous man is born in the Pure Land, so without question is the man who is evil."

[From Hirota, trans., *Tannishō*, pp. 22–24]

RENNYO: RENNYO'S RULES

As the True Pure Land (Shinshū) movement spread through the creation of local congregations, each group developed rules of conduct to define proper belief and behavior. In 1473, Rennyo composed the following rules, which became the standard for all Shinshū communities to follow in their relationships with the rest of society. Whereas his predecessors framed their teachings in somewhat exclusive terms, Rennyo is noteworthy for his tolerant and compromising attitude, especially in regard to the Shinto deities and practices.

ITEMS TO BE PROHIBITED AMONG TRUE PURE LAND ADHERENTS

1. Do not denigrate the various *kami* or the Buddhas and Bodhisattvas.
2. Never slander the various teachings or the various schools.
3. Do not attack other schools by comparing them to the practices of our own school.
4. Though taboos (*monoimi*) are not something to be adhered to by Buddhists, observe them scrupulously before public officials and [members of] other schools.

5. Do not proclaim the Buddhist teachings while arbitrarily adding alongside them words that have not been handed down in our school.

6. As *nembutsu* adherents, do not denigrate the provincial governor (*shugo*) or the steward (*jitō*).

7. In a state of ignorance, do not display your own ideas to other schools or proclaim the teachings of your own school without any sense of discretion.

8. If you yourself are not yet established in faith (*anjin ketsujō*), do not proclaim the teachings of faith (*shinjin*) using words you have heard from other people.

9. Do not eat fish or fowl when you meet for *nembutsu* services.

10. On the day that you assemble for *nembutsu* services, do not drink liquor and lose your senses.

11. Among *nembutsu* adherents, indulgence in gambling is prohibited.

Concerning these eleven items, you should expel from your assembly any people who turn their backs on these regulations.

[Dobbins, *Jōdo Shinshū*, pp. 141–142]

NEMBUTSU AS GRATITUDE

In his many letters to his followers, Rennyo repeated the theme of the *nembutsu* as an expression of gratitude to Amida. Since salvation, which is affirmed through faith, is a gift of Amida, the only necessary response is thankfulness.

If we have deep faith in the principal vow of the Tathāgata Amida, if we rely with single and undivided heart on the compassionate vow of the one Buddha Amida, and if our faith is true at the very moment that we think of him to please save us, then we will definitely be received into the salvation of the Tathāgata. Over and above this, what should we take to be the meaning of reciting the *nembutsu*? It is a response coming from one's indebtedness [to the Buddha] (*goon hōsha*), thanking him that one is saved through birth in [the] Pure Land by the power of faith in the present. As long as we have life in us, we should say the *nembutsu*, thinking of it as a response of thankfulness. It should be said by the person of faith (*shinjin*) who is established in the faith (*anjin*) of our tradition.

[Dobbins, *Jōdo Shinshū*, p. 145]

IPPEN: SELECTIONS FROM *A HUNDRED SAYINGS*

Despite his conviction that Amida's compassion and the power of the *nembutsu* made religious practices and even faith unnecessary, Ippen was a prolific writer of aphorisms, sayings, and precepts that defined proper conduct for ordinary people. The tension between restrictive prescriptions and unrestrained freedom is a common theme for those whom Buddhist liberation still demands moral responsibility. Ippen's *Hundred Sayings* speaks to the side of an untrammeled freedom reminiscent of some types of Zen and Daoist emancipation.

> To reach the borders of the unconditioned
> Just let go! This is the real repayment of your debt of gratitude.
> Make an offering of your *nembutsu* chant
> To living beings everywhere.
> This is your eternal home;
> With no abode fixed in any place
> Your houses are many
> And keep you from being soaked by rain.
> . . .
> A single straw mat laid down
> Is not thought to be small.
> The rising sound of the *nembutsu*
> Is a dwelling where wicked thoughts do not arise.
> I have no use for practice halls
> Walking, standing, lying, or sitting
> Are all I need for reciting *namu Amida Butsu,*
> The central object of my devotion.
> Having no mind for profit or desire
> I am not a monk soliciting donations.
> Though I am not free from the four impurities of preaching,[8]
> I promise not to teach the dharma.
> . . .
> Were it not for the sake of all living beings
> There is no point to traveling about the world.
> On a pilgrimage to Kumano one year
> I worshiped at the Hall of Confirming Truth
> And received a revelation in my dream.
> Trusting in it I pass my days
> Not relying on it for my next life
> But for the equal benefit of all.

[From Ōhashi et al., eds., *Ippen Shonin goroku,* pp. 294–296; GT]

---

8. Including the claim to complete knowledge, deviating from the sūtras, doubting the teachers according to personal opinions, and preaching for personal gain.

THE REVIVAL OF EARLIER BUDDHISM

MYŌE: SMASHING THE EVIL CHARIOT

The new interpretations of Buddhism by Hōnen and other remarkable leaders of the Kamakura period were so unprecedented that they comprise what scholars call the New Buddhisms. Their challenge to the older Buddhisms of the Shingon, Tendai, and other schools did not, however, go unanswered, and the result was a renewed flaring of controversies and debates. When Hōnen died in 1212 and his *Choosing the Original Vow for the Recitation of the Buddha's Name* was made public, the reaction was swift. Myōe's primary criticism of Hōnen was that he rejected the aspiration or vow to gain enlightenment (*bodaishin*). Hōnen's *Choosing the Original Vow* was an "evil chariot" that had to be "smashed" because a religion without enlightenment as its goal could no longer be called Buddhism. In Myōe's view, Hōnen's understanding of the *nembutsu* was at odds with not only traditional Pure Land teachings but also Buddhism itself.

In the fifth section of this work, I will give my interpretation and detailed explanation of the passage from the *Commentary to the Sūtra on Meditation* in which the Chinese Pure Land master Shandao says that although the benefits of both meditation and moral actions have been taught since ancient times, the intention of the Buddha according to his original vow was to make people recite the name of Amida Buddha with single-minded devotion. At this point, let me speak in general terms and point out that the meditation of mindfulness on the Buddha is not taught solely in the *Sūtra on Meditation* but is widely praised in many other doctrinal writings. This meditative practice of the *nembutsu* is nothing short of being the most direct cause of rebirth into the Pure Land. The meaning of the term for meditation is as I have already dealt with earlier. Moral acts such as the three services of caring for others, following the precepts, and engaging in practices leading to enlightenment are not the same as the meditative practices. The meditation on the sun as taught in the *Sūtra on Meditation*, for instance, is a companion to the meditation of mindfulness on the Buddha.

Now one of the methods of practicing this meditation of mindfulness on the Buddha is to call on the name of Amida single-mindedly. This is as it is explained in the writings on the wisdom of Mañjushrī. This is also explained in terms of all methods which are useful aids. What is mentioned here as single-minded recitation, however, is a practice that succeeds only by means of making the vow to attain enlightenment (*bodaishin*). If you separate single-minded recitation from the vow for enlightenment, then it will become entirely meaningless. Therefore all of the sections of the *Sūtra of Infinite Life*, which explain the single-minded recitation for the three classes of people, specify that the vow for enlightenment is fundamental. This is what is said in the sūtra. Concerning the superior class, it says, "Make the vow for enlightenment and recite the name of Amida with single-minded devotion." For the mediocre class, it says, "You must have a mind for the unsurpassed enlightenment and recite the name of the Buddha of Infinite Life with single-minded devotion." For the inferior class, it says, "You should have a mind for the unsurpassed enlightenment and recite the name of the Buddha of Infinite Life with single-minded devotion ten times."

My explanation of this is that the vow to become enlightened is the primary cause for attaining the way of the Buddha and is like the subject of a sentence. Calling on Amida single-mindedly is a separate practice for gaining rebirth and is like the direct object in a sentence. For you [Hōnen] to discard the subject and keep the object is like looking for smoke where there is no fire. What a joke! What a joke!

You should know that these interpretations in the commentaries sometimes leave aside the vow to attain enlightenment without discussing it and simply elaborate on all of the practices that arise from the vow. Why do you say that all of the other practices such as the vow to attain enlightenment are not found in Amida's original vows? The nineteenth vow says, "Make the vow to attain enlightenment and put all virtues into practice." Is this not the original vow? The phrase "make the vow to attain enlightenment" appears in many places, not just one. But even if the phrase "vow to become enlightened" is not to be found in Amida's forty-eight vows, it still is the primary cause for attaining the Buddha's way and therefore does not have to be explained for the first time in the vows. There are other words for referring to the vow to become enlightened. Ah, what a sad case you are!

. . .

On this basis, we can say that those who make their own sincere vows can be regarded as practitioners of the vow to gain the great enlightenment. You should understand clearly that the words "sincere mind and joy in faith" mean that priority should be given to making the vow to gain the great enlightenment. The fact that the vow to become enlightened is the fundamental cause for all of the three classes of people in the Sūtra of Infinite Life to be reborn in the Pure Land is made explicitly clear in these interpretations. This being the case, it is entirely incorrect for you, Hōnen, to hold up the names of all the other practices apart from the recitation of Amida's name and say that they are not in the original vow.

Next, you argue that the recitation of Amida's name is the primary practice and is that which is assisted, while the vow to become enlightened is a secondary practice and is that which assists. There is no support for this. If it pleases you to set up this distinction between primary and secondary and between that which is assisted and that which assists, then I must tell you that you have it backwards. I say to you that the vow to become enlightened is primary and is that which is assisted, while recitation is secondary and that which assists. I say to you that the vow to become enlightened is the foundation for the practices for rebirth into the Pure Land. Therefore, in order to nurture single-mindedly the vow to become enlightened, you should renounce the life of a householder, become a disciple, and concentrate on calling on the name of Amida Buddha. I say to you that the vow to become enlightened is the very basis of all acts of morality and is the respected director of all actions. This is the reason why in all of the sūtras and commentaries of Exoteric and Esoteric Buddhism, the vow to become enlightened is praised as the genesis of Buddhism. The textual proofs for this are as profuse as clouds and dew, as plentiful as thick hair.

. . .

In your *Choosing the Original Vow*, you say, "The recitation of Amida's name is a practice to be carried out over a long time period [of many rebirths] without losing any progress that has already been made, while the vow to become enlightened is a temporary, initial act that obstructs and destroys recitation." What in the world are you saying in this passage? First of all, what you call the practice of recitation is really meditation on the Buddha. In the five traditional kinds of meditations on the Buddha, there is no distinction made between them and the vow to become enlightened. If you take the practice of recitation and say that it is a practice to be carried out over a long period of time without losing any progress that has already been made, you are really making recitation into an expedient device for producing meditative visions. Once such expedient devices achieve their basic objectives, they can be abandoned. For instance, when you count your breaths while meditating, this technique is but an expedient device for entering into deep meditation. Once that state of meditation is achieved, you can stop counting your breaths.

Furthermore, recitation is significant only up to the end of your present life. Shandao explains what is important in our lives before we die in terms of those who go through the trouble of making initial vows and reciting Amida's name. This being the case, once we die and are reborn in the Pure Land and spiritually progress until the final stage of becoming a buddha, why would we want to make a point of clutching our rosaries and reciting Amida's name?

The vow to attain enlightenment, on the other hand, continues from the beginning until the final objective of becoming a buddha is reached. All virtuous deeds result in nothing if they are divorced from the vow to attain enlightenment. This vow is fundamental all the way up to the final stage. This is what is said in the *Essay on the Lack of Distinctions in the World of the Buddha's Truth*: "Because the vow to attain enlightenment is the supreme means for not losing any progress that has already been made, every act of virtue can be perfected and will result in achieving the final stage, which is nothing other than the world of nirvana."

Fazang, the Chinese master of the Flower Garland (Huayan) school, explained this by saying, "Not losing any progress that has already been made is not only the supreme basis for the final end of becoming a buddha but is also the reason why the progress made through practices one engages in along the way to that end will not be lost." This is because progress made with all practices will be lost if they are divorced from the vow to attain enlightenment. In the Flower Garland school, it is said that the practice of all good deeds apart from the vow to attain enlightenment is to be considered the work of the devil.

. . .

This being the case, the practice of reciting Amida's name should also be perfected through the vow to be enlightened. But, you, Hōnen, say that the vow obstructs the recitation of Amida's name. Are you crazy? This is not the teaching of the Buddha. This is what the devil preaches!

[Kamata and Tanaka, eds., *Kamakura kyū Bukkyō*, NST, vol. 15, pp. 80–89; GT]

THE MEANING OF THE KEGON PRACTICE OF MEDITATION, CLARITY OF INSIGHT, AND ENTRY INTO THE GATE OF DELIVERANCE

Myōe agreed with Hōnen that Shākyamuni was indeed long gone and far away and that the age was one of the dharma's decline, but he vigorously opposed Hōnen's consequent rejection of traditional practices. To reject meditation was to cast off the most viable way of recreating and experiencing the living presence of the Buddha, not to speak of attaining enlightenment. Using a wide variety of rituals and methods drawn from all schools of Buddhism, Myōe repeatedly found himself in an intensely personal relationship with Shākyamuni and other divine beings. Despite the common criticism that Kegon and other forms of traditional Buddhism were abstruse philosophies and not viable religions, he devoted much of his energies to reviving Kegon to show that the complex doctrines were rooted in meditative and ritual experiences that were still available to all.

I devote myself
To Vairochana, King of the Teaching;
To the inexhaustible corpus of the teaching, the precious storehouse of the
 law;
To the congregation in the great sea of Mañjushrī and Samantabhadra; and
To all the great masters who have revealed exquisite meanings.
I pray for divine grace;
For the increase of mindfulness and wisdom; and
For the opening of this deeply profound gate of deliverance
So that we may be able to spread blessings widely among ourselves and
 others, and lead each other hereafter
 without obstructions.

Now a snake and a cow both drink water, but one transforms it into poison, the other into medicine. The wise and the foolish both hear the teachings and transform them into right and wrong views. Do not confuse harm with benefit when you rely on a single tasting of water. You must obtain the teaching that is not divisible and then speak of its merits and defects. If you are interested in only fame and profit, of what use is the sacred teaching of the Buddha? If you are interested only in eloquence, then the historical writings of Confucius and Laozi should suffice.

The most important consideration, however, is that we are ordinary beings living after the Buddha's death. Furthermore, ours is a small country in a peripheral land. Even a person who has reached the age of eighty cannot say that he has bowed in the presence of the Buddha's holy visage. Those who have traversed the seven paths of transmigration still have not walked upon his remaining footsteps. There is no one to whom we can relate our sorrow; no prospect for consoling this grief. For what kind of leisure do you seek the pleasures of fame and profit? What joy is there in forgetting the Buddha's last instructions? We should remove ourselves from the frenzy of the five desires, simply firm up our thoughts in quiet forests, and compose ourselves in meditation halls for the purpose of engaging in the exquisite practice of deep contemplation.

[*Kegon shuzen kanshō nyūgedatsumon gi*, TD 72, no. 2331, pp. 74a–b; GT]

JŌKEI: *GEDATSU SHŌNIN'S PETITION FOR REVIVING THE PRECEPTS*

Like Myōe, Jōkei (1155–1213), also known as Gedatsu Shōnin, was a critic of the innovators. He, too, affirmed the efficacy of meditation and called for a revival of the precepts as the primary means for living the life that Shākyamuni had lived. The precepts, in other words, were a set of regulations and prohibitions, a guide for achieving the kind of spiritual intimacy with Shākyamuni that others claimed was no longer possible. In the pan-Buddhist spirit of his friend Myōe, Jōkei, a Hossō monk, regarded the precepts as the common property of all Buddhists, including the Precepts school. What was important about the precepts was not slavish obedience but the understanding that it defined the teachings of the Buddha as well as the lifestyle of a Buddhist. The age was surely degenerate—the innovators and the indolent proved to Myōe and Jōkei that spiritual corruption was widespread—but it afforded an opportunity to practice what had always been valued: right mindfulness and correct living.

Since the death of Shākyamuni, our master is the precepts. Is there anyone among lay people, clergy, or the seven classes of disciples who does not revere them? *The Ten Recitations of the Precepts* says, "The World Honored One often rebuked the monks who simply recited the scriptures and the doctrines without studying the precepts. It is because of the existence of the precepts that the Buddha's teaching exists in the world." Little do we know how many other passages there are like this.

It is, however, an inevitable truth that a slow decline sets in with the passage of time. I, too, am in the dark; other people are also in the dark. We neither study nor practice the precepts. After the eight different sects were established and the distinctions among the precepts, meditation, and wisdom were made, our temple, Kōfukuji, passed down the ancient traditions of the Hossō and Kusha sects. The monks in the eastern and western halls of Kōfukuji were specialists in the precepts. Those who regarded Master Ganjin as their founder and looked to Dharmagupta's precepts for their main teaching put on the robes of the precepts and formed what was called the Precepts school. They had restrictions about the advancement of the ten major and minor teachers, and the highest rank was that of master of the precepts.

Now, however, the Buddhist teaching in this degenerate age is not free from those who pursue fame and profit. If there is to be a foundation for the precepts, it must be found in courageous effort. In ancient times, the performance of rituals prescribed by the precepts was the condition for residence in all of the temples. Successful participation in the Grand Ceremony on the Vimalakīrti Sūtra set the stage for ecclesiastical advancement. Both of these activities have been discontinued. What are we to make of this?

Those who uphold the One Vehicle, as did the past masters of the eastern and western temples, should be revered; they are all medicines for the world. That is why the faith people commit to them is not misplaced. The approach to the single path of the precepts was most admirable in the past.

Even though we now lament and say that there is no benefit in upholding the precepts, this is just a matter of our own times and may be due in part to a certain lack of compatibility with our circumstances. I shall, however, lay aside other considerations and speak no more about this.

The administration of the precepts in Nara was carried out in all of the seven great temples and was the particular responsibility of the ten preceptors of the eastern and western halls of Kōfukuji. They carried out the rituals according to imperial decrees, and the ceremonies there were exceedingly dignified. Three officiating monks and seven witnessing monks were required for receiving the precepts. Even if the monks were impure or the rituals were not carried out in the prescribed manner, as long as there were one or two monks who knew the teachings, the conditions for the ceremony were excellent and sufficient. How can it be null and void? If there is no one to continue the precepts in our time, what will be done in future? This is not a matter of the decline of only one sect but would be a tragedy for all monks, nuns, and novices. Although some expedient means might be used as a temporary remedy, the elder monks of the eastern and western halls must still put an end to their tiresome complaints and lay out some plans for making progress. Even one book of the precepts will serve as a constant foundation for younger monks; even one section of a doctrinal outline should be recommended for reading and recitation. It is most urgent that they take the time to teach them, make them understand, and give to the world this immense benefit. In our main temple of Kōfukuji and also in our subsidiary temples at the present time, we are not without experts in the teachings, nor are we lacking in books. What difficulty would there be in promoting the precepts again and transmitting them forever?

My only request is that my humble petition be looked upon with favor by the bodhisattvas and wise men living in this world and by all of the good deities who protect the Buddhist teachings and that the vitality of Buddhism be thereby maintained.

[Kamata and Tanaka, eds., *Kamakura kyū Bukkyō*, NST, vol. 15, pp. 10–11; GT]

Chapter 11

NEW VIEWS OF HISTORY

The Japanese learned from the Chinese how to write history sometime during the seventh and eighth centuries. In addition, the calendar that they imported taught them how to keep track of the passage of time in an orderly manner, and the great classics of Chinese history, including the *Spring and Autumn Annals (Chunqiu)*, *Commentary on the Spring and Autumn Annals (Zuozhuan)*, *Records of the Historian (Shiji)*, *History of the Former Han Dynasty (Han shu)*, and *History of the Latter Han Dynasty (Hou Han shu)*, provided models for organizing records of the past. Prince Shōtoku (574–622) is said to have compiled or co-compiled two histories, *Chronicle of Emperors (Tennō-ki)* and *Chronicle of the Country (Kokki)*, but neither has survived. The oldest extant history of Japan by the Japanese is the *Chronicles of Japan (Nihongi* or *Nihon shoki).*[1]

The Chronicles of Japan, completed in 720, was a product of a historiographical project inaugurated by Emperor Tenmu (r. 673–686) in the late seventh century. Written in Chinese, it begins with an account of the creation of the world (conceived primarily as Japan) and the "age of the gods." This is followed by annals of the reigns of Japan's emperors and empresses starting with Jinmu,

---

1. The *Kojiki*, whose narrative ends in the late fifth century, is a work mainly of mythology and hence is not regarded as history for the purpose of this survey of history writing in ancient and medieval Japan.

who was believed to have founded the Japanese state in 660 B.C., to Jitō (r. 686–697), Tenmu's wife and successor. The first half of the Nihongi, covering up to about the late sixth century, is essentially myth. But as it progresses, the second half becomes increasingly reliable as history. Thus when we speak of the Nihongi as Japan's first history, we refer to the work's second half, covering the period of about a century or so from the late sixth century until the Nihongi's termination date of 697. Apart from scattered accounts of relations with Japan in Chinese and Korean records, the Nihongi is our sole written source of knowledge about Japan during this crucial age of the late sixth and seventh centuries when, as a result of extensive borrowing from the continent, it became a land of advanced civilization within the China-centered cultural sphere of East Asia.

Of the two principal Chinese models of history writing, the "chronicle" model (J: hennen-tai) and the "annals and biographies" model (J: kiden-tai), the Nihongi is primarily a chronicle, that is, a narrative arranged in chronological order with precise (although not always accurate) dating throughout. But the Nihongi also partakes of the annals and biographies model because, as just noted, it is divided from the time of Jinmu into the chronology of the passing years and also the reigns of emperors and empresses. This division of the Nihongi after the age of the gods into imperial reigns is, in fact, one of the work's most distinguishing features.

The annals and biographies model of history, originated by Sima Qian in Records of the Grand Historian (Shiji), was used in China primarily for compiling dynastic histories, that is, histories arranged according to the division of time into dynastic periods or cycles of history generated by the founding, flourishing, and fall of successive ruling dynasties. Each dynasty, it was believed, began when it received the Mandate of Heaven and fell when Heaven, judging the dynasty no longer worthy, withdrew the mandate. Although there are occasional references to the Mandate of Heaven in Japan's early writings about emperorship, the Japanese never adopted this Chinese idea as a theory for imperial succession. On the contrary, they firmly grounded the succession to their emperorship in another mandate: the one that the Sun Goddess bestowed on her grandson Ninigi when she sent him from Heaven to rule the land of Japan. As related in the Nihongi, the mandate was: "Do thou, my August Grandchild, proceed thither and govern it. Go! and may prosperity attend thy dynasty, and may it, like Heaven and Earth, endure for ever."[2] To the Japanese of later times, this mandate was the basis for the idea of bansei ikkei, "one dynasty [to rule] a myriad generations." Imperial rule in Japan was not to be governed by moral laws or cyclical forces; instead, the founding dynasty would rule forever.

After the Nihongi, the court compiled five more histories, also in Chinese, that cover the period from 697 through the reign of Emperor Kōkō (r. 884–887)

---

2. Aston, Nihongi, I, p. 77.

and are known as the "Five National Histories" (*gokokushi*). Combined with the *Nihongi*, they are called the "Six National Histories" (*rikkokushi*). The Five National Histories are, however, works quite different from the *Nihongi*. First, whereas the *Nihongi* extensively uses myths, oral stories, and foreign (Chinese and Korean) records, the *gokokushi* are compilations based entirely on Japanese government documents. In this sense, they are better, more reliable histories than the *Nihongi*. They also are examples of "objective" history, although one may question the value of that. In contrast to the *Nihongi*, which is lively, imaginative, and readable, the Five National Histories are dry-as-dust, bare-bones chronologies of court events—coronations, marriages, the changing of calendrical eras (*nengō*), the appointment of ministers, the promulgation of decrees, reports of omens, and so forth.

One distinctive feature of Chinese history writing that is almost entirely missing from the Five National Histories is the personal evaluations (J: *ronsan*) of the emperors made at the end of their reigns and those of other important people in their biographies. These evaluations were a crucial means by which Chinese historians performed the Confucian function of judging morality or the lack of it in emperors and others. Neglect of the *ronsan* by the *gokokushi* authors appears to reflect a general disinterest by the Japanese at this early stage of their history in the force of individual morality in government and society.

The length of time covered by the Five National Histories decreases almost steadily as the series progresses. Whereas the first, *Chronicles of Japan Continued* (*Shoku Nihongi*), covers nine reigns and nearly a century, 697 to 791, the second, *Later Chronicles of Japan* (*Nihon kōki*), spans only four reigns and forty-one years, 793 to 833, and the third and fourth, *Later Chronicles of Japan, Continued* (*Shoku-Nihon kōki*) and *True Records of Emperor Montoku of Japan* (*Nihon Montoku tennō jitsuroku*), deal with only one reign each (Ninmyō, 833–850, and Montoku, 850–858). Only the last, *True Records of Three Japanese Reigns* (*Nihon sandai jitsuroku*), goes against the trend, increasing its coverage slightly to become a record of three brief reigns (Seiwa, Yōzei, and Kōkō, 858–887). Thus we see that even during the years in the early Heian period when the Fujiwara rose to dominance at court as imperial regents and the emperors steadily lost political power, the authors of the Five National Histories devoted their attention ever more intensely to the imperial succession and the lives of individual emperors. As a result, these works, although important as sources of basic court data and activities, became less and less relevant as records of the events and developments that were really shaping Japanese history at this time.

HISTORICAL TALES (*REKISHI MONOGATARI*)

Japan sent its last mission to Tang China in 838. For some two and a half centuries, the Japanese had borrowed from China, first from the Sui dynasty and later from the Tang. The end of the missions in the mid-ninth century—and hence the end of the borrowing—coincided with the dawn of a new age, the age of the Fujiwara regency. Although the Japanese had borrowed a great deal from China, they borrowed selectively, as we can clearly see in retrospect. In many important ways, the Japanese rejected or modified their Chinese models. Thus, for example, although the ostensible aim of the Japanese court in the seventh and early eighth centuries had been to shape its government into a Chinese-style imperial bureaucratic state with ministerial preferment based on merit, this kind of state did not take firm root in Japan. With few exceptions, merit was never accepted as the primary criterion for appointments and promotions at court: the courtier aristocracy remained a privileged elite whose statuses (in the form of ranks and offices) were defined almost entirely by birth. With the rise of the Fujiwara, many of the bureaucratic offices at court lost their power, and the actual functions of government were transferred to the private family councils of the Fujiwara. Another example of a major Chinese institution that failed in Japan was the equal-field system of landholding adopted from the Tang. Beginning in at least the eighth century, this system gradually fell into abeyance (as it had in China as well) and was eventually replaced by a countrywide structure of privately held agricultural estates (*shōen*).

Changes in the aims and forms of history writing in the new age of the Fujiwara regency also reflected a rejection of Chinese models. These changes emerged not so much from the decisions of historians as from important new developments in the realm of language and literature. Most fundamental was the evolution, from about the late ninth and early tenth centuries, of the *kana* syllabaries, which enabled the Japanese, with two notable exceptions, to write their native language for the first time.[3] The availability of *kana* encouraged the composition of prose literature, which appeared initially in the form of introductory or explanatory passages written as accompaniments to *waka* poetry. We see this, for example, in the *uta monogatari* or "poem tales," the most important of which was the tenth-century *Tales of Ise (Ise monogatari)*.

The *monogatari* (the word means "to talk about or narrate things") provided a flexible format by means of which the Japanese, employing a mixture of Chinese characters and *kana* as an orthography for their language, could write prose with a freedom impossible when using Chinese, both because Chinese was a foreign language and because it carried the weight of China's own great literary tradition. As prose fiction, the *monogatari* attained its highest development in the early-eleventh-century novel *The Tale of Genji (Genji monogatari)*. But the Japanese did not restrict their use of the *monogatari* to fiction: they

---

3. The compilers of both the *Kojiki* and the *Man'yōshū* used Chinese characters to represent the sounds of Japanese.

adapted it also to history, and in the process, they blurred the line usually thought to distinguish history from literature.

A TALE OF FLOWERING FORTUNES
(EIGA MONOGATARI)

This blurring of history and literature seems at least in part to have resulted from the success of *The Tale of Genji*, which became enormously popular and highly esteemed as literature among readers at the Heian court almost immediately upon its composition by Lady Murasaki. Evidence of this can be found, for example, in the fact that the author of the first "historical tale"(*rekishi monogatari*), *A Tale of Flowering Fortunes* (*Eiga monogatari*), written in the mideleventh century in the wake of *Genji*, looked up to *Genji* as a model of style and composition and in many ways shaped *Eiga* to resemble it.

The thinking that brought history and literature together in the format of the *monogatari* is well expressed by Lady Murasaki herself in a passage in *Genji*. The hero of the novel's first half, Genji the Shining One, visits Tamakazura, a lady much younger than he whom he is courting without noticeable success. Tamakazura, we are told, is the most avid reader of tales among all the ladies living at Genji's residence in Kyoto. Genji teases her by saying that women like her seem to enjoy being deceived by stories they know perfectly well are not true. But then becoming serious, he says: "Amid all the fabrication [in *monogatari*] I must admit that I do find real emotions and plausible chains of events. . . . [The *monogatari*] have set down and preserved happenings from the age of the gods to our own. *The Chronicles of Japan* and the rest are a mere fragment of the whole truth. It is your [*monogatari*] that fill in the details."[4] The *Chronicles of Japan* (*Nihongi*) and the other great records of Japan (i.e., the "national histories"), according to Genji, tell only one part of history: the major developments and happenings. The details about how individuals actually lived, thought, and felt had to be filled in by an author's (a historian's?) imagination in a "plausible" manner. In keeping with Genji's conception of history, the historical tales as a genre, beginning with *Eiga monogatari*, took the form of "embellished histories."

Flowering Fortunes (*Eiga monogatari*), it is generally agreed, was written by a court lady named Akazome Emon (ca. 957–1041). That its author was a woman was in one sense fitting, since women were the ones who made the first and best use of the new means (*kana*) for writing in the native language. As is well known, many of the finest works of Heian-period prose literature, including *The Tale of Genji* and Sei Shōnagon's *Pillow Book* (*Makura no sōshi*), were

---

4. Murasaki Shikibu, *The Tale of Genji*, trans. Edward Seidensticker, vol. 1, p. 437.

written by court ladies. Here we see that a woman took the lead also in the writing of a new kind of history.

In addition to its composition in Japanese rather than Chinese, *Flowering Fortunes (Eiga)* differs from the *Nihongi* and the other Six National Histories in not having court sponsorship or multiple authorship (e.g., a board of compilers at court); rather, its author was an individual writing privately. *Eiga* resembles the Six National Histories in being organized in the chronicle (*hennen-tai*) form, but whereas the Six National Histories are also divided into imperial reigns, *Eiga* is not. Akazome Emon was certainly attentive to the succession of emperors and their affairs, but her real focus was on the Fujiwara family and especially Fujiwara no Michinaga (966–1027), who is usually regarded as the greatest of the imperial regents. *Eiga* begins about 946, during the reign of Emperor Murakami (r. 947–967), and ends in 1028, the year of Michinaga's death. The bulk of the book deals with the age of Michinaga.

Largely descriptive with little analysis, *Flowering Fortunes (Eiga)* is essentially a woman's-eye view of events and affairs in the life of the Heian court, including marriages, births, deaths, personal rivalries, and romantic liaisons (what Genji called the "details" of history). This is hardly surprising inasmuch as court ladies led sheltered lives that prevented them from moving about freely and strictly limited their range of personal associations. Akazome Emon and her kind were not likely to have had the opportunity to hear, much less engage in, serious discussions about the larger issues and developments of their times or to have been privy to the workings and decision-making processes of court government.

FUJIWARA NO MICHINAGA: FLOWERING FORTUNES

One way in which Akazome Emon demonstrated her admiration for *The Tale of Genji* was by dividing the contents of *A Tale of Flowering Fortunes* into chapters with *Genji*-like titles, such as "The Moon-Viewing Banquet," "Unfinished Dreams," and "Radiant Fujitsubo." The following passage, which appears in "Doubts," tells of the extraordinary flowering fortunes of Michinaga, the greatest of the Fujiwara regents. In the first two-thirds of the passage, Emon speaks in typically Buddhist terms of the impermanence of all things. She then asserts that this most fundamental of Buddhist principles does not apply to Michinaga, whose fortunes will flourish for a "thousand years"—that is, for the period of time that she may have chosen to signify "forever." This assertion contributes to the "cult of personality" developed for Michinaga in both *The Tale of Flowering Fortunes* and the next historical tale to be discussed, *The Great Mirror* (*Ōkagami*).

There is a difference between fact and aspiration for people in this world, regardless of their status. Though a tree may wish to remain motionless, winds never cease to blow; though a son may intend to be filial, parents do not live forever.[5] Whatever lives dies. A life span may be immeasurably long, but there is always a limit. Those who prosper must decline; where there is meeting, parting will follow. All is cause and effect; nothing is eternal. Fortunes that prospered yesterday may decline today. Even spring blossoms and autumn leaves are spoiled and lose their beauty when they are enshrouded by spring haze and autumn mist. And after a gust of wind scatters them, they are nothing but debris in a garden or froth on the water. It is only the flowering fortunes of this lord [Michinaga] that, now having begun to bloom, will not be hidden from sight during a thousand years of spring hazes and autumn mists. No wind disturbs their branches, which grow ever more redolent with scent—rare and splendid as *udumbara*[6] blossoms, peerlessly fragrant as the blue lotus, fairest of water-flowers.

[McCullough and McCullough, trans., *A Tale of Flowering Fortunes*, II, pp. 515–516; PV]

THE GREAT MIRROR (*ŌKAGAMI*)

Glorification of the Fujiwara, and Michinaga in particular, is the main theme also of *The Great Mirror* (*Ōkagami*), the second of the historical tales, which was probably written by a courtier in the late eleventh or early twelfth century. In *The Great Mirror*, we encounter for the first time use of the word "mirror" in the title of a work dealing with Japanese history. In China, history was regarded metaphorically as a mirror or reflector of past events. Implicit was the belief that looking into a mirror (i.e., reading history) would enable one to learn the lessons of the past, especially those concerning proper, ethical rule. No such didactic meaning, however, was intended for the word as it was used in the title *The Great Mirror*. One of the two implausibly ancient raconteurs (they are, respectively, 150 and 140 years old) who narrate the story of *The Great Mirror* suggests in verse this idea of history as a mirror:

Akirakeki	Now that I have chanced upon
Kagami ni aeba	This clear mirror,
Suginishi mo	I can see the past,
Ima yukusue no	The present,
Koto mo miekeri.	And what is to come.[7]

---

5. This and the following three sentences are paraphrased from the popular Pure Land tract *Ōjōyōshū*, pp. 43, 39.

6. A legendary Indian tree said to bloom once in every three thousand years.

7. McCullough, trans., *Ōkagami*, p. 85.

The raconteur claims that history as a mirror informs us not only about the past but also about the present and even the future. So far as the past is concerned, *The Great Mirror* was not composed with the thought of recording or "reflecting" in any comprehensive way—as we might expect of a mirror—the course of times gone by. Indeed, many of the major events of the period covered by *The Great Mirror* (from the late ninth century until 1025, two years before Michinaga's death), including rebellions and power struggles at court, are either totally ignored or only briefly noted. Rather, *The Great Mirror's* author carefully selected and arranged his materials to record and celebrate the history of the Fujiwara family's rise and its enjoyment of greatest prosperity under Michinaga.

In order to highlight the Fujiwara and especially Michinaga, *The Great Mirror's* author chose to use the annals and biographies (*kiden*) form for his work rather than the chronicle (*hennen*) form in which all previous histories of Japan, including *A Tale of Flowering Fortunes*, had been written. The annals of the emperors begin with Montoku (r. 850–858), at the end of whose reign the Fujiwara regency was established. Uniformly brief, the annals occupy only about 10 percent of *The Great Mirror*. And once the older of the raconteurs completes his narration of the annals, he apologizes for having taken so much time, commenting: "You may wonder why I have talked about all these reigns . . . but how can I explain Michinaga's success without discussing the Emperors and Empresses who made it possible?"[8] The bulk of *The Great Mirror* is devoted to biographies, all twenty of which deal with the lives and careers of Fujiwara ministers.

In view of how extensively the Japanese borrowed from China over a period of many centuries and specifically (for the purpose of this discussion) how much they admired and studied the great Chinese histories, such as the *Chunqiu* and *Shiji*, the reader of *The Great Mirror* must marvel at the near absence of any discussion in it of rule by ethical men—that is, of the central Confucian theme that runs like a mighty river through the Chinese histories. In fact, the influence of Confucianism as a whole on *The Great Mirror*—and *A Tale of Flowering Fortunes*—is, at best, minimal.

If a minister like Michinaga was not regarded as great because of his morality or virtue, then where was his greatness? As the following readings show, *The Great Mirror's* author suggests a variety of reasons for Michinaga's having become a great ruler, the first of which is good fortune. (By good fortune, the author sometimes seems to mean pure luck, whereas at other times he attributes the fortune to divine favor.) Second to good fortune as an explanation for Michinaga's success and greatness is resourcefulness, that is, doing what is necessary in any situation to come out ahead. As Helen McCullough, commenting on

---

8. Ibid.

Michinaga, has put it: "The question in [the] mind [of *The Great Mirror's* author] is not whether Michinaga is good, but whether he is able."[9]

Still other reasons given for Michinaga's success and greatness are his physiognomy, his mastery of poetry and other polite arts, and his ability to appear resplendent in great public celebrations and rituals. Last but not least, Michinaga of all the Fujiwara regents was able to ensure his success as a ruler by producing many able sons and daughters and skillfully placing them in high positions at court (in the case of sons) and marrying them to emperors and other prominent persons (in the case of daughters).

FUJIWARA NO MICHINAGA: *FLOWERING FORTUNES, CONTINUED*

The setting for the narration of *The Great Mirror* is Urin'in Temple outside Kyoto, where a group of people are waiting for a priest to arrive and present an enlightenment sermon. Two incredibly old men (150 years old and 140 years old) begin talking, and one, Ōyake no Yotsugi (the name Yotsugi means the "passage of generations"), suggests passing the time by his telling "a story about the old days."

"I have only one thing of importance on my mind," he went on, "and that is to describe Lord Michinaga's unprecedented successes to all of you here, clergy and laity of both sexes. It is a complicated subject, so I shall have to discuss a fair number of Emperors, Empresses, ministers of state, and senior nobles first. Then when I reach Michinaga himself, the most fortunate of all, you will understand just how everything came about. They tell us that the Buddha began by expounding other sutras when he wanted to explain the *Lotus*, which is why his sermons are called the teachings of the five periods.[10] That is how it is with me, too; I need to 'expound other sutras' in order to describe Michinaga's successes."

. . .

"I suppose you youngsters nowadays think every Regent, minister of state, and senior noble in history has been very much like Michinaga. That is far from true. Of course, they have all been descendants of the same ancestor and members of the same family, but the family has produced many different kinds of people in the process of branching out.

"The first Japanese sovereign after the seven divine generations was Emperor Jinmu; and there have been sixty-eight Emperors from Emperor Jinmu to our

---

9. Ibid., p. 46.

10. The division of the Buddha's teachings into five periods, allegedly representing five successive phases of his fifty-year career (see chapter 6).

present ruler. I ought to discuss each of them in turn, from Emperor Jinmu on, but that would take us far back into unfamiliar history, so I had better confine myself to the recent past.

"There was an Emperor called Montoku. From that Emperor to the present, there have been fourteen reigns. To put it in terms of years, 176 have elapsed since the accession of Emperor Montoku in the third year of Kashō [850]. Awesome as it is to speak the names of those August sovereigns." . . .

And so he went on to tell the following story. [pp. 68–69]

In this passage, Yotsugi refers to the fact that two of Michinaga's older brothers "luckily" died prematurely to allow Michinaga to become the leading Fujiwara minister. Michinaga dominated the court from the time of the death of his second brother in 995 until his own death in 1027, although he chose to occupy the office of regent only briefly (1015–1017).

"In my opinion, the explanation for all those deaths is simply that Michinaga is a supremely lucky man. He would never have risen so high if others had kept the offices to which they were entitled by seniority."

. . .

"Michinaga held the offices of Major Counselor and Master of the Empress's Household then. On the eleventh of the Fifth Month, at the age of thirty—a time when he was still very young and could look forward to a long career— he received the Imperial decree naming him Regent, and thereafter he began to prosper in earnest. The regency has never left his house, and we may assume that it never will." [p. 185]

In the following passage, Yotsugi begins by observing that owing to "boundless good fortune," Michinaga produced many children, all of whom were "perfect." Then after describing Michinaga's steady rise in court rank and office to the highest levels, he emphasizes the extraordinary fact that Michinaga was at the same time able to make empresses of no fewer than three of his daughters. (Since the source of Fujiwara power always lay in their marital ties to the imperial family, this was no mean feat.) Picking up steam with his words of adulation for Michinaga, Yotsugi suggests that as a poet he may have been superior to Bo Zhuyi, the Chinese poet most admired by the Heian-period courtiers, and such Japanese masters of the past as Kakinomoto no Hitomaro and Ki no Tsurayuki (d. 946). Pulling out all the stops, Yotsugi goes on to recount that on a certain imperial visit to the Kasuga Shrine, Michinaga's bearing and appearance in the imperial train were so dazzling and resplendent that the crowds viewing the visit may even have mistaken him for a buddha.

"Michinaga is the father of twelve children. None has died, and all of them, whether sons or daughters, are quite certain to get whatever offices and ranks they want. There is not one who is at all inadequate or open to criticism in disposition or character, or who lacks accomplishments and elegance. I am sure it is due solely to His Lordship's boundless good fortune that this should be so. Although his predecessors produced children, were all of them so perfect? By no means! Regardless of sex, some were good and some were bad—that is only natural."

. . .

"Michinaga was named *kanpaku* [regent for an adult emperor] in his thirtieth year. After governing as he pleased during the reigns of Emperors Ichijō and Sanjō, he became the present Emperor's *sesshō* [regent for an emperor who has not attained adulthood] when His Majesty ascended the throne at the age of nine. He was then fifty-one. During that same year, he assumed the office of Chancellor, ceding the regency to [his son] Yorimichi. He took Buddhist vows on the Twenty-First of the Third Month in the third year of Kannin [1019], when he was fifty-four. On the Eighth of the Fifth Month, the Court made him equivalent to the three Empresses in status, with annual ranks and offices, even though he was a monk. He is the grandfather of the Emperor and the Crown Prince, and the father of three Empresses, of the Regent Minister of the Left, of the Palace Minister, and of many Counselors; and he has governed the realm for approximately thirty-one years. Since this year is his sixtieth, people say there will be a celebration for him after the birth of Kishi's child. What a magnificent affair that will be, with so many great personages present!

"No other minister of state has ever been able to make three of his daughters Empresses at the same time. It must be counted a rare blessing that Michinaga's house has produced three Imperial ladies—Senior Grand Empress Shōshi, Grand Empress Kenshi, and Empress Ishi. Our other Empress, Seishi, was the only one who belonged to a different house, but she was also descended from [Fujiwara no] Tadahira, so we certainly can't think of her as an outsider. We may indeed call Michinaga the supreme ruler of the land, particularly since Empress Seishi's death this spring has left his three daughters as the sole surviving Empresses.

"The Chinese and Japanese poems Michinaga has composed on various occasions are so ingenious that I am sure not even Bo Zhuyi, Hitomaro, Mitsune, or Tsurayuki could have thought of them. For example, there was the Imperial visit to Kasuga Shrine, a custom inaugurated in the reign of Emperor Ichijō. Since Emperor Ichijō's precedent was considered inviolable, our present sovereign made the journey in spite of his youth, with Senior Grand Empress Shōshi accompanying him in his litter. To call the spectacle brilliant would be trite. Above all, what can I say about the bearing and appearance of Michinaga, the Emperor's grandfather, as he rode in the Imperial train? It might have been disappointing if he had looked anything like an ordinary man. The crowds of country folk along the way must have been spellbound. Even sophisticated city dwellers, dazzled by a resplendence like that of the Wheel-Turning Sacred Monarchs,[11] found themselves, in perfectly natural confusion, raising their hands to their foreheads as though gazing on a buddha." [pp. 190–191]

Yotsugi continues to heap extravagant praise on Michinaga, associating him in this passage with the gods and buddhas and also two of ancient Japan's great culture heroes, Prince Shōtoku and Kōbō Daishi (Kūkai, 774–835). In the second half of the passage, Yotsugi makes a rare reference to the effect of Michinaga's glorious rule on the people. If Michinaga were a great Chinese ruler, we would expect to be informed (in a Chinese history) of something to the effect that he had pacified the realm by means of his virtue and that as a result, the people were content and prosperous. But here in Ōkagami we find not a word about what Michinaga the Japanese ruler has done of a positive or exemplary nature for the welfare of the people. At best he may have clamped down on some of the human predators, including those in the employ of "noblemen and princes," who have been making the people's lives miserable by dunning them for services, seizing their belongings, and squeezing them for money.

"[Michinaga] is in a class by [himself]. He is a man who enjoys special protection from the gods of heaven and earth. Winds may rage and rains may fall day after day, but the skies will clear and the ground will dry out two or three days before he plans anything. Some people call him a reincarnation of Shōtoku Taishi; others say he is Kōbō Daishi, reborn to make Buddhism flourish. Even to the censorious eye of old age, he seems not an ordinary mortal but an awesome manifestation of a god or buddha.

"A nation is bound to be perfectly happy with a ruler like Michinaga. In the old days, cattle drivers and horse herders in the employ of noblemen and Princes were always dunning us for festivals and spirit services.[12] They wouldn't even let anyone cut grass in the fields and hills. But now the minor functionaries of the great no longer seize a man's belongings, and there is no more talk of local headmen and village magistrates who pester people to defray the expenses of fire festivals and so forth.[13] Can we ever hope to enjoy such safety and peace again?"

[From McCullough, trans., Ōkagami, pp. 68–69, 185, 190–191, 208–209; PV]

---

11. Tenrinjōō. In Buddhism, supernaturally endowed kings who rule the world by turning the wheel of righteous political power bestowed by heaven.

12. Spirit services (goryōe) were designed to placate the pestilence gods, curse-laying spirits of the dead, and other supernatural troublemakers.

13. Fire festivals (himatsuri) are conjectured to have been folk events held for the purpose of preventing fires.

MEDIEVAL USES OF THE PAST

The shogunate's founding in 1185 did not mean that warrior rule immediately and completely supplanted courtier rule (for purposes of this discussion, the imperial family is included with the courtiers). Instead, the shogunate was a new, separate government that never entirely displaced the court. What emerged was a dyarchy of court (Kyoto) and camp (Kamakura), and only gradually did Kamakura assume all of the court's traditional ruling powers. Even when this was accomplished by the late Kamakura period (1185–1333), the courtiers as a class remained an economic force to be reckoned with by virtue of their continued possession of vast wealth in revenue-producing agricultural estates (*shōen*).

Because the court remained at least potentially a viable government, some of its members periodically dreamed of regaining actual ruling powers by either overthrowing the shogunate and carrying out an "imperial restoration" or seeking a more intimate accommodation with the military. It was in the context of such dreaming that the two most important histories of the medieval age were written, *Gukanshō* by Jien (1155–1225) and *Jinnō shōtōki* (*Chronicle of the Direct Descent of Gods and Sovereigns*) by Kitabatake Chikafusa (1293–1354). In composing these works, Jien and Chikafusa, both of whom came from high-ranking court families, opened new avenues of inquiry into the study of Japanese history. They stand apart from earlier historians of Japan in at least two important respects:

1. Unlike the earlier historians, who were content to narrate events of the past more or less on a straight continuum of time with little attempt to discern larger processes of cause and effect or long-term change, Jien and Chikafusa divided Japanese history into periods and were at pains to analyze and explain the reasons for the transitions from one period to another.

2. Although their histories have been labeled, in the case of one (*Gukanshō*), a "Buddhist" history and, in the case of the other (*Jinnō shōtōki*), a "Shinto" history, Jien and Chikafusa appear to have been inspired to take up their brushes primarily to argue politics. Viewing the past in terms of the central issues of the times in which they lived and the interests of the class to which they belonged, as well as their personal political allegiances, they sought to interpret and use the past with the express aim of influencing and directing the course of the country in the present and future.

JIEN

Jien was born into the Kujō branch of the Fujiwara family in 1155. A year later, 1156, armed conflict erupted in Kyoto for the first time in three and a half centuries. Known after the calendrical era as the Hōgen conflict, it centered on a factional dispute involving an emperor, a retired emperor, and leading Fujiwara ministers and was fought by members of the Taira and Minamoto warrior families. To Jien, writing in *Gukanshō*, the Hōgen conflict marked the start of the "age of warriors." In 1159, another, similar conflict in Kyoto (the Heiji conflict) broke out. This time, however, the Taira and Minamoto were more clearly pitted against each other in the fighting, and when the Taira emerged victorious, they began, under their leader Kiyomori (1118–1181), a dramatic rise to power at court. By the late 1170s, Kiyomori, who married his daughter into the imperial family and installed his infant grandson as emperor, had become a virtual dictator in Kyoto. But Kiyomori and the Taira were not to remain at this pinnacle of power for long. Beginning in 1180, chieftains of the Minamoto rose in rebellion in the provinces and provoked a five-year war (the Minamoto-Taira or Genpei War) that ended in the complete destruction of the Taira (Kiyomori himself died in 1181) and the establishment in 1185 of the Kamakura shogunate by Minamoto no Yoritomo (1147–1199).

Backed by Yoritomo, Jien's older brother Kujō no Kanezane (1149–1207) was appointed imperial regent at court in 1186, and in 1192 Jien, who had entered Buddhist orders, became head abbot of the Tendai temple of Enryakuji on Mount Hiei (thus embarking on the first of four terms as the head of the Enryakuji). With Kanezane serving as ranking minister at court and Jien occupying one of the highest positions in the Buddhist ecclesiastical world, the Kujō family flourished during these years. But in 1196 Kanezane, embroiled in political battle at court and no longer enjoying Yoritomo's strong support, was dismissed as regent, and at the same time, Jien was ousted as the abbot of Enryakuji. For the next thirteen years, the Kujō were, for the most part, outshone at court by the rival Konoe branch of the Fujiwara family.

Then in 1219, two developments gave rise to what Jien hoped would be a great revival of Kujō fortunes. First, it seemed that the Kujō would soon regain the office of regent, and second, Jien's two-year-old great grandnephew Yoritsune (1218–56) was adopted into the warrior family of Minamoto in order to become the shogun. This adoption was engineered by the Hōjō family, which during the years after Yoritomo's death in 1199 had emerged as the new power holders in the shogunate. Wielding their power through the office of shogunal regent (*shikken*), the Hōjō sought in Yoritsune a figurehead leader who would bring a fresh aura of legitimacy to the shogunate by virtue of his Kujō (Fujiwara) family origins. Jien, however, saw the pending appointment of Yoritsune as shogun in a very different light. He professed to believe that the appointment was the work of the "Great Hachiman Bodhisattva," who intended that once Yoritsune had attained his majority, he would become a ruler in fact as well as name. Jien was convinced that Yoritsune was destined to bring together court and camp to form a new, truly national government.

It is doubtful that many others at the time shared Jien's grandiose expectations for Yoritsune, least of all the retired emperor Go-Toba (1180–1239), who even then was plotting to overthrow the Kamakura shogunate. To Jien, such plotting was reckless adventurism that might jeopardize Yoritsune's chances to become the unifier of the country in the future. It was primarily to dissuade Go-Toba from pursuing the collision course on which he appeared to be set that Jien took up his brush in 1219 to write *Gukanshō*. But Jien's effort came to naught. In 1221 Go-Toba launched his "rebellion" against the Kamakura regime, which responded by dispatching a huge army westward that speedily and thoroughly defeated the ragtag force that Go-Toba had assembled to oppose it. As a result of this brief conflict, known as the Jōkyū war, Go-Toba was sent into exile, and the Kyoto court was left far weaker and more firmly under Kamakura's control than before. Yoritsune did become shogun, although not until 1226. He held the office for nearly twenty years (until 1244) but never became more than the figurehead the Hōjō intended him to be.

GUKANSHŌ

Gukanshō has two parts: a history of Japan from the first emperor, Jinmu, until 1219, and a detailed chronology of names, dates, titles, court appointments, and the like for the same period.[14] The first part, the history, is divided approximately in half at 1156, the year of the Hōgen conflict. Thus, fully half of *Gukanshō* is devoted to Jien's own lifetime, which he identifies as the "military age."

Although Jien follows the chronology of historical events, dividing Japanese history into seven periods (the first four go to 1156 and the last three go from 1156 to 1219), his presentation of these events is not always orderly, and he is frequently repetitious. But even more daunting for the reader is that in seeking to explain why certain key events occurred and how and why history moved from one period to another, Jien relies heavily on a single concept: *dōri*, "principle." In effect, he attempts to analyze the course of Japanese history in terms of a great variety of principles, some of which he does not clearly or convincingly explain. At times, indeed, his discussion of principles collapses into confusion, as in the following passage dealing with his third period of Japanese history (571–1027, from the introduction of Buddhism to Japan through the age of Fujiwara no Michinaga):

> [This was the] period of the principle by which people of the visible world did not act in accord with the will of invisible beings, although everyone felt that what he was doing was actually a requirement of a principle [created by invisible beings]. This was a situation in which something that was thought to be good would certainly be regretted later on. In this

---

14. The chronology actually precedes the history, but this discussion follows the order in Brown and Ishida's *The Future and the Past*.

period people who thought of something as a requirement of principle came to realize, later on and upon reflection, [that it was not in accord with the will of invisible beings].[15]

We can discern in *Gukanshō*, however, two general types of principles whose characteristics and interactions with each other tell us a great deal about the thinking of intellectuals in Jien's day. The first type is destructive principles, derived from the *mappō* ("end of the [Buddhist] Law") thought discussed earlier. *Gukanshō* is based on the belief that history is a process of long-term decline or deterioration in accordance with the Mahāyāna Buddhist notion of its passing through three downward-moving stages from the time of the death of the historic Buddha, Gautama. The third and final stage, *mappō*, by Japanese calculation, began in 1052.[16] The *mappō* interpretation of history provided the principal means by which Jien, who was not a trained or professional historian, became the first writer of Japanese history to interpret Japan's past in terms of cause and effect and to periodize it accordingly. This interpretation also gave rise to the popular conception of *Gukanshō* as a "Buddhist" history. But the second type of principles described in *Gukanshō*, constructive principles, derives from both Buddhism and Shinto, and indeed, those of Shinto often appear to be the more important. For this reason, we might well describe *Gukanshō* as *both* a Buddhist and a Shinto history. Then too, the Song Neo-Confucian concept of "principle" in human affairs may also be at work here, though not in systematic ways.

Constructive principles can bring about historical "improvement" or upward movement. Nothing can ultimately prevent long-term deterioration from running its course, but there can be occasional and partial reversals of that course. The introduction of Buddhism to Japan in the late sixth century, for example, caused such a reversal and brought temporary improvement when the Buddhist Law (*buppō*) became the protector of the Imperial Law (*ōhō*). But the constructive principle that interests Jien most in *Gukanshō* is that the Sun Goddess, Amaterasu, and the Great Hachiman Bodhisattva ordained that the Fujiwara family should assist emperors in ruling. Although Hachiman, with the designation Bodhisattva, is identified here as both a Shinto and a Buddhist deity, the principle to which Jien refers is clearly Shintoist, since its locus classicus is in the age of the gods section of the mythology. When the Sun Goddess sent her grandson, Ninigi, to Japan with the mandate to rule it forever, she had Ame no Koyane no Mikoto, the ancestral *kami* of the Fujiwara family, accompany him,

---

15. Brown and Ishida, *The Future and the Past*, pp. 206–207.

16. For a discussion of the various stages in the decline of the Buddhist Law and how the Japanese arrived at the date 1052 for the commencement of the age of *mappō*, see Ishida, "Structure and Formation of *Gukanshō* Thought," in ibid., pp. 423–425.

ordering the *kami* to assist Ninigi in his rule.[17] The order to Ame no Koyane became the scriptural basis, so to speak, for the establishment of the Fujiwara regency.

Let us return to Jien's periodization of Japanese history in *Gukanshō*. We have noted that he divided it into seven periods. But more important, he also conceived of it in terms of three broad ages: ancient (*jōko*), medieval (*chūko*), and modern (*kindai*). In this he was not entirely original, for by the late Heian period, courtiers in general had come to think of Japanese history as progressing through such ages. Jien does not try to pinpoint the transition from the ancient age to the medieval age, but like other late-Heian courtiers who referred to it in their writings, he believed the transition occurred about the time when the Fujiwara consolidated their power as regents at court in the early tenth century. In regard to the transition to the modern age, however, Jien is precise: it occurred in 1156, the year of the Hōgen conflict, which, as we noted, he also calls the starting date of the age of warriors. In his thinking, "modern age" and "age of warriors" (or "military age") were synonymous.

Of the three ages, ancient, medieval, and modern, the medieval represented the ideal to Jien. In the ancient age, emperors (and some empresses) had been able to rule unaided. But by the medieval age, as history continued on its inexorable course of decline, it became necessary to enforce the Sun Goddess's order that the descendants of Ame no Koyane—the Fujiwara—help the emperors rule. The result was what Jien regarded as a brilliant, albeit temporary, revival of history, especially during the time of the greatest regent, Michinaga, in the late tenth and early eleventh centuries. Jien hoped that the spirit of the medieval age might be revived in the early Kamakura period with the appointment of his great-grandnephew, Kujō no Yoritsune, as ruler of the Kamakura shogunate.

ONE HUNDRED KINGS

In addition to the *mappō* theory of historical decline, Jien also subscribed to the belief that Japan would be ruled by only one hundred kings (or emperors; *hyakuō*). An idea received from China, "one hundred kings" seems originally to have meant simply many or an indefinite number of kings. But by the late Heian period, courtiers like Jien, under the influence of *mappō* thought, came to interpret "one hundred kings" literally as exactly one hundred. As Jien points out, only sixteen kingly reigns remained

---

17. The Sun Goddess also ordered the ancestral *kami* of the Imbe family to assist Ninigi (Aston, *Nihongi*, I, p. 83). But the Imbe lost out politically to the Fujiwara during the early Heian period and declined into insignificance at court, thus enabling the Fujiwara to claim that they alone had been mandated by the Sun Goddess to be imperial assistants.

at the time he wrote *Gukanshō*. He tells us nothing about what would happen after the one-hundredth reign.

I have become keenly aware of principles that have been changing since ancient times. I do not know how it was in the Age of the Gods but I hear that after the beginning of the age of man and the enthronement of Emperor Jinmu, Japan is to have only one hundred reigns. Now that we are in the 84th reign not many more are left. . . .

Even [Prince Shōtoku's] Seventeen Article Constitution has become inef-fective during these final reigns because the "principles of things" exist only faintly and unfamiliarly in the hearts of men. Persons of high position have no sympathy for those below, and those below have no respect for those above. Turning against the civil and penal codes (and their supplements) compiled long ago—with the Seventeen Article Constitution as their source—the state is simply going to ruin. It is sad to be thinking only about what can be done about such deterioration. All that can be done until the 100th reign is to rely upon the blessings of the Gods worshipped at the Imperial shrines of Ise and Iwash-imizu, and Kashima and Kasuga, and upon the divine grace of the Three Bud-dhist Treasures and deities of the various Heavens.

[Adapted from Brown and Ishida, *The Future and the Past*, pp. 19, 82–83; PV]

HELPING EMPERORS RULE

In the following passages, Jien refers to the Sun Goddess's directive to the descendants of Ame no Koyane to help emperors rule. He also alludes to what was apparently a second, similar order issued by the Sun Goddess and the Great Hachiman Bodhisattva.

It is desirable to have an Emperor whose behavior as an Emperor is good, but Japan is a country that has had the tradition, since the Age of the Gods, that no person should become Emperor who is not in the Imperial line of descent. It is also the tradition of the country to want an Emperor from that line who will be a good Emperor. But since it has necessarily become difficult for an Emperor to govern the state well by himself, it was established that a Great Imperial Chieftain [i.e., regent] would be appointed and used as Imperial guardian, and that the state would be governed in consultation with this min-ister. . . .

An instruction from the Sun Goddess and the Great Hachiman Bodhisattva created an arrangement . . . by which it would be deemed improper for an Emperor to be the least bit estranged from his guardian. Whether the empire is governed well or becomes chaotic depends on whether that instruction is respected. Long ago, the Sun Goddess made a divine agreement with Ame no

Koyane no Mikoto [the ancestral God of the Fujiwara clan] that the latter was to reside in, and guard the Imperial Palace. The descendants of Ame no Koyane no Mikoto grasped the implications of this Principle, which was not to be violated one iota. . . .

But nothing was amiss in governmental affairs during this Medieval Age, because the abilities of Fujiwara regents were superb and because they assisted Imperial rule and had the state governed well. . . . The reason why governmental affairs came to be handled in this way was that in the Age of the Gods the Sun Goddess had said to the ancestral Gods of the Fujiwara clan: "You will guard the Imperial Palace well." She did so because she realized that Emperors in the Medieval Age would not be like sovereigns in the Ancient Age. Therefore one descendant of the ancestral Gods of the Fujiwara clan after another was born with appropriate ability. . . . [The principle that Emperors would not be able to rule unassisted and the principle that the descendants of the ancestral Gods of the Fujiwara were to assist Emperors] were created together.

[Adapted from Brown and Ishida, *The Future and the Past*, pp. 210–211, 213; PV]

AN APPEAL TO RETIRED EMPEROR GO-TOBA

In this appeal, Jien refers to the retired emperor Go-Toba as both "sovereign" and "His Majesty." The purpose of the appeal is to dissuade Go-Toba from plotting against the Kamakura shogunate because of the possibilities for peace and national unity enabled by the adoption of Jien's great-grandnephew, Kujō no Yoritsune, into the Minamoto in order to become shogun. Jien suggests that Yoritsune will—or at least should—also be made imperial regent in the future in order to preside administratively over both the court and the shogunate. There is no evidence, however, that the court ever considered Yoritsune for the position of regent.

Under the conditions of this Age, the [mistakes] of people will not be rectified unless an honest Shogun emerges. But such a Shogun *has* emerged, because the Great Hachiman Bodhisattva planned to produce a person from the regental house who would protect the state and guard the sovereign with the prestige and power of both learning and military might. And yet the sovereign does not understand that Yoritsune was born for the benefit of state, man, and the sovereign. A very serious matter indeed! It was definitely a divine decision that it would be good for the sovereign to have the same person serve as Shogun and Regent. The ancestral Gods decided to provide the sovereign with a guardian who would also be powerful and prestigious. It would be best if His Majesty understood that Yoritsune's birth and appointment were brought about in this way. . . . By rejecting the plan for Yoritsune to be both Shogun and Regent, the sovereign will be acting contrary to the will of the Sun Goddess and Hachiman. But by accepting it, he will become enlightened. . . .

It has come to my attention that the sovereign is making short-sighted plans [to oppose the shogunate] because he does not understand either the principle of deterioration alternating with improvement from the beginning to the end of the present small kalpa, nor the principle—granted by the ancestral Gods of the Imperial House and of the Fujiwara and Minamoto clans—for this Final Age, a principle that has come down to us from the ancient past. The principles of things, and the history of our country, will surely be stabilized if the sovereign acts according to these principles.

[Brown and Ishida, *The Future and the Past*, pp. 210–211, 213, 225–226; PV]

KITABATAKE CHIKAFUSA AND THE SOUTHERN COURT

The Kamakura shogunate was overthrown in 1333 by warrior forces that rallied to the loyalist cause of Emperor Go-Daigo (r. 1318–1339). Go-Daigo interpreted the shogunate's overthrow as a mandate to revive what he believed had been government by direct imperial rule before the rise, from about the mid-Heian period, of, first, the Fujiwara regents, second, politically powerful retired emperors, and, third, the military (the Kamakura shogunate). This "imperial restoration," known as the Kenmu Restoration, lasted until 1336.

Japan at the time of the Kenmu Restoration was entering a turbulent new age of regionalism in which warrior chieftains throughout the country contended against one another for land and power. The restoration government, whatever its good intentions, was unable to deal either promptly or satisfactorily with the multitude of problems and demands presented to it by contentious warriors. It was bedeviled in particular by a personal struggle for power between Nitta Yoshisada (1301–1338) and Ashikaga Takauji (1305–1358), leaders of the main branches of the Minamoto. In 1335, fighting broke out between these two leaders in which Yoshisada championed the restoration government and Takauji and his army were stigmatized as rebels. In 1336, Takauji defeated Yoshisada in a key battle and captured Kyoto. Go-Daigo, unwilling to accept Takauji as the new military hegemon, fled to Yoshino in the mountainous region to the south. He proclaimed Yoshino the new seat of the court and himself still the rightful sovereign. Takauji, meanwhile, had a member of another branch of the imperial family chosen as emperor in Kyoto, creating a situation in which, for the first time in Japanese history, there were two emperors. Takauji also established a new shogunate, known in history as the Ashikaga or Muromachi shogunate (1336–1573), with its headquarters in Kyoto. During the first half-century of its existence, 1336 to 1392, the shogunate was embroiled in conflict with forces of the Yoshino regime in what came to be called the War Between the Northern (Kyoto) and Southern (Yoshino) Courts.

Kitabatake Chikafusa, scion of a high-ranking noble family (the Murakami

Genji or Minamoto) and formerly a prominent minister at court, did not play a significant role in the Kenmu Restoration. He may have assisted in the arrangements made for Go-Daigo's flight to Yoshino in 1336, but the records remain largely silent about his activities until 1338. In that year, he joined a group that went by sea to the Kantō region in an effort to rally support among eastern warriors for the Southern Court. While in the Kantō, Chikafusa made a particularly intense effort to recruit the chieftain Yūki Chikatomo to the Southern Court's side. The nearly seventy remaining letters from Chikafusa to Chikatomo constitute the largest correspondence from one person to another still extant from the medieval age. In the end, however, Chikafusa was unsuccessful, for in 1343 Chikatomo joined the side of the Ashikaga and the Northern Court. Early the following year, 1344, Chikafusa returned to Yoshino. From then until his death in 1354, he served as one of the Southern Court's leading ministers under Emperor Go-Murakami (r. 1339–1368), the successor to his father, Go-Daigo, who died in 1339.

DIRECT SUCCESSION OF GODS AND SOVEREIGNS (JINNŌ SHŌTŌKI)

Chikafusa began writing his *Direct Succession* (*Jinnō shōtōki*) in 1339 in the Kantō, using, we are told, an imperial genealogy as his only reference. He revised it in 1343. Chikafusa appears to have written the *Direct Succession* at this time as part of his effort to attract Yūki Chikatomo and other eastern warriors to the cause of the Southern Court. The work, like *Gukanshō*, is both a history and a political tract.

As a history, the *Direct Succession* was a product of a Shinto revival that began in the Kamakura period. One premise of this revival was that the gods of Shinto were the true protectors of the country, not the deities of Buddhism who had been thought to perform that function since at least the late seventh century. The effectiveness of the gods' protection appeared to be confirmed when the *kamikaze*, "divine winds," arose to annihilate the enemy fleets during the two Mongol invasions of Japan in 1274 and 1281. In the words of Chikafusa, "the gods, revealing their awesome authority and manifesting their form, drove the invaders away. Thus a great wind suddenly arose and the several hundreds of thousands [*sic*] of enemy ships were all blown over and demolished. Although people speak of this as a degenerate later age, the righteous power displayed by the gods [of Shinto] at this time was truly beyond human comprehension."[18]

Belief that the gods of Shinto held primacy as protectors of the country derived from the concept of Japan as a divine land or "land of the gods" (*shin-*

---

18. Varley, *A Chronicle of Gods and Sovereigns*, p. 234.

koku), which was first expressed in the mythology as found in the *Kojiki* and the *Nihongi*. Used by Chikafusa as a key concept in his interpretation of Japanese history, *shinkoku* first appears in the *Jinnō shōtōki* in its famous opening lines: "Great Japan is the divine land. The heavenly progenitor founded it, and the Sun Goddess bequeathed it to her descendants to rule eternally. Only in our country is this true; there are no similar examples in other countries. This is why our country is called the divine land."[19] Whereas belief in the gods as the true protectors of the country was emphasized in divine-land thought during the late thirteenth century when the Mongols threatened Japan, by Chikafusa's time—or more precisely, because of Chikafusa—the emphasis, as succinctly but powerfully articulated in the preceding lines, was shifted to faith in the mandate of the Sun Goddess that the imperial dynasty would rule forever.

In writing *Gukanshō*, Jien began with the reign of the first emperor, Jinmu. But Chikafusa, in his *Direct Succession*, partly reflecting a revival of interest during the middle and late medieval age in the age of the gods before Jinmu, starts with the story of the creation of the land (Japan) and then describes the reigns of five godly rulers before entering into his main narrative of "human sovereigns," spanning the reigns from Jinmu through Go-Daigo and Go-Murakami.

In their overall views of Japanese history, Jien and Chikafusa differed markedly. Whereas Jien believed that history was following a fundamentally unalterable path of decline and deterioration that might possibly end in the destruction of the world (or at least Japan, as in the theory of one hundred kings), Chikafusa asserted that the Sun Goddess's mandate guaranteed that Japan and its ruling family would continue forever. To Chikafusa, the course of Japanese history was essentially a straight, "direct," and correct (*shō*) line. There might be periodic deviations, but these would always be rectified by a return to the direct line. Chikafusa also discerned a direct line within the imperial succession. Although in fact there had been occasional shifts away from the succession's direct line, all were straightened out with the passage of time. It was precisely the succession's capacity to return invariably to its direct course that guaranteed its legitimacy and ensured its eternal continuance, setting Japan apart from—and making it superior to—countries like India and China: "In our country alone, the imperial succession has followed in an unbroken line from the time when heaven and earth were divided until the present age. Although, as is inevitable within a single family, the succession has at times been transmitted collaterally, the principle has prevailed that it will invariably return to the direct line."[20]

---

19. Ibid., p. 49.
20. Ibid., pp. 60–61.

Jien's and Chikafusa's views of history from the perspective of what might be called the short term, on the other hand, were quite similar. Both, for example, regarded history—especially recent history—from the same class perspective, that of the upper echelon of courtiers. Jien, of course, was one of the bluest of the blue-blooded courtiers by virtue of his birth into the regental branch of the Fujiwara. But Chikafusa was not far behind: he came from a ministerial family descended from Murakami (r. 946–967), one of the most illustrious emperors, that had rivaled the Fujiwara for ministerial power from at least the early years of the Kamakura period. Both Jien and Chikafusa were also imperial restorationists. But their idea of imperial restoration focused more on the return of actual governing power from the military to the hands of the Fujiwara and Murakami Genji in the service of "restored" emperors than to the emperors themselves. As Chikafusa put it: "First [in undertaking decisive administration], there is the selection and appointment of people to the offices of central government. Once the ruler has appointed the proper people to these offices, he need interfere no further in their activities."[21]

The *Direct Succession* is often believed to be a tract arguing the legitimacy of the Southern over the Northern Court, as suggested in the translation of its title into English as the "Chronicle of the Legitimate Succession of Divine Sovereigns (or Gods and Sovereigns)."[22] But Chikafusa has little to say directly about imperial legitimacy in the *Jinnō shōtōki*. He tacitly accepts the legitimacy of all the recognized sovereigns from Jinmu through Go-Daigo, including those from the branch of the imperial family that later provided emperors for the Northern Court. He does claim that Go-Daigo never willingly relinquished the emperorship in 1336, and hence the Northern Court, founded at that time with Ashikaga backing, was illegitimate. But Chikafusa does this in a way suggesting the point did not require arguing. And indeed, other records from the period make clear that the Ashikaga themselves privately believed that Takauji had acted improperly in establishing the Northern Court. Throughout the half century of the War Between the Northern and Southern Courts, the Ashikaga consistently sought not to destroy the Southern Court but to persuade its emperor to return to Kyoto in order to remove the stain of "illegitimacy" from the Northern Court.[23]

---

21. Ibid., p. 251.

22. "Divine Sovereigns" and "Gods and Sovereigns" mean the same thing, since the former phrase includes the five godly rulers who preceded the first human sovereign, Jinmu.

23. In 1392, when the Southern Court had lost most of its capacity to continue fighting, the Ashikaga finally persuaded its emperor to return to Kyoto with the promise that his line would be allowed to provide emperors alternately with the line of the Northern Court. But this promise was never honored, and the Southern Court line sank into historical oblivion.

FUJIWARA AND MURAKAMI GENJI AS ASSISTANTS TO EMPERORS

Chikafusa here discusses the historical rise of the Fujiwara as assistants to emperors, based on the Sun Goddess's mandate to the family's godly forebear, Ame no Koyane (or Ama no Koyane). He then lays claim to a similar "right to assist the throne" for the Murakami Genji because of their descent from Emperor Murakami and the outstanding and virtuous service of many Murakami Genji ministers over the years. Chikafusa also recalls the selection of men in the remote past to serve as both army commanders and ministers at court, combining the functions of the civil (*bun*) and the military (*bu*). He himself became such a minister-commander during the War Between the Courts, and his son Akiie (1318–1338), qualified by birth to be a minister, gave his life fighting as a general in the service of Go-Daigo and the Southern Court.

The imperial family certainly stands apart from other families, yet in our country there has been a mandate since the Age of the Gods stating that while the sovereign, as a descendant of the Sun Goddess, rules over the land, those subjects in the line of Ame-no-Koyane are also mandated to assist the sovereign in his administration of affairs. The [Murakami] Genji are subjects who have recently branched off from the imperial family. Should they, without virtue or merit, rise to high offices and lord it over people, they will surely be visited with punishment by the two great deities, the Sun Goddess and Ame-no-Koyane.

In the ancient age many princes and other royal descendants were given official positions in the provinces and were even appointed as generalissimos. The first to assign such generalissimos [shoguns] was Emperor Sujin who, in the tenth year of his reign, appointed four, all of whom were members of the imperial family, and sent them to the four circuits. Emperor Keikō, in the fifty-first year of his reign, inaugurated the practice of designating a chief among his ministers. The person he selected was Takeuchi-no-Sukune. In the third year of Emperor Seimu's reign, Takeuchi was further advanced to the position of ō-omi. (This marked the beginning of the office of ō-omi or daijin [great minister] in our country.) A great-grandson of Emperor Kōgen, Takeuchi served as an administrator of government during six reigns.

Things changed, however, when Fujiwara no Kamatari revitalized his clan and Yoshifusa ultimately established an imperial regency. For this marked a return to the arrangement decided upon in the age of the gods whereby the descendants of Ame-no-Koyane were to serve as assistants to the throne. Fuyutsugu also contributed much to this reassertion of the divinely mandated rights of the Fujiwara. Lamenting the decline of his clan, Fuyutsugu not only engaged ceaselessly in good works and accumulated great merit, but also prayed to the gods and devoted himself to Buddhism.

Prince Tomohira was indeed a man of great ability and virtue. His son Morofusa, who received the [Murakami] Genji surname and joined the ranks of subjects, also possessed talent in no way inferior to the noted officials of ancient times and achieved fame that spread throughout the land. Morofusa was appointed counselor at the age of seventeen. Devoting himself over a period of decades to the study of ancient court precedent and ceremonial, he rose to the positions of great minister and general of the inner palace guards and served the court until the age of seventy.

. . .

From Morofusa's time, the Murakami Genji have devoted themselves to both Chinese and Japanese learning and have been dedicated with total sincerity to loyal service to the state. Perhaps it is because of this that only the Morofusa line of Genji ministers has continued to thrive over many generations. Although within the line there have been some ministers of doubtful achievement and questionable virtue, their branch families have inevitably declined and died out. Genji in the future should carefully reflect upon the fate of such families as these.

Even though the intent of this book is mainly to record the affairs of sovereigns, I have also spoken several times about the origins of the Fujiwara clan. Moreover, in view of the longevity of the Murakami Genji line, I have wished to record something of the direct succession of ministers to which they are the inheritors. Emperor Murakami's line of sovereigns has continued through seventeen generations, and we note with great admiration and reverence that, thanks to Murakami's enduring virtue, the subject line of Murakami Genji, which he spawned, has continued to serve at court throughout this same sequence of reigns.

[Varley, A Chronicle of Gods and Sovereigns, pp. 188–189; PV]

ON IMPERIAL RESTORATION

In this very revealing passage, Chikafusa sharply criticizes retired emperor Go-Toba for trying to overthrow the Kamakura shogunate in the Jōkyū war of 1221 when the time for doing it "had not yet arrived." In his analysis of the course of recent Japanese history, Chikafusa acknowledges the inevitability of the rise of the military and even praises Minamoto no Yoritomo and the early Hōjō for restoring and maintaining order when the court could not do so. But ultimately, he believes, there had to be a return to "direct" imperial rule. Ever the formalistic conservative in his social thinking, Chikafusa sees disorder occurring in the country when "those who are socially inferior seek to prevail over their superiors." His idea of the ideal military ruler is Hōjō no Yasutoki (1183–1242), who not only "knew his place" and did not himself take high (court) rank or office but also impressed on "the other members of his family and the warrior class in general" not to seek them. Although the Direct Succession, as noted, is often labeled a "Shinto history," Chikafusa in fact has a great deal to say also about both Buddhism and Confucianism. In this passage, as in many others, the Confucian tone is particularly strong, as Chikafusa repeatedly refers to virtuous rule and the welfare and contentment of the people.

In reflecting upon the disturbance of the Jōkyū era, one's mind is indeed apt to be bewildered about the course and meaning of events in this later age. One thing discernible is the beginning of a pattern of behavior whereby those who are socially inferior seek to prevail over their superiors.[24] It is essential, therefore, to assess the events of this time as carefully as possible. Minamoto no Yoritomo's achievements were beyond compare with anything since earliest times in history; yet we can understand why, as Yoritomo sought to gather all the power of the country into his own hands, the imperial family felt uneasy. It is even more understandable why, after Yoritomo's line came to an end and his widow (the nun [Hōjō no] Masako) and the rear vassal [Hōjō no] Yoshitoki took control of the country, Go-Toba should wish to do away with the Bakufu [shogunate] and rule directly himself.

Since the age of Shirakawa and Toba, the ancient way of government had declined steadily,[25] and in Go-Shirakawa's time armed rebellions occurred and treacherous subjects threw the country into disorder. The people of the land fell into almost total misery. Minamoto no Yoritomo restored order by his own force of arms; and, although the imperial house was not returned to its former state, the fighting in the capital was quelled and the burdens of the people were eased. High and low were once again at peace, and people everywhere submitted to Yoritomo's virtue. Apparently it was because of this submission that no one rebelled against the Bakufu, even at the time of Sanetomo's assassination. How then could the Kyoto court expect so readily to overthrow the Bakufu, if it did not have an administration of merit equal to that of Kamakura? Let us suppose the Bakufu had been destroyed. If the people were not thereby made content, Heaven would surely not assent to such a change in governance to the country. The sovereign's army chastises only those who have committed offenses, not the blameless.

It was strictly by means of the royal directives of retired monk-emperor Go-Shirakawa that Yoritomo rose to high offices and received appointment as constable-general of the country. One can scarcely say that he selfishly seized these offices for himself.

After Yoritomo's death, Masako took charge of affairs at Kamakura, and later Yoshitoki wielded power for a long while. But since Masako and Yoshitoki did

---

24. This is the concept of *gekokujō* (those below overthrow those above) that was so aptly used to characterize social upheaval at various levels during the medieval age.

25. The ancient (and proper) way of government was, in Chikafusa's mind, that prevailing during the heyday of the Fujiwara regents: rule by the sovereign assisted by a small group of his highest ministers at court. The assumption of power by Shirakawa and Toba as retired emperors was a perversion of such government.

not go against the hopes of the people, they committed no transgressions as subjects "from below." We may indeed say that the attempt by Go-Toba to overthrow the Kamakura Bakufu for insufficient reason was a transgression "from above."

The Jōkyū incident cannot be likened to a conflict in which enemies of the throne rise in rebellion and are victorious. Since the time for opposing the Kamakura regime had not yet arrived, Heaven clearly would not permit Go-Toba's action to succeed. Nevertheless, it is the greatest of offenses for social inferiors to exceed their superiors, and ultimately the day must come when all people submit to the imperial sway. Until that time it is essential to understand that the proper course for the court is to begin by establishing a truly virtuous government and asserting its royal authority. Only then can those subjects who do not submit be overthrown. And even at that point the state of order or disorder in the country must be carefully assessed and the final decision to take up arms or set them aside must be based not on personal desire but on the will of Heaven and the hope of the people.

Eventually the imperial succession did return to the direct line, and in the time of Go-Toba's descendant, Go-Daigo, unity was restored to the country under direct imperial rule. Go-Toba's wish was thus ultimately fulfilled. But how regrettable it is that even for a brief while the throne was visited with such misfortune.

. . .

Yoshitoki was succeeded by Yasutoki, who conducted government virtuously and codified strict laws. Not only did he know his own place, Yasutoki admonished the other members of his family and the warrior class in general, so that there was none among them who coveted high office and rank. Later, when Hōjō rule gradually declined and finally was destroyed, it was because the family's stock in heaven's fate ran out. The Hōjō, however, had little to complain of, since the residue of Yasutoki's virtue had sustained their rule for as long as seven generations.

[Varley, A Chronicle of Gods and Sovereigns, pp. 224–226, 229; PV]

Chapter 12

THE WAY OF THE WARRIOR

Sometime in the late seventh century, as part of its long-term effort to construct a centralized, bureaucratic state on the Chinese model, the Japanese court developed a countrywide military system by establishing militia units in the provinces under the command of the provincial governors. These units, known as *gundan*, were made up of (1) foot soldiers conscripted from the peasantry as part of the corvée labor tax imposed under the Taika reform's equal-field system of landholding and (2) horse-mounted officers drawn from locally powerful families.

The origins of fighting on horseback in Japan are obscure, although it is possible that this form of combat was either introduced or greatly advanced by the importation of military technology, weapons, and equipment from the Asian continent—especially Korea—during the late fourth and fifth centuries. Terra cotta figurines (*haniwa*) of armor-clad, mounted warriors and their battle-ready mounts found on the surfaces of tombs from the fifth century suggest that by that time, if not earlier, a class of formidable equestrian warriors, armed with bows and swords, had evolved in Japan. The bow was the primary weapon, a fact reflected in the later description of the way of the warrior as the "way of the bow and horse" (*kyūba no michi*).

In addition to establishing *gundan* in the various provinces (usually one to a province), the court placed extra units in northern Kyushu to defend against possible invasion from the continent. Soldiers from some units were also assigned to perform guard duty in the capital, which from 710 on was Nara. When necessary, larger armies could be organized by mobilizing troops from two or more *gundan*. During such mobilizations, commanders favored men from the eastern provinces of the Kantō, which from earliest times was regarded as the home of Japan's best equestrian fighters. Kantō men had ready access to the finest horses, which were bred in the Kantō and in Mutsu Province just to the north, and these fighters were trained from infancy in riding, archery, and the other military skills.

The real test of the *gundan*'s effectiveness came during the campaigns that the court conducted against the Emishi in northern Honshu during the last decades of the eighth century and the opening years of the ninth. In 801, the redoubtable commander Sakanoue no Tamuramaro (758–811) succeeded in conquering the Emishi and incorporating their land, which comprised Mutsu and Dewa Provinces, into the Japanese state. For this, Tamuramaro, who was the first to hold the title of *sei-i tai-shōgun* or "great general for subduing the eastern barbarians," has also been celebrated as the first great warrior chief in Japanese history. Thus we read in an eleventh-century war tale:

> Our court in ancient times often sent forth great armies. Although these armies destroyed many barbarians within the provinces [of Mutsu and Dewa], they never completely defeated them. Then Sakanoue no Tamuramaro was called upon to go down to Mutsu-Dewa, and he bequeathed his fame to myriad generations by conquering the barbarians throughout the six districts. He was like an incarnation of the god of the northern heavens, a general of distinction rarely to be seen.[1]

Although the Emishi were finally defeated, it took a long time and a number of campaigns. Whereas the Emishi were excellent horsemen and tough fighters, specializing in hit-and-run guerrilla tactics, the Japanese armies proved cumbersome and were often outwitted and embarrassed. The peasant foot soldiers, organized along Chinese lines and relying on the crossbow as their principal weapon, were largely ineffective fighters. Because of this and also because the conscription system as a whole had proved excessively burdensome to the peasantry, in 792—nearly a decade before Tamuramaro's great campaign—the court abandoned conscription. Although foot soldiers continued to be used in armies in the ninth and even tenth centuries, they were gradually eliminated, and warfare became almost exclusively the preserve of mounted warriors from locally powerful families. By the tenth century, a distinct warrior class drawn from these families had emerged in the provinces.

Much of our knowledge about the warrior class during its early centuries of

---

1. *Mutsu waki*, in Hanawa, comp., *Gunsho ruijū*, vol. 20, p. 32.

evolution comes from a genre of writing called "war tales" (*gunki-mono*). The first of these tales, *The Chronicle of Masakado* (*Shōmonki*), which deals with the rebellion of Taira no Masakado (d. 940) in the Kantō in 939–940, was probably written in the late tenth century. Although war tales continued to be composed from this time until the seventeenth century, the finest of them recount the fighting that accompanied (1) the transition from the ancient age to the medieval age (or from the Heian period to the Kamakura period) in the late twelfth century and (2) the overthrow of the Kamakura shogunate and the ensuing War Between the Courts (1336–1392) in the fourteenth century.

Focused primarily on warriors and warfare, the war tales are based on historical events but have been embellished to various degrees. Hence they are mixtures of history and fiction. Little is known about the authorship of any of the tales, although in some cases, such as the two most important tales, *The Tale of the Heike* (*Heike monogatari*) and *Taiheiki*, they clearly are the products of more than one author. As the principal repositories of information about warriors, their values, behavior, and exploits for at least the tenth through the fourteenth centuries, the war tales are indispensable sources for historians investigating the early stages in the evolution of a warrior ethos in Japan. But historians also must be cautious, for when studying the tales, they constantly need to judge between fact and fiction.

Beginning with *The Chronicle of Masakado*, the early war tales were written in Chinese and therefore lack some of the flavor of the later tales (i.e., those from about the twelfth century), which were composed in a Japanese vernacular rich in the special vocabulary and lingo of the warriors. But even in *Masakado* and the other early tales in Chinese, we can see the essential character and style of the provincial warrior who was to dominate fighting in Japan for centuries to come. He was a man on horseback who specialized in archery and fought in a highly individualistic manner. When armies of warriors clashed, those on each side sought out opponents of equal or higher status on the other side with whom to engage in one-to-one combat. *The Chronicle of Masakado* tells us little about the relationships among the warriors of the same side or army, but in tales from the eleventh century we learn that they were bound by superior-inferior ties as lords and vassals and that the armies themselves were made up of bands of warriors, each consisting of a lord and his vassals.

The lord-vassal relationship, which became the central feature of what we call feudalism, is idealized in the war tales as a reciprocal compact bound by the highest degree of loyalty on the part of the vassal and by parent-like, loving care by the lord. Thus we read in *A Tale of Mutsu* (*Mutsu waki*), the story of a war fought in Mutsu Province in northern Honshu in 1056–1062, that because the chieftain Minamoto no Yoriyoshi (998–1075) "cared for [his vassals] and saw to their needs, more than half of the men of bow and horse east of Osaka became his followers." And after a particular battle in the Mutsu war, Yoriyoshi is said to have fed his soldiers and put their equipment in order. He personally went around the camp, tending to the wounded. The soldiers were deeply moved and all said: "We will repay our obligations (on) with our bodies. We consider our lives as nothing compared to loyalty [or honor, gi]. If it is for the general, we do not in the least regret dying now.[2]

As portrayed in the war tales, the vassal warrior is typically motivated by great loyalty for his lord, but he is also highly sensitive to his personal honor and to the honor of his house. In this regard, warrior society in this age—and indeed throughout the premodern centuries—can aptly be described as a "shame" society, inasmuch as the maintenance of honor required that the warrior avoid shame above all or, if he has been shamed, that he avenge the insult and redeem his honor. And therein lay a problem, for the demands made on the warrior by loyalty to his lord on the one hand and personal honor on the other could easily lead to a clash of interests in which the warrior was obliged to choose between the two—that is, between loyalty (lord) and honor (self). Although the loyalty-honor clash is not, in fact, a theme found often in the war tales, it was always a potentially powerful issue among warriors. Thus, for example, in the tumultuous years of the Sengoku age (Age of the Country at War, 1478–1568), territorial chiefs known as daimyō staked their capacities to administer and maintain their domains largely on their success in preventing or stamping out the personal feuds over honor among their almost paranoically "face"-conscious vassals.

The war tales are celebrations of the warrior's way and life, and much of their focus is on the portrayal of great warrior heroes. In some cases, these heroes are historically authentic fighters or chieftains of note; in other cases, they are fictional creations of the tales' authors. In virtually all cases, however, the great heroes of the war tales have been inflated into larger-than-life—sometimes superhuman—champions. One of the earliest examples of such a champion is Minamoto no Yoshiie (1041–1108), the son of the aforementioned Yoriyoshi, who was in fact an eminent chief and probably also a very good combat warrior but who is described in A Tale of Mutsu in the following implausibly hyperbolic terms:

[Yoriyoshi's] oldest son, Yoshiie, was a warrior of peerless valor. He rode and shot arrows like a god. Defying naked blades, he broke through the rebel's encirclements, appearing first on their left and then on their right. With his large-headed arrows, he shot the rebel chieftains in rapid succession. He never wasted an arrow, but mortally wounded all those he attacked. Known throughout the land for his godly martial ways, Yoshiie

---

2. Ibid., p. 29.

rode like thunder and flew like the wind. The barbarians scattered and fled before Yoshiie, not one willing to confront him. The barbarians called . . . him Hachiman Tarō, the firstborn son of the war god Hachiman.[3]

An example of a fictional champion or superhero in the war tales is Minamoto no Tametomo (1139–1177), who appears in *The Tale of Hōgen* (*Hōgen monogatari*), the story of a clash of arms in Kyoto in 1156. There was, in fact, a real Minamoto no Tametomo, but almost nothing is known about him. In *The Tale of Hōgen*, however, Tametomo almost single-handedly holds off an entire army during a nighttime attack. His credentials for doing this are stated in the *Hōgen* in these words:

More than seven feet tall, Tametomo exceeded the ordinary man's height by two or three feet. Born to archery, he had a bow arm that was some six inches longer than the arm with which he held his horse's reins. . . . [He used] a bow that was more than eight and a half feet in length.[4]

Elsewhere in the *Hōgen*, Tametomo is described as "unlike a human being" and "a demon or monster."

TAIRA AND MINAMOTO

As warrior bands took shape in the provinces in the middle and late Heian period, they drew their leadership largely from the great Taira (or Heike) and Minamoto (or Genji) clans. Taira and Minamoto were the surnames of former imperial princes who, beginning in the ninth century, had taken up posts in the provincial governments, become warriors, and established positions of power in the regions where they served. By the time of the revolt by Taira no Masakado in the mid-tenth century, many branches of both Taira and Minamoto were scattered throughout the Kantō and elsewhere. One reason that these clans branched out so rapidly and widely was that many men not related by blood joined them in order to call themselves Taira and Minamoto and share in the high prestige of these names.

In the late eleventh century, one branch of the Minamoto gained great fame through their participation in two wars in the Mutsu-Dewa region of northern Honshu. The first of these wars, fought in 1056–1062 and known as the Former Nine-Years War (although the fighting spanned only six years), pitted the Minamoto under Yoriyoshi against the Abe, independent-minded local officials who

---

3. Ibid., p. 25.
4. Nagazumi and Shimada, eds., *Hōgen monogata*ri, p. 81.

had flouted the orders of the Kyoto court. In the second war, the Later Three Years War, which actually lasted only two years, 1086 to 1087, Yoriyoshi's son Yoshiie, who helped his father defeat the Abe (in the process of which he was dubbed, according to A Tale of Mutsu, the "Firstborn Son of Hachiman" because of his fighting prowess), intervened in his capacity as governor of Mutsu in a dispute within the Kiyowara family. Although Yoshiie was able, under harsh climatic conditions and with great difficulty, to achieve victory for the Kiyowara chief he backed, he gained nothing personally from the Later Three Years War except enhanced status as a military commander. This, however, proved to be considerable: from this time on, Yoshiie was widely recognized as the first among warriors in the land.

Not long after Yoshiie gained renown in warfare in Mutsu-Dewa in the late eleventh century, members of a branch of the Taira family from Ise Province came into prominence in the service of senior retired emperors in Kyoto. During the twelfth century, both the Ise Taira and Yoshiie's line of the Minamoto became increasingly involved in court politics, the Taira as agents of the retired emperors and the Minamoto as armed guards or "claws and teeth" of the Fujiwara regents. In 1156, a factional dispute broke out between Emperor Goshirakawa (1127–1192) and Retired Emperor Sutoku (1119–1164), Goshirakawa's older brother. Fujiwara ministers lined up on both sides, as did Taira and Minamoto (some Taira and some Minamoto on each side). This dispute soon escalated into the first clash of arms in Kyoto since the early ninth century. Known in history as the Hōgen conflict, it lasted only one night and was won by Goshirakawa's side. Although brief, the Hōgen conflict was important because, in the words of a contemporary historian, it ushered in the "age of warriors."

THE TALE OF HŌGEN (HŌGEN MONOGATARI)

On the night of the Hōgen conflict, Retired Emperor Sutoku and the courtiers and warriors who backed him gathered in the Shirakawa Palace in Kyoto, while Emperor Goshirakawa and his followers established themselves in the nearby Takamatsu Palace. In the following passage, the Sutoku side listens first to Minamoto no Tametomo on how to conduct the coming battle. Tametomo recommends that they attack the Takamatsu Palace and burn it. But Minister of the Left Fujiwara no Yorinaga (1120–1156), the ranking minister present, haughtily dismisses this advice as youthful impulsiveness and not at all appropriate to a situation in which men are fighting for an emperor and a retired emperor. Even assuming that this exchange between Tametomo and Yorinaga is apocryphal, it nicely contrasts the thinking of representatives of two ages: a courtier of the fast-vanishing ancient age, who looks with disdain on warriors as a lesser breed and does not hesitate to chide one for suggesting a breach of what he regards as the proper conduct of war, and a warrior chief from the provinces who, exemplifying the spirit of the advancing medieval age, cares nothing for "proper conduct" but thinks only of what must be done to win. His advice rejected, Tametomo grumbles as he withdraws from the audience with the retired emperor that surely his older brother Yoshitomo (1123–1160), one of the chiefs on Emperor Goshirakawa's side, will seize the opportunity to attack and burn *their* palace, the Shirakawa Palace. And in the central irony of *The Tale of Hōgen,* that is exactly what Yoshitomo does.

Retired Emperor Sutoku and all the people with him gathered to see the celebrated Minamoto no Tametomo. When the Great Minister of the left, Fujiwara no Yorinaga, then ordered, "State your plan as to the conduct of battle," Tametomo replied respectfully: "Tametomo has lived long in the Chinzei [Kyushu], and he has engaged in I do not know how many battles, great and small, in bringing under subjection the people of the Nine Provinces [of Kyushu]. Among them more than twenty required special effort. Whether to break strong positions though surrounded by enemy, or to destroy the enemy when attacking a fortified place, in any case there is nothing equal to night attack to achieve victory. Therefore if we bear down on the Takamatsu Palace immediately, set fire to it on three sides and hold them in check on the fourth side, those who escape the fire cannot escape the arrows, and those who fear the arrows cannot escape the fire. The warriors on the emperor's side are not awfully good. But only let my brother Yoshitomo and his kind try to rush out, I'll shoot them through the middle. All the more so with weak shots like Taira no Kiyomori. They are not likely to count for much; I'll sweep them away with my armor sleeve or kick them away. If the Emperor moves to another place, if it is clear that, begging his pardon, the people with him are going to get shot up a little, it is certain that the bearers will abandon the palanquin and try to escape. At that time Tametomo will come up and conduct the Emperor to this palace; putting our sovereign, Retired Emperor Sutoku, on the Throne should be like turning over my hand. Meeting and receiving the Emperor being only a matter of Tametomo letting off two or three arrows, what doubt can there be of settling the issue before dawn?"

When Tametomo had spoken thus freely, the Great Minister of the Left thereupon said: "What Tametomo proposes is a crude scheme which is quite out of the question. Perhaps it is something one does when one is young—a thing like a night attack is a private matter in a fight among you warriors, which involves only ten or twenty. In a struggle for the realm befitting the Emperor and Retired Emperor, when the issue is to be decided with every member of the Taira and Minamoto on one side or the other, it is completely out of the question. Besides, the Retired Emperor has summoned the soldier-monks from Nara. . . . We must wait for them, effect our joint arrangement of troops, and then engage the enemy." . . .

Tametomo gave in to superior authority, but leaving the audience he grumbled to himself: "Since this is a matter in no way resembling either previous precedents in Japan or China, or the traditional rules for conduct of Court ceremonial, he ought to leave the conduct of fighting to fighting men, but since he doesn't, what can one do about this senseless scheme? Since Yoshitomo is a man well versed in the stratagems of war, he must certainly intend to come at us tonight. If he postpones until tomorrow, the lay-monks from Yoshino and the soldier-monks from Nara will join us. If he advances now and sets fires upwind of us how can we possibly win, even if we fight? If the enemy follows up his advantage, not one of us is likely to escape."

[Wilson, trans., *Hōgen monogatari*, pp. 26–28; PV]

THE NIGHT ATTACK ON THE SHIRAKAWA PALACE

Until Yoshitomo resorts to arson, Tametomo the superhero almost single-handedly fends off all attackers from the Goshirakawa side during the night attack on the Shirakawa Palace. In this passage, Taira no Kiyomori (1118–1181), leading a force that includes three members of the Itō family (Itō no Kagetsuna, Itō no Roku, and Itō no Go), prepares to attack the palace gate defended by Tametomo. Itō no Kagetsuna, representing Kiyomori, advances and identifies himself and his two kin and demands that Tametomo also identify himself—that is, perform the traditional "name announcing" (*nanori*) that was common among warriors before and even during battle. In the typical name announcing, a warrior recited his family genealogy, listed the honors and battle accomplishments of his ancestors and himself, and taunted his adversary. In this case, Tametomo, stating that he does not regard either Kiyomori or Kagetsuna to be "worthy enemies," simply summarizes his genealogy and tells Kagetsuna to "clear out." Reflecting the acute status consciousness of warriors of his time, Tametomo considers Kagetsuna in particular to be far too low socially to deserve the honor of fighting with him. But when Kagetsuna boasts in his name announcing about himself and insults Tametomo by calling him a "rebel against the Imperial Mandate," Tametomo accepts the challenge. Brushing off an arrow shot by Kagetsuna, he launches one of his own that goes clear through the armor and body of Itō no Roku and lodges in the sleeve of Itō no Go. In awe, Kagetsuna likens this prodigious feat of strength to a similar feat by Tametomo's ancestor Yoshiie, who, at the time of the Later Three Years War, shot an arrow through three suits of armor hung on a tree branch. Hearing this and other, similar comments, Kiyomori suggests that they leave Tametomo alone and attack another gate of the Shirakawa Palace.

Taira no Kiyomori had paused facing the west side of the east bank of the riverbed at Nijō. Fifty horsemen of his force went forward and advanced as vanguard. "What men are holding this place? Name yourselves! We who speak are dwellers in Ise province, of the band of the Lord of Aki, Taira no Kiyomori. We are the warrior Itō no Kagetsuna of Furuichi, and Itō no Go and Itō no Roku of the same family."

Minamoto no Tametomo, hearing this, said, "I think even Kiyomori, the master of you fellows, is an unworthy enemy. Though the Taira are descendants of Emperor Kanmu, over the years they have degenerated. As for the Minamoto, who does not know about them? It is nine generations from Emperor Seiwa to Tametomo. I am Chinzei Hachirō no Tametomo, eighth son of the Rokujō Hōgen no Tameyoshi, grandson of Lord Hachiman (Yoshiie), seventh generation from Prince Rokuson. If you are Kagetsuna, clear out!"

Kagetsuna: "From ancient times, both houses, Minamoto and Taira, have furnished military commanders to the realm, and in striking those who rebel against the Imperial mandate, followers of both houses have had occasion to shoot down commanders on the other side. While I am of the same company, I have the honor of being known by the Court. For I am Kagetsuna who received the Imperial appointment as vice-commander-in-chief, having captured and bound Ono no Shichirō, the bandit ring-leader of Suzukayama in the province of Ise. See whether an arrow shot by a base fellow hits or not!"

So saying, he drew to the full and shot, but Tametomo made nothing of this. "Though I think you are an unworthy enemy, for the charm of your words I will give you an arrow; have it! And make it an honor in this life or a remembrance in the next!" With this he fitted one to his bowstring, of three-year-old close-jointed bamboo rubbed down a little, fletched with copper pheasant tail-feathers, and with a seven-and-a-half-inch round-edged broad head with tang more than a half-shaft in length. Pausing a moment, he let it off whistling. Piercing unchecked the breastplate of Itō no Roku who was in the lead, the arrow passed on the other side through the left sleeve of Itō no Go and stuck in the lining of his armor. Roku fell dead on the spot.

Itō no Go broke off the arrow and went before his commander, "Look at Tametomo's arrow! One cannot feel this the act of an ordinary man. Roku is already dead!" When he said this the Lord of Aki (Kiyomori) and all the warriors who saw the arrow wagged their tongues in fright.

Kagetsuna spoke: "[A]t the time of the Later Three Years War [my ancestor, Kiyowara no Takenori, said to Lord Hachiman (Yoshiie):] 'When struck by my lord's arrow, there is no such thing as impenetrable helmet or armor. May I see for certain the power of my lord with the bow?' Yoshiie piled up three suits of armor of good leather and hung them on a tree branch, and when he shot through all six layers, they feared him as the manifestation of a demon. From that time the warriors were all the more devoted to him, it is said, but I have only heard it told. Is such strength with the bow now before my eyes? Dreadful!" He spoke in terror.

Subjected to talk in this vein from many mouths, the commander said, "It is not that I, Kiyomori, have received orders to attack this particular gate without fail. It is only by chance that I have charged against it. Orders were only to charge in somewhere. So how about the east gate?"

[Wilson, trans., *Hōgen monogatari*, pp. 36–37; PV]

THE TALE OF HEIJI (HEIJI MONOGATARI)

The chieftain primarily responsible for victory in the Hōgen conflict was Min-amoto no Yoshitomo, Tametomo's older brother. But the court chose to reward Taira no Kiyomori far more generously than he for his participation in the conflict. Disgruntled and resentful, Yoshitomo was drawn by the minister Fu-jiwara no Nobuyori (1133–1159), who was also dissatisfied with the court's recent actions, into a scheme to overthrow Kiyomori and the leaders at court. Choosing a time in 1159 when Kiyomori was absent from Kyoto on a religious pilgrimage, Yoshitomo and Nobuyori made their move, attacking and burning the Sanjō Palace, residence of the retired emperor Goshirakawa, and transporting Goshi-rakawa to the emperor's palace, where they placed him in confinement. But Kiyomori returned quickly to Kyoto and managed to smuggle Goshirakawa's son, Emperor Nijō, out of the palace disguised as a lady-in-waiting and to escort him to the main Taira residence at Rokuhara in the southeastern part of the capital. Kiyomori and the Taira now claimed that they were the "emperor's army" and branded their Minamoto adversaries "rebels." The Heiji conflict, as this clash came to be called, reached its climax soon thereafter in a battle that began at one of the gates of the imperial palace and ended in a decisive triumph for the Taira. Yoshitomo, the defeated Minamoto commander, tried to escape to the eastern provinces but was murdered on the way by a treacherous vassal.

THE BURNING OF THE SANJŌ PALACE

Arson played a dramatic role in the Heiji conflict, as it had in the Hōgen conflict. The description in *The Tale of Heiji* of the burning of the Sanjō Palace, which started the Heiji conflict, is memorable as one of the few scenes in the war tales (at least before *Taiheiki* in the fourteenth century) that conveys some of the true brutality and horror of warfare. For the most part, though, the war tales romanticize militarism and warrior behavior, and most battle scenes are not graphic. Warriors and others are killed, to be sure, but there is very little description of the blood, gore, and suffering that must have accompanied such killing. The *Heiji*'s description of the burning of the Sanjō Palace is doubly shocking because in a capital city that had not witnessed the bloodshed of war in two and a half centuries (except for the one-night Hōgen conflict, which seems to have involved only the combatants), "nobles, courtiers and even ladies-in-waiting" were wantonly "shot down or slashed to death." In their terror, some of these nonwarriors even jumped into wells where "the bottom ones in a short time had drowned, those in the middle had been crushed to death by their fellows, and those on top had been burned up by the flames themselves." There could be no more striking proof of how Japan's world was changing in the transition from rule by courtiers to rule by warriors. In samurai history, the burning of the Sanjō Palace is highlighted in the account of it in *The Tale of Heiji* and also in a magnificent visual re-creation of the burning in the first scroll of the *Picture Scrolls of the Tale of Heiji (Heiji monogatari ekotoba)*. This first scroll was obtained by Ernest Fenollosa in the late nineteenth century and placed in the Boston Museum of Fine Arts. It remains one of the most valuable of Japanese art treasures held outside Japan.

At this time, on the night of the ninth day of the same moon, just at the hour of the rat [midnight], Lord Nobuyori, with Yoshitomo, the Director of the Stables of the Left, as his general and with more than five hundred of his mounted men, advanced on the Sanjō Palace, the residence of the Retired Emperor Goshirakawa. They secured the gates on all four sides, and Nobuyori, the Colonel of the Gate Guards of the Right, while mounted said, "Though I have received Your Majesty's favor for years, I have heard that because of Shinzei's slanderous statements, I, Nobuyori, am to be stricken down.[5] Therefore, in order to save my life for a while, I am going down to the eastland."

The Retired Emperor was greatly surprised at this and said in amazement, "Who would do away with you?" The Fushimi Middle Counselor, Lord Minamoto no Moronaka, then brought up the Imperial carriage and told him to hasten to get into it, while voices cried, "Hurry and set the fires." The Retired Emperor mounted into the carriage in confusion, and his younger sister, Jōsai-mon'in, who was in the same palace, got into the carriage and the others surrounded them in front and rear and on the right and left and took them to the Imperial Palace. . . .

The situation at the Sanjō Palace was beyond description. Soldiers were guarding all the gates, and flames were shooting up here and there. Wild flames filled the heavens, and a tempestuous wind swept up clouds of smoke. The nobles, courtiers and even the ladies-in-waiting of the women's quarters were shot down or slashed to death, for it was thought that they perhaps constituted the whole of Shinzei's family. When they rushed out, so as not to be burned by the fire, they met with arrows. When they turned back, so that they would not be struck by the arrows, they were consumed by the flames. Those who were afraid of the arrows and terrified by the flames even jumped into the wells in large numbers, and of these, too, the bottom ones in a short time had drowned, those in the middle had been crushed to death by their fellows, and those on top had been burned up by the flames themselves. The palace buildings, built one beside the other, were swept by a fierce wind, and ashes spewed forth upon the ground. How could anyone at all have saved himself? The Imperial consorts and the ladies-in-waiting were not destroyed in the burning

---

5. Fujiwara no Shinzei was an ally of Taira no Kyomori and Nobuyori's chief ministerial rival at court.

of the A-fang palace, but the loss of life among the "moon nobles" and "cloud courtiers" in the burning of this retreat of a Retired Emperor was indeed terrible.

[Reischauer and Yamagiwa, trans., *Translations from Early Japanese Literature*, pp. 301–302; PV]

THE TALE OF THE HEIKE (HEIKE MONOGATARI)

Victory in the Heiji conflict set the stage for the further rise of Kiyomori and the Ise Taira at court. Although warriors, the Taira now devoted themselves primarily to court politics and advancement within courtier society. Kiyomori, in particular, acquired steadily higher court ranks and offices, finally becoming chancellor (*daijō daijin*), the court's highest appointive position. Having married his daughter into the imperial family, Kiyomori in 1180 capped his rise to supremacy at court by crowning his infant grandson as Emperor Antoku (1178–1185).

The rapid, and sometimes ruthless, advance of the Ise Taira incurred the resentment of many in Kyoto, including the retired emperor Goshirakawa, Kiyomori's chief rival for power at court. In 1177, Kiyomori suppressed a plot against him to which Goshirakawa was privy. Three years later, in 1180, a prince who had been passed over in the imperial succession to make way for Antoku dispatched an edict to Minamoto chieftains in the provinces, calling on them to take up arms and overthrow Kiyomori and the Ise Taira. Among those who responded to the edict was Minamoto no Yoritomo (1147–1199), who had been exiled as a youth to the Kantō twenty years earlier in the wake of the Minamoto defeat in the Heiji conflict. In the five-year war (Genpei War, 1180–1185) that was sparked by the prince's edict, Yoritomo gradually emerged as the supreme Minamoto commander, and it was under his orders that the Minamoto forces finally defeated and annihilated the Ise Taira at the naval battle of Dannoura in the straits between Honshu and Kyushu in 1185. Yoritomo himself remained at his headquarters at Kamakura in the Kantō throughout the Genpei War, simultaneously directing the Minamoto in battle from afar and establishing the offices of what became Japan's first warrior government, the Kamakura shogunate.

"THE MIGHTY FALL AT LAST, THEY ARE DUST BEFORE THE WIND"

Like *The Tale of Hōgen* and *The Tale of Heiji*, *The Tale of the Heike* was first written in the early thirteenth century and subsequently underwent a long process of embellishment, primarily by guilds of blind monks who traveled the country telling its stories to the accompaniment of a lute-like instrument called a *biwa*. The most widely disseminated version of the *Heike* was completed in 1371, nearly two hundred years after the events it covers.

More than any other war tale, the *Heike* is a work unified throughout by a single theme, the rise and fall of the Ise Taira. This theme is dramatically enunciated in the *Heike's* opening lines, in which we learn that the Ise Taira, full of arrogance and hubris, have risen to dizzying heights at court and in courtier society but, because of their very success, are in for a great fall. The Taira are led by Kiyomori, whom the *Heike* ranks among the most heinous villains of Chinese and Japanese history. This demonization of Kiyomori—and, by association, the entire Taira clan—provides the main "reason" that the Taira will surely fall, but in the larger scheme of things, the fall of the Taira symbolizes the inevitable decline of the world as a whole in the dark and disastrous age of *mappō*, the "end of the Buddhist Law."

The sound of the Gion Shōja bells echoes the impermanence of all things; the color of the *sala* flowers reveals the truth that the prosperous must decline. The proud do not endure, they are like a dream on a spring night; the mighty fall at last, they are dust before the wind.

In a distant land [China], there are examples set by Zhao Gao of Qin, Wang Mang of Han, Zhu Yi of Liang and Lushan of Tang, all of them men who prospered after refusing to be governed by their former lords and sovereigns, but who met swift destruction because they disregarded admonitions, failed to recognize approaching turmoil, and ignored the nation's distress. Closer to home [Japan], there have been Masakado of Shōhei, Sumitomo of Tengyō, Yoshichika of Kōwa and Nobuyori of Heiji, every one of them proud and mighty. But closest of all, and utterly beyond the power of mind to comprehend or tongue to relate, is the tale of Taira no Ason Kiyomori, the Rokuhara Buddhist Novice and Former Chancellor.

[McCullough, trans., *The Tale of the Heike*, p. 23; PV]

EASTERN WARRIORS

We have noted that from early times, the warriors of the eastern provinces of the Kantō were regarded as the best fighters in Japan. In the Genpei War, as narrated in the *Heike*, the eastern warriors (the Minamoto) are portrayed as so superior to the western warriors (the Taira) in martial ability that there is never any doubt about the war's outcome. We are made aware of this discrepancy in fighting ability at the very beginning of the war when the commander of a Taira army sent to chastise the rebel Yoritomo in the east asks one of the warriors in his army, Saitō no Sanemori, who is from the east and was previously a follower of the Minamoto, "How many men in the Eight Provinces [of the Kantō] can wield a strong bow as well as you do?"

Sanemori uttered a derisive laugh. "Do you think I use long arrows? They barely measure thirteen fists.[6] Any number of warriors in the east can equal that: nobody is called a long-arrow man there unless he draws a fifteen-fist shaft. A strong bow is held to be one that requires six stout men for the stringing. One of those powerful archers can easily penetrate two or three suits of armor when he shoots.

"Every big landholder commands at least five hundred horsemen. Once a rider mounts, he never loses his seat; however rugged the terrain he gallops over, his horse never falls. If he sees his father or son cut down in battle, he rides over the dead body and keeps on fighting. In west-country battles, a man who loses a father leaves the field and is seen no more until he has made offerings and completed a mourning period; someone who loses a son is too overwhelmed with grief to resume the fight at all. When westerners run out of commissariat rice, they stop fighting until after the fields are planted and harvested. They think summertime is too hot for battle, and wintertime too cold. Easterners are entirely different."

[McCullough, trans., *The Tale of the Heike*, pp. 188–189; PV]

THE TAIRA AS COURTIER-WARRIORS

A major phenomenon in the history of the samurai was the merging of the *bu* (the military) and the *bun* (the courtly)—that is, the assumption of courtly tastes and the adoption of courtly ways by warriors. This phenomenon was especially marked during times when samurai leaders and their followers lived in Kyoto in proximity to the court, for example, during the Ise Taira's residence there in the decades leading up to the Genpei War and during the entire Ashikaga or Muromachi period, 1336–1573, when the Ashikaga shogunate was situated in the imperial capital. In the *Heike*, the Taira are portrayed as no match militarily for the Minamoto, in part because they have lived so long in Kyoto, enjoying the elegance of court life and becoming soft and "courtly." There are countless scenes in the *Heike* that portray the Taira as what can be described as courtier warriors. Probably the most famous such scene is "The Death of Atsumori," in which, after killing the young Taira commander Atsumori, a Minamoto adherent, Kumagai no Naozane, is astonished to find a flute in a bag at Atsumori's waist. Observing that no one in the Minamoto army would think of bringing such a thing as a flute into battle, Naozane observes, "These court nobles are refined men!" In his sense of awe and admiration for the socially and culturally superior, Naozane goes so far as to refer to the Taira as court nobles.

Kumagai no Jirō Naozane walked his horse toward the beach after the defeat of the Heike. "The Taira nobles will be fleeing to the water's edge in the hope

---

6. Arrows were measured by units determined by the width of a fist.

of boarding rescue vessels," he thought. "Ah, how I would like to grapple with a high-ranking Commander-in-Chief!" Just then, he saw a lone rider splash into the sea, headed toward a vessel in the offing. The other was attired in crane-embroidered *nerinuki* silk *hitatare*, a suit of armor with shaded green lacing, and a horned helmet. At his waist, he wore a sword with gilt bronze fittings; on his back, there rode a quiver containing arrows fledged with black-banded white eagle feathers. He grasped a rattan-wrapped bow and bestrode a white-dappled reddish horse with a gold-edged saddle. When his mount had swum out about a hundred and fifty or two hundred feet, Naozane beckoned with his fan.

"I see that you are a Commander-in-Chief. It is dishonorable to show your back to an enemy. Return!"

The warrior came back. As he was leaving the water, Naozane rode up alongside him, gripped him with all his strength, crashed with him to the ground, held him motionless and pushed aside his helmet to cut off his head. He was sixteen or seventeen years old, with a lightly powdered face and blackened teeth—a boy just the age of Naozane's own son Kojirō Naoie, and so handsome that Naozane could not find a place to strike.

"Who are you? Announce your name. I will spare you," Naozane said.

"Who are you?" the youth asked.

"Nobody of any importance: Kumagae no Jirō Naozane, a resident of Musashi Province."

"Then it is unnecessary to give you my name. I am a desirable opponent for you. Ask about me after you take my head. Someone will recognize me, even if I don't tell you."

"Indeed, he must be a Commander-in-Chief," Naozane thought. "Killing this one person will not change defeat into victory, nor will sparing him change victory into defeat. When I think of how I grieved when Kojirō suffered a minor wound, it is easy to imagine the sorrow of this young lord's father if he were to hear that the boy had been slain. Ah, I would like to spare him!" Casting a swift glance to the rear, he discovered Sanehira and Kagetoki coming along behind him with fifty riders.

"I would like to spare you," he said, restraining his tears, "but there are Genji warriors everywhere. You cannot possibly escape. It will be better if I kill you than if someone else does, because I will offer prayers on your behalf."

"Just take my head and be quick about it."

Overwhelmed by compassion, Naozane could not find a place to strike. His senses reeled, his wits forsook him and he was scarcely conscious of his surroundings. But matters could not go on like that forever; in tears, he took the head.

"Alas! No lot is as hard as a warrior's. I would never have suffered such a dreadful experience if I had not been born into a military house. How cruel I was to kill him." He pressed his sleeve to his face and shed floods of tears.

Presently, since matters could not go on like that forever, he started to remove the youth's armor *hitatare* so that he might wrap it around the head. A brocade bag containing a flute was tucked in at the waist. "Ah, how pitiful! He must have been one of the people I heard making music inside the stronghold just before dawn. There are tens of thousands of riders in our eastern armies, but I am sure none of them has brought a flute to the battlefield. Those court nobles are refined men!"

When Naozane's trophies were presented for Yoshitsune's inspection, they drew tears from the eyes of all the beholders. It was learned later that the slain youth was Tayū Atsumori, aged seventeen, a son of Tsunemori, the Master of the Palace Repairs Office.

After that, Naozane thought increasingly of becoming a monk.

The flute in question is said to have been given by Retired Emperor Toba to Atsumori's grandfather, Tadamori, who was a skilled musician. I believe I have heard that Tsunemori, who inherited it, turned it over to Atsumori because of his son's proficiency as a flautist. Saeda [Little Branch] was its name. It is deeply moving that music, a profane entertainment, should have led a warrior to the religious life.

[McCullough, trans., The Tale of the Heike, pp. 315–317; PV]

THE MONGOL INVASIONS OF JAPAN

During the thirteenth century, Japan was subjected to the only two attempts in premodern times to invade its islands. These occurred in 1274 and 1281 when huge expeditions ordered by Kublai Khan, the Mongol ruler of China, and composed of recruits from both China and Korea (which was then under Mongol control) overran the islands of Tsushima and Iki in the Korean Strait and landed at points in northern Kyushu and its offshore islands.

In 1268, Kublai sent a letter to Japan demanding that it enter into a tributary relationship with China, a relationship that the Japanese, alone among the peoples of East Asia, had refused to accept from at least the time of Prince Shōtoku in the early seventh century. Acting on behalf of Japan, the Kamakura shogunate chose to ignore both this and a number of subsequent demands made by Kublai. Infuriated, the Mongol leader in 1274 dispatched his first invasion force, comprising some ninety thousand troops and sailors in two armadas, one from Korea and one from China, that made its main landing at Hakata Bay.[7]

The defending warriors of Japan, accustomed to fighting one against one, were confronted by invaders who were organized into trained units that re-

---

7. Although we speak of the "Mongols" invading Japan, the invading forces included Mongols, Chinese, and Koreans.

sponded to signals from drums and gongs. In addition, the Japanese were exposed to weapons, including exploding balls and poisoned arrows, that were entirely new to them. But if the Mongols with their trained units and various weapons enjoyed superiority as fighters on the battlefield, as traditionally believed, they did not get much opportunity to exploit it, for on the very day they landed in Kyushu—again, according to traditional belief—a typhoon arose that forced them back into their ships and out into open water, where many of the ships were sunk and those remaining were obliged to straggle back to the continent.

Scholars continue to raise many questions about the Mongol invasions. For example, could the first invasion force have really been as large as ninety thousand (140,000 are said to have participated in the second invasion), and if so, how many actually fought? Also, the date of the first invasion was November 19, which is after the typhoon season has ended, so could Kyushu really have been struck by one at this time?

One question that is of particular interest to us in regard to the "way of the warrior" is whether the Japanese were as ineffectual in fighting against the Mongols as is usually thought.[8] However one evaluates the relative fighting merits of the Mongols and Japanese during the brief first invasion, the Japanese success in parrying and frustrating the Mongols during the much longer 1281 invasion suggests that the Japanese warriors—all of whom were from Kyushu— got the better of the fighting. In preparation for this invasion, the Japanese constructed stone walls (about three meters high) at Hakata Bay and other possible landing sites in northern Kyushu and prepared a navy of small ships to harass the large Mongol troop carriers. As a result of these preparations and, it appears, the Japanese warriors' aggressive fighting style, the Mongols overran several islands during their six weeks or more in the waters north of Kyushu but were finally unable to land on Kyushu proper.

Unlike the first invasion, the second invasion took place during the typhoon season, and there is no question that a great storm destroyed many ships of the Mongol armadas (again from China and Korea). The Japanese believed that this typhoon and the one said to have occurred during the 1274 invasion were *kamikaze* or "divine winds" that would protect Japan in times of its greatest peril. Accordingly, belief in such divine winds of protection was resuscitated in the last, desperate days of World War II with the establishment of special forces (*kamikaze*) units of suicide pilots.

---

8. For a discussion of the various questions raised here concerning the Mongol invasions, see Thomas Conlan's *In Little Need of Divine Intervention*.

THE MONGOL SCROLLS

We have an important visual record of the Mongol invasions of Japan in the Mongol scrolls, which are narrative picture scrolls (*emakimono*) commissioned by a local warrior of northern Kyushu named Takezaki Suenaga to commemorate his participation in both the 1274 and 1281 defenses against the Mongols. The following passage from the text of the Mongol scrolls is Suenaga's first-person account of how he and four followers fought during the 1274 invasion. On the day of the invasion, Suenaga and his men gathered with other warriors as a group under Shōni Kagesuke, their commander. But Suenaga, who yearned to be first in battle in order to receive reward, became impatient waiting for the commander to assemble his force and so finally set off alone with just his four followers toward Hakata Bay, where the Mongols had landed. In conjunction with his great wish to fight against the Mongols, Suenaga was much concerned about having someone witness his heroics. Yet when he confronted the Mongol invaders, he ignored the advice of one of his men to wait for witnesses and insisted, instead, that the "way of the bow and arrow" demanded that a warrior who wished to be deserving of reward should charge the enemy immediately. In the fighting that ensued, Suenaga and several of his men were wounded. Most fortunately for them, a larger group of Japanese warriors appeared on the scene just in time both to save them and to serve as witnesses. According to Suenaga's account, the Japanese warriors clearly outfought the Mongols.

I set off to attack before knowing how many warriors had assembled at Okinohama. Of all the members of my clan (*ichimon*), Eda Matatarō Hideie begged me to stand as his witness. We traded helmets so that we could recognize each other. Just at that time, we heard that the foreign pirates had set up a camp at Akasaka. As the warriors of our clan set off for battle, we saw the commander (*taishōgun*), Dazai no Shōni Saburō Saemon Kagesuke.[9] He dispatched Noda Saburō Jirō Sukeshige, who came up to Eda Hideie and said: "In order to be seen [we] should fight together. As Akasaka has poor terrain, you should pull back here. When the enemy attacks, as they most certainly will, bear down on them, firing at once." Determined to keep our word [to fight with Kagesuke, we all] pulled back. Nevertheless, I Suenaga said: "Waiting for the general will cause us to be late to battle. Of all the warriors of the clan, I Suenaga will be first to fight from Higo," and set off to attack.

I passed by the hills where Shōni Kagesuke, the commander of the day, had fortified his encampment. [Kagesuke's] retainer Ōta Saemon told me to dismount, but because I intended to attack [text missing] . . . I said: "We five horsemen are going to fight before you. We won't limit ourselves to merely

---

9. Dazai refers to the Dazaifu, the Office of the Imperial Court established centuries earlier to handle overseas intercourse through the port of Hakata. Shōni was an office in the Dazaifu but later became the surname of a warrior family.

shooting down the enemy! I have no purpose in my life but to advance and be known [text missing]. I want [my deeds] to be known by his lordship." Kagesuke said: "I don't expect to survive tomorrow's battle but if I do I will stand as a witness for you [text missing]." "I am ashamed to speak to you on horseback," I said but Kagesuke merely replied: "As you were." I followed his command and set off to attack Akasaka [text missing], first of all the warriors in my clan. From the Hakozaki encampment I made my way to Hakata.

Thinking that I was first to battle of all the warriors from Higo, I set off from the Hakata encampment. On my way to Akasaka, after passing the *torii* of the Sumiyoshi Shrine, I met a warrior on a dapple gray horse at Komatsubara. He wore purple armor with a reverse arrowhead design, and a crimson billowing cape (*horo*) and, having just defeated the invaders in their encampment, was returning with a hundred horsemen. The pirates had fled. Two had been taken. He looked most brave and had two retainers walking before him on his left and right carrying heads—one pierced on a sword, the other on a *naginata*.[10] "Who passes here looking so brave?" I asked, and he replied, "I am Kikuchi Jirō Takefusa of Higo province. Who are you?" I am Takezaki Gorō Hyōe Suenaga of the same province. Watch me attack!" Saying so, I charged.

Defeated by Takefusa at Akasaka, the invaders fled their encampment in two groups. The larger force retreated to Sohara; the smaller one fled to Tsukahara in Beppu. From Tsukahara, the smaller force attempted to link with the larger force at Shiohikata in Torikai. While pursuing the smaller force, my horse was slowed by the mud flats of the ebb tide and could not gain on the fleeing enemy. The invaders established their camp at Sohara and planted many battle flags. Shouting a battle cry, I charged. As I was about to attack, my retainer Tōgenda Sukemitsu said: "More of our men are coming. Wait for reinforcements, get a witness and then attack!" I replied: "The way of the bow and arrow is to do what is worthy of reward. Charge!" The invaders set off from Sohara and arrived at the salt-house pines of Torikai beach. There we fought. My bannerman was first. His horse was shot and he was thrown down. I Suenaga and my other three retainers were all wounded. Just after my horse was shot and I was thrown off, Shiroishi Rokurō Michiyasu, a houseman (*gokenin*)[11] of Hizen province, attacked with a formidable squad of horsemen and the Mongols retreated toward Sohara. Michiyasu charged into the enemy, for his horse was unscathed. I would have died had it not been for him. Against all odds, Michiyasu survived as well, and so we each agreed to be a witness for the other. Also a houseman of Chikugo province, Mitsumoto Matajirō, was shot through his neck bone with an arrow. I stood as a witness for him.

[Conlan, trans., *In Little Need of Divine Intervention*, pp. 37, 53, 64, 77; PV]

---

10. A pole-shaped weapon with a curved blade.
11. A vassal of the Kamakura shogunate.

CHRONICLE OF GREAT PEACE (TAIHEIKI): THE
LOYALIST HEROES

The Kamakura shogunate was overthrown in 1333 by "loyalist" forces supporting Emperor Go-Daigo (1288–1339). Triumphant over the shogunate, Go-Daigo proclaimed the "restoration" of governing power to the imperial court in Kyoto. But Go-Daigo's restoration, known as the Kenmu Restoration, lasted a brief three years, until 1336. Ashikaga Takauji (1305–1358), a leading chieftain of the great Minamoto clan who had earlier helped Go-Daigo to power, turned against him and forced him to flee to Yoshino in the mountainous region south of the capital. There Go-Daigo, still claiming to be the rightful sovereign, founded the Yoshino, or Southern Court. Meanwhile, Takauji installed a member of another branch of the imperial family as emperor in Kyoto and, at the same time, founded a new military government, the Ashikaga or Muromachi shogunate (1336–1573), in the same city. The first half century of the Muromachi period, 1336–1392, is also known as the age of War Between the Northern (Kyoto) and Southern (Yoshino) Courts.

The protracted War Between the Northern and Southern Courts resulted from the only major dynastic schism in the history of the Japanese imperial family. In a way not seen in earlier or later conflicts during premodern times, imperial legitimacy was a central issue. The principal war tale that narrates the fighting between, first, the supporters of Go-Daigo and of the Kamakura shogunate and, later, after the failure of the Kenmu Restoration, those of the Northern and Southern Courts is the *Taiheiki* (*Chronicle of Great Peace*). The *Taiheiki* is often thought to be a tract whose anonymous author or authors argue that the Southern, and not the Northern, Court was the legitimate seat of imperial authority between 1336 and 1392. But the *Taiheiki* does not explicitly declare the Southern Court to be legitimate; rather, it portrays a group of warrior heroes whose loyalty to Go-Daigo and, subsequently, the Southern Court was of such a superbly self-sacrificing, admirable character that later generations of Japanese believed the Southern Court was legitimate in large part because they could not believe that such heroes could have fought and died for an "illegitimate" cause. Foremost among the *Taiheiki's* loyalist heroes—and indeed, the man regarded as Japan's greatest hero until at least the end of World War II— was Kusunoki Masashige (d. 1336).

In the following passage from the *Taiheiki*, we read how Masashige appeared almost magically to become the guiding spirit of Go-Daigo's loyalist movement in the early days of the emperor's opposition to the Kamakura shogunate. A consummate fighter in the new style of guerrilla warfare that had developed in the central and western provinces by the fourteenth century, Masashige speaks to Go-Daigo of using a "carefully devised strategy" to overcome the superior strength of the Kamakura shogunate's armies. He also tells the emperor, in words that were to become famous in Japanese history, that as long as he, Masashige, lived, the emperor's cause would prevail.

On the twenty-seventh day of the eighth month of Genkō,[12] Emperor Go-Daigo went to Kasagi Temple and made the temple's main hall his temporary palace. For several days, not a single person came to support His Majesty, because all feared the military might of Kamakura. But upon learning that an army from Rokuhara[13] had been defeated in battle at Higashi-Sakamoto at the foot of Mount Hiei, the monks of Kasagi and warriors from nearby provinces rode in from all directions. Even so, not a single noted fighter or great chieftain (*daimyō*) at the head of a force of one or two hundred riders had yet appeared. The emperor feared that the contingent that had gathered might be insufficient even to guard his temporary palace.

Dozing off, the emperor had a dream. The place of the dream appeared to be the garden in front of the Shishinden,[14] within which stood a giant evergreen tree whose branches grew densely. Those spreading southward were especially luxuriant. Beneath the tree, the three great ministers of state and all the other ministers were seated in rows according to their ranks. But the main seat, piled high with cushions, remained unoccupied. The dreaming emperor thought wonderingly, "For whom has this seat been prepared?" As he stood there, two youths with their hair parted in the middle and tied on each side, suddenly appeared. Kneeling before the emperor and drenching their sleeves with tears, the youths said, "There is no place in the land where Your Majesty can hide, even for a moment. But in the shade of that tree is a south-facing seat. It has been prepared as a throne for you, so please sit there awhile." So saying, the youths seemed to ascend high into heaven. Soon the emperor awoke from his dream.

The emperor believed that the dream was a message to him from heaven. Considering the written characters for what he had seen, he observed that, by placing the character for "south" next to that for "tree," together they formed a third character, *kusunoki*, or camphor tree. Hopeful, the emperor interpreted his dream this way: "The instructions of the youths to sit in the south-facing seat in the tree's shade meant that I will once again rule with sovereignly virtue and will draw the warriors of the land into the service of the court. This has been divinely revealed by the bodhisattvas Nikkō and Gekkō." When dawn broke, the emperor summoned Jōjubō, a priest of the temple.

The emperor asked Jōjubō, "Is there a warrior in these parts called Kusunoki?" The priest replied, "I have not heard of anyone with that name around

---

12. 1331.

13. Rokuhara was in the southeastern section of Kyoto. The deputies of the Kamakura shogunate who administered Kyoto had their offices there.

14. One of the halls at the imperial palace in Kyoto.

here. But west of Mount Kongō in Kawachi Province is a man renowned as a wielder of bow and arrow named Kusunoki Tamon[15] Hyōe Masashige. Although he is said to be a descendant of the Ide Minister of the Left, Lord Tachibana no Moroe (himself a descendant in the fourth generation from Emperor Bidatsu), Masashige has long lived in the provinces. I hear that his mother, when young, worshiped Bishamon on Mount Shigi for one hundred days and gave birth to a child after receiving an oracle in a dream. She named the child Tamon." The emperor, regarding this as confirmation of the oracle he had received in his dream the night before, ordered, "Summon Kusunoki Masashige immediately." Lord Madenokōji Chūnagon Fujifusa, upon receiving the imperial edict, promptly summoned Masashige.

The imperial messenger, bearing the emperor's wishes, proceeded to the Kusunoki residence and explained everything to Masashige. Believing there was no greater honor for a man of bow and arrow, Masashige, without any hesitation, went secretly to Mount Kasagi. The emperor, speaking through Lord Fujifusa, said to Masashige, "When I dispatched an imperial messenger to call upon you to subjugate the eastern barbarians,[16] you rode here immediately. I am most pleased. So, what plans do you have to undertake unification of the country? How can you win a decisive victory and bring peace to the four seas? Speak your thoughts freely, without omitting anything."

Masashige respectfully replied, "The eastern barbarians, in their recent treasonous behavior, have drawn the censure of Heaven. If we take advantage of their weakness, resulting from the decline and disorder they have caused, what difficulty should we have in inflicting Heaven's punishment upon them? But the goal of unifying the country must be carried out by means of both military tactics and carefully devised strategy. Even if we fight them force against force and although we recruit warriors throughout the more than sixty provinces of Japan to confront the men of the two provinces of Musashi and Sagami,[17] we will be hard-pressed to win. But if we fight with clever scheming, the military force of the eastern barbarians will be capable of no more than breaking sharp swords and crushing hard helmets. It will be easy to deceive them, and there will be nothing to fear. Since the aim of warfare is ultimate victory, Your Majesty should pay no heed to whether we win or lose in a single battle. So long as you hear that Masashige alone is alive, know that your imperial destiny will in the end be attained." After delivering these earnest words, Masashige returned to Kawachi.

[Gotō and Kamada, eds., *Taiheiki*, vol. 1, pp. 96–98; PV]

---

15. Another name for the Buddhist guardian deity Bishamon.

16. The men of the Kamakura shogunate.

17. These two provinces of the Kantō constituted the principal base of the Hōjō regents, who were the main power holders in the Kamakura shogunate.

In narrating the warfare that resulted in the overthrow of the Kamakura shogunate in 1333, the *Taiheiki* describes Kusunoki Masashige's innovative and brilliant methods for defending fortresses against attacks and sieges by huge shogunate armies. Indeed, the *Taiheiki* attributes much of the ultimate success of Go-Daigo's loyalist movement to the failure of the shogunate to deal promptly and effectively with Masashige. He kept the fires of antishogunate revolt burning until larger forces under Ashikaga Takauji and Nitta Yoshisada (1301–1338) could finally destroy the Kamakura regime.

After failure of the Kenmu Restoration in 1336, Go-Daigo, as we see in the first passage, rejects Masashige's advice about strategy and insists that he and Nitta Yoshisada, the leading loyalist general, meet in a showdown battle with Ashikaga Takauji at Minatogawa in Hyōgo. Masashige obeys with the knowledge that he will die in this battle, and symbolically, so also will Go-Daigo's cause.

The second passage relates the suicide of Masashige and his brother at Minatogawa after the battle has been lost.

As Lords Takauji and Tadayoshi headed toward the capital in command of a great army, Yoshisada sent a messenger on a fleet horse to the palace to report that he was pulling back to Hyōgo in order to establish a position from which to defend against the Ashikaga. The emperor, greatly alarmed, sent for Kusunoki Masashige. "Go quickly to Hyōgo to join forces with Yoshisada and do battle," he ordered.

Respectfully, Masashige replied, "Since Lord Takauji is already on his way up to the capital in command of an army from the nine provinces of Kyushu, his might will surely be as vast as clouds and mist. I fear that if a small, tired force like ours were to engage such a giant enemy army in high spirits, it would, by fighting in the conventional manner, undoubtedly be defeated. I recommend that Your Majesty recall Lord Yoshisada to Kyoto and have him accompany you again to Mount Hiei. I will go down to Kawachi and, with a contingent from the central provinces, defend Kawajiri. If we press Kyoto from two directions, north and south, and force the Ashikaga to exhaust their supplies, they will gradually tire and their numbers will dwindle. Meanwhile, our side will increase in strength day by day. Then, if Lord Yoshisada advances down from Mount Hiei and Masashige attacks from the rear, we can destroy the enemies of the court in a single battle. Lord Yoshisada undoubtedly agrees with me. But he is ashamed by the thought that he will be seen as cowardly if he avoids a battle while in the field. Hence he has decided to take a stand at Hyōgo. What matters most in war is who wins the final battle. I urge the court to make its decision after the most careful deliberation.

"Truly, war should be entrusted to warriors," the courtiers agreed. But Bōmon no Saishō Kiyotada again spoke out: "What Masashige says is not without merit. Yet to have His Majesty abandon the capital and proceed for a second time in the same year to Mount Hiei before an army, commissioned to pacify the country, has even fought one battle is tantamount to demeaning the imperial position. It also goes against the way of an imperial army. Although Takauji is advancing toward the capital in command of a Kyushu army, it surely does not exceed the force he brought to Kyoto last year after conquering the eight eastern provinces. At that time, our side, although small, never failed to prevail over the larger enemy in each battle, from the start of fighting until the final victory. This had nothing to do with superior military strategy but was thanks entirely to the imperial destiny. Therefore, if you engage the enemy in decisive battle away from the capital, what difficulty should there be in emerging victorious? Masashige must go at once to Hyōgo."

"I have no further objections," said Masashige. On the sixteenth day of the fifth month, he left the capital and, with five hundred riders, went down to Hyōgo.

Because he knew that this would be his final battle, Masashige stopped, as he had planned, at Sakurai Station to send his oldest son, Masatsura, age eleven this year, who had been accompanying him, back home to Kawachi. As he bid farewell to Masatsura, Masashige gave these instructions to him, "It is said that three days after the lioness gives birth to a cub, she throws it off a stone wall several thousand *jō* high.[18] But because the cub has a lion's nature, it is able, without having been taught, to right itself in midair and avoid being killed. The moral of this story applies even more to you, a young man who has passed his tenth birthday. You must heed my words and never disobey the advice I give you. The coming battle will decide the fate of the country. I fear this is the last time I will see your face in this life. If you hear that Masashige has died in battle, you will know with certainty that the country has fallen into the hands of the shogun, Takauji. But you must never surrender, and thus forsake years of unswerving loyalty by our family to the emperor, merely to preserve your transient life. So long as even one of the young men of our family survives, he must fortify himself in the vicinity of Mount Kongō and, if the enemy attacks, be prepared to expose himself to the arrows of Yang Yu[19] and fight with a devotion comparable to the loyalty of Ji Xin.[20] This will be your most important filial duty to me." After Masashige had tearfully delivered these words, father and son parted, one going east and the other west.

Long ago, when Mu Gong attacked the state of Jin, Bai Lixi, realizing that defeat was inevitable, went to his son, General Meng Mingshi, and sadly bid him a final farewell.[21] In this age, Kusunoki Masashige, upon hearing that the

---

18. The source of this story is not known. But "several thousand *jō*" is an implausibly great height.

19. Yang Yu was a famous archer of the Spring and Autumn period of early Chinese history.

20. Ji Xin was a loyal follower of Emperor Han Gaozu who, on one occasion, took the emperor's place during an attack in order to enable him to escape.

21. This is a story found in Watson, trans., *The Records of the Grand Historian (Shiji)*, vol. 1, *Qin Dynasty*, pp. 14–15.

enemy army was approaching the capital from the west and realizing, with great regret, that the country would surely be overthrown, left his son Masatsura behind with the admonition that he remain loyal to the emperor until his own death. Bai Lixi was a splendid subject of another land, and Masashige was a loyal subject of our country. Although separated in time by a thousand years, they were as one in their sageliness both in this life and the next. They were wise men rarely to be found.

When Masashige arrived in Hyōgo, Nitta Yoshisada immediately came to inquire about what the emperor had said. After Masashige explained in detail both his own thinking and the decision of the emperor, Yoshisada said, "Indeed, a small army that has suffered defeat cannot hope to win against a great army full of spirit. But ever since losing the battle for the Kantō last year and then failing to hold the line against the enemy on the way back up to the capital, I have been unable to avoid the derision of people. On top of that, I was not able to reduce a single enemy fortification when I was recently sent down to the western provinces. If now, upon learning that the enemy has a great army, I should withdraw to Kyoto without fighting even one battle, it would be a humiliation I could not bear. Victory or defeat do not concern me. I wish only to display my loyalty in the coming battle."

Masashige replied, "It has been said, 'Listen not to the biased views of the many who are fools, but heed the opinion of one wise man.'[22] Do not pay attention to the slander of those who do not know the way of war. The superior commander advances only when he judges the situation right for battle and retreats when he knows it is not. Thus Confucius admonished Zilu with these words, 'Do not follow the lead of one who would fight tigers with his bare hands and ford great rivers on foot, regretting not that he might be killed.'[23] Although it is said that destroying Hōjō Takatoki's violent rule at one stroke at the beginning of Genkō and forcing Takauji and the other rebels to retreat to Kyushu this spring were due to the imperial destiny, in fact they were entirely because of your outstanding strategy. In the way of war, who is there to deride you? Especially now, in returning to the capital region from the western provinces, your actions have been exemplary at each and every stage." At this, Yoshisada's face brightened. Throughout the night he and Masashige talked, raising their sake cups many times. Thinking about it later, Yoshisada was saddened to realize that this was his final meeting with Masashige. [pp. 149–152]

Kusunoki Masashige, facing his younger brother Masasue, said: "The enemy is blocking us, front and rear, and has cut us off from our allies. There seems no way to escape now. I suggest that we first attack those in the front, drive

---

22. Words similar to these can be found in several ancient Chinese texts, including *Shiji*.

23. "I would not take with me anyone who would try to fight a tiger with his bare hands or to walk across the River and die in the process without regrets"(*Analects* 7:11).

them away, then take on those in the rear." "That's fine!" said Masasue approvingly.

Aligning their force of seven hundred riders, the brothers drove into the center of the great enemy host. Ashikaga Tadayoshi's men, seeing the Chrysanthemum and Water standard[24] and realizing that the attackers were worthy foes, sought to surround and smash them. But Masashige and Masasue struck the Ashikaga from east to west and drove them from north to south. Whenever they saw worthy foes, they rode up, grappled with them, and took their heads. When they encountered foes they considered unworthy, they drove them away with their swords. During the course of battle, Masasue and Masashige met up seven times, and seven times they were separated. Their only thought was to reach Tadayoshi, grapple with him, and kill him. At length, however, Tadayoshi's force of five hundred thousand drove the Kusunoki seven hundred back, forcing them to retreat again toward Ueno in Suma.

The horse Tadayoshi was riding stopped, having picked up an arrowhead in its hoof. As it stood there lamely, favoring its right leg, the Kusunoki drove forward. Tadayoshi, it seemed, was about to be killed. But just then a single horseman, Yakushiji Jūrōjirō slashed the chests of the oncoming horses, felling one after another. In all, he cut down seven or eight riders. Tadayoshi, meanwhile, had changed mounts and fled far from the scene.

The shogun, Takauji, observing Tadayoshi's retreat in the face of the Kusunoki attack, issued an order: "Bring in fresh troops, and make sure Tadayoshi is not killed." Whereupon some six thousand riders of the Kira, Ishitō, Kō, and Uesugi galloped to the east of Minatogawa and surrounded the Kusunoki in order to cut them off from retreat. Turning back, Masashige and Masasue charged into the encircling horde, clashing with them, grappling them down, and killing them. During six hours they fought sixteen times but gradually their force was diminished until only seventy-three remained. Even then, if they had tried to break through the enemy and escape, they could have. But Masashige had decided when he left the capital that this would mark the end of his time in this world. So the Kusunoki fought without retreating a step, until their energy was exhausted. They then went north of Minatogawa and rushed into a house in one of the villages.

Masashige stripped off his armor in order to cut his belly. Examining himself, he found that he had suffered sword wounds in eleven places. Among the other seventy-two men, not one had fewer than three to five wounds.

The thirteen members of the Kusunoki family and their sixty retainers aligned themselves in two rows in the six-bay reception hall. Reciting the *nembutsu* ten times in unison, they cut their bellies as one. Masashige, occupying the seat of honor, turned to his brother Masasue. "Well now, it is said that one's

---

24. The standard of the Kusunoki family.

last thoughts in this life determine the goodness or evil of one's next incarnation. Into which of the nine realms of existence would you like to be reborn?" Laughing loudly, Masasue replied: "It is my wish to be reborn again and again for seven lives into this same existence in order to destroy the enemies of the court!" Masashige was greatly pleased. "Although it is deeply sinful, it is also my wish. Let us therefore be born again into this life to fulfill our cherished dream!" Stabbing each other, the brothers fell down on the same pillow.

Sixteen men from prominent families, including Hashimoto Hachirō Masakazu, the governor of Kawachi, Usami Masayasu, Jingūji Tarō Masamoro, and Wada Gorō Masataka, along with fifty of their followers, lined up in a row, each in his own way, and cut their bellies.

Kikuchi Shichirō Taketomo had come as the emissary of his older brother, the governor of Hizen, to observe the fighting at Suma-guchi and happened upon Masashige's *seppuku*. How, he thought, could he shamelessly forsake Masashige and return home? And so he too committed suicide and fell into the flames.[25]

From the Genkō era, tens of millions of people graciously came forth in response to His Majesty's call, served loyally, and distinguished themselves in battle. But since this rebellion erupted, people ignorant of the way of benevolence have flouted the imperial favor and joined the enemy. Feckless individuals, hoping to escape death, have surrendered and, contrary to their expectations, have been executed. Other ignorant people, not comprehending the trend of the times, have gone against the Way. In the midst of this, Masashige, a man combining the three virtues of wisdom, benevolence, and courage, whose fidelity is unequaled by anyone from ancient times to the present, has chosen death as the proper way. His and his brother's deaths by suicide are omens that a sagely sovereign has again lost the country and traitorous subjects are running amok. [pp. 158–160]

[Gotō and Kamada, eds., *Taiheiki*, vol. 2, pp. 149–152, 158–160; PV]

---

25. This is the first mention of fire or flames.

Chapter 13

NICHIREN: THE SUN AND THE LOTUS

The story of Nichiren (1222–1282) is that, to use his own words, of "a son of the shūdras (lowest caste)" on the seacoast of Japan, who was destined to become "the pillar of Japan, the eye of the nation and the vessel of the country." Like most of the great religious leaders of that age, this son of a humble fisherman spent years in study and training at the great monastic center of Mount Hiei. Unlike many others, however, he found new faith not by turning away from the teachings of its Tendai founder, Saichō, but by turning back to them. In doing so, he was forced to depart from Mount Hiei itself, which had long since become a stronghold of Esoteric Buddhism, and to embark on a preaching career of unceasing hardship, conflict, and persecution. But through it all, he became ever more convinced of his mission to save his country and Buddhism.

For Nichiren, the Lotus Sūtra, on which the Tendai teaching was based, was the key to everything. It is the final and supreme teaching of the Buddha Shākyamuni, revealing the one and only way of salvation. In this sūtra, the three forms of the Buddha—his Universal or Law Body (Dharmakāya), Body of Bliss (Sambhogakāya), and Transformation Body (Nirmānakāya)—are seen as one and inseparable, and the prevailing schools of Buddhism emphasized one form at the expense of the others. Esoteric Buddhism stressed the Universal Buddha, Vairochana, or Dainichi; and Amidism worshiped the Body of Bliss, Amitābha. By thus dispensing with the historical Buddha, Shākyamuni (the Transformation Body), they committed the inexcusable crime of mutilating Buddha's perfect body. Conversely, Zen Buddhism and the Vinaya school, which was undergoing something of a revival at that time, ignored the universal and eternal aspect of the Buddha in favor of the historical or actual Buddha. That is, the Lotus Sūtra alone upholds the truth of the triune Buddha, and only in this trinity is the salvation of all assured.

So it is the name of the Lotus Sūtra, not the name of Amida Buddha, which should be on the lips of every Buddhist. "All praise to the Lotus Sūtra of the Wondrous Law" (*namu myōhō rengekyō*) is the Buddha's pledge of salvation, which Nichiren often called out to the beat of a drum—"dondon dondoko dondon." Like Shinran, Nichiren was a man of no slight intelligence, and he spent his years of exile or enforced seclusion in an intensive study of scripture and doctrine. But this erudition served only to adorn a simple conviction, arrived at early in life and held to with single-minded devotion throughout his stormy career, that faith in the Lotus of the Wondrous Law was all that one needed for salvation.

Unlike Shinran, Nichiren stressed the importance of one's own efforts and became ever more deeply convinced that he himself was destined to fulfill a unique mission in the world. A man of active temperament who commanded attention because of his forceful and magnetic personality, Nichiren thought the Lotus Sūtra should be "read by the body" and not just with the eyes. To him, among its most significant passages were those describing the saints destined to uphold and spread abroad the truths of the Lotus. One of these was the Bodhisattva of Superb Action,[1] who was to be a stalwart pioneer in propagating the Perfect Truth. Another was the Bodhisattva Ever-Abused,[2] who suffered continual insults from others because he insisted on saluting everyone as a buddha-to-be, convinced that every man was ultimately destined to be such. The Lotus's account of these two saints he regarded as prefiguring his own mission, and often he referred to himself as a reincarnation of them, especially of the Bodhisattva of Superb Action. Nichiren also found special meaning in the vows taken by Buddha's disciples when his eternal aspect was revealed to them at the climax of the Lotus Sūtra. In these vows, they promised to proclaim the supreme scripture in evil times and to endure all the injury and abuse that were certain to descend on them. In this, too, Nichiren saw a prophecy of his own sufferings.

The immediate cause of his sufferings was Nichiren's unrelenting attack on the established sects and his outspoken criticism of Japan's rulers for patronizing these heretics. The repeated calamities suffered by the country at large and the threat of foreign invasion, which he hinted at ten years before the Mongol fleet appeared in Japanese waters, he regarded as the inevitable retribution for the

---

1. Vishishtachārita (Viśistacāritra).
2. Sadāparibhūta.

false faith of the nation's leaders, both ecclesiastical and political. Contrasted to this sad state of affairs was Nichiren's vision of Japan as the land in which the true teaching of the Buddha was to be revived and from which it was to spread throughout the world. The name Nichiren, which he adopted, symbolizes this exalted mission and his own key role in its fulfillment. *Nichi*, "the sun," represents both the Light of Truth and the Land of the Rising Sun, and *ren* stands for the Lotus.

To accomplish this aim, Nichiren urged all his followers to imitate the bodhisattva ideal of perseverance and self-sacrifice. In an age of utter decadence, as understood in terms of the theory concerning the Latter Day of the Law (*mappō*), everyone must be a man of Superb Action, ready to give his life if necessary for the cause. Nichiren himself was sentenced to death for his bold censure of the Hōjō regency in Kamakura and was saved only by miraculous intervention, according to his followers, when lightning struck the executioner's blade. Banished then to a lonely island in the Sea of Japan, Nichiren wrote, "Birds cry but shed no tears. Nichiren does not cry, but his tears are never dry." Ever after his narrow escape at the execution ground, Nichiren regarded himself as one who had risen from the dead, who had been reborn in the faith. "Tatsunokuchi is the place where Nichiren renounced his life. The place is therefore comparable to a paradise; because all has taken place for the sake of the Lotus of Truth. . . . Indeed every place where Nichiren encounters perils is Buddha's land."[3] In this way, Nichiren made suffering into a glorious thing and set an example for his disciples that did more to confirm their faith in the Lotus than could volumes of scripture.

At least three of Nichiren's adherents followed in his footsteps as Bodhisattvas of Superb Action. One was Nichiji (1250–?), who undertook foreign missionary work at the age of forty-six, going first to Ainuland in Hokkaido and thence, it is said, to Siberia, from which he never returned. A stone monument he erected in northern Japan testifies to his indefatigable zeal for spreading faith in the Lotus among the heathen of unknown lands. In his youth, he had accompanied his master into exile off the Sea of Japan coast, opposite Siberia. Known as a master of prose and poetry, who wrote for Nichiren in the latter's old age, Nichiji might have settled down to a quiet life of study and writing but chose instead a strenuous life exploring the unknown with only his faith to sustain him.

A later follower of Nichiren, named Nisshin (1407–1488), went to Kyushu at the other end of Japan and was made superintendent of the mission there. But he, too, was a Bodhisattva of Superb Action, and, dissatisfied with the easy life of a successful missionary, returned alone to Kyoto. In this stronghold of tradition and conservatism, Nisshin started out as a street-corner evangelist, calling out the name of the Lotus Sūtra to the beat of a drum, "dondon dondoko

---

3. Anesaki, *Nichiren*, pp. 58–59.

dondon." He openly challenged the ruling shogun to suppress all other Buddhist sects and recognize the Lotus alone. When the shogun, who had left the religious life to become a military dictator, was persuaded by his former clerical associates to command Nisshin to keep silent, the evangelist only beat his drum louder. Thrown into jail and tortured, he still would not yield to the shogun's order. Finally a brass pot was jammed down over his head so as to keep him from talking, and thus he became known as the "pot-wearer" (*nabe-kaburi*). Among the converts that he made through his almost superhuman endurance under such suffering were Prime Minister Konoe, the master craftsmen of the Hon-ami family, and also the head of the eminent Kano school of painting.

Last is Nichiō (1565–1630), who led a group of the Nichiren sect known as the Fuju-fuse, from their slogan "Accept nothing [from nonbelievers] and give nothing." So uncompromising was Nichiō in regard to all other schools of Buddhism that upon unifying the country, when Hideyoshi invited all sects to send delegates for a festival of celebration, Nichiō refused on the ground that the conqueror was not a follower of Nichiren. This incident was repeated when the shogun Ieyasu unified the country, but this time Nichiō's refusal of such an invitation led to his banishment for more than ten years. Thereafter the Fuju-fuse school was subjected to repeated persecutions by the Tokugawa shogunate, and yet it somehow managed to survive into the twentieth century.

NICHIREN: "RECTIFICATION FOR THE PEACE OF THE NATION" (*RISSHŌ ANKOKU RON*)

In this famous tract, which led to his banishment from Kamakura for his attacks on the shogun's authority, Nichiren speaks as a prophet condemning the faithlessness of Japan's rulers and people in abandoning the true teaching of the Lotus, to which they must return if the peace and security of the state and nation (*ankoku*) are to be restored. Later, it was this theme of "rectification"—that is, restoration of religious orthodoxy as a means of protecting the state and nation—that led to Nichiren's being honored by the Taishō Emperor in 1922 as "great teacher of rectification" (*risshō daishi*).

In the following, Nichiren reasserts what had earlier been Saichō's two main aims for Mount Hiei: Buddhism as protector of the state and nation, and the Lotus Sūtra as central to Mahāyāna Buddhism. The main focus of Nichiren's attack on false teachings is Hōnen's *Choosing the Original Vow* (*Senchakushū*), which set aside all other Buddhist scriptures and practices in favor of exclusive devotion to Amida. Other principal targets are Zen and Shingon.

The original text is in dialogue form, abbreviated here to focus on Nichiren's main argument, which starts with a lament for the disorders and disasters besetting Japan. Readers should be aware that such editorial abbreviation necessarily omits much of Nichiren's lengthy argument based on Buddhist scriptures, which he says the Pure Land and Zen sects have abandoned.

Once there was a traveler who spoke these words in sorrow to his host:

In recent years, there are unusual disturbances in the heavens, strange oc-currences on earth, famine and pestilence, all affecting every corner of the empire and spreading throughout the land. Oxen and horses lie dead in the streets, the bones of the stricken crowd the highways. Over half the population has already been carried off by death, and in every family someone grieves. [13]

All the while some put their whole faith in the "sharp sword"[4] of the Buddha Amida and intone this name of the lord of the Western Paradise. . . . There are also those who follow the secret teachings of the Shingon sect and conduct esoteric rituals, while others devote themselves entirely to Zen-type meditation and perceive the emptiness of all phenomena as clearly as the moon. . . .

Yet despite these efforts, they merely exhaust themselves in vain. Famine and disease rage more fiercely than ever, beggars are everywhere in sight and scenes of death fill our eyes. Cadavers pile up in mounds like observation platforms, dead bodies lie side by side like planks on a bridge. . . .

The host then spoke: I have been brooding alone upon this matter, indignant in my heart, but now that you have come, we can lament together. . . . I have pondered the matter carefully with what limited resources I possess, and have searched rather widely in the scriptures for an answer. The people of today all turn their backs upon what is right; to a man, they give their allegiance to evil. This is the reason that the benevolent deities have abandoned the nation, that sages leave and do not return. And in their stead come devils and demons, disasters and calamities that arise one after another. I cannot keep silent on this matter. I cannot suppress my fears. . . . [14]

Nichiren proceeds to invoke the Golden Light Sūtra and the Sūtra of the Humane Kings (see chapter 5) on the important role of Buddhism as "protector of the nation."

The Sūtra of the Humane King (Ninnō kyō) states: "When a nation becomes disordered, it is the spirits which first show signs of rampancy. Because these spirits become rampant, all the people of the nation become disordered. In-vaders come to plunder the country and the common people face annihilation. The ruler, the high ministers, the heir apparent, and the other princes and government officials all quarrel with each other over right and wrong. Heaven and earth manifest prodigies and strange occurrences; the twenty-eight con-stellations, the stars, the sun and the moon appear at irregular times and in irregular positions, and numerous outlaws rise up." . . . [20]

In the reign of Emperor Gotoba there was a monk named Hōnen who wrote a work entitled *Choosing the Original Vow (Senchakushū)*.[5] He contradicted

---

4. A sword that would cut off earthly desires, karma, and suffering.
5. See chapter 10.

the sacred teachings of Shākyamuni and brought confusion to people in every direction. The *Senchakushū* states: "The Chinese priest Daochuo[6] distinguished between the Shōdō or Sacred Way teachings and the Jōdo or Pure Land teachings and urged men to abandon the former and immediately embrace the latter. . . . We may assume that the esoteric Mahāyāna doctrines of Shingon and the true Mahāyāna teachings of the Lotus Sūtra are both included in the Sacred Way. If that is so, then the present-day sects of Shingon, Zen, Tendai, Kegon, Sanron, Hossō, Jiron, and Shōron—all these eight schools are included in the Sacred Way that is to be abandoned [according to Hōnen]." . . . [22]

Hōnen also says: "The Chinese monk Shandao distinguished between correct and sundry practices and urged men to embrace the former and abandon the latter. Concerning the first of the sundry practices, that of reading and reciting sūtras, he states that, with the exception of the recitation of the Contemplation of Limitless Life Sūtra (Kammuryōju kyō) and the other Pure Land sūtras, the embracing and recitation of all sūtras, whether Mahāyāna or Hīnayāna, exoteric or esoteric, is to be regarded as a sundry practice." . . .

Finally, in a concluding passage, Hōnen says: "If one wishes to escape quickly from the sufferings of birth and death, one should confront these two superior teachings and then proceed to put aside the teachings of the Sacred Way and choose those of the Pure Land. And if one wishes to follow the teachings of the Pure Land, one should confront the correct and sundry practices and then proceed to abandon all those that are incorrect and devote one's entire attention to those that are correct." . . . [23]

And on top of that, he groups together all the sage monks of the three countries of India, China, and Japan as well as the students of Buddhism of the ten directions, and calls them a "band of robbers," causing the people to insult them! . . .

But because of this book written by Hōnen, this *Senchakushū*, the Lord Buddha Shākyamuni is forgotten and all honor is paid to Amida, the Buddha of the Western Land. The Lord Buddha's transmission of the Law is ignored and Yakushi, the Buddha of the Eastern Region, is neglected. All attention is paid to the three works in four volumes of the Pure Land scriptures, and all other wonderful teachings that Shākyamuni proclaimed throughout the five periods of his preaching life are cast aside. . . . As a result, the halls of the Buddha fall into ruin, scarcely a wisp of smoke rises above their mossy tiles; and the monks' quarters stand empty and dilapidated, the dew deep on the grasses in their courtyards. And in spite of such conditions, no one gives a thought to protecting the Law or to restoring the temples. . . . If people favor

---

6. Daochuo (562–645) is traditionally held to be the second patriarch of the Pure Land school in China.

perverse doctrines and forget what is correct, can the benevolent deities be anything but angry? If people cast aside doctrines that are all-encompassing and take up those that are incomplete, can the world escape the plots of demons? Rather than offering up ten thousand prayers for remedy, it would be better simply to outlaw this one evil doctrine that is the source of all the trouble! . . . [25]

Though I may be a person of little ability, I have reverently given myself to the study of the Mahāyāna. A blue fly, if it clings to the tail of a thoroughbred horse, can travel ten thousand miles, and the green ivy that twines around the tall pine can grow to a thousand feet. I was born as the son of the one Buddha, Shākyamuni, and I serve the king of scriptures, the Lotus Sūtra. How could I observe the decline of the Buddhist Law and not be filled with emotions of pity and distress? . . . [29]

The Lotus Sūtra says: "One who refuses to take faith in this sūtra and instead slanders it immediately destroys the seeds for becoming a Buddha in this world. . . . After he dies, he will fall into the hell of incessant suffering." . . .

If we accept the words of the Lotus Sūtra, then we must understand that slandering the Mahāyāna scriptures is more serious than committing the five cardinal sins. Therefore one who does so will be confined in the great fortress of the hell of incessant suffering and cannot hope for release for countless kalpas. . . .

The Lotus and the Nirvāna sūtras represent the very heart of the doctrines that Shākyamuni preached during the five periods of his teaching life. Their warnings must be viewed with the utmost gravity. Who would fail to heed them? And yet those people who forget about the Correct Way and slander the Law put more trust than ever in Hōnen's *Senchakushū* and grow blinder than ever in their stupidity. . . . [35]

In conclusion, Nichiren's opposite number in this dialogue concedes to him but, even more, is moved to take up the cause of warning and converting others to the correct teaching. Thus the prophetic warning prompts active proselytization among the people (in contrast to meditative praxis or esoteric rituals).

The guest said: Now when I examine the passages you have cited from the sūtras and see exactly what the Buddha has said, I realize that slandering is a very grave offense indeed, that violating the Law is in truth a terrible sin. I have put all my faith in one Buddha alone, Amida, and rejected all the other Buddhas. I have honored the three Pure Land sūtras and set aside the other sūtras. . . . [41]

But now I realize that to do so means to exhaust oneself in futile efforts in this life, and to fall into the hell of incessant suffering in the life to come. The texts you have cited are perfectly clear on this point and their arguments are detailed—they leave no room for doubt. . . . But it is not enough that I alone should accept and have faith in your words—we must see to it that others as well are warned of their errors.

[Yampolsky, Writingss of Nichiren, pp. 13–41]

THE EYE-OPENER

The following excerpts from *The Eye-Opener* (*Kaimoku shō*) were written in 1272 when Nichiren was in exile on the forbidding island of Sado on Japan's northwest coast. Experiencing great physical suffering and alarmed that his followers back in Kamakura were abandoning their faith under persecution, he wrote this work to encourage his disciples as if it were a last will and testament.

Nichiren begins this essay with the words "There are three categories of people that all men and women should respect. They are the sovereign, the teacher, and the parent." These three categories are equated with the three virtues that are the attributes of the sovereign, teacher, and parent and in turn are the qualifications of a Buddha. The virtue of the sovereign is the ability to protect all living beings; the virtue of the teacher is the ability to lead all to enlightenment; and the virtue of the parent is the possession of a compassion that will nurture and maintain them. These three virtues constitute a theme that runs throughout this essay and concludes the second volume of this work. Nichiren declares: "I, Nichiren, am sovereign, teacher, father, and mother to all the people of Japan."

At the conclusion of this treatise, Nichiren explains that there are two ways to propagate the Lotus Sūtra: *shōju*, gentle arguments, and *shakubuku*, strong refutation. Here Nichiren argues that both methods should be used because there are two kinds of countries, those whose people are ignorant and those whose people deliberately go against the Law. Japan, as a nation that slanders the Lotus Sūtra, requires the strong method.

Already over two hundred years have passed since the world entered the Latter Day of the Law. I was born in a remote land far from India, a person of low station and a monk of humble learning. During my past lifetimes through the six paths, I have perhaps at times been born as a great ruler in the human or heavenly worlds, and have bent the multitudes to my will as a great wind bends the branches of the small trees. And yet at such times I was not able to become a Buddha.

I studied the Hīnayāna and Mahāyāna sūtras, beginning as an ordinary practitioner with no understanding at all and gradually moving upward to the position of a great bodhisattva. For one kalpa, two kalpas, countless kalpas I devoted myself to the practices of a bodhisattva, until I had almost reached the state where I could never fail to attain Buddhahood. And yet I was dragged down by the powerful and overwhelming influence of evil, and I never attained Buddhahood. . . . [78]

Over a period of countless lifetimes, men are deceived more often than there are sands in the Ganges, until they [abandon their faith in the Lotus Sūtra and] descend to the teachings of the provisional Mahāyāna sūtras, abandon these and descend to the teachings of the Hīnayāna sūtras, and eventually abandon even these and descend to the teachings and scriptures of the non-Buddhist doctrines. I understand all too well how, in the end, men have come in this way to fall into the evil states of existence. . . . [79]

I, Nichiren, am the only person in all Japan who understands this. But if I utter so much as a word concerning it, then parents, brothers, and teachers will surely criticize me and the government authorities will take steps against me. On the other hand, I am fully aware that if I do not speak out, I will be lacking in compassion. I have considered which course to take in the light of the teachings of the Lotus and Nirvana sūtras. If I remain silent, I may escape harm in this lifetime, but in my next life I will most certainly fall into the hell of incessant suffering. If I speak out, I am fully aware that I will have to contend with the three obstacles and the four devils. But of these two courses, surely the latter is the one to choose. . . .

The Buddha decided the time [when the votary of the Lotus Sūtra should appear], describing it as a "fearful and evil age," "a latter age," "a latter age when the Law will disappear," and "the final five hundred years," as attested by both [of] the Chinese versions of the Lotus Sūtra, Shō-hokke kyō and Myōhō-renge-kyō. At such a time, if the three powerful enemies predicted in the Lotus Sūtra did not appear, then who would have faith in the words of the Buddha? If it were not for Nichiren, who could fulfill the Buddha's prophecies concerning the votary of the Lotus Sūtra? . . . [84]

Prince Shōtoku of Japan was the son of Emperor Yōmei, the thirty-second sovereign of Japan. When he was six years old, elderly men came to Japan from the states of Paekche and Koguryŏ in Korea and from the land of China. The six-year-old prince thereupon exclaimed, "There are my disciples!" and the old men in turn pressed their palms together in reverence and said, "You are our teacher!" This was a strange happening indeed. . . . [100]

The Great Teacher Dengyō[7] was the patriarch of both esoteric and exoteric Buddhism in Japan. In his *Exemplary Passages from the Lotus (Hokke Shūke)* he writes: "The sūtras that the other sects are based upon give expression in certain measure to the mother-like nature of the Buddha. But they convey only a sense of love and are lacking in a sense of fatherly sternness. It is only the Tendai sect, based upon the Lotus Sūtra, that combines a sense of both love and sternness. The sūtra is a father to all the worthy men, sages, those in the stages of learning and beyond learning, and those who have awakened in themselves the mind of the bodhisattva." . . . [106]

---

7. That is, Saichō.

In view of these facts, I believe that the devotees and followers of the various [provisional] sūtras such as the Flower Garland Sūtra (Kegon kyō), Contemplation of Limitless Life Sūtra (Kammuryōju kyō), and Vairochana Sūtra (Dainichi kyō) will undoubtedly be protected by the Buddhas, bodhisattvas, and heavenly beings of the respective sūtras that they uphold. But if the votaries of the Vairochana, Contemplation of Limitless Life, and other sūtras should set themselves up as the enemies of the votary of the Lotus Sūtra, then the Buddhas, bodhisattvas, and heavenly beings will abandon them and will protect the votary of the Lotus Sūtra. It is like the case of the filial son whose father opposes the ruler of the kingdom. The son will abandon his father and support the ruler, for to do so is the height of filial piety. . . . [109]

I, Nichiren, am the richest man in all of present-day Japan. I have dedicated my life to the Lotus Sūtra, and my name will be handed down in ages to come. If one is lord of the great ocean, then all the gods of the various rivers will obey him. If one is king of Mount Sumeru, then the gods of the various other mountains cannot help but serve him. . . .

Moreover, the Great Teacher Dengyō of Mt. Hiei is honored by monks throughout Japan as master of ordination into the priesthood. How could any monks turn their hearts toward a person like Hōnen, who is possessed by the Devil of the Sixth Heaven, and reject the Great Teacher Dengyō, who established the very ordination ceremonies that these monks themselves underwent? . . . [120]

In volume five of the *Great Calming and Contemplation* (*Maka shikan*) Tiantai [Zhiyi] says: "There is a type called Zen men, but their leaders and disciples are blind [to the truth] and lame [in practice], and both leaders and disciples will fall into hell." In the seventh volume, we read: "[I have set forth ten ways of meditation.]" But the ninth way has nothing in common with the ordinary monks of the world who concentrate on the written word, nor does it have anything in common with the Zen masters who concentrate on practice. Some Zen masters give all their attention to meditation alone. But their meditation is shallow and false, totally lacking in the rest of the ten ways. . . . [131]

We are living in an evil country and an evil age. I have discussed all this in detail in my work entitled *Rectification for the Peace of the Nation* (*Risshō ankoku ron*). This I will state. Let the gods forsake me. Let all persecutions assail me. Still I will give my life for the sake of the Law. . . . [137]

Whether tempted by good or threatened by evil, if one casts aside the Lotus Sūtra, he destines himself for hell. Here I will make a great vow. Though I might be offered the rulership of Japan if I will only abandon the Lotus Sūtra, accept the teachings of the [Amidist] Sūtra of Limitless Life (Kammuryōju kyō, and look forward to rebirth in the Western Pure Land, though I might be told that my father and mother will have their heads cut off if I do not recite the Nembutsu—whatever obstacles I might encounter, so long as men of wisdom do not prove my teachings to be false, I will never yield! All other troubles are no more to me than dust before the wind.

I will be the Pillar of Japan. I will be the Eyes of Japan. I will be the Great Ship of Japan. This is my vow, I will never forsake it! . . . [138]

I, Nichiren, am sovereign, teacher, father, and mother to all the people of Japan. But the men of the Tendai sect [who do not refute the heretical sects] are all great enemies of the people. As Zhangan has noted, "He who makes it possible for an offender to rid himself of evil is acting like a parent to him."[8] [147]

[Yampolsky, *Writings of Nichiren*, pp. 52–147]

THE TRUE OBJECT OF WORSHIP (*KANJIN HONZON SHŌ*)

This work, dated 1273, was written after the preceding *Eye-Opener* while Nichiren was still in exile on the island of Sado. It opens with a long explanation of the Tendai doctrine of "the three thousand worlds encompassed in a single thought." That "single thought" in which Zhiyi saw all the multiplicity of experience (i.e., on the level of provisional truth) as mystically identified with the higher truth of Emptiness is represented here by the simple invocation of the Lotus Sūtra. In effect, this formula provides a theoretical (exoteric) basis for the Lotus invocation similar to the one earlier Tendai teachers like Genshin had provided for the *nembutsu* as an esoteric mantra.

After a lengthy discussion of the stages by which Shākyamuni gradually revealed his teaching, Nichiren concludes with the establishment of the true and definitive object of worship, represented graphically by his new mandala, centered on the characters for the invocation of the Lotus Sūtra. The beginning of the phase known as the Latter Day of the Law—that is, the fifth half millennium following Shākyamuni's death—is the time when Nichiren was destined to appear.

Now is when the Bodhisattvas of the Earth will appear and establish in this country the supreme object of worship on the earth which depicts Shākyamuni Buddha of the essential teaching attending [the original Buddha]. This object of worship has never appeared in India or China. Its time had not come when Prince Shōtoku in Japan constructed the Shitennō-ji,[9] so he could only make a statue of Amida, a Buddha in another world, as the object of worship. When Emperor Shōmu[10] erected Tōdai-ji, he made a statue of the Buddha of the Kegon Sūtra [Vairochana Buddha] as the object of worship but could not manifest the true meaning of the Lotus Sūtra. The Great Teacher Dengyō almost revealed the truth of the sūtra, but because the time had not yet come, he

---

8. From a commentary on the Nirvana Sūtra, TD(?), 38, 80b.

9. The Shitennōji was founded in 587 and is located in present-day Osaka.

10. Emperor Shōmu (701–756) was the forty-fifth emperor of Japan. He established *kokubunji* (state-established provincial temples) in each province as well as the Tōdaiji in Nara.

constructed a statue of Yakushi Buddha, who dwells in an eastern realm of the universe, but he did not represent the Four Bodhisattvas of the Earth in any form.

Thus the revelation of the true object of worship has been entrusted only to the Bodhisattvas of the Earth. They have been waiting for the right time to emerge from the earth and carry out the Lord Buddha's command. . . .

When the skies are clear, the ground is illuminated. Similarly, when one knows the Lotus Sūtra, he understands the meaning of all worldly affairs. Showing the profound compassion for those ignorant of the gem of "the three thousand worlds comprised in a single thought," the Buddha wrapped it within the five-character phrase [*myōhō-renge-kyō*], with which he then adorned the necks of those living in the Latter Day.

[Yampolsky, *Writings of Nichiren*, pp. 178–179]

Nichiren as the Bodhisattva of Superb Action

I, Nichiren, a man born in the ages of the Latter Law, have nearly achieved the task of pioneership in propagating the Perfect Truth, the task assigned to the Bodhisattva of Superb Action (Vishisishtachāritra). The eternal Buddhahood of Shākyamuni, as he revealed himself in the chapter on Life-duration, in accordance with his primeval entity; the Buddha Prabhūtaratna, who appeared in the Heavenly Shrine, in the chapter on its appearance, and who represents Buddhahood in the manifestation of its efficacy; the bodhisattvas who sprang out of the earth, as made known in the chapter on the Issuing out of Earth—in revealing all these three, I have done the work of the pioneer [among those who perpetuate the Truth]; too high an honor, indeed, for me, a common mortal! . . .

I, Nichiren, am the one who takes the lead of the Bodhisattvas of the Earth. Then may I not be one of them? If I, Nichiren, am one of them, why may not all my disciples and followers be their kinsmen? The scripture says, "If one preaches to anybody the Lotus of Truth, even just one clause of it, he is, know ye, the messenger of the Tathāgata, the one commissioned by the Tathāgata, and the one who does the work of the Tathāgata." How, then, can I be anybody else than this one? . . .

By all means, awaken faith by seizing this opportunity! Live your life through as the one who embodies the Truth, and go on without hesitation as a kinsman of Nichiren! If you are one in faith with Nichiren, you are one of the Bodhisattvas of the Earth; if you are destined to be such, how can you doubt that you are the disciple of the Lord Shākyamuni from all eternity? There is assurance of this in a word of Buddha, which says: "I have always, from eternity, been instructing and quickening all these beings." No attention should be paid to the difference between men and women among those who would propagate the Lotus of the Perfect Truth in the days of the Latter Law. To utter the Sacred Title is, indeed, the privilege of the Bodhisattvas of the Earth. . . .

When the Buddha Prabhūtaratna sat in the Heavenly Shrine side by side with the Tathāgata Shākyamuni, the two Buddhas lifted up the banner of the Lotus of Perfect Truth and declared themselves to be the commanders [in the coming fight against vice and illusion]. How can this be a deception? Indeed, they have thereby agreed to raise us mortal beings to the rank of Buddha. I, Nichiren, was not present there in the congregation, and yet there is no reason to doubt the statements of the scripture. Or, is it possible that I was there? Common mortal that I am, I am not well aware of the past, yet in the present I am unmistakably the one who is realizing the Lotus of Truth. . . . The present, future, and past cannot be isolated from one another. . . .

In this document, the truths most precious to me are written down. Read, and read again; read into the letters and fix them into your mind! Thus put faith in the Supreme Being, represented in a way unique in the whole world! Ever more strongly I advise you to be firm in faith and to be under the protection of the threefold Buddhahood. March strenuously on in the ways of practice and learning! Without practice and learning, the Buddhist religion is nullified. Train yourself and also instruct others! Be convinced that practice and learning are fruits of faith! So long as, and so far as, there is power in you, preach, if it be only a phrase or a word [of the scripture]! "All Praise to the Lotus Sūtra of the Wondrous Law" *Namu Myōhō-renge-kyō! Namu Myōhō-renge-kyō!* [pp. 83–85]

His Destiny to Convert Japan

So far as, and so much as, my—Nichiren's—compassion is vast and comprehensive, the Adoration of the Lotus of the Perfect Truth shall prevail beyond the coming ages of ten thousand years, nay, eternally in the future. This is the merit I have achieved, which is destined to open the blind eyes of all beings in Japan [the world] and to shut off the ways to the nethermost avīchi hell. These merits surpass those of Dengyō and Tendai and are far beyond those of Nāgārjuna and Kāshyapa. Is it not true that one hundred years' training in a heavenly paradise does not compare with one day's work in the earthly world and that all service done to the truth during the two thousand years of the ages of the Perfect Law and the Copied Law is inferior to that done in one span of time in the age of the Latter Law?[11] All these differences are due, not to Nichiren's own wisdom, but to the virtues inherent in the times. Flowers bloom in spring, and fruits are ripe in autumn; it is hot in summer and cold in winter. Is it not time that makes these differences? Buddha announced, "This Truth shall be pro-

---

11. That is, the present degenerate times, in which Buddha's teaching has almost been lost.

claimed and perpetuated in the whole Jambudvīpa [world], in the fifth five hundred years after my death; and it will avail to save all kinds of devils and demons, celestial beings, and serpent tribes," etc. If this prediction should not be fulfilled, all other prophecies and assurances will prove false, the Lord Shāk-yamuni will fall to the avīchi hell, and the Buddha Prabhūtaratna will be burned in the infernal fires while all other Buddhas in the ten quarters will transfer their abodes to the eight great hells and all bodhisattvas will suffer from pains, one hundred and thirty-six in kind. How should all this be possible? If it is not, the whole of Japan [the world] will surely be converted to the "Praise to the Lotus Sūtra of the Wondrous Law."

[Anesaki, *Nichiren*, pp. 83–85, 119–120]

Chapter 14

ZEN BUDDHISM

While most schools of Buddhism cite particular scriptures in support of their own special form of Buddhist practice, the Zen school, in contrast, rejects claims of scriptural authority and embraces many different practices. Its legitimacy rests on claims to an exclusive ancestral lineage that has been passed from teacher to disciple in an unbroken succession from Shākyamuni, the historical Buddha, down to the present day.

Zen legend says that one day on Vulture Peak, Shākyamuni Buddha preached a sermon not with words but by holding up a flower. Mahā Kāshyapa was the only one of Shākyamuni's many disciples who grasped the true significance of this wordless teaching, which he expressed by a slight smile. Mahā Kāshyapa thereby inherited Shākyamuni's robe and lineage as the second Zen ancestor. The Zen lineage was faithfully transmitted in India through twenty-eight generations until Bodhidharma (J: Daruma) brought it to China sometime in the sixth century. According to Zen teachers, certification in this lineage ensured that Zen monastics and their disciples practiced Buddhism correctly as living embodiments of the Buddha's awakened wisdom. Thus, regardless of whatever types of Buddhist practices Zen monks performed, they always would have more religious power than the exact same practices engaged in by other monks not affiliated with Zen. Because Zen orthodoxy rests on the teacher-disciple lineage alone, instead of issues of doctrine or practice, Zen clerics have historically enjoyed great flexibility in adapting a wide variety of activities, from tantric (esoteric) rituals to Pure Land chanting, to their Zen practice.

The development of the Zen lineage is difficult to determine on the basis of the extant historical evidence. During the Tang Dynasty (618–907), several competing Zen (Ch: Chan) lineages emerged, each with distinct unilinear genealogical claims and each seeming to advocate a different approach to Buddhist practice. Regardless of the relative importance any particular lineage afforded meditation exercise (the literal meaning of *zen* or *chan*), scriptural study, or other monastic routines, each insisted that all of their ancestors and teachers had attained full awakening to the wisdom of the Buddha Mind. Some of these Tang-dynasty lineages were transmitted to Japan, most notably by Saichō (767–822), the founder of the Tendai establishment on Mount Hiei. But in Heian-period Japan, when any accomplished practitioner of meditation or esoteric rituals could be called "Zen master" (*zenji*), teacher-disciple Zen lineages were not maintained.

During the Song dynasty (960–1279), a more comprehensive vision of the Zen lineage became dominant, a multibranched one encompassing five or more family lines to which almost any ordained cleric could find affiliation. Hagiographical compendiums, known as "flame records" (*tōroku*),[1] compiled during the Song dynasty, depicted the Zen ancestors of all lines as expressing the activity of Buddha awakening in novel ways, with shouts or gestures and strikes and with enigmatic and sometimes impious language. Collections of these individual episodes, known as *kōan* (Ch: *gongan*),[2] were compiled so that they could be studied as guidelines for Buddhist practice. Song-dynasty records explained the significance of these seemingly bizarre stories in a pithy verse, attributed to Bodhidharma, which summarizes the Zen message: "A special transmission outside the scriptures, not relying on words or letters; pointing directly to the human mind, seeing true nature is becoming a Buddha."

It is important to note that this emphasis on going outside the orthodox scriptures did not displace the traditional Buddhist monastic practices of chanting, meditation, and scriptural study. Rather, it revitalized them and charged them with increased soteriological significance by insisting that they must be performed as meaningful expressions of individual awakening realized in the here and now. The effectiveness of Zen rhetoric in promoting strict monastic practice was recognized by the Song government when it officially designated most state-recognized monasteries (i.e., public institutions, open to any legally

---

1. The term *tōroku* is commonly rendered as referring to the "transmission of the lamp," but the basic metaphor is one in which the flame of wisdom burning in one lamp is used to ignite other lamps. It is the flame that is transmitted, not the lamps.

2. Literally, "public cases" but better understood as "test cases."

ordained monk, that offer prayers for the long life of the emperor) as being Chan (Zen) cloisters. These temples housed the monastic elites, the monks with the best education (in both Buddhist scriptures and Confucian classics), the most sincere religious motivation, the strictest discipline, and the strongest ties to powerful political patrons. It was natural, therefore, that Japanese monks who traveled to Song-dynasty China in search of a new model of Buddhist vitality, as well as Chinese émigré monks who subsequently came to Japan, would identify themselves with the Zen lineage.

ZEN IN JAPAN

Japanese Zen tradition customarily cites Eisai (aka Yōsai, 1141–1215) and Dōgen (1200–1253) as the first teachers of Song-dynasty Zen in Japan and as the founders of the Rinzai (Ch: Linji) and Sōtō (Ch: Caodong) Zen lineages, respectively. Certainly Eisai and Dōgen were important Zen pioneers who laid the foundation for subsequent developments, but their Zen teachings had little immediate impact. Even the wave of Chinese émigré Zen teachers who fled to Japan from the advancing Mongol armies and found new patrons among the military rulers of Kamakura immediately before and after the first Mongol invasion attempt of 1274 remained largely isolated from cultural currents. These Chinese monks provided the Hōjō regents and the new military government with a cosmopolitan aura otherwise lacking in the provincial town of Kamakura. But overall, the Kamakura warlords continued to sponsor established Buddhist schools and to join Pure Land and Nichiren movements as well. It was not until the second- and third-generation Japanese disciples of this first wave of Zen pioneers found new patrons among rival warlords and among members of the royal family that Zen became prominent in Japan.

Eisai was a Tendai monk who traveled to China twice (in 1168 and from 1187 to 1197). He was especially impressed by the resolute discipline of Chinese monasteries, which contrasted markedly with the moral laxity so common among Japanese clerics. Eisai believed that Zen would breathe new life into Japanese Tendai by reviving strict observance of the Buddhist precepts and the norms of monastic decorum. But Eisai's agenda was opposed by the Tendai establishment on Mount Hiei. He also had to contend with competition from the Darumashū, a rival Zen group founded by another Tendai monk named Nōnin, who never went to China but who had received mail-order certification in a Chinese Zen lineage. The Darumashū (named after Bodhidharma) promoted ideas completely opposite from Eisai's goals. They taught that no monastic discipline was required, since Buddha awakening could be expressed in any activity. In 1194, the court in Kyoto banned the Zen teachings of Eisai and the Darumashū. Eisai's most important work, the *Propagation of Zen for the Protection of the State* (*Kōzen gokokuron*, 1198), is an eloquent defense of Chinese Zen training that shows how it differs from normative Japanese Tendai and Darumashū practices.

Dōgen also began his monastic career in Tendai but soon switched to Zen under the guidance of one of Eisai's disciples. Dōgen spent four years in China (1223–1227), but unlike Eisai he was not edified by what he saw as political corruption in Song monasticism. Upon returning to Japan, he did not try to reform Tendai or promote Zen among the ruling elite. Instead, he established a small Zen temple on the outskirts of Kyoto. After a group of former Darumashū monks joined his community, Dōgen moved deep into the wilderness of Echizen (Fukui Prefecture), where his potential audience was even smaller. Although Dōgen died in relative obscurity, in modern times his writings have achieved wide recognition as works of religious and philosophical genius. His *How to Practice Buddhism* (*Bendōwa*, 1231) remains to this day a widely studied primer for Zen practice. And his *True Dharma Eye Treasury* (*Shōbōgenzō*, unfinished) is celebrated for the novel ways in which it analyzes *kōan* stories to express the wordless truth of Zen awakening in language.

Eisai's and Dōgen's very limited success at propagating Zen illustrates a crucial issue in our understanding of medieval Japanese religion. The religious life of the age often has been explained almost exclusively in terms of the so-called New Buddhism of the Pure Land, Nichiren, and Zen traditions that first appeared during the Kamakura period and remain the dominant forms of Japanese Buddhism to this day. Recent scholarship has emphasized, however, that these new schools for a long while remained relatively marginal movements with little political power or cultural influence compared with the orthodox mainstream of mixed exoteric and tantric (*kenmitsu*) Buddhism represented by the major landholding monasteries of Nara, Kyoto, and Mount Hiei. This Esoteric Buddhism was a dominant force in all aspects of medieval Japanese culture: politics, economics, literature, arts, and religion, including the worship of local gods (i.e., the *honji suijaku* forms of Shintō). To survive, the new forms of Kamakura Buddhism either had to move into the countryside beyond the reach of Esoteric Buddhist control or compromise with the preexisting Buddhist power structure or both.

Japanese Zen developed along both lines. Zen found a home in the state-recognized Buddhist establishment in the form of the Five Mountain (Gozan) temple networks of Kamakura and Kyoto. Although the title "Five Mountain" had been awarded to some Zen temples by the Hōjō regents, initially it was just an honorary designation. Through the political machinations of, first, Emperor Go-Daigo (1288–1339) and, subsequently, the Ashikaga military rulers, the Five Mountain system eventually consisted of some three hundred Zen monasteries, ranked into three tiers, that provided crucial income to the royal family and the military rulers. At the top tier were the large urban monasteries in Kyoto that performed tantric rites for the benefit of the state, sponsored foreign trade with China, managed the military government's estates, and, most of all, promoted the latest styles of Chinese culture. Five Mountain temples became centers of learning for the study of Neo-Confucian metaphysics, Chinese poetry, painting, calligraphy, and material arts such as printing, architecture, garden design, and ceramics. The role of Five Mountain Zen temples in introducing new styles of Chinese arts into medieval Japan has helped foster an indelible association between Zen and medieval forms of artistic expression.

At the center of the development of the Five Mountain system stood Musō Soseki (1275–1351), probably the most famous monk of his time, who achieved the unique distinction of receiving the title of "national teacher" (*kokushi*) from seven different emperors. Musō's career illustrates the precarious political waters that Zen abbots of his day had to navigate. He first rose to prominence under the sponsorship of the Hōjō regents, but when they finally selected him to become abbot of a Zen monastery in Kamakura, he refused to accept the post. In 1325, however, when Go-Daigo appointed him abbot of a Zen monastery in Kyoto, he accepted. But Musō resigned the following year and returned to Kamakura, where he finally served as abbot of Hōjō-sponsored Zen temples. Then, after forces loyal to Go-Daigo overthrew the Hōjō regents in 1333, Musō returned to Kyoto, where Go-Daigo again appointed him abbot. Musō nurtured close ties as well to the warrior Ashikaga Takauji (1305–1358), who, in 1336, removed Go-Daigo from power and established a new military government in Kyoto. At the time of Go-Daigo's death in 1339, Musō persuaded Takauji to sponsor the establishment of a new Zen monastery, Tenryūji, in order to pray for the late emperor's salvation. Naturally, Musō himself was appointed abbot. This event signaled the apex of the new Zen institution's identification with the ruling powers. Musō's sermon "Reflections on the Enmity Between Go-Daigo and the Shogun, Ashikaga Takauji" speaks volumes not only about church-state relations in medieval Japan but also about how little prestige Go-Daigo then commanded.

The other main branch of Zen in medieval Japan was the Rinka (literally, "forest") monasteries found primarily in the countryside. In contrast to the emphasis on Chinese learning found in the Five Mountain Zen temples, the Rinka generally housed less-educated monks who devoted more of their energies to the practices of "sitting Zen" (*zazen*) meditation and *kōan* study than to the writing of Chinese poetry. Rinka temples flourished among nouveau riche merchants of emerging trading centers and among the lower-ranked landed warriors and peasants, whose economic wealth and military power increased throughout the medieval period. For these merchants, warriors, and peasants, Rinka Zen monks performed simplified rites for worldly benefits, lay precept ordinations, and funerals and exorcized evil spirits and ghosts. When the Ashikaga shogunate declined in power, especially following the devastation of the Ōnin War (1467–1477), the Five Mountain system also declined in prestige and lost control of its lands, the source of its wealth. At this time, the Rinka temples' lack of political connections to the governing elites, which initially had left them less wealthy than the Five Mountains, proved to be a blessing in disguise. Many of the new warrior leaders who rose to power during the sixteenth century came from rural families who supported Rinka temples. The present-day Sōtō and Rinzai lineages also emerged from Rinka Zen.

Considering the Five Mountain Zen monks' pride in their poetry, it is ironic that two of the most celebrated Zen poets in Japanese history came out of the Rinka: Ikkyū Sōjun (1394–1481) from the Ō-Tō-Kan lineage of Daitokuji and Daigu Ryōkan (1758–1831) from Dōgen's Sōtō lineage. Although Ikkyū, or "Errant Cloud" (Kyōun), as he styled himself, had been thoroughly schooled in the orthodox Chinese prosody of the Five Mountain Zen monasteries, he later abandoned Five Mountain Zen and developed his own distinctive and deeply personal approach to Chinese verse. In contrast to Five Mountain poetry's conventional secular themes expressed in rigid adherence to established form, Ikkyū seems to delight in violating Chinese grammar and rhymes in novel ways as he discusses religious themes (laden with Buddhist technical vocabulary) in unconventional ways. Because of his pronounced iconoclasm, Ikkyū became the subject of many entertaining folktales and, like Ryōkan, is a well-known character ("Little Ikkyū") in the popular culture of modern Japan.

Japanese Zen establishments, both the Five Mountain and the Rinka, owed much of their success to the strict discipline of their monks and to their teaching of traditional virtues, especially loyalty to one's lord. Warriors, court officials, and merchants alike patronized Zen monks for their stern moralizing sermons. As demonstrated by figures such as Nōnin or Ikkyū, however, Zen also has antinomian tendencies. The liberated lifestyle and free literary expression still had its serious side as a means of manifesting deeper insight or protesting abuses in institutionalized Zen and, in this, can be seen the interactions between two dominant themes in Zen: discipline and liberation.

EISAI: *PROPAGATION OF ZEN FOR THE PROTECTION OF THE STATE* (*KŌZEN GOKOKURON*)

Eisai compiled this anthology in 1198, four years after the court had prohibited the establishment of independent Zen institutions in an attempt to persuade the court not merely to lift its ban but also to promote Zen in order to revitalize Japanese Buddhism. Since Eisai's chief adversaries at the Kyoto court were the monks of Mount Hiei monastery, which Saichō had founded, Eisai selected quotations primarily from scriptures and commentaries favored in the Tendai school to argue that Zen is the essence of true Buddhism. He points out that Saichō himself belonged to a Zen lineage and asserts that if Zen is illegitimate, then Saichō and the Tendai school he founded must also be illegitimate. In the following excerpts, Eisai equates Zen with the essence of mind, whose clarification is the goal of Buddhist practice. He asserts that mind is understood only by members of the special Zen lineage and emphasizes that the master-to-disciple transmission of the Zen lineage preserves the correct forms of monastic discipline as well as strict adherence to the precepts. He further attacks the Darumashū as false Zen, defends Zen's rejection of language, and attempts to show how Zen practice will reform wayward Japanese Buddhist monasticism.

Preface

So great is Mind! Heaven's height is immeasurable, but Mind goes above it. Earth's depth is unfathomable, but Mind extends beneath it. The light of the sun and moon cannot be outdistanced, yet Mind reaches beyond them. Galaxies are as infinite as grains of sand, yet Mind spreads outside them. How great is the empty space! How primal is the ether! Still Mind encompasses all space and generates the ethereal. Because of it, Heaven and Earth treat us with their coverage and support. The sun and moon treat us with their circuits, and the four seasons treat us with their transformations. The myriad things treat us with their fecundity. Great indeed is Mind! Of necessity we assign it names: the Supreme Vehicle, the Prime Meaning, the True Aspect of Transcendental Wisdom [Prajñā], the Single Dharma Realm of Truth, the Unsurpassed Awakened Wisdom [Bodhi], the Heroic Concentration [Shūrangama samādhi], the True Dharma Eye Matrix, the Marvelous Mind of Nirvāna. All scriptures of the Three Turnings of the Dharma Wheel and eight canons, as well as all the doctrines of the Four Shāla Trees and Five Vehicles fit neatly within it.[3]

The Great Hero Shākyamuni's having conveyed this Mind Dharma to his disciple the golden ascetic Mahā Kāshyapa is known as the special transmission outside the scriptures. From their facing one another on Vulture Peak to Mahā Kāshyapa's smile in Cockleg Cave, the raised flower produced thousands of shoots; from this one fountainhead sprang ten thousand streams. In India the proper succession was maintained. In China the dharma generations were tightly linked. Thus has the true dharma as propagated by the Buddhas of old been handed down along with the dharma robe. Thus have the correct ritual forms of Buddhist ascetic training been made manifest. The substance of the dharma is kept whole through master-disciple relationships, and confusion over correct and incorrect monastic decorum is eliminated. In fact, after Bodhidharma, the great master who came from the West, sailed across the South Seas and planted his staff on the banks of the East River in China, the Dharma-eye

---

3. The Three Turnings of the Dharma Wheel correspond to the Flower Garland Scripture (Buddhāvatamsaka), the provisional scriptures, and the Lotus Scripture (Saddharma puṇḍarīka). The "eight canons" is a catchall term for all genres of Buddhist scripture. The Four Shāla Trees, a reference to the four trees among which Shākyamuni passed away into nirvāna, symbolize impermanence. The Five Vehicles refer to Buddhist practices that lead to human rebirth, heaven, or the spiritual attainments of the *arhat*, solitary Buddha, or bodhisattva (i.e., full Buddha realization).

Zen lineage of Fayan Wenyi was transmitted to Korea and the Ox-head Zen lineage of Niudou Farong was brought to Japan. Studying Zen, one rides all vehicles of Buddhism; practicing Zen, one attains awakening in a single lifetime. Outwardly promoting the moral discipline of the Nirvāna Scripture while inwardly embodying the wisdom and compassion of the Great Perfection of Wisdom Scripture is the essence of Zen.

In our kingdom the sovereign shines in splendor and his honor extends far and wide. Emissaries from distant fabled lands pay their respects to his court. Ministers conduct the affairs of the realm while monastics propagate the path of renunciation. Even the dharma of the Four Hindu Vedas finds use. Why then discard the five family lineages of Zen? Nonetheless, many malign this teaching, calling it the Zen of blind trance. Others doubt it, calling it the evil of clinging to emptiness. Still others consider it ill-suited to this latter age of dharma decline, saying that it is not needed in our land. Or they disparage my capacity, saying that I lack sufficient power. They belittle my spiritual ability, saying that it is impossible for me to revive what was already abandoned. Whoever attempts to uphold the Dharma Jewel in such a way destroys the Dharma Jewel. Not being me, how can they know my mind? Not only do they block the gateway through the Zen barriers, but they also defy the legacy of Saichō, the founder of Mount Hiei. Alas, how sad, how distressing. Which of us is right? Which of us is wrong?

I have compiled an anthology of the Buddhist scriptures that record the essential teachings of our lineage for consideration by today's pundits and for the benefit of posterity. This anthology is in three fascicles consisting of ten chapters, and it is entitled *Propagation of Zen for the Protection of the State* in accordance with the basic idea of the Sutra for Humane Kings. As my humble fictive words accord with reality, I ignore the catcalls of ministers and monastics. Remembering that the Zen of Linji benefits his later generations, I am not embarrassed by their written slanders. I merely hope that the flame of wisdom transmitted in Zen verse will not be extinguished until the arrival of Maitreya and that the fountain of Zen will flow unimpeded until the future eon of the Thousand Buddhas.

[Ichikawa, *Chūsei zenke*, pp. 8–9; WB]

ZEN AND PRECEPTS

QUESTION: Some criticize you, asking what makes you think this new Zen lineage will cause Buddhism to flourish forever?

ANSWER: Moral precepts and monastic discipline cause Buddhism to flourish forever. Moral precepts and monastic discipline are the essence of Zen. Therefore, Zen causes Buddhism to flourish forever. Zhiyi's *Calming and Contemplation* states: "Worldly desires of ordinary people are denounced by all the holy ones. Evil is destroyed by pure wisdom. Pure wisdom arises from pure Zen. Pure Zen arises from pure precepts."

[Ichikawa, *Chūsei zenke*, pp. 35–36; WB]

THE DARUMASHŪ

QUESTION: Some people say that the Zen teaching of "not relying on words and letters" means the evil of clinging to emptiness and the practice of blind trance. If so, then Tendai opposes it. In Zhi-yi's *Calming and Contemplation*, where it explains contemplation of the inconceivable object, it says: "This cannot be known by the Zen teachers of blind trance or the dharma masters of scriptural chanting." In Zhiyi's *Profound Meaning of the Lotus Scripture* it says: "If those who contemplate Mind think that their own mind is it, equate themselves with the Buddha, and ignore the scriptures, then they fall into the error of arrogance. It is like holding a torch so as to burn oneself." Likewise, Zhanran's commentary on this passage says: "Grasping the torch of blind trance burns the hand of cavalier meditator." How do you respond to these criticisms of not relying on words and letters?

ANSWER: This Zen lineage despises teachers of blind trance and hates people who practice the evil of clinging to emptiness. They are as repugnant as corpses sunk to the bottom of the ocean. We solely rely on the Perfect Teaching, cultivating the perfect and the sudden. Outwardly we observe the precepts to eliminate vice, inwardly we employ compassion to benefit others. This is called the Zen teaching. This is called the Buddha dharma. Those who practice blind Zen and cling to evil not only lack our teaching but are thieves of the dharma. Yongming Yanshou's *Zen Mirror Record* says: "Principle truly responds to conditions. No practice obstructs principle. Practice rests on principle. No practice exists without principle. Those people who do not enter the Perfect Teaching but disparage others as being beneath them and regard themselves as spiritually advanced have not only lost the practice but completely lack principle. One must merely awaken to the essence of the One Mind free from all obstructions, in which principle and practice fuse together naturally, in which the worldly and the ultimate merge completely. If one clings to practice and mistakes principle, then one sinks into eons of *samsāra*. If one awakens to principle but neglects practice, then one lacks perfect realization. How can principle and practice not be products of the mind? How could essence and appearance not correspond? If one enters the Zen

Mirror and suddenly awakens to the True Mind, then even the words 'principle' or 'practice' do not exist, much less the clinging to principle or practice. But after attaining the fundamental, one must not abandon perfect cultivation. How can those practitioners of the Zen of blind trance even know of the Six Identities between Buddha and Humans? How can the crazed chanters of the scripture even be aware of the One Mind?" . . .

QUESTION: But what about those who mistakenly refer to the Zen lineage as the Dharumashū? They teach: "There is nothing to practice, nothing to cultivate. Originally afflictions (*klesha*) do not exist. From the beginning, afflictions are *bodhi*. Therefore, moral precepts and monastic rituals are of no use. One should merely eat and sleep as needed. Why must anyone labor to recall the Buddha (*nembutsu*), to worship relics, or to observe dietary restrictions?" What about their teaching?

ANSWER: There is no evil that such people will not do. They are the ones the scriptures denounce as nihilists. One must not talk with such people nor even sit with them. One must avoid them by a thousand *yojana* [about 8,500 miles].

[Ichikawa, *Chūsei zenke*, pp. 39–41; WB]

LANGUAGE

"Scriptures," or "Zen" are merely names. "Investigate," or "study" likewise are merely provisional designations. "Self," "other," "living beings," "*bodhi*," "nirvāna," and so forth are just words, without any real existence. Similarly, because the dharma preached by the Buddha is just such words, in reality nothing was preached.

For this reason Zen lies beyond the details of words and letters, outside mental conditions, in the inconceivable, in what ultimately cannot be grasped. "So-called Buddha dharma consists of the dharma that cannot be preached." So-called Zen is exactly the same. If anyone says the Buddha's Zen exists in words, letters, or speech, then that person slanders the Buddha and slanders the dharma. For this reason our ancestral teachers did not rely on words and letters, pointed directly at the human mind, saw nature, and became Buddhas. Such is Zen practice. Whoever clings to words loses the dharma, whoever clings to appearances becomes topsy-turvy. Fundamentally inactive, without a thing to grasp, is seeing the Buddha dharma. The Buddha dharma consists of merely walking, standing, sitting, and lying down. Adding even a single fine hair to it is impossible. Subtracting even a single fine hair from it is impossible. Once one attains this understanding, then expend not even the least effort. With even the slightest attempt at being clever, one has already missed it. Therefore, activity gives rise to *samsāra* while quietude leaves one in a drunken stupor, and avoiding both activity and quietude displays ignorance of Buddha nature. If one does none of the above, then what? This point lies outside clarification of doctrine. It cannot be fathomed through words. Look ahead and see! Get up and go! Once the arrow leaves the bow, there is no art that can bring it back. Even the thousand Buddhas could not grab it. As long as it has not hit the ground, no matter how much one might rue the crooked shot, one merely seizes air. Even if one tried until the last days of one's life, there is no grasping it.

[Ichikawa, *Chūsei zenke*, pp. 62–63; WB]

TEN FACILITIES FOR ZEN MONASTICISM

Facilities for Zen Monasticism consist of ten items, which I describe in accordance with the *Pure Rules for Zen Cloisters* and other Chinese standards.

First, the monastery: Monasteries can be large or small, but all should conform to the layout of the Buddha's Jetavana Vihāra (Gion Shōja) in India. Along the four sides there are walls without side gates. There is only one main gate, which the gatekeeper shuts at dusk and opens at dawn. Nuns, women, and inauspicious people must not be allowed to stay the night. The decline of the Buddha dharma always results from women.

Second, ordinations: The distinction between Hīnayāna precepts and Mahāyāna precepts exists only in the hearts of men. Because one must merely embody sentiments of great compassion for the benefit of others, Zen does not choose between Mahāyāna or Hīnayāna precepts but merely focuses on living a pure life.

Third, observing the precepts: After ordination, if one violates the precepts, it would be the same as obtaining a precious jewel only in order to smash it. Therefore one must strictly observe the two hundred fifty *bhiksu* [monk] precepts, as well as the bodhisattva's three groups of pure precepts, ten major precepts, and forty-eight minor precepts. Twice each month during the *uposatha* ceremony, these precepts must be reviewed as explained in the precept scriptures. Anyone who violates the precepts must be kicked out. Such a one can be likened to a corpse cast into the ocean.

Fourth, academic study: Learning that spans the entire Buddhist canon and conduct that accords with the Mahāyāna and Hīnayāna precepts as well as proper monastic decorum constitute being a field of merit for gods and men. Inwardly embodying the great compassion of the bodhisattvas constitutes being a benevolent father to all living beings. In this way we become a valued jewel to the sovereign and a good physician to the country. To these goals we must aspire.

Fifth, ritual conduct: monastics observe dietary restrictions, practice chastity, and obey the Buddha's words. The schedule for each night and day are as follows: At dusk all monks assemble in the Buddha Hall to offer incense and worship. At evening they practice sitting Zen (*zazen*). During the third watch of the night (about 2:00 A.M.) they sleep. During the fourth watch they sleep. At the fifth watch they practice sitting Zen. At cockcrow they assemble in the Buddha Hall to offer incense and worship. At dawn they eat morning gruel. At the hour of the dragon (about 8:00 A.M.) they chant scriptures, study, or attend elder monks. At midmorning they practice sitting Zen. At noon they eat their daily meal. Afterwards they bathe or wash. During midafternoon they practice sitting Zen. Late afternoons are free time. The four periods of sitting Zen must be diligently practiced. Each moment of sitting Zen repays one's debts to the state; each act commemorates the sovereign's long life. These rituals truly cause the imperial reign to long prosper and the dharma flame to shine forever.

Sixth, monastic decorum: Old and young must always wear full robes. When they encounter one another, they must first place the palms of their hands together and then bow their heads to the ground in harmonious expressions of respect. Also, all meals, all walking exercises, all sitting Zen, all academic study, all chanting, and all sleeping must be performed as a group. Even if a hundred thousand monks are together inside one hall, each of them must observe correct monastic decorum. If someone is absent, the group leader (*inō*) must investigate and must not forgive even the slightest transgression.

Seventh, robes: Both inner and outer wear should conform to Chinese designs. These imply circumspection. One must be prudent in all affairs.

Eighth, disciples: Those who embody morality and wisdom without lapse should be admitted to the assembly. They must possess both mental and physical ability.

Ninth, economic income: As they say, "Do not cultivate the fields, since sitting Zen leaves no time for it; Do not hoard treasures, since the Buddha's words alone suffice." Aside from one cooked meal each day, eliminate all other needs. The dharma of monks consists of being satisfied with as little as possible.

Tenth, summer and winter retreats: The summer retreat begins on the fifteenth day of the fourth moon and ends on the fifteenth day of the seventh moon. The winter retreat begins on the fifteenth day of the tenth moon and ends on the fifteenth day of the first moon. Both of these two retreats were established by the Buddhas. Do not doubt it. In our land these retreats have not been practiced for a long time. In the great land of Song-dynasty China, however, not a single monk fails to participate in the two retreats. From the standpoint of the Buddha dharma, the Japanese practice of calculating one's monastic seniority in terms of the retreats without actually participating in them is laughable.

[Ichikawa, *Chūsei zenke*, pp. 80–83; WB]

ESSENTIALS FOR MONASTICS (*SHUKKE TAIKŌ*)

Unlike *Propagation of Zen for the Protection of the State*, which was directed toward a wide audience of court officials and ecclesiastical officials, Eisai wrote this treatise for his own followers as a guide to the proper lifestyle for Buddhist monks and nuns. In it, he confesses that before his trip to China he had, like most other Japanese monks, ignored the Buddhist prohibitions against eating meat and drinking alcohol. Eisai's vigorous advocacy for observing the Buddhist precepts is remarkable not just because it goes against the currents of Japanese Buddhist history but also because it stresses such elementary points (e.g., the distinctions between Buddhist robes and secular clothing) that the reader is left with the impression that clerics of Eisai's time completely lacked any firsthand knowledge of traditional Buddhist monastic norms. The opening section gives an overview of the treatise.

The Buddha dharma is the boat that ferries one across the sea of death, the chariot that traverses the roads of delusion, the good medicine that cures our eternal afflictions, the torch that illuminates our long night. The depth of its merit cannot be fathomed. Now that the degenerate and evil age has finally arrived, our ability to know suffering must develop. Now that we have entered the beginning of the latter five hundred years, the number of people who study precepts must increase. The Great Perfection of Wisdom Scripture's prophecy that it will be propagated in northeastern lands during the latter age must refer to today's Japan. Likewise, how could the Nirvāna Scripture's goal of promoting moral discipline during the latter age have been intended for any other time? The same applies to the Lotus Scripture's four peaceful practices for the evil age and to the *Calming and Contemplation*'s encouragement of *samādhi*. What is essential for this age is merely to follow the Buddha's own words, namely, "promoting moral discipline by preaching the permanent."

The life essence of the Buddha dharma is moral purity. You must comprehend this life essence. The five-thousand scrolls of scriptures are called the Buddha dharma. How can you chant them without practicing what they teach? The sixty scrolls of Zhiyi's commentaries are known as the Tendai Perfect Doctrine. How can you discuss them without following their principles? You must know that Buddha dharma consists of the Buddha's wondrous decorum. Only a person who knows the Buddha dharma's meaning, who understands its principles, and who practices its decorum can be called a Buddhist.

In this treatise I outline the practice of Buddhist decorum in order to save people during this latter age. The Buddhist canon of discourses, discipline, and treatises resembles a contract. They record the principles of the threefold study (meditation, morality, and wisdom) of the Buddha dharma. For example, contracts for estates (*shōen*) are preserved in a ledger to show how much profit can be derived from planting, weeding, and harvesting a piece of land. Similarly, chanting the discourses, discipline, and treatises and practicing their teachings show you how to rectify body and mind and how to follow the Buddha's footsteps.

The *Seven Past Buddhas' Precept Verse* says: "Refrain from all evil; Perform every manner of good; Purify your own mind; This is the teaching of all Buddhas." All the doctrines preached by the Buddha throughout his teaching career are summed up in this one verse. How can you rely on the Buddha's teaching to leave your home as a renunciant monk, yet not follow the Buddha's admonition? The time to uphold the precepts has arrived. How can you imagine that observing the precepts is tiresome? Isn't the wheel of suffering around your neck more bothersome? When impermanence strikes you in the face, don't be caught lackadaisically napping.

When I, Eisai, was in Great China, I studied the holy scriptures, recorded the main points of the discipline, and then returned to Japan. Once here, I knew that the time was ripe and that people's spiritual capacities were ready for me to promote the precepts. When so many monks responded to my encouragement, I experienced joy a thousand times over. Since my twenty-first year until my fiftieth year, I have trained as a Buddhist monk in Japan and in China for a full thirty years. During that time I never before experienced any miracles. Now, however, I have the miracle of all of you following me. Based on the notes that I took in China, I have written this treatise on precepts for the latter age. Anyone who wishes to attain moral purity should follow its exhortations. The essentials for monastics are written herein.

Maintaining moral purity consists of two main types of practices. The first concerns robes and meals. The second concerns practice and decorum. First, robes cover the body while meals nourish the body. Second, practice means observing the Buddhist precepts while decorum means proper etiquette. Each of these consists of two types. There are secular robes and dharma robes. There are invitations to banquets and begging for food. There are *bhiksu* precepts and bodhisattva precepts. There are secular forms of etiquette and the universal norms of the Way. . . .

[from the 1789 woodblock edition]

DŌGEN: HOW TO PRACTICE BUDDHISM (BENDŌWA)

Dōgen wrote this treatise in 1231 at the beginning of his ministry as a basic introduction to Zen Buddhism. In the following excerpts, Dōgen argues that true Buddhism has been preserved only by members of the Zen lineage and can be learned only by studying under a fully initiated Zen teacher. True Buddhism consists of practicing sitting Zen (*zazen*), which Dōgen identifies as self-actualizing *samādhi* or, in other words, the concentration that transforms both self and the world experienced by self into its original state of awakened Buddha activity. According to Dōgen, other Buddhist practices lack this kind of spiritual efficacy.

After arousing dharma-seeking mind, I traveled throughout our kingdom searching for a good teacher. Finally I met Master Myōzen at Kenninji monastery. I followed him for nine swift years as I heard about the Rinzai family lineage. Master Myōzen was the foremost disciple of ancestor Eisai, from whom he alone received correct transmission of the supreme Buddha dharma. No one else compared to Myōzen.

Later I journeyed to the Great Song-dynasty China and visited various good teachers along both sides of the Qiantang River, where I learned the ways of the five family lineages of Zen. Finally, I met Zen Master Rujing on the Great White Peak of Mount Tiandong and completed the great goal of my lifelong study. Thereafter, I returned home in 1227 to save living beings by propagating the dharma. I felt as if I shouldered a heavy responsibility.

Yet I put aside my burden, and waiting for a favorable opportunity, I moved about like a cloud or tumbleweed, all the while wanting to teach in the style of my former mentor. I thought there must be a few student monks unconcerned with fame and fortune who consider the Buddha Way of first importance in their sincere study. What if they were led astray by false teachers who obscure correct understanding and thereby became self-deluded or sunk in *samsāra*? When would they ever sprout the true seeds of Prajñā [awakened wisdom] and attain the Way? As long as I move about like a cloud or tumbleweed, how can they cross the mountains or rivers to visit me? Out of concern for these monks, I have written about the practices that I saw and heard in the Zen monasteries of Great Song-dynasty China and about the abstruse import that my good teacher [Rujing] taught me. I dedicate this treatise to all students devoted to the Way so that they may know the true dharma. Here is the genuine initiation.

We teach: The Great Master, Lord Shākyamuni, atop Vulture Peak in India transmitted the dharma to Mahā Kāshyapa. Correctly transmitted from ancestor to ancestor, it subsequently reached the venerable Bodhidharma. Venerable Bodhidharma traveled to China and transmitted the dharma to Master Huike. Thus was the Buddha dharma first transmitted to China.

In this same manner the dharma was directly transmitted to Huineng, the sixth ancestor, also known as Great Mirror Zen Master. From him the authentic Buddha dharma spread throughout China without divisions. He produced two fabulous disciples: Nanyue Huairang and Qingyuan Xing-si. Both of them transmitted and preserved the Buddha-mind Seal (*mudra*), and both were teachers of gods and men. From these two disciples, five family lineages emerged: the Fayan line, the Guiyang line, the Caodong line, the Yunmen line, and the Linji line. Today in Song-dynasty China only the Linji lineage is widespread. Although the five family lineages differ, there is just one Buddha-mind Seal.

In China, since the Later Han dynasty [first century], various Buddhist scriptures had been translated repeatedly, but no one could separate the grain from the chaff. When Bodhidharma came from the West, he cut through the confusion, and since then the single pure Buddha dharma spread everywhere. We must try to do the same in our land.

We teach: For all the Buddha dharma–preserving Zen ancestors and Buddhas, sitting upright in the practice of self-actualizing (*jijuyū*) *samādhi* [concentration] is the true path of awakening. Both in India and in China, all who have attained awakening did so in this way. Because in every generation each teacher and each disciple intimately and correctly transmitted this marvelous art, I learned the genuine initiation.

In the correctly transmitted Zen lineage we teach: This directly transmitted, authoritative Buddha dharma is the best of the best. Once you start studying under a good teacher, there is no need for lighting incense, worshipful prostrations, recalling the Buddha (*nembutsu*), repentance, or chanting scripture. Just sit (*shikan taza*) and slough off body-mind (*shinjin datsuraku*).

If you, for however short a while, imprint all your activities with the Buddha-mind Seal by sitting upright in *samādhi*, then all things in the entire dharma realm become imprinted with the Buddha-mind Seal, and the entire cosmos becomes awakening. Thereupon all Buddhas and Tathāgatas increase their fundamental essence of dharma joy, and the adornments of the way of awakening are revitalized. Moreover, at this very moment all living beings in the six courses of rebirth throughout all dharma realms of the ten directions simultaneously purify their body-minds, realize great liberation, and discover their original faces. All things realize complete awakening, all creatures access Buddha bodies, transcend the boundaries of awakening, sit as Buddhas at the base of the tree of awakening, and simultaneously turn the incomparable Dharma Wheel that expresses deep, ultimate, unconditioned Prajñā.

Because the Fully Awakened Ones [Buddhas] provide mysterious assistance, when you practice sitting Zen, you will definitely slough off body-mind, eliminate habitually defiled thought patterns, and realize divinely genuine Buddha dharma. You will aid all Buddha activity in all Buddha wayfaring sites as infinite as atoms. You will encourage the aptitude for practicing beyond Buddha and promote the dharma beyond Buddha. At that moment all lands, plants, fences, and roof tiles throughout the dharma realms of the ten directions also engage in Buddha activity, causing everyone to obtain the Buddha's inconceivable mysterious assistance in attaining awakening as easily as they receive natural blessings like wind and water. Just as everyone makes use of water and fire, so too you will circulate the innate realization of Buddha deliverance so that everyone living or talking with you will all embody inexhaustible Buddha-virtue. As it unfolds and widens without end, without break, the inconceivable, infinite Buddha dharma will flow throughout the entire cosmos and beyond. The fact that the one who practices sitting Zen is unaware of the Buddha's mysterious assistance is because it is direct realization of nondeliberative quiescence. If, as ordinary people suppose, cultivation and realization are two separate processes, then it would be possible to be aware of each in isolation. But what interacts with our awareness cannot be fundamental realization because fundamental realization is beyond deluded human thoughts.

Moreover, although both subject and object disappear and reappear during the practice of quiescent realization, because it is the realm of self-actualizing *samādhi*, they become expansive Buddha activity and profound, miraculous Buddha deliverance without moving a single speck of dust or blemishing a single image. All the lands and plants reached by this path of Buddha deliverance radiate great brilliance and preach the profound, wondrous dharma endlessly. Plants and fences sermonize for humans, for Buddhas, and for all living beings. Humans, Buddhas, and all living beings expound the dharma for the sake of plants and fences. Because this realm of self-awakening and awakening others is permeated with the quality of universal Buddha realization, fundamental realization occurs ceaselessly.

Therefore, whenever you practice sitting Zen, for however short a while, you mysteriously merge with all existence, you completely permeate all time, and throughout the infinite dharma realm, you eternally perform past, present, and future Buddha deliverance. Each and every one equally performs the same cultivation and the same realization. It is so not just during seated cultivation. Echoes of emptiness sound during the intervals both before and after the temple bell is struck because it continues to vibrate due to its marvelous resonance. In this same manner, the original cultivation of original face possessed by each one of the infinite individual beings reverberates beyond all measurable calculation.

Know that even if all the Buddhas as infinite as grains of sand used all their Buddha wisdom in an attempt to sum up the amount of merit generated by just one person practicing sitting Zen, they could never reach the end of it.

> QUESTION: Now I know how immense must be the merit of sitting Zen. But stupid people will doubt you by asking: "Since there are many different ways to practice Buddhism, why do you recommend sitting Zen alone?"
>
> ANSWER: Because it is the main way to practice Buddhism.
>
> QUESTION: Why is it alone the main practice?
>
> ANSWER: Because the great master Shākyamuni transmitted this marvelous art of attaining the Way, and because all Tathāgatas of the past, present, and future all attained the Way by sitting Zen. For this reason every generation transmits sitting Zen as the main practice. Not only that, but all the Zen ancestors of India and China attained the Way through sitting Zen. For this reason, I am teaching sitting Zen to gods and men.

QUESTION: This practice, whether correctly transmitted by the Tathāga-tas or handed down by the Zen ancestors, truly is beyond the ability of ordinary people. Chanting scriptures or recalling the Buddha (*nem-butsu*), however, easily leads to awakening. How can just sitting vainly without doing anything lead to awakening?

ANSWER: If you say that the *samādhi* of the Buddhas, the unsurpassed great dharma, is vainly sitting without doing anything, then you are a heretic who slanders the Mahāyāna. Yours is a very deep delusion, the same as someone in the middle of the ocean denying the existence of water. Fortunately for you, all Buddhas already sit in self-actualizing *samādhi*. Have you not benefited from their great merit? How pitiful you are, with your wisdom eye closed and your drunken wits.

The realm of the Buddhas is inconceivable. It is beyond our un-derstanding. How could it be known by someone who lacks faith or intelligence? Only someone of proper faith and Mahāyāna aptitude can approach it. Those who lack faith will not believe even if taught, just like those who left Vulture Peak when Shākyamuni was about to preach the Lotus Scripture. To generate a mind of proper faith, you must practice Buddhism and study Buddhism. If you cannot believe, then you should give up and merely regret your not having inherited any karmic link to the dharma from your previous lives.

Moreover, how do you know if you have acquired any merit from chanting the scripture or recalling the Buddha? How futile to think that the merit of Buddha activity can be produced merely by moving the tongue aloud. If you regard such practices as Buddha dharma, then you are far from the truth. You should open the scriptures only to clarify what the Buddha taught about the fundamentals of gradual and sudden cultivation and to practice in accordance with the teach-ing so as to attain realization. No intellectual deliberations could ever produce merit leading to *bodhi* [awakened wisdom]. To foolishly pur-sue the Buddha Way by chanting is like pointing your cart north while wanting to go south to the tropics. It is the same as trying to put a square peg in a round hole. To read the words without knowing the practice is the same as having the recipe for a medical prescription but forgetting to mix the medicine. Where is the benefit? Chanting without interruption resembles the frogs in the spring paddy fields croaking day and night. Ultimately it produces no merit. Those de-luded by ambitions for fame and fortune cannot abandon chanting. Their greed runs too deep. As they were in ancient time, so they still are today. How pitiful!

Just know that the wondrous dharma of the past seven Buddhas is preserved and taught in its legitimate import only when there occurs the correct transmission between a student monk who merges his mind in realized understanding with that of a master teacher who has attained the bright mind of the Way. This dharma lies beyond the knowledge of preachers who merely study the words of the scriptures. In short, you should put a stop to this nonsense, follow the teachings of a true teacher, practice the Way of sitting Zen, and attain realization of the self-actualizing *samādhi* of all the Buddhas.

QUESTION: Nowadays in our kingdom we already have the doctrines of the Lotus and Flower Garland Scriptures, both of which constitute the pinnacle of Mahāyāna. And the esoteric (Shingon) rituals have been transmitted from Mahā Vairochana through the Vajrasattva to the present in an unbroken lineage. They teach: "this very mind is Buddha" and "this very body becomes Buddha," so that even without eons of cultivation, one will be able to attain the supreme awakening of the Five Buddhas in the Central Assembly of the Womb Mandala. Surely this is the most marvelous Buddhist practice. What superlative features of Zen cultivation cause you to recommend it alone to the exclusion of these other practices?

ANSWER: Know that Buddhists must not engage in debates over the superiority or inferiority of the teachings and must not choose between profound and shallow doctrines. Just know whether the practice is authentic or not. Grass, flowers, the landscape itself, have brought some people into the Buddha Way. Merely grasping earth or sand has caused others to receive and preserve the Buddha-mind Seal. This means that the greatest words are the ones whose abundant meanings overflow from every existing thing. The Great Dharma Wheel of preaching turns in every speck of dust. In light of this, a phrase like "this very mind is Buddha" is just the moon reflected in water. "This very sitting becomes Buddha" is just a reflection in a mirror. Do not be misled by clever slogans. I now recommend the practice of direct realization of *bodhi* because I teach the marvelous Way directly transmitted by the Buddhas and Zen ancestors and because I want you to become a true man of the Way.

The transmitting and acceptance of Buddha-dharma require both a fully realized student and a teacher in the Zen lineage. Do not rely on instruction from a scholar concerned with book learning. That would be like the blind leading the blind. In this lineage that has been directly transmitted by the Buddhas and Zen ancestors the Buddha dharma is maintained and preserved by venerating all the skilled Zen masters who attained the Way through embodied realization. For this reason, visible and invisible spirits (*shintō*) take refuge in them. Arhats who realize Mahāyāna Buddhahood ask them for the dharma. And each and every one receives mental clarification from them. Other

lineages have never known these accomplishments. Disciples of the
Buddha should just study this [Zen] Buddhist practice.

[Ichikawa, *Chūsei zenke*, pp. 80–83; WB]

THE FULLY APPARENT CASE (*GENJŌ KŌAN*)

The term *kōan* originally referred to case law or legal precedents that provided guidelines for subsequent affairs. In Zen, *kōan* record the sometimes enigmatic sayings or
actions of Zen ancestors that should be studied as guidelines for Buddhist practice. A
fully apparent (*genjō*) *kōan* is one that we might call an open-and-shut case, a matter
whose settlement (or meaning) should be perfectly obvious. For Dōgen, it does not imply that something hidden becomes obvious but refers to the actualization of each moment of reality on its own terms, in the here and now, without the distortion of human
biases. The fascicle entitled *Genjō kōan* is the first essay in Dōgen's *True Dharma Eye
Treasury* (*Shōbōgenzō*) because it defines the agenda, namely, self-realization through
Zen practice, for the entire work. The essay begins with the fundamental issue of life
and death, the inescapable *kōan* of human life. Dōgen's seemingly paradoxical use of
language rests on a logic of affirmation in which any single aspect of reality is completely true in the totality of itself, even though its exact opposite must also be
completely true in its own totality.

In the synchronicity of all things as Buddha dharma, there is delusion and
awakening, there is religious cultivation, there is birth, there is death, there is
Buddhahood, and there is humanity. In the synchronicity of all existence un-
connected to yourself, there is no delusion, no awakening, no Buddhahood, no
humanity, no birth, and no death.

Because the Buddha Way ultimately transcends all surplus or dearth, the
Buddha Way is both birth and death, both delusion and awakening, both humanity and Buddhahood. Even as the Buddha Way is thus, nonetheless flowers
wilt and die in spite of our attraction while weeds sprout and live in spite of
our rejection.

The individual self striving to realize all things is delusion; all things striving
to realize the individual self is awakening.

Those who awaken to delusion are Buddhas, while those who are deluded
about awakening are humanity. Furthermore, others attain awakening beyond
awakening, and delusion deludes others.

When Buddhahood is truly Buddhahood, there is no individual self aware
of Buddhahood. Nonetheless Buddhahood is realized as each activity is Buddha
realization.

If you see sights with your whole body-mind, if you hear sounds with your whole body-mind [if you perceive objects with your whole body-mind], then you will comprehend them intimately, not in the way a mirror harbors a reflection [of an object outside itself], not in the way the moon appears in water. Illuminating one side obscures the other side.

To study the Buddha way is to study the individual self. To study the individual self is to forget the individual self. To forget the individual self is to be realized by all things. To be realized by all things is both the individual self's body-mind and the other selves' body-mind sloughing off.

[When body-mind sloughs off,] the afterglow of awakening fades away and this faded-away afterglow of awakening fades and fades away forever.

A person, at the moment when he first starts to seek dharma, departs far beyond the boundaries of the dharma. The dharma, when it is correctly transmitted, is fully embodied by that person.

A person who travels down a river on a boat and who gazes out into the distance will mistakenly see the riverbanks as moving. But if he shortens his gaze and looks down at the boat, then he will know that it is the boat that is moving. In this same manner, when you ignore your body-mind in examining things of the world, then you will mistakenly believe your own personality and own nature to be immortal. But if you return your awareness to an attentive intimacy with your own travails, then the truth that all beings lack a permanent self becomes obvious.

Firewood becomes ashes, and afterward it can never return to being firewood. Nonetheless, do not see ashes as its future or see firewood as its past. Know that because firewood dwells eternally in its dharma aspect of firewood it experiences both past and future. While both past and future exist, in the present moment there is neither past nor future. As ash dwells eternally in its dharma aspect of ash, it experiences both past and future. Just as this firewood that has become ashes can never again return to being firewood, likewise a person who has died can never again become alive. In contrast, the established teaching of the Buddha dharma does not say that the living die. It teaches the Not Living [life that transcends living and dying]. In turning the Dharma Wheel, the Buddha did not preach that the dead return to life. He taught the Not Dying [death that transcends living and dying]. Life is a single moment in time; death is a single moment in time. For example, it is like winter and spring. Don't think that winter turns into spring; don't say that spring turns into summer.

[Nishio, Shōbōgenzō, vol. 1, pp. 101–102; WB]

BUDDHA NATURE (BUSSHŌ)

Buddha nature is sometimes explained as the spiritual potential to become a Buddha that is possessed by some or all living beings. In this treatise, Dōgen rejects any substantive conception of Buddha nature as a permanent innate characteristic or meta-physical reality. Dōgen emphasizes that Buddha nature is the "no-ness" (i.e., empti-ness, void, or nonsubstantiality) of all things, which is realized only through the true practice of Buddhism (what he calls "doing Buddha"). The following excerpt is char-acteristic of Dōgen's style of *kōan* study in which he reads his own interpretations into the texts of *kōan*, often by ignoring the rules of Chinese grammar in favor of an overly literal, word-by-word translation.

Hui-neng, the sixth Zen ancestor of China, also known as Great Mirror Zen Master of Mount Caochi, began his study of Buddhism by going to the mon-astery on Mount Huangmei. When he arrived there, Hongren, the fifth Zen ancestor, asked him: "You came here from where?"

The sixth ancestor replied: "I am a Lingnan person from the south."

The fifth ancestor asked: "You came here seeking to do what?"

The sixth ancestor replied: "I seek to do Buddha."

The fifth ancestor said: "Lingnan People No Buddha Nature. How Can Do Buddha?"

This utterance "Lingnan People No Buddha Nature" does not say that peo-ple in Lingnan lack Buddha nature nor does it say that they possess Buddha nature. It says, "Lingnan People No Buddha Nature" [i.e., the emptiness of Buddha nature]. The utterance "How Can Do Buddha" means what kind of Doing Buddha will you do?

Overall only a few spiritual guides have clarified the truth of Buddha nature. Teachers of the *āgama* scriptures and of the Mahāyāna scriptures do not know it. Only descendants in the lineage of the Buddhas and Zen ancestors have transmitted this knowledge. The truth of Buddha nature is that it is not some-thing we are endowed with before becoming a Buddha. We are endowed with it only after becoming a Buddha. Buddha nature and becoming a Buddha necessarily co-participate. Investigate and struggle with this truth well. If nec-essary, study and struggle with it for twenty or thirty years. Even holy celestial bodhisattvas have not clarified this truth. This truth is expressed by saying "Liv-ing Beings Exist Buddha Nature" and "Living Beings No Buddha Nature." The correct object of study is the truth that Buddha Nature is what we are endowed with since becoming Buddhas. If you do not study in this way, then you are not studying the Buddha dharma. Without this kind of study, Buddhism would not have survived until the present. If you do not clarify this truth, then you will not clarify becoming a Buddha, you will not even hear of it. This is why the fifth ancestor faced the sixth ancestor and said: "Lingnan People No Buddha Nature." When you first meet a Buddha and hear him preach the dharma, the most difficult words to understand are "Living Beings No Buddha Nature." Whether learning from a good teacher or learning from the scriptures, however, the most joyous words to hear are "Living Beings No Buddha Nature." If you do not fully embody the knowledge of seeing and hearing "Living beings No

Buddha Nature," then you have not yet seen nor heard of Buddha nature. For the sixth ancestor to attain Doing Buddha and for the fifth ancestor to help the sixth ancestor attain Doing Buddha, there was nothing else to say, no other method could have been as skillful. The only thing he could say is "Lingnan People No Buddha Nature." Know that the saying and the hearing of "No Buddha Nature" is itself the direct path of Doing Buddha. In other words, that very moment of No Buddha Nature is Doing Buddha. If you have not yet seen or heard No Buddha Nature, if you have not yet said No Buddha Nature, then you have not yet practiced Doing Buddha.

The sixth ancestor said: "People Exist North and South, but Buddha Nature No North or South." Let's take this utterance and struggle with its inner meaning. The words "north and south" seem quite innocent. The sixth ancestor's words, however, convey vital religious significance. That is to say, they imply the position that while people can practice Doing Buddha, Buddha nature cannot practice Doing Buddha. Did the sixth ancestor know this or not?

[Nishio, *Shōbōgenzō*, vol. 3, pp. 118–119; WB]

MUSŌ SOSEKI: "SERMON AT THE DEDICATION OF TENRYŪ-JI DHARMA HALL" (FROM MUSŌ KOKUSHI GOROKU)

The following sermon was delivered at the dedication of the Dharma Preaching Hall when Musō became the founding abbot of Tenryūji monastery, founded in memory of Go-Daigo. The dedication coincided with the anniversary of the Buddha's birthday. Musō used this occasion to remind his audience that the truth preached by the Buddha, the truth proclaimed by the Zen ancestors, and the truth taught by Musō were all the very same truth. Thus, Shākyamuni's message of salvation is not ancient history but must be realized in this present moment at this very spot.

(In the tenth month of the second year of the Rekiō period [1339] a court decree ordered the conversion of the detached palace of Kameyama *tennō* [emperor] into a monastery dedicated to the memory of Go-Daigo *tennō* and also nominated Musō to be its founding abbot. In the fourth year of Kōei [1345], fourth month, eighth day, the Dharma Preaching Hall was opened for the first time, with their lordships Shogun Ashikaga Takauji and Vice-Shogun Tadayoshi in attendance. Musō first performed the ceremony celebrating the Buddha's birth and then proceeded to say:)

The appearance in this world of all Buddhas, past, present, and future, is solely for the purpose of preaching the dharma that saves living beings. The Buddha used the arts of oratory and eight types of eloquence as the standards for his preaching the dharma, and the Deer Park and Vulture Peak both served as his halls of salvation. Our lineage of the Zen ancestors stresses the method of individual instruction directed toward the essential endowment, thus distinguishing itself from doctrinal schools. But examination of our aims reveals that we too focus solely on transmitting the dharma that saves the deluded. Thus all the ancestors, from the twenty-eight in India through the first six in China, each signaled his succession to the lineage with a dharma-transmission verse. The Great Master Bodhidharma said, "I came to China in order to transmit the dharma that saves deluded people." So it is clear that Huike's cutting off his arm in the snow and the conferring of the robe at midnight upon Huineng were both meant to signify the transmission of the marvelous dharma.[4] In all kinds of circumstances, whether under a tree, upon a rock, in the darkness of a cave, or deep in a glen, there is no place where the dharma banner has not been erected and no place where the Mind Seal has not been transmitted to whoever possessed the spiritual capacity. Ever since Baizhang Huaihai founded the first Zen cloister, China and Japan have seen numerous grand Zen monasteries erected. All of them, whether large or small, have included a Dharma Preaching Hall for proclaiming the message of salvation. . . .

As for this mountain monk appearing before you today on this platform, I have nothing special to offer as my own interpretation of the dharma. I merely join with my true master, Shākyamuni Buddha, and with all others throughout infinite empty space, all Buddhas, bodhisattvas, holy ones, assembled clerics, patrons, and officials, the very eaves and columns of this hall, lanterns, and posts, as well as all the people, animals, plants, and seeds in the boundless ocean of existence to turn in unison the great Dharma Wheel. At this very moment, what is happening?

(Musō raised his staff high into the air.)

Look! Look! Shākyamuni is here right now on top of my staff. He takes seven steps, points to heaven and to earth, announcing to all of you:

> Today I am born again here with the completion of this new Dharma Preaching Hall. All the holy ones are assembled here; people and gods mingle together. Every single person here is precious in himself, and everything here—plaques, paintings, square eaves and round pillars— every single thing is preaching the dharma. Wonderful, wonderful it is, that the true dharma lives and never dies. At Vulture Peak, indeed, this dharma was transmitted to the right man!

It is thus that Lord Shākyamuni, the most venerable, instructs us here. It is the teaching that comes down to men in response to their needs. But perhaps,

---

4. According to Zen legends, Huike, the second Zen ancestor of China, gained Bodhidharma's attention by cutting off his own arm as a gesture of his sincerity, and Huineng, the sixth Zen ancestor of China, visited his teacher in secret at midnight so as to avoid incurring the wrath of a jealous monk senior to him.

gentlemen, you wish to know the state of things before Shākyamuni ever entered his mother's womb.

(Musō tapped his staff on the floor.)

Listen, Listen!

[TD 80, no. 2555; 460c–461a; WB]

"REFLECTIONS ON THE ENMITY BETWEEN GO-DAIGO AND THE SHOGUN, ASHIKAGA TAKAUJI" (FROM *MUSŌ KOKUSHI GOROKU*)

This extract is from a sermon delivered by Musō upon resuming the office of abbot of Tenryūji in 1351, in which he reflects on the reasons for dedicating this monastery to the memory of Go-Daigo and analyzes the causes of the rupture between the latter and Ashikaga Takauji, his erstwhile supporter. He attributes the break to jealousy, which blinded Go-Daigo and estranged him from his obedient servant. Musō's frank censure of the deceased sovereign shows both how low the prestige of the imperial house had fallen and how little awed by it was this Zen prelate, who considered it a purely human institution and not divine.

In the realm of True Purity, there is no such thing as self or other. How much less can friend or foe be found there! But the slightest confusion of mind brings innumerable differences and complications. Peace and disorder in the world, the distinction between friend and foe in human relationships, follow upon one another as illusion begets delusion. A person of spiritual luminosity will immediately recognize false thought and eliminate it, but the shallow-minded person will be enslaved by his own delusion so that he cannot put an end to it. In such cases one's true friend may seem a foe and one's implacable enemy may appear a friend. Enmity and friendship have no permanent character; both of them are illusions.

During the disorders of the Genkō period [1331–1334] the shogun, acting promptly on the court's order, swiftly subdued the foes [the Hōjō regents] of the state, as a result of which he rose higher in court rank day by day and his growing prestige brought a change in the attitude of others toward him. Ere long, slander and defamation sprang up with the violence of a tiger, and this unavoidably drew upon him the royal displeasure. Consider now the reasons for this turn of events. It was because he performed a meritorious task with such dispatch and to the entire satisfaction of his sovereign. There is an old saying that intimacy invites enmity. That is what it was. Thereupon, the auspicious clouds of goodwill were scattered to the winds, and the august dragon [Go-Daigo] had to take refuge in the mountains to the south, where the music of the court was no longer heard and whence his royal phoenix palanquin could never again return to the northern court.

With a great sigh the military leader [Takauji] lamented, "Alas, due to slander and flattery by court ministers, I am consigned to the fate of an ignominious rebel without any chance to explain my innocence." Indeed his grief was no perfunctory display, but without nurturing any bitterness in his heart, he devoutly gave himself over to spiritual reflection and pious works, fervently praying for the Buddhahood of Go-Daigo and subsequently constructing [in Go-Daigo's memory] this grand monastery for the practice of great Buddha activity. . . .

The virtuous rule of Go-Daigo *tennō* accorded with Heaven's will and his holy wisdom equaled that of the ancient sage-kings of China. Therefore the royal family's fortunes rose high as reign and military power were unified. The phoenix reign inaugurated a new period of magnificence and splendor. Barbarians beyond the four borders were submissive and all within the borders were earnest. People compared his Yao-like reign to the wind, which always blows without end.[5] Who, then, would have thought that his Shun-like sun would appear for only a moment and then immediately disappear behind the clouds? And what are we to make of it—was it merely a random turn of events? No, the fact that Go-Daigo expended all his karmic connections to this defiled world and straightaway joined the happy assembly of the Pure Land was not because his august reign lacked luck. It was because he caused the people so much suffering and distress. As a result, from the time of his passing right up to the present there has been no peace, clergy and laity alike have been displaced, and there is no end to the complaints of the people.

What I have expounded above is all a dream within a dream. Even though it actually happened, there is no use finding fault with what is past and done—how much less with what has happened in a dream! We must realize that a Wheel-Turning Monarch (*cakravartin*), the highest position among humans, is itself but something cherished in a dream. Even Brahmā, the highest king of the gods, knows only the pleasure of a dream. This is why Shākyamuni forsook the option of becoming a Wheel-Turning Monarch and entered the mountains to practice austerities. What was his purpose? To teach all people that the King of Awakening [Buddha] far surpasses the highest rank of human society. Although the four social classes differ, each member of them is like every other in being a disciple of the Buddha, and should behave accordingly.

I pray therefore that our late sovereign will instantly transform his defiled capacity, escape from the bondage of delusion, bid farewell to his karma-producing consciousness, and realize luminous wisdom. May he pass beyond the distinctions of friend and foe and attain the luminous region wherein delusion and awakening are one. May he not forget that the dharma transmission of Vulture Peak lives on and extend his protection to this monastery, so that without ever leaving this spot his blessings may extend to all living beings.

This is indeed the wish of the military leader [Takauji]. He bears no grudge

---

5. Yao is remembered as a sage ruler in ancient China who chose Shun as his successor.

toward Go-Daigo but merely wishes for him to develop favorable karmic causes, which is no trifling affair. The Buddhas in their great compassion will surely respond by bestowing mysterious blessings. In this way may the warfare come to an end, all the land within the four seas enjoy true peace, and all the people rest secure from disturbances and calamities. May [Takauji's] military success pass on to his heirs, generation after generation. Our earnest prayer is that it should wash over all opposition.

[TD 80, no. 2555; 463c–464b; WB]

IKKYŪ SŌJUN: THE ERRANT CLOUD COLLECTION (KYŌUNSHŪ)

Ever the eccentric, Ikkyū wrote religious poetry about seemingly irreligious topics, including his personal feelings, brothels, drinking parties, diatribes against false Zen, and especially attacks against his compatriot Yōsō Sōi (1376–1458), whom Ikkyū accused of currying political favor and selling initiations into Zen secrets. Ikkyū more than once vowed to quit Zen in protest of such corrupt practices.

[38]   Anniversary of the Buddha's Birthday
Past, Present, and Future: One person with many names.
Today, who knows his alias?
Appearing in this polluted Sahā world eight thousand times,
As a horse, as an ass, as a shākya.

[39]   Anniversary of the Buddha's Awakening
Among gods and humans, only one person is venerable.
Attaining the way in today's kingdom, receiving whose benefaction?
This wise monk with the shooting-star eyes,
I am Gautama's legitimate progeny.

[40]   Anniversary of the Buddha's Parinirvāna
The complete extinguishing of that Indian, old Shākyamuni;
For his next life in whose family will he appear?
Two thousand three hundred years ago they wept;
And here in Japan we scatter second-month flower petals.

[45]   Yunmen, lecturing the assembly, said: "The old Buddha and the bare pillar intermingle. What functioning is this?" Speaking for himself he answered: "In the southern mountains, clouds arise; in the northern mountains, rain falls."

How did Mount Xiaogu wed the water spirit Peng-lang?
Clouds raining love tonight, that's the dream.
From morning at northern Mount Tiantai to evening at southern Mount Nanyue,
I do not know from where to view Yunmen Mountain.

[76]   Puppets
The stage presents their whole bodies,
Some as nobility, some as commoners.
Forgetting the guide-sticks in front of their eyes,
Ignorant fools regard them as their original selves.

[153]   The Austerities of Shākyamuni
For six years starvation and cold pierced his bones.
Austerities are the essential secret of Buddha and ancestors.
Believe me when I say that Shākyamunis are made, not born,
All of you rice-hungry worthless monks.

[165]   Holding Up the Flower, Slight Smile
From the assembly on Vulture Peak to the here and now;
From the cave in Cockleg Mountain to the eons yet to come;
A poisoned person certainly knows poison's use.
In India and in this land: the same tricky fox.

[171]   Attacking False Zen
Gautama's forty-nine years of teaching:
Look at his silence in Vaishālī! Look at his silence in Magadha!
False teachers distorting his words with *kōan* phrases,
See if Yama, King of Hell, doesn't yank out your tongues.[6]

[175]   In Honor of Daitokuji Abbot Yōsō Sōi of the Great Function Hermitage (Daiyūan) Receiving an Imperial Purple Robe and the Title of Great Illuminator of Religious Wisdom Zen Master (Sōe daishō zenji)

Purple robes and the title of "master" cannot conceal your spiritual poverty.
The edict alone cost three hundred strings of cash.
Your great function is perfectly obvious, you counterfeit abbot.
Look! Here he comes! A real Szechuanese thief.

[203]   Chōroku period, 4th year [1460], 8th moon, last day, a typhoon brought floods to everyone's distress. That night there were customers enjoying themselves with singing and music. Unable to endure listening to them I composed this verse to comfort myself.

---

6. Vimalakīrti preached a wordless sermon on the meaning of nonduality in the town of Vaishālī, and Shākyamuni preached a wordless sermon by holding up a flower on Vulture Peak in the kingdom of Magadha.

Typhoons and floods: everyone's miserable.
Singing, dancing, music: who's enjoying the night?
The dharma flourishes and declines; the times prosper and deteriorate.
And now that bright moon has dipped below the western rooftops.

[205]   The celebrated poet Bo Juyi asked the Bird Nest Zen master: "What is the ultimate teaching of Buddhism?" Bird Nest replied: "Refrain from all evil; perform every manner of good." Bo Juyi, in disappointment, responded: Even a three-year-old child knows how to recite that verse. Bird Nest said: "A three-year-old child can say it, but even a man of eighty cannot accomplish it." Master Lingshan always instructed: "But for Bird Nest's words, my students would be corrupted by sayings like 'originally there is not a single thing,' 'do not think of good, do not think of evil,' 'the nonduality of good and evil,' 'the oneness of false and true,' and my students thereby would deny the moral truth of karma." In today's world there are many false teachers who engage in impure actions daily. Therefore I wrote the following verse for my disciples.

Student monks who deny karma sink into *samsāra*.
That old Zen teacher's words are worth a thousand pieces of gold:
"Refrain from all evil; perform every manner of good."
Isn't that a line in drunken Bo Ju-yi's singing?

[226]   Say nothing; the *kōan* is perfectly complete;
The eight-sided stone mortar is stuck in my mind.
During a chance encounter, it's difficult to smell the stench of one's
own shit,
But the other person's faults are as obvious as one's own face in a
mirror.

[227]   Years past I reverently gazed upon the portrait of Daitō Kokushi. I have now changed my robe and joined the Pure Land school. For this reason I dedicate this poem to that old master dwelling amid the clouds.

I have left the Zen lineage, the supreme vehicle,
And changed my robe to become a priest in the Pure Land school.
How foolish I was to lightly join Ryōzen Tettō's monastery [Daitokuji].
Alas! So many years wasted in the Daitō lineage!

[228]   Errant Cloud [Ikkyū] is Daitokuji's very own Demon Pāpiyas:
Within the temple grounds fighting with an *Asura*'s titan-like anger.
Old *kōan* phrases—of what use can they be?
So much elation and suffering just to count up someone else's wealth.[7]

---

7. Pāpiyas is the name of a demon who murders innocent victims. By extension, it refers to any exceedingly evil person. Asura refer to a class of Indic demigods, similar to the Titans of Greek mythology, who compete against the true gods.

[254]   Two poems for a painting of an *arhat* visiting a brothel[8]
An *arhat* in this polluted world lacks human feelings;
A brothel's patrons, however, overflow with feeling.
On this side, "no"; On that side "yes":
Monks struggling with demonic Buddha feelings.

[255]   In this polluted world an *arhat* is far from the Buddha land;
One trip to a brothel, however, will arouse his great wisdom.
Deeply laughing Mañjushrī recites the *Shūrangama Dhāranī*,
Reminiscing the long eons since his own youthful frolics.[9]

[Ichikawa, *Chūsei zenke*, pp. 285–341; WB][10]

---

8. An *arhat* is a Buddhist saint who has eliminated the taints of human passions. Although some Mahāyāna scriptures disparage the *arhat* as inferior to the bodhisattva, in others he is seen as the protector of Buddhism who will remain on earth until the time of the future Buddha Maitreya.

9. According to a famous story in the Shūrangama Sūtra, the Bodhisattva Mañjushrī, the Crown Prince of Wisdom, first recited the Shūrangama Dhāranī (magical spell) to rescue the Buddha's disciple Ānanda from the clutches of a prostitute who was about to seduce him.

10. The poems are numbered in accordance with this edition, which is based on the Okumura manuscript.

Chapter 15

SHINTO IN MEDIEVAL JAPAN

The introduction of Buddhism and its subsequent acceptance by the Japanese court resulted in the submergence of Shinto, the native religion, for many years. It was said of Emperor Kōtoku (who reigned at the time of the Great Reform of 645) that he "honored the religion of Buddha and despised the Way of the Gods."[1] Other sovereigns generally had more respect for Shinto, although the brilliant Buddhist ceremonies that marked the Nara and Heian periods occupied the court far more than did the simple observances of the native religion. The ethical values of the indigenous tradition—later the subject of much attention by scholars of the native learning—were seldom articulated in early Japan. Except for a few prayers (*norito*), Shinto did not produce religious writings, and anything resembling a theology had to be inferred from myths and legends.

But Shinto was not entirely absent from the scene in early Japan. The gods had their functions and rituals, chiefly concerned with particular localities and natural phenomena—rain, drought, earthquakes, and the like. This meant that among the peasants (and, in general, most people living away from the capital in the provinces), the local cults of Shinto continued to be the prevailing religion even when Buddhism was triumphant at the court. But even the court

---

1. Aston, *Nihongi*, II, p. 195.

recognized the importance of the gods. Over and over in the *Chronicles of Japan*, we find such entries as the following (for 599 C.E.): "There was an earthquake which destroyed all the houses. So orders were given to all quarters to sacrifice to the God of Earthquakes."[2] An entry for 689 contains the first mention of a state "department of Shinto," and in the eleventh month of 691 we are told that "the festival of first-fruits was held. Ōshima, Nakatomi no Ason, Minister of the Department of the Shinto religion, recited the prayers invoking the blessing of the Heavenly Deities."[3]

By the early tenth century, when the Institutes of the Engi Era were completed, more than six thousand Shinto shrines were enumerated where annual offerings were to be made by the court or the provincial governments. This official recognition of Shinto represented a great landmark in the systematization of the native cults, which until then had tended to remain loosely connected local shrines. In this attempt to systematize Shinto, we can detect the influence of Chinese-style administration and Buddhist practices. Indeed, already in the late Nara period (in 765), Buddhist monks and nuns had participated in the Great Thanksgiving Festival, one of the most sacred Shinto celebrations, and Empress Shōtoku declared on that occasion that she considered it her duty (having returned to the throne as a nun), "first to serve the Three Treasures, then to worship the Gods, and next to cherish the people."[4] The union of the two religions was further promoted in 768 when a Buddhist temple was erected next to the Ise Shrine, the holiest imperial shrine and Shinto sanctuary, and from this time on, many Shinto shrines included temples and Buddhist priests who served both religions.

The idea of fusing Buddhism with another religion did not originate in Japan. In India, Buddha himself had recognized the popular gods, the *devas*, as deities possessing powers far less considerable than his own but superior to those of ordinary men. The early texts frequently refer to the conversion of the Indian gods (*devas*) to Buddhism after they heard Buddha preach. In later Buddhist writings, Brahmā and the lesser deities were described as avatārs of Buddha and the bodhisattvas who had appeared on earth to save humankind. This concept was later adopted by the Mahāyāna sects. It is found in such works as the *Saddharma Puṇḍarīka*, the Vimalakīrti, and Vairochana Sūtras, and the Shingon mandalas.

In China, Buddhists sometimes claimed that Confucius, Laozi, and other famous philosophers were sent by Buddha to help humankind. By the middle of the Tang dynasty, we find the first mention of the phrase "manifest traces of

---

2. Ibid., p. 124.

3. Sansom, *Japan, a Short Cultural History*, p. 135.

4. Aston, *Nihongi*, II, p. 404. The Nakatomi family, later renamed Fujiwara, was one of the chief supporters of Shinto.

the original substance" (*honji suijaku*) that figured so prominently in Japan. In an explanation of the Vairochana Sūtra, a commentator stated that the spirits and gods were avatārs of Vairochana—traces on earth of the original substance of divinity.

Although Buddhism had also joined the native religions in both India and China, it was in Japan that this fusion assumed its most significant form. Kūkai is often mentioned as the originator of *honji suijaku*, but despite the numerous forged works on the subject attributed to him, nothing indicates that the *honji suijaku* formula was known in his time. Later supporters tended to invoke Kū-kai's name to lend greater authority to *honji suijaku*, a fact that may also explain the tales of how Kūkai taught Emperor Saga about the mysteries of Shinto or such supposed quotations as "Unless one studies Shinto, one will not understand the profundities of my school of Buddhism." Whether or not we believe such stories, it is certain that both Saichō and Kūkai did pay considerable attention to the gods. When he built his temple on Mount Kōya, which had been known as the seat of various gods, Kūkai called out to them:

All evil spirits and gods, who may be to the east, south, west, above, or below this monastery: you hinderers and destroyers of the True Law, hie you seven leagues hence from my altar! If however there be any good spirits and gods who are beneficial to the Buddhist Law and protect it, you may dwell as you choose in this monastery and protect the Buddhist Law.[5]

The first clear evidence of *honji suijaku* thought in Japan seems to date from 937, when two gods were declared to be manifestations of bodhisattvas. In time, every god was established as a manifestation of one or another Buddha or bodhisattva. Most of the "original substances" of the different gods proved to be the thirteen Buddhas of Shingon, a fact indicative of the special affinity between this sect and Shinto. Shinto adopted the incantations, ritual fire ceremonies, charms, signs, and methods of instruction of Shingon, and these alien features soon became so much a part of Shinto that even purists later considered them to be part of the religion in its pristine form. The most important form of union between Buddhism and Shinto was called "Dual Shinto" (Ryōbu Shintō), a term derived from the equation between the two mandalas of Shingon Buddhism and the Inner and Outer Shrines at Ise. The Tendai monasteries of Mount Hiei and Miidera, which had become strongholds of Esoteric Buddhism, consummated their union with Shinto by adopting local tutelary deities,

---

5. *Kōbō Daishi zenshū*, III, *Shōryōshū*, pp. 530–531.

as had the Shingon center of Mount Kōya.[6] But Shingon was considered by most Shinto scholars to be the Buddhist sect closest to the native religion. Kitabatake Chikafusa declared that the "traditions from the age of the gods tally most closely with the teachings of this sect [Shingon]. That is probably why, though it [Shingon] enjoyed only brief popularity in China, it has persisted in Japan."

In medieval Japan, the fusion of Buddhist and Shinto ceremonies became almost invariable. Many of the nation's shrines were controlled by Buddhists. Within the shrines themselves, Buddhist images were worshiped as representations of the gods, and Buddhist implements (principally Shingon) were used alongside the traditional paper streamers and ropes of Shinto. The pantheism of Tendai and the cosmotheism of Shingon easily incorporated Shinto beliefs and legends, and even in the remote regions of Japan, where the Way of the Gods remained strongest, the two religions regularly intertwined. Although it is true that monks were not allowed to enter the Inner Shrine at Ise and certain Buddhist sects failed to show much interest in Shinto, by and large the union of Buddhism and Shinto, usually stated in *honji suijaku* terms, became a general feature of Japanese religious life and remained such at least until the Meiji Restoration of 1868.

At first, Shinto's part in the combined religion was relatively minor, but with the downfall of the court aristocracy at the end of the Heian period, the men from the outlying provinces brought to power retained a strong attachment to Shinto. Thus, the Taira clan proclaimed its loyalty to the goddess Itsukushima, and the Minamoto clan worshiped Hachiman, sometimes spoken of as the god of war. As early as the year 750, Hachiman is reported to have paid his respects to the Great Statue of the Buddha in Nara, and it was not many years afterward that he acquired the title of "great Bodhisattva." Later, the Minamoto shoguns adopted Hachiman at their headquarters in Kamakura, just as the imperial house had established his worship in Nara and Kyoto. Hachiman was considered a manifestation of Amida Buddha, while Itsukushima (at Miyajima) was the "manifested trace" of Kannon (Avalokiteshvara), further examples of *honji suijaku*.

The Mongol invasions of 1274 and 1281 aroused in the Japanese a strong national consciousness. The "divine winds" (*kamikaze*) that drove off the invaders were interpreted as signs of the protection afforded to Japan by the native gods (the Sun Goddess and Hachiman). Less than fifty years afterward Chikafusa wrote his *Records of the Direct Succession of the Divine Sovereigns*, in which

---

6. At Mount Kōya, it was either the deity Nifu Myōjin (or Tanjō) or Kōya Myōjin who allegedly turned the mountain over to Kūkai; at Mount Hiei it was the mountain god Sannō; and at Miidera, the Korean goddess Shiragi Myōjin (Korean influence was pervasive in this region).

he proclaimed the supremacy of Japan over China and India because of Japan's single line of emperors descended from the gods. Chikafusa's work was primarily political, but at about the same time (or somewhat earlier), the Five Classics of Shinto appeared, forgeries purporting to have been composed in remote antiquity. The Five Classics are concerned mainly with the history of the Ise Shrine and attempt to set forth a Shinto philosophy and ethics. Whatever philosophical or ethical significance these books possess was borrowed from Buddhism, but the adherents of the "Prime Shinto" (Yuiitsu Shintō) school of the fifteenth century and later referred to the Five Classics as a treasury of pure Shinto teachings.

The chief figure in the Prime Shinto school was Yoshida Kanetomo (1435–1511). Kanetomo did not attempt, as did certain later Shinto scholars, to discredit Buddhism; instead, he tried to shift the emphasis in the combined religion from Buddhism to Shinto while maintaining the union. He interpreted *honji suijaku* as meaning that the Japanese gods were the original substance and Buddha and the bodhisattvas were the manifest traces. (This is comparable to a similar switch in India, where Hindus came to consider Buddha as the ninth avatār of Vishnu, or in China, where the Daoists thought of Buddha as an avatār of Laozi.) Kanetomo relied heavily on the forged Five Classics, and when they were insufficient to meet his needs, he appears not to have been above forgery of his own. In one of Kanetomo's works, we find his most famous statement, attributed to Prince Shōtoku, that Japan was the root of all civilization, China its branches and leaves, and India its flowers and fruit; thus all foreign doctrines were offshoots of Shinto. In this way, Kanetomo boldly attempted to turn the tables on Buddhism and Confucianism and assert the primacy of Shinto after centuries of subservience.

Kanetomo revealed his indebtedness to Buddhism, particularly Esoteric Buddhism, at every point in his exposition of Shinto principles; indeed, it often appears as if he has merely substituted a Shinto word in an otherwise Buddhist context:

> *Kami* or Deity is spirit, without form, unknowable, transcending both cosmic principles, the yin and the yang . . . changeless, eternal, existing from the very beginning of Heaven and Earth up to the present, unfathomable, infinite, itself with neither beginning nor end, so that the so-called "Divine Age" is not only in the past but also in the present. It is, indeed, the eternal now.[7]

This is an enunciation of the Shingon doctrine of *aji hompushō* (the eternity of creation) decked out in Shinto garments, and in the following passage we find Shingon cosmotheism expressed in the characteristic three aspects:

---

7. Kanetomo, *Shindaishō*, trans. in Holtom, *The National Faith of Japan*, pp. 39–40.

With reference to the universe we call it *kami,* with reference to the interactions of nature we call it spirit *(rei),* in man we call it soul *(kokoro).* Therefore, *kami* is the source of the universe. He is the spiritual essence of created things. *Kami* is soul *(kokoro)* and soul is *kami.* All the infinite variety of change in nature, all the objects and events of the universe are rooted in the activity of *kami.* All the laws of nature are made one in the activity of *kami.*[8]

The most significant result of Kanetomo's teachings was that by his time the long period of Shinto apprenticeship to alien ideologies had ended; the Shinto spokesmen not only knew the intricacies of Buddhism and other foreign doctrines but also were adept at rewriting them in Shinto terms with ease and vigor. Kanetomo was a member of the Urabe family, one of the oldest and most important Shinto families of diviners. For centuries, this family had experienced all the tribulations that had befallen Shinto during its period of subservience to Buddhism, but when Kanetomo appeared, Shinto once more came into its own, and the Urabe family's persistent devotion was justified.

EMPRESS SHŌTOKU: *EDICT ON THE GREAT THANKSGIVING FESTIVAL*

The following edict from the Nara period illustrates the early tendency toward Shinto/Buddhist syncretism.

Today is the day of plenteous feasting attendant on the Great Thanksgiving Festival.[9] This occasion differs from the usual celebrations in that we, as a disciple of Buddha, have received the bodhisattva ordination. Therefore, deeming that we should serve the Three Treasures with our highest devotion, should next reverence the gods of the shrines of heaven and earth and should next cherish and love the princes, the ministers, the officials of the hundred departments, and all the people of this land who serve us, we have returned [to the throne] and again rule over the nation. . . .[10]

Some people believe that the gods shun and will not touch the Three Treasures. However, it may be seen in the sūtras that it is the gods who protect and exalt the Law of Buddha. For this reason we consider that there can be no

---

8. Adapted from ibid., p. 40.

9. Held on the twenty-third day of the eleventh moon of 765, or January 8, 766. This was a traditional celebration held after the accession to the throne of a new sovereign. Shōtoku had recently reascended the throne.

10. A few lines dealing with the wines and food offerings of the ceremony have been omitted here.

objection to both Buddhist monks and ordinary laymen joining together in the service.

Hearken all ye people to the imperial command: we do direct that on the occasion of this Great Thanksgiving Festival that which has hitherto been avoided should not be avoided.[11]

[*Rikkokushi, Shoku Nihongi*, II, p. 126]

THE MIRACLES OF THE KASUGA DEITY

The following selections are from a collection of miracle tales about the god of the Kasuga Shrine, the principal Shinto shrine in the old capital Nara, which was tutelary to the Fujiwara clan and closely associated with its clan temple, the Kōfukuji. These tales illustrate the interpenetration and mutual assimilation of Buddhism and Shinto in what became known as Dual Shinto and also suggest something of the conflict among temples and shrines—not so much over doctrinal issues as over political and social vested interests.

Prefatory Note of the Minister of the Left (Saionji Kinhira, 1264–1315)

As a descendant of the Fujiwara ancestors, I place my trust entirely in the protection of this shrine. Unable to restrain my zeal to honor the Deity, I have gathered this collection together to the best of my ability, so as to increase the faith of all men. Now that the work is in its final form, I have only to add these words. After I conceived this gesture of devotion, great good fortune blessed my house, and by this I knew that my plan had met with divine approval. May those who come after me be inspired by it to ever greater reverence and faith!

The Bamboo Grove Hall

In the village of Yama, in Heguri country of Yamato Province,[12] there is a sacred place named Chikurin-den [Bamboo Grove Hall] where the Great Guardian God of Kasuga (Daimyōjin) appeared.

Of old, Fujiwara no Mitsuhiro, an Assistant Keeper of the Right Imperial Stables, lived at Kichinan-den in Hirose county. Every night he saw a spot shining on the north bank of the Yamato River. A noble lady came there, and told him that this was where his descendants would flourish.

"Who are you, and where are you from?" Mitsuhiro asked.

---

11. That is, the participation of Buddhist priests in the ceremony. The word here translated as "avoid" has the implication of "to be tabooed."

12. Now Meyasu, a locality in eastern Ikaruga-chō in Ikoma-gun, Nara-ken.

The lady said:

Waga yado wa	I make my home
Miyako no minami	south of the Capital
Shika no sumu	in the floating cloud palace[13]
Mikasa no yama no	on Mikasa-Yama
Ukigumo no miya	the haunt of deer[14]

Then she vanished.

This dream inspired Mitsuhiro to begin building on the 25th day of the 2nd month on Tenryaku 2.[15] Then, after informing Emperor Murakami, he moved in on the 16th day of the 6th month of the same year.

Later, in Shōryaku 3, Fujiwara no Yoshikane[16] dreamed that a noble lady flew down to the bamboo grove southwest of the house.

"I am the Great Guardian God of Kasuga, your Clan God," she said. "I have come to live here because your house is so high and your bamboo grove so thick that the place is like the Bamboo Grove Garden.[17] As long as the bamboo grows fine and strong, your descendants will prosper."

Yoshikane immediately erected a shrine and worshiped the God, and he wrote a pledge that this sacred bamboo should never be cut. They say the bamboo now grows very tall there, so the spot is just like the Ryō Garden.[18]

[Tyler, *The Miracles of the Kasuga Deity*, pp. 159–169]

KŌFUKUJI GOES TO WAR IN THE EIKYŪ ERA

The following episode concerns the rivalry between the Tendai temple of Enryakuji on Mount Hiei and the Hossō temple of Kōfukuji in Nara over control of the famous Kiyomizu Temple of Kyoto. A retired emperor was also involved on the side of Mount Hiei in the conflict between armed monks of the temples, during which the Kiyomizu Temple was burned down. The guardian god of Kasuga is portrayed here as protecting Kōfukuji from the emperor's retaliation.

---

13. Probably the Kasuga Shrine.

14. Deer are sacred to the shrine at the foot of Mount Mikasa.

15. Tenryaku 2 (948).

16. Apparently the heir of Mitsuhiro but otherwise unknown.

17. Chikurin'en. Possibly an allusion to the bamboo grove near the royal palace in which Karanda (Skt: Kalanda) built a monastery for the Buddha. The monastery was named Chikurin shōja (Skt: Venuvana).

18. Ryōen (Ch: Liang-yuan), a famous garden created by King Xiao of Liang to entertain guests. References to it can be found in Chinese poetry.

In Eikyū 1 the monks of Enryaku-ji burned Kiyomizu Temple to the ground. Kōfuku-ji was furious, since Kiyomizudera is its dependency,[19] and the Kōfuku-ji monks set forth to war. The Court sent troops to stop them. Undaunted by the imperial authority, however, the monks joined the battle with these troops at Kurikoma-yama. The Retired Emperor,[20] outraged, declared that the Southern Capital[21] was to be punished.

At this point Akisue, the Master of Palace Repairs and an officer in the Retired Emperor's Household, dared to observe: "It is to the Guardian God of Kasuga's supernatural help that you owe all your good fortune, My Lord. How could you forget Kasuga's divine virtue?"

"What do you mean?" asked His Majesty.

"When you were young, My Lord," Akisue replied, "the ceiling of your residence shook, greatly startling you. Then a voice said, 'By the will of the Grand Shrine of Ise I guard the Imperial Person. I am the Guardian God of Kasuga.' Your Majesty should show more gratitude."

The Retired Emperor did not answer, but in the end he called off the campaign against Kōfuku-ji.

SANETSUNE

The Kasuga Overseer Sanetsune[22] was Hidetsura's successor in the sixth generation.[23] He had been under arrest for several days, on order from the outraged Lord Chisokuin, when Lord Chisokuin fell ill.

At first the Regent suffered from a fever every other day, as though he had an ague; but in time the fever came upon him daily. Zōyo, the Grand Prelate of Ichijō-ji,[24] was among the healers His Excellency summoned. When the fever arose as usual, despite his prayers, Zōyo dedicated to His Excellency all the merit he had gained from having practiced the *goma* of Fudō, so as to abolish

---

19. Enryakuji is the Tendai establishment on Mount Hiei. Kiyomizudera, dangerously close to Enryakuji's territory, was officially a Hossō temple and a dependency of Kōfukuji. Conversely, Tōnomine (the site of the mausoleum of Kamatari), dangerously close to Kōfukuji territory, was a dependency of Enryakuji. The result was the repeated destruction of both.

20. Shirakawa.

21. In the writings of this period, "Southern Capital" (Nara) often means simply "Kōfukuji."

22. Nakatomi (Ōhigashi) no Sanetsune (1038–1123). Appointed overseer in 1091, Sanetsune resigned in favor of his son, Nobutoshi, in 1115. In 1122 he was reappointed and died the next year.

23. Nakatomi no Hidetsura (713–807) came with Takemikazuchi from Kashima to Kasuga. He is the ancestor of the Ōhigashi line of Kasuga priests.

24. Zōyo (1032–1116), a grandson of the regent Michitaka, was a famous healer and *shugendō* adept. He served as the head monk of Miidera, Enryakuji, and other great temples.

every sin, during his three thousand days at the Nachi waterfall.[25] Then he begged the Great Holy One[26] for help, and His Excellency began to look much better. The fever seemed to be gone. Zōyo was rewarded before he withdrew.

The next day the fever arose again at the usual hour. Having now been ill for a long time, His Excellency was very weak, and the new attack was more severe than ever. At last his breathing became so feeble, and the color of his nails so bad, that he seemed to be dying. The whole household was naturally aghast. Grand Prelate Zōyo was summoned again, and despite his ignominious failure, he came.

Zōyo went to His Excellency, looked into his eyes, then drew far back and bowed very, very low. "No words can describe my incompetence," he said. "The healer's first duty is to grasp the nature of the disorder. He must discriminate between the curse of a living person and that of someone deceased, and discern whether a great or minor divinity is at work; and it is upon this understanding that he must found all his prayers and protective rites. But I was inattentive, and missed the truth. This is extremely serious. Clearly, a very great God has come down upon you. It was an awful blunder for a fool like me to have prayed on your behalf."

By "a very great God," he meant the God of Kasuga.

His Excellency summoned Sanetsune, in case it was his holding Sanetsune under arrest that had provoked the divine displeasure.

Sanetsune accordingly appeared: a bent old man over seventy, with white hair and eyebrows, who came tottering in wearing a rumpled white robe.[27] He might as well have been an ancient of Shōzan[28] in days of yore, and was obviously old and venerable—the mere sight of him made that plain. Lord Hosshōji[29] gave him a direct audience.

"Well," said Lord Hosshōji, "how many days is it now that you have been confined?"

---

25. Since the longest period of sustained practice recognized in *shugendō* is one thousand days, Zōyo had apparently done three one-thousand-day retreats. The Nachi Waterfall, one of the three Kumano shrines, was a major center of such ascetic practice, and the wrathful Fudō is a common object of devotion in *shugendō*. *Goma* (from the Sanskrit *homa*) is a fire rite most commonly associated with Fudō. Zōyo, like other ascetics, practiced it to achieve *metsuzai* ("destruction of sins").

26. That is, Fudō.

27. Sanetsune had on "pure raiment" (*jōe*), white clothing worn by persons who are in special contact with the sacred.

28. Shangshan, a mountain in Shensi Province in China, where four ancient, white-haired advisers to the Qin court took refuge when the dynasty fell. According to the *Records of the Historian (Shiji)*, they were eventually persuaded to come forth and serve the Han court. *Kara monogatari* 17 also tells the story.

29. Tadamichi.

He had not finished speaking before Sanetsune burst into tears and hung his head. "This is already the one hundred and thirtieth day," he replied after a pause.

"What have you been thinking about all this time?"

The weeping Sanetsune took a moment to answer. "This and only this," he said at last. "My mother and father told me that for the first six months after I was conceived, they went every day on a pilgrimage—and I therefore with them—to the Great Guardian God, Daimyōjin, and that after I was born, they had my wet-nurse take me every day, in her arms, to walk on the Mountain.[30] As an adult I have gone before the Daimyōjin every day, except when I was ill, and each time have sat against the Shrine fence.[31] But for one hundred and thirty days now, ever since My Lord placed me under arrest this spring, I have drifted on the waves of my seventy years and more, separated from the Daimyōjin. Old as I am, I am not ill, but still, each breath I draw may be my last; and how much more so now, in the stifling heat of summer! It is really more than I can bear. If I pass away here in the Capital, I will never go home, and will never worship the Daimyōjin again. That thought is so painful that I grieve over nothing else, day or night." Here he broke off and sobbed aloud.

Lord Hosshōji was in tears himself as he relayed all this to the Regent.

"I do feel sorry for him," Lord Chisokuin said. "Let him pray to the Daimyōjin and heal this sickness of mine."

At a word from Lord Hosshōji, Sanetsune faced south and, with tears in his eyes, wrung his hands in supplication. "Please Daimyōjin," he prayed, "heal His Excellency's affliction, and set my face once more toward your Mountain!"

Even as he spoke, Lord Chisokuin recovered completely. Deeply moved, he had Lord Hosshōji present Sanetsune with a sword, and Her Ladyship[32] sent him a robe. Sanetsune then withdrew, with two gentlemen leading him by the hand.

Sanetsune received Daigō in Harima province[33] as a fee for his prayers.

[Tyler, *The Miracles of the Kasuga Deity*, pp. 172–182]

YOSHIDA KANETOMO: PRIME SHINTO

The following excerpts are taken from Yoshida Kanetomo's *Essentials of Prime Shinto* (*Yuiitsu Shintō myōbō yōshū*), written about 1485 and expounding in catechistical style

---

30. Mount Mikasa.

31. Literally, "I have never failed to warm the Shrine fence."

32. Shishi, the second daughter of Minamoto no Akifusa. *Kokonchomonjū* no. 13 tells how once when a distressed Tadazane prayed to the Kasuga deity, the deity possessed this lady in order to assure him, "You will come into your own again."

33. According to *Koshaki*, an estate worth 500 *koku*.

what Kanetomo considered the key terms and teachings of Prime Shinto. These passages deal with the three main forms or divisions of Shinto and their relation to Buddhism; the scriptural bases for each; key terms, texts and rituals; the three Imperial Regalia; the divine origins and spiritual lineage of Prime Shinto; and the basic regulations governing the transmission and practice of the teachings. Much of Kanetomo's exposition is couched in the then widely current language of Esoteric Buddhism as if to establish that the real meaning of the latter derives from a primordial Shinto, which should now be followed to the exclusion of all "foreign" excrescences.

Q: Into how many categories is it possible to divide Shinto?

A: The Shinto formulated through "Co-dependent origination of essence and hypostasis" (Honjaku-engi Shintō); the Shinto devised around the "Twofold mandala combinations" (Ryōbu-shūgō Shintō); and the Shinto called "Original and Fundamental" (Gempon-sōgen Shintō). Hence the term of three "lineages" (*ke*) of Shinto.

Q: What is the Shinto formulated through "Co-dependent origination of essence and hypostasis"?

A: It may also be called "Shinto based on the scriptural transmissions of shrines." It is the object of various secret transmissions and of oral interpretations occurring in a particular shrine and concerning its history since the first manifestation (*kegen*), descent (*kōrin*), or ritual invocation (*kanjō*) of the kami of that shrine. Sacerdotal lineages are defined as the generations of those who have received these oral transmissions of secret knowledge. Furthermore, the various practices leading to an appreciation of the true character of the Essence are determined according to the doctrine and teachings that belong to what is called Inner Purification. By contrast, the various rituals and ceremonies are determined by rites that belong to what is called Outer Purification.

Q: What is the form of Shinto devised around the "Twofold mandala combinations"?

A: It appears to have received this name by virtue of an assimilation of the Diamond and Womb Mandalas to the Outer and Inner Shrines of Ise and of the associations between the various divinities of those mandalas and various kami.

Q: Who established those associations?

A: The four Great Masters Dengyō (Saichō), Kōbō (Kūkai), Jikaku (Ennin), and Chishō (Enchin). What is the reason for this? Each of these masters has authored Shinto scriptures because their complete understanding of the arcane meanings of Shingon enabled them to awaken to the secret meaning of Shinto. They were able to realize that the term Dai-Nippon-koku (Great Japan) was an adequate appellation for the True Residence of Mahāvairochana (Dainichi) and were thereby inspired to compose secret interpretations based on mythology. Every lineage of Esoteric and Exoteric Buddhism has thereafter entered [the realm of] Shinto, [and this has led to the composition of] well over five hundred scriptures. That is why that form of Shinto is also called "Shinto of the Great Masters." . . .

Q: What is the form of Shinto called "Original and Fundamental"?

A: The term *gen* designates the origin of origins predating the appearance of yin and yang. The term *hon* designates the state predating the appearance of thought processes. Hence the following verse:

> Taking the Origin as such, one penetrates the origin of origins;
> Taking the Original State as such, one sees the heart-mind.

Q: What do the terms *sō* and *gen* mean?

A: The term *sō* designates the original spirit predating the diversification of energy. All phenomena return to that single origin. The term *gen* designates the divine function referred to as "mingling with the dust and softening one's radiance."[34] This provides the basis of benefit for all living beings. Hence the following verse:

> *Sō* indicates that all phenomena return to the One;
> *Gen* reveals the source of all bonds between living beings.
> Such is Yuiitsu-Shinto, which has been transmitted since the creation of our Nation.

Q: On what scriptural evidence is this claim founded?

A: Three Primordial Texts form the basis of the Exoteric Doctrine, and Three Divine Scriptures form the basis of the Esoteric Doctrine. Yuiitsu-Shinto is made up of those two doctrines.

Q: What are the Three Primordial Texts?

A: They are *Tendai-kuji-hongi*, compiled by Shōtoku Taishi;[35] *Kojiki*, compiled by Ō no Yasumaro;[36] and *Nihon shoki*, compiled by Toneri Shinnō upon imperial order.[37]

Q: What are the Three Divine Texts?

A: They are the Subtle Sacred Scripture of the Divine Metamorphoses

---

34. The term *wakō*, originally taken from the Daodejing, came to qualify in Japan the use of expedient means (Skt: *upāya*, J: *hōben*) on the part of those buddhas and bodhisattvas who would have manifested themselves in the form of *kami*. It is rendered as "soften the glare," as in Lau, trans., *Lao Tzu*, pp. 60, 117.

35. *Tendai kuji hongi* is found in vol. 8 of *Shintō taikei*.

36. See chapter 2.

37. Ibid.

of the Heavenly Foundation, the Subtle Sacred Scripture of the Divine Supernatural Powers of the Earthly Foundation, and the Subtle Sacred Scripture of the Divine Powers of the Human Foundation.[38]

Q: Were those Scriptures revealed by the kami or authored by wise men?

A: They were revealed by [the kami] Ame-no-koyane-no-mikoto. In later generations they were translated into Chinese by the True Lord of the Polar Star. Thus did they come to be called the Three Divine Scriptures.

Q: What is meant by "the Primordial Texts form the basis of the exoteric doctrine"?

A: In those scriptures one can find information concerning the cosmogony, the events and origins of the generations of kami, and the genealogies of emperors and ministers. This information forms the exoteric aspects of the doctrine.

Q: What is meant by "the esoteric doctrine is built upon the Divine Scriptures"?

A: The esoteric doctrine based on the Divine Scriptures offers the noumenal correspondences responsible for the activities of Heaven, Earth, and Humanity; the three types of empowerment; the three types of subtle treasures; and various teachings connected to those. Hence the following verse:

> Denominations (*myō*) and rites (*hō*) of the esoteric doctrine
>   are called Inner Purification;
> Practical teachings and rites of the exoteric doctrine are
>   called Outer Purification.

Q: What is meant by Inner and Outer Purification?

A: There are two broad interpretations of these terms. The first one concerns the terms "peripheral abstinence" and "central abstinence"; the second concerns the terms "sacred space" and "sacred site" in which rituals are performed.

Q: What is meant by peripheral abstinence and by central abstinence?

A: Peripheral abstinence (*sansai*) refers to those acts of purification that are observed prior to a ritual and upon its completion. They are termed initial and final peripheral abstinences, and correspond to the rites of outer [physical] Purification. Central abstinence (*chisai*) is the observance and performance of a rite with an undisturbed mind, and the observance of the sextuple taboo as determined by the codes and

---

38. Kanetomo wrote these three short texts.

edicts. This corresponds to the rites of Inner [mental] Purification. Hence the following verse:

> Peripheral abstinence corresponds to Outer Purification,
> Central abstinence corresponds to Inner Purification.

Q: What is meant by sacred space and sacred site?

A: The place of practice of Inner Purification is called sacred space (*saijō*); it is also called "Inner Space." The place of practice of Outer Purification is called sacred site [*saitei*]; it is also called "Outer Site." Hence the verse:

> Sacred space, inner space: Inner Purification.
> Sacred site, outer site: Outer Purification.

Q: What do the terms *yuki* and *suki* refer to?

A: These are the original denominations of the sacred halls in which the kami of Heaven and Earth are invoked. Hence the verse:

> The sacred space for the kami of Heaven is the *yuki* hall;
> The sacred space for the kami of Earth is the *suki* hall.

Q: What is the origin of these two halls called *yuki* and *suki*?

A: These halls are erected by the Department of State at the time of the Enthronement Ceremony performed once in each imperial genera-tion, a ritual without par in this nation. *Yuki* is the divine hall of the altar of Original Spirits of the Ten Thousand Phenomena (*bansōdan*); *suki* is the divine hall of the altar of Sources of All Living Beings (*shogendan*). Hence the verse:

> The *yuki* hall is the altar of Original Spirits,
> The *suki* hall is the altar of Sources.

Q: What is meant by the terms "altar of Original Spirits" and "altar of Sources"?

A: These denominations correspond to the twofold aspect (*ryōbu*) of Yuiitsu-Shinto. Since these denominations are not current in the pro-fane world, allow me to use a comparison with Shingon Buddhism in order to interpret them. The term "altar of Original Spirits [of the ten thousand phenomena]" corresponds to the mandala of the Realm of Diamond. The term "altar of Sources [of all living beings]" corre-sponds to the mandala of the Realm of the Womb. These two altars correspond to the original design (*genzu*) of Heaven and Earth, to yin and yang, to the fundamental representation (*honzō*) of the Outer and

Inner Shrines of Ise, to the external appearance (*hyōsō*) of the Inner and Outer Heavens, and to the Seal Inscription on the Ocean Floor (*kaitei inmon*). . . .

Q: What are the Three Imperial Regalia?

A: First is the divine mirror kept in the Onmeiden [Hall] of the imperial palace. Second is the Grass-cutting sacred sword. Third is the sacred seal of Yasakani.

Q: Is there a difference between these three kinds and the ten kinds?

A: These three kinds are different. Thus one reads in the fifth book of *Nihon shoki*:

> Then Amaterasu-ō-Kami gave to Ninigi-no-mikoto the curved stone of Yasakani, the Yata mirror, and the Kusanagi sword.

These are the treasures in question.

Q: But is it possible to say that there is a distinction of relative versus absolute, or of superior versus inferior between the three and ten treasures?

A: There is a distinction of relative and absolute, but no distinction of superior and inferior. The ten kinds represent a spiritual treasure and pervade the universe; being of the relative kind, they manifest the absolute. Of the three kinds, the first one is endowed with a spirit perfect and complete like that of the ten kinds; it is the Yata mirror. The second one is a treasure endowed with the same properties as the ten kinds: that is the curved-stone of Yasakani. These three treasures represent the absolute, but are endowed with the relative. Therefore it is said that there is a distinction of relative and absolute but that there is no distinction of inferior and superior. The spiritual efficacy that dwells in the three and ten treasures is, ultimately, that which allows one to govern. Therefore they are called the sacred space (*iwasaka*) where the support (*himorogi*) of the kami is located. This is what is meant by the term "Unsurpassable Spiritual Treasure." Hence the verse:

> The ten kinds represent perfection, correspondence, completion,
> All contained within the three kinds; the ten and the three,
> Ultimately, a repository of divine presence, unsurpassable spiritual treasures.

Q: What proof do you have of this unsurpassable quality?

A: A seal-inscription transmitted within the lineage of Yuiitsu-Shinto. It is said in the last book of the Mythology Section of *Nihon shoki*:

Ame-no-koyane-no-mikoto was the first kami charged with liturgical matters. Takami-musubi-no-kami accordingly gave command, saying: "I will set up a heavenly divine fence (*himorogi*) and a heavenly rock-boundary (*iwasaka*) wherein religious abstinence shall be practiced on behalf of my descendants. Do ye, Ame-no-koyane-no-mikoto and Futo-dama-no-mikoto, take with you the *himorogi* and go down to the Central Land of Reed Plains."[39]

Such is the evidence for the tradition according to which Ame-no-koyane-no-mikoto's descendants are the sole recipients of this secret transmission.

Q: What is the meaning of the term "Shinto"?

A: The term *shin* denotes the foundation of the ten thousand things in Heaven and Earth. Therefore, it is also qualified as unfathomable yin and yang. The term *tō* denotes the rationale of all activities. Therefore it is said, "The Way is not the constant way."[40] As a consequence there is nothing in the material world, nor in the worlds of life, of animate and inanimate beings, of beings with energy and without energy, that does not partake of this Shinto. Hence the verse:

> *Shin* is the heart-mind of all beings,
> *Tō* is the source of all activities.
> All animate and inanimate beings of the triple world are
>   ultimately nothing but Shinto only.

Q: What is the meaning of the terms "substance," "function," and "aspect"?

A: Substance is represented by the term "three subtleties." Aspect is represented by the term "three types of active aspects."

Q: What is meant by the three foundations?

A: Shinto is the foundation of Heaven, it is the foundation of Earth. It is also the foundation of Humanity. Hence the term. . . .

Q: If this is so, then are the Way of Heaven, the Way of Earth, and the Way of Humanity all endowed with Shinto?

A: If the Way of Heaven did not possess Shinto, there would not be any sun, moon or stars, nor would there be any seasons. Without Shinto, the Way of Earth would be deprived of the five active aspects and of the ten thousand phenomena. Without Shinto, Humanity would have neither life nor order. Hence the verse:

---

39. *Nihongi*, II, 2; Aston, *Nihongi*, II, pp. 81–82.
40. The first line of the *Laozi*. See de Bary and Bloom, eds., *Sources of Chinese Tradition*, 2d ed., vol. 1, chap. 5.

> The great kami of the beginnings ordered that there be
>   Shinto in Heaven;
> Hence the sun, the moon, and the stars, the four seasons.
> Ordered that there be Shinto on earth;
> Hence the five active aspects and the ten thousand
>   phenomena.
> Ordered that there be Shinto in Humanity;
> Hence the five elements and the six sense organs.

Q: What is meant by the term "Eighteenfold Shinto"?

A: Heaven, Earth, and Humanity each have a sixfold Shinto.

Q: What is the sixfold Shinto of Heaven?

A: Heaven is endowed with a Shinto of perfect fundamental energy. Add to this the five active aspects of Heaven, and you have this sixfold aspect.

Q: What is the sixfold Shinto of Earth?

A: Earth is endowed with a Shinto of perfect correspondence [to the energy of heaven]. Add to this the five active aspects of Earth, and you have this sixfold aspect.

Q: What is the sixfold Shinto of Humanity?

A: Human powerment through the divine metamorphoses.
    Add the five active aspects: this is the sixfold Shinto.
    Perfect correspondence is realized by empowerment
        through supernatural powers.
    Add the active aspects: this is the sixfold Shinto.
    Completion of life is realized by empowerment through
        divine powers.
    Add the active aspects: this is the sixfold Shinto.
    Yuiitsu-Shinto is made up of three foundations and of
        eighteen parts.
    All activities are a function of Shinto in the heart-mind.

Q: Would a kami refuse its grace if, in the case of a minor reverence to the kami, the subtle altars of the threefold, ninefold, and eighteenfold Shinto were missing?

A: Any single reverence with folded hands is necessarily endowed with the triple altar. Even more so in the case of a reverence to a kami!

Q: I will defer my question on the three types of active aspects to a later opportunity. For now I would like to know the meaning of the term "empowerment."

A: The term *kaji* (here translated as empowerment) is itself an utterance made by the kami. A long time ago, during the age of the kami, the kami Takemikatsuchi and Iwainushi acted as guides and messengers for the kami of Heaven and descended to earth in order to pacify all

evil spirits. Thereafter, the august descendant of the solar kami descended. In virtue of this, these two kami have received the hypostasis
(*suijaku*) name of Kashima and Katori, this last one being alternatively
written with graphs meaning "helmsmen" and pronounced Kajitori.
Such was the beginning of imperial rule in this realm according to
secret techniques. Therefore, when Jingū Kōgō went on an expedition
to conquer a foreign land, she put upon the vast ocean a fleet of ships.
It was then that, upon reception of a divine oracle, a rudder (*kaji*) was
first created; the ships could then move in any desired direction. The
orthograph that I use to write the term *kaji* was realized when the
names of these two kami were cleverly combined. In this one artifact
(*kaji* = rudder = empowerment), the entirety of the empowerment
of the three foundations is revealed. For instance, to take this rudder
into the hand is to manifest empowerment through divine powers; to
move this rudder is to manifest empowerment through supernatural
powers; to be able, thanks to those two aspects of empowerment, to
change one's direction at will is to manifest empowerment through
divine metamorphoses. . . .

Does the *kaji* used by the Buddhists correspond in any way to this
Shinto term? This would not be the first time one finds the same words
in the languages of India, China, and Japan. . . .

Q: In this connection, what is meant by the term "empowerment of the
body through the three treasures"?

A: The first one is longevity; the second is good health; the third is mental/
material happiness. This is what is called the three treasures of the
body. The first and second are within the body; the third is extraneous
to the body. The reason why longevity comes first is that one wants to
cure oneself simply because one is alive. And it is because one is alive
that one looks for material possessions. The reason why good health
comes second is that those who fall ill fear for their lives, and that
those who are gravely sick forget the importance of material possessions. The reason why mental/material happiness comes third is that
longevity is the foundation of life, its trunk and roots. The various
diseases are the body's branches and leaves. Mental/material happiness
is the body's flowers and fruit. . . .

Q: Since when did the people of our sacred nation revere the law of the
Buddha, and why are they searching for foreign doctrines?

A: An infinity of time after the creation of our sacred nation, the venerable
Shākyamuni appeared in that other nation [India]. One must emphasize that the transmission of his doctrine to our nation occurred only
in the recent past, in the reign of the thirtieth emperor, Kimmei, and
already five hundred years after the Buddha had died. Buddhism was
transmitted to our nation only after four hundred and some years of

development within China. But the people of our nation did not originally believe in that new doctrine. During the reign of the thirty-fourth ruler of our nation [Empress Suiko], Shōtoku Taishi made to her the following secret declaration:

Japan produced the seed, China produced the branches and leaves, India produced the flowers and fruit. Buddhism is the fruit, Confucianism is the leaves, and Shinto is the trunk and the roots. Buddhism and Confucianism are only secondary products of Shinto. Leaves and fruit merely indicate the presence of the trunk and roots; flowers and fruit fall and return to the roots. Buddhism came east only to reveal clearly that our nation is the trunk and roots of these three nations.[41]

Since then, Buddhism has remained in our nation. From Emperor Jinmu on and for more than two thousand years Buddhism and Confucianism have never interfered in our history; all they did was to protect the root of this sacred nation and thus implement the fundamental vow of the kami. That is why it is common these days in the course of Shinto ceremonies to abandon the contemplation of the buddhas and the recitation of Buddhist scriptures. It is written in the text titled *Yamatohime no Mikoto Seiki*:[42]

Respect Heaven and serve Earth, revere the kami and respect the ancestors, continue the rites of adoration of the imperial ancestors, follow the heavenly teachings and abandon Buddhism, adore instead the kami of Heaven and Earth! . . .

Q: Are there any more details about this term "Yuiitsu"?
A: There are three types of interpretation of this term. First, there is only one doctrine and not two. Second, there is only one lineage and not two. And third is the demonstration that it is One-and-Only in Heaven.
Q: What is meant by "there is only one doctrine and not two"?
A: This Shinto is a most subtle and obscure transmission that has taken place between Kuni-no-tokotachi-no-mikoto, who is the origin of the incommensurable yin and yang, and Amaterasu-ō-kami. This kami then transmitted it to Ame-no-koyane-no-mikoto. Since that time all the way down to this degenerate age of decadence, this Shinto has

---

41. This statement, attributed to Shōtoku Taishi by Japanese tradition since Jihen, is an adaptation of an earlier Chinese concoction.

42. *Yamato-hime no Mikoto Seiki* is found in Jingū, ed., *Daijingū sōsho*, vol. 14, pp. 61–92. For an edited version, see Ōsumi, *Chūsei Shintō*, pp. 8–38; the quotation is from p. 30.

drawn on the primeval water of chaos and has not even once been corrupted by a single drop of the Three Teachings [Confucianism, Daoism, Buddhism]. That is why it is said that there is only one doctrine and not two.

THE LINEAGE OF YUIITSU-SHINTO

G: What is meant by the demonstration that it is One-and-only in Heaven?

A: This country is a Sacred Land (*shinkoku*). Its way is the kami Way (*shintō*). The ruler of this country is the Sacred Emperor (*jinnō*). The Great Ancestor is Amaterasu-ō-kami. The awesome light of this one kami pervades billions of worlds, and its will shall forever be transmitted along an imperial way laden with ten thousand chariots. Just as there are not two suns in heaven, there are not two rulers in a country. That is why, when the sun is in the sky, the light of the stars and planets cannot be seen. Such is the demonstration that it is One-and Only in Heaven. . . .

REGULATIONS OF YUIITSU-SHINTO

Caution shall be exercised when transmitting the doctrine.

Concerning the above. If within the true lineage of the Urabe one finds an adequate recipient of the doctrine, he shall be trained from a young age and with particular care. If it is someone from another lineage, it must be ensured that his capabilities are in accordance with the demands of the duty, and the degree to which he shares our purpose must be evaluated before he be accepted as a disciple.

It is absolutely forbidden to transmit the doctrine to priests of other shrines.

Concerning the above. The history of this shrine must be studied in depth, the rites of Outer and Inner Purification must be strictly observed; a candidate shall be deemed worthy to receive the transmissions only if he comes from a demonstrably adequate background.

Monks shall not readily be given the transmissions.

Concerning the above. This order does not apply to monks who have studied in depth the arcane meanings of the doctrine of their own school, and who are capable because they have shown that they observe their own regulations.

Taboos shall be observed.

> Concerning the above. The taboo of pollution caused by death shall be determined by the length of a moon. The categories of mourning dress shall be determined according to the five categories of parentage. Taboo in the case of death in the family is a rite that has been transmitted since the age of the kami. The categories of mourning dress, however, have been established by the codes. That is why the Yuiitsu-Shinto tradition observes a taboo on pollution but not on dress.

One shall not pay homage to the kami without attaching the *yufu*.

> Concerning the above. The term *yufu* denotes the ritual binding of mulberry bark strips to the ceremonial hat. Hence its extension to refer to the ceremonial robes. Ceremonial robes are classified in two categories of extended taboo and minute taboo. If no ceremonial dress is put on, but the *yufu* is used, any dress becomes ceremonial. . . . Within Yuiitsu-Shinto, those who have received the First Transmission [exoteric teaching] are restricted to one single strip [of mulberry bark]. Those who have received the Second Transmission [exoteric and esoteric teachings] use a combination of eight. Those who do not attach the *yufu* may absolutely not perform services in front of the kami.

One shall not search for the doctrines and teachings of foreign countries.

> Concerning the above. Yuiitsu-Shinto is a direct transmission by the kami, the one doctrine expounded at the time of the creation of the cosmos. Thus it is reported that the Daishokkan [Kamatari] said as follows: "Heaven and Earth are the scriptures of Shinto. The Sun and Moon are its demonstration." Such is the ultimate esoteric and pure meaning of the doctrine. That is why one should not search for the teachings of Confucianism, Buddhism, or Daoism. But as I have said, there is no objection to deeply studying the meanings of the three teachings as long as the purpose is to increase the flavor of Yuiitsu-Shinto, to enrich the beauty and light of Shinto, and to explore the depths of our Way.

The paper strips (*kirigami*) follow face-to face transmissions.

> Concerning the above. All transmissions beyond third face-to face transmissions are classified as most secret. Once the contents of a transmission on paper strips (*kirigami*) have been learned by heart, the *kirigami* ought

to be returned to the priestly lineage. The contents of oral transmissions may not be put on paper.

The first two levels of transmissions must be written on white paper. The second two levels of secret transmissions must be written on ornate paper (*suiunshi*).

[Ōsumi, *Chūsei Shintō ron*, pp. 209–251: trans. and adapted from Grapard, "Yoshida Kanetomo," pp. 137–61; AG]

KITABATAKE CHIKAFUSA: *CHRONICLE OF THE DIRECT DESCENT OF GODS AND SOVEREIGNS* (*JINNŌ SHŌTŌKI*)

As noted in chapter 11, Kitabatake Chikafusa's *Chronicle* is both a history of Japan from the creation of the country by the gods to the reign of Emperor Gomurakami, who succeeded Godaigo in 1339, and a political tract intended primarily to draw supporters to the Southern Court during the fourteenth-century War Between the Courts. *Jinnō shōtōki* is also one of the most important documents of the Shinto revival of the medieval age. Thus in its opening lines (quoted in chapter 11), Chikafusa proclaims Japan to be a "divine land" (*shinkoku*), different from and superior to all other lands, because it has always been ruled by an unbroken line of emperors descended from the Sun Goddess.

In these first three passages from the *Chronicle*, Chikafusa discusses the various names that have been used for Japan, its position in the universe according to Buddhist geographical concepts, and the differing Indian, Chinese, and Japanese accounts of the creation of the universe and its evolution. Chikafusa's preoccupation in the first passage with names and their etymologies is characteristic of writers on Shinto, who have never wearied of tracing the origins of names and words, such as Yamato and *kami*.

In the second and third passages, Chikafusa displays his familiarity with Indian (Buddhist) and Chinese writings. He does not reject them but attempts to show that they are incomplete—if not misleading—because they do not reveal the highest and most important truth: the uniquely divine character of Japan based on its unbroken line of sovereigns.

In the fourth passage, Chikafusa discusses the imperial regalia of mirror, sword, and jewel, seeking to show that they are symbols of both the Sun Goddess's mandate that one line descended from her will rule Japan forever and the morality with which that rule is invested.

Japan is the divine country. The heavenly ancestor it was who first laid its foundations, and the Sun Goddess left her descendants to reign over it forever and ever. This is true only of our country, and nothing similar may be found in foreign lands. That is why it is called the divine country.

The Names of Japan

In the age of the gods, Japan was known as the "ever-fruitful land of reed-covered plains and luxuriant ricefields."[43] This name has existed since the creation of heaven and earth. It appeared in the command given by the heavenly ancestor Kunitokotachi to the Male Deity and the Female Deity.[44] Again, when the Great Goddess Amaterasu bequeathed the land to her grandchild, that name was used; it may thus be considered the prime name of Japan. It is also called the country of the great eight islands. This name was given because eight islands were produced when the Male Deity and the Female Deity begot Japan. It is also called Yamato, which is the name of the central part of the eight islands. The eighth offspring of the deities was the god Heavenly-August-Sky-Luxuriant-Dragonfly-Lord-Youth [and the land he incarnated] was called Ō-yamato, Luxuriant-Dragonfly-Island. It is now divided into forty-eight provinces. Besides being the central island, Yamato has been the site of the capital through all the ages since Jinmu's conquest of the east. That must be why the other seven islands are called Yamato. The same is true of China, where All-Under-Heaven was at one time called Zhou because the dynasty had its origins in the state of Zhou, and where All-Within-the Seas was called Han when the dynasty arose in the territory of Han.

The word Yamato means "footprints on the mountain." Of old, when heaven and earth were divided, the soil was still muddy and not yet dry, and people passing back and forth over the mountains left many footprints; thus it was called Yama-to—"mountain footprint." Some say that in ancient Japanese *to* meant "dwelling" and that because people dwelt in the mountains, the country was known as Yama-to—"mountain dwelling."

In writing the name of the country, the Chinese characters Dai-Nippon and Dai-Wa have both been used. The reason is that when Chinese writing was introduced to this country, the characters for Dai-Nippon were chosen to represent the name of the country, but they were pronounced as "Yamato." This choice may have been guided by the fact that Japan is the land of the Sun Goddess, or it may have thus been called because it is near the place where the sun rises. . . .

Japan's Position Geographically

According to Buddhist scriptures, there is a mountain called Sumeru which is surrounded by seven gold mountains. In between them is the Sea of Fragrant

---

43. Toyoshihara no Chiihoaki no Mizuho no Kuni. Translations of ancient names of places and deities are only approximate.

44. The Male Deity (Izanagi) and the Female Deity (Izanami) were ordered to descend to Earth and produce the terrestrial world.

Waters, and beyond the gold mountains stretch four oceans which contain the four continents. Each continent is in turn composed of two smaller sections. The southern continent is called Jambu (it is also known as Jambudvīpa, another form of the same name) from the name of the jambu tree. In the center of the southern continent is a mountain called Anavatapta, at the summit of which is a lake. A jambu tree grows beside this lake, seven yojanas in circumference and one hundred yojanas in height. (One yojana equals forty *li*; one *li* equals 2,160 feet.) The tallest of these trees grows in the center of the continent and gives it its name. To the south of Anavatapta are the Himālayas, and to the north are the Pamirs. North of the Pamirs is Tartary; south of the Himālayas is India. To the northeast is China, and to the northwest, Persia. The continent of Jambu is seven thousand yojanas long and broad; that is, 280,000 *li*. However big China may seem, when compared with India it is only a remote, minor country. Japan is in the ocean, removed from China. Gomyō Sōjō of Nara and Saichō of Hiei designated it as the Middle Country, but should not that name refer to the island of Chāmara, which lies between the northern and southern continents? When, in the Kegon Sūtra, it states that there is a mountain called Kongō [diamond], it refers to the Kongō Mountain in modern Japan, or so it is believed. Thus, since Japan is a separate continent, distinct from both India and China and lying in a great ocean, it is the country where the divine illustrious imperial line has been transmitted.

Japan's Position Chronologically

The creation of heaven and earth must everywhere have been the same, for it occurred within the same universe, but the Indian, Chinese, and Japanese traditions are each different. According to the Indian version, the beginning of the world is called the "inception of the kalpas." (A kalpa has four stages—growth, settlement, decline, and extinction—each with twenty rises and falls. One rise and fall is called a minor kalpa; twenty minor kalpas constitute a middle kalpa, and four middle kalpas constitute a major kalpa.) . . .

In China, nothing positive is stated concerning the creation of the world, even though China is a country which accords special importance to the keeping of records. In the Confucian books nothing antedates King Fuxi.[45] In other works they speak of heaven, earth, and man as having begun in an unformed, undivided state, much as in the accounts of our age of the gods. There is also the legend of King Pangu,[46] whose eyes were said to have turned into the sun

---

45. Fuxi was the legendary founder of Chinese culture, being credited, among other things, with establishing the laws of marriage, inventing writing, and preparing the first instruction in hunting and fishing.

46. The legend of Pangu was apparently of Central Asiatic origin and was not "naturalized" by the Chinese until post-Han times.

and the moon and whose hair turned into grasses and trees. There were afterward sovereigns of Heaven, sovereigns of Earth, and sovereigns of Man, and the Five Dragons, followed by many kings over a period of ten thousand years.

The beginnings of Japan in some ways resemble the Indian descriptions, telling as it does of the world's creation from the seed of the heavenly gods. However, whereas in our country the succession to the throne has followed a single undeviating line since the first divine ancestor, nothing of the kind has existed in India. After their first ruler, King People's Lord, had been chosen and raised to power by the populace, his dynasty succeeded, but in later times most of his descendants perished, and men of inferior genealogy who had powerful forces became the rulers, some of them even controlling the whole of India. China is also a country of notorious disorders. Even in ancient times, when life was simple and conduct was proper, the throne was offered to wise men,[47] and no single lineage was established. Later, in times of disorder, men fought for control of the country. Thus some of the rulers rose from the ranks of the plebeians, and there were even some of barbarian origin who usurped power. Or some families after generations of service as ministers surpassed their princes and eventually supplanted them. There have already been thirty-six changes of dynasty since Fuxi, and unspeakable disorders have occurred.

Only in our country has the succession remained inviolate from the beginning of heaven and earth to the present. It has been maintained within a single lineage, and even when, as inevitably has happened, the succession has been transmitted collaterally, it has returned to the true line. This is due to the ever-renewed Divine Oath and makes Japan unlike all other countries.

It is true that the Way of the Gods should not be revealed without circumspection, but it may happen that ignorance of the origins of things may result in disorder. In order to prevent that disaster, I have recorded something of the facts, confining myself to a description of how the succession has legitimately been transmitted from the age of the gods. I have not included information known to everyone. I have given the book the title of *The Chronicle of the Direct Descent of the Gods and Sovereigns*. . . .

The Imperial Regalia

Then the Great Sun Goddess conferred with Takami-musubi and sent her grandchild to the world below. Eighty million deities obeyed the divine decree to accompany and serve him. Among them were thirty-two principal deities, including the gods of the Five Guilds—Ame no Koyane (the first ancestor of the Nakatomi family), Ame no Futodama (the first ancestor of the Imbe family),

---

47. This refers to the decisions of the legendary emperors Yao and Shun to hand over the throne to wise men rather than to their own sons.

Ishikoridome (the first ancestor of the mirror makers), and Tamaya (the first ancestor of the jewel makers). Two of these deities, those of the Nakatomi and the Imbe, which received a divine decree specially instructing them to aid and protect the divine grandchild, uttered these words of command, "The reed-plain-of-one-thousand-five-hundred-autumns-fair-rice-ear land is where my descendants shall reign. Thou, my illustrious grandchild, proceed thither and govern the land. Go, and may prosperity attend thy dynasty, and may it, like Heaven and Earth, endure forever."

Then the Great Goddess, taking in her own hand the precious mirror, gave it to her grandchild, saying, "When thou, my grandchild, lookst on this mirror, it will be as though thou lookst at myself. Keep it with thee, in the same bed, under the same roof, as thy holy mirror." She then added the curved jewel of increasing prosperity and the sword of gathered clouds, thus completing the three regalia. She again spoke, "Illumine all the world with brightness like this mirror. Reign over the world with the wonderful sway of this jewel. Subdue those who will not obey thee by brandishing this divine sword." It may indeed be understood from these commands why Japan is a divine country and has been ruled by a single imperial line following in legitimate succession. The Imperial Regalia have been transmitted [within Japan] just as the sun, moon, and stars remain in the heavens. The mirror has the form of the sun; the jewel contains the essence of the moon; and the sword has the substance of the stars. There must be a profound significance attached to them.

The precious mirror is the mirror made by Ishikoridome, as is above recorded. The jewel is the curved bead of increasing prosperity made by him to the Great Goddess. The goddess's commands on the Three Regalia must indicate the proper methods of governing the country. The mirror does not possess anything of its own but, without selfish desires, reflects all things, showing their true qualities. Its virtue lies in its response to these qualities and, as such, represents the source of all honesty. The virtue of the jewel lies in its gentleness and submissiveness; it is the source of compassion. The virtue of the sword lies in its strength and resolution; it is the source of wisdom. Unless these three[48] are joined in a ruler, he will find it difficult indeed to govern the country. The divine commands are clear; their words are concise, but their import is far-reaching. Is it not an awe-inspiring thing that they are embodied in the Imperial Regalia?

The mirror stands first in importance among the regalia and is revered as the true substance of ancestor worship. The mirror has brightness as its form: the enlightened mind possesses both compassion and decision. As it also gives

---

48. Compare the *Classic of Documents* (*Hongfan*); Legge, *Shoo-King*, p. 333: "The three virtues: The first is correctness and straightforwardness; the second, strong rule; and the third, mild rule."

a true reflection of the Great Goddess, she must have given her profound care to the mirror. There is nothing brighter in heaven than the sun and the moon. That is why, when the Chinese characters were devised, the symbols for the sun and for moon were joined to express the idea of brightness. Because our Great Goddess is the spirit of the sun, she illuminates with a bright virtue which is incomprehensible in all its aspects but dependable alike in the realm of the visible and invisible. All sovereigns and ministers have inherited the bright seeds of the divine light, or they are descendants of the deities who received personal instruction from the Great Goddess. Who would not stand in reverence before this fact? The highest object of all teachings, Buddhist and Confucian included, consists in realizing this fact and obeying in perfect consonance its principles. It has been the power of the dissemination of the Buddhist and Confucian texts which has spread these principles.[49] It is just the same as the fact that a single mesh of a net suffices to catch a fish, but you cannot catch one unless the net has many meshes. Since the reign of the Emperor Ōjin, the Confucian writings have been disseminated, and since Prince Shōtoku's time Buddhism has flourished in Japan. Both these men were sages incarnate, and it must have been their intention to spread a knowledge of the way of our country, in accordance with the wishes of the Great Sun Goddess.

[*Jinnō shōtō-ki*, pp. 1–22]

---

49. That is, Buddhist and Confucian texts have helped spread a knowledge of Shinto because they contain the same essential principles.

Chapter 16

THE VOCABULARY OF JAPANESE AESTHETICS II

Late in the twelfth century, the war fought between two powerful military clans, the Taira and the Minamoto, brought an end to the Heian period, four hundred years after the founding of the capital in Kyoto. The ensuing medieval period also lasted some four hundred years until a new order was created at the end of the sixteenth century.

The victory of the Minamoto clan, which established its capital at Kamakura in the east, did not cause the aristocratic society of the Heian capital to collapse immediately. Members of the emperor's court led much the same lives as before, as we know from their diaries and the poetry they composed, whether on the conventionally admired sights of nature or bittersweet memories of love. But with the foundation of the new capital by the shogun Minamoto Yoritomo, warriors (*bushi*) now dominated the scene, and the literature of the medieval period came to be characterized by accounts of the warfare that the samurai waged rather than by the writings of the court.

Aesthetic attitudes soon changed in similar ways, and the new masters of Japan imposed their own criteria of taste. Nonetheless, these changes tended to be softened by the influence of *miyabi*, and even the fiercest warlord was much more likely to compose poetry on the beauty of falling cherry blossoms than on the joys of victory in battle. After Minamoto Sanetomo, the third of the Kamakura shoguns, studied with Fujiwara Teika, he composed *tanka* poetry of traditional elegance that earned him a reputation as a major poet. Other warlords with less poetic talent than Sanetomo also sought to acquire the trappings of the aristocratic culture. Poets from the capital who could tutor such men and guide them in the rules of *tanka* composition were eagerly welcomed to the strongholds of the different warring factions.

The distinctive aesthetic standards in literature and art that eventually emerged did not represent a sharp break with the past so much as an intensifying and darkening of Heian ideals. The seemingly endless warfare gave new meaning to the uncertainty of life, which also was a frequent theme in the writings of the Heian courtiers, who saw death in the falling of blossoms or in a moment of parting, but still there was a difference. The court lady who in the past had brooded over a lover's neglect was now likely to suffer more immediate grief on learning he had been killed in battle. In some diaries, women described their emotions on seeing their lover's head on a pike being paraded through the streets.

The aesthetic ideals that pervaded the poetry, drama, painting, gardens, tea ceremony, and many other artistic activities of the medieval period cannot be evoked by one single word, but *yūgen* is perhaps the most characteristic. The term *yūgen* was used to evoke the profound, remote, and mysterious, those things that cannot easily be grasped or expressed in words. In some ways, *yūgen* resembles Western symbolism, not the obvious symbolism of a flag for a country or a bird in a cage for a captive spirit, but what Poe called "a suggestive indefiniteness of vague and therefore of spiritual effect." The Japanese of the medieval period courted ambiguity, leaving empty spaces in their compositions for readers or spectators to fill in according to their intuitive understanding of the ultimate meaning of the poem or play.

Yūgen and the Heian *aware* also differed. The Heian poet felt *aware* when, seeing wrinkles in the mirror, she realized with a pang that time was passing by, that the years of her youth had ended. But this realization was generally the end of the emotion; it did not bring the poet to the dark and mysterious region of *yūgen*. When a nō actor slowly raises his hand in a gesture, it corresponds to words of the text he is performing, but it also must suggest something beyond mere representation, something eternal—in T. S. Eliot's words, a "moment in and out of time." Although the gesture is in itself beautiful, it is the gateway to something beyond as well, as the hand points to depths as profound as the viewer is capable of seeing. It is a symbol not of any one object or conception but of an eternal region, an eternal silence. Again, in T. S. Eliot's words,

> . . . Words, after speech, reach
> Into the silence. Only by the form, the pattern,
> Can words or music reach

The stillness, as a Chinese jar still
Moves perpetually in its stillness.[1]

To suggest the stillness, a form or pattern is necessary. If that form or pattern is beautiful, it is enough for most people, and they do not feel a need for a deeper meaning. Others, though, might doubt whether such a thing as silence beyond the form exists and whether one can seriously consider anything like *yūgen*, which defies definition or description.

Such doubts are not peculiar to our time. A work written in the year 1430 observed:

> *Yūgen* may be comprehended by the mind, but it cannot be expressed in words. Its quality may be suggested by the sight of a thin cloud veiling the moon or by autumn mist swathing the scarlet leaves on a mountainside. If one is asked where in these sights lies the *yūgen*, one cannot say, and it is not surprising that a man who does not understand this truth is likely to prefer the sight of a perfectly clear, cloudless sky. It is quite impossible to explain wherein lies the interest or the remarkable nature of *yūgen*.[2]

Even though it may be impossible to explain *yūgen*, we can intuitively sense it. "It is just as when we look at the sky of an autumn dusk. It has no sound or color, and yet, though we do not understand why, we somehow find ourselves moved to tears."[3] *Yūgen* is the quality of the highest realm of art, an absolute domain to which all forms point. It tends to be expressed in bare and simple terms as if to keep the mind from dwelling too long on the beauty of the form presented and thereby to allow it to leap to that realm. There is *yūgen* in the simple perfection of the Chinese jar that "moves perpetually in its stillness" but not in the Dresden figurine. There is *yūgen* in the sound of the nō flute, which stirs us imprecisely yet with an almost painful urgency to an awareness of the existence of something beyond the form, but not in the ravishing melodies of the sextet from *Lucia*. There is *yūgen* in the sight of a tea master dipping water into a kettle with simple movements that have about them the lines of eternity.

Although *yūgen* may be discovered in many forms of Japanese medieval art, the nō theater was the medium that carried it to the highest degree. It was, in fact, the effect at which the masters of the nō, and particularly the great Zeami (1363–1443), consciously aimed. From what little we know of the nō before

---

1. Eliot, "Burnt Norton," in *Four Quartets*, p. 7.

2. *Shōtetsu monogatari*, in *Zoku gunsho ruijū*, bk. 16, p. 929.

3. *Mumyō hisho*, in *Gunsho ruijū*, bk. 13, p. 366.

Zeami's day, it seems clear that it was essentially a representational theater, with the attempt being made in a manner not very different from that employed in the West to portray on the stage the actions of dramatic personages. Zeami, however, chose to make the nō a symbolic theater in which the most important actions were not represented but suggested. The central character in many of his plays is a ghost, someone from a world beyond our own that can only be symbolized. Often this ghost returns in his former appearance in the second part of the play, and during the interval between the first and second parts harsh music and inarticulate cries from the musicians suggest the distance of the world of the dead and the pain of being born. The climax of the play is the final dance symbolizing and resolving the character's anguish.

Zeami wrote that spectators of the nō sometimes found the moments of "doing nothing" the most enjoyable when it was not any gesture of the actor that suggested the eternity beyond the gestures but only his own unconsciously revealed spiritual strength. Usually, however, *yūgen* was achieved through the means of beautiful forms, and in deciding what was beautiful Zeami was guided by the Heian principle of *miyabi*. He says, for instance, that "the *yūgen* of discourse lies in a grace of language and a complete mastery of the speech of the nobility and the gentry so that even the most casual utterance will be graceful." This is another instance of how *yūgen* was achieved by using Heian aesthetic means and not by denying them. But what had stopped at the level of being "charming" or "touching" in the Heian period became in the medieval period the profoundly moving *yūgen*. It is tempting to speculate that in an age of painful changes and destruction like the Japanese medieval period, the need for eternal incorruptible values might well have given rise to such an aesthetic ideal as *yūgen*.

During the medieval period, another aesthetic ideal, *sabi*, joined *yūgen*. *Sabi* is a very old word, found as far back as the *Manyōshū*, in which it has the meaning of "to be desolate." It later acquired the meaning of "to grow old" and is related to the phrase "to grow rusty." In *The Tale of the Heike*, we find it used in the sentence "It was a place *old* with moss-covered boulders, and he thought it would be pleasant to live there." It seems likely that already by this time (the thirteenth century), *sabi* suggested not only "old" but the taking of pleasure in what was old, faded, or lonely. To achieve *yūgen*, art had sometimes been stripped of its color and glitter lest these externals distract. For instance, a bowl of highly polished silver reflects more than it suggests, but one of oxidized silver has the mysterious beauty of stillness, as Zeami realized when he used for stillness the simile of snow piled in a silver bowl. Or one may prize such a bowl for the tarnished quality itself, its oldness and its imperfection, and this is the point at which we feel *sabi*.

We find a beautiful statement of *sabi* in *Essays in Idleness* (*Tsurezuregusa*) by Yoshida Kenkō (1283?–1352?) when he asks

Are we to look at cherry blossoms only in full bloom, the moon only when it is cloudless? To long for the moon while looking on the rain, to lower the blinds and be unaware of the passing of the spring—these are even more deeply moving. Branches about to blossom or gardens strewn with faded flowers are worthier of our admiration. . . . People commonly regret that the cherry blossoms scatter or that the moon sinks in the sky, and this is natural; but only an exceptionally insensitive man would say, "This branch and that branch have lost their blossoms. There is nothing worth seeing now."

The appreciation of the fallen flower, the moon obscured by the rain, and the withered bough are part of *sabi*. Unlike *yūgen* (to which, however, it is not opposed), *sabi* does not necessarily find in these things symbols of remoter entities, for in themselves they can give deep pleasure. *Sabi* also differs from the gentle melancholy of *aware*: when moved by a sense of *sabi*, one does not lament the fallen blossoms, one loves them. This quality is superbly captured in the haiku of Bashō (1644–1694). Although he lived after the medieval period, he was heir to its aesthetic traditions, and many of his haiku express a love for old and faded things.

> *Kiku no ka ya*   Scent of chrysanthemums—
> *Nara ni wa furuki*   In Nara, all the many
> *Hotoketachi*   Ancient Buddhas.

In this haiku, a correspondence is suggested between the impressions of *sabi* received through different senses, an example of the principle of synesthesia advocated by the Symbolist poets. The scent of chrysanthemums, astringent and somewhat musty, blends into the visual impression of statues in the old capital of Nara—dark, with flaking gold leaf and faded colors. The *sabi* found in the scent of the chrysanthemums and the ancient statues may also be contrasted with the Heian love of the fragrance of plum blossoms, recalling the memories of past springs, and for richly colored Buddhist images, or with the Western preference for the heavy perfume of the rose and the polish of white marble statues.

In *sabi*, art is valued as a refuge, a haven of tranquillity, as is not surprising when we read the early history of the tea ceremony, born amid the terrible warfare of the medieval period. Even when the warfare ceased in the seventeenth century, the need for spiritual peace continued to be met largely by the *sabi* aspects of beauty.

Yūgen can probably be understood only by a person of developed aesthetic perceptions who is spiritually capable of seeing beyond symbols to the eternal things adumbrated, but *sabi* has become very much a part of Japanese life. Like every other people, the Japanese love bright colors, but they are unusual in that they also like the old, the faded, and the underdecorated. When the Golden Pavilion was rebuilt in Kyoto, its dazzlingly gilded walls reflected in the temple pond brought delight to tourists, but the people of Kyoto said, "Wait ten years, wait until it acquires some *sabi.*" Indeed, this love for the old and unobtrusive may be the best defense the Japanese have against the harsher aspects of mechanization that are all too apparent today.

ZEAMI: ENTERING THE REALM OF *YŪGEN*

Yūgen is a term that is difficult either to define or to translate. It primarily means "mystery" and, however loosely used in criticism, generally retains something of the sense of a mysterious power or ability. The term was employed as a standard of criticism long before Zeami, but it was only with him that it attained its full meaning as the unifying aesthetic principle underlying all parts of the nō. In this section of a longer essay, he describes some of the ways of attaining *yūgen*. He concludes, however, by insisting that it is not enough for an actor to learn about *yūgen* from others—he must discover it through his own efforts.

The aesthetic quality of *yūgen* is considered the highest ideal of perfection in many arts. Particularly in the *nō*, *yūgen* can be regarded as the highest principle. However, although the quality of *yūgen* is manifested in performance and audiences give it high appreciation, there are very few actors who in fact possess that quality. This is because they have never had a taste of the real *yūgen* themselves. So it is that few actors have entered this world.

What kind of realm is represented by what is termed *yūgen*? For example, if we take the general appearance of the world and observe the various sorts of people who live there, it might be said that *yūgen* is best represented in the character of the nobility, whose deportment is of such a high quality and who receive the affection and respect not given to others in society. If such is the case, then their dignified and mild appearance represents the essence of *yūgen*. Therefore, the stage appearance of *yūgen* is best indicated by their refined and elegant carriage. If an actor examines closely the nobility's beautiful way of speaking and studies the words and habitual means of expression that such elevated persons use, even to observing their tasteful choice of language when saying the smallest things, such can be taken to represent the *yūgen* of speech. In the case of the chant, when the melody flows smoothly and naturally on the ear and sounds suitably mild and calm, this quality can be said to represent the *yūgen* of music. In the case of the dance, if the actor studies until he is truly fluent, so that his appearance on stage will be sympathetic and his carriage both unostentatious and moving to those who observe him, he will surely manifest the *yūgen* of the dance. When he is acting a part, if he makes his appearance beautiful in the Three Role Types, he will have achieved *yūgen* in his performance. Again, when presenting a role of fearsome appearance, a demon's role for example, even should the actor use a rough manner to a certain extent, he must not forget to preserve a graceful appearance, and he must remember the principles of "what is felt in the heart is ten"[4] and "violent body movements, gentle foot movements," so that his stage appearance will remain elegant. Thus he may manifest the *yūgen* of a demon's role.

An actor must come to grasp those various types of *yūgen* and absorb them within himself; for no matter what kind of role he may assume, he must never separate himself from the virtue of *yūgen*. No matter what the role—whether the character be of high or low rank, a man, a woman, a priest or lay person, a farmer or country person, even a beggar or an outcast—it should seem as though each were holding a branch of flowers in his hand. In this one respect they exhibit the same appeal, despite whatever differences they may show in their social positions. This flower represents the beauty of their stance in the *nō*; and the ability to reveal this kind of stance in performance represents, of course, its spirit. In order to study the *yūgen* of words, the actor must study the art of composing poetry; and to study the *yūgen* of physical appearance, he must study the aesthetic qualities of elegant costume, so that, in every aspect of his art, no matter how the role may change that the actor is playing, he will always maintain one aspect in his performance that shows *yūgen*. Such it is to know the seed of *yūgen*.

However, it may well happen that an actor will put such an importance on his impersonation of the particulars of his role, regarding this aspect of his performance as the highest of his art, that he will neglect to maintain the beauty of the stance he has properly assumed. Thus he will fail to enter the world of *yūgen*. And if he does not enter into the world of *yūgen*, he cannot approach the level of Highest Fruition. And unless he reaches this highest level of accomplishment, he will never be recognized as a great actor. There are indeed few masters who have attained those heights. Thus an actor must rehearse with the utmost diligence on this critical point of the representation of *yūgen*.

This Highest Fruition of an actor represents precisely the appearance of this deeply beautiful posture. I cannot repeat too often that an actor must rehearse with the need for the proper preparation of his body always in mind. Thus it is of crucial importance that, beginning with the Two Basic Arts down to the specifics of any role that may be played, the stance of the actor be attractive so as to represent this Highest Fruition in every circumstance. If the actor's posture is unattractive, his art will invariably appear vulgar. In any case, whatever ges-

---

4. As explained elsewhere in Zeami's writings, the superior actor does not expend all his energy, so that "what is felt in the heart is ten, what appears in the movement is seven" (i.e., only seven-tenths of what is thought or felt).

tures may be seen or music may be heard, however great the variety, the fact that the actor's stance is beautifully assumed represents the true attainment of *yūgen*. An actor may be said to have entered the world of *yūgen* when he has of his own accord studied these principles and made himself master of them. If an actor does not work to fulfill them and thinks that, without mastering every aspect of his art, he can still try to attain this *yūgen*, he will, in fact, never know it during his entire lifetime.

[Adapted from Rimer and Yamazaki, *On the Art of the Nō Drama*, pp. 92–95]

CONNECTING THE ARTS THROUGH ONE INTENSITY OF MIND

The influence of Buddhism, and especially Zen, is particularly apparent in the "mind-lessness" that transcends mind, the moments of "doing nothing" that excite greater interest than those of deliberate action, and the mind that controls all the powers.

It is often commented on by audiences that "many times a performance is effective when the actor does nothing." Such an accomplishment results from the actor's greatest, most secret skill. From the techniques involved in the Two Basic Arts down to all the gestures and the various kinds of Role Playing, all such skills are based on the abilities found in the actor's body. Thus to speak of an actor "doing nothing" actually signifies that interval which exists between two physical actions. When one examines why this interval "when nothing happens" may seem so fascinating, it is surely because of the fact that, at the bottom, the artist never relaxes his inner tension. At the moment when the dance has stopped, or the chant has ceased, or indeed at any of those intervals that can occur during the performance of a role, or, indeed, during any pause or interval, the actor must never abandon his concentration but must keep his consciousness of that inner tension. It is this sense of inner concentration that manifests itself to the audience and makes the moment enjoyable.

However, it is wrong to allow an audience to observe the actor's inner state of control directly. If the spectators manage to witness this, such concentration will merely become another ordinary skill or action, and the feeling in the audience that "nothing is happening" will disappear.

The actor must rise to a selfless level of art, imbued with a concentration that transcends his own consciousness, so that he can bind together the moments before and after that instant when "nothing happens." Such a process constitutes that inner force that can be termed "connecting all the arts through one intensity of mind."

"Indeed, when we come to face death, our life might be likened to a puppet on a cart [decorated for a great festival]. As soon as one string is cut, the creature crumbles and fades."[5] Such is the image given of the existence of man, caught in the perpetual flow of life and death. This constructed puppet, on a cart, shows various aspects of himself but cannot come to life of itself. It represents a deed performed by moving strings. At the moment when the strings are cut, the figure falls and crumbles. *Sarugaku* too is an art that makes use of just such artifice. What supports these illusions and gives them life is the intensity of mind of the actor. Yet the existence of this intensity must not be shown directly to the audience. Should they see it, it would be as though they could see the strings of a puppet. Let me repeat again: the actor must make his spirit the strings, and without letting his audience become aware of them, he will draw together the forces of his art. In that way, true life will reside in his *nō*.

In general, such attitudes need not be limited to the moments involved in actual performance. Morning and night alike, and in all the activities of daily life, an actor must never abandon his concentration, and he must retain his resolve. Thus, if without ever slackening, he manages to increase his skills, his art of the *nō* will grow ever greater. This particular point represents one of the most secret of all the teachings concerning our art. However, in actual rehearsal, there must be within this concentration some variations of tension and relaxation.

[Rimer and Yamazaki, *On the Art of the Nō Drama*, pp. 96–98]

THE NINE STAGES OF THE NŌ IN ORDER

The *Nine Stages* is a summary and systematization of Zeami's aesthetic principles found in his various other writings. It appears to be a late work and, of all his works of aesthetic criticism, is the most difficult to understand, partly because of the unexplained technical terms and partly because of its Zen form of expression. As the leading authority on the work, Nosé Asaji, wrote,

In order to understand this work properly one must have had considerable experience with Zen practices and have discovered how to decipher the Zen riddles (*kōan*). One must have also studied Zeami's aesthetic criticism thoroughly. Unless this work is approached with the wisdom gained from both aspects of it, it will not be possible to give any definitive explanation of the text.

Nevertheless, thanks mainly to Nosé's work, we can now understand much of what Zeami was seeking to express in his deliberately elusive manner.

Most of the sentences or phrases used to characterize the different stages of the nō

---

5. A saying attributed to a priest of the Rinzai sect of Zen Buddhism in Japan, Gettan Sōkō (1316?–1389).

are taken from poems written by Japanese Zen monks, and the use of such symbols itself is a typical Zen device. But the general structure, synthetic character, and much of the terminology of this essay are reminiscent of Tendai and Shingon doctrine, and Daoist and Confucian works are also quoted.

The Higher Three Stages

1. The flower of the miraculous
   "At midnight in Silla the sun is bright."[6]
   The miraculous transcends the power of speech and is where the workings of the mind are defeated. And does "the sun at midnight" lie within the realm of speech? Thus, in the art of the *nō*, before the *yūgen* of a master actor all praise fails, admiration transcends the comprehension of the mind, and all attempts at classification and grading are made impossible. The art which excites such a reaction on the part of the audience may be called the flower of the miraculous.
2. The flower of supreme profundity
   "Snow covers the thousand mountains—why does one lonely peak remain unwhitened?"
   A man of old once said, "Mount Fuji is so high that the snow never melts." A Chinese disagreed, saying, "Mount Fuji is so deep. . . ."[7] What is extremely high is deep. Height has limits but depth is not to be measured. Thus the profound mystery of a landscape in which a solitary peak stands unwhitened amidst a thousand snow-covered mountains may represent the art of supreme profundity.
3. The flower of stillness
   "Snow piled in a silver bowl."
   When snow is piled in a silver bowl, the purity of its white light appears lambent indeed. May this not represent the flower of stillness?

The Middle Three Stages

1. The flower of truth
   "The sun sinks in the bright mist, the myriad mountains are crimson."

---

6. From a Chinese Zen work also paraphrased in Japan by Musō Kokushi. The reason for mentioning Silla (Korea) here is uncertain, but since Korea is east of China, it may signify that the sun is already rising there while it is still night in China—a typical device in Daoism and Zen to show that nothing is impossible but only appears so due to limitations of time and place of the individual.

7. Both the "man of old" and the Chinese are as yet unidentified. The meaning is apparently that height can be measured but depth cannot.

A distant view of hills and mountains bathed in the light of the sun in a cloudless sky represents the flower of truth. It is superior to the art of versatility and exactness and is already a first step towards the acquisition of the flowers of the art.

2. The art of versatility and exactness

"To tell everything—of the nature of the clouds on the mountains, of moonlight on the sea."

To describe completely the nature of clouds on the mountains and of the moonlight on the sea, of the whole expanse of green mountains that fills the eyes, this is indeed desirable in acquiring the art of versatility and exactness. Here is the dividing point from which one may go upward or downward.

3. The art of untutored beauty

"The Way of ways is not the usual way."[8]

One may learn of the Way of ways by traveling along the usual way. This means that the display of beauty should begin at the stage of the beginner. Thus the art of untutored beauty is considered the introduction to the mastery of the nine stages.

The Lower Three Stages

1. The art of strength and delicacy

"The metal hammer flashes as it moves, the glint of the precious sword is cold."

The movement of the metal hammer represents the art of strong action. The cold glint of the precious sword suggests the unadorned style of singing and dancing. It will stand up to detailed observation.

2. The art of strength and crudity

"Three days after its birth the tiger is disposed to devour an ox."

That the tiger cub only three days after its birth has such audacity shows its strength; but to devour an ox is crude.

3. The art of crudity and inexactness

"The squirrel's five talents."

Confucius said,[9] "The squirrel can do five things. He can climb a tree, swim in the water, dig a hole, jump and run: all of these are within its capacities but it does none well." When art lacks delicacy it becomes crude and inexact.

---

8. Paraphrased from the opening of the *Laozi*, but the meaning given by Zeami to the phrase is not the one generally accepted.

9. Said by Xunzi and not Confucius.

In the attainment of art through the nine stages, the actor begins with the middle group, follows with the upper group, and finally learns the lower three. When the beginner first enters the art of the *nō*, he practices the various elements of dancing and singing. This represents the stage of untutored beauty. As the result of persistent training, his untutored style will develop into greater artistry, constantly improving until, before he is aware of it, it reaches the stage of versatility and exactness. At this stage if the actor's training is comprehensive and he expands his art in versatility and magnitude until he attains full competence, he will be at the stage of the flower of truth. The above are the stages from the learning of the Two Disciplines to the master of the Three Roles.

Next the actor progresses to the stage of calm and the flower that arouses admiration. It is the point where it becomes apparent whether or not he has realized the flower of the art. From this height the actor can examine with insight the preceding stages. He occupies a place of high achievement in the art of calm and the realization of the flower. This stage is thus called the flower of stillness.

Rising still higher, the actor achieves the ultimate degree of *yūgen* in his performance and reveals a degree of artistry which is of that middle ground where being and nonbeing meet.[10] This is the flower of supreme profundity.

Above this stage, words fail before the revelation of the absolute miracle of the actor's interpretation. This is the flower of the miraculous. It is the end of the road to the higher mysteries of the art.

It should be noted that the origin of all these stages of the art may be found in the art of versatility and exactness. It is the foundation of the art of the *nō*, for it is the point where are displayed the breadth and the detail of performance which are the seeds of the flowers of the highest forms of the art. The stage of versatility and exactness is also the dividing line where is determined the actor's future. If he succeeds here in obtaining the flower of the art, he will rise to the flower of truth; otherwise he will sink to the lower three stages.

The lower three stages are the turbulent waters of the *nō*. They are easily understood and it is no special problem to learn them. It may happen, however, that an actor who has gone from the middle three stages to the upper three stages, having mastered the art of calmness and the flower of the miraculous, will purposely descend and indulge in the lower three stages.[11] Then the special qualities of these stages will be blended with his art. However, many of the excellent actors of the past who had mounted to the upper three stages of the

---

10. Expression used in Tendai philosophy of a region "which is not being and not nonbeing and is being and nonbeing."

11. Suggested by the Mahāyāna doctrine of the bodhisattva who voluntarily leaves the highest rank to go down to save those at the bottom.

art refused to descend to the lower three. They were like the elephant of the story who refused to follow in the tracks of a rabbit. There has been only one instance of an actor who mastered all the stages—the middle, then the upper, and then the lower: this was the art of my late father.[12] Many of the heads of theaters have been trained only up to the art of versatility and exactness, without having risen to the flower of truth, have descended to the lower three stages, thus failing in the end to achieve success. Nowadays there are even actors who begin their training with the lower three stages and perform with such a background. This is not the proper order. It is therefore no wonder that many actors fail even to enter the nine stages.

There are three ways of entering the lower three stages. In the case of a great master who has entered the art by the way of the middle stages, ascended to the upper stages of the art, and then descended to the lower stages, it is quite possible to give a superb performance even within the lower stages. Actors who have dropped to the lower stages from the level of versatility and exactness will be capable only of parts which call for strength with delicacy and crudity. Those actors who have wilfully entered the art from the lower three stages have neither art nor fame and cannot be said even to be within the nine stages. Although they have taken the lower three stages as their goal, they fail even in this, to say nothing of reading the middle three stages.

[Nosé, *Zeami jūroku bushū hyōshaku*, I, pp. 547–583]

THE TRUE PATH TO THE FLOWER (*SHIKADŌ SHO*)

In this piece, Zeami sets forth the criteria for mastering the performance of the nō. "Flower" here signifies "beauty" or "perfection," a meaning that derives from the use of the Lotus as a symbol of supreme truth or perfection in Buddhism, especially as represented in the Lotus (Hokke) and Flower Wreath (Kegon) Sūtras.

Zeami was chiefly instrumental in defining and shaping the nō drama, and his views reflect the synthetic character of the art form that he and his father, Kan'ami, helped develop. In it, elements from earlier dance-drama forms, especially shrine and folk dances, were combined to produce an art of the greatest refinement and sophistication. Much of the nō's subtlety and striking simplicity reveal the influences of Shinto and Zen. But its extreme stylization, precision, and gorgeous costuming also reveal the deep and lasting influence of Esoteric Buddhism on Japanese art, although today this is less generally appreciated. The elaborate symbolism, conventionalized movements, and stylized gestures of the nō relate it closely to the mandala, that typical expression of the esoteric teaching in the field of painting, which, like the nō, is not accessible to those who are ignorant of the conventions and mystic rituals that have

---

12. Kan'ami (1333–1384), the first great master of the nō.

surrounded these arts from the beginning. To them, Esoteric Buddhism has contributed not so much the conventions themselves as the essential concern for proper form in the representation of sacred mysteries and the performance of symbolic acts. Through the exercise of all one's faculties, not just one's intellect, Esoteric Buddhism has made the widest use of all the riches of the natural world to enhance the efficacy of its secret formulas and thus achieve the unity of matter and spirit in the perfection of Buddhahood. To accomplish this was a great art, requiring perfect mastery. Zeami's conception of mastery in the nō, his insistence on prolonged training in orthodox disciplines and in imitation of one's teacher, as well as his neat numerical formulations and philosophical categories all attest to the formative influence of this earlier tradition. Zeami served his apprenticeship in Nara, the stronghold of traditional Buddhism, which left its seal on the fundamentals of his art. Only later in the Ashikaga court at Kyoto did he find in Zen the final quickening insight that brought these dramatic elements into sharp focus and raised his mature art to the threshold of perfect ease and freedom.

1. Two Basic Arts, Three Role Types

There are various important elements to be mastered in our art. Among them, an actor who is beginning his training must not overlook the Two Basic Arts and Three Role types. By the Two Basic Arts, I mean dancing and chanting. By the Three Role Types, I refer to the human forms that constitute the basis of role impersonation [an old person, a woman, a warrior].

A beginning actor must follow his teacher and study dancing and chanting as thoroughly as possible. From the ages of ten to seventeen, however, it is necessary to study the Three Role Types. The young actor may perform any sort of role using his natural, childlike appearance. He need not wear a mask, nor attempt any actual role playing; even if he does assume various roles in name only, he should retain his own youthful appearance. In the case of *bugaku* dances as well, the same procedure should be followed — in such dances as *ryōō* and *nasori*,[13] the child should perform them in name only, preserve his natural appearance and wear no mask. Following such a method of avoiding any banality will insure that, at a later stage in the development of the actor's art, his basis for creating *yūgen* will be established. In *The Great Learning*, it says that "it cannot be, when the root is neglected, that what should spring from it will be well ordered."[14]

---

13. *Ryōō* and *nasori* are two ancient court dances in which masks are employed. Both are derived from Chinese models. For details, see Inoura, *A History of Japanese Theater I*, and Harich-Schneider, *A History of Japanese Music*.

14. The quotation, slightly altered in Zeami's text, occurs in *The Great Learning* (*Daxue*). See de Bary and Bloom, eds., *Sources of Chinese Tradition*, vol. 1, chap. 10.

From the time that an actor comes of age and his appearance becomes that of a fully grown man, he can wear a mask and should begin to change his appearance in order to perform in various roles. Although he may perform a wide variety of parts, his only successful beginning must lie in his study of the Three Role Types if he wishes to succeed in creating an acting style of the Highest Fruition. These three are: the old person, the woman, and the warrior. An actor must master the study of what is required for the imitation of an old man, a woman, and a man of strength. Then, adding to this what he has already learned as a youth concerning the Two Basic Arts of chanting and dancing, he can create the specifics of any particular role; if he can manage this, no other method of study will be required.

As for the various other kinds of roles, all of them grow naturally out of the Two Basic Arts and the Three Role Types, and therefore the actor will have them at hand. The style of acting appropriate to a quiet and solemn god is adapted from the style of the old man; roles requiring great taste and elegance come naturally from the style of women's roles, and roles requiring powerful body movements and foot stamping grow from warrior roles. Therefore, whatever the actor's artistic intentions, he will be able to find a means to manifest them in his performance. Then too, even if he does show some shortcomings in his artistic abilities and cannot produce the technique appropriate to certain roles, his mastery of the Two Basic Arts and Three Role Types, if he has attained it, will still make him a superior actor. In sum, the Two Basic Arts and Three Role Types provide the proper means to achieve the correct style in acting.

Observing the method of training used for *sarugaku* players these days, however, it seems clear that the actor's basic training does not begin with the Two Basic Arts and Three Role Types; rather, all kinds of roles are studied, as well as techniques not central to our art. Thus the actor's style does not seem assured, and his performances are insecure and lack interest. Indeed, it seems that artists of the first rank are no longer performing. To repeat again, those who do not begin their training with the Two Basic Arts and Three Role Types will only succeed in committing themselves to the creation of mere scattered elements in their Role Playing, trees and leaves without any trunk. Yet the elegant beauty of the child performer does remain in the Three Role Types of the mature performer, and the skill arising from a mastery of the Three Role Types can permit the actor to manifest his own vision, no matter what the play.

2. An Art That Remains External

In terms of the *nō*, art that remains External is to be despised. This point must be fully understood. First, if an actor is born with the proper natural character, and gifted with talent, he can surely become a master. As he polishes and practices his art, his natural abilities will manifest themselves of their own accord.

In terms of dancing and chanting, an actor has not yet achieved a fluent mastery at the stage when he is still imitating what he has learned from his teacher. On the surface, the imitation may be effective, but he will not yet have assimilated the art unto himself, his artistic powers will be insufficient, and his real skill in *nō* will not increase—such is the actor who remains at the level of Externals. A real master is one who imitates his teacher well, shows discernment, assimilates his art, absorbs his art into his mind and in his body, and so arrives at a level of Perfect Fluency through a mastery of his art. A performance by such an actor will show real life. An actor who adds strength to his natural abilities through constant practice and rehearsal, understands quickly and puts himself totally into the object of his role is one who can truly be said to have achieved Internalization. To repeat again, a performer must truly grasp the distinction between true mastery and its opposite. "To do something is not hard; but to do it well is very difficult indeed."[15]

3. Perfect Freedom

It happens in our art that an actor who has mastered every secret and has attained the pinnacle of artistic maturity does occasionally perform in an unorthodox manner, and young actors may attempt to copy this style of performance. Yet a style that grows out of true mastery is no simple matter to imitate. Why should they try to do so?

The art that achieves Perfect Freedom requires thorough practice of the elements of the *nō* appropriate to the actor's whole career, from his beginnings as a young actor through his period of full maturity; the actor must assemble all these elements, remove their impurities, and achieve self-mastery. Such attainments are revealed in performance through the force of the actor's skills. The actor can accomplish this by mixing in his performance some of the impure elements that in years past he has learned to exclude from his art through training and practice. It may be asked why a skillful player should introduce such elements of improper style into his performance. Certainly, such means constitute a strategy available only to the most experienced actors. Generally, all that remains for such actors are the pure and orthodox techniques. As there are no novel elements in a perfect performance, then on those occasions when the audience has become accustomed to an actor's art, the actor who is truly a master may include something unorthodox, in order to introduce again the element of novelty. Thus, in this manner, bad art can indirectly serve the cause of good art. The power of the artist's personality can thus transform impurity into purity, and so make such art exciting for his audiences.

---

15. Zeami's text attributes the text to Mencius, where it does not appear. A similar phrase occurs in the *Classic of Documents* (*Shujing*) and was quoted and paraphrased in a variety of texts in Japan before and during Zeami's time.

Beginning actors, of course, only see this technique as out of the ordinary and think of it as something that can be imitated; but when they do so, since their own technique is naturally insufficient, the mixing in of these unusual elements in an art based on such immature foundations is like adding brushwood to the fire of error. Such young actors doubtlessly believe that Perfect Freedom is a matter of mere technique, rather than something that grows out of the artistic maturity of the master actor. This is a matter that must be thoroughly considered. The master actor can use such techniques with the knowledge that they are impure; but insofar as the novice mistakes them for true art and imitates them, these two ways of thinking will remain as different as black and white. And without a long development of self-mastery, how can a beginner hope to achieve a level of Perfect Freedom? Thus, when a beginner tries to imitate an actor who has reached a level of true proficiency, he will merely copy what is incorrect and will never improve. As is written in Mencius, "to achieve what one wants by following one's own desires, rather than following the Way, is like climbing a tree to find a fish, no great harm is done. But it is a great loss to follow one's will rather than the Way."[16]

The art of an actor who has attained the highest level, by turning bad art into good, will allow him to manifest his precise meaning. A clumsy actor does not have the ability to do this. An unskilled actor, performing with the amount of artistic skill he has available to him, thinks to emulate the strength of a performance that lies beyond him. He will fail absolutely. This situation is just the same as [the saying of Mencius that] it is dangerous to try to accomplish something by using merely the means you yourself choose. Thus, if a young actor wishes to copy something beyond his ability and yet which lies within the realm of true art, there will be no great harm done even if he fails in his attempt. This is merely to climb a tree to try to find a fish. To repeat again, one must not copy the performance of an actor who has attained the highest mastery and who performs in an unorthodox fashion. Such a practice serves only as a means to seek out failure. Take careful note of this.

Rather, a beginner must follow his teacher, ask concerning what he cannot grasp, and make every effort to achieve an understanding appropriate to the level of his own art. And, even though he sees the art of one who has mastered its secrets, he must first strive himself in order to master the fundamental elements of the Two Basic Arts and the Three Role Types. As the Lotus Sutra says, "be careful of those who say that they have attained what they have not."[17]

---

16. For this passage in context, see Dobson, Mencius, p. 12.

17. A slightly altered version of a phrase from the Lotus Sūtra, bk. II. For the passage in context, see Watson, trans., The Lotus Sūtra, p. 30.

4. Skin, Flesh, and Bone

In the performance of *nō* there are three basic elements: Skin, Flesh, and Bone. The three are almost never found together in the same actor. In the art of calligraphy, it is said that the three have never been found together except in the work of Kūkai.

When it comes to explaining the elements of Skin, Flesh, and Bone in terms of the *nō*, then what can be described as Bone represents that exceptional artistic strength that a gifted actor shows naturally in his performance and which comes to him of itself through his inborn ability. Flesh can doubtless be defined as that element visible in a performance that arises from the power of the skills of the actor that he has obtained by his mastering of the Two Basic Arts of chant and dance. Skin, on the other hand, may be explained as a manner of ease and beauty in performance that can be obtained when the other two elements are thoroughly perfected. To put it another way: when considering the art that comes from Sight, the art that comes from Sound, and the art that comes from the Heart, it can be said that Sight should be equated with Skin, Sound with Flesh, and the Heart to the Bone. Within the category of the chant itself, these three qualities can be seen to exist. The beauty of the voice of the actor represents the Skin, the interest of the melody is the Flesh, and the techniques of breathing employed represent the Bone. These are matters to be pondered over with great care.

On this point, when I look at the artists who are performing today, I find that not only are there no artists who can truly manifest these three principles in performance, but indeed there are none who even know that such conceptions exist. My father taught me such things privately, and I have taken his lessons to heart. From what one can observe in the performances of actors these days, they are only able to manage certain elements of Skin. And yet such is not the true Skin [which has behind it the Flesh and the Bone]. It is only the Skin that they attempt to imitate. Such actors have not gained a fluent mastery.

Then again, even if an actor should manage to possess all three of these qualities, there is still more that he must understand. Even if he possesses them (Bone, his naturally inherited talent; Flesh, his acquired skills in chant and dance; and Skin, the elegance of his outward appearance on stage), these three have, of themselves, no greater significance than each of these individual qualities may possess. It is difficult to describe the qualities of an actor who has truly fused them together. To speak of such a level of achievement involves, for example, a true mastery of those artistic principles that have already reached a high degree of perfection, to a level where the artist moves beyond his means of expression to produce a performance of profound ease. The spectators, witnessing his performance, will be caught up in his mastery and will forget themselves; only afterward will they reflect on the performance, realizing that they found no weak spots whatsoever. Such, for the audience, represents the sensation of having seen an actor whose years of training have added to the Bone of his natural skills. Secondly, they will find in him one whose art, no matter how often it is observed, will seem inexhaustible. Such is the effect of the Flesh of an artist who exhibits the mastery of the skills that are highly developed to the point of rare mastery. Thirdly, the audience will always find the actor elegant. This quality derives from his attainment of the skills represented by Skin. When the actor himself can naturally reflect those emotions felt in mutuality with the audience, it can be said that he has truly blended Skin, Flesh, and Bone.

5. Substance and Function

One must know the elements of Substance and Function in the nō. If Substance can be compared to a flower, then Function can be compared to its odor. The moon and its light make a similar comparison. If the concept of Substance is fully understood, then the nature of Function will be naturally comprehensible of itself.

When it comes to observing the nō, those who truly understand the art watch it with the spirit, while those who do not, merely watch it with their eyes. To see with the spirit is to grasp the Substance; to see with the eyes is merely to observe the Function. Thus it is that beginning actors merely grasp the Function and try to imitate that. Although they do not understand the real principle of Function [i.e., the fact that it derives from Substance], they attempt to copy. Yet Function cannot be imitated. Those who truly understand the nō, since they grasp it with their spirit, are able to imitate its Substance. Thus in a performance, Function comes of itself from a successful attempt to assimilate Substance. Yet those who do not understand this principle try to master Function and imitate it as a principle of their art; they do not realize that as they do so they rob Function of its proper role. And since Function can never become Substance, the art of nō therefore becomes broken and confused, possessing neither Substance nor Function. Under such circumstances, there is no proper path for the nō, and our art has no meaning.

Substance and Function may seem to represent two independent elements. But in fact, without Substance there can be no Function. Therefore, there are no means with which to imitate it directly [as it cannot exist independently]. Thus it is foolish for an actor, thinking that there is something there to be copied, to attempt to imitate it. One must understand that it is precisely by attempting to reproduce Substance that the actor can manage to create naturally the appropriate Function. To repeat again, if one truly comes to understand the principle that the imitation of Function cannot become an end in itself, he will evolve into an actor able to grasp this crucial distinction between the two. It has been said that "everyone wishes to resemble a master actor, yet no one should try to imitate him."[18] Here, imitation refers to Function, resemblance to Substance.

In previous times, such attention was not given to these various theoretical terms. Among those performing before, in the old style, however, there were quite a few who managed of themselves to gain high artistic power. At that time, the nobility and the people of high rank took note only of what was good in various performances, but they did not make it a point to observe the defects. These days, however, their eyes are highly skilled and so audiences have come to observe even the slightest fault, so that if a presentation is not as elegant as a polished gem or a bouquet of flowers, it cannot meet the expectations of a cultured group of spectators. Therefore, there are few artists who are considered to have attained the highest level of success. Because the *nō* is entering into a period of decline, I am concerned that if our training loses its rigor, our art will cease to be, and it is for this reason that I have written here an outline of my own understanding of our art. As for the rest, it will depend on the intelligence and artistic skills of the individual actor and should be transmitted directly through oral teaching.

Ōe 27, [1420] the Sixth Month Zeami

[Rimer and Masakazu, *On the Art of the Nō Drama*, pp. 64–73]

CONVERSATIONS WITH SHŌTETSU

19. Of recent poems on the topic "Snow on the Mountains at Dusk," I think this one of mine reads well:

Watarikane	Hesitant to cross,
Kumo mo yūbe o	Even the clouds feel their way along,
Nao tadoru	Searching the dusk—
Ato naki yuki no	Where the steep path over the peaks
Mine no kakehashi.	Lies beneath the trackless snow.[19]

Now it is unlikely that the clouds should be unable to cross the trackless snow in actuality, but as it is the way in poetry to attribute feelings to insentient things,[20] I have treated the clouds as if deliberately crossing the mountains at morning and evening. In the brightness of the snow piled up deep and white, they cannot tell that evening has come, making it seem as if even they are

---

18. Doubtless an expression current at the time. No source has been located.

19. *Sōkonshū* 3986.

20. "Insentient things" is the translation of *mushin naru mono*, "things without human feeling," particularly animals and natural phenomena, which were often personified in poems.

feeling their way and hesitating to cross the peaks. Such might be one's impression on gazing out at the gathering dusk on mountains deep in snow and seeing the clouds slowly drifting across. Attributing feelings to the clouds in this way makes plausible the poetic idea that they are hesitating to cross. Also, since I say there is no sign of human footprints among the drifts, one can imagine that even the clouds have difficulty in getting across. Now, one might think that it would have been better if I had said, "There are no tracks upon the snow" (*yuki ni ato naki*), but that would have been unsuitable. The phrase "the trackless snow" has a good deal more poetic effect for the reason that since there are no such things as footprints left by clouds, my "feel their way along . . . the trackless snow" also suggests that the clouds leave no tracks. So it is more elegant to have said "the trackless snow" instead of "there are no tracks upon the snow."

Thus it is that the styles of "moving clouds" and "swirling snow"[21] — the snow blown about by the wind, or the spring haze drifting past the cherry blossoms — have an ineffable charm and elegance. A poem that has this indescribable something hovering over it is a superior poem. Such a poem has been compared to a beautiful lady who grieves over something but does so in silence. To say nothing despite one's sadness is impressive. The same thing happens when a little child of two or three brings something to a person, saying, "This, this" — knowing what it wants to say but unable to express itself clearly. The best poems are those that leave something unsaid.

20. There are poems that leave out whole lines of meaning. Narihira's[22] poem

Tsuki ya aranu	Is this not the moon?
Haru ya mukashi no	And is this not the springtime,
Haru naranu	The springtime of old?
Waga mi hitotsu wa	Only this body of mine
Moto no mi ni shite.	The same body as before.

seems incomprehensible unless one understands the context. The poem was composed when, thinking of his love affair with the Nijō empress the previous year, he went to the western wing of her palace. What it means is, "Is the moon not there? Is the spring not the same spring as ever? I alone am the same as I always was, but tonight the one I used to meet here is gone." So it is that in the text where it says of Narihira's poetry that it "tries to express too much content in too few words, resembling a faded flower with a lingering fragrance," this

---

21. The styles of "moving clouds" (*kōun*) and "swirling snow" (*kaisetsu*) are treated as subcategories of *yūgen* in a number of earlier critical works, particularly in those mistakenly attributed to Teika in Shōtetsu's day.

22. Ariwara no Narihira (d. 880), one of the "Six Poetic Immortals" (*rokkasen*).

poem is given as an example.[23] Narihira deliberately left out the line, "Tonight the one I used to meet here is gone" (*koyoi aitaru hito koso nakere*). Yet for this very reason the poem is also interesting.

JAKUREN'S[24] POEM

Uramiwabi	Worn out with bitterness
Mataji ima wa no	I vow to have an end of it
Mi naredomo	and wait no longer—
Omoinarenishi	And yet there is the evening sky
Yūgure no sora.	That always made me think of him.

is incomplete. The poem implies the thought, "So then, what can I do about the sky at evening?" Thus it has left out the line, "So then, what can I do?" (*sate ika ni sen*).

21. This poem of mine on the topic "Cicadas in Late Summer" might be said to be similar to the preceding ones:

Mori no ha mo	In the forest grove
Aki ni ya awan	The leaves, too, must have their autumn:
Naku semi no	Just like the crying cicadas
Kozue no tsuyu no	Whose fragile husks must vanish
Mi o kaenu tote.	Like the dew upon the branches.

The lines "In the forest grove / The leaves, too, must have their autumn" mean that although the leaves may now have spread forth in their lush green, when autumn comes it will be their time to fall; by the lines, "Just like the crying cicadas / Whose fragile husks must vanish / Like the dew upon the branches," I mean that although the cicadas have shed their shells and transformed themselves, hope is vain, since in autumn they must inevitably die and become nothing. Thus I suggested the lines "Just because they have changed their shells, does that mean they have more time to live? It is futile to hope." The word "too" in the line "The leaves, too, must have their autumn" is very important. Some people will be able to comprehend the poem just on the basis of this one word, "too." I had originally thought to use the word in the last two lines, as in *tsuyu no / Mi o kaenu tomo*, but since I had already used it in the

---

23. The characterization of Narihira comes from the preface to *Kokinshū*, by Ki no Tsurayuki (872?–945). The poems—among them Narihira's given as illustrations of Tsurayuki's criticisms— were added later, anonymously.

24. Lay name Fujiwara no Sadanaga (d. 1202). He took the tonsure in 1172 after beginning a career in the official ranks but continued to participate actively in the literary life of the court.

first part of the poem, I decided to write "*kaenu tote*" instead—though it might be easier to understand if it were *tomo* instead of *tote*.[25]

22. On the topic "Praying for Love," the poem:

Yūshide mo	Even the prayer strips
Ware ni nabikanu	Refuse to incline toward me
Tsuyu zo chiru	As dewdrops scatter.
Ta ga negigoto no	Whose orisons so stir the autumn wind,
Sue no akikaze.	Presaging the death of our love?

The lines "Whose orisons so stir the autumn wind, / Presaging the death of our love?" are somewhat obscure and may be a bit difficult to understand. They must mean that the beloved, knowing that the speaker is praying, is also making his own prayers to the gods. If the wind fails to blow toward her the sacred strips that the speaker has offered to the gods, and if the dew scatters in the wrong direction, then the beloved must be praying that they not meet again—which is what is meant by the lines, "Whose orisons so stir the autumn wind / Presaging the death of our love?" The word "orisons" means the same as "prayers."

Now, a person might object to this kind of expression, saying that he would write instead, "Can it be that he has prayed / Never to see me any more?" (*Ware ni awaji to / Hito ya inorishi*) and protesting that there is no point in putting it into such difficult language. This may be very true, of course, but let such critics look at the collected poems of Teika. There is not a single flat verse[26] to be found among them. On the other hand, this simple poem by Tameko[27] works very well:

Kazu naranu	The cruel man
Misogi wa kami mo	Must have prayed first to the gods,
Uke so to ya	Saying, "No—forebear!
Tsurenaki hito no	Pay no heed to the devotions
Mazu inoriken.	Of one of so little account."[28]

[Brower and Carter, *Conversations with Shōtetsu*, pp. 71–75]

---

25. In other words, he used *tote* instead of *tomo* because he had already ended a line with *mo* and wanted to avoid an unpleasant rhyme.

26. "Flat verse" is the translation of *tada mahira naru uta*, "dull or ordinary verse." Shōtetsu's point seems to be that poetic language should not be as straightforward as prose.

27. Kyōgoku Tameko (d. 1316?), elder sister of Tamekane and a major poet in the court of Retired Emperor Fushimi.

28. *Shoku GSIS* 787 (Love) Headnote: "Praying Not to Meet a Lover."

KAMO NO CHŌMEI: CONCERNING MYSTERIOUS BEAUTY

The following is in answer to a question concerning mysterious depth (*yūgen*):

Every poetic style is difficult to master. Even the old collections of oral traditions and guides to composition only explain such difficulties as it is possible to resolve by taking someone by the hand and leading him along, as it were, and when it comes to poetic effects we find nothing at all precise. This is all the more true of the style of mystery and depth, whose very name is enough to confound one. Since I do not understand it at all well myself, I am at a loss as to how to describe it in any satisfactory manner, but according to the views of those who have developed the skill necessary to penetrate its mysteries, the qualities deemed essential to the style are overtones that do not appear in the words alone and an atmosphere that is not visible in the configuration of the poem. When both conception and diction are full of charm, these other virtues will be present of themselves. On an autumn evening, for example, there is no color in the sky nor any sound, yet although we cannot give any definite reason for it, we are somehow moved to tears. The average person lacking in sensibility finds nothing at all impressive in such a sight—he admires only the cherry blossoms and the scarlet autumn leaves that he can see with his own eyes. Or again, it is like the situation of a beautiful woman who, although she has cause for resentment, does not give vent to her feelings in words, but is only faintly discerned—at night, perhaps—to be in a profoundly distressed condition. The effect of such a discovery is far more painful and pathetic than if she had exhausted her vocabulary with jealous accusations or made a point of wringing out her tear-drenched sleeves to one's face. . . .

By these two analogies it should be evident that this is a matter impossible for people of little poetic sensibility and shallow feelings to understand. . . . How can such things be easily learned or expressed precisely in words? The individual can only comprehend them for himself. Again, when one gazes upon the autumn hills half-concealed by a curtain of mist, what one sees is veiled yet profoundly beautiful; such a shadowy scene, which permits free exercise of the imagination in picturing how lovely the whole panoply of scarlet leaves must be, is far better than to see them spread with dazzling clarity before our eyes. What is difficult about expressing one's personal feelings in so many words—in saying that the moon is bright or in praising the cherry blossoms simply by declaring that they are beautiful? What superiority do such poems have over mere ordinary prose? It is only when many meanings are compressed into a single word, when the depths of feeling are exhausted yet not expressed, when an unseen world hovers in the atmosphere of the poem, when the mean and common are used to express the elegant, when a poetic conception of rare beauty is developed to the fullest extent in a style of surface simplicity—only then, when the conception is exalted to the highest degree and "the words are too few," will the poem, by expressing one's feeling in this way, have the power of moving Heaven and Earth within the brief confines of a mere thirty-one syllables, and be capable of softening the hearts of gods and demons.

[Brower and Miner, *Japanese Court Poetry*, p. 269]

THE WAY OF TEA

Tea was introduced to Japan sometime during the early Heian period, probably by monks such as Saichō (767–822) and Kūkai (774–835) returning from study in China. Tea drinking had become widespread in China by at least the seventh or eighth century and was brought to Japan in the wave of cultural borrowing from the continent that spanned the late sixth through early ninth centuries. In 815, Emperor Saga (r. 809–823) ordered that tea be grown in various provinces around Kyoto and that some of the annual harvest in leaves be presented as tribute to the court.

Tea drinking appealed primarily to two elite groups in Japan: nobles at the emperor's court, who, in emulation of their Chinese counterparts, drank tea and composed poetry (in Chinese) extolling the tea's taste and the elegant ways in which it could be prepared and served; and monks in Buddhist temples, who esteemed tea mainly for its medicinal value. But tea drinking at court declined from the late ninth century, when the Japanese ceased sending missions to China and lost at least some of their enthusiasm for Chinese culture. Although tea continued to be consumed at Buddhist temples and also Shinto shrines, there is no indication that people outside these establishments adopted it as a beverage during the remainder of the Heian period.

Tea was reintroduced to Japan from China in the late twelfth century (the early Kamakura period) by the monk Yōsai (aka Eisai, 1141–1215), who in *Kissa yōjō ki* analyzes and describes tea's medicinal efficacy. The kind of tea that Yōsai brought to Japan was unfermented, powdered green tea (called *matcha* in Japanese). During the Song period—mid-Heian times in Japan—the Chinese invented the tea whisk, which they used to dissolve powdered tea in hot water. Later, the Chinese abandoned the whisk and returned to their earlier practice of steeping or infusing tea (i.e., flavoring hot water by placing or dipping tea leaves into it). Most people today, including the Japanese in their everyday lives, drink infused tea, whether fermented (black tea), partially fermented (oolong tea), or unfermented (green tea). But the tea ceremony, *chanoyu*, which evolved in Japan in the late fourteenth through sixteenth centuries, has always used powdered green tea and the whisk.

Some of Yōsai's tea was planted at Toganoō, located in the mountains to the northwest of Kyoto. As the popularity of tea drinking spread among all classes

during the thirteenth and fourteenth centuries, Toganoō tea came to be regarded as the finest in Japan. In tea-tasting contests held at Kyoto social functions of the new warrior elite of the Muromachi period, Toganoō tea was called
"real tea" (*honcha*) and the products of other places "non-tea" (*hicha*). In later
times, the tea of Uji, some ten miles south of Kyoto, became especially favored
and remains today the preferred—and most expensive—of Japanese teas.

Tea-tasting contests were a form of *monoawase*, "comparisons of things,"
popular among the Japanese from at least the Heian period. The *Tale of Genji*
and the *Pillow Book*, for example, refer to a variety of *monoawase* among courtiers involving the comparing or judging of things such as seashells, flowers,
incense, perfume, poetry, and pictures. During the Muromachi period, many
of these *monoawase*, which were essentially games, were transformed into serious pursuits described as the "way of flowers," the "way of incense," and so
forth. Drawing on Buddhism, the devotees of these ways (*michi*) even regarded
them as paths to religious enlightenment.

When it took form in about the late fourteenth or early fifteenth century,
the tea ceremony had four principal components: rules, setting (the tea room),
behavior (among host and guests), and aesthetic taste. All these components
either derived from or were strongly influenced by Zen or the Zen establishment of Muromachi Japan.

The tea ceremony was born when rules were adopted to govern the preparation, serving, and drinking of tea, rules that distinguished the "ceremony" of
tea drinking from the casual, everyday consumption of the beverage. The inspiration for the tea ceremony's rules were the monastic rules (J: *shingi*) that
had been compiled in China to govern the daily lives of monks in Zen temples.
Zen places great emphasis on mundane, quotidian acts such as scrubbing floors,
cleaning latrines, or preparing tea as ways of pointing to or achieving enlightenment, and the procedures for carrying out these acts were described in detail
in the *shingi* brought to Japan by Chinese Zen monks during the Kamakura
period.

The tea room evolved as a variant of the *shoin*-style room, which took shape
during the fifteenth and sixteenth centuries and was itself derived from the
libraries (*shoin*) used by monks in Zen temples. The *shoin* became the proto-
typical Japanese room, having *tatami* matting, *shōji* and *fusuma* sliding doors,
an alcove, asymmetrical shelves, and a low built-in desk. Among the special
features that set a tea room apart from the regular *shoin* is the "crawling-in
entrance" (*nijiriguchi*) and the hearth, a recessed space in the floor designed to
accommodate a kettle in winter.

Behavior among the participants in the tea ceremony as it evolved in the
medieval age was based on the spirit of Buddhism and especially Zen. By the
late sixteenth century, when the tea ceremony reached the height of its development, tea masters were wont to say that "tea and Zen have the same flavor"
(*cha-Zen ichimi*). The tea ceremony may also have been influenced at this time

by the rituals of the Christian mass that were brought to Japan by European missionaries. Later, during the Tokugawa period, some tea masters based their practice of the tea ceremony on the ritual principles of Confucianism. Throughout its long history, the tea ceremony has been associated mainly with Buddhism, but many of its practices, such as those stressing simplicity, purity, and purification (e.g., the constant cleaning of utensils by the host and his or her careful selection and handling of water), derive from Shinto. Thus as a synthesis of native tastes and foreign influences, the tea ceremony evolved as a quintessentially Japanese art and ritual.

Aesthetic taste in the tea ceremony comes into play in both the construction of the tea room and the selection, handling, and display of utensils and other articles, such as scrolls and flowers, during tea gatherings. In the first form of the tea ceremony, which emerged in the Higashiyama cultural epoch of the late fifteenth century, the tea ceremony employed only "Chinese things" (*karamono*): objects of art and craft imported from China, including tea bowls and caddies, flower vases, incense burners, Song-style monochrome ink paintings (to be displayed in alcoves), and the portable stands known as *daisu* that were used to hold utensils. *Karamono* had been imported from the early medieval age, many of them by Zen monks who journeyed to China.

While the tea ceremony based on the aesthetics of *karamono* was maturing during the Higashiyama epoch, a new variation, *wabicha*, or *chanoyu* inspired by the *wabi* aesthetic, began to evolve. The person regarded as the founder of *wabicha* was Murata Shukō (or Jukō, d. 1502), who in his "Letter of the Heart" (*Kokoro no fumi*) wrote: "In pursuing this way of tea, great care should be taken to harmonize Japanese and Chinese tastes." By Japanese taste, Shukō meant taste for "Japanese things" (*wamono*), that is, for tea utensils made by Japanese artisans, especially ceramicware, that, in contrast to technically perfect Chinese things, were often crude, rough, and misshapen. These qualities did not reflect the incompetence of Japanese artisans. Rather, they were deliberately sought to satisfy the *wabi* aesthetic that, during the sixteenth century, was elevated to the highest level of taste in the tea ceremony.

Professor Haga Kōshirō has defined *wabi* as three kinds of beauty: a simple, unpretentious beauty; an imperfect, irregular beauty; and an austere, stark beauty. According to *Nanpōroku*, Takeno Jōō (1502–1555) selected the following poem by Fujiwara no Teika to convey the *wabi* spirit in the tea ceremony:

Miwataseba	Looking about
Hana mo momiji mo	Neither flowers
Nakarikeri	Nor scarlet leaves.
Ura no tomaya no	A bayside reed hovel
Aki no yūgure.	In the autumn dusk.

Jōō's student Sen no Rikyū (1522–1591), who became the greatest of all the tea masters, chose this poem by Fujiwara no Ietaka to illustrate his sense of *wabi*:

> Hana o nomi
> Matsuran hito ni
> Yamazato no
> Yukima no kusa mo
> Haru o misebaya.

> To those who wait
> Only for flowers
> Show them a spring
> Of grass amid the snow
> In a mountain village.[29]

Professor Haga analyzes this last poem and surmises Rikyū's reasons for selecting it:

> We can imagine a mountain village in the depths of winter when the seven wild grasses of autumn have withered and the brilliant scarlet leaves have scattered. It is a lonely, cold, and desolate world, a world that is even more deeply steeped in the emptiness of non-being than that of "a bayside reed hovel in the autumn dusk." At first glance this may seem like a cold, withered world at the very extremity of *yin*. It is not, of course, simply a world of death. As proof, we have these lines: "When spring comes it turns to brightness and amid the snow fresh grass sprouts, here two, there three blades at a time." This is truly "the merest tinge of *yang* at the extremity of *yin*." Ietaka expressed this notion as a "spring of grass amid the snow." And Rikyū found in it the perfect image of *wabi*. Thus Rikyū's *wabi*, viewed externally, is impoverished, cold, and withered. At the same time, internally, it has a beauty which brims with vitality. While it may appear to be the faded beauty of the passive recluse, or the remnant beauty of old age, it has within it the beauty of non-being, latent with unlimited energy and change."[30]

Wabicha was created mainly by members of the wealthy merchant class of the three cities of Kyoto, Nara, and Sakai in the central provinces. Merchant tea masters from Sakai, including Jōō and Rikyū, played especially important roles during the sixteenth century in molding this form of the tea ceremony. Although *wabicha* was spiritually based on the rejection of materialism, a serious pursuit of it in fact required a great deal of money, primarily because of the enormous cost of the best tea articles. In pursuing the tea ceremony in general and *wabicha* in particular, Sakai tea masters had the double advantage of personal wealth and ready access to Chinese articles (*karamono*), since Sakai

---

29. Varley and Kumakura, eds., *Tea in Japan*, pp. 199–200.
30. Haga Kōshirō, "The Wabi Aesthetic," in Varley and Kumakura, *Tea in Japan*, p. 200.

played a leading role in the trade with China during the sixteenth century. It was said that a person of this age could not be considered a true tea master (*meijin*) unless he owned at least one "famous [tea] article" (*meibutsu*)—that is, a tea article, whether Chinese or Japanese, that was judged to be of superior quality. With their wealth and connections, Sakai tea masters could compete even with the daimyo, the military lords of the country, in the acquisition of "famous articles."

When Oda Nobunaga (1534–1582) entered Kyoto in 1568 and began the military campaigning that unified Japan before the end of the century, he used the tea ceremony as one means to ritually legitimize his rule. Conducting a "hunt for famous tea articles" (*meibutsu gari*), he amassed, through both purchase and confiscation, the largest collection of tea articles in the land. In addition, he took into his employ the three leading tea masters of Sakai, the youngest of whom was Sen no Rikyū. By displaying his vast collection of "famous articles" and his Sakai tea masters, Nobunaga sought to confirm his right to rule in cultural (*bun*) as well as military (*bu*) terms.

When Nobunaga was assassinated in 1582, the job of unification was completed by his former lieutenant, Toyotomi Hideyoshi (1536–1598). Displaying even greater enthusiasm for the tea ceremony than Nobunaga had, Hideyoshi took possession of both his predecessor's *meibutsu* collection and his tea masters, and it was in the service of Hideyoshi that Rikyū rose to become Japan's foremost arbiter of taste and man of culture. Rikyū also became a confidant of Hideyoshi and came to exercise great political influence. Indeed, his involvement in the affairs of Hideyoshi's government may have contributed to his downfall. Although historians still dispute the reason or reasons, Hideyoshi ordered Rikyū to commit suicide in 1591. Later apotheosized as a god of the tea ceremony, Sen no Rikyū had brought the way of tea to its highest development.

In cultural history, Rikyū's age is known as the Momoyama epoch. It was a heroic time, witnessing the rise of the great warlords who strode across the country trying to unify it. Grandeur and show, including the erection of lofty castles and the mass display of tea articles, were the hallmarks of the epoch. In contrast to the monochromatic and quietistic art of the medieval age, Momoyama painting was dynamic and bursting with brilliant colors, especially gold. Hideyoshi, the parvenu hegemon and consummate showman of the age, had a portable, gilded tea room constructed for his use, and he furnished it with gold-plated utensils.

But Hideyoshi also had a rustic tea room, fashioned like a hut in a mountain village (*yamazato*), in which he practiced the subtleties of *wabicha* with Rikyū. Hideyoshi's two tea rooms, the rustic and the golden, symbolized the extremes of Momoyama taste, one epitomizing the highest spiritual and aesthetic values of the medieval age and the other heralding what scholars call the early modern age. It was an exciting time in Japanese history, and the tea ceremony and its masters, led by Sen no Rikyū, played central roles in the cultural—and also political—events that determined the direction that the country would take.

DRINK TEA AND PROLONG LIFE

From its earliest use in China, tea was appreciated probably above all for its medicinal value, and the tradition of tea as good "medicine" accompanied the beverage on its transmission to Japan in the early Heian period (although, as noted, the Heian courtiers also very much esteemed tea as a feature of Chinese higher culture). When the Zen monk Yōsai reintroduced tea to Japan in the late twelfth century, at the beginning of the medieval age, he did so primarily to promote good health. Referring to "these degenerate times" (i.e., the age of *mappō*), Yōsai observed that "man has gradually declined and grown weaker, so that his four bodily components and five organs have degenerated." Of the five organs, the heart is "sovereign": its condition determines the well-being of all the organs. And because the heart craves the bitter taste found in tea, drinking it will "put the heart in order and dispel all illness." Drinking tea, a stimulant, was also an excellent means for Zen monks and others to fight drowsiness during meditation. Still another use for tea was as a cure for hangover, as Yōsai publicly demonstrated during a visit to Kamakura, when he provided relief for the shogun Sanetomo the morning after one of Sanetomo's frequent drinking bouts.

Tea is the most wonderful medicine for nourishing one's health; it is the secret of long life. On the hillsides it grows up as the spirit of the soil. Those who pick and use it are certain to attain a great age. India and China both value it highly, and in the past our country too once showed a great liking for tea. Now as then it possesses the same rare qualities, and we should make wider use of it.

In the past, it is said, man was coeval with Heaven, but in recent times man has gradually declined and grown weaker, so that his four bodily components and five organs have degenerated. For this reason even when acupuncture and moxa cautery are resorted to, the results are often fatal, and treatment at hot springs fails to have any effect. So those who are given to these methods of treatment will become steadily weaker until death overtakes them, a prospect which can only be dreaded. If these traditional methods of healing are employed without any modification on patients today, scarcely any relief can be expected.

Of all the things which Heaven has created, man is the most noble. To preserve one's life so as to make the most of one's allotted span is prudent and proper [considering the high value of human life]. The basis of preserving life is the cultivation of health, and the secret of health lies in the well-being of the five organs. Among these five the heart is sovereign, and to build up the heart the drinking of tea is the finest method. When the heart is weak, the other organs all suffer. It is more than two thousand years since the illustrious healer Jīva passed away in India, and in these latter degenerate days there is none who can accurately diagnose the circulation of the blood. It is more than three thousand years since the Chinese healer Shennong disappeared from the earth, and there is no one today who can prescribe medicines properly. With no one to consult in such matters, illness, disease, trouble, and danger follow one another in endless succession. If a mistake is made in the method of healing, such as moxa cautery, great harm may be done. Someone has told me that as medicine is practiced today, damage is often done to the heart because the drugs used are not appropriate to the disease. Moxa cautery often brings untimely death because the pulse is in conflict with the moxa. I consider it advisable, therefore, to reveal the latest methods of healing as I have become acquainted with them in China. Accordingly I present two general approaches to the understanding of diseases prevalent in these degenerate times, hoping that they may be of benefit to others in the future.

I. Harmonious Functioning of the Five Organs

According to the esoteric scripture known as the Conquest of Hell the liver likes acid foods, the lungs pungent foods, the heart bitter ones, the spleen sweet, and the kidney salty. It also correlates them with the five phases and five directions as follows:

Organ	Direction	Season	Element	Color	Spirits	Sensory Organs
Liver	East	Spring	Wood	Blue	Soul	Eyes
Lungs	West	Autumn	Metal	White	Soul	Nose
Heart	South	Summer	Fire	Red	Spirit (*shin*)	Tongue
Spleen	Center	Between Seasons	Earth	Yellow	Will	Mouth
Kidney	North	Winter	Water	Black	Imagination	Ears

Thus the five organs have their own taste preferences. If one of these preferences is favored too much, the corresponding organ will get too strong and oppress the others, resulting in illness. Now acid, pungent, sweet, and salty foods are eaten in great quantity, but not bitter foods. Yet when the heart becomes sick, all organs and tastes are affected. Then eat as one may, one will have to vomit and stop eating. But if one drinks tea, the heart will be strengthened and freed from illness. It is well to know that when the heart is ailing, the skin has a poor color, a sign that life is ebbing away. I wonder why the Japanese do not care for bitter things. In the great country of China they drink tea, as a result of which there is no heart trouble and people live long lives. Our country is full of sickly looking, skinny persons, and this is simply because we do not drink tea. Whenever one is in poor spirits, one should drink tea. This will put the heart in order and dispel all illness. When the heart is vigorous, then even if other organs are ailing, no great pain will be felt.

Then follows a section explaining how the five organs correlate with the various Buddhas, symbols, gestures, and regions of the esoteric mandalas (see chapters 7 and 8), together with the esoteric secrets of healing disorders in each.

In regard to the Five Tastes: acid foods include oranges, lemons, and other citrus fruits; pungent foods include onions, garlic, and peppers; sweets include sugar, etc. (all foods are sweet by nature); bitter foods include tea, herb teas, etc.; salty foods include salt, etc.

The heart is the sovereign of the five organs, tea is the chief of bitter foods, and bitter is the chief of the tastes. For this reason the heart loves bitter things, and when it is doing well all the other organs are properly regulated. If one has eye trouble, something is wrong with the liver, and acid medicine will cure it. If one has ear trouble, something is wrong with the kidney, and salty medicine will cure it. [And so forth, running through the preceding table of correspondences.] When, however, the whole body feels weak, devitalized, and depressed, it is a sign that the heart is ailing. Drink lots of tea, and one's energy and spirits will be restored to full strength.

[*Kissa yōjōki*, pp. 899–901; PV]

MURATA SHUKŌ: "LETTER OF THE HEART"

Murata Shukō (or Jukō), the late-fifteenth-century tea master from the merchant class of Nara, occupies a lofty position in tea history as the putative founder of the *wabicha* form of the tea ceremony. Yet we know little about Shukō. On the basis of the records that have come down to us, his reputation is based almost entirely on the brief "Letter of the Heart" (*Kokoro no fumi*) that he wrote to a disciple, the petty daimyo Furuichi Chōin. Terse and in places difficult to interpret, the letter is especially remembered, as noted, for its injunction "to harmonize Japanese and Chinese tastes"—that is, to develop an aesthetic appreciation for "Japanese things" (*wamono*) as well as "Chinese things" (*karamono*). To illustrate Japanese taste, Shukō speaks of the "cold," "withered," and "emaciated," using terms from the aesthetic vocabulary of the medieval age that appear to have been introduced to the tea ceremony (especially *wabicha*) from linked verse (*renga*) poetry. Shukō is concerned that people inexperienced in the tea ceremony will become so enamored of these qualities, which are the hallmarks of Bizen and Shigaraki ceramicware, that they will ignore others and thus fail to *harmonize* Japanese and Chinese tastes. Reflecting the influence of Buddhism on the tea ceremony, Shukō also speaks of the dangers of egotistical self-assertion and attachment. Warning practitioners of the tea ceremony to avoid these "faults," he enjoins them to pursue mastery of the way of tea with humility and sensitive awareness of their own limitations.

The worst faults in this way of tea are self-assertion and attachment. To envy the skilled and look down upon those seeking to learn is reprehensible in the extreme. You should approach the skilled to learn from them, conscious of your own limitations, and do your best to nurture those who are just beginning.

In pursuing this way of tea, great care should be taken to harmonize Japanese and Chinese tastes. Mark these words carefully and do not be negligent.

Nowadays those who are inexperienced speak of the "cold" and "withered" and covet Bizen and Shigaraki ware. Though lacking the recognition of others, they assume airs of being knowledgeable and experienced. This is unspeakably bad. "Withered" means to possess good utensils and understand their qualities thoroughly, and thus to attain knowledge and experience within the core of one's heart. What one does thereafter will manifest the "cold" and "emaciated," and will have the power to move. (One not in a position to appraise and acquire fine utensils should not vie with others in collecting them, but should use what one has.)

However cultivated one's manner, a painful self-awareness of one's shortcomings is crucial. Remember that self-assertion and attachment are obstructions. Yet the way is also unattainable if there is no self-esteem at all. A dictum of the Way states: "Become heart's master, not heart mastered"—the words of an ancient.

[Adapted from Hirota, *Wind in the Pines*, p. 198; PV]

THE SPIRITUAL BASIS OF THE TEA CEREMONY
(FROM *NANPŌROKU*)

In these passages, Rikyū speaks of the tea ceremony as an almost purely spiritual exercise. Material values are ignored, if not rejected, and the path to Buddhist enlightenment seems to be opened by the simple, mundane acts of preparing, serving, and drinking tea. These passages, and others in *Nanpōroku*, express an ideal of tea sought especially in the practice of *wabicha*. But most of *Nanpōroku* is a detailed analysis of the complexities of the tea ceremony, with more than a little attention given to the quest for and employment of fine tea articles. In reality, the tea ceremony has almost always been strongly governed by the tension between art and aesthetics (having and using fine articles), on the one hand, and the religious rejection of materialism, on the other.

Once when Rikyū had been speaking of the tea ceremony at Shūun-an,[31] I asked, "You often remark that, although the tea ceremony has its roots in the formal tea employing the *daisu* stand, when considering the deeper attainment of its spirit, nothing surpasses the informal tea held in a small room. Why should this be so?"

---

31. A hermitage at Nanshūji Temple in Sakai.

Rikyū responded: "The tea ceremony of the small room is above all a matter of performing practice and attaining realization in accord with the Buddhist path. To delight in the refined splendor of a dwelling or the taste of delicacies belongs to worldly life. There is shelter enough when the roof does not leak, food enough when it staves off hunger. This is the Buddhist teaching and the fundamental meaning of the tea ceremony. We draw water, gather firewood, boil the water, and make tea. We then offer it to the Buddha, serve it to others, and drink ourselves. We arrange flowers and burn incense. In all of this, we model ourselves after acts of the Buddha and the past masters. Beyond this, you must come to your own understanding." . . .

Someone once asked Rikyū to explain the hearth and the brazier, revealing the proper bearing of the spirit and the crucial points in performing tea in summer and winter. Rikyū replied: "In summer, impart a sense of deep cool-ness, in winter, a feeling of warmth; lay the charcoal so that it heats the water, prepare the tea so that it is pleasing—these are all the secrets." Dissatisfied with this answer, the man remarked, "That is something everyone knows." Then Rikyū said, "If so, try performing in accord with what I have stated. I will be your guest, and perhaps become your student."

[*Nanpōroku*, in Hirota, *Wind in the Pines*, pp. 217, 223; PV]

PURITY AND PURIFICATION IN THE TEA CEREMONY
(FROM *NAMPŌROKU*)

The great attention given in the tea ceremony to water, its quality and handling, reveals one aspect of the influence of Shinto on tea practice. Rinsing the hands as the first act of the guests at a tea ceremony, for example, is taken directly from a Shinto rite of purification observed when preparing to enter a shrine. At the same time, the passages given here reflect the influence also of Buddhism ("[washing] off the stains of worldly dust") and the yin-yang cosmology on the use of water in the tea ceremony.

Whenever I go to have tea with Rikyū, he unfailingly brings water to fill the stone basin (*chōzubachi*) in a bucket and pours it in himself. I once asked the significance of this. He replied: "In the *roji*,[32] the host's first act is to bring water; the guests' first act is to use this water to rinse their hands. This is the very foundation underlying the use of the *roji* and thatched hut. It is precisely so that the person who calls and the person called on can together wash off the stains of worldly dust in the *roji* that the stone basin is placed there. In the depths of the cold season, one draws and carries the water without aversion to

---

32. Literally, the "dewy path," the garden that leads to a teahouse.

the cold; in summer heat, one does so imparting a crisp feeling of coolness. In either case, providing this water is an act of attentiveness to the guests." . . .

Always use water drawn at dawn for tea, whether the gathering be in the morning, at noon, or at night. This is a matter of the alertness of the practitioner of the tea ceremony—of making ready sufficient water for the whole day's tea from dawn into night. Just because it is a night gathering does not mean one uses water drawn after noon. During the period from dusk to midnight *yin* prevails; the water's spirit subsides, and poisons are present. Dawn water belongs to the beginning of the *yang*, when its pristine spirit surfaces; it is "the flower of the well." This water is vital for tea and demands careful attention on the part of the practitioner.

[Hirota, *Wind in the Pines*, pp. 217–219, 224; PV]

Chapter 17

WOMEN'S EDUCATION

In the formal sense of the term "education" as schooling through a defined curriculum such as existed in the Confucian College in Nara or the kind of instruction designed by Saichō for his monks on Mount Hiei or by Kūkai for his Academy of Arts and Sciences, there was no formal education for women in early Japan. Nevertheless, women clearly did learn enough to take a prominent part in the life of the country, and especially in its cultural life. Great writers like Murasaki Shikibu and Sei Shōnagon were highly literate, and the court life of Nara and Heian Japan, in which literary culture figured so prominently, could not have been so brilliant had it not been for the participation of women at the highest levels.

Women obviously had access to learning in the home and at court, just as women did in Han and Tang China, even though they were somewhat disadvantaged in its pursuit. Especially among the upper classes with the leisure to devote to the cultural refinements they so prized, women had available not only a considerable body of classical literature but also some of the same primers and texts as the Han and Tang Chinese: the *Classic of Filiality* (Ch: *Xiao jing*) and the *Admonitions for Women* (Ch: *Nüjie*) of Ban Zhao, the *Household Instructions of the Yan Family* (Ch: *Yan-shi jiaxun*), the *Analects for Women* (Ch: *Nü lunyu*), and *The Learning Quest* (Ch: *Meng qiu*).[1]

---

1. See de Bary and Bloom, eds., *Sources of Chinese Traditions*, vol. 1, chaps. 18 and 23.

In this section we present three early Japanese texts for the edification of women in Buddhism. They were specifically intended for a female audience and spoke to the situation and condition in which women found themselves. Nevertheless, instead of emphasizing the social roles of women or addressing their specific problems or potentialities, these works propose a way of spirituality common to men and women (the one exception being the reference to the particular moral and spiritual failings of women as seen in traditional Buddhism). The fundamental spiritual problems addressed in these writings are those of all humankind, and most of the guidance offered would apply equally well to men.

The first of these texts, *Illustrations of the Three Jewels*[2] (*Sanbōe*) by Minamoto Tamenori (984), was addressed to a young nun; the second, *A Companion in Solitude* (*Kankyo no tomo*), by a Tendai monk to a court lady; and the third, *Mirror for Women* (*Tsuma kagami*), by the Zen monk Mujū Ichien in 1300, to lay women. In its adaptation of a secular genre (the illustrated narrative scroll or *emaki*), the first work is strikingly reflective of Heian culture in that although it was written for a woman who had already entered the religious life, it cautions her against the continuing powerful attraction of, and emotional involvement with, the same aesthetic culture she has supposedly renounced. There is great similarity here to the problems of the spiritual and religious life as revealed in *The Tale of Genji* and *The Pillow Book* and to the need for the religious message to be adapted to the same cultural features, that is, literary and artistic genres, that might otherwise distract one from it. In this respect, despite the ostensible distinction between lay and religious life, in practice it was somewhat blurred.

Illustrations of the Three Jewels was an illustrated collection of Buddhist tales in three volumes, compiled for and presented to an imperial princess, Sonshi Naishinnō, who had recently taken vows as a nun, and it was written to serve as her guide to Buddhism. Tamenori offered her an array of exemplary tales that showed how merit generated through good deeds and practices would yield rewards in both this life and the next. He included stories from the lives of Buddhas, based on scriptural sources; tales of Japanese Buddhists and miracles produced through their devotions, adapted from other Japanese sources, chiefly a *Japanese Chronicle of Miracles* (*Nihon ryōiki*); and accounts of the origins, organization, and benefits of various Buddhist rites, for which he drew on court and monastic documents, scripture, and, in one or two cases, personal observation. Tamenori then added a general preface and three other prefaces to bind the tales together in three volumes, or fascicles.[3]

---

2. Rendered elsewhere in this series as Three Treasures.

3. The preceding paragraph and the following introductory material on the *Sanbōe* are from Kamens, *The Three Jewels*, pp. 3–4.

Tamenori's stated purpose was to give Sonshi information helpful to her spiritual advancement, but he also believed that by providing such guidance and rejoicing in her accomplishments, he would simultaneously augment his own store of merit and increase the likelihood of his own salvation. He claimed that this particular kind of literature—which literally chastised evil and encouraged good and was based on the irrefutable teachings of the Buddha—was superior to the fanciful romances (*monogatari*) favored by women of Sonshi's day and Sonshi's class. But to convey his message most effectively, Tamenori adapted the form of the illustrated *monogatari* for his own purposes and thus devised a special book designed to fulfill his special goals and particularly suited to the needs and capacities of his intended reader.

Tamenori wrote, "I have had illustrations of several exemplary stories made, and I submit them to you together with these words from the scripture and from other works." Accordingly, he prepared for Sonshi a book that was unlike any of its acknowledged sources and unlike any of its known models in the genre of Buddhist tale collections. It was, instead, an *emaki*, a text combined with pictures, like many of the books read at court and in the private quarters of aristocratic women in mid-Heian Japan.

GENERAL PREFACE TO *ILLUSTRATIONS OF THE THREE TREASURES*

Tamenori's innovative choice of the *emaki* format for *Sanbōe*, a serious didactic and devotional work, made its content all the more accessible and palatable to Sonshi; yet in its author's view, its content and purpose made it a far better book than those whose form it imitated. In a passage of the "General Preface" that is the most quoted portion of the whole work, Tamenori condemns the *monogatari* and criticizes their readers for allowing themselves to be taken in by so much of what he considered to be make-believe. He approaches the subject by imagining how Sonshi will spend her time now that she has left her old way of life for that of a nun. Concerned about the temptations to which she may yield in her idleness, he warns her against too much enjoyment of games of *go* and *koto* practice before moving in for the real attack.

> Then there are the so-called *monogatari*, which have such an effect upon ladies' hearts. They flourish in numbers greater than the grasses of Ōaraki Forest, more countless than the sands on the Arisomi beaches. They attribute speech to trees and plants, mountains and rivers, birds and beasts, fish and insects that cannot speak; they invest unfeeling objects with human feelings and ramble on and on with meaningless phrases like so much flotsam in the sea, with no two words together that have any more solid basis than does swamp grass growing by a river bank. *The Sorceress of Iga, The Tosa Lord, The Fashionable Captain, The Nagai Chamberlain,*

and all the rest depict relations between men and women just as if they were so many flowers or butterflies, but do not let your heart get caught up even briefly in these tangled roots of evil, these forests of words.

Long ago it was written:

> Contemplate the body:
> it is but rootless grass
> lying on the riverbank;
> As for this life:
> it is but a small boat
> drifting at the channel's edge.[4]

And elsewhere:

> To what shall I compare this life?
> To white waves of foam trailing behind
> a boat putting out at break of day.[5]

Thus, in both China and Japan, people who understood the essence of things expressed the same thought. Indeed, in the teachings of the truly enlightened, universally compassionate Buddha we find these words: "This world is absolutely insubstantial, like the bubbles on the water, the shadow of the mist. You must reject this world as soon as possible and free yourselves from it." . . .[6]

One thousand nine hundred and thirty-three years have passed since Buddha Shākyamuni left this world. We may now be in the Period of the Imitated Teaching but surely only a few years of this interim period remain to us.[7] Those who have the misfortune to be born as human beings at this time have less chance of receiving the Buddha's teaching than a thread dangled from heaven has of going through the eye of a needle in the middle of the sea. Even if they manage to free themselves from this life, they will never have any assurance of what will become of them hereafter. At this time there is nothing to do but contemplate the Buddha, hear his Teachings, and revere his Clergy.

---

4. This Chinese verse appears in the same form in *Wakan rōeishū*, in a section with other poems on the topic of "Impermanence" (see *NKBT* 73:254), where it is attributed to Louwei, which may be a mistranscription for Yenwei.

5. This verse appears in slightly different form in the *Manyōshū* 3 (no. 351), where it is attributed to the monk Mansei (*NKBT* 4:179).

6. A verbatim quotation from the sixth chapter of the Lotus Sūtra (TD 9, no. 262:47b).

7. If the year A.D. 984 is the starting point for Tamenori's calculation, this places the Buddha's demise in the year 958 B.C.E. The "Period of the Imitated Teaching" (*zōhō*) is the second of the "Three Periods." It was widely believed that this period would end in 1052.

Have you not heard of the elder of Rājagrha[8] who gathered treasures and rejoiced in the flourishing of his household, only to die and become a snake whose lot it was to guard his former mansion and storehouse? And do you not know of the lady of Shrāvastī who constantly gazed into her mirror in order to admire her own beauty, only to become an insect at the end of her life and dwell in what was formerly her own skull?[9] While they lived they never thought they would become a snake or an insect, but they took inordinate pride in wealth and beauty, and so they brought their fate upon themselves. So, a flourishing household is a likely site for sinning; you must abandon it and seek out the Buddha's Country. Have no second thoughts for your worldly beauty; forget it and pray that you may attain the Buddha's Body. . . .

The second daughter of my liege, the Retired Emperor Reizei, whose beauty puts the spring flowers to shame and silences even the cool wind in the pines, was chosen to live in the Ninefold Palace, but now she despises and seeks release from this world with its Five Pollutions.[10] Shrīmālā, the daughter of Prasenajit, needed no one to inspire her faith.[11] Candraprabhā was the wife of King Udāyi, and she voluntarily shaved her head, without anyone having suggested that she do so. They were born into noble families and achieved high station, but since their sacred destiny was to be reborn upon the lotus, they made haste to plant the seeds of the Law; since they nurtured lofty intentions of becoming as perfect as the full moon, they strove constantly toward the light that shines on those who take the Buddha's vows. When we compare the present age to the ancient past, the time may seem different, but the act is essentially the same. Jeweled blinds and brocade curtains may have graced your former abodes, but now you shall tend to the dew on the flower and the perfumed incense.[12] Even so, the spring days linger, with nightingales warbling softly in the grove, and the autumn nights seem endless, as the light from your candle and its shadow on the wall grow dim. Go may seem like a pleasing way to pass the time, but there is no profit to be had in challenging others to games of skill. The *koto* may also serve as your companion for the night, but you should not let yourself become too attached to its sound.

[Kamens, trans., *The Three Jewels*, pp. 91–93]

---

8. Rājagrha (Ōshajō) was one of the great Indian cities at the time of Shākyamuni.

9. This story is quoted from *Gengukyō* (TD, no. 242:4:378b).

10. "The second daughter" is Sonshi Naishinnō. The "Five Pollutions" are marks of a degenerate age, during which (1) life spans are shortened; (2) kalpas are shortened; (3) ignorance and evil are shortened; (4) ignorance and evil desires proliferate; (5) heretical views prevail; and (6) human life is extremely corrupt.

11. Shrīmālā (Shōman), the daughter of King Prasenajit, is the subject of the Shrīmālā Sūtra.

12. The "jeweled blinds and brocade curtains" are poetic emblems of a royal lady's chamber which, in Sonshi's case, have now been replaced by emblems of a nun's way of life.

A *Companion in Solitude* (*Kankyo no tomo*) is believed to have been written in 1222 by the monk Keisei (1189–1268), of the Fujiwara Kujō branch, whose religious associations were with Tendai esotericism and who was a friend of the Kegon monk Myōe (see chapter 10). The *Companion* is a collection of stories written for a high-ranking court lady for her spiritual edification, moving from accounts of prominent monks to ones of ordinary monks and laymen and then, down the scale, to women.

The stories excerpted here reveal the ambivalence of Mahāyāna Buddhism and Japanese religiosity with regard to the life of the senses and human emotions. In the first story, such attachments are seen as at once sinful and compelling in their emotional appeal, reflecting the same ambivalence in Heian literature. From this point of view, even the impurities traditionally attached to womanhood can be seen, in the light of the equation of Nirvana and Samsara, as instruments of salvation.

About the Religious Awakening of the Nun Who Lived in the Mountains of Tsu Province

Long ago there was a nun who built herself a rough straw hut in the depths of the mountains in Tsu province. She abstained from eating the five cereals, and would pluck the seeds from a yew tree and use them for making her food. . . . The nun had a pale complexion and her appearance had declined to such an extent that it would be impossible to know whether she was good-looking or ugly.

A certain person met her by chance and asked her why she was living in such a place. She replied, "When I was at the height of my youth, I lost my husband. After completing the religious services of the forty-ninth day,[13] I shaved my head and entered the mountains. I have never returned to my village since. I loved my husband deeply, but when he died so suddenly I realized that the relationship between man and wife is but ephemeral, and so I became what I am today. I have several children. I owned a great deal of land and other possessions. Realizing, however, that all these are merely companions of one's dreams, I cast them all away." . . .

A woman's nature is such that whether of high rank or low birth, she pins her hopes on all sorts of things, but in the end is unable to realize her expectations. The depth of this lady's heart that made her decide to receive the tonsure was, by contrast, truly profound.

In truth we hear of many instances of couples who want to grow old together, pledging that they would be buried in the same grave and praying that they

---

13. The period after death and before rebirth in a new life, believed to last for forty-nine days, was known as *chūin*, or the intermediate state between death and the next life.

may be together again in the next world. Their acts are full of expectations for the future, but in fact these constitute a deep crime.[14] . . .

Throughout their lives people constantly think about love. Comparing their love to the flames of Mt. Fuji,[15] they display a heart that is tortured by love. How they must suffer during their lives! The sorrow of those who are endowed with great sensitivity must become greater and deeper, depending on the time and situation they are in. . . .

Then again there was the case of the person who compared his life with the ephemeral dew and said that he would gladly exchange it for one meeting with his lover. The bond that tied these lovers must have been truly hard to bear. These relationships are at once pitiable and shamelessly unmindful of the Buddha's Dharma.

[Pandey, *"Kankyo no tomo,"* pp. 335–337]

The "adaptive means" by which the passions might be made to serve enlightenment are illustrated by several stories in the *Companion in Solitude*. In one account, the author cites a high councillor at court as an impressive example of enlightenment for, after becoming passionately involved with a court lady, having deserted her "in order to bring home to her the ephemeral nature of such attachments, which she could not have understood by herself."[16] However one interprets this last comment, the following serves as a contrasting case of how a court lady turned the passionate advances of a monk into a lesson in disillusionment/enlightenment.

How a Noble Lady Serving at Court Displayed Her Impure Form

Long ago there was a certain monk of high standing who fell in love with a lady-in-waiting of royal birth. He must have been unable to keep silent, for he fervently revealed his feelings and the depth of his heart to her.

The lady hesitated a while and said, "Why do you torment yourself so? When I return home from the court, I shall certainly let you know." The monk had thought that his interest in the lady was in no way out of the ordinary, but now his feelings quite surpassed those he had held for her before.

Not long after, the lady informed him that she had returned to her home and that she would be there that night. The monk made the necessary preparations and set off to meet her.

When he arrived, the lady appeared before him and said, "What I wanted

---

14. *Tsumi fukaku*, or deeply sinful, as a violation of Buddhist precepts.

15. The fire and smoke that rose from Mount Fuji were popular symbols of the ardor and passion of a person in love.

16. Pandey, "Women, Sexuality, and Enlightenment," p. 339.

to say was so important that it could not be done lightly, and so I came back here.

"This body of mine is an indescribably smelly and foul object. The inside of my head is filled to overflowing with gray matter. Inside the skin, bones and flesh are coiled together. Blood and pus flow through the whole body, and there is not a single thing in the body that one would want to get close to. Despite this, I have somehow made this body appear attractive by decorating it and using all kinds of perfumes. If you were to see my true form, you would undoubtedly find it most repulsive and frightening. It was to tell you this in some detail that I invited you here to my home."

The lady then called to one of her servants to bring in a light, which was burning bright red on a stand. She then removed the partition between them and showed herself to the monk. She said, "This is what I look like. How can you bear to look at me?"

Her hair was standing up, extremely disheveled like that of a demon. Her face, once so refined, was blue in some places and yellow in others. Her legs had lost their former color and were filthy. Her robes were covered here and there with blood, and smelled unbearably repulsive. She came forward and, weeping without restraint, continued her lament.

"What would happen if I stopped using cosmetics and adorning myself? If I no longer took care of my body and let it follow its natural course? Then both my physical form and my clothes would undoubtedly look like this. As you are a person who is closely associated with the Buddha's Way, I was afraid of showing you my false form, and so I have dropped all pretenses and showed you my real appearance."

The monk was dumbfounded and, shedding tears, he told her, "I have indeed met a true friend who has guided me to reform myself."

[Pandey, "Women, Sexuality, and Enlightenment," pp. 349–50]

MUJŪ ICHIEN: *MIRROR FOR WOMEN*

Mirror for Women was written in 1300 by Mujū Ichien (1226–1312), a monk with broad theoretical interests who ultimately allied himself with Rinzai Zen's Enni Ben'en (Shōichi, 1202–1280), founder of the Tōfukuji in Kyoto. In 1262, he restored the Chōboji in Miya (now Nagoya), where he lived until his death a half century later. Here he wrote a noteworthy collection of Buddhist "tales" (*setsuwa*), *Sand and Pebbles* (*Shasekishū*, 1279–1283), the *Mirror for Women*, *Collection of Sacred Assets* (*Shōzaishū*, 1299), and *Casual Digressions* (*Zōtanshū*, 1305). The prominent role of women in the early days of the Chōboji and their continuing support during Mujū's tenure there may help explain his concern for women's salvation.

Nevertheless, although Mujū often refers to the types of religious devotionalism popular among women (especially Amida and the Pure Land), for the most part his argument is addressed to the human condition in general, not in ways that are gender specific. He quickly relativizes all moral, social, and cultural values, which become insignificant in comparison to the fundamental need to detach oneself from all worldly, even human, concerns and apply oneself to the "one great life and death matter": to rise beyond suffering and illusion to realize one's inherent Buddha-nature.

One of several specific references to women—quite late in the work and not a high priority—is his recital of a traditional formula concerning the faults and failings of women propounded by Daoxuan, the seventh-century founder of the Chinese disciplinary sect noted for his codifications of monastic rules. Without further elaboration, Mujū characteristically relates a couple of moral anecdotes with a humorous twist and then comments that "there are among women many instances of deep compassion and religious aspiration. The Sūtra of Meditation on the Buddha Amitayus contains the account of Lady Vaidehi, and the Lotus Sūtra speaks of the daughter of the Dragon King attaining Buddhahood." Then, abruptly, he once again returns to the non-gender-specific issues of the human condition and liberation from all worldly involvements.

Difficult to attain is birth in human form, but although we may now have attained it and we may have seen with our eyes the impermanence of the cycle of birth-and-death, we may not feel this in our hearts; then we are like trees and stones. Difficult to encounter is the Buddha's teaching, but although we have now encountered it, it may merely move our ears and we do not learn from it; then we are just beasts in human skin. . . . For the sake of our bodies we cut short the lives of living beings, savoring them on the tongue. Blindly we covet material goods, devising schemes to obtain clothing and food. But these material goods are like a sweet drug which intoxicates us so that we do not practice the Law of Buddha. . . . Throughout life we tend to encourage evil and neglect good, and so we produce and accumulate only evil karma in our hearts. Covetousness is the karmic cause for rebirth as a hungry ghost. Anger is the karmic cause for rebirth in the hells; at our death it becomes the fires of hell to scorch us. And ignorance is the karmic cause for rebirth as an animal; in the future life we assume the form of a beast, and as a result we are subjected to the agony of being slaughtered. . . .

We say that a man is wise who takes care of himself, looks after others, visits his parents' birthplace, and acts to requite the benefits which have accrued to him over several lifetimes. The household of a man who accumulates good deeds prospers, while the family of one who cultivates wickedness is destroyed. When a man has committed no evil, why should he worry? They tell of men who spend a considerable portion of their wealth performing acts of merit in the discharge of filial obligations toward parents, teachers, and superiors. Nevertheless, only a seventh part of the merit redounds to the advantage of the deceased, while six-sevenths benefits the doer of the action. A man may neglect the Buddha's Law himself from the mistaken notion that he has descendants who will pray for his deliverance. But not to seek the Way of the Buddha oneself is foolishness indeed. . . .

Our actions may be of such merit as to help the blessed spirits of parents, teachers, and superiors, the objects of our solicitude. But although we may transform their grave crimes into minor ones or change a life of misfortune to happiness, our own actions cannot become the infallible road to birth in the Pure Land for either donor or recipient. . . .

Thus one's own practice of the *nembutsu* results in one's own birth in the Pure Land rather than another's. Nor are we to imagine that having another person call upon the name of Buddha or recite the scriptures can be a direct cause of our own birth in the Pure Land and attainment of Buddhahood, or that of our parents, teachers, or superiors who are the object of solicitude. The fact is that even though a deep determination to transfer merit to others, substituting light for heavy retribution, may result in felicitous karma through which those other people receive rebirth into a good life, at one moment they rise, only to fall in the next, for the karma of retribution is not exhausted. . . .

People ordinarily think that wisdom consists in cleverly figuring out the ways of the world and diligently manipulating others to consolidate their estate, passing it on to heirs and later generations, that is, setting themselves up and teaching others to act in this way. But since we err in attaching importance to mundane affairs and in becoming estranged from the Buddha's Law, this worldly wisdom is thought to be one of the Eight Impediments to spiritual progress, an enemy who invites us to rebirth in the Evil Directions. The disposition to store up treasure is called "covetousness," and it is a serious offense drawing down upon us karma which results in transmigration. . . .

The mind of the sage is completely untroubled by the problem of good and bad karma, nor is he vexed by the cleanness or impurity of the water in the great ocean [i.e., he is tolerant of all men and conditions]. It is as though he does not mind the impurity of the land. Within the general defilement, he employs delusion to attain what is of primary importance. . . .

Prince Shōtoku was a manifestation of the Kuse Kannon and manifested himself in our country in order to propagate Buddhism. Nevertheless, he had five children. Moreover, although he attacked Moriya and committed the crime of murder, we cannot speak of him as the "immoral prince." All of these actions were the exalted behavior of the bodhisattvas, virtuous deeds performed in the state of Buddhahood, skillful means to help sentient beings. Having noted that karma and liberation are one, the sage understands and manifests the principle that good and bad are inseparable, and he realizes the identity of illusion with enlightenment. . . .

People venerate as a Buddha anyone who, in the eyes of ordinary men and fools, excels in religious exercises and is endowed with honor and virtue. But there is no certainty that release from birth-and-death and the attainment of enlightenment will follow from his actions and character, nor from his wisdom and cleverness. . . .

The mass of men sink or float in the sea of birth-and-death in accordance with their state of mind. The man of deep resolve who would escape the round of birth-and-death will certainly realize enlightenment, while the man without this resolve continues to transmigrate, receiving the retribution of rising and falling in the sea of mortality. Those who do not make use of the way things operate are stubborn and incorrigible, wretched people who nullify the efforts of the various Buddhas to help sentient beings and who behave carelessly as regards the skillful devices of the patriarchs. . . .

Even if a man is lord of a province, compared to the king of the whole country he is like an ordinary person with respect to his superior. So also, although the results of a man's actions bring him to the level of the great rulers Indra and Brahmā, yet compared to the highest levels of enlightenment, it is as mud to a cloud. The gods in the heavens see the span of human life as even more evanescent than that of the May fly that is born in the morning and does not live till evening; they see the human body as inferior to that of an ant or a frog. . . .

Many serious instances of the sins of women, among the unregenerate who are all deluded, are cited in sacred scriptures and commentaries. Because of their abundance, there is no time to discuss these sins in detail. The Preceptor Daoxuan[17] said, "Basically these are the seven grave vices of women. First of all, like the myriad rivulets flowing into the sea, they have no compunction about arousing sexual desire in men. Secondly, when we observe women in a house, we see that their jealous disposition is never idle. Friendly in speech, in their hearts is malice; with no thoughts for others, they are concerned only with their own affairs. Thirdly, on account of a disposition prone to deceit, they smile at a man even before he has said anything. In their speech, they say that they empathize, while in their hearts they are distant and cherish thoughts of envy. A person who faces you but whose thoughts look the other way is said to be prone to deceit. Fourthly, neglecting their religious practices and concentrating on how they may deck themselves with fine clothes, they think of nothing but their appearance and desire for the sensual attentions of others. Their hearts are attached to desire without regard to whether the object of their attention is closely related or distant. Fifthly, they take deceit as their guide and their honest words are few. They often vow to bring evil to others without fearing that they are piling up sins for themselves. Sixthly, burning themselves in the fires of desire, they have no shame toward others. Their hearts deluded, they fear not

---

17. Daoxuan (J: Dōsen, 596–667) is noted for his codification of monastic rules. Mujū's Japanese rendering of these seven grave vices is from *Rules to Purify Mind and Maintain Insight* (*Jing xin jie guan fa*, TD 45, no. 1893:1893).

the tip of the sword; as though drunk, they know no shame. Seventh, their bodies are forever unclean, with frequent menstrual discharges. Seeing that both pregnancy and childbirth are both foul and the afterbirth unclean, the evil demons vie for possession while the good deities depart. The foolish find these things attractive, but the wise are repelled." . . .

When the Buddha was still in this world, there was a woman named Ciñcā, who from the first had belonged to a family of unbelievers and was deeply jealous of him. With the idea of bringing shame to the Buddha, she attached a cord to a bowl which she hung around her neck and down over her stomach beneath her clothes, and then went to where the Buddha was expounding the Law. Wending her way into the area where bodhisattvas, disciples, and beings from the heavenly world were as thick as dense vegetation, she faced the Buddha and stroked her stomach. "Look at this! I am pregnant with the Buddha's child," she cried, abusing him and declaring that she would give birth and disgrace the Buddha. Now one of the Buddha's disciples, the holy Maudgalyāyana, excelled in supernatural powers. Seeing what was taking place, he transformed himself into a mouse and chewed through the cord holding the bowl, which then fell before the Buddha. As the woman's stomach vanished, the Buddha's shame was transferred to Ciñcā and she paled with vexation.[18]

Again in India there lived a woman called Yajñadattā, whose mind was as restless as a monkey's. Once when she held up a mirror that she might admire her face, she became extremely agitated at not being able to see herself. "I have lost my head! What has happened?" she cried. Utterly distraught she shrieked at the heavens and pounded the earth, but in the end she was never able to see her head. All sentient beings possess the Buddha-nature, which can never leave us even for a short time. But because we do not show forth the moon of our inner nature, for it is obscured from view by dense clouds of delusive thought, we are regarded as the unregenerate, forever sunk in the mire. Although Yajñadattā did not actually lose her head, she lost it in the sense that in the agitation of her heart her mind clouded over.[19]

In China national calamities are said to have originated with three women. And in our own country Emperor Go-Toba fomented the [Jōkyū] Insurrection at the instigation of a woman [Kamegiku] and was ultimately sent into exile. Such cases are common, it is true, but there are also among women many instances of deep compassion and religious aspiration. The Sūtra of Meditation on the Buddha Amitayus[20] contains the account of Lady Vaidehi, and the Lotus

---

18. This story and its variants appear in several early texts, especially the *Treatise on Great Wisdom* (*Daichidoron*, TD 25, no. 1509), which Mujū had studied in his youth.

19. Ennyadatta, that is, Yajñadattā, is sometimes referred to as a man (Yajñadatta), although the anecdote is similar; compare the Shūrangama Sūtra (Ryōgonkyō), T 945).

20. *Kammuryōjukyō*, TD 12, no. 365.

Sūtra speaks of the daughter of the Dragon King attaining Buddhahood.[21] If a woman is aware of the great burden of sin which women bear, she will revise her attitudes and reject the business of fame and fortune in this world of a single dream, betaking herself to the practice of the Buddha's Law, which helps us from life to life and from world to world. Throughout life, evil advances and the good retreats; there are actions which simply take us "from darkness to darkness" and from the depths submerge us into even lower depths. Karma is like a balance — it pulls to the heavier side. We may weigh and determine which was greater between the good and bad of a person's life, between the good and bad karma which one generates during a year, a month, a day, a moment. When evil is dominant, one will fall into Evil Paths; when virtue is dominant, one will attain good rebirth. The recording angels meticulously note the smallest error on their tablets.

Mujū was broadly familiar with the other schools of Buddhism and, like many others of his age, readily accepted Buddhist-Shinto syncretism. His tolerance of other schools follows the pattern already set forth in the Lotus Sūtra and Tendai doctrine, which he had studied in his youth. The final, unqualified "truth" was an immediate experience transcending all rational formulations. In the prologue to Collection of Sand and Pebbles (Shasekishū) *he states: "There is not just one method for entering the Way, the causes and conditions for enlightenment being many. Once a person understands their general significance, he will see that the purport of the various teachings does not vary. And when he puts them into practice, he will find that the goal of the myriad religious exercises is the same."*

Inasmuch as natural dispositions are not all identical, the teaching has a myriad differences. The Mahāyāna, Hīnayāna, provisional and absolute teachings are all discourses of the one teacher Shākyamuni. This is to attract those who have an affinity for the Buddhist teaching by sampling and suggesting a partial version of what has been said. When a man who practices one version of the Way of the Buddha vilifies another because it differs from his own sect, he cannot avoid the sin of slandering the Law. It has been said that a man who slanders the methods of another out of attachment to his own beliefs will surely suffer the pains of hell even though he observes the commandments.[22] However, if there is an occasion to promote Mahāyāna by persuading people to convert, there is great advantage in breaking their attachment to the Hīnayāna and drawing them into the Mahāyāna. But under no circumstances should one

---

21. Lotus Sūtra, 12. See de Bary and Bloom, eds., *Sources of Chinese Tradition*, vol. 1, chap. 16.

22. Mujū here apparently paraphrases a verse from chapter 26 of the Lotus Sūtra. See Watson, trans., *The Lotus Sūtra*, p. 310.

reject the Mahāyāna and enter the Hīnayāna. The difficult and painful practices are for the foolish; easy conduct and practice are for the wise. . . .

The greatest fruits of Buddhahood to be realized from the Hīnayāna are considered to be far inferior by the Buddhas of the Mahāyāna. The *Explanation of Mahāyāna* (*Shakuron*) says

> Attaining the name of Buddha "by self-cultivation is later viewed as a joke."[23] That is, although a man may be called a Buddha according to the Hīnayāna, when viewed later from the standpoint of the Mahāyāna, he becomes a thing of amusement. A man who would practice the Way of the Buddha should never stop along the way saying that he has attained what in fact he has not attained, or that he has realized what in fact he has not realized. . . .

The *Calming and Contemplation*[24] says: "The Great Sages in their wanderings all sought the Law without respect to the source. The youth of the Himalayas[25] took half a verse from an *asura*, and Indra venerated an animal, taking it as his teacher." Just as their resolve to practice the Buddha's teachings was so great, we too should take advantage of our youth and not neglect religious practice. It will do us no good to regret having ignored the One Great Matter and to have vainly passed our span of life in the karma of transmigration. To place the obsessions of the deluded mind before all else is not to know how to distinguish jewels from seaweed.

I do not care about the laughter of those who will come later and read this. Nor does it benefit me at all that I have collected together these leaves of words like free-floating grasses, diverting myself with a water-soaked reed which traces my thoughts as they ripple through my mind. But should a woman make these precepts her constant companion [as she would a mirror], she will show herself to be a person of sensibility, a follower of the Way. And so I give this work the title, *Mirror for Women*.

[Morrell, "Mirror for Women," pp. 51–75]

---

23. The quotation actually appears in Kūkai's *Precious Key to the Sacred Treasury* (*Hizō hōyaku*), not in the *Shaku[makaen]ron* (TD 32, no. 1668), a commentary on the *Awakening of Faith in the Mahāyāna* (*Daijō kishinron*, TD 32, no. 1666) by a certain Nāgārjuna other than the great Mādhyamika philosopher.

24. *Maka shikan*, chap. 4B.

25. That is, Gautama.

Chapter 18

LAW AND PRECEPTS FOR THE WARRIOR HOUSES

The Kamakura shogunate is perhaps best remembered in history as a regime of law and justice, although for most of its first half century, it had no law of its own with which to dispense justice. When the regime was founded in 1185, it was administered autocratically by its leader, Minamoto Yoritomo, the lord of Kamakura, who made no significant effort to establish new laws for warrior society but, rather, accepted in general the jurisdiction of the country's two existing bodies of law: the law of the imperial court of Kyoto and the customary law compiled by the independent estates (*shōen*) that by this time controlled most of Japan's agricultural lands.

As noted in earlier chapters, after Yoritomo's death in 1199, a power struggle lasting several decades ensued in Kamakura that was finally won by the Hōjō, who were related to Yoritomo by marriage. By establishing the office of shogunal regent (*shikken*), the Hōjō became the real rulers of the young warrior government under figurehead shoguns (first Fujiwara and, later, imperial princes). In 1221 in a brief clash of arms, the Hōjō put down an attempt by the retired emperor Go-Toba to overthrow the shogunate (discussed in chapter 11). Victorious in this clash, which was known as the Jōkyū war, the Hōjō were able to assert Kamakura rule over the country far more extensively than before.

In 1224, the Hōjō established the Council of State (Hyōjōshū), which under their leadership became the shogunate's principal decision-making body. Through this council, assembly rule superseded the one-man governance of

Yoritomo, the shogunate's founder. In 1232, Hōjō Yasutoki (1193–1242), generally regarded as the finest of the shogunal regents, issued a document known as the Jōei Code,[1] comprising fifty-one articles, that was intended as a guide for the conduct of the Council of State but that also became the starting point for the development of warrior law, distinct from both court law and estate law.

To prepare the Jōei Code, Yasutoki consulted legal specialists from Kyoto and studied court law assiduously. But as he made clear, the Jōei Code was designed exclusively for warriors and would not compete with or seek to displace the older law. In letters he wrote to his brother at this time, Yasutoki stated that his primary aim was to set standards for the fair and equitable handling of suits, and he vowed to rectify the practices of the past that had enabled the powerful to prevail over the weak and those of higher status to defeat their social inferiors through favoritism, bribery, and the like. Yasutoki said he feared that the courtiers in Kyoto would ridicule attempts by the "eastern barbarians" to establish their own law. But he noted that in the provinces not one person in a thousand—or even ten thousand—could understand court law. Hence to apply such law to suits arising among provincial warriors was like luring animals into traps. In addition to being fair and equitable, therefore, the code he was preparing would be written in a manner readily understandable by everyone.[2]

The Jōei Code is not a formal set of laws. Rather, it establishes certain rules, identifies categories of legal concern, and provides standards for warrior behavior. Yasutoki clearly intended the code to be only a starting point for the creation of warrior law, stating that if anything were found to be missing from it, the code should be amended through the addition of supplementary articles (tsuika-hō). In practice, the Council of State and other bodies of the Kamakura shogunate passed judgment on accusatorial suits (suits brought by plaintiffs against defendants), and their judgments or decisions became supplementary articles to the Jōei Code. Some seven hundred of these articles survive, many if not most dealing with land disputes, the area of greatest concern to warriors.

Yasutoki's aim in the Jōei Code was to base law primarily on precedent and principle (dōri). By precedent, he had in mind especially the decisions made in Yoritomo's time. Thus, for example, in article 3 of the code, in which he discusses the duties of the provincial constables (shugo), Yasutoki observes that these duties were permanently established by Yoritomo himself. In article 8, dealing with deeds to land, he decrees that the precedent established in Yoritomo's time was to recognize as legitimate the claim to a holding, even in the absence of a deed, if the holder could prove that he had been in possession of the land for at least twenty years.

---

1. Jōei was a period that lasted only one year (1232). The formal name of the Jōei Code is *Goseibai shikimoku* (Formulary of Adjudications).

2. Satō et al., eds., *Chūsei hōsei shiryō shū*, vol. 1, pp. 56–59.

When no precedents could be applied in adjudicating a suit, Yasutoki held that the judgment should be based on principle (*dōri*). We observed in chapter 11 that Jien, writing in *Gukanshō*, used the term *dōri* to indicate the various "principles" that he believed governed the course of Japanese history. For countless readers of *Gukanshō*, Jien's use of *dōri* has hindered rather than helped in seeking to understand the text. But the term as more generally employed had the meaning of "reasonableness," "common sense," or "rightness," and this is how Yasutoki, a younger contemporary of Jien, intended it to be applied to warrior law. In short, *dōri* was to be the real basis for dispensing fair and equitable decisions in legal cases brought before the Kamakura shogunate.

THE JŌEI CODE

The fifty-one articles of the Jōei Code deal with a broad range of topics, including the granting and holding of land, the duties of shogunate officials, the bestowal and receipt of estate property, the rights of inheritance, and the apprehension and punishment of criminals. The following is a sampling of these articles, chosen to illustrate some of the distinctive features of the new warrior law promulgated by the Kamakura shogunate. Among the distinctive features are the limitations placed on the duties and rights of the shogunate's own principal officers in the provinces and estates, that is, the constables and stewards (articles 3 and 5); the recognition of the continuing, independent jurisdictions of both court-appointed officials (governors) and estate holders (article 6); the twenty-year rule applied to the possession of land (article 8); and the granting and holding of land and adoption of heirs by women (articles 18, 21, and 23). The articles dealing with women are particularly interesting because they show that women enjoyed considerable rights of ownership and privileges of family membership in Kamakura warrior society based on the practice of divided inheritance, that is, the division of estate property to all offspring, female as well as male. But within a century or so, most of these rights and privileges were lost, as warrior society shifted to the practice of single inheritance or the exclusive inheritance of both economic wealth and political authority by the male successor to a family's headship.

Article #1. The shrines of the gods must be kept in repair; and their worship performed with the greatest attention. . . .

Article #2. Temples and pagodas must be kept in repair and the Buddhist services diligently celebrated. . . .

Article #3. Concerning the duties of the constables (*shugo*) in the provinces. It was decided in the time of Lord Yoritomo[3] that these duties should be: 1. providing for guard duty at the imperial capital [Kyoto]; 2. suppressing rebel-

---

3. Here and elsewhere in the Jōei Code, Yoritomo is referred to as "Great General of the Right (*utaishō*)," which is an abbreviation of the highest court title he held, *ukon'e taishō*.

lions; and 3. tracking down and apprehending murderers. But of late, deputies (*daikan*) of the constables have been dispatched to districts and towns (*gunkō*), where they have imposed levies. Although not provincial governors (*kokushi*), they have interfered in the provinces' administration. Although not stewards (*jitō*), they have coveted profits from the land. Such behavior is utterly unprincipled. . . .

Article #5. Concerning the withholding by a steward (*jitō*) of the assessed amount of the annual rent (*nengu*). If a complaint is submitted to the central proprietor (*honjo*) of an estate that the annual rent has been withheld by a steward, an accounting will be made at once and the complainant will receive a certificate specifying the balance that may be due him. . . .

Article #6. Governors of the provinces and estate holders (*ryōke*) may continue to exercise their usual jurisdiction without reference to the Kantō [i.e., the Kamakura shogunate]. . . .

Article #8. Concerning a fief that a plaintiff, although holding a deed of investiture, has not possessed over a period of years. If the current holder has been in possession of the fief in question for more than twenty years, then, in accordance with a precedent established in Lord Yoritomo's time, it will not be transferred to the plaintiff, whatever he may claim in seeking to obtain it. . . .

Article #11. Whether, because of a husband's crime, the landholding of a wife should be confiscated or not. In the case of serious crimes, such as rebellion and murder, as well as banditry, piracy, night attacks and burglary, the husband's guilt will extend also to the wife. But if, as the result of a sudden dispute, the husband wounds or kills someone, the wife will not be held responsible. . . .

Article #18. Whether or not parents, having given a daughter a holding in land, may reclaim it because of a later falling out with the daughter. Legal scholars have held that, although sons and daughters differ in gender, they are equal in terms of the benefits bestowed upon them by their parents. Hence, a gift to a daughter should be as irrevocable as one to a son. But if a gift to a daughter were irrevocable, she might rely upon that fact and not scruple to go against her filial duties. Parents therefore must, when thinking of bestowing a gift of land on a daughter, consider whether or not there might later occur a dispute between them and the daughter. . . .

Article #21. Whether or not a wife,[4] having received a grant of land from her husband, can retain that grant after divorce. If the wife has been rejected because of a serious transgression, she will not be allowed to retain the grant even if she possesses written documentation for it from an earlier time. But if the wife has been virtuous and innocent of any fault and was discarded by the husband in favor of something new, then the grant given her cannot be revoked. . . .

---

4. It states here "wife or concubine," but the remainder of the article refers only to "wife."

Article #23. Concerning the adoption of heirs by women. The intent of earlier law was not to allow adoption by women. But from the time of Lord Yoritomo to the present day it has been a fixed rule to allow a childless woman to bequeath her land to an adopted child. . . .

[Adapted from Hall, "Japanese Feudal Law," pp. 37–45; PV]

THE LAW OF THE MUROMACHI SHOGUNATE

When Ashikaga Takauji overthrew the government of Emperor Go-Daigo's Kenmu Restoration in 1336 and established the Muromachi shogunate (see chapter 12), he faced formidable problems. Go-Daigo himself fled to Yoshino in the mountainous region south of Kyoto, proclaimed that he was still the rightful emperor, and founded what came to be known in history as the Southern Court. Takauji and his followers were accordingly obliged to contend not only with the disorder and dislocations caused by the recent fighting against the Restoration government but also with a new, rival regime in the Southern Court whose warrior supporters launched a war against them that lasted for more than half a century (until 1392).

One of Takauji's first concerns was where to place the seat of his shogunate. Although he finally decided on Kyoto because of the geographical advantages it offered in fighting the Southern Court, he apparently passed over Kamakura, the capital of the previous military regime, only with great reluctance. As observed by Nikaidō Ze'en, head of a group of legal scholars and others whom Takauji consulted about policies and principles of governance, Kamakura had been a site of both glory and disgrace for the country's military. It was a site of glory when Yoritomo established the first shogunate there and when Hōjō Yoshitoki "seized the empire during the Jōkyū era" (i.e., foiled the former emperor Go-Toba's "rebellion" against the Kamakura shogunate in 1221), but it was a site of disgrace when the later Hōjō regents "accumulated evil unceasingly by their arrogance and selfish desires" and the shogunate had to be destroyed. In Ze'en's thinking, what mattered most was how a government was run and not the location of its seat; therefore Kyoto would serve as well as Kamakura. In his words, "The rise and fall of a capital . . . depends on the quality of a government. . . . [M]an's misfortune is not to be found in the bad luck of his dwelling place."[5]

In the eleventh month of 1336, Ze'en and seven others presented to Takauji the Kenmu Code (Kenmu *shikimoku*), a document in seventeen articles that Ze'en called an "opinion" to guide the shogun in rule. The decision to have the code divided into seventeen articles was clearly made with Prince Shōtoku's famous Seventeen-Article Constitution in mind, and indeed, the Kenmu Code

---

5. Grossberg and Kanamoto, trans. and eds., *The Laws of the Muromachi Bakufu,* p. 15.

bears some similarity to that constitution. Both are sets of maxims or principles for proper rule; but whereas the constitution, which is derived almost entirely from Confucian thought, offers very general, universalistic principles, the Kenmu Code is much more specific in applying these or similar principles to the particular problems of the disordered and dangerous time in which it was composed. Thus, for example, article 1 of the code calls for "the need for enforcing frugality" (whereas article V of the constitution speaks about "ceasing from gluttony and abandoning covetous desires") and then refers immediately to specific "extravagance[s] and excess[es]" that have recently become fashionable, such as "the wearing of twill damask and brocade, ornamental silver swords and elegant attire to dazzle the eyes."

The Kenmu Code served the same historical role for Muromachi warrior law that the Jōei Code served for Kamakura warrior law, becoming the starting point for the creation of new laws through "supplementary articles." Thus, as during Kamakura times, the judgments or decisions made in cases brought before the courts of the Muromachi shogunate became laws and were added as supplements to the Kenmu Code.[6] There are more than five hundred of these supplementary articles.

THE KENMU CODE

A number of the articles in the Kenmu Code seem to address the particular problems of Kyoto in 1336 as the city swelled in size with the influx of warriors and others that accompanied the founding of the Muromachi shogunate. This appears clearly to be the case, for example, in articles 1 through 3, which call for the control of "extravagance and excess," "drinking in crowds and carousing," "gambling and sporting with women," and general lawlessness, including "breaking into buildings in broad daylight, burglary at night, [and] murder." No doubt these problems could also be found elsewhere in Japan, but we know from other records of the time that, as described in the Kenmu Code, they were primarily the problems of Kyoto, now the seat of both the imperial court and the shogunate.

Prince Shōtoku's Seventeen-Article Constitution is echoed in several articles of the Kenmu Code (e.g., articles 1 and 13, which discuss frugality and decorum), and article 15 about "hearing suits brought by poor and weak vassals" reminds us of Hōjō Yasutoki's wish, expressed in a letter to his brother as the Jōei Code was being compiled, to prevent the powerful and the socially elite from winning cases against those of lesser social standing through bribery, favoritism, and the like.

Two other points of note in the code are the calls to (1) select men of political

---

6. See ibid., p. 8, for a discussion of how suits were handled, according to category, by various organs of the Muromachi shogunate.

ability to be constables (article 7) and (2) reward those who are upright and loyal (article 14). We may wonder whether much heed was actually paid to selecting constables from among men of ability, since the constable positions continued to be held almost exclusively by men on the basis of birth into powerful families. But the call to reward warriors who are upright and loyal is worth noting because the Kenmu Code's precursor, the Jōei Code—which decrees what warriors should or should not do—says almost nothing about ethical behavior per se. In the late fifteenth and sixteen centuries, as we will see, loyalty in particular becomes a central issue in the laws and precepts of that age's warrior chieftains.

Article #1. The need for enforcing frugality. Recently, fashion has been used as an excuse to indulge in extravagance and excess, such as the wearing of twill damask and brocade, ornamental silver swords and elegant attire to dazzle the eyes. This has become a mania. While the rich swell with pride, the poor are ashamed because they cannot match them. This is the major reason for the poverty of the population, and it must be severely suppressed.

Article #2. The need for suppressing drinking in crowds and carousing. As stated in the imperial supplementary laws, these must be strictly controlled. This also applies to gambling and to excessive sporting with women. In addition, large wagers are made at tea parties and linked-verse meetings, and incalculable sums of money are lost in this way.

Article #3. The need for suppressing lawlessness. Breaking into buildings in broad daylight, burglary at night, murder and highway robbery cause the cry for help to be heard incessantly. The shogun must take strenuous measures against these crimes.

Article #4. The need for prohibiting the commandeering of private houses [by warriors].

Article #5. The need for returning vacant lots in Kyoto to their former owners. . . .

Article #6. The need for reviving mutual financing associations and moneylenders. . . .

Article #7. The need for selecting men of political ability to fill the posts of constable (*shugo*) in the provinces. Constables are presently appointed on the basis of accumulated military service, and award lands are granted to them from among the estates (*shōen*). The office of constable is equivalent to the old office of provincial governor, and since the peace of the provinces depends on this office, stable rule for the people will be realized if the most able men are appointed.

Article #8. The need for preventing powerful courtiers, as well as women and Zen priests, from meddling [in government].

Article #9. The need for admonishing official negligence, and for selecting officials carefully. . . .

Article #10. The need for firmly prohibiting bribery. . . .

Article #11. The need for returning gifts which have been presented to the shogun and members of his court.

Article #12. The need for selecting the shogun's personal bodyguard. . . .

Article #13. The need for emphasizing decorum. An overriding concern for etiquette and decorum is most important for ruling the country. The lord must observe his own proper conduct and his vassal his own. High and low must each bear in mind their proper station, and strenuously observe decorum in both speech and conduct.

Article #14. The need for granting special rewards to those who have reputations for uprightness and loyalty. This is the way of advancing men of quality and removing those who are harmful. The shogun must bestow special praise in such cases.

Article #15. The need for hearing suits brought by poor and weak vassals. The government of Yao and Shun considered this very important. As it is written [in *The Classic of Documents*], ordinary people treat such petitions lightly, but sages treat them as important. The shogun must pay special attention to this, and show compassion for his poor vassals. His most important duty is to listen to their petitions.

Article #16. The need for listening to or rejecting suits presented by temples and shrines, depending on the merits of the cases. . . .

Article #17. The need for establishing fixed days and hours for judging suits. There is nothing which people complain of more than delays [in processing their suits]. But one must not neglect searching for the truth simply in order to speed up the procedure. The shogun must hand down his decision so that there is no cause for complaint either with respect to speed or thoroughness of the investigation.

> [Adapted from Grossberg and Kanamoto, trans. and eds., *The Laws of the Muromachi Bakufu*, pp. 16–21; PV]

THE LAW OF THE WARRIOR HOUSES IN THE AGE OF WAR IN THE PROVINCES

Even at its peak in the late fourteenth and early fifteenth centuries, the Muromachi shogunate presided over only a loose territorial hegemony based on a balance of power between the shogun and those chieftains who held appointment to the office of constable. (One constable was appointed to each province, but some chieftains held more than one constableship.) The hegemony, moreover, did not extend over the entire country. Northern Honshu and the island of Kyushu, for example, were largely beyond the shogunate's effective control, and even the eastern provinces of the Kantō, administered by a rival branch of the Ashikaga family, frequently resisted shogunate rule.

The shogunate's hegemony weakened steadily from about the fifth decade of the fifteenth century as some leading constable families floundered and the shogunate itself suffered from weak leadership and internal conflict. In 1467, a succession dispute within the Ashikaga family provoked a decade-long war (the Ōnin War, 1467–1477), fought largely in Kyoto, that not only destroyed most of that venerable city but also shattered the shogunate's hegemony and plunged the country into a century of war and disorder known as the Age of War in the Provinces (Sengoku, 1478–1568).

Almost all the pre–Ōnin War constable families were overthrown or declined during and in the aftermath of the war, and the shogunate itself was reduced to near impotence as a central government. Beginning about the end of the fifteenth century, a new class of territorial rulers emerged in the provinces whom historians call Sengoku lords (daimyo). Many of these daimyo held the title of constable, although it was not essential to their rulership. For the most part, they were military commanders who carved out and defended their domains by their own military might and administered the domains as totally independent entities.

Living in a brutal age when "might made right," the Sengoku daimyo assembled armies of vastly greater size—up to fifty thousand or more—than any seen before in Japanese history. Although concerned first and foremost with military power, the daimyo also pursued policies—such as the encouragement of greater agricultural yields, the development of commerce, and the exploitation of mining resources—that were part of their overall endeavors to enrich their domains in every way possible.

Among the most important steps taken by the Sengoku daimyo to formalize control over their domains and enhance their personal rule was the compilation of legal formularies or house codes (*kahō*). Although they were called "house" codes, the *kahō*, ten of which have come down to us,[7] are not simply sets of rules for the daimyo's own houses. Rather, they prescribe law for all the warrior houses and for the general populace as well. Their articles deal with a wide range of matters, including relations between the daimyo and his vassals and among vassals, land disputes, judicial procedures, the payment and nonpayment of taxes, borrowing and lending, crime and the punishment of criminals, intercourse with other domains, and drinking and gambling. The great majority of the articles in the house codes, however, concern relations between the daimyo and his vassals, and it is to these that we turn next.

As far as relations with his vassals were concerned, a daimyo's main purpose in promulgating a house code was to assert his authority over them. As noted, the Sengoku daimyo were far more powerful and independent territorial rulers

---

7. The ten are the codes of the Sagara, Ōuchi, Imagawa, Date, Takeda, Yūki, Rokkaku, Miyoshi, Chōsōkabe, and Kikkawa houses.

than the pre–Ōnin War constables. But they lived in a precarious and harsh age, and they could be—and not infrequently were—overthrown either in war with rival daimyo or through internal treachery and rebellion by vassals and even kin. Yet despite these dangers, the daimyo display through their house codes an unusually forceful authoritarianism toward their vassals that at least some may in fact have had difficulty enforcing. A possible explanation for this authoritarianism is that the daimyo were, in a sense, gamblers. The strict control of vassals was a matter of life and death for them; hence, they either enforced strong rules for vassals or, if unable to do so, probably did not long survive as daimyo.

At the heart of the problem of controlling vassals was the nature of honor in warrior society. The war tales, discussed in chapter 12, contain countless examples of vassals motivated by a self-abnegating loyalty that leads them to forfeit their lives without hesitation in the service of their lords. Such loyalty, however, was an ideal to which probably few actually subscribed. But if the loyalty of some, if not most, warriors toward their lords had its limitation, all seem to have been committed without reservation to maintaining their personal honor. Indeed, the records strongly suggest that it was honor rather than loyalty that served as the warrior's chief ethical guide. Any loss of face, including that incurred by a lord's poor performance or any slight or offense that might cause shame and stain his honor, was intolerable to the warrior and demanded reprisal or revenge.

Professor Katsumata Shizuo described the kind of world in which matters of honor, face, and shame could stir men so profoundly:

Japan's medieval age was a time when private revenge ruled. The entire social lives of medieval people were darkly shrouded by primitivism. If we try to understand from today's perspective the actions of people of that time—for example, their hypersensitivity to personal insult, their potential for explosive anger, their instinct for violent conflict, their sense of impending death carried to the point of despair—we are bound to be baffled, even though we may acknowledge the great significance of these feelings to them. Fights among people born into this kind of world, even if the result of trifling causes, quickly escalated into private clashes and private battles in which blood could only be cleansed by blood. Fights were propelled by personal anger and personal resentments. Far from joining battle for reasons of loyalty (*chū*) or rightness (duty) (*gi*), medieval warriors gambled their lives in combat as though responding to some great manliness that rose from deep within them. Moreover, exacting revenge for harm suffered in fights was their overriding ethical concern. Conflicts among them, regardless of the rights or wrongs of the combatants, were prolonged until the desire for retaliation on both sides was subjectively satisfied. Fights, in this sense, were conflicts over honor.[8]

This warrior society's preoccupation with honor was accompanied by the belief that warriors possessed a fundamental right of self-redress (*jiriki kyūsai*) and that such self-redress, which permitted reprisal for even the most trifling offense, was part of what Sengoku writers called "the manly way" (*otokodō*). But the exercise of self-redress by a vassal not only might go against the loyalty he owed his daimyo, it might also threaten the very order the daimyo was trying to maintain in his domain. Not surprisingly, therefore, the daimyo took steps to restrain their vassals from pursuing self-redress. Chief among these steps was the inclusion in their house codes of articles—known as *kenka ryō-seibai*, or articles "dealing with both/all parties to a fight" (henceforth referred to simply as *kenka* articles)—that threatened punishment, without regard for who might be right or wrong, of any vassals who entered into a dispute or fight.

A classic example of a *kenka* article can be found in the house code of the Imagawa: "If any warriors [i.e., vassals] engage in fighting, both parties will be executed regardless of who may be right or wrong."[9] Not all daimyo prescribed such severe punishment for fighting as execution, but all *kenka* articles were military enactments designed to demonstrate the daimyo's authority to summarily mete out punishment to their vassals without any reference to such principles as reasonableness (*dōri*) and justice, which had been fundamental guides to warrior law from the time of the Jōei Code in the Kamakura period.

THE YŪKI HOUSE CODE[10]

The authoritarianism of Sengoku law is clearly observed in the following articles from the house code of the Yūki family of Shimōsa Province in the Kantō. Articles 3 and 4 are, for example, typical *kenka* laws (although the revocation of family names is not a typical form of punishment found in the house codes as a whole). Strict authoritarianism also informs article 22, prescribing execution for disloyal vassals and their families; article 23, disallowing vassal marriages without the Yūki's permission; and article 72, prohibiting vassals from "making plans" without first consulting the Yūki daimyo.

The articles dealing with warriors setting out for battle (articles 26, 67, and 68) appear to be efforts by the Yūki to break the habit of their vassals, typical of warriors

---

8. Katsumata Shizuo, "Sengoku-hō," in Iwanami shoten, ed., *Iwanami kōza Nihon rekishi*, vol. 8, p. 189.

9. Satō et al., eds., *Chūsei hōsei shiryō shū*, vol. 3, p. 117.

10. The formal name of the Yūki Code is Yūki-shi shin-hatto. It contains 104 articles and two supplementary (*tsuika*) articles.

from earliest times, of fighting one against one. One of the notable developments in Sengoku warfare was the gathering of warriors (as officers) and peasant soldiers (as "men") into disciplined armies whose success did not allow the kind of one-against-one fighting tactics and individual heroics so common in pre-Sengoku battling.

Article 3. If a fight (*kenka*) or quarrel should arise, for whatever reason, and the participants should call upon relatives and associates to come together with them and form bands, those who form those bands will be punished without regard for the reason or reasons that provoked the fight or dispute. Be attentive to this. . . .

Article 22. Hereafter, those who are disloyal to the Yūki will be executed along with their families. They will also have their names revoked and their lands confiscated and assigned to others. . . .

Article 23. Henceforth, there will be no marriages without Yūki permission. This applies not only to marriages with people from other houses but also from one's own house. . . .

Article 26. Wherever it may be to, you must not gallop forth as a lone rider without receiving orders from the Yūki. But when summoned by the Yūki, you must not be tardy. If you have business that must be attended to or are sick, send a replacement. . . .

Article 28. No matter how distinguished his family background may be in terms of loyalty to the Yūki, a person who is indiscreet and neglects his duty as a warrior will have his family name revoked and his lands confiscated. . . . No matter how loyal his family has been, a person who is disloyal will be punished without leniency. . . .

Article 51. In a dispute between a parent and child, the child will be considered to have acted without justification. . . . But if a parent alienates his oldest son and heir and replaces him with a younger son and, in the process, is himself disloyal and induces the younger son to be disloyal too, then the parent is in the wrong. . . .

Article 53. No matter how many times a child may serve the Yūki loyally while both his parents are alive, if he should die the parents are not to interfere. The successor to his family will be decided from here by the Yūki. . . .

Article 65. There is a great deal of talking these days. You must not speak badly of people of this house or other houses while on the verandah of the Yūki fort. Slander among men of the Yūki is also strictly forbidden. . . .

Article 66. The warrior who works land worth five *kan* will report to camp wearing armor and helmet. He will be provided with an outfitted horse. The warrior possessing land worth ten *kan* will report to camp with a suit of armor and a horse. Warriors with land worth fifteen *kan* or more will report to camp with retainers.

Article 67. To gallop forth heedlessly and without thought because you hear the sound of the conch shell from the main fort that signals taking to the field is quite unpardonable. If the shell sounds, you should go to a village and quickly dispatch some underling or servant to the main fort and have him inquire into where you should go. Only then should you gallop forth. . . .

Article 68. No matter what the emergency, you should not dash off to a battlefield without your armor. Regardless of how brave and prompt you may be, you should not ride out as a lone rider. Wait, form a unit, and then proceed to the battlefield.

Article 69. To undertake surveillance without orders is to act like someone not involved in a battle. In leaving your force to undertake surveillance, you are not acting loyally, no matter what you achieve. . . .

Article 72. Men of the horse units (*umamawari*)[11] should obviously not join an outside group, nor should they join a different group within the Yūki house. No matter how well they may perform, it will not be acceptable and they will lose face. The horse units should always act in conjunction with ten or twenty other riders and not mingle with other groups.

Article 73. Even though it may be for my [the Yūki daimyo's] benefit, vassals are not to make plans without informing me. . . .

[Satō et al., eds., *Chūsei hōsei shiryō shū*, vol. 3, pp. 229–246; PV]

PRECEPTS OF THE WARRIOR HOUSES

The house precepts (*kakun*) are documents—sometimes referred to as "testaments"—that were written by the heads or patriarchs of houses as guides for the deportment, behavior, and cultural (including religious) training of younger family members of both present and future generations. The idea for such precepts was originally received from China, probably during the seventh century. In the eighth century, Kibi no Makibi (693–775), a high-ranking official and leading scholar of the Nara court who had studied in China, wrote a treatise on a famous set of Chinese precepts entitled "Family Instructions for the Yan Clan" (*Yan-shi jiaxun*); and during the Heian period, a number of courtiers wrote precepts for their families. The best known of the Heian *kakun* is Fujiwara no Morosuke's "The Testament of Lord Kujō" (*Kujō-dono go-ikai*).

The first two sets of warrior precepts came from the brush of Hōjō Shigetoki (1198–1261), younger brother of Yasutoki who served as Kyoto or Rokuhara deputy (Rokuhara *tandai*)[12] for the Kamakura shogunate and, later, as "cosigner" (*rensho*) or cochairman of the shogunate's Council of State.[13] Shigetoki wrote his first *kakun* sometime between

---

11. *Umamawari* were mounted horse guards whose duty was to protect the daimyo.

12. There were two *tandai* or deputies, and they were known as Rokuhara deputies because their offices were located in the Rokuhara section of southeastern Kyoto. The deputies were the shogunate's representatives in Kyoto.

13. The *rensho* (literally, "cosigner") served with the shogunal regent as cochairman of the Council of State and ranked just below the regent in the shogunate's hierarchy of offices.

1237 and 1247, during his term as Rokuhara deputy. Often called the "Letter to Na-gatoki," it was prepared for the edification and training of his son Nagatoki (1230–1264), who was preparing to succeed his father in the Kyoto deputyship.

Comprising a preamble and forty-three precepts, the Letter to Nagatoki is primarily a collection of practical advice on how Nagatoki should comport himself and how he should deal with others, including social inferiors, both while he was deputy and afterward.

1. Fear the Buddhas, the Gods, your feudal lord, and your father . . . act with imperturbable courage . . . [and] never be considered a coward . . . constantly train in bow and arrow . . . try to be charming; when facing others, see to it that they come to think well of you. . . .

3. However profitable an undertaking might be, desist from it, though the gain be huge, if your reputation is at stake; stick to your respectability. . . .

5. When otherwise well-behaving retainers or foot-soldiers commit some mi-nor fault, calm down and let them off with a scolding, but do not be so strict as to punish them.

6. Never think big of yourself. You should always consider, "What do others think of the things I do?" Deliberately take a low posture. Be polite even to persons of no consequence. . . .

12. Never drink *sake*, even a single jar, alone. . . .

22. Let no person of discernment—not even a servant—ever see you with loosened topknot or in your underwear. . . .

[Steenstrup, *Hōjō Shigetoki*, pp. 143–151; PV]

Shigetoki wrote his second kakun between 1256, when he retired from his last official position (cosigner), and his death in 1261. Called the "Gokurakuji Letter" after Shige-toki's retirement residence at Gokurakuji in Kamakura, which was constructed in the style of a Buddhist temple, it contains ninety-eight precepts and was intended for the benefit of all Shigetoki's sons and future descendants. The Gokurakuji Letter is similar in content to the much shorter Letter to Nagatoki but differs considerably in tone. Whereas the Letter to Nagatoki appears to have been composed with the thought of encouraging and promoting Nagatoki's career in every way possible and places what we may regard as an excessive emphasis on formalities and appearances, the Gokurakuji Letter is more reflective and seems to be more concerned with cultivating true character than focusing on just what was necessary to get ahead. We can observe this concern with the cultivation of character, for example, in the following precepts.

6. When you see somebody rejoice or grieve, you should meditate on the meaning of the impermanence of worldly things. In this connection, you should

reflect on the law of cause and effect, and meditate on the mutability of life. . . .

13. Right contains elements of wrong, and vice versa. . . .

35. You should assist others even against your own interests. But you should not ask other people's help unless it is absolutely necessary. . . .

38. Learn from the teachings and advice of others. . . .

[Steenstrup, *Hōjō Shigetoki*, pp. 165–174; PV]

Although the preceding was cited to illustrate Shigetoki's wish to cultivate character, the Gokurakuji Letter contains other precepts that are very different in kind. Indeed, like its predecessor, the Letter to Nagatoki, the Gokurakuji Letter is not a carefully ordered or intellectually consistent piece of writing. Rather, it is a collection of thoughts that its author may simply have jotted down, much in the manner of the literary "miscellany" (zuihitsu), without particular regard for how they might hold together as a whole. Thus, along with such elevated thoughts as "You should assist others even against your own interests," we find the rather paranoiac injunction, "When you enter somebody's house, behave as though there are people there peeping at you through cracks in the wall. . . . [Because] 'walls have ears and Heaven eyes,' be on your guard and do not relax!" (precept 29) and the parsimonious advice that "though someone may have given you a splendid fan, use a plain one, one of those of which you get three for a hundred coppers" (precept 18)

HOUSE PRECEPTS IN THE SENGOKU AGE

One of the most striking features of Hōjō Shigetoki's letters, especially when compared to most of the warrior house precepts of the Sengoku age, is the paucity of references to military matters. The letter to Nagatoki contains several precepts that refer to horses (although not in regard to how they should be used in battle), another that encourages Nagatoki to be courageous and "constantly train in bow and arrow" (precept 1), and still another that cautions him not to let his "short sword get rusty" (precept 30). Otherwise, the Nagatoki letter says nothing about military or martial behavior. And the Gokurakuji letter, which is more than twice the length of Nagatoki's, is totally silent on these matters.

The Sengoku house precepts, on the other hand, are full of martial references, as we can see, for example, in these precepts from the "Ninety-Nine Article Testament" (*Iken kyū-jū-kyū-ka-jō*) of Takeda Nobushige, younger brother of the famous Sengoku daimyo Takeda Shingen (1521–1573):

2. You must not show the slightest cowardice on the battlefield.

4. You must devote yourself to military training and to the cultivation of a martial spirit.

39. Do not neglect to keep your weapons prepared.

44. When you are victorious in battle, do not hesitate [and allow the enemy to recoup]. Attack him again.

Although Nobushige's testament deals with many other matters, including etiquette, learning, and moral cultivation, many of its precepts concern the art of war and the proper conduct of a warrior.

The Sengoku age was, of course, a time of constant conflict, and hence we should not be surprised to find the authors of house precepts preoccupied with military matters. Such matters, as we have seen, are also the main focus of the Sengoku house codes, especially in regard to the relationship between the lord (the Sengoku daimyo) and his vassals. There is, however, a significant difference between how the house codes and the house precepts approach the lord-vassal relationship. Whereas the daimyo in their house codes, as noted, seek to assert their authority by summarily demanding that vassals be obedient and loyal, the authors of the house precepts (some of whom were daimyo) attempt to promote and sustain vassal loyalty primarily through persuasion. The principal form of persuasion advocated by the precepts is strong leadership. Thus a number of Sengoku house precepts devote much of their attention to instructing daimyo and other warrior chiefs how to behave as great leaders, especially wartime leaders, who will inspire their vassals to brave—and loyal—deeds in their service.

The testament of Asakura Sōteki, son of the daimyo of Echizen province and a leading battle commander of his family, is probably the richest source of precepts aimed at promoting great leadership. Here are some of the precepts:

3. When it comes to military matters, the commander must never say that anything is impossible. He will reveal his inner weakness.

9. When fighting a major battle or managing a difficult retreat, the commander's warriors will test him by observing his conduct with particular care. The commander must not show the slightest weakness at these times, and should not speak.

10. Call the warrior a dog, call him a beast: winning is his business.

53. For a person who aspires to be a commander, it is essential to earn a reputation as a man of bow and arrow inferior to none.

[Hanawa, ed., *Zoku zoku gunsho ruijū*, vol. 10, pp. 1–9; PV]

THE "SEVENTEEN-ARTICLE TESTAMENT OF ASAKURA TOSHIKAGE" (*ASAKURA TOSHIKAGE JŪ-SHICHI-KA-JŌ*).

Asakura Toshikage was a leading vassal of the Shiba, a collateral family of the Ashikaga that held constable appointments to several provinces. Taking advantage of a great succession dispute that fractured the Shiba in the mid-fifteenth century and plunged it into the turmoil of the Ōnin War, the Asakura under Toshikage seized control of one of the Shiba provinces, Echizen. Appointed the new constable of Echizen by the shogunate in 1471, Toshikage became one of the first Sengoku daimyo and the founder of a family dynasty that ruled Echizen for a century.

Toshikage's testament, which contains seventeen precepts (in imitation, perhaps, of the seventeen articles of Prince Shōtoku's constitution), is often considered to be a house code. In content, however, it is much more like a set of house precepts. In the first two precepts, Toshikage presents one of the earliest and most forceful assertions that, in the Sengoku age, warriors should be judged more on ability than status. Yet, although he thus places ability ahead of status, Toshikage seems to be ambivalent when choosing between ability and loyalty. In precept 9, for example, he says that those warriors "who are unskilled and lack ability, but are steadfast in spirit [that is, are loyal], deserve special attention." But the most distinguishing characteristic of Toshikage's testament is its overall rationality. The highlighting of ability in the first two articles is itself an example of this, as is the advice to heirs and followers in precept 4 that they should not covet famous—and expensive—weapons. A sword worth a thousand *hiki*, he observes, is no match for a hundred spears worth one hundred *hiki* each.

Most impressive of all from the standpoint of rationality is Toshikage's criticism of the commander who, in his preparation for and conduct of battle, wastes time worrying about auspicious days and favorable directions (precept 114). Other records of the Sengoku age attest that many if not most commanders did, in fact, waste much of their time worrying about such things as auspicious days and favorable directions. Some Sengoku daimyo even hired special advisers, called "*gunpai* men" because they carried a fanlike object called a *gunpai*,[14] whose jobs included making decisions about days and directions, judging the workings of the yin and the yang, and consulting the *Classic of Changes* (*Yijing*).

1. In the Asakura domain you must not appoint people on the basis of seniority. They should be chosen for ability and loyalty.

2. You must not assign people without ability to lands or positions just because they have served the Asakura family for generations.

3. Even though the country may be at peace, station spies in domains far and near and always keep abreast of conditions in them.

4. You should not covet famous swords and dirks. The reason for this, to use an example, is that a single sword worth one thousand *hiki* cannot win out against a force of a hundred men supplied with spears costing one hundred *hiki* each. . . .

---

14. The *gunpai* were also sometimes carried by daimyo and other chiefs as symbols of command in battle. Today, *gunpai* are wielded by the referees in sumō matches.

5. We should not eagerly invite troops of the four schools of *sarugaku*[15] down from Kyoto for the pleasure of viewing them. With the money saved, we could select talented people from our domain, send them to Kyoto for dance training, and take pleasure in them ever after.

6. There will be no performances of *nō* at night within the fort precincts.

7. There will be no dispatching of agents to Date and Shirakawa for fine horses, falcons, and the like on the grounds that they are for the use of samurai. . . .

8. At the time of the first attendance of the year, all who are in the service of the domains, beginning with those bearing the Asakura surname, should wear coats made of wadded cotton; and all coats, without exception, should bear the Asakura crest. If some, claiming consideration of status, should wear elegant clothing, lesser samurai of the domain will be reluctant to attend those occasions that are given to show and display. If these lesser samurai, falsely citing illness, should fail to appear for a year or two, the number of samurai attending upon the Asakura will decrease to a small number.

9. Among the men who serve the Asakura house: those fellows who are unskilled and lack ability but are steadfast in spirit deserve special attention. But this does not apply to those who, although of splendid appearance and manner, are weak-spirited. . . .

10. If you treat one who has neglected his duty and one who has served faithfully the same way, how can you expect the one who has served faithfully to maintain his spirit?

11. Make every effort not to employ *rōnin* and similar types from other provinces as secretaries.

12. No one skilled in an art, whether clergy or lay person, should be sent to another domain. However, a person who relies solely on his ability and neglects duty is of no use.

13. It is extremely regrettable if a commander, when fighting a battle that can be won or laying siege to a castle that can be taken, should change his time schedule after choosing an auspicious day and considering which directions are good and which are bad. But if a commander, disregarding auspicious days and favorable directions, assesses in detail the realities of the military situation, lays detailed plans for attacking, responds flexibly to circumstances as they present themselves, and maintains his basic strategy, he is sure to be victorious.

14. About three times each year you should direct three vassals, known for their ability and honesty, to travel around the domain and inquire into the views of the four classes of people. . . .

---

15. *Sarugaku* is a theatrical form from which nō is derived. As used here, *sarugaku* may mean nō.

15. Other than the Asakura fort at Ichijōnotani, no other fortifications are to be constructed in the domain. All major vassals, without exception, are to move to Ichijōnotani.

16. When traveling around to visit shrines and temples or markets, stop your horse occasionally and offer some praise for an unusual place or express a few words of sympathy for one that is run down.

17. When you receive direct reports, you should not permit the slightest discrepancy in regard to truth or falsehood. If you hear that some functionary is seeking to enrich himself, you should firmly impose suitable punishment.

[Satō et al., eds., *Chūsei hōsei shiryō shū*, vol. 3, pp. 339–343; PV]

TAKEDA NOBUSHIGE: THE "NINETY-NINE-ARTICLE TESTAMENT"

Of all the sets of Sengoku house precepts, Takeda Nobushige's "Ninety-Nine-Article Testament" is probably the most concerned with personal ethics. The influence of Confucian ethical thought is clear in a number of its precepts. But we should also note the advocacy of ethical behavior toward vassals that derives from the custom, traceable to earliest times in Japanese warrior history, of treating the lord-vassal relationship in fictive kinship terms. According to this custom, the lord is thought to be like a parent who loves his vassals as he would his own children. Nobushige refers to such love when, for example, he calls on Takeda chiefs to be compassionate toward their retainers (precept 20) and to visit them when they are sick (precept 21).

In his many precepts advising warriors how to behave as warriors, Nobushige offers a broad range of advice from canny—at times cynical—military strategy, much of which is taken from Sun Zi's *Art of War* and other Chinese military classics, to such humanitarian injunctions as not to take lives needlessly (precept 78). We also see in a few of Nobushige's precepts the kind of authoritarianism that is more characteristic of the Sengoku house codes than house precepts, for example, the demand that Takeda family members never entertain thoughts of rebellion against the daimyo, Shingen (precept 1), and that they obey Shingen's orders in all matters, great and small (precept 17).

1. You must never entertain thoughts of rebellion against Lord Shingen. . . .
2. You must not show the slightest cowardice on the battlefield. . . .
4. You must devote yourself to military training and to the cultivation of a martial spirit. . . .
5. You must never lie. . . .
6. You must not be in the slightest unfilial to your father or mother. . . .
9. You should not be in the least disrespectful to people. . . .
10. It is essential to cultivate and train horses. . . .
11. You must not neglect learning. . . .
12. You should have a liking for poetry. . . .

13. Do not neglect the various rites. Cultivate them. . . .

14. Do not overdo the pursuit of pleasure. . . .

15. Whenever you are asked about something, do not reply rudely. . . .

16. In all matters, keep in mind the word "forbearance" . . . .

17. In all matters, great and small, you must not disobey the orders of Lord Shingen. . . .

20. It is essential to be compassionate to the retainers of the house. . . .

21. When a retainer is sick you definitely must visit him, even though it may be inconvenient.

22. You must not ignore the loyal follower. . . .

24. You must not go against the honest admonition. . . .

32. No matter how coldly you may be treated by Lord Shingen, you must not be distressed. It is said that: "although the lord does not behave like a lord, the subject must continue to serve as a subject." . . .

35. You must never speak, to one from another house, of bad things about his house. . . .

38. In employing a person, you should assign him duties in accordance with his ability. . . .

39. Do not neglect to keep your weapons prepared. . . .

42. When ally and enemy face each other, strike before the enemy has prepared his forces. . . .

44. When you are victorious in battle, do not hesitate [and allow the enemy to recoup]. Attack him again. But if the enemy's allies have still not been defeated, be careful. . . .

46. Do not speak approvingly about the enemy's strength, good preparation, and the like in front of people. . . .

47. Warriors [under your command] must not speak badly toward the enemy. It is said: "If you stir bees and arouse them, they become dragons."

48. Do not reveal weakness, even in front of parents and retainers with whom you are otherwise at ease. . . .

53. Even though a father should punish them without thinking, his children should serve him loyally, bearing no resentment. . . .

55. It is absolutely wrong to try to settle everything by fighting. . . .

78. You should never take lives for no reason. . . .

83. Rather than confront the enemy with a thousand men, it is more effective to attack him from the flank with a hundred men. . . .

85. There are many occasions when, although you may know nothing about the secrets of military strategy, it is best to pretend that you do. . . .

86. Listen carefully to the criticism of those below you. No matter how angry the criticism may make you, restrain yourself and secretly make your plans accordingly. . . .

[Yoshida, ed., *Buke no kakun*, pp. 191–241; PV]

Chapter 19

THE REGIME OF THE UNIFIERS

Midway into the sixteenth century, the traditional Japanese state was in crisis and approaching collapse. Its structure had been shaken to the foundations by decades of social upheaval. The two main pillars of its edifice of authority, the imperial institution and the shogunate, had been undermined and weakened, apparently beyond repair. The tide of *gekokujō*, the overthrow of superiors by subordinates, seemed to be irresistible. By the end of the century, however, that tide had been reversed, and a new order had emerged.

One of the architects of Japan's political and social reconstruction, Toyotomi Hideyoshi (1537–1598), stressed in a document included in this chapter that for many years before his advent, "the country was divided, the polity disturbed, civility abandoned, and the realm unresponsive to imperial rule." He was presumptuous to take sole credit for the country's unification, as his predecessor, Oda Nobunaga (1534–1582), had cleared the ground for it, but his descriptive phrases certainly express the historical truth. Not for nothing is the period between 1467 and 1568 called Sengoku, "the country at war." The nation broke up into innumerable fragments, each of them a small-scale polity. At every level, society was divided. Great warlords, called *daimyō*, fought over provincial domains; petty barons (*kokujin*) contended not only with one another but also with the daimyo for territory; the rural gentry (*jizamurai*) resisted being submerged from the top or washed away from the bottom; and farmers defended the newly gained independence of their villages by forming leagues (*ikki*) to protect their interests against their supposed betters. Country folk violently pressed their demands on townspeople, and religious institutions maintained military forces and engaged in attacks on secular lords or on one another.

The extraordinary variety of the types of contention is perhaps illustrated best by the so-called Daishō Ikki (Big League–Little League War) of 1531. This was a civil war between two factions of what was no doubt the Sengoku period's most powerful ecclesiastical organization, the Honganji branch of the Buddhist True Pure Land sect, fought over control of that religious monarchy's provincial domain in Kaga. It may be superfluous to add that neighboring daimyo, local samurai, and True Pure Land sectarians from other provinces participated in this conflict. In 1532, the very next year, the Honganji pontiff's head temple at Yamashina on the outskirts of Kyoto was destroyed, together with the town that had grown up about it, by an alliance of daimyo and a league of Kyoto towns-men mobilized under the banners of the Nichiren sect. The Honganji then moved to Osaka.[1] There the temple formed the heart of what developed into a great citadel. From that supposedly impregnable stronghold, the religious mon-archy's pontiff continued to issue calls for his adherents to rise in arms against the enemies of their faith. True to its reputation, the fortress held to the end of the bitter ten years' war fought between Nobunaga and the Honganji from 1570 to 1580. The terms of a negotiated peace called for it to be handed over to the hegemon, but it was burned down in the process of being transferred. The Honganji's provincial adherents continued to fight.

Conditions being so, great determination, tactical skill, and strategic vision— not to speak of the military wherewithal—were required on the part of a leader who set out to pacify the country and stabilize society. Oda Nobunaga, the daimyo of Owari and Mino, demonstrated this ambition and showed that he had the capacity to pursue those goals.

As early as 1565, the year of Shogun Ashikaga Yoshiteru's assassination, No-bunaga began using a stylized form of the Chinese character *rin* (for the myth-ical beast camelopard) as his monogram, that is, his signature cypher. The camelopard is a prodigy that announces the coming of a ruler who will bring order to the realm—a strikingly evocative emblem of Nobunaga's aspirations. By 1567, a seal bearing the device *tenka fubu*, "the realm subjected to the military," started appearing on documents issued by him. In Confucian terms, the word *tenka* signified humankind living under the moral aegis of Heaven. In conventional sixteenth-century Japanese, two meanings of that word were current: the nominal Japanese empire and, in a more limited geographical sense, the region of the capital city (i.e., Kyoto and the Kinai area), the heartland of Japan. Nobunaga later appropriated this term for the realm that he built and governed, a polity he identified with himself.

---

1. Then known as Ozaka.

This provincial warlord attained national prominence by embracing the cause of the political fugitive Ashikaga Yoshiaki and marching on Kyoto, where he installed his protégé as shogun in the autumn of 1568. From the beginning, the relationship between the two was uneasy. While professing reverence for Nobunaga, the new shogun sought to subordinate him by offering him the positions of vice shogun (*fuku-shōgun*, a new office) or deputy shogun (*kanrei*). Nobunaga turned him down, refusing to be encumbered with offices under the shogunate and reduced to the status of one of its functionaries. Strictly speaking, this refusal left Nobunaga as an outsider without a designated role to play on the central stage of national politics. As far as he was concerned, however, there was no doubt that he, the man of power, took precedence over Shogun Yoshiaki, who was only nominally the pillar of the military (*buke no tōryō*). Not only did Nobunaga preserve his independence, but he also presumed to dictate rules of behavior to the shogun. Nobunaga was to be the boss and Yoshiaki merely the figurehead in their unequal condominium.

Although the shogun was complaisant on the surface, he continued to make overtures to provincial lords despite Nobunaga's insistence that he cease his diplomatic activities or submit his correspondence to censorship. Nobunaga therefore had reason to suspect that the shogun was involved in a coalition of his secular and religious enemies. In March 1573, as that coalition's plans to destroy Nobunaga appeared to be on the verge of succeeding, Yoshiaki finally flung down the gauntlet to his overweening partner. But the shogun's "treason," as Nobunaga called it, was doomed to fail. In early May, Nobunaga surrounded Kyoto with a huge army which first burned the periphery of the capital city and then devastated its northern half. Overwhelmed by this show of force, Yoshiaki sued for peace. Saved for the time being by the imperial court's intervention, the shogun broke the peace again in August. This time, Nobunaga decided that their partnership had outlived its usefulness and chased Yoshiaki into exile. Legally, the Ashikaga shogunate continued to exist until 1588, when Yoshiaki, a wanderer through the provinces, finally renounced his office. But in fact, the shogunate had been demolished in 1573. The implacable hegemon who destroyed this vestige of the medieval political order meant to rule his realm by himself, on his own terms, by the grace of Nobunaga. In 1576 he ordered a majestic new castle to be built for him at Azuchi on Lake Biwa as a symbol of his ascendancy.

Nobunaga sought to dominate the imperial court, too, but found Emperor Ōgimachi more difficult to intimidate than Shogun Yoshiaki. Until 1578, Nobunaga continued to accept imperial titles and ranks, rising to the position of minister of the right (*udaijin*), the third highest office in the court hierarchy. That year, however, he resigned his imperial appointments, stating that the pacification of the country demanded his full attention. In 1582, when he conquered the great eastern domain of the Takeda, Nobunaga appeared to be well on his way to achieving that goal. On his return from that campaign to Azuchi

Castle, in May of that year, the court therefore decided to send him an embassy and offer him "any rank at all" in recognition of his latest triumph. The court's preference may have been to appoint Nobunaga shogun, but that cannot be said with certainty. Nobunaga, of course, could consider other options, including creation of an entirely unprecedented system of government. In any event, he refused to take up the matter with the imperial envoys in Azuchi, deferring the discussion until his next visit to Kyoto. Nobunaga arrived in Kyoto on June 19, 1582, on his way to a campaign against the great western domain of the Mōri. Two days later, he was killed there by a treacherous vassal, Akechi Mitsuhide. The court's proposal was thus left unanswered and the question of Nobunaga's preferred type of rulership unresolved. It is, however, difficult to avoid the conclusion that whatever form his regime might have taken, Nobunaga would have retained supremacy in it.

At the time of Nobunaga's violent death, the realm carved out by him in a series of ruthless military campaigns covered thirty of the traditional Japanese empire's more than sixty provinces and overflowed into three others, stretching across the Japanese heartland from Kōzuke (now Gunma Prefecture) in the east beyond the borders of Bizen (now part of Okayama Prefecture) in the west, and occupied a third of the landmass of Honshu, Japan's main island. He had delegated those territories to men who were subjected to him in a command relationship. He had made daimyo and unmade them, dispossessing even his oldest vassals for failing to "meet the standards of the Way of Arms." He had dragooned his own sons. His pride was so flagrant and his drop from the heights so spectacular that Christian missionaries, who had cheered him on and broadcast the glory of his accomplishments to Europe during his lifetime, portrayed him as Lucifer-like and doomed him to hell after his fall. In his oft-cited moral tale on the death of the tyrant, the Jesuit priest Luís Fróis dramatically depicted Nobunaga's endeavor "to be adored by all, not as a human being of this earth, and a mortal, but as if he were divine, or the lord of immortality." In the absence of supporting contemporary Japanese sources, however, there is no reason to put trust in this highly imaginative writer and give credence to his story of Nobunaga's self-deification.

Both Japanese and Jesuit sources contain ample evidence of Nobunaga's disdain for traditional religious forms and institutions. The most persistently invoked example of his sacrilegious destructiveness is the sack of the Enryakuji in 1571. That temple of the Tendai sect traced its origins to the year 785 and was the very symbol of orthodox Buddhism's entrenched power. Not surprisingly, its destruction was one of the most notorious acts of Nobunaga's violent career. Traditionalists at the imperial court of Kyoto described it at the time as the ruin of Buddha's Law and a disaster for the realm. Contrary to their fears and to the wishful thinking of those Jesuit observers who praised Nobunaga for his deed, he was not a vehement enemy of Buddhism as such. Rather, he was determined to crush all hostile Buddhists—as, indeed, he gave no quarter to anyone who opposed him. On the contemporary scale of atrocity, the burning of the Enryakuji does not rank high. In this regard, Nobunaga outdid himself by far on a number of other occasions when he took the field against combative adherents of the Honganji; he butchered them by the tens of thousands. For that matter, Hideyoshi's sack of Negoro Temple, a great medieval institution, in 1585 was just as bloody an act as Nobunaga's assault on Mount Hiei, although it is not nearly so notorious. Hideyoshi is sometimes portrayed as a patron of the restoration of Buddhism after Nobunaga's devastating attacks, but such a representation is misleading. Both unifiers pursued the same policy: to reduce organized religion to subservience. That policy was perfected under the Tokugawa shogunate, which made Buddhist temples into agents of the state in the surveillance of the populace.

The principle that religion must be kept under state control was only one part of the legacy bequeathed by Nobunaga to his successor, Hideyoshi, and to the third of the great unifiers, Tokugawa Ieyasu (1543–1616). Some of Hideyoshi's most famous national policies—the transfers of daimyo from one domain to another, the demolition of provincial forts, the land survey, and even the sword hunt—were in fact initiated on a provincial or even regional scale in Nobunaga's realm. Hideyoshi's career owed its start to Nobunaga in more senses than one.

Hideyoshi's origins are obscure. After ascending to de facto power over Japan, he tried to exalt his pedigree literally to the skies, by describing his conception as a miraculous one brought about by the wheel of the sun. He is known to have used five family names, none properly his own. The first, Kinoshita, probably did not belong to his father, who was most likely too lowly to have a family name; instead, it appears to have been borrowed by Hideyoshi from his wife's genealogy. The fifth, Toyotomi, means "Bountiful Minister" and is self-descriptive; it was commissioned by Hideyoshi from the imperial court, which created the name of a new "aristocratic" house for the parvenu after his appointment as imperial regent (*kanpaku*) in 1585. Unlike Nobunaga, whose father was a daimyo of some significance (though the Oda were, astonishingly enough, of priestly stock), Hideyoshi had no traceable provenance at all. Legitimizing himself and his regime was therefore a problem that he appreciated keenly, and he resolved it ingeniously. Unlike Nobunaga, who refused to be entangled in the designs of the shogunate or the court, Hideyoshi avidly sought access to the imperial institution, the most hallowed if mummified vessel of authority in Japan. In the event, he found the ideal way to make himself the emperor's master and snatch away whatever prerogatives the court had left. The upstart appropriated the cultural capital of the elite. He had himself appointed to offices for which only members of the "Nine Ministerial Families" were qualified, insinuated himself by a forced adoption into the "Regency" lineage, translated his military liege men into the imperial aristocracy—and Kyoto was his oyster. In the process, he managed to revivify the imperial order of government. By holding its offices, he infused it with his actual power. The title of *kanpaku*—for a long time meaningless except in the court's inner circle—became synonymous with national public authority under Hideyoshi.

For all that dignity and splendor, we must not forget that Hideyoshi began his career under Nobunaga as a menial attendant. He rose in Nobunaga's service to the status of a daimyo and the function of a general charged with conducting important campaigns. After Nobunaga's violent death in 1582, Hideyoshi avenged his lord by destroying his assassin, Akechi Mitsuhide, in battle near Kyoto. Having seized the main chance, he established himself as the lead player on the central stage of Nobunaga's realm, and he confirmed his role as Nobunaga's heir by ordering a funeral for the fallen hegemon to be held with great pomp and circumstance later that year. In 1583, Hideyoshi destroyed those of Oda's paladins who resisted what they considered his unjustifiable assumption of power, in particular the daimyo of Echizen, Shibata Katsuie, and Nobunaga's son, Oda Nobutaka. Hideyoshi marched from one victory to another until he was stopped by Tokugawa Ieyasu in the inconclusive Komaki-Nagakute campaign of 1584. In January of the next year, the two reached an accommodation, and Hideyoshi's march of conquest resumed. In 1585, he subjected the island of Shikoku to the realm of unification; in 1587, he subdued Kyushu; in the summer of 1590, he and a great army of his vassal daimyo destroyed the last great independent power of the Kantō region, the Hōjō of Odawara, and extended the realm across the core area of eastern Japan.

There followed the last act of the drama of unification—the pacification of the vast provinces Dewa and Mutsu, Japan's Far North. There Sengoku conditions persisted. Vicious fighting between daimyo and within daimyo families had continued unabated despite the *kanpaku's* prohibitions of "private quarrels" and his orders for peace in the realm. Hideyoshi was intent on having the northern daimyo accept his mediation, thereby demonstrating allegiance to his regime. When he ordered a general mobilization of his vassals against the Hōjō, he did so with an eye to making all the daimyo submit to his public authority as far as northernmost Japan. Those he found unregenerate or slow to accede to him would be deprived of their domains.

Soon after accepting the surrender of the Hōjō, Hideyoshi himself headed north along a new road built especially for his progress. He made his dispositions on the spot, confiscating some territories. The daimyo who were confirmed in their possessions, however, were ordered to observe three conditions: They were to send their wives and children to reside in Kyoto, Hideyoshi's capital city. They were to destroy all forts save one in their domains, each of them keeping only his own castle, where his retainers' wives and children would take up residence. Each was to undertake a cadastral survey of his fief. In other words, while Hideyoshi forced the northern daimyo to submit to him, he also coerced their samurai into recognizing that daimyo authority was something delegated by the central power and that they therefore had to bend before it. The Sengoku daimyo of the northern provinces would not have been able to attain such a concentration of authority without Hideyoshi's intervention. To be sure, when they received Hideyoshi's vermilion-seal letters of investiture in 1591, they lost their character as independent regional rulers. They had been integrated into the realm of the unification regime.

The last act of the drama was not yet over, however, because uprisings broke out in the northern provinces as soon as Hideyoshi's occupation army was withdrawn toward the end of 1590. According to one daimyo's plea for help to Hideyoshi, "all the samurai and peasants in the entire district hate the Kyoto rule," which was depriving them of their accustomed freedoms. By the autumn of 1591, however, the local leagues (*ikki*) had been wiped out with the assistance of another intervention force. Japan was unified. It was time to plan external exploits.

What did Hideyoshi accomplish? In a remarkably astute analysis of the means by which Hideyoshi governed the realm, written in Kyoto in 1594, the Jesuit priest Organtino Gnecchi-Soldo offered, among other things, the following:

[1] If he give his word of security to any after he has conquered a [province], they shall have no harm, which was not observed by Nobunaga, who never conquered any town or [province] but that he put all the governors thereof to the sword. . . .

[2] He has so impoverished all the rude and rustical multitude (which were they that chiefly caused and procured the tumults and hurly-burly of all these kingdoms) that they have scarcely enough whereon to live, taking from them beside all their armor and weapons.

[3] He has taken away all their private quarrels and questions, which gave always occasions of their farther risings and tumults. Whosoever is now found in any of these risings and tumults, he is sure to die therefore. . . . And it happens often that many do suffer that are not culpable, lest some other might escape that were guilty. By which severity it is brought to pass that you shall seldom hear of any of those former stirs and broils in all *Japonia*.

[4] He uses indifference and equality with all men in ministering justice, not sparing his own kinsfolk and chiefest captains although they be of the blood imperial.

[5] He will not suffer any of his soldiers or gentlemen to live in idleness, setting them [to] work with buildings and repairing of his forts . . . so as they have no time, nor leisure to procure or practice any treasons or rebellions.

[6] He uses [his power] to change the people and potentates of one [province] and place them in another far off.[2]

After making these points, Father Organtino observed that Hideyoshi had hitherto been successful in all of his endeavors, "saving only the enterprise of *China*, which far exceeded his power to compass." He meant the invasion of Korea, where Hideyoshi was stubbornly maintaining forces, even though he had lost any real prospect of victory.

There is something preposterous about Hideyoshi's grandiloquent explanation of his reason for starting a totally unprovoked war. His mission in invading the mainland, he stated, was to spread Japanese culture to China. For Korea, the country in between, his pretensions had tragic consequences. Hideyoshi's armies invaded that country in 1592 and devastated it all the way to the Yalu and Tumen rivers. But by the spring of the following year, they had been chased back south by the Chinese, stalemated, and forced to take up a garrison existence in a string of fortresses along the southern edge of the peninsula. In 1597, Hideyoshi decided to take the offensive again. Again, his armies ravaged the countryside; again, they were forced to withdraw to a string of forts along the sea; again, Hideyoshi stubbornly kept them there, refusing to admit failure until he died on September 18, 1598. His Five Great Elders, the executors of his heritage, brought the Japanese troops back from the earth they had scorched. Hideyoshi's attack on Korea—the tragic overseas export of his drive to mobilize and dominate the daimyo of Japan—proved to be the climacteric of this man of power.

Hideyoshi died imploring the grandees and the chief administrators of his state "again and again" to safeguard the interests of his five-year-old son, Hideyori, and to ensure his succession. Two years later, in 1600, the greatest of the Five Elders, Tokugawa Ieyasu, wrested the hegemony for himself. In 1603 he gave form to the new order in Japan by founding the Tokugawa shogunate. Hideyori had been reduced to the status of one of many daimyo, but he still occupied what was considered Japan's most formidable fortress, the nonesuch his father had erected in Osaka. In 1615, however, Ieyasu stormed Osaka Castle. Hideyori died in its defense, and the house of Toyotomi did not survive the fall of its mighty citadel. In one sense, however, strong traces of Hideyoshi's heritage did survive, as the foundations of the Tokugawa peace, a stable edifice that lasted for two and a half centuries, were built from the blueprint of his—and, more distantly, Nobunaga's—policies.

---

2. "The Coppie of a Letter written from Fa: Organtine one of the Societie of the name of Jhs to the Fa: generall of the same Societie from Meaco in JAPONIA," September 29, 1594, ff. 3v–4v; in "Seven unrecorded contemporary English translations of Jesuit letters from Japan," MS. Jap 3, Houghton Library, Harvard University; orthography modernized by JSAE.

ODA NOBUNAGA

THE HUMILIATION OF THE SHOGUN

THE ARTICLES OF 1570

Not even three months after Ashikaga Yoshiaki's formal investiture as shogun, he was humiliated by the man who had made possible his accession. On January 30, 1569, Nobunaga imposed his will on Yoshiaki by making the shogun accept a set of regulations for the shogunal residence dictated by him. That document both prescribed what types of persons were to be allowed into the shogun's presence and made stipulations regarding the judicial activities of Yoshiaki and his entourage. Evidently unsatisfied with Yoshiaki's measure of compliance during the previous year, Nobunaga in February 1570 issued the following "Articles" to the shogun. Yoshiaki acknowledged the legality of the document by imprinting his seal at the head of the text. He thereby formally submitted to Nobunaga's tutelage, acquiescing in the circumscription of his right to conduct correspondence with the daimyo and the cancellation of authoritative instructions issued by him. Yoshiaki acknowledged that the competency to govern the realm had "in fact" been taken over by Nobunaga. The part left for the shogun to play was the largely ceremonial one of looking after the imperial court.

The document is addressed to the priest Asayama Nichijō and Akechi Mitsuhide, who at the time were in the service both of Yoshiaki and Nobunaga and acted as liaison officers between them. The term *gogeji* refers especially to documents issued by the shogun to grant or confirm landed proprietorships. The important political concept *kōgi*, rendered as "the public authority" throughout this chapter, may, depending on the context, signify the official polity or the common weal. Because it is often personalized, it can also stand for the ruler who has been invested with official authority or, for that matter, one who has arrogated that authority to himself.

Black Seal [Shogun Yoshiaki] Articles

[1]. Should there be occasion for the shogun to send orders to the provinces in the form of a letter issued over his signature (*gonaisho*), he shall inform Nobunaga, who will append his letter of endorsement.

[2]. All prior shogunal directives (*gogeji*) are void. His Highness shall make new dispositions on this basis, after careful consideration.

[3]. Should it happen that His Highness wishes to recognize or reward those who have given loyal service to the public authority (*kōgi*; i.e., the shogun) without there being estates available for that purpose, Nobunaga will allot such, if must be from his own domains, as the shogun may require.

[4]. Since the affairs of the realm (*tenka*) have in fact been put in Nobunaga's hands, he may take measures against anyone whomsoever according to his own discretion and without the need to obtain the shogun's agreement.

[5]. As the realm is at peace, His Highness shall unfailingly attend to the affairs of the imperial court. That is all.

Eiroku 13.I.23 (27 February 1570)   VERMILION SEAL *[Nobunaga]*
[To]
Nichijō Shōnin
Lord Akechi Jūbyōe no Jō

[Okuno, *Zōtei Oda Nobunaga monjo no kenkyū*, I, pp. 343–345, no. 209; JSAE]

THE REMONSTRANCE OF 1572

This seventeen-article remonstrance, which bears no date but is known to have been made public by the early part of November 1572, was issued against the background of a gathering storm. That year had not been a triumphant one for Nobunaga. He was stalemated by a coalition consisting of Asakura Yoshikage, the daimyo of Echizen; Azai Nagamasa, the lord of Odani Castle in northern Ōmi Province; Kennyo, the pontiff of the Osaka Honganji, and the armed leagues (*ikki*) of his provincial adherents; and a variety of other enemies. Nobunaga expected the powerful eastern daimyo Takeda Shingen also to enter the ranks against him. It is possible and even likely, though not proven, that Shogun Yoshiaki was a covert participant in this coalition. It is clear from the following document that Nobunaga distrusted Yoshiaki. Hence he sought to defame and discredit the shogun. Impeached before the people of the realm, Yoshiaki would be deprived of his public authority.

The document opens and closes with unsubtle allusions to the fate that awaits malfeasant shoguns—Yoshiaki's own brother, Ashikaga Yoshiteru, assassinated in 1565, and Ashikaga Yoshinori, killed in 1441. Recriminations regarding Yoshiaki's failure to keep the agreement forced on him in 1570 initiate the argument. There follows a long list of articles indicting the shogun for "improper" and "outrageous" behavior. Yoshiaki is stamped as an unjust, niggardly, and greedy ruler, one so blinded by ill judgment and favoritism that he cannot even make the elementary distinction between loyal and disloyal. This derogation of the shogun is justified by repeated appeals to public opinion. For instance, according to Nobunaga it was "the talk of the entire realm" that "the era name Genki is unpropitious." Since that era name had been adopted on Yoshiaki's initiative, this statement was just another way of declaring the shogun unfit to rule. (The articles omitted from this translation cite particular cases of Yoshiaki's alleged underhandedness, failure to reward merit, disregard of legality, obstinacy, vindictiveness, and extortionate misfeasance in pecuniary matters. They reinforce the general charge of greed.)

Nobunaga inferred that Yoshiaki was amassing funds in preparation for taking military action against his sometime patron. True to Nobunaga's suspicions, the shogun openly joined the coalition of his enemies in March 1573. But that decision was ill timed. A mere two months later, the death of Takeda Shingen, the strongest of those enemies, freed Nobunaga to attack the others. In August 1573, Nobunaga expelled the hapless Yoshiaki from the capital and its region, in effect putting an end to the Ashikaga shogunate.

[1]. The imperial court was neglected by Lord Kōgen'in [Shogun Yoshiteru], so in the end he met misfortune; this is an old story. Accordingly, from the time of your entry into the capital, I have advised Your Highness never to be remiss in your attention to His Majesty's affairs. Nevertheless, you quickly forgot your resolution, and there has been a decline in recent years. I find this inexcusable.

[2]. You have sent letters over your signature to various provinces, requesting horses and such. You should have had the foresight to consider what would be thought of such behavior. In cases absolutely requiring the issuance of orders, however, I had stated beforehand that you should let Nobunaga know and that I would add my endorsement. You agreed, but did not so act; instead, you have been sending such letters and issuing instructions to distant provinces. This is contrary to the previous agreement. I stated a long time ago that if you heard of suitable horses and so forth wherever, Nobunaga would arrange to have them presented to you. You have not acted accordingly but have instead been issuing instructions in secret. I find this improper.

[3]. You have failed to make appropriate awards to a number of lords who have attended you faithfully and have never been remiss in their loyal service to you. Instead, you have awarded stipends to some who, to this day, have nothing much to their credit. That being so, the distinction between loyal and disloyal becomes irrelevant. What will people think? I find this improper.

[4]. You have reacted to recent rumors by initiating the removal of your household goods. This news has not escaped the notice of town or country. Indeed, I hear that it has caused extreme disquiet in Kyoto, and I am shocked. I exerted my utmost efforts in building and equipping a residence for you. You can live there in peace and comfort; instead, you are moving your goods. Where do you then intend to move? This is a sad affair. When such a thing happens, it means that all of Nobunaga's exertions have been to no purpose. . . .

[6]. I am grieved to hear of your harsh treatment of men who enjoy Nobunaga's friendship, and even of their women and other dependents. If, having learned that someone is on friendly terms with me, you were to treat that person with special consideration—now, that is something I would certainly be grateful for. What could be the reason for your being so contrary? . . .

[10]. That the era name Genki is unpropitious and ought to be changed was the talk of the entire realm. Accordingly, the imperial court made the arrangements necessary to change it, but you failed to provide the mere pittance required, and the delay continues. This is a matter that concerns the realm's interests, so I find this sort of negligence on your part improper. . . .

[12]. It is a patent fact that provincial rulers present gold and silver to you by

way of a salute or a gratuity. You hide these gifts away, not putting them to any use. What could your purpose be? . . .

[14]. I hear that this past summer you sold your castle's rice supply for gold and silver. That a shogun should engage in trade is something unknown until now. The times being what they are, it would, I think, be good for your reputation to keep commissary supplies on hand in your storehouses. I am astonished at this state of affairs.

[15]. Should you wish to reward the boys you retain for night duty, anything will do as long as it is insubstantial. To appoint one of them shogunal intendant or arrange for another to profit from extraordinary imposts is, however, to invite notoriety throughout the realm. I find this outrageous.

[16]. It has come to my attention that the lords of your entourage care nothing for such accomplishments as wielding arms or managing the commissary and are interested solely in the pursuit of trade, that is, of gold and silver. These appear to be preparations for exile. Is not Your Highness amassing gold and silver so that you can leave your residence at the slightest rumor? Even the populace will have noted that your intention is to abandon Kyoto. To be sure, looking out for number one is nothing so unusual.

[17]. You are steeped in avarice through and through. It is well known that you show no concern either for ethics or for your own reputation. Down to the crudest of peasants and dirt farmers, everyone calls you the evil shogun. I understand that Lord Fukōin [Shogun Yoshinori] was also called that, but that is another story. Why do people speak ill of you behind your back? Should you not reflect on this?

[Okuno, Zōtei Oda Nobunaga monjo no kenkyū, I, pp. 565–576, no. 340; JSAE]

THE ASSAULT ON MOUNT HIEI AND
THE BLESSINGS OF NOBUNAGA

As this extract from The Chronicle of Lord Nobunaga (Shinchō-Kō ki) seeks to demonstrate, Nobunaga's assault on the Enryakuji was not so much a wanton act of sacrilege as retaliation against a military adversary. The temple had permitted the strategic position it occupied on Mount Hiei between Kyoto and Lake Biwa to be used by the armies of the daimyo Asakura Yoshikage and Azai Nagamasa, enemies who had fallen on Nobunaga's rear and forced him to abandon a campaign in the area of Osaka in 1570. Sakamoto, the Enryakuji's rich municipality on Lake Biwa, became one of their bases, and they were given succor by the monks when Nobunaga counterattacked. In short, Nobunaga had ample justification when he took his revenge on the Enryakuji in September 1571. To consolidate his position on Kyoto's eastern flank, he then installed his own man, Akechi Mitsuhide, in Sakamoto, assigning him landed properties from the temple's extensive domains.

The author of *The Chronicle of Lord Nobunaga* (*Shinchō-Kō ki*), Nobunaga's old vassal Ōta Gyūichi (1527–after 1610), went on to serve Hideyoshi in important administrative capacities and after Hideyoshi's death entered the service of his son Hideyori. Ōta's elaborate chronicle, partially based on his diaries, was completed in 1610. It is composed of an introductory book and fifteen books covering year by year the period 1568 to 1582, "the fifteen years Lord Nobunaga ruled the realm." The introductory book has serious flaws, but the rest of the work is meticulous and highly reliable; indeed, it is an indispensable source for that period of Japanese history. Ōta is, on the whole, a factually oriented and dry, not florid, writer. In these two passages, however, he permits himself a certain level of rhetorical embellishment, juxtaposing the tale of Nobunaga's brutality with a gushing account of his generosity toward the imperial court and the blessings brought upon the realm by the hegemon. Needless to say, Nobunaga cultivated the court with a view toward manipulating it. The restoration of the imperial palace, begun in 1569, was a project through which Nobunaga sought to display his munificence, bring into prominence his contributions to revitalizing the political order, and establish his own claim to public authority.

Ōta and other sixteenth- and seventeenth-century writers frequently refer to Tentō, the Way of Heaven, in seeking to explain history. Their notion of Tentō conveys the sense of a governing natural order that is impersonal yet exerts a moral force, guiding the endeavors of the virtuous to success while ensuring the downfall of the wicked. The Jesuit missionaries found the term to be related to their own concept of Heavenly Providence and used it as a synonym for God while stressing that pagans meant something else by it.

(5) On the 12th of the Ninth Month [September 30, 1571], Nobunaga attacked Mount Hiei. The reason was as follows: The previous year, Nobunaga had laid siege to Noda and Fukushima. As those castles were about to fall, the Asakura of Echizen, joined by Azai Bizen, moved on Sakamoto. Realizing that things would get untidy if they forced their way into Kyoto, Nobunaga withdrew from Noda and Fukushima. Straightaway, he crossed Ausaka, confronted the Echizen and Ōmi forces, and chased them up Mount Tsubokasa with the intention of letting them starve there. Nobunaga then summoned the monk soldiers from the Enryakuji and promised, striking steel on steel,[3] that if the monks were to give him loyal service on this occasion, he would restore all of the Enryakuji's domains in the provinces under his rule, with their original privileges intact. Moreover, he sent the monks a vermilion-seal document to that effect. But if their religious principles prevented them from supporting one side exclusively,

---

3. To emphasize the solemnity of his pledge, a samurai might strike the blade of his sword or the sword guard with a piece of metal.

he reasoned, then they should not interfere at all. Nobunaga also made it clear to the monks that if they violated these conditions, then he would burn down the whole mountain from the Central Hall (Konponchūdō) and the Twenty-One Shrines of the Mountain King (Sannō) on down.

Was it that their time had come? Mount Hiei was the guardian of the imperial capital. Nevertheless, the monks who lived on the mountain and at its foot cared nothing for penances, ascetic exercises, and religious customs and felt no shame at the derision of the realm. Heedless of the Way of Heaven (Tentō) and its terrors, they gave themselves over to lewdness, ate fish and fowl, and became habituated to bribes in gold or silver. They took the side of the Azai and Asakura, and while they did as they pleased, Nobunaga restrained himself and let them be for the moment, because he was wont to adjust himself to the times and the circumstances. To Nobunaga's regret, he had to withdraw his army. In order to dispel his resentment, this day, the 12th of the Ninth Month, he invested Mount Hiei. Surging round in swarms, Nobunaga's troops in a flash set fire to a multitude of holy Buddhas, shrines, monks' quarters, and sūtra scrolls; they spared nothing, from the Central Hall and the Twenty-One Shrines of the Mountain King on down. How miserable it was to see it all reduced to ashes! At the foot of the mountain, men and women, young and old ran about panic-stricken. In feverish haste, barefooted, they all fled up Mount Hachiōji, seeking refuge in the precincts of the inner Hie Shrine. Soldiers shouting battle cries advanced up the mountain from all sides. One by one they cut off the heads of monks and laymen, children, wise men and holy men alike. They presented the heads to Lord Nobunaga, saying: "Here is an exalted prelate, a princely abbot, a learned doctor, all the men of renown at the top of Mount Hiei." Moreover, they captured countless beautiful women and young boys and led them before Nobunaga. "We don't care about the evil monks," they shrieked, "but spare us!" Nobunaga, however, absolutely refused to reprieve them. One by one, they had their heads chopped off, a scene horrible to behold. Thousands of corpses lay scattered about like so many little sticks, a pitiful end. Thus Nobunaga dispelled years of accumulated rancor. Shiga District was now given to Akechi Jūbyōe, who took up residence in Sakamoto.

On the 20th of the Ninth Month, Lord Nobunaga returned from his campaign to Gifu in Mino Province.

On the 21st of the Ninth Month, acting on Nobunaga's orders, Kawajiri Yohyōe and Niwa Gorōzaemon invited Takamiya Ukyō no Suke and all prominent members of his family to Sawayama and killed them. The Takamiya put up a fight but were finished off without difficulty. The reason for this measure was that during the previous year's Noda and Fukushima campaign, the Takamiya had acted in concert with the Honganji in scheming to cause an uprising. Halfway through the campaign they had deserted their post at Kawaguchi, an outpost of Nobunaga's fort in Tenmagamori, and had gone over to the side of Osaka.

(6) The imperial palace had long gone to ruin and nothing was left of its former splendor. Thinking that it would bring blessings, Nobunaga had in a previous year appointed Nichijō Shōnin and Murai Sadakatsu as superintendents of a project to repair it. At length, after three years' work, the Shishiiden, the Seiryōden, the Naishidokoro, the Shōyōsha, and various other palace quarters were all finished. Lord Nobunaga moreover thought of a plan that would unfailingly provide for the imperial court's income for all times to come. He gave out a loan in rice to the townsmen of Kyoto and ordered that the interest be presented to the court every month. At the same time, Nobunaga also brought the maintenance of impoverished nobles in order, amply securing their family succession. The satisfaction of all the people of the realm could not have been greater. One could not possibly measure Nobunaga's glory and the dignity of his family in our empire.

Furthermore, Nobunaga abolished all duties at toll barriers throughout the provinces under his control. The realm was at peace. Travelers could come and go as they pleased, thanks to Nobunaga's benevolence. As his compassion was exceedingly profound, so did his blessings and his good fortune surpass the ordinary. This was the foundation of his ever-increasing prosperity. But the cause of it all was Nobunaga's desire to "study the Way, rise in the world, and gain fame in future generations."[4] How auspicious! How auspicious!

[Ōta, Shinchō-Kō ki, bk. 4, sec. 5–6, pp. 126–129; JPL]

NOBUNAGA IN ECHIZEN

LETTERS FROM THE BATTLEGROUND

Nobunaga shows his true face in these letters to Murai Sadakatsu, an old and valued vassal whom he had made governor of Kyoto (tenka shoshidai) upon Shogun Yoshiaki's expulsion from the capital. Rather than a military campaign, the conquest of Echizen is made to appear like a ruthless head-hunting expedition. In part, the ferocity is made explicable by Nobunaga's rancorous frustration: He had conquered Echizen once before by defeating its daimyo, Asakura Yoshikage, the lord of Ichijōdani, in 1573, but he could not hold the province; it had been taken over by militant sectarians of the Osaka Honganji, his most indefatigable foe. Without a doubt, however, it was even more the nature of the enemy—peasants mobilized by the religious motive—that called forth such terrifyingly matter-of-fact expressions of joy at the slaughter. To be sure, Nobunaga sheds no tears for the hundreds of "proper Ichijō samurai" who also fell victim to his search parties.

The grisly piece of banter about Wakabayashi's cognomen that Nobunaga permits

---

4. Classic of Filiality, I.

himself vis-à-vis Murai, who shared the title Nagato no Kami with that famous captain of the Honganji's forces, is truly startling. In spite of Nobunaga's double-sure assurance about his death, Wakabayashi had escaped to fight another day. Shimotsuma Chikugo Hokkyō, the Honganji's governor of Echizen, was less fortunate. In disguise, he tried to flee but was discovered and killed by adherents of a rival branch of the True Pure Land sect.

Nobunaga deployed massive forces against Echizen. These letters show many of his most important generals in action: Koretō Hyūga no Kami, as Akechi Mitsuhide was known at the time; Hashiba Chikuzen no Kami, later to become famous under the name Toyotomi Hideyoshi; Takikawa Kazumasu and Korezumi Gorōzaemon (i.e., Niwa Nagahide); Sakuma Kuemon and his son Jinkurō; Shibata Katsuie; and Maeda Toshiie. As a result of their efforts, Nobunaga felt confident enough to boast that not a single enemy was left in Echizen. Insofar as the provinces of Kaga, Noto, and Etchū were concerned, however, his repeated trumpeting of success amounted to no more than empty vaunting. The Honganji's Kaga domain was not subdued until the very end of 1580, Noto not integrated into Nobunaga's realm until 1581, and Etchū not fully pacified until 1582.

Your letter of the 15th arrived this morning, the 17th, and I have read it.

[1]. News about this front: I arrived at camp in Tsuruga on the 14th inst. and on the 15th distributed the troops for the advance, some by the Kinome approach and others along the seaside or by other routes. But first I attacked and destroyed two forts on the seaside, Sasanoo and Suizu, took many heads, and amused myself thoroughly.

[2]. These are the tactics I ordered. I was to move out yesterday, the 16th, by the Kinome approach. As part of the plan, Koretō Hyūga no Kami was to proceed from the seaside to the town of Fuchū and lie in wait for the enemy troops sure to run that way once I broke through at Kinome and scattered the defenders. Hashiba Chikuzen no Kami, still smarting from having lost Kinome Castle in last year's fighting, coordinated with Koretō, and both of them advanced on Fuchū the night of the 15th. As their forces, deployed in two contingents, lay in wait there, sure enough groups of five hundred or three hundred stragglers came fleeing straight at them. In the town of Fuchū itself we took as many as one and a half thousand heads, and in the environs we took in all two thousand more. We killed three ranking captains: Saikōji, Shimotsuma Izumi, and Wakabayashi. I should have written down Wakabayashi's cognomen but did not, as it would not do to have it mistaken for yours; in any event, he was such a villain that it surely is anything but unknown. In short, I pacified the province in two days. The town of Fuchū is nothing but corpses, with not a clear spot anywhere around; I'd like to show it to you! Today I shall search every mountain and every valley, and I shall kill them all.

[3]. Having subjugated Echizen like this, I am now at leisure to make my dispositions in all regards as intended, so rest your mind at ease. You should

pass all of this along to Araki Shinano no Kami, Miyoshi Yamashiro no Kami, and all the others; it will gladden their hearts. I shall be sure to write more. Respectfully,

[Tenshō 3].VIII. 17 (21 September 1575)   Nobunaga VERMILION SEAL
[To]
Lord Murai Nagato no Kami.

P.S. As I was about to send you a special courier, your messenger came, and I shall take advantage of it. So this is how it is.
. . .
Your letter of the 20th arrived in Fuchū today, the 22nd, and I have read it.

[1]. I understand that you have received the letter I sent you on the 17th with news of this front.

[2]. After smashing the enemy defenses at Kinome and Hachibuse and de-capitating Saikōji, Shimotsuma Izumi Hokkyō, and Wakabayashi as well as Toyohara Saihōin, Asakura Saburō and their ilk, I divided the troops into four contingents and had them search every mountain and every valley without exception, cutting heads. On the 17th, more than two thousand heads were delivered; seventy or eighty were taken alive, so their heads were cut off. On the 18th, five or six hundred heads at a time arrived from various places, quite impossible to tell how many in all. On the 19th, more than six hundred arrived from the detachment of Chasen, Sanshichirō, and Kōzuke no Suke [Nobun-aga's sons Nobukatsu and Nobutaka and his brother Nobukane] reinforced by Harada Bitchū no Kami and Takikawa Sakon; from Ujiie and Mutō's detach-ment, more than three hundred, proper Ichijō samurai. Shibata Shuri no Suke and Korezumi Gorōzaemon no Jō attacked and destroyed the stronghold held by Asakura Yozō. They killed more than six hundred men of standing; more than a hundred were taken alive, so their heads were cut off. On the 20th I sent [Sakuma] Kuemon no Jō, Maeda Matazaemon, as well as men of the Horse Guards to a mountain called Hinagatake, where they cut down more than a thousand. More than a hundred were taken alive, so their heads, too, were chopped off. Chasen and Takikawa's detachment made a clean sweep of enemy places of refuge in Ōtaki and Hakusan; more than six hundred. Apart from that, [the units led by] Hirano Tosa and Asami each cut down fifty or sixty, as did the musketeers. Those taken alive arrived in groups of ten or twenty at a time, hard to tell how many in all. On the 21st, from Sakuma Jinkurō's detachment, more than five hundred; more than ten were taken alive, so their heads were cut off.

[3]. Asakura Magosaburō held out at the fort of Kazao. He made various assurances of future friendship, but I refused to pardon him. Yesterday, the 21st, I made him commit suicide. His retainers, from the Kaneko brothers on down, had their heads chopped off.

[4]. On the 21st, Shibata and Korezumi reported cutting down more than a

thousand. On the same day, Ujiie and Mutō reported wiping out a countless number in two valleys. Thirty-six were taken alive, including Ryōgen, the Honganji's deputy in Kōno; so their heads, too, were cut off.

[5]. Today, the 22nd, a few prisoners have arrived. Apart from that, there have been no reports as yet. With the enemy more or less killed off like this, I am now at leisure. Tomorrow, the 23rd, I shall move camp to Ichijōdani. I shall follow up with another sweep through the province, and I shall search them out and kill them all.

[6]. It was previously reported that Shimotsuma Chikugo had been driven into a river; actually, he was making his way to Kazao, supporting himself on a bamboo cane and wearing a bamboo hat. An individual loyal to me cut off his head. When it was delivered here, I must say I relished the sight.

[7]. Regarding Kaga: The two gateway districts [Enuma and Nomi] are totally beaten! More than ten personages of the Kahoku and Ishikawa districts have sent me a pledge over their joint signatures, making various assurances of future friendship. They say that they will put all the [deputies] sent there by Osaka to death and will present themselves before me to show their loyalty. I sent them a vermilion-seal document to the effect that I shall pardon them if what they say proves true. So that is settled. Needless to say, once Kaga Province is settled, Noto and Etchū are, too.

[8]. Regarding this province: The year before last, Azai was still to be reckoned with in Odani, so I dealt with this place hastily and hurried back. This time my attention is demanded nowhere else, so I shall take my time and sojourn here for a while. I want to make the dispositions that will ensure Echizen does not rise again. For that reason my plan is to stay here another month or two.

[9]. You have not had the chance to see this province yet, I believe. First of all I should like to show you the guard posts and other fortifications erected on difficult terrain such as Kinome and other key spots. I am making ready a place for you to stay, and the building is just about finished, so do make the trip down here.

Let me assure you again: Not a single enemy is left in this province. That being also the case with Kaga, Noto, and Etchū, no urgent matters occupy my attention. Rather, I am staying here to make sure I order the proper dispositions to be taken regarding punitive measures in the province, and so forth. If there is the slightest sign of an enemy's stirring in the East or in the West, wherever it may be, know that I am prepared to move out.

Respectfully,
Nobunaga

[Tenshō 3]. VIII. 22 (26 September 1575)
[To]
Lord Murai Nagato no Kami

[Okuno, *Zōtei Oda Nobunaga monjo no kenkyū* II,
pp. 61–64, no. 533, pp. 66–70, no. 535; JSAE]

REGULATIONS FOR THE PROVINCE OF ECHIZEN

After completing the conquest of Echizen, Nobunaga appointed his general Shibata Katsuie governor of the province. Shibata is the unnamed addressee of the "Regulations" that follow. His functions are different from those of a medieval military governor (*shugo*), and he may be more aptly described as the custodian of the province on behalf of Nobunaga. Shibata's overlord orders him to be a firm but fair administrator yet leaves him few discretionary powers. Indeed, three overseers (*metsuke*) are assigned to Echizen to report on his conduct in office, just as he is to report on theirs. Nobunaga remains in firm command: "You must resolve to do everything as I say." The public and private aspects of Nobunaga's government of his realm merge into one as he demands reverence for his person. This document is an excellent example of his imperious presumption.

Two of the so-called Echizen Triumvirs named in the supplementary paragraph were to become daimyo over entire provinces themselves. (Fuwa Mitsuharu, who died in early 1581, was the exception.) In the autumn of 1581, Maeda Toshiie was assigned the newly conquered province of Noto, and Sassa Narimasa was allotted Etchū. These are early examples of the policy of daimyo transfers, later to be applied methodically by Hideyoshi and by the Tokugawa shogunate. To be transferred to a new domain was not an unmixed blessing, even if the move brought with it a rise in status and an increase of income. When the lord was uprooted, his vassal band had to be restructured as well.

[1]. No extraordinary imposts shall be levied on the province. Should there be cogent reasons for doing so, however, refer the matter to me for a decision.

[2]. Provincial samurai who have been left in place shall not be treated willfully but rather with unstinting courtesy. For all that, do not let the reins slip. Make sure you keep a close eye on fortifications and other such matters. Scrupulously turn over estates to the recipients [designated by Nobunaga].

[3]. Adjudication must be fair and just. Do not ever take sides or play favorites when you sit in judgment. Should it happen that the two sides remain unsatisfied, the case shall be settled by referring it through an agent to me.

[4]. The estates of Kyotoite proprietors shall be returned to them, insofar as they actually held proprietary authority before the disturbances, in accordance with [Nobunaga's] vermilion-seal letter. However, I reserve the right of refusal.

[5]. Toll barriers have been abolished throughout my domains, and the same shall obtain in this province.

[6]. A large province is being left in your hands. Guard it carefully; negligence will be considered miscreant. Take care of Arms above all. Stockpile weapons and commissary supplies, so that you are certain the province can be held against attack for five or even ten years. In any event, do not be greedy; determine what is due, ascertain that it is paid. Stay away from young boys;

abstain from amateur theatricals, parties and promenades, and other such diversions.

[7]. Do without falconry, unless it be to scout terrain; otherwise it profits you nothing. There is no objection to children's engaging in it.

[8]. Although this depends on the domain's productivity, two or three places shall be left without designated recipients, to be kept in custody by you with the explanation that it is land reserved for future award to individuals in proportion to their loyal service. If men observe that no estates are available for rewarding even those most exemplary in their dedication to Arms, their spirits and their loyalty are apt to sink. Act with prudence in this matter! As long as no holder is appointed, the property remains [Nobunaga's] direct domain.

[9]. At the risk of repeating myself: You must resolve to do everything as I say. For all that, do not flatter me when you feel that I am unreasonable or unjust. If anything should trouble you in this regard, tell me, and I may comply with your request. In any event, you shall revere me and shall bear me no evil thought behind my back. Your feelings toward me must be such that you do not even point your feet in the direction where I am. If you act that way, then you will be blessed with good fortune forevermore, as befits the proper samurai. Good sense is all-important.

Tenshō 3.IX. [5]

Echizen Province is for the most part left at Shibata's disposal. You three, however, shall act as Shibata's overseers and are assigned two districts. Hence you shall report without duplicity on the good and bad points of his conduct, and Shibata shall report on the good and bad points of yours. Above all, act with due care that you sharpen each other's efficiency. Permissiveness will be considered miscreant.

Tenshō 3.IX. (1575)
[To]
Lord Fuwa Kawachi no Kami
Lord Sassa Kura no Suke
Lord Maeda Matazaemon

[Ōta, *Shinchō-Kō Ki*, bk. 8, sec. 7, pp. 197–200; JSAE]

---

5. The "Regulations" and their supplementary paragraph are included in *Shinchō-Ki* under the entry for Tenshō 3.IX.14 (October 17, 1575).

NOBUNAGA IN AZUCHI

THE PROUD TOWER

At the end of 1575, the year of his conquest of Echizen, Nobunaga made a show of turning over the affairs of the house of Oda to his eldest son, Nobutada, whom he installed as the daimyo of Mino and Owari Provinces in Gifu Castle, his own headquarters since 1567. At the beginning of 1576, Nobunaga ordered the construction of a new fortress for himself at Azuchi in Ōmi Province, and he moved to the site in March. These actions underlined his claim to being more than a regional ruler. Azuchi Castle was to be the visible sign of his supremacy as the lord of the Tenka, the realm subjected by his military might and governed by virtue of his prowess.

Azuchi occupied a strategic position between the Sea of Japan and the Pacific Ocean, permitting the rapid deployment of forces throughout central Japan. It also offered easy access to the Inland Sea and western Japan. Above all, Azuchi was close, but not too close, to Kyoto (or Miyako, as the city was commonly called then)—about fifty-three kilometers away by the most convenient land route from the imperial palace, the seat of a court that Nobunaga wanted to dominate while avoiding unwanted entanglements in its ceremonial affairs. Especially because of its relative proximity to the imperial capital, Azuchi was preferable to Gifu, some eighty kilometers farther off to the east along roads apt to be blocked in the winter.

Nobunaga built his castle atop a hill called Azuchiyama, then a promontory jutting out into Lake Biwa but now, owing to reclamation work, no longer near the water. As its summit is no more than 199 meters above sea level (and only 114 meters above the level of the lake), this is not a "large mountain," contrary to the following account. Indeed, Azuchi Castle marks a transition between the medieval mountain fort (*yamajiro*) and the residential castle built on level ground (*hirajiro*) that became common in the early modern period. At the apex rose the donjon (*tenshu*) that was the figurative axis of Nobunaga's realm. This tower was completed and became his official residence in June 1579. Further building works continued until Nobunaga's assassination on June 21, 1582, put an end to his project. The fortress survived its master by less than two weeks. Everything went up in flames; who set the fire is still not known.

Contemporary observers exhausted their stock of superlatives in describing Azuchi Castle. The following account is taken from the annual report for 1581 submitted by the head of the Christian mission in Japan, Padre Gaspar Coelho, to the general superior of the Society of Jesus in Rome. Coelho's description of Azuchi was incorporated—with emendations and additions—in the *History of Japan* written between 1583 and 1594 by his fellow Jesuit Luís Fróis, whose text is excerpted here [between square brackets] to supplement the more contemporary account. Fróis is known for creative embellishment, but there is no reason to question his impressions of the palace built by Nobunaga in the castle's main enceinte (*honmaru*), one level below the donjon. The extraordinary opulence of this complex of buildings and gardens, which included a hall meant to host an imperial visit, is attested in Ōta Gyūichi's "Chronicle of Lord Nobunaga." Ōta, who noted that "in these chambers all is gold," could not restrain his admiration for the imaginativeness of the landscapes and other striking designs with which Kano Eitoku decorated the palace's interior. Eitoku, the premier painter of his day, also was responsible for the elaborate decorative program of the donjon, which culminated on the top story with portrayals of Chinese sages and paragons of good government, evoking the Confucian ideal of the Mandate of Heaven. Eitoku's aesthetic direction combined with his uncompromising patron's demand for perfect workmanship guaranteed that Nobunaga's castle was not only replete with luxury but also governed by taste.

Although Nobunaga is lord of Miyako and of the Tenka (for that is how the Japanese call the monarchy of Japan), he nonetheless resides ordinarily in the kingdom of Ōmi, in the town of Azuchiyama, which is located fourteen leagues from Miyako. . . . There Nobunaga built a new town [with] a fortress—a town that is now the most imposing sight in Japan, excelling all others in its site, its pleasant air, the nobility of its residents, and the opulence of its buildings.

This town is situated on a level tract of land which has on one side a large and breezy lake (. . .) with many inlets into the settlement; on the other side are very large, cultivated fields. It lies at the foot of a large mountain, one divided into three parts, that is, three smaller hills covered with groves of trees and made pleasant by the refreshing verdure that occupies their entire surface. The lake glides round about these hills, making the site not only beautiful but strong. Nobunaga determined to display his glory and magnificence by erecting a lavish, beautiful, and impregnable fortress on the highest of the three hills.

At its foot was built the township for the common people [and artisans] to reside, adorned by very broad and straight streets. By now it will have five or six thousand inhabitants. Elsewhere at the foot of the mountain, in a place separated by an arm of the lake from the township, Nobunaga ordered the lords and noblemen to build their houses. As all were eager to comply with his wishes, the lords of the kingdoms subject to him at once built very noble and rich edifices there. All their houses are encircled by graceful, high stone walls, topped by parapets, in such a manner that each in itself is a fine fortress. Thus the houses clamber up the mountain, surrounding the highest of the three hills on all sides.

At the top of that hill is Nobunaga's fortress, which in its opulence, order, and architectural design can compete with the noblest and most sumptuous of Europe. Not to speak of its graceful and very stout stone walls, more than fifty spans in height, the buildings within are very large, handsome, and splendid, being embellished with gold. Indeed, they have been rendered as immaculate and elegant as human industry alone could ever accomplish. At the center is a kind of tower—more proud and noble in its appearance, to be sure, than our towers. This tower [which they call Tenshu] has seven stories and is distinguished inside and out by a marvelous architecture. The pictures inside are all of gold and fine colors, applied with the greatest of artistry. On the exterior each story is painted in different colors, some in white with their windows varnished black in the Japanese fashion—something delightful and charming—others in red or blue; and the top story is gilt. Both this tower and all the other buildings are covered with blue tiles which, it seems to me, must be the strongest in use anywhere in the world. The tile rows are all fitted at the forepart with round crowns covered with gold and the roof ridges appointed with proud figureheads, which contribute much to the beauty and nobility of the edifice. Thus these building works maintain a rich and proud character in their entirety; and although everything is made of wood, neither inside nor out does the fabric appear to be anything other than stout stone and lime. Such, to conclude, are these works that they can stand the comparison with the most sumptuous edifices of Europe.

[On one side of this fortress Nobunaga built another palace, one separate from his own, even though the two are connected by corridors. It excels his own by far in exquisiteness and perfection, being endowed with extraordinarily pleasant, majestic gardens that are almost in every respect different from ours. The magnificence of the chambers, the harmony and technical perfection of design, the rare wood, the immaculacy, the ingenious layout of the structure— everything about this palace revealed a singular wealth of emotion and had its own fascination.]

[Coelho, in *Cartas*, pt. 2, ff. 35v–36; also Fróis, *Historia*, III, pp. 256–258; JSAE]

THE FREE MARKET OF AZUCHI

To ensure that the town he called into being below his castle would prosper, Nobunaga made it a free market (*rakuichi*), safeguarding it from restraints on trade exercised by guilds—monopolistic organizations of merchants and transporters—and granting its residents various immunities. To be sure, the patent of privileges he conferred on Azuchi was not the first such decree issued by a daimyo. As early as 1549, the Rokkaku, masters of southern Ōmi until Nobunaga destroyed them in 1568, had proclaimed a free market at Ishidera beneath their mountain fort Kannonji, just a few kilometers from Azuchi. In 1567 Nobunaga himself had declared Kanō, the settlement below newly conquered Gifu Castle, to be a free marketplace, and the next year he also specified that the place was free from guilds (*rakuza*). But no similar decree issued previously was as detailed, comprehensive, or innovative as the following "Regulations."

Merchants were diverted from the inland Upper Highway (Kamikaidō, a portion of the Nakasendō trunk road), one of two routes that ran in parallel on the east side of Lake Biwa, to the shoreline Lower Highway (Shimokaidō), and were made to stop over in Nobunaga's castle town. This constraint, however, was overshadowed by the many positive inducements to trade and settle in Azuchi. Residents were exempted from the multitude of dues and duties customary in the period and were assured that no extraordinary imposts would be levied on them. (The exactions burdening the populace of sixteenth-century Japan were heavy. Indicative of their onerousness is the term *tenma*, "remount duties"—that is, providing horses from one stage to another at a lord's command—was used as a metaphor for futile labor performed without pay.) Creditors living in Azuchi were protected against the debt cancellation edict, a common device of medieval authorities seeking to give relief to subjects in financial distress or to appease remonstrating groups; but debtors, too, received a measure of protection against aggressive collection agents. Surrogate liability, an imposition that in effect made one a hostage against the repayment of obligations incurred by a fellow countryman, was another medieval practice abolished in Azuchi. Particularly remarkable was Nobunaga's suspension or at least diminution of a cardinal principle of medieval daimyo law, namely, shared culpability in cases of fire or crime.

Contrary to the typical policy of late medieval daimyo, who distrusted "foreigners" from other provinces, Nobunaga affirmed his indifference to where a new settler might come from or whose retainer he might be. Encouraging artisans and traders to settle in the immediate vicinity of the lord's castle was uncommon as well. To be sure, the distinction between men serving in the armed forces and those performing other kinds of service was not as clear-cut in Nobunaga's day as it later became under Hideyoshi.[6] Thus the identity of the servicemen (*hōkōnin*) mentioned in this text is ambiguous, as it was still possible for a military man to pursue one of the trades and live next to tradesmen. It is clear, however, that those who served Nobunaga directly could expect no exemption from duties but were always at his beck and call.

Regulations for the Township Below Mount Azuchi

[1]. This place is decreed to be a free market. Accordingly, it is immune from all guilds (*za*), duties (*yoku*), and taxes (*buji*).

[2]. The Upper Highway is closed to traveling merchants. Whether heading in the direction of the capital city or away from it, they shall take lodging in this township. However: In the case of goods being forwarded, this will be left up to the consignor.

---

6. See "Restrictions on Change of Status" in this chapter.

[3]. Immunity from construction duties. However: A contribution shall be made when His Lordship leaves on a campaign, must be absent in Kyoto, or is otherwise called away unavoidably.

[4]. Immunity from remount duties.

[5]. Regarding fires: In case of arson, the householder will not be held liable. In case of an accidental fire, he is to be banished, on completion of an inquiry. However: Depending on the circumstances, the degree of severity may vary.

[6]. Regarding criminal offenders: Even if a tenant or someone living in the same house commits a crime, if the householder was unaware of the particulars and not in a position to intervene, then the householder will not be blamed for it. The perpetrator shall be brought to justice for his offense on completion of an inquiry.

[7]. Regarding the purchase of various goods: Even if they are stolen goods, the purchaser will not be held culpable if he was unaware of that. But if a judicial confrontation is thereupon held with the thief, then the purloined goods shall be returned [to their rightful owner] in accordance with the ancient law.

[8]. Even if a cancellation of debts (*tobusei*) is put into effect throughout the subject provinces, this place shall be exempted.

[9]. Those who come from other provinces or other localities to settle in this place shall be treated the same as long-standing residents. No objections will be raised to their being the retainers of anyone whatsoever. No one claiming to be an enfeoffed recipient will be permitted to levy extraordinary imposts on them.

[10]. Fights and quarrels, as well as coercion to stand surety for debtors from the same province or the same locality, forced sales, forced purchases, forced rents, and the like are all prohibited.

[11]. Regarding debt collectors and other intruders into the township: The matter shall be reported to Fukutomi Heizaemon no Jō and Kimura Jirōzaemon no Jō, an inquiry conducted, and the appropriate measures ordered.

[12]. Those living in the residential quarters, whether they be in service or artisans, are exempted from duties ordinarily imposed on each household. Add: Except for those residents who are under His Lordship's orders and receive his stipend, as well as artisans in his employ.

[13]. Regarding horse traders: The horse trade of this province shall be conducted entirely in this place.

Any violator of the above articles shall be swiftly brought to justice for his grave offense.

Tenshō 5.VI.[7]

BLACK SEAL *[Nobunaga; on reverse]*

[Okuno, *Zōtei Oda Nobunaga monjo no kenkyū*, II, pp. 300–304, no. 722; JSAE]

TOYOTOMI HIDEYOSHI

DOMESTIC POLICIES

THE DISARMAMENT OF THE POPULACE

It is no accident that the following two documents were promulgated on the same date, which corresponds to August 29, 1588, in the Gregorian calendar. They both address the same fundamental aims of the unifiers' regime: to deprive the common populace of the means to armed resistance and to guarantee that arms bearing became the exclusive preserve and privilege of the samurai class. The target of the "Decree" is the maritime population of fishermen and traders who occasionally metamorphosed into pirates. The "Articles" are directed at farmers. Commonly known as Hideyoshi's Sword Hunt Edict, this is arguably the most famous document issued on his orders. To be sure, the sword hunt was not his original idea. A well-known Japanese precedent is the sweep for weapons conducted in Echizen by Shibata Katsuie in 1576, the year after Nobunaga assigned him to govern that province. Under Hideyoshi, however, the disarmament of the populace was to be carried out as a nationwide policy.

The unstated purport of the "Articles" is that the samurai are to have a monopoly on the means to exercise violence. In exchange, the populace is promised peace and prosperity, security and happiness. Hideyoshi has the temerity to make the additional offer of rewards in the life to come: The "useless instruments" of mayhem collected from the farmers are to be put to a pious use, their scrap metal earning them a meritorious bond with the Buddha whose colossal image is to be erected in a temple complex being built in southeast Kyoto. (The foundation stone of the Kyoto Daibutsu project had been laid not quite three months earlier, on Tenshō 16.V.15, or June 8, 1588.) The Confucian vision of a well-ordered realm is also invoked by Hideyoshi, who does not hesitate to put himself on a level with Yao, one of the greatest culture heroes in all of Chinese myth.

Note that *seibai*, a word often seen in the documents of the unifiers' regime and translated here as "to punish," frequently but not always means "to put to death" and is indeed defined in the authoritative Japanese-Portuguese dictionary published in Nagasaki by the Jesuit mission in 1603 only as "to kill or to execute" and "to kill in the exercise of justice." Ambiguity is the spice of sixteenth-century Japanese documentary style, but there is little doubt what is meant to happen, for instance, to unregenerate pirates under the following "Decree."

---

7. The Sixth Month of Tenshō corresponds to June 16 to July 15, 1577, according to the Julian calendar.

Decree

[1]. His Highness has banned pirate vessels from the seas of the various provinces with the utmost rigor. Nevertheless, sea robbers have recently been reported on Itsuki Island, between the provinces of Bingo and Iyo. Their activity has come to the attention of His Highness, who considers it miscreant.

[2]. The sea captains and fishermen of the provinces and the seashores, all those who go in ships to the sea, shall immediately be investigated by the local land steward or administrative deputy [of the lord's demesne; *daikan*] and made to subscribe jointly to written oaths, forswearing the slightest piratical activity henceforward. The provincial lords shall collect these pledges and forward them to His Highness.

[3]. From now on and hereafter, should the enfeoffed recipient of a domain prove so negligent that pirates are found [under his jurisdiction], the pirates shall be punished (*seibai*) and the fief containing the miscreant locality confiscated with its goods and chattels in all perpetuity.

These articles shall be enforced rigorously. Any transgressor shall swiftly be brought to justice for his offense.

Tenshō 16.VII. 8   VERMILION SEAL *[Hideyoshi]*

Articles

[1]. The farmers of the various provinces are strictly forbidden by His Highness to have swords, daggers, bows, spears, firearms, or other kinds of weapons in their possession. The reason is as follows: Those who stockpile useless implements, evade the payment of rents and dues, plot to band together in leagues (*ikki*), and commit criminal actions against the recipients of fiefs must of course be punished. As a consequence, however, the fields lie fallow and the fief goes to waste. Hence the provincial lords, recipients of fiefs, and administrative deputies shall collect all such weapons and forward them to His Highness.

[2]. The swords and daggers thus to be collected will not go to waste. They are to be made into nails and cramp irons for the Great Buddha building project recently begun by His Highness. Consequently, the farmers will benefit not only in this world but even unto the world to come.

[3]. As long as farmers have agricultural tools and devote themselves exclusively to tilling the fields, they and the generations of their children and children's children will prosper. It is out of compassion with the farmers that His Highness has issued these orders. This is truly the foundation of the country's security and the people's happiness. It is said that in deepest antiquity, when Yao, the lord of Tang, pacified all under Heaven, treasured swords and sharp

blades were turned into farm tools, but that was in a foreign land. In our empire there can surely be no precedent. Let all who enforce these orders fully realize their purport and farmers put all their energies into agriculture and sericulture.

The aforesaid implements shall be collected and forwarded immediately.

Tenshō 16.VII. 8   *VERMILION SEAL [Hideyoshi]*

[*Dai Nihon komonjo, iewake* 11: *Kobayakawa-ke monjo,* I,
pp. 478–481, nos. 502–503; JSAE]

REGULATIONS FOR THE MUNICIPALITY OF THE HONGANJI

In the background of these regulations issued to the Honganji's municipality (*jinai*, "temple precincts," in that temple's own parlance) in Nakajima, directly across the Yodo River from Hideyoshi's Osaka Castle, is an incident that had severely affronted the hegemon. Graffiti containing unflattering references to Hideyoshi had been posted on one of the gates leading to his Kyoto palace, Juraku no Tei. One of the seven people incriminated fled to Nakajima, where he was decapitated. Hideyoshi, however, chose to use this opportunity to demonstrate that giving refuge and comfort to his enemies could never be tolerated. His special emissaries, Ishida Mitsunari and Mashita Naga-mori, arrested other persons who were in ill odor with the regime and destroyed all the houses in two residential wards condemned for harboring rebels. As if to add emphasis, 113 men, women, and children—not only members of the Honganji community but also some merchants from other provinces who had just been passing through—were crucified.

In the aftermath, loyalty oaths were extracted from the inhabitants of the temple precincts—priests, samurai, and townspeople—and the regime issued these "articles" designed to keep the townspeople's quarters (*machi*) and their inhabitants under control. Particularly noteworthy is the prohibition of the free movement of one's abode from one place to another.

The two addressees, Shimotsuma Yorikado and Shimotsuma Nakayasu, were members of a family of hereditary retainers of the Honganji. What is truly remarkable about their appointment as township magistrates (*machi bugyō*) by Hideyoshi is that the Honganji's pontiff had already assigned his own administrators for the municipality. That Hideyoshi should have gone over the pontiff's head, ignoring the arrangements made by the Honganji, shows just how much he was in control not only of his own castle town, Osaka, but also of the nominally autonomous community, Nakajima.

The Honganji, brought back from provincial exile in 1585 and located in Nakajima on grounds assigned to it by Hideyoshi, was transferred by him to Kyoto in 1591. It may, however, be assumed that the order set down for its residential quarters remained as an institutional model and that a regimen similar to the one established in the

Nakajima *jinai* was introduced and continued in the rest of the townspeople's areas of Osaka.

Articles

[1]. It is strictly forbidden to give employment and sustenance to rōnin drifters who have incurred the displeasure of His Highness (that much goes without saying) or even to tolerate their presence.

[2]. Uncompromising measures shall be taken to root out thieves and evildoers.

[3]. No samurai owing service and allegiance to a master shall be given employment in the townspeople's residential quarters.

[4]. In the townspeople's quarters, all residents, regardless of whose retainers they may be, shall be subject to the ordinary dues and duties levied on their township.

[5]. Townspeople or farmers from another locality or village shall not be given employment and shelter insofar as they are under some restriction from the enfeoffed recipient or the administrative deputy of their place of origin; in case permission to take up residence is granted unknowingly, they shall be turned back immediately upon receipt of notice. Add: It shall be considered miscreant for townspeople with a fixed abode to move to any other place.

The above having thus been ordered, any transgressors of these regulations shall be reported to us. You two have been appointed township magistrates by His Highness. If you stay silent in case of a misfeasance, that shall be considered public misconduct, on orders from His Highness.

[Tenshō 17].III.13 (27 April 1589)   *Ishida Jibu no Shō* CYPHER
       Mashita Uemon no Jō CYPHER

To
Shimotsuma Gyōbukyō Hōin
Shimotsuma Shōshin Hōin

[*Tokitsune-Kyō ki*, III, pp. 200–201; JSAE]

RESTRICTIONS ON CHANGE OF STATUS

This decree is the unification regime's fundamental determination regarding social status. It fixes the positions of four orders of society—samurai, farmers, merchants, and artisans—and may therefore be considered the blueprint of the Tokugawa period's rigid class system. The samurai class is defined broadly to include everyone in military service down to miscellaneous attendants or varlets (*komono*) and men engaged in rough, nonmilitary duties (*arashiko*). Membership in that class is frozen as of the date of the brief expedition that Hideyoshi undertook to Mutsu, Japan's northernmost province, after defeating the powerful Hōjō family of Odawara, that is, conquering the Kantō region, in the summer of 1590. That expedition turned into a triumphal progress as the northern barons bent before Hideyoshi, submitted to his rearrangement of their territorial holdings, sent hostages to Kyoto, and began implementing the land survey, the sword hunt, and his other policies in the domains with which he had invested the lucky ones among them (a significant number of them were dispossessed). With the conquest of the Kantō and the subjugation of the north, the unification of Japan could be considered complete. Actually, revolts started breaking out throughout the north country, particularly in those areas confiscated by Hideyoshi, within weeks of his departure from the scene. A huge army was still engaged in their suppression even as this decree was issued. Nevertheless, 1590 remains the epochal date. With the formal integration of the eastern and northern provinces into his realm in August and September that year, the decrees ordained by Hideyoshi became the law throughout Japan.

Not only are samurai restrained from leaving their status group, they are prevented by a draconian rule from changing affiliations within it. The vassal bands of the daimyo houses are kept closed and intact. Farmers are tied to their fields. Townspeople are confined to their townships. Social mobility is virtually negated. Collective responsibility is the mechanism used to coerce the populace into compliance.

Decree

[1]. Servicemen (*hōkōnin*), samurai, grooms, varlets, on down to ancillaries on fatigue duty, all those who may have newly turned themselves into townsmen or farmers since His Highness's expedition to Mutsu Province in the seventh month of last year shall be rooted out by the residents of the township or village concerned. None shall be permitted to remain. Should any be harbored in secret, the entire township or village shall be punished.

[2]. Any country farmer who abandons his fields and takes up either trade (*akinai*) or paid employment (*chin shigoto*, i.e., artisanship) shall of course be punished and, with him, also his community. Add: Those who neither are in service nor farm the fields shall be rigorously rooted out by the administrative deputies or the recipients of fiefs and shall not be permitted to remain. Should any recipient fail to take the proper measures in this regard, the locality in question shall be confiscated from him for his negligence. Should townspeople or farmers secretly harbor such persons, the entire village and the entire township shall be considered miscreant.

[3]. Samurai or varlet regardless, no one who has taken his departure without asking for his master's leave shall be taken into service. Employ only those who provide a guarantor, and only after careful inquiry. However: If it proves that the new retainer already has a master and is reported missing, then it is a shared

responsibility. Accordingly, he shall be put in bonds and delivered to his former master. Should anyone contravene this regulation of His Highness, permitting such a one to go free, then in place of that individual he shall have the heads of three others cut off and delivered to the other party. Should he fail to dispose thus of the three substitutes, there will be no choice but to have the new master punished.

These articles are ordained by decree as above.

Tenshō 19.VIII.21 (8 October 1591)　　　　　*VERMILION SEAL [Hideyoshi]*

[*Dai Nihon komonjo, iewake* 11: *Kobayakawa-ke monjo,* I,
pp. 481–482, no. 504; JSAE]

THE LAWS AND REGULATIONS OF THE TAIKŌ

In February 1592 Hideyoshi passed on the office of imperial regent (*kanpaku*) to his nephew and adopted son Hidetsugu, seeking to demonstrate that the ruling power over Japan would thereafter be held by successive members of the Toyotomi family. In August 1593, however, Hideyoshi's natural son Hideyori was born, and Hideyoshi faced the quandary of how to regulate the succession in his favor. In the event, he decided to extirpate Hidetsugu's progeny. Hidetsugu himself was forced to commit suicide on August 20, 1595, and more than thirty members of his family were executed the day before these "Regulations" and their "Supplement" were issued. The post of *kanpaku* was left open, but Hideyoshi continued to rule under the title of Taikō, which applies to an imperial regent who has handed over his charge to his son.

Immediately upon Hidetsugu's suicide, Hideyoshi exacted oaths of loyalty to Hideyori and adherence to "the laws and regulations of the Taikō" from the leading daimyo. The most notable of these were Maeda Toshiie, appointed Hideyori's guardian; Ukita Hideie, who was to assist Maeda in that all-important task; Tokugawa Ieyasu, entrusted with enforcing Hideyoshi's laws and regulations in the east; Mōri Terumoto and Kobayakawa Takakage (d.1597), charged with keeping the peace in the west; and Uesugi Kagekatsu, the daimyo of the great Echigo domain on the coast of the Sea of Japan. The issuance of these documents over their names in Hideyoshi's behalf signals the emergence of the group popularly known as the Five Great Elders (*gotairō*), a council that acted as the top executive organ of Hideyoshi's regime toward the end of his life.

First and foremost, these decrees seek to deprive the daimyo of the capability to form coalitions; even the freedom to select a marriage partner is taken from them. Hideyoshi is to be the ultimate arbiter of quarrels among them, and they are admonished regarding various aspects of their private behavior. But the daimyo and their samurai retainers are not the only social category being addressed. Indeed, comprehensiveness is these documents' most conspicuous and significant feature. They inform the imperial aristocracy that the pursuit of the arts is to be their principal mission in life, tell priests to be faithful to their calling, and remind the farmers that 67 percent is the basic tax rate on the harvest under Hideyoshi. The Taikō's regime lays down the law to all without exception, prefiguring the Tokugawa shogunate's arrogation of power to dictate to all orders of society.

His Highness's Regulations

[1]. Daimyo shall contract marriages only upon obtaining His Highness's permission and in conformity with his directions.

[2]. It is strictly forbidden by His Highness for daimyo great or small to enter into solemn agreements, exchange written compacts, and the like.

[3]. In case of an accidental fight or quarrel, forbearance shall be exercised and reason made to prevail.

[4]. Should anyone claim that a false accusation has been made against him, both parties shall be summoned and a strict investigation conducted by His Highness.

[5]. Those privileged by His Highness to ride in a litter are Ieyasu, Toshiie, Kagekatsu, Terumoto, and Takakage, as well as members of the old imperial aristocracy, high prelates, and ranking abbots. Apart from these, the young shall ride on horseback, even if they are daimyo. Those aged fifty or older will be permitted to ride in a palanquin if the distance is one league or more. Those who are sick will also be permitted the use of a palanquin during their illness.

Any transgressor of the above articles shall be swiftly brought to justice for his grave offense.

Bunroku 4.VIII.3 (6 September 1595)   *Ieyasu* CYPHER
                                               Hideie CYPHER
                                              Toshiie CYPHER
                                            Terumoto CYPHER
                                            Takakage CYPHER

Supplement to His Highness's Regulations

[1]. Members of the imperial aristocracy and heads of imperial abbacies shall apply themselves to the pursuit of the Ways (*michi*) fostered by their respective houses and shall devote themselves wholeheartedly to serving the public authority (*kōgi*, i.e., Hideyoshi).

[2]. Buddhist temples and Shinto shrines shall observe their temple rules and shrine rules in accordance with precedent, shall keep their buildings in good repair, and shall never be remiss in their pursuit of learning and their devotion to religious practice.

[3]. In fiefs of the realm, dues shall be collected on the basis of an inspection of the harvest: two-thirds for the steward, one-third for the farmers. In all events,

dispositions shall be taken that fields do not lie fallow.

[4]. In addition to his wife, one who is of low rank may keep one housemaid in his service. However: He may not set up a separate household. Even one of high rank is not permitted more than one or two concubines.

[5]. Your conduct shall be commensurate with the size of your fief.

[6]. The procedure for entering direct pleas is as follows. When an ordinary petition is presented, it is first brought before the Ten.[8] The Ten (*jūninshū*) will then cooperate with the petitioner in summoning both contending parties and will carefully hear their plaints. A direct petition (*jikiso meyasu*), however, follows a different procedure. It is brought before the six undersigned. If upon discussion we determine that it should be presented to the ears of His Highness, it shall so be done.

[7]. Unless it be by special privilege from His Highness, neither the chrysanthemum nor the paulownia shall be used as a crest on articles of dress. One who has been bestowed a garment by His Highness may wear it as long as he owns it. He is, however, not permitted to dye another garment and furnish it with His Highness's crest.

[8]. Drink according to your capacity. However: Drinking to excess is forbidden by His Highness.

[9]. To go about masked is strictly prohibited by His Highness.

Any transgressor of the above articles shall be brought to justice for his grave offense.

Bunroku 4.VIII.3

Ieyasu CYPHER
Hideie CYPHER
Kagekatsu CYPHER
Toshiie CYPHER
Terumoto CYPHER
Takakage CYPHER

[*Dai Nihon komonjo, iewake* 2: *Asano-ke monjo*, pp. 477–480, nos. 265–266; JSAE]

THE KOREAN WAR

LETTER TO THE KING OF KOREA

On Tenshō 18.XI.7 (December 3, 1590), some two months after returning to Kyoto from his expedition to subjugate the Kantō region and the northern provinces, Hideyoshi received there a Korean embassy that presented him with a letter of state congratulating him on having unified Japan. This was his response.

---

8. Who the Ten were is uncertain. It is likely that this was a specially constituted judicial board composed of specialists, but their identities are unknown.

This letter's arrogant and pompous tone speaks for itself. Evidently, it suited Hideyoshi to pretend that the Korean ambassadors had brought him a message not of felicitations but of submission from their ruler. The envoys objected to Hideyoshi's breaches of diplomatic propriety, in particular to the condescending form of address "His Excellency" (*kakka*) in reference to the king of Korea and to the phrase "attending on our court" (*nyūchō*, in other words, demonstrating submission). Their complaints went unheard, and they were forced to take back with them to their country this rodomontade in which Hideyoshi not only announces his plan to invade Ming China, Korea's suzerain, but also intimates ominously that when the time came, Korea was expected to play a significant part in his enterprise.

This is not the only document issued over Hideyoshi's name in which there is mention of a miracle attendant on his conception or birth. The message of intimidation he sent to the Spanish colonial governor of the Philippine Islands in 1591 alludes to it, and the 1593 letter demanding the submission of Taiwan describes it in words similar to those found here. Indeed, he rehearses the story in the instructions he gave his own envoys on what to tell the Ming ambassadors in the Korean peace negotiations of 1593. The lowborn Hideyoshi used such legends to mystify his origins, insinuating that he was of a transcendently lofty lineage. His stated desire to spread his fame throughout the "Three Countries"—Japan, China, and India—is but another indication that Hideyoshi's ambitions were unbounded.

Hideyoshi, the Imperial Regent of Japan, sends this letter to His Excellency the King of Korea.

I read your epistle from afar with pleasure, opening and closing the scroll again and again to savor the aroma of your distinguished presence.

Now, then: This empire is composed of more than sixty provinces, but for years the country was divided, the polity disturbed, civility abandoned, and the realm unresponsive to imperial rule. Unable to stifle my indignation at this, I subjugated the rebels and struck down the bandits within the span of three or four years. As far away as foreign regions and distant islands, all is now in my grasp.

As I privately consider the facts of my background, I recognize it to be that of a rustic and unrefined minor retainer. Nevertheless: As I was about to be conceived, my dear mother dreamt that the wheel of the sun had entered her womb. The diviner declared, "As far as the sun shines, so will the brilliance of his rule extend. When he reaches his prime, the Eight Directions will be enlightened through his benevolence and the Four Seas replete with the glory of his name. How could anyone doubt this!" As a result of this miracle, anyone who turned against me was automatically crushed. Whomever I fought, I never failed to win; wherever I attacked, I never failed to conquer. Now that the realm has been thoroughly pacified, I caress and nourish the people, solacing the orphaned and the desolate. Hence my subjects live in plenty and the revenue produced by the land has increased ten-thousand-fold over the past. Since this empire originated, never has the imperial court seen such prosperity or the capital city such grandeur as now.

Man born on this earth, though he live to a ripe old age, will as a rule not reach a hundred years. Why should I rest, then, grumbling in frustration, where I am? Disregarding the distance of the sea and mountain reaches that lie in between, I shall in one fell swoop invade Great Ming. I have in mind to introduce Japanese customs and values to the four hundred and more provinces of that country and bestow upon it the benefits of imperial rule and culture for the coming hundred million years.

Your esteemed country has done well to make haste in attending on our court. Where there is farsightedness, grief does not come near.[9] Those who lag behind [in offering homage], however, will not be granted pardon, even if this is a distant land of little islands lying in the sea. When the day comes for my invasion of Great Ming and I lead my troops to the staging area, that will be the time to make our neighborly relations flourish all the more. I have no other desire but to spread my fame throughout the Three Countries, this and no more.

I have received your regional products as itemized. Stay healthy and take care.

Tenshō 18.XI.   *Hideyoshi*
Imperial Regent of Japan

[*Zoku zenrin kokuhō ki*, XXX, in *Zoku gunsho ruijū*, demivol. 1, fasc. 881, 404; JSAE]

KOREA DAY BY DAY

Keinen (1534?–1611), the author of *Chōsen hinikki* ("Korea Day by Day"), was a priest of the True Pure Land sect in Usuki, a castle town in Kyushu. In the summer of 1597, he was ordered to accompany the daimyo of Usuki, Ōta Hida no Kami Kazuyoshi, to Korea as his personal chaplain and physician. Hida no Kami (or Lord Hishū, as he is called here) was one of the inspectors-general (*yokome bugyō*) of the Japanese field armies during Hideyoshi's second campaign in that country. Keinen was an innocent abroad in this company, an unwilling eyewitness aghast at what he saw.

The vast majority of the writers who produced the voluminous Japanese literature of Hideyoshi's invasion of Korea gloried in the war of aggression. Keinen is the striking exception. No trace of bombast is found in his record of "Korea Day by Day," which is instead a remarkable outpouring of human compassion from what the author called the arena of demonic violence and described through the metaphor of hell. Keinen's

---

9. *Analects* 15:12.

memoir is a thoroughly honest historical source, but it is also a conscious literary product, written in the time-honored form of a poetic diary (*uta nikki*). The running account of his experiences is interspersed with hundreds of simple but affecting epigrams written in poetic meter.

Keinen's diary entries cover, day by day, the seven months from Keichō 2.VI.24 (August 7, 1597), when he left his home, to Keichō 3.II.2 (March 9, 1598), the day of his return to Usuki. The excerpt translated here deals with the three and a half weeks from the disembarkation of Japanese troops in Chŏlla Province, called here by its Japanese code name "Red Country" (Akaguni), to their receipt of orders to invade the "Blue Country" (Aoguni), that is, Ch'ŭngch'ŏng Province. It includes an account of one of the second campaign's major battles, the assault on Namwŏn, a strategic fortress in northern Chŏlla Province. Although heavily reinforced with troops of the Ming expeditionary force in Korea, Namwŏn fell rapidly to a concentric attack mounted by the combined armies of several daimyo. Having thus secured the road north, the Japanese then marched and countermarched through Chŏlla and Ch'ŭngch'ŏng, but they were held on the borders of Kyonggi Province and never reached Seoul during their second Korean campaign.

Eighth Month, 4th day (September 15, 1597). Everyone is trying to be the first off the ship; no one wants to lag behind. They fall over each other in trying to get at the plunder, to kill people. It is a sight I cannot bear to see.

toga mo naki	A hubbub rises
hito no zaihō	as from roiling clouds and mist
toran tote	where they swarm about
unka no gotoku	in their rage for the plunder
tachisawagu tei	of innocent people's goods.

VIII.5. They are burning the houses. As I watched them go up in smoke, I thought that my own existence was like this and was seized by sympathy.

Akaguni to	The "Red Country" is
iedomo yakete	what they call it, but black is
tatsu keburi	the smoke that rises
kuroku noboru wa	from the burning houses
homura to zo miru	where you see flames flying high.

VIII.6. The very fields and hillsides have been put to the fire, not to speak of the forts. People are put to the sword, or they are shackled with chains and bamboo tubes choking the neck. Parents sobbing for their children, children searching for their parents—never before have I seen such a pitiable sight.

no mo yama mo	The hills are ablaze
yakitate ni you	with the cries of soldiers
musha no koe	intoxicated
sanagara shura no	with their pyrolatry—
chimata narikeri	the battleground of demons.

VIII. 7. Looking at the various kinds of plunder amassed by them all, I formed a desire for such things. Could I really be like this, I thought, and felt ashamed. How can I attain salvation like this, I thought.

hazukashiya	How ashamed I am!
miru monogoto ni	For everything that I see
hoshigarite	I form desires—
kokoro sumazaru	a creature of delusions,
mōnen no mi ya	my mind full of attachments.

On the same day, as I exerted myself in reflections on my spiritual state, I felt myself more and more ashamed. And yet the Buddha has vowed not to give weight to the weightiest of evil deeds, not to abandon the most abandoned and intemperate!

osoraku wa	Unless it be through
Mita no chikai o	reliance on the vow of
tanomazu wa	Amida Buddha,
kono akushin wa	who could obtain salvation
tare ka sukuwan	with such wicked thoughts as mine?

VIII.8. They are carrying off Korean children and killing their parents. Never shall they see each other again. Their mutual cries—surely this is like the torture meted out by the fiends of hell.

aware nari	It is piteous;
shichō no wakare	when the four fledglings parted,[10]
kore ka to yo	it must have been thus—
oyako no nageki	I see the parents' lament
miru ni tsuketemo	over their sobbing children.

VIII.11. As night fell, I saw people's houses go up in smoke. They have lost everything to the fire, all their grain and all their property.

---

10. An allusion to the proverbial tale of a mother bird's sorrow at her fledglings' departure to the four directions; *Kongzi jiayu*, 18.

asamashiya	How wretched it is!
gokoku no tagui	Smoke lingers still where the grain
yakisutsuru	was burned and wasted;
keburi no ato ni	so that is where I lay my
hitoyo fushikeri	head tonight: on the scorched earth.

VIII. 12. We are heading for Namwŏn. The high mountains along the way are like nothing I have seen in Japan. The huge rocks are sharp as swords. There also are terrifying waterfalls; just looking at them makes my hair stand on end. This deserves to be called the traverse of the Mountain of Death or the crossing of the River of Hell. There is no place for a man to set his feet here or a horse its hooves.

osoroshiya	How fearsome, worthy
Shide no Yama tomo	to be called the traverse of
iitsubeshi	the Mountain of Death—
kumo ni sobiyuru	this journey along the ridge
mine o koso yuke	of mountains that pierce the clouds.

VIII.13. His Lordship has set up camp about five leagues this side of Namwŏn. Unless this fortress is taken, our prospects are dubious; so we are to close in and invest it this evening. The word is that fifty or sixty thousand soldiers from Great Ming are garrisoning the place.

Akaguni no	We'll solve the challenge
shiro mo kotaete	posed even by this fortress
ari to kikeba	of the Red Country!—
shojin yorokobi	The troops rejoice to hear this,
ashi o yasumuru	and they rest their weary feet.

VIII.14. Rain has been falling steadily since the evening. It comes down in sheets, like a waterfall. We have put up a makeshift tent covered with oil paper only, and it is frightening how the rain pours in. It is impossible to sleep. I had to think of the story "The Devil at One Gulp" in *Tales of Ise*.[11] The night described in that tale must have been just like this.

nasake naku	Inexorably,
furishiboritaru	fearsome torrents beating down

---

11. See *Ise monogatari*, 6, the story of an abduction that ends badly. The lady in question, sequestered in a broken-down storehouse to keep her safe from the elements on a dark and stormy night, is devoured "at one gulp" by an ogre who dwells there.

ame ya somo	remind me of that
oni hitokuchi o	dreadful night when the devil
omoi koso yare	at one gulp ate his victim.

VIII. 15. The fortress is to be stormed before dawn tomorrow. Fascines of bamboo have been distributed to the assault troops. The sun was about to set as they worked their way close in, right up against the edge of the castle's bulwarks, and gunfire opened up from the several siege detachments, accompanied by arrows shot from short-bows. Unthinkable numbers of men were killed. As I saw them dying:

shiro yori mo	From the fortress, too,
hanatsu teppō	comes gunfire; arrows fly
hankyū ni	from their short-bows, too.
omoiyorazu no	How many killed? Beyond count
hito zo shinikeru	is the number of the dead.

The castle fell to the assault in the course of the night. Lord Hishū's troops were the first inside the walls. Needless to say, he is to get a vermilion-seal letter of commendation.

VIII.16. All in the fortress were slaughtered, to the last man and woman. No prisoners were taken. To be sure, a few were kept alive for exchange purposes.

muzan ya na	How cruel! This world
shiranu ukiyo no	of sorrow and inconstancy
narai tote	does have one constant—
nannyo rōshō	men and women, young and old
shi-shite usekeri	die and vanish; are no more.

VIII. 17. Until yesterday they did not know that they would have to die; today, they are transformed into the smoke of impermanence, as is the way of this world of constant change. How can I be unaffected by this!

tare mo miyo	Look! Everyone, look!
hito no ue to wa	Is this, then, to be called the
iigatashi	human condition?—
kyō o kagiri no	a life with a deadline, a
inochi narikeri	life with a limit: today.

VIII.18. We displace camp deeper into the interior. As I looked at the surroundings of the fortress at daybreak, I saw corpses numberless as grains of sand scattered along the roadsides. It was a sight I could not bear to see.

Nanmon no	Leaving behind the
shiro o tachiide	fortress of Namwŏn,
mite are wa	I look about me,
me mo aterarenu	and I witness a sight that
fuzei narikeri	my eyes cannot bear to see.

VIII. 19. This place, too, appears to have been built as a fort, but everyone has fled to the hills and the moors.

kyō wa mata	Once again today
shiranu tokoro no	I lie down in a strange place
akiie ni	in an empty house
hitoyo o akasu	to spend the night in sadness
koto oshi zo omou	at the transience of it all.

VIII.20. His Lordship has now arrived in the capital of the Red Country, and we shall be staying here for at least three days. He is to meet the courier officers sent by His Highness from Kyoto and consult on plans for the ongoing campaign. The word is that we are to move on the capital city [Seoul], but the routes to be followed by the several detachments are still to be assigned. In any event, we shall be going into action soon, before the onset of cold weather.

VIII.28 (October 9, 1597). We break camp in the middle of the night. Our next assignment is the Blue Country.

[Keinen, *Chōsen hinikki*, in *Chōsen gakuhō*, 35:69–75; JSAE]

BIBLIOGRAPHY

ABBREVIATIONS

AG: Allan Grapard

BD: *Bukkyō daijiten*. Ed. Mochizuki Shinkō. 10 vols., rev. ed. Kyoto: Sekai seiten kankō kyōkai, 1955–1963.

CO: Charles Orzech

dB: W. T. de Bary

DS: Daniel Stevenson

DT: Denis Twitchett

GT: George Tanabe

JSAE: Jurgis S. A. Elisonas

LH: Leon Hurvitz

PG: Paul Groner

PV: Paul Varley

WB: William Bodiford

NKBT: Nihon koten bungaku taikei. 100 vols. Tokyo: Iwanami shoten, 1958–1968.

NST: Nihon shisō taikei. 67 vols. Tokyo: Iwanami shoten, 1970–1982.

TD: Taishō shinshū daizōkyō. Ed. Takakusu Junjirō and Watanabe Kaigyoku. 85 vols. Tokyo: Taishō issaikyō kankōkai, 1924–1932.

SOURCES

Analects. In James Legge, trans., *Confucian Analects*, vol. 1 of *The Chinese Classics.* Hong Kong: Hong Kong University Press, 1960.

Anesaki, Masaharu. *History of Japanese Religion; with Special Reference to the Social and Moral Life of the Nation.* London: Kegan Paul, Trench, and Trübner, 1930.

———. *Nichiren, the Buddhist Prophet.* Cambridge, MA: Harvard University Press. 1916.

Annen Oshō no kenkyū. Comp. Eizan gakkai. Kyoto: Dōmeisha, 1979.

Aoki, Michiko Y. *Izumo no kuni fudoki.* Tokyo: Sophia University Press, 1971.

Aston, W. G., trans. *Nihongi. Chronicles of Japan from the Earliest Times to* A.D. 697. 2 vols. Transactions and Proceedings of the Japan Society, supp. 1. London: Kegan Paul, Trench and Trübner, 1896.

Azuma Kagami. In *Kokushi taikei*, vol. 33. Tokyo: Kokushi taikei kankō-kai, 1935.

Brower, Robert H., and Steven D. Carter. *Conversations with Shōtetsu.* Ann Arbor: Center for Japanese Studies, University of Michigan, 1992.

Brower, Robert H., and Earl Miner. *Japanese Court Poetry.* Stanford, CA: Stanford University Press, 1961.

Brown, Delmer, and Ichirō Ishida. *The Future and the Past: A Translation and Study of the Gukanshō, an Interpretive History of Japan Written in 1219.* Berkeley and Los Angeles: University of California Press, 1979.

Buke no kakun. See Yoshida Tōyō.

Bukkyō daijiten. Ed. Mochizuki Shinkō. 10 vols., rev. ed. Tokyo: Sekai seiten kankō kyōkai, 1958–1963.

Bunkashijō yori mitaru Kōbō Daishi den. See Moriyama Shōshin.

"Burnt Norton." *See* T. S. Eliot.

Chamberlain, Basil Hall, trans. *Ko-ji-ki or Records of Ancient Matters.* Transactions of the Asiatic Society of Japan, supp. to vol. 10. Yokohama, 1882.

Chōsen nichinichi ki. See Keinen.

Chūsei hōsei shiryō shū, vols. 1 and 3. *See* Satō Shin'ichi et al.

Chūsei karon shū. See Hisamatsu Sen'ichi.

Chūsei zenke no shisō. Ed. Ichikawa Hakugen and Iriya Yoshitaka. In *Nihon shisō taikei*, vol. 16. Tokyo: Iwanami shoten, 1976.

Classic of Documents. In James Legge, trans., *The Shoo King*, vol. 3 of *The Chinese Classics.* Hong Kong: Hong Kong University Press, 1960.

Coates, Havelock Harper, and Ryugaku Ishizuka. *Hōnen, the Buddhist Saint.* Kyoto: Chionin, 1925.

Coelho, Gaspar, SJ, to General SJ, Nagasaki, February 15, 1582. *Cartas qve os Padres e Irmãos da Companhia de Iesus escreuerão dos Reynos de Iapã & China.* Evora, 1598.

The Collected Works of Shinran. Vol. 1. Kyoto: Jōdo shinshū hongwanji-ha, 1997.

Conlan, Thomas, trans. *In Little Need of Divine Intervention: Scrolls of Mongol Invasions of Japan.* Ithaca, NY: Cornell East Asian Series, Asia Program, Cornell University, 1999.

Cowell, E. B., et al., eds. *The Buddhist Mahayana Texts.* Sacred Books of the East 49. Delhi: Motilal Banarsidass, 1965.

Dacheng zhiguan famen. TD 46, no. 1924.

Dai Nihon komonjo, iewake 11: *Kobayakawa-ke monjo*, vol. 1. Ed. Tōkyō daigaku shiryō hensanjo. Tokyo: Tōkyō daigaku shuppankai, 1979.

Daijingū Sōsho. See Jingū Shichō.

de Bary, William Theodore, and Irene Bloom, eds. *Sources of Chinese Tradition.* Vol. 1, 2nd ed. New York: Columbia University Press, 1999.

De Visser, M. W. *Ancient Buddhism in Japan.* Paris: P. Geuthner, 1928–1935.

Dengyō Daishi zenshū. 4 vols. Tokyo: Tendai-shū shūten kankō-kai, 1912.

Dengyō Daishi zenshū. 5 vols. Tokyo: Sekai seiten kankō kyōkai, 1989.

Dobbins, James. *Jōdo Shinshū: Shin Buddhism in Medieval Japan.* Bloomington: Indiana University Press, 1989.

Dobson, W. A. C. H., trans. *Mencius.* Toronto: University of Toronto Press, 1963.

Dykstra, Yoshiko Kurata. "Jizō, the Most Merciful: Tales from *Jizō Bosatsu Reigenki.*" *Monumenta Nipponica* 33, no. 2 (1978): 179–200.

———, trans. *Miraculous Tales of the Lotus Sūtra from Ancient Japan: The* Dainihonkoku hokekyōkenki *of Priest Chingen.* Hirakata City, Japan: Intercultural Research Institute, 1983.

Eika taigai. In *Chūsei karon shū.* Iwanami bunko, nos. 968–970. Tokyo: Iwanami shoten, 1934.

Eliot, Sir Charles. *Japanese Buddhism.* London: Arnold, 1935.

Eliot, T. S. "Burnt Norton." In *Four Quartets.* New York: Harcourt Brace, 1943.

Fanwang jing. TD 24, no. 1484.

Fróis, Luís SJ. *Historia de Japam.* Ed. José Wicki, SJ. Vol. III. Lisbon: Presidencia do conselho de ministros, secretaria de estado da cultura, direccao-geral do patrimonio cultural, Biblioteca nacional de Lisboa, 1976–1984.

Gedatsu Shōnin kairitsu kōgyō gansho. Eds. Kamata Shigeo and Tanaka Hisao. Vol. 15 of *Kamakura kyū bukkyō, NST.* Tokyo: Iwanami shoten, 1971.

Gotō Tanji, ed. *Taiheiki,* 6 vols. Tokyo: Asahi shinbunsha, 1961.

Grapard, Allan G. "The Shinto of Yoshida Kanetomo." *Monumenta Nipponica* 47, no. 1 (Spring 1992): 27–58.

———, trans. "*Yuiitsu Shintō Myōbō Yōshū.*" *Monumenta Nipponica* 47, no. 2 (Summer 1992): 137–161.

Grossberg, Kenneth, and Kanamoto Nobuhisa, trans. and eds. *The Laws of the Muromachi Bakufu.* Tokyo: Monumenta Nipponica, 1981.

Guanxin lun shu. TD 46, no. 1921.

Gunsho ruijū. See Hanawa Hokiichi.

Hakeda, Yoshito S. *The Awakening of Faith.* New York: Columbia University Press, 1967.

———. *Kūkai: Major Works.* New York: Columbia University Press, 1972.

Hall, J. C. "Japanese Feudal law (*Go Seibai Shikimoku*)." Transactions of the Asiatic Society of Japan, 1st ser., no. 34 (1907): 1–44.

Hanawa Hokiichi, comp. *Gunsho ruijū.* 21 vols. Tokyo: Nagai shoseki, 1928–1932.

———, comp. *Zoku gunsho ruijū.* 33 vols. Tokyo: Zoku gunsho ruijū kansei-kai, 1923–1928.

———, ed. *Zoku zoku gunsho ruijū.* Vol. 10. Tokyo: Kokusho kankō kai, 1907.

Harich-Schneider, Eta. *A History of Japanese Music.* Oxford: Oxford University Press, 1973.

Hirota, Dennis. *Tannishō: A Primer.* Kyoto: Ryūkoku University, 1982.

——. *Wind in the Pines.* Fremont, CA: Asian Humanities Press, 1995.

Hisamatsu Sen'ichi. *Chūsei karon shū.* Iwanami bunko, nos. 968–970. Tokyo: Iwanami shoten, 1934.

Hōgen monogatari. In *Nihon koten bungaku,* vol. 31. Tokyo: Iwanami shoten, 1961.

Hōgen monogatari. See Wilson, William R.

Hōkyōshō. TD 77, no. 2456.

Holtom, D. C. *The National Faith of Japan.* New York: Dutton, 1938.

Hurvitz, Leon, trans. *Scripture of the Lotus Blossom of the Fine Dharma.* New York: Columbia University Press, 1976.

——. *Wei Shou — Treatise on Buddhism and Taoism.* Kyoto: Jimbunkagaku kenkyū-sho, Kyoto University, 1956.

Ichikawa Hakugen, Iriye Yoshitaka, and Yanagida Seizan, eds. *Chūsei zenke no shisō.* Vol. 16 of NST. Tokyo: Iwanami shoten, 1972.

Inoura Yoshinobu. *A History of Japanese Theater.* Vol. 1. Tokyo: Kokusai bunka shin-kōkai, 1971.

Ippen Shōnin goroku. In Ōhashi Shunnō et al., eds., *Hōnen — Ippen.* Vol. 10 of NST. Tokyo: Iwanami shoten, 1971.

Ishii Kyōdō, ed. *Shōwa shinshū Hōnen Shōnin zenshū.* Kyoto: Heirakuji shoten, 1974.

Iwanami kōza Nihon rekishi. Ed. Iwanami shoten. 26 vols. Tokyo: Iwanami shoten, 1975–1977.

Jing xin jie guan fa. TD 45 , no. 1893.

Jingū Shichō, ed. *Daijingū Sōsho.* Kyoto: Rinsen, 1976.

Jinnō shōtō-ki. Dokushi yoron, Sanyō shiron. Yūhō-dō bunko. Tokyo: Yūhō-dō shoten, 1927.

Kamata Shigeo and Tanaka Hisao, eds. *Kamakura kyū Bukkyō.* Vol. 15 of NST. Tokyo: Iwanami shoten, 1971.

Kamens, Edward, trans. *The Three Jewels: A Study and Translation of Minamoto Tamenori's Sanbōe.* Ann Arbor: University of Michigan Press, 1988.

Katsumata Shizuo. "Sengoku-hō." In Iwanami shoten, ed., *Iwanami kōza Nihon rekishi,* vol. 8. Tokyo: Iwanami shoten, 1976.

Keene, Donald. *Anthology of Japanese Literature: From the Earliest Era to the Mid-Nineteenth Century.* New York: Columbia University Press, 1955.

Kegon shuzen kanshō nyūgedatsumon gi, TD 72, no. 2331.

Kegonkyō. TD 10, no. 279.

Keinen. *Chōsen nichinichi ki.* Comp. Naitō Shunpo. In *Chōsen gakuhō* 35 (May 1965): 55–167.

Kissa yōjōki. In Hanawa Hokiichi, comp., *Gunsho ruijū.* 21 vols. Tokyo: Nagai shoseki, 1928–1932.

Kōbō Daishi den zenshū. Ed. Hase Hōshū. 10 vols. Tokyo: Pitaka, 1977.

Kōbō Daishi zenshū. Ed. Sofū sen'yō-kai. 5 vols. Tokyo: Yoshikawa kōbunkan and Kyoto: Rokudai shimpō-sha, 1910.

[Shinshū] *Kōgaku sōsho.* Ed. Mozumi Takami. 12 vols. Tokyo: Kō-bunko kankōkai, 1927–1931.

[Shintei zōho] *Kokushi taikei.* Ed. Kuroita Katsumi. 60 vols. Tokyo: Kokushi taikei kankō-kai, 1935.

Konishi Jin'ichi. *A History of Japanese Literature*. Princeton, NJ: Princeton University Press, 1984.

Lau, D. C., trans. *Lao Tzu: Tao Te Ching*. Baltimore: Penguin Books, 1963.

Legge, James, trans. *The Sacred Books of China: The Texts of Confucianism*. Vol. 2: *The Yi King*. Oxford: Oxford University Press, 1899.

———. *The Chinese Classics*. 5 vols. Hong Kong: Hong Kong University Press, 1960.

Li chi. Trans. James Legge. New Hyde Park, NY: University Books, 1967.

Makra, Mary Leila, trans. *The Hsiao Ching*. New York: St. John's University Press, 1961.

McCullough, Helen Craig, trans. *Ōkagami, the Great Mirror: Fujiwara Michinaga (966–1027) and His Times*. Princeton, NJ: Princeton University Press, 1980.

———, trans. *The Taiheiki*. Rutland, VT: Tuttle, 1979.

———, trans. *The Tale of the Heike*. Stanford, CA: Stanford University Press, 1988.

McCullough, William H., and Helen Craig, trans. *A Tale of Flowering Fortunes: Annals of Japanese Aristocratic Life in the Heian Period*. Stanford, CA: Stanford University Press, 1980.

Mencius. In James Legge, trans. *The Works of Mencius*, vol. 2 of *The Chinese Classics*. Hong Kong: Hong Kong University Press, 1960.

Mohe zhiguan. TD 46, no. 1911.

Moriyama Shōshin, ed. *Bunkashijō yori mitaru Kōbō Daishi den*. Tokyo: Buzanha shūmusho, 1931.

Morrell, Robert E.. "Mirror for Women: Mujū Ichien's *Tsuma Kagami*." *Monumenta Nipponica* 35, no. 1 (Spring 1980): 45–75.

Morris, Ivan. *The World of the Shining Prince*. Tokyo: Kodansha International, 1994.

Mouzi. Ed. Bing-jin guan cong-shu. Wuxian, Suzhou: Privately published, 1885.

Mozumi Takami, ed. [Shinshū] *Kōgaku sōsho*. 12 vols. Tokyo: Kō-bunko kankō-kai, 1927–1931.

Mumyō Hisho. In Hanawa Hokiichi, comp., *Gunsho ruijū*. 21 vols. Tokyo: Nagai shoseki, 1928–1932.

Mumyō sōshi shinchū. Ed. Tomikura Jirō. Tokyo: Ikuei shoin, 1937.

Musō kokushi goroku. TD 80, no. 2555.

Mutsu waki. In Hanawa Hokiichi, comp., *Zoku zoku gunsho ruijū*, vol. 10. Tokyo: Kokusho kankō kai, 1907.

Nagazumi Yasuaki and Shimada Isao, eds. *Hōgen monogatari*. Vol. 31 of *Nihon koten bungaku taikei*. Tokyo: Iwanami shoten, 1961.

Nihon bukkyō shi. See Tsuji Zennosuke.

Nishio Minoru. *Shōbōgenzō zuimonki*. In *Nihon koten bungaku taikei*, vol. 8. Tokyo: Iwanami shoten, 1968.

Nosé, Asaji. *Zeami jūroku bushū hyōshaku*. Tokyo: Iwanami shoten, 1966.

Ōhashi Shunnō et al., eds. *Ippen Shōnin goroku*. In *Hōnen—Ippen*, vol. 10. Tokyo: Iwanami shoten, 1971.

Okuno Takahiro. *Zōtei Oda Nobunaga monjo no kenkyū*, vol. 1. Tokyo: Yoshikawa kōbunkan, 1994.

Ōsumi Kazuo, ed. *Chūsei Shintō Myōbō Yōshū*. Vol. 10 of NST. Tokyo: Iwanami shoten, 1997.

Ōta Gyūichi. *Shinchō-Kō ki*. Ed. Okuno Takahiro and Iwasawa Yoshihiko, *Kadokawa bunko*, vol. 254. Tokyo: Kadokawa shoten, 1970.

Pandey, Rajyashree. "Women, Sexuality, and Enlightenment: *Kankyo no Tomo.*" *Monumenta Nipponica* 50, no. 3 (Fall 1995): 325–356.

Philippi, Donald L. *Norito: A New Translation of the Ancient Japanese Ritual Prayers.* Tokyo: Institute for Japanese Culture and Classics, Kokugakuin University, 1959.

———. The *Kojiki.* Tokyo: University of Tokyo Press, 1975.

Reischauer, Edwin O. *Japan: The Story of a Nation.* New York: Knopf, 1970.

Reischauer, Edwin O., and Joseph K. Yamigawa, trans. *Translations from Early Japanese Literature.* Cambridge, MA: Harvard University Press, 1951.

Reischauer, Edwin O., John K. Fairbank, and Albert Craig. *East Asia: The Great Tradition.* Boston: Houghton Mifflin, 1958.

Reischauer, Robert Karl. *Early Japanese History (ca. 40 B.C.–A.D. 1167),* pt. A. Princeton, NJ: Princeton University Press, 1937.

Rikkokushi. See Saeki Ariyoshi.

Rimer, Thomas, and Masakazu Yamazaki. *On the Art of the Nō Drama: The Major Treatises of Zeami.* Princeton, NJ: Princeton University Press, 1984.

Saeki Ariyoshi, ed. *Rikkokushi.* 12 vols. Tokyo: Asahi shimbun-sha, 1940.

Sansom, G. B. "The Imperial Edicts in the *Shoku-Nihongi.*" Transactions of the Asiatic Society of Japan, 2d ser., vol. 1 (1923–1924): 5–39.

———. *Japan, a Short Cultural History.* London: Cresset, 1946.

———, trans. "Tsuredzure-gusa." Transactions of the Asiatic Society of Japan, 1st ser., vol. 39 (1911): 1–146.

Satō Shin'ichi et al., eds. *Chūsei hōsei shiryō shū.* Vols. 1 and 3. Tokyo: Iwanami shoten, 1955–1965.

Seidensticker, Edward, trans. *The Tale of Genji.* 2 vols. New York: Knopf, 1976.

"Sengoku-hō." See Katsumata Shizuo.

"Seven Unrecorded Contemporary English Translations of Jesuit Letters from Japan." MS Jap. 3, Houghton Library, Harvard University.

[Shinsen] *Meika shishū.* See Tsukamoto Tetsuzō.

Shintō taikei hensankai, ed. *Shintō taikei seikoshū.* Tokyo: Seikosha, 1984.

Shoku Nihongi. In Saeki Ariyoshi, *Rikkokushi.* 12 vols. Tokyo: Asahi shimbun-sha, 1940.

Shōtetsu monogatari. In *Zoku gunsho ruijū,* vol. 16. Tokyo; Zoku gunsho ruijū kanseikai, 1923–1928.

Shōtoku taishi shū. In Ienaga Saburō and Tsukishima Hiroshi, eds., vol. 2 of *NST.* Tokyo: Iwanami shoten, 1976.

Shōwa shinshū Hōnen zenshū. See Ishii Kyōdō.

Steenstrup, Carl. *Hōjō Shigetoki (1198–1261).* Scandinavian Institute of Asian Studies monograph series, no. 41. London: Curzon Press, 1979.

Tendai kuji hongi. In Shintō taikei hensankai, ed., *Shintō taikei,* vol. 8. Tokyo: Seikosha, 1984.

Tokitsugu-Kyō-ki. Vol. 3. Ed. Dai Nihon kokiroku. Tōkyō daigaku shiryō hensanjo. Tokyo: Iwanami shoten, 1962.

Tso chuan. In James Legge, trans., *The Ch'un Ts'ew, with the Tso Chuen,* vol. 5 of *The Chinese Classics.* Hong Kong: Hong Kong University Press, 1960.

Tsuji Zennosuke, ed. *Nihon bukkyō shi.* 10 vols. Tokyo: Iwanami shoten, 1944–1955.

Tsukamoto Tetsuzō, comp. [Shinsen] *Meika shishū.*Yūhō-dō bunko. Tokyo: Yūhō-dō shoten, 1927.

Tsunoda Ryusaku, and L. Carrington Goodrich. *Japan in the Chinese Dynastic Histories*. Perkins Asiatic Monograph no. 2. South Pasadena, CA: P. D. and Ione Perkins, 1951.

Twitchett, Denis. "How to Be an Emperor. " *Asia Major*, 3d ser., no. 9, pts. 1 and 2 (1996): 1–102.

Tyler, Royall. *The Miracles of the Kasuga Deity*. New York: Columbia University Press, 1990.

Varley, Paul, trans. *A Chronicle of Gods and Sovereigns: Jinnō shōtōki of Kitabatake Chikafusa*. New York: Columbia University Press, 1980.

———. *Warriors of Japan, As Portrayed in the War Tales*. Honolulu: University of Hawaii Press, 1994.

Varley, Paul, and Isao Kumakura, eds. *Tea in Japan: Essays on the History of Chanoyu*. Honolulu: University of Hawaii Press, 1989.

Waley, Arthur, trans. *The Analects of Confucius*. London: Allen & Unwin, 1938.

Watson, Burton, trans. *The Lotus Sūtra*. New York: Columbia University Press, 1993.

———. *Records of the Grand Historian*. 3 vols. New York: Columbia University Press, 1992.

———. *The Vimalakirti Sūtra*. New York: Columbia University Press, 1997.

Wilhelm, Richard, and Cary F. Baynes, trans. *The I Ching*. Princeton, NJ: Princeton University Press, 1967.

Wilson, William R., trans. *Hōgen monogatari: Tale of the Disorder in Hōgen*. Tokyo: Sophia University Press, 1971.

Xunzi. Trans. John Knoblock. 3 vols. Stanford, CA: Stanford University Press, 1988–1994.

Yampolsky, Philip. "The Essentials of Salvation." Master's thesis, Columbia University, 1948.

———, ed. *Selected Writings of Nichiren*. Trans. Burton Watson et al. New York: Columbia University Press, 1996.

Yamatohime no Mikoto Seiki. In Jingū Shichō, ed., *Daijingū Sōsho*. Kyoto: Rinsen, 1976.

Yoshida Tōyō. *Buke no kakun*. Tokyo: Tokuma shoten, 1972.

Zoku zenrin kokuhō ki. In *Zoku gunsho ruijū*, vol. 30. Tokyo: Zoku gunsho ruijū kanseikai, 1925.

Zoku zoku gunsho ruijū. See Hanawa Hokiichi.

INDEX

Translated selections from the Japanese sources are indicated by italicized page numbers.

Acknowledgments (from page iv)

Allan G. Grapard. "The Shinto of Yoshida Kanetomo." *Monumenta Nipponica* 47.1 (1992), pp. 137–161.

Kenneth Grossberg and Kanamoto Nobuhisa, trs. *The Laws of the Muromachi Bakufu*. Tokyo: Monumenta Nipponica, 1981, pp. 16–21.

Dennis Hirota. *Wind in the Pines*. Fremont, CA: Asian Humanities Press, 1995, pp. 198, 217–219.

From pp. 91–93 of *The Three Jewels: A Study and Translation of Minamoto Tamenori's Sanbôe*, by Edward Kamens, Michigan Monograph Series in Japanese Studies, Number 2 (Ann Arbor: Center for Japanese Studies, The University of Michigan, 1988). Used with permission.

Reprinted from *The Tale of the Heike*, translated by Helen Craig McCullough with the permission of the publishers, Stanford University Press. © 1988 the Board of Trustees of the Leland Stanford Junior University.

Helen Craig McCullough. *Okagami, the Great Mirror: Fujiwara Michinaga and His Times*. Copyright © 1980 by Princeton University Press. Reprinted by permission of Princeton University Press.

Reprinted from a *Tale of Flowering Fortunes*, translated, with an introduction and notes, by William H. and Helen Craig McCullough with the permission of the publishers, Stanford University Press. © 1980 the Board of Trustees of the Leland Stanford Junior University.

Robert E. Morrell. "Mirror for Women: Mujû Ichien's Tsuma Kagami." *Monumenta Nipponica* 35.1 (Spring 1980), pp. 51–75.

Ivan Morris. *The World of the Shining Prince*. Tokyo: Kodansha International, 1994, pp. 308–310.

Rajyashree Pandey. "Women, Sexuality, and Enlightenment." *Monumenta Nipponica* 50.3 (Fall 1995), pp. 335–337, 349–350.

Donald L. Philippi. *Norito: A New Translation of the Ancient Medieval Japanese Ritual Prayers*. Copyright © 1990 by Princeton University Press. Reprinted by permission of Princeton University Press.

Edwin O. Reischauer and Joseph K. Yamagawa, trs. *Translations from Early Japanese Literature*. Cambridge University Press, 1951, pp. 301–302.

Thomas Rimer and Masakazu Yamazaki. *On the Art of the No Drama: The Major Treatises of Zeami*. Copyright © 1984 by Princeton University Press. Reprinted by permission of Princeton University Press.

Carl Steenstrup. *Hôjô Shigetoki*. Scandinavian Institute of Asian Studies, Monograph No. 41. London: Curzon press, 1979.

Denis Twitchett. "How to Be an Emperor." *Asia Major*, 3rd series, 9.1–2 (1996), pp. 50–92.

William R. Wilson, tr. *Hōgen Monogatari: Tale of the Disorder in Hōgen*. Tokyo: Sophia University Press, 1971, pp. 26–28, 36–37.

OTHER WORKS IN THE

COLUMBIA ASIAN STUDIES SERIES

The Platform Sutra of the Sixth Patriarch, tr. Philip B. Yampolsky. Also in paperback ed. 1967

Essays in Idleness: The Tsurezuregusa of Kenkō, tr. Donald Keene. Also in paperback ed. 1967

The Pillow Book of Sei Shōnagon, tr. Ivan Morris, 2 vols. 1967

Two Plays of Ancient India: The Little Clay Cart and the Minister's Seal, tr. J. A. B. van Buitenen 1968

The Complete Works of Chuang Tzu, tr. Burton Watson 1968

The Romance of the Western Chamber (Hsi Hsiang chi), tr. S. I. Hsiung. Also in paperback ed. 1968

The Manyōshū, Nippon Gakujutsu Shinkōkai edition. Paperback ed. only. 1969

Records of the Historian: Chapters from the Shih chi of Ssu-ma Ch'ien, tr. Burton Watson. Paperback ed. only. 1969

Cold Mountain: 100 Poems by the T'ang Poet Han-shan, tr. Burton Watson. Also in paperback ed. 1970

Twenty Plays of the Nō Theatre, ed. Donald Keene. Also in paperback ed. 1970

Chūshingura: The Treasury of Loyal Retainers, tr. Donald Keene. Also in paperback ed. 1971; rev. ed. 1997

The Zen Master Hakuin: Selected Writings, tr. Philip B. Yampolsky 1971

Chinese Rhyme-Prose: Poems in the Fu Form from the Han and Six Dynasties Periods, tr. Burton Watson. Also in paperback ed. 1971

Kūkai: Major Works, tr. Yoshito S. Hakeda. Also in paperback ed. 1972

The Old Man Who Does as He Pleases: Selections from the Poetry and Prose of Lu Yu, tr. Burton Watson 1973

The Lion's Roar of Queen Śrīmālā, tr. Alex and Hideko Wayman 1974

Courtier and Commoner in Ancient China: Selections from the History of the Former Han by Pan Ku, tr. Burton Watson. Also in paperback ed. 1974

Japanese Literature in Chinese, vol. 1: Poetry and Prose in Chinese by Japanese Writers of the Early Period, tr. Burton Watson 1975

Japanese Literature in Chinese, vol. 2: Poetry and Prose in Chinese by Japanese Writers of the Later Period, tr. Burton Watson 1976

Scripture of the Lotus Blossom of the Fine Dharma, tr. Leon Hurvitz. Also in paperback ed. 1976

Love Song of the Dark Lord: Jayadeva's Gītagovinda, tr. Barbara Stoler Miller. Also in paperback ed. Cloth ed. includes critical text of the Sanskrit. 1977; rev. ed. 1997

Ryōkan: Zen Monk-Poet of Japan, tr. Burton Watson 1977

Calming the Mind and Discerning the Real: From the Lam rim chen mo of Tsoṇ-kha-pa, tr. Alex Wayman 1978

The Hermit and the Love-Thief: Sanskrit Poems of Bhartrihari and Bilhaṇa, tr. Barbara Stoler Miller 1978

The Lute: Kao Ming's P'i-p'a chi, tr. Jean Mulligan. Also in paperback ed. 1980

A Chronicle of Gods and Sovereigns: Jinnō Shōtōki of Kitabatake Chikafusa, tr. H. Paul Varley 1980

Among the Flowers: The Hua-chien chi, tr. Lois Fusek 1982

Grass Hill: Poems and Prose by the Japanese Monk Gensei, tr. Burton Watson 1983

Doctors, Diviners, and Magicians of Ancient China: Biographies of Fang-shih, tr. Kenneth J. DeWoskin. Also in paperback ed. 1983

Theater of Memory: The Plays of Kālidāsa, ed. Barbara Stoler Miller. Also in paperback ed. 1984

The Columbia Book of Chinese Poetry: From Early Times to the Thirteenth Century, ed. and tr. Burton Watson. Also in paperback ed. 1984

Poems of Love and War: From the Eight Anthologies and the Ten Long Poems of Classical Tamil, tr. A. K. Ramanujan. Also in paperback ed. 1985

The Bhagavad Gita: Krishna's Counsel in Time of War, tr. Barbara Stoler Miller 1986

The Columbia Book of Later Chinese Poetry, ed. and tr. Jonathan Chaves. Also in paperback ed. 1986

The Tso Chuan: Selections from China's Oldest Narrative History, tr. Burton Watson 1989

Waiting for the Wind: Thirty-six Poets of Japan's Late Medieval Age, tr. Steven Carter 1989

Selected Writings of Nichiren, ed. Philip B. Yampolsky 1990

Saigyō, Poems of a Mountain Home, tr. Burton Watson 1990

The Book of Lieh Tzu: A Classic of the Tao, tr. A. C. Graham. Morningside ed. 1990

The Tale of an Anklet: An Epic of South India—The Cilappatikāram of Iḷaṅkō Aṭikaḷ, tr. R. Parthasarathy 1993

Waiting for the Dawn: A Plan for the Prince, tr. and introduction by Wm. Theodore de Bary 1993

Yoshitsune and the Thousand Cherry Trees: A Masterpiece of the Eighteenth-Century Japanese Puppet Theater, tr., annotated, and with introduction by Stanleigh H. Jones, Jr. 1993

The Lotus Sutra, tr. Burton Watson. Also in paperback ed. 1993

The Classic of Changes: A New Translation of the I Ching as Interpreted by Wang Bi, tr. Richard John Lynn 1994

Beyond Spring: Tz'u Poems of the Sung Dynasty, tr. Julie Landau 1994

The Columbia Anthology of Traditional Chinese Literature, ed. Victor H. Mair 1994

Scenes for Mandarins: The Elite Theater of the Ming, tr. Cyril Birch 1995

Letters of Nichiren, ed. Philip B. Yampolsky; tr. Burton Watson et al. 1996

Unforgotten Dreams: Poems by the Zen Monk Shōtetsu, tr. Steven D. Carter 1997

The Vimalakirti Sutra, tr. Burton Watson 1997

Japanese and Chinese Poems to Sing: The Wakan rōei shū, tr. J. Thomas Rimer and Jonathan Chaves 1997

Breeze Through Bamboo: Kanshi of Ema Saikō, tr. Hiroaki Sato 1998

A Tower for the Summer Heat, Li Yu, tr. Patrick Hanan 1998

Traditional Japanese Theater: An Anthology of Plays, Karen Brazell 1998

The Original Analects: Sayings of Confucius and His Successors (0479–0249), E. Bruce Brooks and A. Taeko Brooks 1998

The Classic of the Way and Virtue: A New Translation of the Tao-te ching of Laozi as Interpreted by Wang Bi, tr. Richard John Lynn 1999

The Four Hundred Songs of War and Wisdom: An Anthology of Poems from Classical Tamil, The Puranāṇūṟu, eds. and trans. George L. Hart and Hank Heifetz 1999

Original Tao: Inward Training (Nei-yeh) *and the Foundations of Taoist Mysticism*, by Harold D. Roth 1999

Lao Tzu's Tao Te Ching: *A Translation of the Startling New Documents Found at Guodian*, Robert G. Henricks 2000

The Shorter Columbia Anthology of Traditional Chinese Literature, ed. Victor H. Mair 2000

Mistress and Maid (Jiaohongji) by Meng Chengshun, tr. Cyril Birch 2001

Chikamatsu: Five Late Plays, tr. and ed. C. Andrew Gerstle 2001

The Essential Lotus: Selections from the Lotus Sutra, tr. Burton Watson 2002

Early Modern Japanese Literature: An Anthology, 1600–1900, ed. Haruo Shirane 2002

The Sound of the Kiss, or The Story That Must Never Be Told: Pingali Suranna's Kalapurnodayamu, tr. Vecheru Narayana Rao and David Shulman 2003

The Selected Poems of Du Fu, tr. Burton Watson 2003

Far Beyond the Field: Haiku by Japanese Women, tr. Makoto Ueda 2003

Just Living: Poems and Prose by the Japanese Monk Tonna, ed. and tr. Steven D. Carter 2003

Han Feizi: Basic Writings, tr. Burton Watson 2003

Mozi: Basic Writings, tr. Burton Watson 2003

Xunzi: Basic Writings, tr. Burton Watson 2003

Zhuangzhi: Basic Writings, tr. Burton Watson 2003

MODERN ASIAN LITERATURE

Modern Japanese Drama: An Anthology, ed. and tr. Ted. Takaya. Also in paperback ed. 1979

Mask and Sword: Two Plays for the Contemporary Japanese Theater, by Yamazaki Masakazu, tr. J. Thomas Rimer 1980

Yokomitsu Riichi, Modernist, Dennis Keene 1980

Nepali Visions, Nepali Dreams: The Poetry of Laxmiprasad Devkota, tr. David Rubin 1980

Literature of the Hundred Flowers, vol. 1: *Criticism and Polemics*, ed. Hualing Nieh 1981

Literature of the Hundred Flowers, vol. 2: *Poetry and Fiction*, ed. Hualing Nieh 1981

Modern Chinese Stories and Novellas, 1919–1949, ed. Joseph S. M. Lau, C. T. Hsia, and Leo Ou-fan Lee. Also in paperback ed. 1984

A View by the Sea, by Yasuoka Shōtarō, tr. Kären Wigen Lewis 1984

Other Worlds: Arishima Takeo and the Bounds of Modern Japanese Fiction, by Paul Anderer 1984

Selected Poems of Sō Chōngju, tr. with introduction by David R. McCann 1989

The Sting of Life: Four Contemporary Japanese Novelists, by Van C. Gessel 1989

Stories of Osaka Life, by Oda Sakunosuke, tr. Burton Watson 1990

The Bodhisattva, or Samantabhadra, by Ishikawa Jun, tr. with introduction by William Jefferson Tyler 1990

The Travels of Lao Ts'an, by Liu T'ieh-yün, tr. Harold Shadick. Morningside ed. 1990

Three Plays by Kōbō Abe, tr. with introduction by Donald Keene 1993

The Columbia Anthology of Modern Chinese Literature, ed. Joseph S. M. Lau and Howard Goldblatt 1995

Modern Japanese Tanka, ed. and tr. by Makoto Ueda 1996

Masaoka Shiki: Selected Poems, ed. and tr. by Burton Watson 1997

Writing Women in Modern China: An Anthology of Women's Literature from the Early Twentieth Century, ed. and tr. by Amy D. Dooling and Kristina M. Torgeson 1998

American Stories, by Nagai Kafû, tr. Mitsuko Iriye 2000

The Paper Door and Other Stories, by Shiga Naoya, tr. Lane Dunlop 2001

Grass for My Pillow, by Saiichi Maruya, tr. Dennis Keene 2002

For All My Walking: Free-Verse Haiku of Taneda Santōka, with Excerpts from His Diaries, tr. Burton Watson 2003

STUDIES IN ASIAN CULTURE

The Ōnin War: History of Its Origins and Background, with a Selective Translation of the Chronicle of Ōnin, by H. Paul Varley 1967

Chinese Government in Ming Times: Seven Studies, ed. Charles O. Hucker 1969

The Actors' Analects (Yakusha Rongo), ed. and tr. by Charles J. Dunn and Bungō Torigoe 1969

Self and Society in Ming Thought, by Wm. Theodore de Bary and the Conference on Ming Thought. Also in paperback ed. 1970

A History of Islamic Philosophy, by Majid Fakhry, 2d ed. 1983

Phantasies of a Love Thief: The Caurapañcāśikā Attributed to Bilhaṇa, by Barbara Stoler Miller 1971

Iqbal: Poet-Philosopher of Pakistan, ed. Hafeez Malik 1971

The Golden Tradition: An Anthology of Urdu Poetry, ed. and tr. Ahmed Ali. Also in paperback ed. 1973

Conquerors and Confucians: Aspects of Political Change in Late Yüan China, by John W. Dardess 1973

The Unfolding of Neo-Confucianism, by Wm. Theodore de Bary and the Conference on Seventeenth-Century Chinese Thought. Also in paperback ed. 1975

To Acquire Wisdom: The Way of Wang Yang-ming, by Julia Ching 1976

Gods, Priests, and Warriors: The Bhr.. gus of the Mahābhārata, by Robert P. Goldman 1977

Mei Yao-ch'en and the Development of Early Sung Poetry, by Jonathan Chaves 1976

The Legend of Semimaru, Blind Musician of Japan, by Susan Matisoff 1977

Sir Sayyid Ahmad Khan and Muslim Modernization in India and Pakistan, by Hafeez Malik 1980

The Khilafat Movement: Religious Symbolism and Political Mobilization in India, by Gail Minault 1982

The World of K'ung Shang-jen: A Man of Letters in Early Ch'ing China, by Richard Strassberg 1983

The Lotus Boat: The Origins of Chinese Tz'u Poetry in T'ang Popular Culture, by Marsha L. Wagner 1984

Expressions of Self in Chinese Literature, ed. Robert E. Hegel and Richard C. Hessney 1985

Songs for the Bride: Women's Voices and Wedding Rites of Rural India, by W. G. Archer; eds. Barbara Stoler Miller and Mildred Archer 1986

The Confucian Kingship in Korea: Yŏngjo and the Politics of Sagacity, by JaHyun Kim Haboush 1988

COMPANIONS TO ASIAN STUDIES

Approaches to the Oriental Classics, ed. Wm. Theodore de Bary 1959

Early Chinese Literature, by Burton Watson. Also in paperback ed. 1962

Approaches to Asian Civilizations, eds. Wm. Theodore de Bary and Ainslie T. Embree 1964

The Classic Chinese Novel: A Critical Introduction, by C. T. Hsia. Also in paperback ed. 1968

Chinese Lyricism: Shih Poetry from the Second to the Twelfth Century, tr. Burton Watson. Also in paperback ed. 1971

A Syllabus of Indian Civilization, by Leonard A. Gordon and Barbara Stoler Miller 1971

Twentieth-Century Chinese Stories, ed. C. T. Hsia and Joseph S. M. Lau. Also in paperback ed. 1971

A Syllabus of Chinese Civilization, by J. Mason Gentzler, 2d ed. 1972

A Syllabus of Japanese Civilization, by H. Paul Varley, 2d ed. 1972

An Introduction to Chinese Civilization, ed. John Meskill, with the assistance of J. Mason Gentzler 1973

An Introduction to Japanese Civilization, ed. Arthur E. Tiedemann 1974

Ukifune: Love in the Tale of Genji, ed. Andrew Pekarik 1982

The Pleasures of Japanese Literature, by Donald Keene 1988

A Guide to Oriental Classics, eds. Wm. Theodore de Bary and Ainslie T. Embree; 3d edition ed. Amy Vladeck Heinrich, 2 vols. 1989

INTRODUCTION TO ASIAN CIVILIZATIONS
Wm. Theodore de Bary, General Editor

Sources of Japanese Tradition, 1958; paperback ed., 2 vols., 1964; 2d ed., vol. 1, 2001, compiled by Wm. Theodore de Bary, Donald Keene, George Tanabe, and Paul Varley

Sources of Indian Tradition, 1958; paperback ed., 2 vols., 1964; 2d ed., 2 vols., 1988

Sources of Chinese Tradition, 1960; paperback ed., 2 vols., 1964; 2d ed., vol. 1, 1999, compiled by Wm. Theodore de Bary and Irene Bloom; vol. 2, 2000, compiled by Wm. Theodore de Bary and Richard Lufrano

Sources of Korean Tradition, ed. Peter H. Lee and Wm. Theodore de Bary; paperback ed., vol. 1, 1997

NEO-CONFUCIAN STUDIES

Instructions for Practical Living and Other Neo-Confucian Writings by Wang Yang-ming, tr. Wing-tsit Chan 1963